AN INTRODUCTION TO COMPILER CONSTRUCTION

WILLIAM M. WAITE
Department of Electrical and Computer Engineering
University of Colorado-Boulder

LYNN ROBERT CARTER
Software Engineering Institute
Carnegie-Mellon University

HarperCollins*CollegePublishers*

Project Editor: Janet Tilden
Art Direction: Julie Anderson
Cover Design: Jess Schaal
Cover Photo: Hans Blohm/MASTERFILE
Production Administrator: Kathleen Donnelly
Compositor: House of Equations, Inc.
Printer and Binder: R.R. Donnelley & Sons Company
Cover Printer: New England Book Components

An Introduction to Compiler Construction

Copyright © 1993 by HarperCollins College Publishers.

All rights reserved. Printed in the United States of America. No part of this book may be used or reproduced in any manner whatsoever without written permission, except in the case of brief quotations embodied in critical articles and reviews. For information address HarperCollins College Publishers, 10 East 53rd Street, New York, NY 10022.

Library of Congress Cataloging-in-Publication Data

Waite, W. M. (William McCastline)
    An introduction to compiler construction / W. M. Waite, L. R. Carter.
       p. cm.
    Includes bibliographical references and index.
    ISBN 0-673-39822-6
    1. Compilers (Computer programs)   I. Carter, Lynn Robert.
II. Title.
QA76.76.C65W35   1992   91-14518
005.4'53—dc20   CIP

Preface

Compiler construction techniques underlie most of a user's communication with a computer system. They are applied in the implementation of a variety of user interface software, ranging from full programming languages through specialized application programs to operating system command processors. A basic understanding of these pervasive techniques is useful for virtually anyone working in the computer field.

This book is an introduction to compiler construction techniques. Our intent is to give a consistent overall picture, illustrating the important issues with simple but practical examples. You will learn how languages of the complexity of Pascal are translated into reasonable code for machines with standard sequential architectures. Such knowledge will help you to understand many of the peculiarities of specific compilers (including cryptic error reports) and to write programs that are portable and efficient. Compiler construction is also an excellent example of "programming-in-the-large," showing the application of software engineering principles to the solution of a familiar problem.

Compiler construction has extensive theoretical foundations. The subject is often presented in a deductive manner, formally deriving the necessary algorithms from a set of axioms. We feel that this deductive approach is a mistake as an introduction to the subject. Most people are inductive learners, preferring to begin with observations of phenomena and then to move to theoretical explanations. Our presentation is therefore centered on specific examples that, together, characterize the complete compilation problem. We provide systematic, intuitive approaches to solving the compiler subproblems posed by these examples. The approaches used for different subproblems fit together to provide a consistent compiler construction strategy. All of these approaches are grounded in theory, and each chapter provides notes and references pointing the reader to that theory. We strongly believe that it is more important for an introductory text to present a complete, coherent picture of the compilation process than to provide mathematically elegant derivations of individual algorithms.

We also believe that an introductory text for a subject of this complexity cannot provide a survey of competing approaches to particular subproblems. By restricting ourselves to one or two subproblem solutions, we run the risk of having our treatment regarded as a "cookbook" with little attention to basic principles. To counter this perception, we have tried to provide general characterizations of the problems themselves and the concepts upon which solutions must be built. These are reinforced by exercises that point to alternative solutions and encourage the student to compare and contrast.

Parsing is the one task for which we discuss two approaches in detail. One of those approaches (recursive descent—Chapter 5) is most attractive when the compiler is written entirely by hand; the other (shift-reduce parsing—Chapter 6) demands the use of a parser generator. We favor having students in an introductory course write the entire compiler by hand because we believe it gives them a better understanding of the tasks involved. Our experience has been that use of a parser generator does *not* reduce the amount of time spent on the compiler in this course. The student must learn the principles of shift-reduce parser generation in order to be able to deal with errors reported by the generator, as well as learning the input language of the generator itself. Finally, the source grammar must be cast in the proper form and debugged via repeated generator runs. This whole process takes about the same amount of time as learning the principles of recursive descent and coding the parser by hand.

Every reader of this book should have had prior experience with programming in a block-structured high-level language such as Pascal, C, PL/1, or some variant of ALGOL. Many of our algorithms are described in Pascal, and most of the specific examples of translations involve subsets of Pascal. These examples should be understandable to anyone familiar with block-structured languages, but readers with only FORTRAN or BASIC experience may find some of the important concepts foreign.

Our choice of Pascal as a vehicle for describing the compiler's algorithms was determined by its ubiquity in undergraduate computing curricula. We believe it is better to use a familiar language that is widely taught and used for programming exercises than to move to a more modern language such as Modula-2 or Ada, or a systems implementation language such as C. This choice has disadvantages, however, because Pascal is not well-suited to programs of the complexity of a compiler. The major problem is that ISO Standard Pascal does not provide support for decomposing a program into separately-compiled modules. Although we do present the compiler design in terms of a modular decomposition and define interfaces for all of the modules we discuss, we are hampered by the lack of private types that results from Pascal's bias toward monolithic programs. For example, a module cannot make a pointer type available to its clients without making every type used in the data structure accessed by that pointer type visible. This means that if a change is made to any data type accessible from the pointer, every module that uses the pointer must be recompiled. In order to separate the compiler's modules, therefore, we will sometimes use integers where pointers might be more appropriate. One particularly annoying Pascal limitation is in error reporting: We cannot supply a literal character string as a parameter to the error reporting procedure without requiring that all such strings have the same length! Thus, instead of the string, we supply an integer error number that represents the string, and we include the string itself as a comment.

We think that it is important to use a real computer as the target machine in an introductory compiler construction course. Digital Equipment Corporation's VAX architecture is representative of the "general register" class of machines and is widely available in instructional computing facilities. It is relatively free of uninteresting asymmetries, thus simplifying the explanation of code generation. Our experience has been that it is not possible to compare and contrast compilation techniques for several distinct architectures (e.g., general register and single accumulator) in a class at this level. The students become confused and lose track of the important principles in a welter of conflicting details. Thus we have tried to identify the principles and to illustrate them in the context of a single machine. Again, exercises and references to the literature are used to broaden the reader's view and to show how the principles apply to other architectures.

We use this book as a text in a one-semester undergraduate course with a project orientation, covering all but Chapter 6 in the 15 weeks available. (Chapter 6 is omitted because our students write their parser by hand, and we believe that more depth in code generation is preferable to a broader treatment of parsing.) A course given in a 10-week quarter should cover only Chapters 1 through 7, omitting either Chapter 5 or Chapter 6, depending upon the parsing technique to be used. This suggestion has the disadvantage that the relationship between source languages and target machines—one of the general topics best explored in the context of compiler construction—will not be covered. Nevertheless, it provides a coherent treatment of the issues involved in making human-readable text understandable to a computer by creating an annotated internal data structure.

A project for this course should concentrate on the methods by which translation is carried out; it should not require the students to invent the relationships on which that translation is based. Thus, the instructor should define the source language, the structure of the source and target program trees, and the relationship between them. Students can then use these ideas as a basis for designing compilers for other languages and machines. The Appendix contains documentation that forms the basis for a typical project, and a sequence of assignments that constitute the project itself. Such a project improves one's understanding of design methodology as it applies in practice, and provides an opportunity for sharpening programming skills on a piece of software of reasonable size.

Contents

Chapter 1 The Characteristics of a Compiler 1
    1.1 Structuring 4
          1.1.1 Lexical Analysis 5
          1.1.2 Syntactic Analysis 6
    1.2 Translation 6
          1.2.1 Semantic Analysis 8
          1.2.2 Transformation 11
    1.3 Encoding 11
          1.3.1 Code Generation 11
          1.3.2 Assembly 12
    1.4 Summary 13
    Notes 14
    References 15

Chapter 2 The Compiler's Interface 16
    2.1 Modularity 17
    2.2 The Source Module 20
          2.2.1 The Source Text Input Problem 20
          2.2.2 Source Module Interface Specification 22

- **2.3** The Error Module 23
  - **2.3.1** The Error Reporting Problem 23
  - **2.3.2** Error Module Interface Specification 24
- **2.4** The External Value Module 26
  - **2.4.1** The External Value Management Problem 26
  - **2.4.2** External Value Module Interface Specification 28
- **2.5** Summary 33
  - Notes 34
  - References 35
  - Exercises 36

Chapter 3 Lexical Analysis 38

- **3.1** The Lexical Analysis Module 39
- **3.2** Scanning the Source Text for Basic Symbols 41
  - **3.2.1** Syntax Diagrams and Finite-State Machines 42
  - **3.2.2** Regular Expressions 48
  - **3.2.3** How to Implement a Scanner 51
- **3.3** Converting Denotations and Identifiers 56
  - **3.3.1** Denotations 58
  - **3.3.2** Identifiers 59
- **3.4** Summary 61
  - Notes 62
  - References 63
  - Exercises 64

Chapter 4 Syntactic Analysis 69

- **4.1** How to Construct a Tree 70
  - **4.1.1** Representing a Tree 70
  - **4.1.2** Building a Tree 75
- **4.2** How to Specify the Parsing Task 79
  - **4.2.1** Activity Sequences 80
  - **4.2.2** Syntax Diagrams 81
  - **4.2.3** Extended Regular Expressions 87
  - **4.2.4** Context-Free Grammars 90
- **4.3** Operator Precedence and Association 92
- **4.4** Syntactic Error Recovery 98
  - **4.4.1** A General Error Recovery Strategy 99
  - **4.4.2** Implementing the General Strategy 100
- **4.5** Summary 104
  - Notes 105
  - References 107
  - Exercises 107

Chapter 5   Recursive Descent Parsing 110

    5.1   Left Recursion   *111*
    5.2   Decision Making   *115*
    5.3   Error Recovery in a Recursive Descent Parser   *121*
        5.3.1   How to Specify Continuations   *122*
        5.3.2   How to Find an Anchor   *123*
        5.3.3   How to Introduce Generated Symbols   *126*
    5.4   Summary   *133*
            Notes   *134*
            References   *134*
            Exercises   *135*

Chapter 6   Shift-Reduce Parsing 139

    6.1   How to Construct a Shift-Reduce Parser   *140*
    6.2   Shift-Reduce Parser Generators   *145*
    6.3   Error Recovery in a Shift-Reduce Parser   *150*
        6.3.1   How to Specify Continuations   *150*
        6.3.2   How to Find an Anchor   *151*
        6.3.3   How to Introduce Generated Symbols   *152*
    6.4   Summary   *154*
            Notes   *154*
            References   *154*
            Exercises   *155*

Chapter 7   Managing Contextual Information 157

    7.1   How to Gather Contextual Information   *160*
        7.1.1   Computation of Values   *163*
        7.1.2   Tree Traversal   *166*
        7.1.3   Information Storage   *170*
    7.2   The Definition Table   *172*
        7.2.1   The Definition Table Interface   *173*
        7.2.2   Definition Table Design Criteria   *177*
        7.2.3   Implementing the Definition Table Module   *178*
    7.3   The Cost of Gathering Contextual Information   *181*
        7.3.1   A Simple Implementation of the Environment Module   *182*
        7.3.2   A Second Implementation of the Environment Module   *185*
    7.4   Summary   *190*
            Notes   *191*
            References   *193*
            Exercises   *194*

Chapter 8 Types and Data Mapping 198

- 8.1 How to Represent Pascal Data on the VAX *199*
  - 8.1.1 Simple Types *200*
  - 8.1.2 Structured Types *201*
  - 8.1.3 Parameters and Variables *204*
- 8.2 The Compiler's Type System *207*
- 8.3 Type Declarations and Storage Allocation *210*
  - 8.3.1 The Storage Module *210*
  - 8.3.2 Visit Sequence Design *216*
- 8.4 Summary *221*
- Notes *222*
- References *223*
- Exercises *224*

Chapter 9 Action Mapping and the Target Program Tree 228

- 9.1 The Target Program Tree *230*
  - 9.1.1 Resource Allocation Decisions *231*
  - 9.1.2 Instruction Selection Decisions *233*
  - 9.1.3 Execution-Order Decisions *236*
- 9.2 How to Construct a Target Program Tree *241*
  - 9.2.1 Statement Mapping *243*
  - 9.2.2 Expression Mapping *247*
  - 9.2.3 Identifier Mapping *249*
- 9.3 Case Studies in Target Program Tree Design *251*
  - 9.3.1 Array Indexing *251*
  - 9.3.2 Count-Controlled Iteration *256*
  - 9.3.3 Expressions with Alternatives *260*
- 9.4 Summary *262*
- Notes *264*
- References *265*
- Exercises *265*

Chapter 10 Operator Identification 268

- 10.1 Overload Resolution *269*
  - 10.1.1 How to Characterize an Operator *270*
  - 10.1.2 How to Obtain a Consistent Labeling *272*
  - 10.1.3 How to Use the Operator Identification Module *276*
- 10.2 Action Mapping and Operator Identification *282*
  - 10.2.1 How to Interpret an Operator *284*
  - 10.2.2 Jump Cascades *287*
  - 10.2.3 Voiding *291*

- **10.3** Implementing the Operator Identification Computations *295*
  - 10.3.1 The Computation Algorithms *295*
  - 10.3.2 The Underlying Data Structure *299*
- **10.4** Summary *300*
- Notes *301*
- References *302*
- Exercises *302*

Chapter 11 Code Generation *306*

- **11.1** Operand Evaluation Order *307*
  - 11.1.1 Determining the Evaluation Order *308*
  - 11.1.2 Determining the Register Requirements *311*
  - 11.1.3 Determining Operand Classes During Tree Construction *314*
- **11.2** Resource Allocation *320*
  - 11.2.1 Computations for Resource Allocation *321*
  - 11.2.2 Resource Allocation Traversal Strategy *322*
  - 11.2.3 Storage Used During Resource Allocation *324*
- **11.3** Instruction Selection *328*
  - 11.3.1 Rationale for the Assembly Module Interface *328*
  - 11.3.2 How to Select and Encode Instructions *330*
  - 11.3.3 Control Sections *333*
- **11.4** Summary *336*
- Notes *337*
- References *338*
- Exercises *339*

Appendix *343*

Collected Bibliography *379*

Index *385*

1
The Characteristics of a Compiler

A compiler is a program that accepts algorithms described in a given *source language* and produces equivalent algorithms in a given *target language*. The source language is usually one suitable for humans to read and write, while the target language is usually one suitable for controlling the actions of a computer. "Equivalence" refers to the input/output behavior of the algorithm, not the actual method of execution: Source and target algorithms are considered equivalent if they produce equivalent outputs when given equivalent inputs.

BASIC, FORTRAN, and Pascal are typical source languages. Probably you have used at least one of these languages in previous computer courses and are familiar with its general characteristics. Figure 1.1 shows a fragment of a source program written in Pascal. (Declarations of the integer variables m, n, q, and r have been omitted.) The fragment implements Euclid's algorithm for integer division. This algorithm counts the number of times that n can be subtracted from m before the result becomes negative. The count is the quotient of the division. Note that, since the **while** loop pre-tests its exit condition, Figure 1.1 will correctly determine that the quotient of 2 divided by 3 is 0 and the remainder is 2.

Most compilers use the instruction set of some machine as their target language. (Our examples in this book assume that the compiler's target is the Digital Equipment Corporation VAX series.) Your familiarity with machine instruction sets is probably less extensive than your familiarity with typical source

(* $m \geq 0$ and $n > 0$ *)
$q := 0$; $r := m$;
while $r >= n$ **do begin** $r := r - n$; $q := q + 1$ **end**;
(* q = quotient of m/n and r = remainder from m/n *)

Figure 1.1
An algorithm for integer division

languages, so we shall explain their characteristics at the appropriate time. For the moment it is sufficient to know that the VAX has a memory that we can think of as being organized into 32-bit "longwords," each capable of storing one integer. These longwords are operated on by instructions such as CLRL (which sets all of the bits of its operand to 0). Instructions are normally executed in sequence, just like the statements of the source language, but it is possible to break this sequence by transferring to some arbitrary instruction. Figure 1.2 illustrates these points with a possible translation of Figure 1.1. (The comments in Figure 1.2 are for your benefit in reading the example; they would *not* be inserted by a real compiler!)

The compiler might go through the following steps to translate Figure 1.1 into Figure 1.2:

1. Determine the structure of the source program and verify that the source program satisfied the rules of the source language.
2. Transform the structure of the source program to the structure of an equivalent target program, assigning target machine memory locations to source program variables.
3. Decide how to represent intermediate results generated by the target program and select instructions to implement the target program's operations.
4. Output the target program in a form suitable for execution.

```
            CLRL   q        ; (CLeaR q)                              q:=0;
            MOVL   m,r      ; (MOVe m to r)                          r:=m;
            BR     test     ; (BRanch to test)                       while r >= n do
  body:     SUBL2  n,r      ; (SUBtract n from r)                    begin r:=r-n;
            INCL   q        ; (INCrement q)                          q:=q+1 end;
  test:     CMPL   r,n      ; (CoMPare r to n)
            BGEQ   body     ; (Branch to body if Greater or EQual)
```

Figure 1.2
A VAX Translation of Figure 1.1

This general model of compilation describes the behavior of essentially every compiler that exists in the world today. Only the degree of optimization—the cost-reducing transformations of the target program—leads to fundamental differences among them. Minor differences arise from the data structures used to represent the source and target programs, and from whether these representations are physical or conceptual. In many cases, for example, it is not necessary to actually build an internal representation of the source program. Even the target program can be created piecemeal, with no complete internal representation. We believe that the important issues in compiler construction are easier to explain if we assume that the compiler builds explicit internal representations for the source and target programs. Therefore, we shall make that assumption in this book.

The remaining sections of this chapter discuss the components of the compilation model we will use. Our intent here is to give you the big picture, so that you can see how the various pieces we discuss in later chapters fit together. Because a compiler is a relatively large and complex program, you are likely to have difficulty grasping the entire structure on a first reading. Plan to review this chapter often as you read the remainder of the book, in order to fit your newly acquired understanding of various modules into the overall framework shown in Table 1.1.

Table 1.1 outlines the structure of a compiler that makes no attempt to optimize by restructuring the target program. Even without restructuring the target program, however, the compiler can generate respectable code for most source programs.

TABLE 1.1 COMPILER TASKS

Structuring	Lexical analysis	Scanning Conversion
	Syntactic analysis	Parsing Tree construction
Translation	Semantic analysis	Name analysis Type analysis
	Transformation	Data mapping Action mapping
Encoding	Code generation	Execution-order determination Register allocation Instruction selection
	Assembly	Internal address resolution External address resolution Instruction encoding

1.1 STRUCTURING

Structuring accepts the sequence of characters that constitutes the source program and builds a tree that represents it internally. Each node of the tree represents some construct of the language and the children of that node represent the components of that construct. Leaves of the tree represent *basic symbols*—components of the source program that are not further decomposed. Figure 1.3 shows the effect of the structuring task on the **while** statement of Figure 1.1.

A particular structure is chosen so that the meaning of each construct is built up from the meanings of its components. According to the definition of Pascal, for example, the effect of **while** $r >= n$ **do begin** $\cdots$ **end** is that of executing **begin** $\cdots$ **end** until $r >= n$ becomes false. If $r >= n$ is false initially, then **begin** $\cdots$ **end** is not executed at all. A tree is a data structure that embodies a "component" relation: The children of a node represent the components of their parent. Thus constructing a tree is an appropriate way for the compiler to capture the structure of a source program. The tree shown in Figure 1.3c enables the compiler to obtain the components $r >= n$ and **begin** $\cdots$ **end** of the **while** statement and their components in turn.

Language constructs are represented by fragments of the tree consisting of a node and its children. The root node of Figure 1.3c, together with its two children, is a tree fragment representing a Pascal **while** statement. Each of the node names represents a unique source language concept. A Pascal **while** statement is an example of a "statement"—a construct that does not deliver an explicit value but may affect the state of the memory—and therefore the tree fragment is rooted in a *Statement* node. The condition of a **while** statement is an example of an "expression," which is a construct that yields a value, and the controlled statement is another statement. Thus the fragment consisting of the root of Figure 1.3c and its two children defines the structure of Figure 1.3a in terms of the expression $r >= n$ and the statement **begin** $\cdots$ **end**.

Figure 1.3c shows three distinct Pascal constructs that implement the Pascal concept of an expression. One consists of an operator and two operands (e.g., $q + 1$), another is a reference to an identifier (e.g., q), and the third is a reference to an integer (e.g., 1). Each of these constructs yields a value; they differ only in the way that the value is obtained: the operator is applied to the values yielded by its operands to yield a new value, the value described by the identifier is fetched from memory (if the identifier was declared as a variable) or simply delivered (if the identifier was declared as a constant), and the expression that is a reference to an integer yields that integer as its value.

Three distinct Pascal constructs that implement the Pascal concept of a statement are also illustrated in Figure 1.3c. We have already discussed the **while** statement; the other two constructs are the assignment statement (e.g., $r := r - n$) and the compound statement (**begin** $\cdots$ **end**). A compound statement differs from the other constructs mentioned here in that its child is a sequence of arbitrary length.

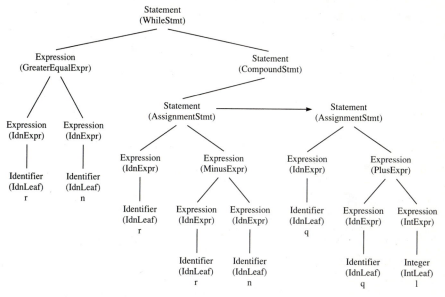

(a) Characters of the **while** statment of Figure 1.1

(b) Division of (a) into basic symbols by the lexical analyzer

(c) The source program tree built by the syntactic analyzer from (b)

Figure 1.3
Structuring

1.1.1 Lexical Analysis

The first step in structuring a source program is the lexical analysis, which accepts a sequence of characters and yields a sequence of basic symbols. Figure 1.3b shows the division of the character sequence of Figure 1.3a into basic symbols. A Pascal lexical analyzer would therefore accept the sequence of 39 characters (including spaces) shown in Figure 1.3a and yield the sequence of 19 basic symbols shown in Figure 1.3b. Illegal characters, such as an occurrence of # outside of a quoted string in Pascal, and ill-formed constants such as .05 (Pascal requires digits both before and after a decimal point) would be reported during lexical analysis.

Lexical analysis can be broken into two subtasks as shown in Table 1.1. The scanner groups characters of the text into basic symbols, ignoring comments and superfluous spaces. It verifies that the basic symbols adhere to the rules of the source language and issues error reports when violations are detected. Each basic symbol is classified by the scanner. This classification is the basic symbol's "part of speech." (Just as a natural language has nouns, verbs, and conjunctions, a programming language has identifiers, plus operators, and semicolons.)

For some basic symbols (such as := or **begin**) the classification is the only information of interest. The scanner can deal completely with such basic symbols. Additional information beyond the classification is needed for other basic symbols (such as identifiers and integers). For example, it is not sufficient in Figure 1.3b to know that the second basic symbol of the sequence is an identifier. The compiler must also know *which* identifier it is. When the scanner classifies a sequence of characters as an identifier, it passes that character sequence to the conversion subtask of the lexical analyzer. The conversion subtask generates the additional information needed to determine which identifier the basic symbol represents. (Character sequences representing literal constants such as 1, 2.3, or 'a' are also passed by the scanner to the conversion subtask.) It is the internal representations generated by the conversion subtask that actually appear at the leaves of the source program tree shown in Figure 1.3c, not the basic symbol's character string.

We cover lexical analysis in detail in Chapter 3.

1.1.2 Syntactic Analysis

The syntactic analyzer accepts the sequence of basic symbols delivered by the lexical analyzer and builds the source program tree. It copies the information attached to constant and identifier basic symbols onto the leaves of the tree as shown in Figure 1.3c, and identifies each interior node by the construct it represents. (Thus the compiler can examine the root node of Figure 1.3c and determine that it represents a **while** statement.) Errors that corrupt the structure of the program, such as unbalanced parentheses, are reported by the syntactic analyzer.

"Parsing" is the subtask that groups the sequence of basic symbols according to the source language structure rules. Whenever the parser has collected a complete construct, it invokes the appropriate operation of the tree construction task to build the subtree that represents the construct. The parser recovers from all syntactic errors and guarantees that the tree constructed during syntactic analysis always represents a legal structure. (If errors are detected, this legal structure may not reflect the programmer's intent.) Since the structure is legal, the compiler can continue in an effort to find semantic errors.

Chapter 4 gives the general properties of syntactic analyzers, and Chapters 5 and 6 present two specific parsing algorithms.

1.2 TRANSLATION

The translator converts the source program, which is an algorithm stated in terms of source language concepts, into an equivalent algorithm stated in terms of target language concepts. For example, the Pascal concepts of "subtraction" and "addition" used in the program of Figure 1.1 are replaced by the VAX concepts of "longword subtraction" and "longword addition" used in Figure 1.2. In carrying out this conversion, the translator is concerned only with the relationship between the source language and the target language, not with the way in which the target language concepts might be realized as machine instructions. Thus it is the translator that decides to convert the subtraction $r := r - n$ (Figure 1.1) into a VAX longword subtraction, but it is the encoder that decides to implement that longword subtraction with a SUBL2 instruction (Figure 1.2). Similarly, the translator converts the addition $q := q + 1$ into a VAX longword addition and the encoder implements that longword addition with an INCL instruction.

Because the translator defers decisions about the implementation of target language to the encoder, it must create a representation of the program that embodies exactly the decisions it has made and provides enough information for the encoder to make the decisions that it has deferred. Table 1.1 shows that in our compiler model the translator defers some decisions about execution order, allocation of target machine registers, and selection of instructions to implement target language operations. The data structure that it uses to describe the target algorithm is a tree. Figure 1.4 shows the translation of our Pascal **while** statement into a target program tree for the VAX.

A *Datum* node represents a VAX construct delivering a value that will be used directly as an operand by some other VAX construct. The translator decides how the values delivered by the *DatumLeaf* constructs will be represented and defers the decision about how values delivered by other *Datum* constructs will be represented. Figure 1.4b indicates that the translator has chosen to represent n by a memory location whose address is 16 bytes lower than the address contained in the VAX frame pointer register FP ("$-16(FP)$" in VAX MACRO assembly code notation), and has chosen to represent the constant 1 by a value stored in the instruction stream ("#1"). The structure of the tree shows the relationships between the constructs that produce values and those that consume them: A value is produced by a child and consumed by the parent. Thus the value produced by subtracting the content of $-16(FP)$ from the content of $-24(FP)$ is used as the first operand of the *MovL* construct that alters the content of $-24(FP)$.

The encoder determines the execution order of the children of a node. Thus, for example, the encoder would decide whether the left child of the *SubL* node in Figure 1.4b would be evaluated before the right child, or vice versa. (The subtrees in Figure 1.4b are so simple that the encoder really has no choice for the execution order in this case.)

Item nodes represent VAX constructs that do not deliver values to be used by other constructs. Figure 1.4b is the sequence of *Item* nodes that describes the algorithm. This sequence is determined by the translator and cannot be altered by the encoder.

Note that the correspondence is relatively close between the trees of Figure 1.4a and Figure 1.4b. This similarity between the trees indicates that the translation will be relatively simple; translation complexity increases as the trees become more dissimilar.

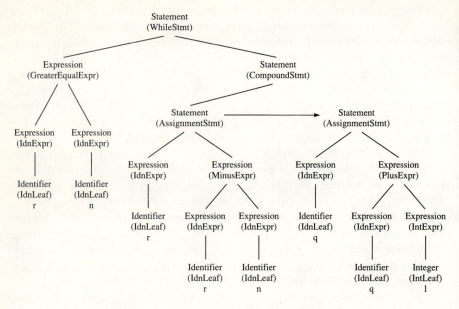

(a) The source program structure from Figure 1.3c

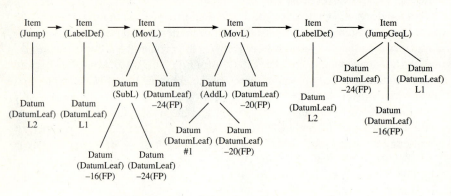

(b) The structure of an equivalent target program

Figure 1.4
Translation

1.2.1 Semantic Analysis

The purpose of the semantic analyzer is to obtain information that is available at certain places in the program (such as identifier declarations) and transport that information to other places in the program (such as identifier uses). It operates on the tree delivered by the structuring task, which defines the source program's structure and has additional information attached to the leaves. Semantic analysis uses this structure and additional information to create a data base called the "definition table." It also attaches information to the nodes of the structure tree in the same way that information was attached to the leaves by the structuring task. The result of semantic analysis is thus a "decorated" structure tree and a definition table. Errors that depend upon contextual information, such as undefined identifiers and operators applied to operands of the wrong type, are reported by the semantic analyzer.

Table 1.1 divides semantic analysis into two subtasks, name analysis and type analysis, that have somewhat different properties. Name analysis associates uses of identifiers with their definitions, according to the structure of the program and the visibility (scope) rules of the language. For example, in Figure 1.5a name analysis would associate the identifier *a* in the first *writeln* call with the parameter of function *f*, and the identifier *a* in the second *writeln* call with the program's integer variable. Identifiers that cannot be associated with any definition are reported as undefined during name analysis. Also, if the visibility rules of the language prohibit multiple definitions of the same identifier in some context, then violations of this constraint are reported by the name analyzer.

Type analysis is responsible for determining the type yielded by each expression and for verifying type consistency. For example, Pascal requires that the argument of the function *round* be an expression that yields a result of type *real*. Therefore in Figure 1.5, the type analyzer must determine the type yielded by the expression $a + 1$ and verify that it is consistent with the use of that expression as an argument to *round*. To do this, it must build on the results of name analysis.

The name analyzer establishes an entry in the definition table data base for each definition and attaches the key for the appropriate definition to each identifier leaf of the source program tree. In Figure 1.5, for example, the name analyzer would establish an entry in the definition table for *f*'s argument. The entry would specify an object that was a value parameter of type *real*, and the entry's key would be attached to the leaf for *a* in $a + 1$ (see Figure 1.5b).

Name analysis is covered in Chapter 7.

Type analysis uses the keys stored in the leaves to access the definition table, from which it can determine the type of object represented by those leaves. Based upon this information, the type analyzer computes the type yielded by each name and expression, attaching an indication of that type to the corresponding node in the tree. In Figure 1.5b, the identifier *a* represents a value parameter of type *real*. Therefore the type analyzer attaches the type *real* to the *expression* node.

An expression that yields the constant value 1 clearly yields an integer. Pascal has three operations (integer addition, real addition, and set union) that are denoted by the operator +. Since one of the operands of this expression yields type *real* and the other yields type *integer*, + must denote real addition and the type yielded by the entire expression must be *real*.

Chapter 8 introduces the compiler's type model and shows how type structure is analyzed. In Chapter 10 we present a very general method for determining the type of value yielded by an expression.

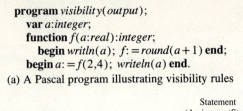

(a) A Pascal program illustrating visibility rules

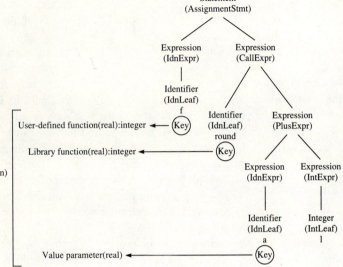

(b) Results of name analysis for $f := round(a+1)$

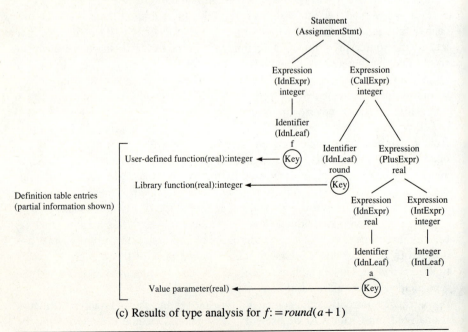

(c) Results of type analysis for $f := round(a+1)$

Figure 1.5
Semantic analysis in Pascal

1.2.2 Transformation

The transformation process builds the target program tree on the basis of the information contained in the source program tree (as decorated during semantic analysis) and the definition table. Information is attached to each leaf, and every node is identified by the construct that it represents. Transformation is generally not carried out if there have been any errors reported by the structuring or semantic analysis tasks.

Data mapping (Table 1.1) is the subtask of transformation that determines how each source data type is to be represented on the target machine. It examines the source program type definitions, lays out composite objects such as records, and enters the results into the definition table. This information will eventually appear at leaves of the target program tree. For example, in Figure 1.4b most of the values attached to the *DatumLeaf* leaves result from mapping the program's variables onto a sequence of contiguous memory locations. (Each value is the offset of the corresponding variable from the top of the memory area.) Data mapping is discussed in detail in Chapter 8.

The actual tree construction is carried out by the action mapping subtask. For each node of the source program tree, the action mapper builds a (possibly empty) subtree of the target program tree. The choice of a particular target subtree is determined by the identity of the source program tree node, the decorations attached to that node and its children, and any relevant information in the definition table. Some of the constructions are quite simple and others are relatively complex. All share the property that they depend only upon local information. Any contextual information needed has been gathered by the semantic analysis and data mapping tasks and either attached to the appropriate node or placed in the definition table under a key that is attached to the appropriate node.

The action mapping task is covered in Chapter 9.

1.3 ENCODING

The target program tree produced by the transformation task defines each target program construct in terms of its components. Encoding determines the order in which the constructs will be executed (subject to the constraints embodied in the tree), allocates machine resources to hold intermediate results, and selects the instructions to carry out the specified operations on the specified resources. It results in a program that is acceptable to the control unit of the target computer. Errors involving target machine memory limitations will be reported during encoding.

1.3.1 Code Generation

Starting with the undecorated target program tree, the code generator constructs an abstract program that is analogous to a program written in symbolic assembly language: the instruction sequence is determined, the operands of each instruction are determined, and the layout of data in memory is determined. Instruction addresses are named, but their values are unknown, and the instructions are not coded by the bit patterns that the target machine needs. Without loss of generality, you may consider the result of code generation to *be* a symbolic assembly code program, although the compiler may not implement it as such. Thus the task of the code generator can be thought of as the task of transforming the tree of Figure 1.4b into the program of Figure 1.2.

Item sequences represent components whose execution order has been determined by the translator. For example, the encoder must ensure that the *Item* sequence of Figure 1.4b is encoded in order from left to right. On the other hand, the operands of *SubL* in Figure 1.4b could be evaluated in either order. Some choices of execution order may require fewer intermediate results than others. Thus the execution-order determination subtask of code generation (Table 1.1) attempts to choose a "good" sequence and decorates the target program tree with information that specifies its choice.

The register allocation subtask attempts to provide machine registers for intermediate results. By using machine registers the compiler both shortens the code and speeds its execution. (No instructions are needed to store results in memory and later retrieve them.) A register allocator must take into account both the number and characteristics of the target machine registers and the characteristics of the intermediate results. It decides upon a machine resource (register, stack, or memory) for every operand and attaches its choice to the appropriate operand node of the target program tree.

Once the target program tree has been decorated with execution-order and resource allocation information, the instruction selection subtask decides upon an encoding for each node. This encoding, like the construction of the target program tree itself, depends only on local information. For example, consider the *Datum* node in Figure 1.4b that describes the *AddL* construct. The register allocation subtask would have decorated the top node with $-20(FP)$, since that is the destination of the assignment. The right child would have been decorated with $-20(FP)$ also, because that is the proper form of access to memory location $-20(FP)$. Finally, the left child would have been decorated with #1—the representation of a literal 1. Since the result and right operand are identical, and the left operand is a constant 1, *AddL* can be implemented by the longword increment instruction INCL operating on the right operand $-20(FP)$.

Code generation is examined in Chapter 11.

1.3.2 Assembly

The assembly task of a compiler carries out essentially the same task as a symbolic assembler (in fact, many compilers simply produce symbolic assembly code and then use the symbolic assembler). It accepts the abstract program created by the code generator, encodes each instruction, determines the value of each address, and creates an executable image. Errors involving code size or addressability will be reported by the assembly task.

The internal address resolution subtask is responsible for determining the size of the code and assigning values to all addresses. On many computers the sizes of certain instructions depend upon how far away their operands are. Internal address resolution usually begins by assuming that all such instructions will take their shortest forms. If some must be lengthened, then certain addresses must be changed and the process iterated.

External address resolution is concerned with linking together separately compiled modules. This subtask is usually carried out by a separate program called a "link editor" or "loader." The compiler prepares for external address resolution by distinguishing certain labels as being "global." Some of the global labels may be defined in the program being compiled and intended to be used elsewhere, while others may be used in the program being compiled but defined elsewhere. *Sqrt* is a typical global label in Pascal programs.

When the size of an instruction depends on how far away its operands are, it must have a different encoding for each size so that the computer's control unit can determine the operand lengths. Since the size of an instruction is determined by the assembly task, there is no way that the code generator could select the proper instruction encoding. Thus the code generator's instruction *selection* subtask will choose a "generic" abstract instruction. Then the assembler's instruction *encoding* subtask will encode that generic abstract instruction properly, depending upon the distance to its operand. The instruction encoding task works on strictly local information, examining only the abstract instruction specified by the code generator and the operands supplied either by the code generator or the internal address resolution subtask of the assembler.

We shall not discuss the assembly task in this book. Assembly is relatively straightforward, but highly machine-dependent. Moreover, the techniques used in assembly are not widely applicable to other tasks. Section 11.3 defines an interface to the assembly module that can be used by the code generator. This interface is sufficiently general that the module can be implemented as a simple symbolic assembly output routine, a relocatable assembler that produces code for subsequent linking and loading, or an absolute assembler that produces executable images directly.

1.4 SUMMARY

A compiler translates a source program into an equivalent target program. This task can be logically decomposed into fourteen subtasks (Table 1.1) related to properties of the source and target languages. The decomposition is a very general one, describing any compiler that does not attempt to transform the target program structure. In any particular compiler, some of the subtasks may be trivial.

The compiler maintains three major data structures: the source program tree, the definition table, and the target program tree. Under some circumstances it may not be necessary to build physical representations of one or the other (or both) of the trees. Generally speaking, however, the compiler design is simplified if both trees are explicitly constructed. (Explicit trees make it easier to separate the subtasks from one another and to retain the information necessary to carry them out.) The definition table is a data base in which information about the source and target language objects is stored. It must always have a physical realization.

NOTES

The compiler-writer's notion of algorithm equivalence can be defined precisely in terms of the diagram shown in Figure 1.6a [4]. It can be applied to the integer division algorithm of Figure 1.1 as shown in Figure 1.6b. The source program, S, transforms some data, D, into some result, R. For the integer division problem, the source program would transform the data (100,75) into the results (1,25). There is a mapping, M, between source language objects and target language objects; D' is an image of D and R' is an image of R under this mapping. Target language objects are 32-bit bit patterns on the VAX, so the image of the data (100,75) under the normal mapping from integers to 32-bit bit patterns is (1100100,1001011) (leading zero bits have been omitted). Similarly, the image of the results (1,25) under this mapping is (1,11001). A target program, T, is equivalent to S if, for all allowable values of D, R' can be obtained *either* by executing S and mapping the result *or* by mapping the data and executing T. Here the target program is given by Figure 1.2. Constraints are placed upon the set of allowable values both by the source program and the mapping. The constraints $m \geqslant 0$ and $n > 0$ are due to the source program, whereas the constraints $m,n < 2^{31}$ are due to the mapping.

In this book we assume that the compiler's target language is the language of some general-purpose computer. Another possibility is to invent an imaginary "abstract machine" that provides the same data types and operations as the source

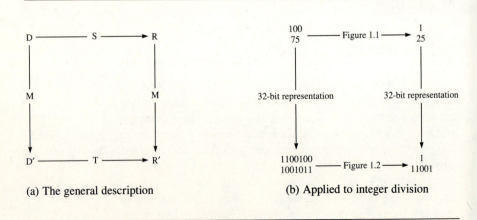

Figure 1.6
Equivalence

language, but whose control structures are chosen for more efficient interpretation. An abstract machine is usually considered when the real target machine is a poor match for the source language. UCSD Pascal for the Intel 8080 used this approach. The only arithmetic provided by the hardware of the 8080 is 8-bit addition and subtraction, which is certainly a poor match for the requirements of Pascal! The target language of the UCSD compiler, called "P-code," was the instruction set of an abstract stack machine that provided exactly the data types and operations Pascal requires [1]. A P-code program was assembled into a byte string and executed by an interpreter running on the 8080. Techniques for coding such interpreters can be found in papers by Bell [2] and Dewar [3].

REFERENCES

1. Ammann, U., Nori, K. V., Jenses, K., Jacobi, C., and Nägeli, H. H., "The Pascal-P Compiler: Implementation Notes," Bericht 10, Eidgenössische Technische Hochschule, Zurich, July 1976.
2. Bell, J. R., "Threaded Code," *Comm. of the ACM 16,* 6 (June 1973), 370–372.
3. Dewar, R. B. K., "Indirect Threaded Code," *Comm. of the ACM 18,* 6 (June 1975), 330–331.
4. McCarthy, J., "Towards a Mathematical Theory of Computation," in *Information Processing 1962,* North-Holland, Amsterdam, 1963, 21–28.

2
The Compiler's Interface

A compiler interacts with its environment in three ways:
- It reads the text of the source program.
- It writes reports about the source program and the compilation process.
- It writes the text of the target program.

The implementation details are not specific to compilation, and may vary widely with the particular environment in which the compiler is embedded. In addition, the compiler must manipulate values defined in the source program and represented in the target program. For example, an integer constant appearing in the source program must be retained by the compiler and introduced into the generated target program, perhaps after being combined with other values. Correct implementation of operations on these "external values" is important but, like the implementation of environment interaction, is not specific to the compilation problem. This chapter shows how it is possible to separate the concerns of compilation from the concerns of providing an environment and operating on external values.

We begin by reviewing the concept of *modularity*, a general structuring method for complex programs. Using this structuring method, we then describe how the compiler can obtain source program text, produce error reports, and manipulate external values. Discussion of how the compiler produces the target program text is deferred until Chapter 11 because it is rather complex and must be motivated by the requirements of code generation.

2.1 MODULARITY

We manage complexity in programming by "modular decomposition": A given problem is decomposed into smaller problems, which are then solved independently of one another. When the solutions of the component problems are available, the original problem is solved by combining those solutions. For example, Table 1.1 divided the compilation problem into structuring, translation, and encoding. These three smaller problems can be solved independently of one another, once the characteristics of the data structures they operate upon have been fixed. Thus, the structuring problem can be solved once the forms of the source text and source tree have been decided upon, and the translation problem can be solved once the forms of the source tree and the target tree have been decided upon.

The solution to each component problem is embodied in a *module*. A module is a collection of routines and data objects that has two properties:

1. You must be able to convince yourself of the correctness of a module, without considering the context of its use in building larger units of software.
2. You must be able to conveniently combine modules into a larger unit without knowledge of their inner workings.

Thus a modular decomposition of the compiler construction problem involves building three major modules, each of which is a collection of routines and data objects. One module reads the source program and constructs a source tree, the second decorates the source tree and then uses its structure and decorations to construct a target tree, while the third decorates the target tree and then uses its structure and decorations to construct the target program.

Each of the three modules satisfies the two properties stated above. You can, for example, convince yourself of the correctness of the translation module without considering how the source tree is constructed and how the target tree is used. This correctness is not affected by whether it is, in fact, embedded in a compiler at all! Thus the translation module satisfies property (1) above. Similarly, you could combine the translation module with a structuring module that reads input from a keyboard, or with one that accepts source programs from a bar-code scanner. There is no need to be concerned about the inner workings of the translation module when combining it with a source module, so property (2) is satisfied as well.

A module will satisfy properties (1) and (2) if, and only if, it adheres to an appropriate *interface specification*. The interface specification (or simply "interface") defines the behavior of the module. It acts as a contract between the implementor and the user. The program using the module (often called a *client* of the module) has access only to the facilities described in the interface; it has no further information about the inner workings of the module. The module's implementor, on the other hand, may make no assumption about the clients' behavior unless that assumption is explicit in the interface specification.

The separation of concerns obtained from a modular decomposition exacts a performance penalty. To reduce the cost of invoking an operation, a programmer needs as much information as possible about both the use and the implementation of that operation—the very antithesis of the interface specification! One criterion in the selection of a modular decomposition is therefore that the operations of a module should "pay for themselves" in the sense that the invocation cost should be a small fraction of the total cost of the operation.

Figure 2.1a shows an interface specification for a simple module that we will use throughout this book. It allows the compiler to manage arbitrary-length strings of characters efficiently: Using the data type defined in Figure 2.1a, strings can be read, written, and passed between modules without being copied, unless a copy is absolutely necessary. Let's examine the components of this interface specification.

One constant, two types and two procedures are defined by Figure 2.1a. We say that the character pool module *exports* these entities because it defines them and makes them available to its clients. Modules may export constants, types, variables, functions, or procedures. Exported constants may be used by any client, but not altered by either the clients or the module exporting them. Exported variables may be used and altered by any client or by the module exporting them. Exported functions or procedures may be invoked by any client or by the module exporting them.

The character pool module has an "internal state" that keeps track of the character buffers currently allocated. Figure 2.1a's *PoolInit* is an *initialization* operation that establishes a consistent initial internal state. *PoolSpace* assumes that the internal state of the module is consistent, so clients must guarantee that *PoolInit* is invoked prior to the first invocation of *PoolSpace*.

Some modules also require a *finalization* operation. The purpose of a finalization operation is to obtain any residual information from the module's internal state, and/or to recover resources used by the module to implement its internal state. The error module (Section 2.3) has a finalization operation.

A data type exported by a module is *public* if the module exports that data type's representation; it is *private* if the representation is not exported. (Pascal provides only public data types, but Modula-2 and Ada support private data types.) Even though a compiler for standard Pascal cannot enforce the privacy of a data type's representation, the concept of a private data type is an important design tool. We shall therefore discuss that concept here, and introduce it into a Pascal program by means of commentary.

CharPool is a public data type of the character pool module. Clients can use any operations of a public data type's representation to manipulate objects of that public data type. Thus a client of the character pool module can use integer

```
const
  BufferSize = 512;

type
  CharPool = ↑CharacterBuffer;        (* General string storage mechanism *)
  CharacterBuffer = record
    n: 0..BufferSize;                 (* Number of characters stored in this buffer *)
    s: packed array                   (* s[1..n] = stored characters *)
      [1..BufferSize] of char
    end;

procedure PoolSpace(var buf: CharPool; len: integer);
  (* Allocate character storage dynamically
    On entry-
      len = number of character positions desired
    On exit-
      buf↑.s[buf↑.n+1..buf↑.n+len] are free character positions
    A deadly error will be reported if len > BufferSize
      or if the requested storage is unavailable
  *)

procedure PoolInit;
  (* Initialize the dynamic storage allocation module *)
```

(a) Interface specification

```
var p: CharPool; i,length: integer;
...
PoolSpace(p,length);                      (* Make sure enough space is available *)
for i:=1 to length do p↑.s[n+i]:= ···;    (* Build the string *)
if not Find(p,p↑.n+1,length) then         (* We need to keep the string *)
  p↑.n:= p↑.n+length;                     (* Claim the string's space *)
```

(b) Sample client code that relies on the interface specification

Figure 2.1
Character pool module

operations to change the value of $buf\uparrow.n$ and can apply character operations to $buf\uparrow.s[i]$. For example, suppose that a string is to be constructed and entered into a table if, and only if, it is not already in that table (Figure 2.1b). The client would first use *PoolSpace* to make storage available for the constructed string, then construct the string and pass it to a table lookup routine (*Find* in Figure 2.1b). Note that the string is passed to the routine without being copied. Finally, if the table lookup routine indicated that the string was not already in the table, the client would retain the string by increasing the count of occupied positions in the character pool. (Presumably the table lookup routine has incorporated the string into the table by storing *Find*'s arguments in the table's data structure.) If the string was already in the table, then there would be no need to retain the characters added to the pool, so the client would not advance the character count.

According to the interface specification of Figure 2.1a, this means that those positions would remain free.

Public data types allow modules to communicate by expressing information in terms of representations understood by both. Those representations might be available because they are defined by the implementation language (as in the case of *CharPool*) or because both communicating modules are clients of the module providing the representation.

Private data types allow a module to manage a set of objects while hiding the implementation of those objects. A module must export operations to create, transform, and extract information from objects of its private data types. No other modules can implement operations to provide these services, because the implementation of the data type is not visible. A client can declare variables of a private type, perform assignments to those variables, compare two objects of the private type for equality, and pass objects of the private type to procedures. If assignment and comparison for equality are not permitted, the private type is *limited* (in Ada terminology). Objects of a limited private type can still be passed to procedures as **var** parameters, so it is possible to update declared variables.

The primary consideration when deciding between making a type public and making it private is information hiding: Must the object carry additional data not obvious to the clients? Are there several ways to represent the object, and is the choice likely to change? If either question can be answered in the affirmative, a private type should be used. A secondary consideration in the public/private decision is performance. We could implement any public data type exported by a module as a private type by exporting a sufficient number of additional operations from the module. Providing simple creation and access operations as procedures exported by a module slows down the program, however, because of the added time spent in procedure calls. What is less obvious is that the *size* of the program is often increased, as well. Setting up a parameter value usually involves storing it in memory, with essentially the same instructions that would be required to store that value directly into the data object.

2.2 THE SOURCE MODULE

As with any programming task, the first step in designing a module interface specification is to understand the subproblem that the module is to solve. Such understanding must encompass not only the logical aspects, but also the likely performance bottlenecks. (Unfortunately, programmers seem almost universally incapable of *predicting* performance bottlenecks; the latter understanding must come from experience with similar problems or actual measurements.) Once the problem has been understood, that understanding is encapsulated in the interface specification for the module that solves the problem.

2.2.1 The Source Text Input Problem

The subproblem that must be solved by the source module is to make the sequence of characters that constitutes the source program available to the scanner subtask of lexical analysis. This character sequence will be examined by the scanner, which will classify contiguous subsequences as basic symbols. Chapter 3 shows that the scanner is simplified if its input is stored in contiguous array elements. Unfortunately, it is usually impractical to allocate an array large enough to hold an entire program.

The source module interface could be designed to deliver a single character. If possible, a longer unit of text should be chosen, however, because the cost of invoking an operation that delivers a character will be a significant fraction of the total cost of that operation. Thus the operation will not "pay for itself" in the sense discussed in Section 2.1. Whether a longer unit of text is feasible depends upon both the definition of the source language and the milieu in which the compiler operates.

According to the definition of Pascal, basic symbols can be classified as special symbols (e.g., :=), identifiers, directives (e.g., forward), unsigned numbers, labels, and character strings. Comments, spaces (except those appearing inside character strings), and the separation of consecutive lines are defined as "token separators." A token separator can never occur *within* a basic symbol. Therefore, a Pascal basic symbol can never start on one line and end on another; would it be feasible to use the line as the unit of text delivered by the source module?

If the source module were to deliver a line, the implementation of that module would place a bound on the maximum line length. The definition of Pascal does not limit the length of a line, so such a bound would mean that the compiler does not conform to the source language. Because machines have finite memory, however, it is inevitable that the compiler will impose constraints that are not part of the language definition. A compiler designer should try to arrange the bounds on internal data structures in such a way that they do not constrain "normal" programs. In other words, decisions on bounds depend upon the milieu in which the compiler operates.

Humans prepare source text using line-oriented devices with relatively short (say, up to 136 character) line lengths. Therefore, if the compiler will be used to process text prepared by humans, a bound of several hundred on the line length is unlikely to constrain "normal" programs. In our case the bound would be *BufferSize* (Figure 2.1a), the maximum length of a contiguous sequence of characters. *BufferSize* is usually related to the size of a system text buffer and typically has values between 512 and 8192.

A compiler may be called upon to process text that is *not* produced by a human. It is quite common to implement an experimental language by building a pre-processor for some available compiler. For example, the RATFOR (RATional FORtran) compiler is really a pre-processor whose output is a subset of FORTRAN. Since there is no need for humans to examine a pre-processor's output, there is no need for the pre-processor to divide that output into lines for display purposes. A pre-processor that did not divide its output into lines of reasonable length would certainly be constrained by a limit placed on the line length by the compiler. We will assume, however, that our compiler is processing text produced by humans.

2.2.2 Source Module Interface Specification

Figure 2.2 shows an interface specification for a source module that embodies the understanding of "obtain source text" summarized in the last section. The module makes available three data objects (*Line*, *LinePtr*, and *LineLng*) and two operations (*SourceLine* and *SourceInit*) to its clients. *SourceLine* delivers a line by setting the data objects appropriately.

The interface specification allows several different implementations of *SourceLine*: Each invocation might result in a line being physically read from the source file into a fixed part of the character buffer. Alternatively, the first invocation might result in many lines being read into the character buffer, with successive invocations simply readjusting *LinePtr* and *LineLng* to specify the next line. Only when the information was exhausted would another physical read be necessary. It might even be that different character buffers are used for successive lines! Thus the client module must regard the values of *Line*, *LinePtr*, and *LineLng* following an invocation of *SourceLine* as being completely new and unrelated to any previous values of these variables.

A free character position is guaranteed at the end of the line by the interface specification "$Line\uparrow.s[LinePtr+LineLng]$ has an unspecified value." This is the character position that would be occupied by the line terminator in ASCII text, and its initial content is determined by the source module implementation. As pointed out in Chapter 3, it is possible to simplify the lexical analyzer by placing an appropriate "sentinel" character in this position.

---

var
  Line: *CharPool*;   (* Character pool containing the source line *)
  LinePtr,*LineLng*: integer;   (* Limits of the line in the character pool *)

function *SourceLine*: boolean;
  (* Obtain the next line of the source program
    If the source program is empty then on exit-
      SourceLine = *false*
      LineLng = 0
      $Line\uparrow.s[LinePtr]$ has an unspecified value
    Else on exit-
      SourceLine = *true*
      $Line\uparrow.s[LinePtr..LinePtr+LineLng-1]$ = next line of the source program
      $Line\uparrow.s[LinePtr+LineLng]$ has an unspecified value
  *)

procedure *SourceInit*;
  (* Initialize the source module
    On exit-
      LineLng = 0
      $Line\uparrow.s[LinePtr]$ has an unspecified value
  *)

Figure 2.2
Source module interface

SourceInit initializes the internal state of the source module, which is encoded in its exported variables. Clients of the source module must invoke *SourceInit* before accessing any of the source module's exported objects and before invoking *SourceLine* for the first time.

2.3 THE ERROR MODULE

Many different situations could be reported by a compiler, ranging from a comment on programming style to an error made by the compiler itself. Error reporting is simplified by providing a single module that accepts *any* report and is responsible for delivering that report to the user. The information making up a report must be quite uniform across the spectrum of situations that might be encountered, or the module interface will be too broad and the operations too varied for reasonable implementation.

2.3.1 The Error Reporting Problem

Violations of the rules of the source language or of the constraints imposed by the compiler may be detected during a particular compilation. Whenever such a violation is detected, the compiler must output a report of the violation and the location at which it occurred. These reports might be examined by the user directly, or a separate process might be used to merge them with a listing of the program or to focus an interactive text editor upon each report in turn. A coordinate system must therefore be provided to permit association of reports with source text positions. The simplest coordinate system makes use of the two-dimensional structure of the source text, specifying a line number and a column number.

A report's position may well not coincide with the actual position of the error that caused the report. Compilers, like medical doctors, can only detect symptoms. Consider, for example, a Pascal assignment statement in which a closing parenthesis is missing. When the compiler reaches the end of the statement, it will note the symptom "unbalanced parentheses"; there is no way for it to know *where* the missing closing parenthesis should be inserted. Thus the position at which the report appears is the position at which the symptom was detected (the end of the statement) rather than the position of the error (the place where the closing parenthesis was actually omitted) or the position of the unmatched opening parenthesis.

Reports can be classified according to the severity of the consequences for the compilation of the situation they report:

- *Information*. Reports of situations that have no consequences for compilation or execution. Examples are the number of lines in the source text or the fact that a particular variable was never used.
- *Warning*. Reports of anomalies that may cause the program's results to be erroneous. The user should be asked for confirmation before the target program is allowed to execute. Examples are detection of a constant 0 as

the right operand of **div** or the fact that a particular variable was used but not set.

- *Fatal*. Reports of errors that preclude a correct compilation. The user must change the source program and recompile it. Examples are programs with undeclared variables or unbalanced parentheses.
- *Deadly*. Reports of errors that make further processing impossible. Examples are programs that exhaust the character pool (see Figure 2.1) or trigger latent bugs in the compiler itself.

The "information" category may be further subdivided to give the user finer control over the reports that are actually output.

The classification by severity is important because it can be used to control the gross behavior of the compiler in response to reports, without requiring this behavior to be keyed to individual situations. For example, the error module can terminate execution immediately upon receipt of a deadly error report, thus preventing the compiler from crashing and possibly losing *all* of the error reports in the process. Abnormal termination is often a tricky thing to get right. By centralizing it in the error module, the compiler designer avoids the problem of ensuring the correctness of many instances.

Reports of compiler errors might not be associated with any particular source text position, but rather with some position in the code of the compiler itself. This information is implicit in the report if it is issued only by one code sequence, but certain errors may be detected at a number of points in the compiler's code. Thus it is useful to be able to associate an *issuer* with each error report. Either a source text position or an issuer, or both, could be relevant for each report.

2.3.2 Error Module Interface Specification

Figure 2.3 gives an error module interface that embodies the error reporting problem as described in Section 2.3.1. Source text coordinates are specified by a record, and report severity by an enumerated type. A running total of the number of reports at each severity level is maintained in the exported array *ErrorCount*. Other modules of the compiler can therefore make decisions based on the number of errors detected so far. For example, the translation module might decide not to transform the source tree if any fatal errors had been reported.

Report requires a position argument, even though Section 2.3.1 pointed out that some reports are not associated with a particular source text position. The error module exports a specific value, *NoPosition*, to be used as an argument to *Report* in those cases. Clearly, the particular representation of this value is a decision dependent upon the implementation of the error module itself. Therefore, that decision should be hidden. Provision of "default" or "dummy" values for objects of an exported type is quite common in module interfaces.

After logging a deadly error, *Report* terminates the compilation abnormally. This should be the *only* abnormal termination, since any other compiler component could cause an abnormal termination by reporting a deadly error. Abnor-

```
type
    position = record         (* Source text coordinates *)
        line: integer;        (* Index of the source line *)
        column: integer       (* Index of the character position *)
    end;

    severity = (              (* Classification of consequences *)
        INFO,                 (* No consequences *)
        WARNING,              (* Target program may be erroneous *)
        FATAL,                (* Source program is erroneous *)
        DEADLY);              (* Compilation cannot continue *)

var
    NoPosition: position;     (* Dummy position argument *)
    ErrorCount:               (* Number of errors detected so far *)
        array [severity] of integer;

procedure Report(s: severity; t: integer; var p: position; i: integer);
    (* Accept a report
        On entry-
            s = severity of the report
            t = number of the report text
            p = source text position (irrelevant if NoPosition)
            i = issuer (irrelevant if 0)
        If s < > DEADLY then on exit-
            The report has been added to the error log
        Else Report terminates abnormally; it does not exit
            The report is added to the error log before termination
    *)

procedure ErrorInit;
    (* Initialize the error module *)

procedure ErrorFinl;
    (* Finalize the error module *)
```

Figure 2.3
Error module interface

mal termination must be defined to include all necessary finalization operations (including that of the error module).

The error module embodies two concepts, the coordinate system for the source text and the reporting mechanism. It is fair to ask why the coordinate system is combined with the error module and not either left on its own or combined with the source module.

The coordinate system is used primarily for error reporting, so it must be available whenever errors can be detected—during the entire compilation—but the source module need be available only to the structuring task. Thus the coordinate system and source text have different visibilities and should not be combined in a single module.

The coordinate system has the same lifetime as the reporting mechanism and forms an integral part of it. No information about the coordinate system can be concealed from the reporting mechanism, and hence no separation of concerns is possible by placing them in separate modules. Thus the coordinate system should not be left on its own.

2.4 THE EXTERNAL VALUE MODULE

Literal constant values appearing in the source program must be retained and possibly manipulated during compilation. These values are "external" in the sense that they do not properly belong to the universe of values defined by the language in which the compiler is written: The source program literals belong to the source language's universe, while the corresponding target program values belong to the target language's universe. Thus we must accept the fact that management of these values may be significantly more complex than management of internal values. Moreover, the complexity does not involve compiler construction issues, but rather issues in numerical analysis and character manipulation.

2.4.1 The External Value Management Problem

Any external value can be described by an integer, a floating-point number or a character string. Although each of these classes is theoretically infinite, they will be bounded in a particular implementation. The bounds must reflect the properties of the source language and the target machine, not the limitations of the compiler implementation language. Thus the external value module interface must allow for arbitrarily large integers, floating-point values with arbitrary range and precision, and character strings of arbitrary length.

Simple computations involving external objects are necessary to analyze the source program and create the target program. For example, consider the following Pascal type constructor:

$$\textbf{array } [LowerBound..UpperBound] \textbf{ of } ElementType \qquad (2\text{-}1)$$

Here *LowerBound* and *UpperBound* are constants that define external values. Pascal requires that the value of *LowerBound* not exceed the value of *UpperBound*. Therefore the compiler must be able to compare the external values defined by *LowerBound* and *UpperBound* in order to verify that the program is correct. Moreover, in order to determine the size of a value of the constructed array type, the compiler must evaluate the expression *UpperBound* − *LowerBound* + 1 to obtain the number of elements.

The range of external integer values must normally exceed the range of target machine integers. Suppose that the compiler translates Pascal to the machine code of a computer with a byte-addressable memory, 16-bit addresses, a two-byte representation of integers, and a 4-byte representation of reals. (The DEC PDP-11 is an example of such a computer, as is the Intel 8086 when single data objects must reside within a single segment.) If *LowerBound* = −5000, *UpperBound* =

5000, and *ElementType* = *real* in type constructor (1) above, then the resulting array has 10001 elements and occupies 40004 bytes. This declaration is perfectly legal, and the declared array fits comfortably within the postulated 65536-byte memory of the target machine. However, the array size cannot be computed by the compiler using the target machine's signed integer arithmetic because *maxint* = 32767 for a two-byte representation of integers.

Decimal (radix 10) representation is used for numbers in most source programs, and binary (radix 2) representation is used internally by most computers. Thus most numeric values must be converted from radix 10 to radix 2 when a program is translated. Integer values can always be converted from one radix to another without loss of information, but this is not true for floating-point values. Consider the decimal value 0.1, for example. If we try to express this value as a binary number, the result requires an infinite number of bits:

$$0.000\ 1100\ 1100\ 1100\ 1100...$$

Since only a finite number of bits can be stored, information will be lost when 0.1 is converted to binary. Unnecessary information loss can be avoided by representing an external floating-point value in the source program radix and carrying out any computations on the value in that radix.

A non-zero floating-point value is completely characterized by four pieces of information: the sign of the value, the radix B of the representation, a fraction f in the range $1/B \leq f < 1$ expressed as a sequence of radix B digits, and a signed integer exponent e. The value characterized is $v = \pm f \times B^e$. Thus the decimal value 12.34 is completely characterized by a positive sign, the radix 10, the sequence of decimal digits 1234 and the signed integer exponent $+2$. In other words, $12.34 = +.1234 \times 10^{+2}$. Note that this characterization is unique; each value v can be characterized in exactly one way. Normal programming language notation is not unique. For example `1.234E1` and `1234E-2` both represent the same value as `12.34` in a Pascal program.

The information needed to characterize a floating-point value must be deduced from the representation of that value in the source program. Usually the radix is understood to be 10. Some programming languages allow use of a different radix, signaling this by a modified number format. For example, `8#1.7#` expresses a radix-8 value in Ada. Here the radix (which must be at least 2 and at most 16) precedes the first # character. The sequence of radix-8 digits is delimited by the two # characters. If desired, an explicit exponent may follow the second # character; a zero value is assumed when no explicit exponent is given. The signed integer exponent of the floating-point value is determined from the explicit exponent and the position of a point that may be embedded in the sequence of radix digits. (When no explicit point is given, one is assumed to follow the last digit.) Several examples of the relationship between source program representations and floating-point values were given above.

Storage must be provided for external values. Two possibilities for allocating this storage exist: the storage may be provided by clients of the external value module, or the external value module may provide the storage. It is advantageous for clients to provide storage because they know the lifetimes of the external values they manipulate. For example, if a client will use an external value only locally, it can store that value in a local variable. If the external value module provides storage, however, then either the client must invoke a special operation to signify that the value is no longer needed, or the external value module must retain the value forever.

A large number of integer external values will normally be created during a compilation. Many of these values, like the values used in the array size calculation above, will have short lifetimes. Storage for integer external values should therefore be provided by the clients of the external value module. On the other hand, only a few string external values will be created while compiling common programming languages. Most of these values will represent source program string constants that must be inserted unchanged into the target program and therefore have long lifetimes. Little would be gained by having clients provide storage for the text of these strings.

The statistics for floating-point values are much harder to predict without detailed knowledge of the compiler and of the application. FORTRAN compilers must cope with many external floating-point values in a scientific environment, whereas C compilers used in a systems programming environment deal with only a few. If the compiler attempts to evaluate floating-point expressions containing only constants, then it will generate additional floating-point values with short lifetimes; otherwise the values will be source program constants to be inserted into the target program, and therefore have long lifetimes.

There are a number of situations in which the compiler will need an external value but be unable to obtain one. For example, suppose the programmer forgets to declare the identifier *LowerBound* in a type constructor like (1). In order to continue the compilation, the compiler must supply a "harmless" value for *LowerBound*. Any valid external value will *not* be harmless in certain contexts. (If the compiler supplied the value "0", and the value of *UpperBound* was "−10", then a puzzling error would be reported to the user.) Thus it is necessary to have a distinguished external value that can be used in all such circumstances and recognized as representing "unknown."

2.4.2 External Value Module Interface Specification

External values are represented by the data structure defined in Figure 2.4. The exported constants are determined by the specific implementation of Pascal's *integer* and *char* data types and by the range of external integer values to be represented. They thus characterize the relationship between the universe of implementation language (in this case, Pascal) values and the universe of external values. Notice that this interface specification gives enough information to determine the storage requirements of an *ExtValue* and to check what kind of value a particular *ExtValue* represents, but it does *not* define the details of how the external values are encoded. All that can be inferred about the encoding is that integers are encoded in some multiple-precision form and character strings are used to encode both floating-point numbers and external strings.

2.4 THE EXTERNAL VALUE MODULE

```
const
    ExtIntegerSize = 2;                         (* Size of an external integer *)
    MaxRadix = 256;                             (* Largest allowable radix *)

type
    ExtType = (                                 (* External value types *)
        ExtInteger,                             (* Integer *)
        ExtFloating,                            (* Floating point *)
        ExtString,                              (* String *)
        ExtUnknown);                            (* Unknown value *)

    ExtValue = record                           (* Description of an external value *)
        case t: ExtType of
            ExtInteger:
                (a: array [1..ExtIntegerSize] of integer);
            ExtFloating, ExtString:
                (v: CharPool;
                 p,l: integer);                 (* v↑.s[p..p+l−1] = data *)
            ExtUnknown:
                ();
    end;
```

Figure 2.4
External value representation

Clients of the external value module can provide storage for *ExtValue* objects, because the storage requirements are visible at the interface. An integer external value is completely represented by an *ExtValue* object. Therefore the storage for integer external objects is allocated completely by the clients, in accordance with the pattern of integer value usage mentioned at the end of Section 2.4.1. Floating-point and string values, on the other hand, are represented by a combination of an *ExtValue* and some character pool storage. The external value module must allocate the character pool storage because the interface does not specify the encoding of the information stored in the character pool.

Because the actual encoding of the external values is hidden from the clients, the external value module must provide encoding and decoding operations. These operations must also allocate appropriate character pool storage for floating-point and string values. The implementor of the external value module may choose to allocate new character pool storage for every floating-point or string value, or to allocate new storage only when the value being encoded differs from all values currently stored. This choice is completely hidden by the encoding and decoding operations, and therefore is no concern of this book. Figure 2.5 gives the interface specification for the encoding and decoding operations of the external value module.

An integer can always be represented as a sequence of digits with a certain radix. For example, an integer constant might appear in the source program as a

function *ExtCodeDigit*(**var** *extval*: *ExtValue*; *digit,radix*: *integer*): *boolean*;
(* Compute *extval*: = *extval* × *radix* + *digit*
  On entry-
    extval is a valid external integer value and $0 \leqslant digit < radix \leqslant MaxRadix$
  If *extval* × *radix* + *digit* is representable then on exit-
    ExtCodeDigit = *true* and *extval* has been updated
  Else on exit-
    ExtCodeDigit = *false* and *extval* is unchanged
*)

function *ExtDecodeDigit*(**var** *extval*: *ExtValue*; **var** *digit*: *integer*; *radix*: *integer*): *boolean*;
(* Compute *digit*: = *extval* **mod** *radix* and *extval*: = *extval* **div** *radix*
  On entry-
    extval is a valid external integer value and $0 < radix \leqslant MaxRadix$
  On exit-
    digit: = *extval* **mod** *radix*
    If *extval* $\geqslant$ *radix* then *ExtDecodeDigit* = *true* and *extval*: = *extval* **div** *radix*
    Else *ExtDecodeDigit* = *false* and *extval* is unchanged
*)

procedure *ExtCodeFloat*(**var** *extval*: *ExtValue*; *v*: *CharPool*; *p,l,radix*: *integer*);
(* Create a floating-point external value
  On entry-
    $v\uparrow .s[p..p+l-1]$ = number to be converted (see text for format)
    radix = radix of $v\uparrow .s[p..p+l-1]$
    $2 \leqslant radix \leqslant 16$
  On exit-
    extval is the corresponding external value
    $v\uparrow .s[p..p+l-1]$ is not referenced by *extval*
*)

procedure *ExtDecodeFloat*(**var** *extval*: *ExtValue*; **var** *v*: *CharPool*; **var** *p,l,radix*: *integer*);
(* Access an external floating-point value
  On entry-
    extval is a valid external floating point value
  On exit-
    $v\uparrow .s[p..p+l-1]$ = number represented by *extval* (see text for format)
    radix = radix of $v\uparrow .s[p..p+l-1]$
    $2 \leqslant radix \leqslant 16$
*)

procedure *ExtCodeString*(**var** *extval*: *ExtValue*; *v*: *CharPool*; *l*: *integer*);
(* Create an external string value
  On entry-
    $v\uparrow .s[v\uparrow .n+1..v\uparrow .n+l]$ = characters of the string
  On exit-
    extval is the corresponding external value
    The state of character pool *v* is undefined
*)

Figure 2.5
Encoding and decoding external values

sequence of decimal (radix 10) digits and need to be inserted into the target program as a sequence of bytes (radix 256 digits). Conversion to and from the external representation is really a radix conversion. The operations *ExtCodeDigit* and *ExtDecodeDigit* perform radix conversion one digit at a time, hiding the radix used by the external representation.

ExtCodeFloat and *ExtDecodeFloat* convert floating point constants between the notations commonly used in programming languages and a unique characterization suitable for arithmetic computation. Most programming languages agree on the notation for representing digit sequences and explicit exponents, although they use a variety of characters as exponent markers. Notation for defining a non-decimal radix varies widely among the languages providing this facility, but there is general agreement that the radix will not exceed 16.

The amount of code specific to each compiler is minimized by allowing clients of the external value module to define floating-point values as triples (radix, digit sequence, optional exponent). The radix is given as an implementation language integer; the digit sequence and optional exponent are given as a single sequence of characters in a character pool. Digits are represented by the characters 0-9 and A-F (either upper- or lower-case). A sign may be prefixed to the digit sequence and a "." may precede any digit or follow the last digit. If the optional exponent is present, it is separated from the digit sequence by "," and consists of an optional sign followed by a sequence of decimal digits. Here are several sample representations of the floating-point value $+.1625 \times 10^{+1}$ using these conventions:

radix 8:	1.5
radix 10:	16250,-4
radix 16:	+.01a,2

An external string value is represented simply by a sequence of characters in a character pool. There is no reason not to allow clients of the external value module to access that character sequence directly, and hence no decoding operation is exported for character strings. Why, then, do we provide an encoding operation? The reason is to hide a particular design decision: whether to store multiple copies of a string.

As discussed in Section 2.4.1, the external value module will provide storage for string values because they have long lifetimes. In some applications, particular string literals will appear over and over in a source program. Thus considerable space could be saved if only one copy of each of these literals were stored. In most applications, however, string literals do not appear repeatedly and the time required to check whether a given literal has appeared before would be wasted.

The decision about string storage policy affects only the *ExtCodeString* operation of Figure 2.5. When only one copy of any string is to be stored, *ExtCodeString* must check whether its argument has already been stored. If so, then it builds an external value that refers to the previously stored copy. Otherwise, it increases the count of occupied positions in the character pool and builds an external value that refers to this new copy. When multiple copies of a string may be stored, *ExtCodeString* does not need to make any tests. It simply increases the count of occupied positions in the character pool and builds the external value. Note that no useless work is done, regardless of the decision.

The client of the external value module places character strings into a character pool before invoking the appropriate encoding operation. However, the interface specifies that the client must *not* retain those character positions by increasing the count of occupied positions in the character pool. (Recall the discussion about retaining characters in the example of Figure 2.1b.) According to the interface specification, the count of occupied characters indicates the start of the relevant information. Moreover, the interface specification asserts that the state of the character pool is undefined on exit from the encoding operation; thus the client can assume nothing about the value of $vt.n$. This allows the external value module to decide whether to claim the character positions currently holding the value, or to use a previously stored representation and allow those character positions to be overwritten.

Figure 2.6 shows the computations provided by the external value module. These operations may or may not be applicable to both integer and floating-point values, depending upon the operation and the implementation of the module. A Pascal compiler must be able to negate both kinds of values in order to process constant declarations, but the remaining operations are needed only for integers. If an operation is applied to an inappropriate value, the module signals a deadly error.

All of the computations in Figure 2.6 are *strict*, with the "bottom" element being an external value of type *ExtUnknown*. This means that if any argument is an external value of type *ExtUnknown*, then the result will also be an external value of type *ExtUnknown*. The computations yield *false* if, and only if, neither operand is of type *ExtUnknown* and the result is unrepresentable. The comparisons yield *false* if either operand is of type *ExtUnknown*.

The external value module also provides some often-used external values, as shown in Figure 2.6. These values are established by *ExtInit*, which would also be responsible for setting up the initial state of any lookup mechanism being used to avoid storing duplicate values.

The definitions of all of the operations listed in Figure 2.5 are independent of both the source language and the target machine. Since the external value module is implemented on a computer, it limits the range of integer and floating-point values that can be represented. In a particular implementation, however, these limits are set so that any computation the compiler might do is valid. Thus, for example, the computation $maxint - (-maxint)$ will be carried out correctly. It is the responsibility of the client to check that values resulting from a computation are valid for the particular source language and target machine and to report appropriate errors. Clients should not *initiate* computations with invalid values. If the limitations of the external value module are exceeded, it will signal a deadly error.

var
  IntegerZero: *ExtValue*;   (* 0 *)
  IntegerOne: *ExtValue*;   (* 1 *)
  FloatingZero: *ExtValue*;   (* 0.0 *)
  NullString: *ExtValue*;   (* Empty string *)
  NoExtValue: *ExtValue*;   (* Invalid external value *)

function *ExtNegate*(**var** *val*: *ExtValue*): *boolean*;
  (* Compute *val*: = − *val*, returning *true* if the result is representable *)

function *ExtAdd*(**var** *v1,v2*: *ExtValue*): *boolean*;
  (* Compute *v1*: = *v1* + *v2*, returning *true* if the result is representable *)

function *ExtSub*(**var** *v1,v2*: *ExtValue*): *boolean*;
  (* Compute *v1*: = *v1* − *v2*, returning *true* if the result is representable *)

function *ExtMpy*(**var** *v1,v2*: *ExtValue*): *boolean*;
  (* Compute *v1*: = *v1* × *v2*, returning *true* if the result is representable *)

function *ExtDiv*(**var** *v1,v2*: *ExtValue*): *boolean*;
  (* Compute *v1*: = *v1* **div** *v2*, returning *true* if the result is representable *)

function *ExtMod*(**var** *v1,v2*: *ExtValue*): *boolean*;
  (* Compute *v1*: = *v1* **mod** *v2*, returning *true* if the result is representable *)

function *ExtLess*(**var** *v1,v2*: *ExtValue*): *boolean*;
  (* Compute *v1* < *v2* *)

function *ExtEqual*(**var** *v1,v2*: *ExtValue*): *boolean*;
  (* Compute *v1* = *v2* *)

procedure *ExtInit*;
  (* Initialize the external value module *)

Figure 2.6
External value computations

2.5 SUMMARY

We attack the implementation of a compiler by dividing the problem into subproblems and assigning each major task and data structure to a module. Modules export operations and data objects to their clients. The behavior of these operations and objects is completely defined by an interface specification. By regarding the interface specification as a binding contract between the implementor and the user of a module, we can provide information hiding and separation of concerns.

Concerns of reading source programs, printing error reports, and manipulating external values are separated from those of compilation by defining source, error, and external value modules. Modules carrying out these tasks represent concepts that are independent of the central issues of compiler construction, and their implementations are ignored in this book.

NOTES

Modularity was recognized early as a mechanism for controlling complexity in programming [3, 5]. The basic criterion for choosing a particular decomposition was to assign a module to each design decision considered difficult or likely to change [11]. Interface specifications were developed to ensure that the design decisions embodied by a module were indeed invisible to that module's clients [12]. Some languages (such as Ada [1] and Modula-2 [14]) incorporate explicit modules, but most do not.

Techniques for implementing programs in a modular fashion regardless of the language are known [6], so this structuring mechanism should be available to everyone. The key is to design using interface specifications, to incorporate these specifications into the code as comments, and to use whatever means are provided for separating name spaces. Documentation must be very detailed in this situation. Otherwise, the modular decomposition will be destroyed during maintenance: The maintainer will simply not understand the program's structure, and will therefore violate that structure when making changes.

We should emphasize that the module interfaces defined in this chapter are independent of the particular environment in which the compiler is embedded. The source, error, and external value modules could be profitably used by *any* compiler written in Pascal. If the implementation language were changed from Pascal to something else, minor adjustments to the interfaces would probably be needed to accommodate the different data types provided by the new implementation language.

Our classification of error severity differs from that of some existing compilers, particularly in the response to warnings. For many compilers, a "warning" message elicits the response we propose for information messages: The target program is executed without requiring any additional action on the part of the user. We believe that it is important to identify a class of anomalies that require user approval before the program is run, but do not require correction. Such anomalies might lead to an incorrect program that could corrupt valuable data files if it were executed; on the other hand they might be perfectly innocuous.

No radix conversion is involved in our floating-point encoding and decoding operations. This is an important point if symbolic assembly code is being produced, because conversion from decimal to binary and back to decimal cannot generally be carried out without loss of information [9, 10]. Real number conversion is a very tricky and interesting business, but it is not really in the mainstream of compiler construction issues. The principles are illustrated by an exhaustive analysis of input/output conversion [4] using the IEEE Floating-Point Standard [7] as an internal representation.

Implementation of the character pool, source, and error modules is straightforward, given the material presented in most elementary programming courses and courses on data structures; the external value module may require some additional background. You can find an exhaustive treatment of multiple-precision integer arithmetic and basic floating-point operations in Volume 2 of *The Art of Computer Programming* [8].

A poorly implemented source module can cause serious performance penalties for a compiler. In one instance, character-oriented Standard Pascal I/O operations were used to implement the source module of a Pascal compiler running on a VAX/780. When they were replaced by a module using VAX System Service routines to obtain full lines, the *entire compilation* sped up by a factor of 10. Even when using system routines, care should be taken to avoid moving the characters in the course of obtaining them from the I/O device and making them available to the compiler [13].

Performance is not an issue for the error module. Even assuming that most compilations result in error reports, the number of reports is small compared to the length of the program. The source code for the P4 compiler [2] occupies 4338 lines, with about 6 basic symbols per line. If there were an average of one error every 10 lines (a rather high error density) then the ratio of basic symbols to error reports would be about 60:1. Even if the cost of processing a report were ten times the cost of processing a basic symbol (which it is not), the total compilation time would only be degraded by about 17%.

REFERENCES

1. "Ada Programming Language," ANSI/MIL-STD-1815A, American National Standards Institute, New York, NY, Feb. 1983.
2. Ammann, U., "The Method of Structured Programming Applied to the Development of a Compiler," in *Proc. of the International Computing Symp. 1973*, North-Holland, Amsterdam, 1974, 94–99.
3. T. O. Barnett, ed., *Modular Programming: Proceedings of a National Symposium, Symposium Preprint,* Information and Systems Press, Cambridge, MA, 1968.
4. Coonen, J. T., Contributions to a Proposed Standard for Binary Floating-Point Arithmetic," Ph.D Thesis, Univ. of California, Berkeley, 1984.
5. Dennis, J. B., Modularity," in *Advanced Course on Software Engineering,* vol. 81, F. L. Bauer (editor), Springer Verlag, Heidelberg, 1973, 128–182.
6. Goos, G. and Kastens, U., "Programming Languages and the Design of Modular Programs," in *Constructing Quality Software,* P. Hibbard and S. Schuman (editor), North-Holland, Amsterdam, 1977, 153–186.
7. "Binary Floating Point Arithmetic," ANSI/IEEE Std. 754–1985, IEEE, New York, NY, 1985.
8. Knuth, D. E., *Seminumerical Algorithms,* Addison Wesley, New York, 1969.
9. Matula, D. W., "In-and-Out Conversions," *Comm. of the ACM II,* 1 (Jan. 1968). 47–50.
10. Matula, D. W., "Base Conversion Mappings," *AFIPS Conf. Proc. 30* (1967), 311–318.
11. Parnas, D. L., "On the Criteria to be Used in Decomposing Systems Into Modules," *Comm. of the ACM 15,* 12 (Dec. 1972), 1053–1058.

12. Parnas, D. L., "A Technique for Software Module Specification with Examples," *Comm. of the ACM 15, 5* (May 1972), 330–336.
13. Waite, W. M., "The Cost of Lexical Analysis," *Software—Practice & Experience 16,* 5 (May 1986), 473–488.
14. Wirth, N., *Programming in Modula-2,* Springer Verlag, Heidelberg, 1985. Third Edition.

EXERCISES

2.1 Suppose that you are writing a module in Standard Pascal to implement a queue of strings. Each string is passed to an operation of your module for enqueuing. Another operation is provided for dequeuing. A third operation is a test for an empty queue. Assume that there is only one queue, and that the *only* access to the queue is via these operations.
   (a) Will your module need an initialization operation? Explain briefly.
   (b) Will your module need a finalization operation? Does your answer depend upon the lifetime of the queue? Explain briefly.
   (c) Define an interface for your module.
   (d) To implement your module, you will need private data. Where would its declaration appear? Explain briefly.
   (e) The behavior of the private data should be described internally by an *invariant*: a condition that is satisfied by the data objects when the program is *not* executing within an operation of the module. Such an invariant constitutes an extra interface specification for all of the operations of the module, because they may assume that it is true on entry and must re-establish its truth on exit. State an invariant for your private data.

2.2 Suppose the error module writes reports to a text file, one per line. Each line contains five integers, separated by spaces. The first two integers are the line and column number, respectively. The third integer is the ordinal of the severity, the fourth is the report number, and the last is the issuer. A second text file contains text for all of the possible reports. Each report occupies one line. The line consists of an integer report number, followed by a space, followed by the text of the report corresponding to that report number.
   (a) Decide upon a modular decomposition of a program to read the file of reports, the file of message texts, and the source program and to produce a listing of the source program with the reports interspersed with the program text. Each report should follow the line for which it was issued, with a mark indicating the character position.
   (b) Use the properties of modules stated at the beginning of Section 2.1 to show that the source module of the compiler can be used in implementing your program.
   (c) Would any of the other modules discussed in this chapter be useful for your listing program? Explain briefly.

2.3 Write a procedure that implements the following interface specification:

      function *ExtCodeInt*(**var** *extval*: *ExtValue*; *value*: *integer*): *boolean*;
        (* Convert an integer to an external value
          On entry-
            value = integer to be converted

>   If *value* is representable then on exit-
>   *ExtCodeInt* = *true* and *extval* has been updated
>   Else on exit-
>   *ExtCodeInt* = *false* and *extval* is undefined
> *)
> external;

2.4 Write a procedure that implements the following interface specification:

> **procedure** *ExtIntegerString*(**var** *p*: *CharPool*; **var** *length*: *integer*; *v*: *ExtValue*);
> (* Convert an external integer to a decimal string
>   On entry-
>   *v* = external integer to be converted
>   On exit-
> $p\uparrow.s[n+1..n+length]$ = (signed) decimal string
> *)

2.5 Write a program that reads sequences of decimal digits from successive lines of a text file, interprets each sequence as an integer, and prints the sum of those integers in binary, octal, decimal, and hexadecimal. Use the external value module to encode each value as an external integer and to accumulate their sum. Finally, modify *ExtIntegerString* (Exercise 2.4) to accept a *radix* parameter and use the modified routine to decode the sum.

2.6 Suppose that the external value module exported *no* variables (i.e., there were no **var** declarations in Figure 2.6).
   (a) Show that it would then be impossible to create any external integer values without violating the interface specification.
   (b) Would it be possible to create external floating-point values? Explain briefly.

2.7 Characterize each of the following decimal values with a sign, a fraction, and an exponent. Use the specified radix and express the fraction with as few digits as possible. If information will be lost, say so.
   (a) 10.10, using radix 10
   (b) 1.25, using radix 4
   (c) 1/3, using radix 9
   (d) 1/3, using radix 16

2.8 Redefine the interfaces for the source, error, and external modules using some language other than Pascal. Evaluate the differences (if any) between your definitions and those given in this chapter. Do you feel that your design is more satisfactory, less satisfactory, or about the same as the one given here? Briefly justify your answer.

3
Lexical Analysis

Basic symbols are the atoms of the source program, the smallest information-bearing units of its structure. A basic symbol may be represented in the text of the source program by a single character or by a character sequence. Whether a particular character is a complete basic symbol, a part of a basic symbol, or unconnected with any basic symbol depends upon its immediate context. For example, consider the following line of Pascal text:

1: **if** $a = 0$ **then** $a := b$; (*entry := default*)

The first occurrences of ":" and "=" are both individual basic symbols. The second occurrences combine to form the basic symbol ":=" and the third occurrences lie within a comment (which carries no meaning) and are therefore unconnected with any basic symbol.

The lexical analyzer accepts the text of the source program (a sequence of characters) as input and produces a sequence of basic symbols as output. It must recognize each basic symbol, extract the information borne by that basic symbol from the source text, and express it in a form appropriate for processing by the rest of the compiler. It must also skip over source text (comments and white space) that is unconnected with any basic symbol and report any invalid characters or ill-formed basic symbols.

Table 1.1 lists two major subtasks of lexical analysis:

- *Scanning*: Recognizing a sequence of characters in the source text as an instance of a particular class of basic symbol.
- *Conversion*: Obtaining the representation of the specific class member that has been recognized.

For example, the scanning subtask of a Pascal lexical analyzer might recognize the character sequence 17 as an instance of a basic symbol in the class "integer." That sequence of digits would then be passed to the conversion subtask, which would obtain the representation of the corresponding integer. Every basic symbol must be scanned, but many basic symbol classes have only one member and therefore need not be converted.

Lexical analysis is a costly process, not because it is complex, but because it must handle a much larger amount of data than most compiler processes. A typical source program has 5-10 times as many characters as basic symbols. The lexical analyzer examines every source character, while the syntactic analyzer examines only the basic symbols.

3.1 THE LEXICAL ANALYSIS MODULE

Basic symbols can be grouped on the basis of the information they carry:

- *Denotation*: A representation of a source language object. Different occurrences of the same denotation all represent the same concept. (Examples: 2, 3.14, 'string').
- *Identifier*: A name for some concept. Different occurrences of the same identifier may name different concepts. (Examples: beta, integer).
- *Delimiter*: A marker that serves to establish the structure of the source program. (Examples: begin, :=, +).

The relationship between an identifier and a concept is established by a declaration that appears in the program or in some "standard" set of declarations. Therefore the meaning of a particular occurrence of an identifier cannot be determined until the structure of the program is known. A denotation's meaning, on the other hand, is fixed by the language definition; the program's structure is irrelevant in determining the meaning of a denotation.

The information carried by each basic symbol is represented internally by a public data type of the lexical analysis module called a *Token* (Figure 3.1). Every basic symbol has a source text position for use in reporting errors, and a classification that determines its properties. Delimiters are completely defined by their classifications, whereas denotations and identifiers carry additional information.

A *Token* corresponding to a denotation specifies the value represented by that denotation as an object of the *ExtValue* data type exported by the external value module (Section 2.4).

A *Token* corresponding to an identifier specifies the particular identifier by giving a unique integer value. Since the meaning of an identifier depends upon

```
type
    SymbolClass = (              (* Classification of Pascal basic symbols *)
        EOPT,                    (* Endmarker *)
        IntegerT,                (* Integer *)
        RealT,                   (* Real Number *)
        StringT,                 (* Character string *)
        CharacterT,              (* Single character *)
        IdentifierT,             (* Identifier *)
        LeftParenT,              (* ( *)
        ...
        AndT,                    (* and *)
        ...
        WithT);                  (* with *)

    DenotId = IntegerT..IdentifierT;   (* Denotations and identifiers *)

    Token = record               (* Representation of a Pascal basic symbol *)
        coord: position;         (* Source text location (see Figure 2.3) *)
        kind: SymbolClass;       (* Basic symbol classification *)
        case DenotId of          (* Required additional information *)
        IntegerT,RealT,CharacterT,StringT:
            (val: ExtValue);     (* Value denoted (see Figure 2.4) *)
        IdentifierT:
            (idn: integer);      (* Which identifier *)
        end;

procedure Lexical(var t: Token);
    (* Build the internal representation of a basic symbol
       On exit-
           t represents the next basic symbol
    *)

procedure LexInit;
    (* Initialize the lexical analysis module *)
```

Figure 3.1
A Pascal lexical analysis module interface

the structure of the program, and the lexical analyzer understands the program only as a sequence of basic symbols, an identifier *Token* cannot carry a meaning. The best that can be done is to distinguish between different identifiers. Thus any *Token* corresponding to the identifier sam might specify the integer 13 (regardless of where it occurred), and any *Token* corresponding to the identifier pete might specify the integer 24.

The state (Section 2.1) of the lexical analysis module is embodied in several variables, as shown in Figure 3.2. *LineNumber* is initialized to 0 and incremented each time a new line is read. Whenever a new line is read, *Current* is set to index the first character of that line; it is advanced as the scanner accepts characters. *Limit* is used to index the character position after the last character of the line. Whenever a new line is obtained from the source module, *Limit* is set from the variables *LinePtr* and *LineLng* (Figure 2.2) as shown in Figure 3.2.

(* The following private objects constitute the internal state of the Lexical Analysis Module *)

const
  EndOfLineMarker = 10;   (* Set the end-of-line marker to ASCII LF *)

var
  LineNumber: *integer*;   (* Line coordinate of *Line*↑.*s*[*LinePtr*] *)
  Current: *integer*;   (* Index of the first uninspected character *)
  Limit: *integer*;   (* Index of the first character position beyond the end of the line *)
                               (* *Line*↑.*s*[*Limit*] = end-of-line marker *)

procedure *LexInit*;
  (* Initialize the lexical analysis module *)

  begin (* LexInit *)
  SourceInit;
  LineNumber: = 0; *Current*: = *LinePtr*; *Limit*: = *LinePtr* + *LineLng*;
  Line↑.*s*[*Limit*]: = *chr*(*EndOfLineMarker*);
  end; (* LexInit *)

Figure 3.2
State variables of the lexical analysis module

Unlike the variables that constitute the internal state of the source module in Figure 2.2, the state variables of Figure 3.2 are *private*; they should be accessible only within the lexical analysis module. A state variable conveys information from one invocation of a module's operation to another, and therefore a description of its behavior should form part of the interface specifications of those operations. If the state variable is private, however, it cannot form part of a contract between the user and the implementor because the user should not know about it! The solution is to provide each private state variable of a module with an *invariant* that governs its value while the locus of execution lies outside of the operations of that module. Every exported routine of a module (other than the initialization routine) may assume that the invariants of the state variables are true on entry, and every exported routine of a module (other than the finalization routine) must guarantee that the invariants of the state variables are true on exit.

The invariants on the private state variables of Figure 3.2, given by the comments associated with each variable, constitute the "private" part of the interface specification for every operation of the lexical analysis module.

3.2 SCANNING THE SOURCE TEXT FOR BASIC SYMBOLS

The purpose of a scanner is to recognize sequences of source characters as instances of basic symbols. It determines the values of the *coord* and *kind* fields of a *Token* (Figure 3.1). A scanner does *not* determine the value specified by a denotation or the integer corresponding to an identifier. Both of these items of information are obtained by converting (Section 3.3) the character sequence that the scanner has recognized. There are two reasons for separating the scanning and conversion tasks: different techniques are used in carrying them out, and the particular conversion algorithm needed depends upon the kind of basic symbol. For some basic symbols, it is necessary to complete the scanning before the conversion algorithm can be chosen.

It is relatively easy to construct scanners for trivial languages by ad hoc methods, but more formal approaches are needed as complexity increases. In the remainder of this section we present a systematic procedure that can be applied to *any* scanning problem, no matter how complex.

The procedure begins with a formal definition of the basic symbols to be recognized. A scanning algorithm can be derived mechanically from that description. Section 3.2.1 describes a graphical notation for defining basic symbols and shows how to derive a scanning algorithm by hand. A textual notation suitable for input to a scanner-generating program is given in Section 3.2.2.

Because of the amount of data a scanner must process, careful implementation of the scanning algorithm is necessary to obtain an economically viable compiler. Section 3.2.3 is therefore concerned with the details of scanner algorithm implementation. These implementation details are independent of the way in which the scanning algorithm was derived.

3.2.1 Syntax Diagrams and Finite-State Machines

You are probably familiar with *syntax diagrams* like those shown in Figure 3.3. Each syntax diagram is a graphical description of a set of character sequences. Those shown in Figure 3.3 describe the character sequences that constitute four kinds of Pascal basic symbols.

A syntax diagram describes a character sequence by giving a procedure to construct it: Each box in the diagram describes a set of characters. To construct a character sequence, start at the left end of the diagram and follow the line until you reach a box. Emit a character from the set described in the box, and follow the line leaving the box. You may turn at a junction, but you may not move along a line in a direction opposite to the arrow on that line. When you reach the right end of the diagram the construction is complete. Thus the diagram for an integer denotation could be used to construct 0 or 123 by selecting different set elements and different turnings.

To recognize a basic symbol, the scanner follows the same path through the syntax diagram that the programmer used to construct the basic symbol. Instead of *emitting* a character at each box, the scanner *accepts* one character. If the scanner reaches the right end of the diagram, all of the characters it has accepted in the process belong to the basic symbol. If it comes to a point other than the right end of the diagram and cannot make any turning that will allow it to accept the next character, then an error must be reported.

Suppose that the scanner attempted to recognize 123 according to the diagram for an integer denotation (Figure 3.3a). Starting at the left end of the diagram, the scanner would accept 1 and follow the line leaving the leftmost

3.2 SCANNING THE SOURCE TEXT FOR BASIC SYMBOLS

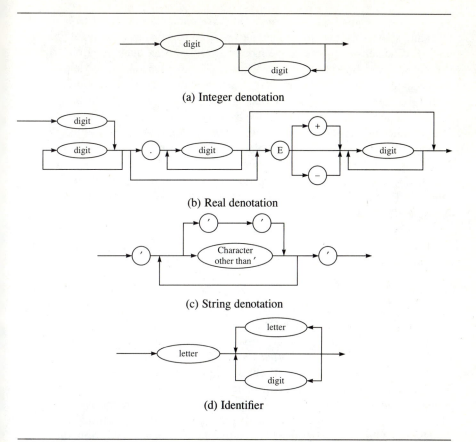

Figure 3.3
Syntax diagrams

"digit" box. It has now reached the right end of the diagram, so all of the characters it has accepted (namely 1) belong to the basic symbol. Thus the scanner has recognized the integer denotation 1—a perfectly legal integer denotation, but certainly not the one intended by the programmer in this case. Instead of asserting that the right end of the diagram had been reached, the scanner should have accepted 2 and followed the line leaving the lower "digit" box. Figure 3.3a is therefore a *nondeterministic* description of an integer denotation. The scanner can recognize 123, but only if it makes the right decision at each turning point.

In Figure 3.3a we can ensure the desired behavior by specifying that the scanner must accept as many characters as possible. Thus it does not have the option of claiming that it has "reached the right end of the diagram" until it can accept no more characters. Later in this section we shall develop a general rule for dealing with nondeterminism.

The only boxes that the syntax diagrams of Figure 3.3 contain are boxes that specify literal character sets. A simple scanning mechanism, the *finite-state machine* (also known as a *deterministic finite automaton*) can be built directly from any syntax diagram whose only boxes are boxes that specify literal character sets. In Chapter 4 we shall define more powerful syntax diagrams from which it is not possible to build finite-state machines. The diagrams discussed in Chapter 4 are capable of describing all of Pascal, whereas the diagrams we are concerned with here are not. Diagrams containing only boxes specifying literal character sets *are* capable of describing all of the basic symbols of Pascal, however.

A finite-state machine has a finite number of *states* that encode its progress through the diagram. The machine starts out in its *initial state*, which corresponds to the left end of the syntax diagram. It is then presented with characters, one at a time. At each step, the combination of a state and a character uniquely determines the output to be produced (possibly none) and the state of the machine after that step.

The behavior of a finite-state machine can be described by a matrix, called a *state table*, with one row per state and one column per character. Each element of the state table specifies the next state and the output for the given combination of current state (row) and input (column). A "state diagram" is a graphical representation of the state table. It has one node for each state. If an input will carry the machine from state i to state j, then the state diagram has an edge directed from the node for state i to the node for state j. The edge is labeled with the input and output, in the form *"input/output"* (if no output occurs on a given transition, the label is simply *"input"*).

Note that state diagrams and syntax diagrams have quite different structures. The boxes of a syntax diagram correspond to input characters, while the boxes of a state diagram correspond to individual states of a finite-state machine. Input characters label the edges of the state diagram, specifying state transitions.

Figure 3.4a gives the state table of a finite-state machine built from the syntax diagram of Figure 3.3a. All of the columns for digit characters are identical in Figure 3.4a, so only one has been shown. Similarly, the columns for all characters that are *not* digits are the same. We shall use the convention of giving only one column of each identical group throughout this book. The heading of such a column will describe the set of characters whose columns the given column represents. "Others" will always be used to describe the set of all characters not described by any of the column headings to its left. If a state table has a column labeled "Others," that column will always be the rightmost.

Each element of the state table specifies the pair (next state, output). If the second member of the pair is missing, the machine does not produce an output for that particular combination of current state and input. The initial state is 1. State 0 is a "trap state," from which the machine can never escape and in which it will produce no outputs.

Two state diagrams corresponding to Figure 3.4a are shown in Figure 3.4b. The two diagrams are equivalent, but the one on the right uses a slightly more complex notation to avoid the clutter associated with state 0. State 0's node is omitted, as are all of the edges incident upon it. By convention, if no edge leaving a node specifies a certain input, then an edge leading to state 0 and specifying that input is assumed. If the node is round, then edges leading to state 0 produce

3.2 SCANNING THE SOURCE TEXT FOR BASIC SYMBOLS

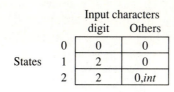

(a) State table

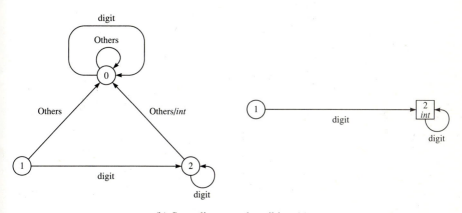

(b) State diagrams describing (a)

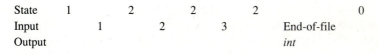

(c) Behavior of (a) for input sequence 123

Figure 3.4
Example of a finite-state machine

no output; if the node is square then edges leading to state 0 produce the output shown in the node.

The behavior of Figure 3.4a when presented with the input sequence 123 is traced in Figure 3.4c: Initially, the machine is in state 1, and the input character is 1. According to the state table, the next state will be 2 and no output will be produced. In state 2, the inputs 23 cause transitions to state 2, and again no output is produced. "End-of-file," which is always assumed to follow the last character of every input sequence, causes the machine to produce output *int* and go to state 0.

If the machine defined by Figure 3.4a is in state 1 and is presented with a character other than a digit, then it cannot make further progress through the syntax diagram. It therefore goes to state 0 without producing any output.

The machine defined by Figure 3.4a scans a character sequence and decides whether some prefix of that sequence fits the definition of a Pascal integer denotation. As soon as it makes this decision, the machine enters its trap state. If the sequence does fit the definition, the machine produces output *int*; otherwise, it produces no output. The output is a "pulse" associated with a specific transition of the machine. Therefore it not only reports the decision, but also marks the input character at which the decision was made.

The scanning problem in lexical analysis is not to recognize a *particular* basic symbol in source text, but to recognize the *next* basic symbol. This means that the scanner must implement a *set* of syntax diagrams rather than a single one. Figure 3.5 shows an example, using Pascal integer and real denotations. A label has been attached to the input of each box and to each diagram exit in Figure 3.5a to simplify the discussion.

Figure 3.5b defines a finite-state machine that implements a scanner for Figure 3.5a. It was derived from Figure 3.5a by considering the steps that such a scanner would have to carry out. The derivation process removes the nondeterminism present in Figure 3.5a, yielding a deterministic finite-state machine.

Each nonzero state, s, in a state table corresponds to a unique set of labels, S, in the syntax diagram from which it was derived. (The column to the left of the state table in Figure 3.5b gives the set of labels in the syntax diagram of Figure 3.5a to which each state corresponds.) The set of labels that corresponds to the initial state is the set of all labels that can be reached from the left end of the chart without passing through any boxes. For example, either the label a or the label d could be reached from the left end of Figure 3.5a without passing through any boxes. Therefore state 1, the initial state of the finite-state machine defined by Figure 3.5b, corresponds to the set of labels {a d}.

State s has a nonzero next state entry in the column for character c if one or more of the boxes whose labels are in S accepts c; otherwise, the next state entry for s is "0". In Figure 3.5b, state 1 has a nonzero next state entry in the "digit" column because both box a and box d accept digits. All other next-state entries are zero because a and d are the only boxes whose labels are in state 1's label set, and they accept only digits.

Let n be the nonzero next state entry for state s in the column for character c. The set of labels that corresponds to state n is then determined by finding all of the labels that can be reached from boxes accepting character c, whose labels are in S, without passing through any other boxes. In Figure 3.5b, 2 is the next state entry for state 1 in the "digit" column. Boxes a and d accept digits, and their labels are in the set of labels corresponding to state 1. Therefore the set of labels corresponding to state 2 consists of all labels that can be reached from box a or box d without passing through any other boxes.

Once the next state entries are available, the output entries can be determined. If S, the set of labels for state s, does not contain labels of any syntax diagram exits, then s will have no output entries. States 0, 1, 3, 4, and 6 of Figure 3.5b have no output entries for this reason.

3.2 SCANNING THE SOURCE TEXT FOR BASIC SYMBOLS

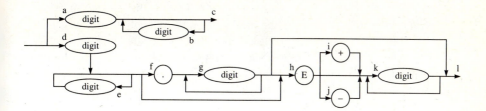

(a) Combining two syntax diagrams

		digit	.	E	sign	Others
	0	0	0	0	0	0
{a d}	1	2	0	0	0	0
{b c e f h}	2	2	3,*int*	4,*int*	0,*int*	0,*int*
{g}	3	5	0	0	0	0
{i j k}	4	7	0	0	6	0
{g h l}	5	5	0,*fpt*	4,*fpt*	0,*fpt*	0,*fpt*
{k}	6	7	0	0	0	0
{k l}	7	7	0,*fpt*	0,*fpt*	0,*fpt*	0,*fpt*

(b) A state table implementing a scanner for (a)

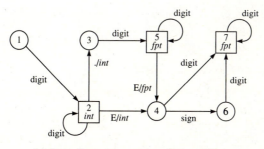

(c) State diagram corresponding to (b)

Figure 3.5
Recognizing the next basic symbol

If S does contain the label of a syntax diagram exit, then one or more of the transitions in state s may specify an output. Let $x \in S$ be the label of an exit from the syntax diagram and let n be the next state entry (possibly 0) for state s in the column for character c. State s has the output corresponding to x in the column for character c if the set of labels that corresponds to state n does not contain x. The label set corresponding to state 2 in Figure 3.5b contains c, which is the label for the exit corresponding to an integer denotation. Of the next state entries for state 2, only the one in the "digit" column has a corresponding label set that contains c. Therefore all columns except the "digit" column specify the output *int* in the row for state 2.

If the rule of the previous paragraph specifies two or more outputs for a particular entry in the state table, then the syntax diagram is ambiguous: A particular character sequence can be classified as two or more different basic symbols. It might be possible to resolve the ambiguity, given information about a broader context than we make available to the scanner, but the methods for doing so are outside the scope of this text.

The machine defined by Figure 3.5b scans a character sequence and decides whether some prefix of that sequence fits the definition of either a Pascal integer denotation or a Pascal real denotation. As soon as it makes this decision, it produces an output. Since an integer denotation is a prefix of a real denotation, the machine may produce more than one output. For example, if the input sequence is 1.10; then the machine will produce *int* when presented with the period and *fpt* when presented with the semicolon. If the input sequence were 1..10; however, the machine would only produce *int* when presented with the first period. The second period would cause a transition to state 0, so no further output could be produced.

A common criterion (which works for Pascal scanners) used to select one of the machine's outputs as the next basic symbol is the so-called principle of the longest match: Select the last output produced by the machine. To apply this criterion, it is necessary to monitor the machine's state as well as its output. When the machine produces an output, the relevant information (the decision and the input character position) are saved in a variable. Subsequent outputs overwrite this variable, so that only the last output information is available. The variable is initialized with an error indication. When the machine enters its trap state the content of the variable defines the longest match.

3.2.2 Regular Expressions

Syntax diagrams are a graphical notation for describing sets of character sequences. *Regular expressions* are a textual notation for describing sets of character sequences. A regular expression is more compact, easier to manipulate, and easier to reason about than a syntax diagram (although many people find it less intuitively appealing). Regular expressions are also important because they are used as the input language for most scanner generation tools. (A scanner generation tool is a program that accepts some description of a set of basic symbols and generates a scanner module that recognizes basic symbols from the set described.)

The meaning of a regular expression is defined in terms of the meanings of its components by six rules:

1. ϵ is a regular expression describing the empty sequence.
2. For any character c, c is a regular expression describing the sequence consisting of a single instance of c.
3. For any two regular expressions e_1 and e_2, $(e_1)(e_2)$ is a regular expression describing the set of sequences consisting of an element of the set described by e_1 concatenated with an element of the set described by e_2.
4. For any two regular expressions e_1 and e_2, $(e_1) \mid (e_2)$ is a regular expression describing the union of the sets described by e_1 and e_2.
5. For any regular expression e, $(e)*$ is a regular expression describing the union of the sets described by ϵ, e, $(e)(e)$, $((e)(e))(e)$, ...
6. For any regular expression e, (e) is a regular expression describing the set of sequences described by e.

Many of the parentheses introduced by these rules can be omitted if the following precedence and association conventions are adopted:

(a) * has the highest precedence.
(b) Concatenation has the middle precedence.
(c) | has the lowest precedence.
(d) All operators are left-associative.

The expression a | b c* is interpreted as (a) | ((b) ((c)*)) according to these conventions.

Each of the first five rules for constructing regular expressions from their components corresponds to a particular composition of syntax diagrams (Figure 3.6). These composition rules show that the regular expression corresponding to Figure 3.3d is

$$letter(letter \mid digit)*$$

Here *letter* stands for the regular expression that describes the set of letters and *digit* stands for the regular expression that describes the set of digits.

Regular expression notation is often extended by introducing a unary + operator, whose precedence is the same as *, defined by:

$$e^+ = ee*$$

Here e is any regular expression. Using this extension, the regular expression corresponding to Figure 3.3c is:

$$'\ ('' \mid (character\ other\ than\ '))^+\ '$$

The atoms of a syntax diagram are boxes representing sets of characters, whereas the atoms of a regular expression are single characters. To describe a set of characters, a regular expression listing all of the characters, separated by "|" operators, must be written. For example, the set of digits is described as follows:

$$0 \mid 1 \mid 2 \mid 3 \mid 4 \mid 5 \mid 6 \mid 7 \mid 8 \mid 9$$

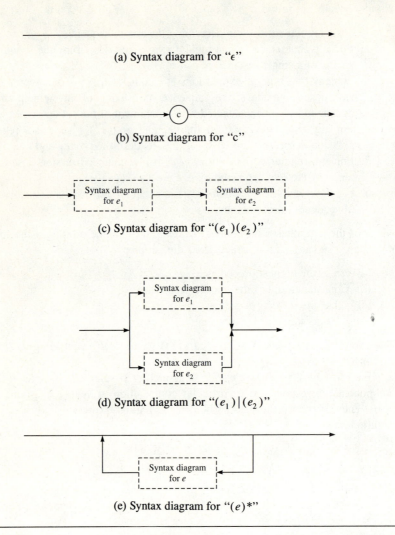

Figure 3.6
Syntax diagrams and regular expressions

The set "character other than '" appearing in Figure 3.3c is a list of every character in the character set, except the apostrophe. Such descriptions are tedious to write and may be system-dependent. (A definition of "character other than '" for a machine using ASCII characters will differ from one for a machine using EBCDIC characters.) These problems can be avoided by providing further notational extensions to describe character sets.

A common extension to regular expression notation is to describe a character set by simply enclosing the elements in square brackets—the set of digits would be described by [0123456789]. Since the letters and digits have a natural ordering, one is allowed to abbreviate sets of letters and digits by separating the first and last with a dash ([0-9]). Using this notation, the complete regular expression corresponding to Figure 3.3d is:

$$[a-zA-Z][a-zA-Z0-9]*$$

(Note that [a-zA-Z]|[0-9] is equivalent to [a-zA-Z0-9].) If the first character is ˆ, then the set contains all characters *except* the ones listed ([ˆ ′] represents "character other than ′").

3.2.3 How to Implement a Scanner

Because the scanner must examine every character of the source text, speed is an important design criterion. Scanning algorithms are simple, but their implementations must be carefully thought out if the scanner is not to become a significant performance bottleneck. Full advantage must be taken of frequently occurring special cases to reduce the amount of processing effort devoted to individual source characters. This means that the scanner designer should have some understanding of the frequency with which basic symbols of various kinds occur in typical source text.

Two design principles are important for scanners:

- Minimize the cost of processing individual source characters. There are 5-10 times as many source characters as basic symbols in a typical program.
- Minimize the cost of skipping *single* spaces. Single spaces (i.e., spaces not forming part of a sequence of spaces) and identifiers are the most common "chunks" of source text in a typical program.

These principles are derived from the characteristics of typical source text for languages such as Pascal and FORTRAN. Other languages *could* have other characteristics, but unless measurements are available to contradict these principles, it would be wise to adhere to them.

The finite-state machine that implements the scanner is embedded in the lexical analysis module's *Lexical* procedure as shown in Figure 3.7. *Lexical* repeatedly seeks a basic symbol in the source text by obtaining a nonblank character and then submitting the character sequence it begins to the finite-state machine that recognizes basic symbols. If the finite-state machine accepts the character sequence as a valid basic symbol, then it will set *SymFound* to *true*, set *t.kind* to the basic symbol's *SymbolClass*, and set *Current* to the index of the first character that does not belong to the basic symbol. If the finite-state machine does not accept the character sequence, then it does not alter *SymFound*, *t.kind*, or *Current*.

Single spaces are skipped at minimum cost by the **repeat-until** statement at the beginning of the loop. It does not need to make a special test for the end of the line because *Line*↑.*s*[*Limit*] is guaranteed not to contain a space (see the invariant on *Limit* in Figure 3.2). This is an example of a general technique for

var
   LineNumber: *integer*;   (* Line coordinate of *Line↑.s[LinePtr]* *)
   Current: *integer*;   (* Index of the first uninspected character *)
   Limit: *integer*;   (* Index of the first character position beyond the end of the line *)
                                  (* *Line↑.s[Limit]* = end-of-line marker *)

procedure *Lexical*(**var** *t*: *Token*);
   (* Build the internal representation of a basic symbol
     On exit-
       t represents the next basic symbol
   *)

   const *SPACE* = ' ';

   var *c*: *char*; *start,temp*: *integer*; *SymFound*: *boolean*;

   function *NextLine*: *boolean*;
     (* Obtain the next source line and establish the lexical analyzer's invariant
       If source text remains then on exit-
          NextLine = true
       Else on exit-
          NextLine = false
          Current = LinePtr = Limit
     *)
     begin · · · **end**;

begin (* *Lexical* *)
SymFound: = *false*;
repeat
   repeat *c*: = *Line↑.s[Current]*; *Current*: = *Current* + 1; **until** *c* < > *SPACE*;
   t.coord.line: = *LineNumber*; *t.coord.column*: = *Current* − *LinePtr*;
   start: = *Current* − 1;
   (* *Line↑.s[start]* = first unaccepted character *)
   (* Implementation of the finite-state machine (uses *temp*) *)
   if not *SymFound* **then**
     if *start* < *Limit* **then** *Report*(*FATAL*,6(*Invalid symbol*),*t.coord*,0)
     else if not *NextLine* **then begin** *SymFound*: = *true*; *t.kind*: = *EOPT* **end**
   (* *Line↑.s[Current]* = first unaccepted character *)
until *SymFound*;
end; (* *Lexical* *)

Figure 3.7
The environment of the finite-state machine

speeding up search loops: Make the data at the end of the search area satisfy the stopping condition. Then the pair of tests (stopping condition, limit) is replaced with a single test at each iteration, and a test for the limit is added after the loop exit. Figure 3.7 assumes that the finite-state machine will not accept a character sequence beginning with the end-of-line marker. Thus *SymFound* will be *false* and *start = Limit* after execution of the finite-state machine. *Lexical* will then

3.2 SCANNING THE SOURCE TEXT FOR BASIC SYMBOLS

attempt to obtain a new source line. If the source text is exhausted, then *SymFound* is set to true and the endmarker basic symbol is reported.

A finite-state machine can be implemented interpretively by means of three arrays and a **case**-statement similar to the Pascal code shown in Figure 3.8b. This code would replace the comment "Implementation of the finite-state machine" in Figure 3.7. The array *next[state,input]* contains the next state entries of the state table shown in Figure 3.8a, while the array *output[state,input]* contains the output entries. Where the output symbol is omitted in the state table, *output* contains *none*.

In practice, many of the possible input characters will have identical columns in the state table. Only one representative of each group of these identical columns will actually be stored. For this reason, the input character cannot be used directly as an index to *next* and *output*. Instead, it is used as an index to *map*. The array *map[character]* gives the index in *next* and *output* of the column that is identical to the column for *character*. For example, *map['3']* would give the index of the "digit" column and *map['E']* would give the index of the E column. Figure 3.8b could be changed to implement a finite-state machine for a

		digit	.	E	sign	Others
{a d}	1	2	0	0	0	0
{b c e f h}	2	2	3,int	4,int	0,int	0,int
{g}	3	5	0	0	0	0
{i j k}	4	7	0	0	6	0
{g h l}	5	5	0,fpt	4,fpt	0,fpt	0,fpt
{k}	6	7	0	0	0	0
{k l}	7	7	0,fpt	0,fpt	0,fpt	0,fpt

(a) The state table of Figure 3.5b with row 0 omitted

```
(* Line↑.s[start] = first unaccepted character *)
state: = 1; temp: = start − 1;
repeat
   temp: = temp + 1;
   case output[state,map[Line↑.s[temp]]] of
   none: ;
   int: begin SymFound: = true; t.kind: = IntegerT; Current: = temp end;
   fpt: begin SymFound: = true; t.kind: = RealT; Current: = temp end;
   end;
   state: = next[state,map[Line↑.s[temp]]];
until state = 0;
(* Line↑.s[Current] = first unaccepted character *)
```

(b) Pascal code to interpret (a)

Figure 3.8
Interpreting a state table

different scanner by changing the **case** statement and the contents of the three arrays *next*, *output*, and *map*.

Some care must be taken to keep the sizes of the *next* and *output* arrays reasonable. One cause of large arrays is the use of the scanner to recognize keywords. Figure 3.9 illustrates this cost for the Pascal keywords **else** and **end**, combined with Pascal identifiers. The cost increase has two components: an increase in the number of states, and an increase in the number of characters that have distinct columns. Pascal identifiers can be recognized by a finite-state machine with two nonzero states and three columns (letters, digits, and Others), while the machine of Figure 3.9 has eight nonzero states and eight columns. A complete machine for Pascal has between 160 and 170 states, depending upon the precise syntax diagrams or regular expressions used. If no distinction is made in the scanner between identifiers and keywords, the number of states is reduced to between 35 and 40. We therefore recommend that the scanner recognize keywords as identifiers, leaving the distinction to the identifier conversion operation discussed in Section 3.3.2.

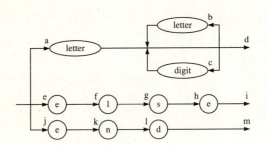

(a) Syntax diagrams for *identifier*, **else** and **end**

		d	e	l	n	s	other letter	digit	Others
{a e j}	1	2	3	2	2	2	2	0	0
{b c d}	2	2	2	2	2	2	2	2	0,*idn*
{b c d f k}	3	2	2	4	5	2	2	2	0,*idn*
{b c d g}	4	2	2	2	2	6	2	2	0,*idn*
{b c d l}	5	7	2	2	2	2	2	2	0,*idn*
{b c d h}	6	2	8	2	2	2	2	2	0,*idn*
{b c d m}	7	2	2	2	2	2	2	2	0,*end*
{b c d i}	8	2	2	2	2	2	2	2	0,*else*

(b) The state table derived from (a)

Figure 3.9
The cost of keywords

3.2 SCANNING THE SOURCE TEXT FOR BASIC SYMBOLS

A finite-state machine can also be expressed as a directly executable program (implemented via **if**, **case**, **while**, and assignment statements), rather than as an interpretive program (implemented as data stored in three arrays and interpreted by **repeat**, **case**, and assignment statements). Direct execution is faster and is usually easier to implement by hand. Most programming languages use very similar sets of basic symbols, so hand construction of a new scanner is often only a matter of making small adjustments to an existing one.

Figure 3.10 defines a finite-state machine for a subset of Pascal assignment statements that allows only integer constants and variables with addition and mul-

	digit	letter	:	=	(	+	*	)	;	Others
1	2	3	4	0	5	6	7	8	9	0
2	2	0,int	0,int	0,int	0,int	0,int	0,int	0,int	0,int	0,int
3	3	3	0,idn	0,idn	0,idn	0,idn	0,idn	0,idn	0,idn	0,idn
4	0	0	0	10	0	0	0	0	0	0
5	0,lpn	0,lpn	0,lpn	0,lpn	0,lpn	0,lpn	0,lpn	0,lpn	0,lpn	0,lpn
6	0,pls	0,pls	0,pls	0,pls	0,pls	0,pls	0,pls	0,pls	0,pls	0,pls
7	0,ast	0,ast	0,ast	0,ast	0,ast	0,ast	0,ast	0,ast	0,ast	0,ast
8	0,rpn	0,rpn	0,rpn	0,rpn	0,rpn	0,rpn	0,rpn	0,rpn	0,rpn	0,rpn
9	0,sem	0,sem	0,sem	0,sem	0,sem	0,sem	0,sem	0,sem	0,sem	0,sem
10	0,asn	0,asn	0,asn	0,asn	0,asn	0,asn	0,asn	0,asn	0,asn	0,asn

(a) State table

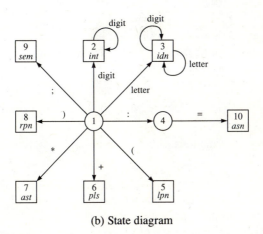

(b) State diagram

Figure 3.10
A simple scanner

tiplication operators only. This machine displays three common characteristics of scanners:

- Many of the successors of the initial state have no successors.
- Only the initial state has many successors.
- Several of the states have themselves as successors.

These three properties can be exploited to simplify the implementation.

Figure 3.10 shows that there is virtually a one-to-one correspondence between the successors of the initial state and the values of type *SymbolClass* (only *EOPT* does not correspond to a successor of the initial state). Figure 3.11 implements state 1 as an array *state*1 containing *SymbolClass* values instead of state numbers. After setting *t.kind* from *state*1, Figure 3.11 uses a **case** statement to select the code corresponding to the next state. Note that the successors of state 1 which have no successors need only *SymFound* set to *true*—*t.kind* has already been set and *Current* has already been advanced.

Case *EOPT* implements the transition to state 0 and the error output in much the same way as was done by Figure 3.7. There is no need to set *t.kind* if the end-of-file is detected, because it has already been set.

Case *ColonEqT* implements state 4. If the next character (indexed by *Current*) is = then it is accepted by incrementing *Current*. Again there is no need to set *t.kind*.

Both the *EOPT* and *ColonEqT* cases in Figure 3.11 must report an invalid character. The "issuer" parameter of *Report* (Figure 2.3) is used to distinguish the two. This information would be most useful during compiler debugging, if an erroneous "illegal symbol" message appeared.

3.3 CONVERTING DENOTATIONS AND IDENTIFIERS

As discussed in Section 3.1, delimiters are completely specified by their classifications, but denotations must be converted into *ExtValue* objects and identifiers must be converted into integers. Both of these conversions involve storage of character sequences:

- The representations of floating-point numbers and strings refer to character pools for their data.
- Character representations must be retained to check whether a newly encountered identifier is distinct from all previously encountered identifiers.

It is important to note that these character sequences must be physically copied from the source line to other locations. Remember that the source module interface (Figure 2.2) leaves the lifetime of the source line unspecified. As a client of the source module, the lexical analyzer can make no assumptions about the source line other than those explicitly stated in the interface. Therefore the conversion modules must obtain storage from the character pool for data that must be retained from one source line to another.

3.3 CONVERTING DENOTATIONS AND IDENTIFIERS

```
type
   SymbolClass = (            (* Classification of basic symbols *)
      EOPT,                   (* Endmarker *)
      IntegerT,               (* Integer *)
      IdentifierT,            (* Identifier *)
      ColonEqT,               (* := *)
      LeftParenT,             (* ( *)
      PlusT,                  (* + *)
      AsteriskT,              (* * *)
      RightParenT,            (* ) *)
      SemicolonT);            (* ; *)
   ...
var
   state1:                    (* Possible class based on first character *)
      array [char] of SymbolClass;
   Digit,LetterOrDigit:       (* Character sets *)
      array [char] of boolean;
   ...
(* Line↑.s[start] = first unaccepted character *)
(* Current = start + 1 *)
t.kind: = state1[Line↑.s[start]];
if t.kind > ColonEqT then SymFound: = true (* States 5-9 of Figure 3.10 *)
else
   case t.kind of
   EOPT: (* Invalid character—State 0 *)
      if start < Limit then Report(FATAL,6(*Illegal symbol*),t.coord,1)
      else SymFound: = not NextLine;
   IntegerT: (* Digit—State 2 of Figure 3.10 *)
      begin SymFound: = true;
      while Digit[Line↑.s[Current]] do Current: = Current + 1;
      end;
   IdentifierT: (* Letter—State 3 of Figure 3.10 *)
      begin SymFound: = true;
      while LetterOrDigit[Line↑.s[Current]] do Current: = Current + 1;
      end;
   ColonEqT: (* :—State 4 of Figure 3.10 *)
      if Line↑.s[Current] = '=' then (* =—State 10 of Figure 3.10 *)
         begin SymFound: = true; Current: = Current + 1 end
      else Report(FATAL,6(*Illegal symbol*),t.coord,2);
   end;
(* Line↑.s[Current] = first unaccepted character *)
```

Figure 3.11
A directly executable scanner

Splitting the recognition of the basic symbol from its conversion violates the design principle "minimize the cost of processing individual source characters" because it requires the compiler to access each character of the basic symbol twice: once to recognize it and once to convert it. Unfortunately, it is not always possible to convert a basic symbol as its characters are being recognized. For example, integer and real denotations are converted in different ways, but they cannot be distinguished from each other until several characters have been passed. Thus the recognition must be completed before the conversion is begun, as assumed in Figure 3.12.

3.3.1 Denotations

Conversion of an integer denotation is a straightforward application of Horner's rule to the polynomial defining positional notation. Let $c_{n-1}c_{n-2} \cdots c_1 c_0$ be the source text character sequence, where c_i is a digit. The value represented is

$$d_{n-1} \times r^{n-1} + d_{n-2} \times r^{n-2} + \cdots + d_1 \times r^1 + d_0 \times r^0$$

Here r is the radix of the notation and $0 \leqslant d_i < r$ is the value represented by the digit character c_i. Horner's rule leads to an iterative evaluation routine by expressing the value polynomial as follows:

$$(\cdots (d_{n-1} \times r + d_{n-2}) \times r + \cdots + d_1) \times r + d_0$$

Each cycle of this iteration is carried out by invoking *ExtCodeDigit* (Figure 2.5) with d_i as the *digit* argument and r as the *radix* argument. The *extval* argument is the value being accumulated; it is modified by the operation.

Conversion of a real denotation is much simpler. After replacing the exponent marker with ``,'' (if an optional exponent is given), all that is needed is an invocation of *ExtCodeFloat* (Figure 2.5). There is no need to copy the denotation, because the interface specification for *ExtCodeFloat* guarantees that the denotation string does not become part of the external value.

Since the conversion operation accesses t as a **var** parameter, it can alter the classification as well as setting the value. This facility is important when the classification of a basic symbol depends upon some property of the value. For example, in FORTRAN the denotation 12.34E5 has type REAL and the denotation 12.34D5 has type DOUBLE. Both denotations have exactly the same form, except for the exponent marker. It may be convenient to recognize the two forms of real number as different basic symbols, but to use the conversion operation to distinguish them, instead of adding extra complexity to the scanner.

A string denotation must be "standardized" by interpreting all special representations of arbitrary characters. Different languages use different conven-

---

procedure *CvtXXX*(*tx*: *CharPool*; *index,length*: *integer*; **var** *t*: *Token*);
   (* Convert a basic symbol of class *XXX*
      On entry-
         $tx\uparrow.s[index..index+length-1]$ = character sequence to be converted
      On exit-
         t = completed representation of the basic symbol
   *)

Figure 3.12
The general form of a conversion operation

tions for representing arbitrary characters within strings, and these conventions determine the structure of the recognizer. If strings were not standardized, the assembly module would become language-dependent because it would need to understand the language-defined representation conventions.

A string delimiter is represented within a Pascal string by doubling it. To standardize a Pascal string denotation, the conversion operation must therefore remove the outermost pair of delimiters and replace any doubled delimiters by single ones—don''t would become don't.

When string and character denotations differ only in length, as in Pascal, the conversion operation differentiates the two cases and sets *t.kind* appropriately. These two possibilities also result in different variants of *t.val*: A character denotation is represented by the ASCII value of the character as an *ExtInteger*, while a string denotation is represented by an *ExtString*.

If an error is noted during the conversion of a denotation, it is reported by the conversion operation. Typical errors might be integer overflow, detection of a digit of the wrong radix in an integer, or exponent overflow in a real. Some of these errors (such as the appearance of a digit of the wrong radix) might be detectable during recognition, but only with a scanner of increased complexity.

3.3.2 Identifiers

In order to convert every instance of a given identifier into the *same* integer, the identifier conversion module must maintain an *identifier table* that associates identifiers with the corresponding integers. Each time the conversion module is invoked, it looks up the specified character sequence in the identifier table. If the character sequence is present, the conversion operation sets *t.idn* (Figure 3.1) to the associated integer. If the character sequence is not in the table, then the module enters it, in association with a new integer, and again sets *t.idn*.

Keyword recognition can be obtained from the identifier conversion operation at almost no cost by storing a *SymbolClass* value in the identifier table along with the character sequence and the associated integer. The table is then preloaded with the keywords, each associated with the proper *SymbolClass* value and an integer. Like many other languages, Pascal specifies certain "predefined" identifiers in addition to its keywords. (The difference between predefined identifiers and keywords is that the former may be redefined within a program but the latter may not.) Predefined identifiers would also be preloaded into the identifier table, since their associated integers must be known at the time the compiler is written. For Pascal, the initial identifier table contents might be as follows:

'and'	*AndT*	1
'array'	*ArrayT*	2
	. . .	
'with'	*WithT*	35
'boolean'	*IdentifierT*	36
'char'	*IdentifierT*	37
	. . .	

If the argument is found in the identifier table, the conversion operation sets *t.idn* to the associated integer and also sets *t.kind* to the associated *SymbolClass* value. If the argument is not in the table, then the module enters it, in association with a new integer and the *SymbolClass* value currently in *t.kind*, and again sets both *t.idn* and *t.kind*. For example, when the scanner invokes the identifier conversion operation with the character sequence `array` and a *Token* with *t.kind* = *IdentifierT*. The operation then returns having set *t.kind* = *ArrayT* and *t.idn* = 2. On the other hand, when the operation is invoked with a new character sequence such as `i`, and a *Token* having *t.kind* = *IdentifierT*, a new entry will be made in the identifier table. Suppose that the identifier table contained 106 entries at the time. Then the new entry would be

$$\text{'i'} \quad IdentifierT \quad 107$$

and the operation would return having set *t.kind* = *IdentifierT* and *t.idn* = 107.

Conceptually, the module's initialization operation preloads the table by invoking the conversion operation for each keyword, passing the keyword's character sequence and a *Token* whose *kind* field is set to the classification of the keyword, and then invoking it for each predefined identifier, passing the identifier's character sequence and a *Token* whose *kind* field is set to *IdentifierT*.

It is important to reduce the number of string comparisons made when recognizing identifiers and keywords, as well as to make those comparisons as fast as possible. Approximately 25% of the characters in a typical Pascal program occur within identifiers and keywords. Suppose that we ignore any setup time and say that comparison of two character sequences is roughly 1.5 times as expensive as simply accessing each character of one. If the average number of candidates with which each character sequence must be compared is between 2 and 3, the total cost of converting identifiers and keywords will be approximately equal to the cost of scanning the entire program.

The number of possible candidates from the identifier table that could match a newly scanned identifier can be reduced by computing some property of the new character sequence and using it as a "filter." There is, of course, a trade-off between the cost of computing the property and its effectiveness in reducing the number of candidates. The usual approach is indicated by Figure 3.13. A *hash function* is applied to the character sequence to yield an integer k in the range $[0, HashConst - 1]$ and the list rooted in that element of *HashTbl* is then searched. The hash function of Figure 3.13c sums the character values and takes the remainder modulo a prime that is not close to any multiple of the character set size. Hash functions that do not use all of the characters in the sequence have worse performance because they are weaker filters, and the cost of searching longer lists offsets the savings from examining fewer characters. Each list should be maintained in order of character sequence length, and only those candidates with lengths equal to that of the new character sequence should be compared. By maintaining this order, the expected search length is reduced to half of the length of the list. If *HashConst* is as least as large as the character set size, then each list can have no more than one character sequence of length 1.

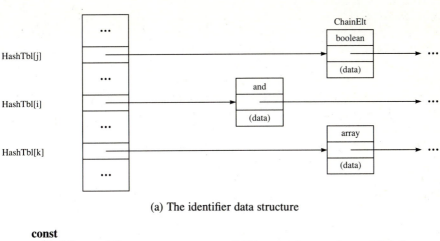

(a) The identifier data structure

const
    HashConst = 421;   (* Prime number not close to 128k *)
    MaxBucket = 420;   (* *HashConst* − 1 *)

type
    Chain = ↑ *ChainElt*;   (* Identifier table entries *)
    ChainElt = **record**
        id: *CharPool*; *p,l*: *integer*;   (* $id\uparrow.s[p..p+l-1] = sequence$ *)
        next: *Chain*;   (* Next entry in the current bucket *)
        class: *SymbolClass*; *key*: *integer*; (* Data *)
    end;

var
    HashTbl: (* Base pointers for the chains *)
    array [0..*MaxBucket*] **of** *Chain*;

(b) Pascal implementation of the identifier table data structure

    sum := 0;
    for $i := p$ **to** $p+l-1$ **do** $sum := sum + ord(tx\uparrow.s[i])$;
    $k := sum$ **mod** *HashConst*;

(c) A simple hash function

Figure 3.13
Identifier table internals

3.4 SUMMARY

Lexical analysis accepts the sequence of characters making up a source program and delivers a sequence of basic symbols to the remainder of the compiler. Its interface provides a single operation—"get next basic symbol"—to its clients.

Every basic symbol returned by this operation is described by a source text position and a classification. Denotations and identifiers carry additional descriptive information.

A lexical analyzer is conveniently divided into two parts, a scanner and a converter. The scanner extracts character sequences from the source text, classifying them and determining their source text positions. It passes the sequences that it classifies as denotations and identifiers to the converter. The converter determines the internal representation of each sequence delivered to it and adds that information to the description of the basic symbol.

Syntax diagrams or regular expressions can be used to describe the lexical structure of the basic symbols. Given such a description, a scanner for the language can be implemented by a finite-state machine. The finite-state machine can be realized either as an interpreter that is controlled by three arrays or as a program whose code embodies the machine description. Generally speaking, the programmed realization is both smaller and faster than the one controlled by arrays.

Denotations are converted into *ExtValue* (Figure 2.4) objects. String denotations are "standardized" by converting all escape sequences to the actual target machine characters. Such standardization makes the *ExtValue* objects completely independent of the source language and allows a particular assembly module to be used in compilers for different source languages.

Identifiers are converted into distinct integers. The cost of the identifier conversion is usually high—approximately equal to the total scanning cost. Thus the identifier conversion module must be carefully coded, using an algorithm that minimizes the number of comparisons and makes each one as fast as possible.

NOTES

Syntax diagrams are widely used in language description, although there is no formal standard for the notation. We have followed the general symbolism of the Pascal User Manual and Report [7]. The syntax diagrams appearing in this chapter, whose boxes specify sets of characters only, are completely equivalent to state transition diagrams of *nondeterministic* finite automata [14, 18]. Each box in the syntax diagram is a representation of a set of edges in the state transition diagram, and each junction of lines in the syntax diagram is a representation of a node in the state transition diagram. Our finite-state machines are all *deterministic*, and the process we describe for converting syntax diagrams into machines is the standard algorithm for converting nondeterministic finite automata into deterministic finite automata [18].

Regular expressions provide a compact textual description of a set of character sequences, and are used to describe search patterns to text editors as well as to lexical analyzer generation tools. Theoretical treatments of regular expressions and their relationship to finite-state machines can be found in almost any book on automata theory, discrete mathematics, or fundamentals of computer science [14, 18].

Tools that generate scanners from regular expressions have a long history [8, 12, 6, 4]. The need for very fast regular expression pattern matching led to early implementations that made creative use of the implementation machine's instruction set [15], but later ones were expressed in higher-level languages [13].

It is important to base design decisions on experience rather than conjecture. The discussion about scanner performance in Section 3.2.3 is based upon extensive performance measurements and analysis of both handwritten and automatically generated scanners [16, 4]. We have tried to explain the rationale behind scanner design and to relate it to the characteristics of typical programs [2, 11]. You should get into the habit of using such criteria and then measuring the characteristics of your product to broaden your experience. Performance is *not* a dirty word, and good performance can almost always be obtained without distorting the program, if you understand the issues.

The identifier table discussed in Section 3.3.2 is an example of a *dictionary*— a module providing lookup and insertion operations. Data structures that implement dictionaries are analyzed in most data structures books, both at the introductory [5] and more advanced [1] levels. A wide variety of hash functions and hash table organizations are surveyed in Volume 3 of *The Art of Computer Programming* [10].

REFERENCES

1. Aho, A. V., Hopcroft, J. E., and Ullman, J. D., *The Design and Analysis of Computer Algorithms*, Addison Wesley, Reading, MA, 1974.
2. Carter, L. R., *An Analysis of Pascal Programs*, UMI Research Press, Ann Arbor, MI, 1982.
3. Cichelli, R. J., "Minimal Perfect Hash Functions Made Simple," *Comm. of the ACM 23*, 1 (Jan. 1980), 17–19.
4. Gray, R. W., "A Generator for Lexical Analyzers That Programmers Can Use," *Proc. USENIX Conf.*, June 1988.
5. Helman, P. and Veroff, R., *Intermediate Problem Solving and Data Structures*, Benjamin/Cummings, Menlo Park, CA, 1986.
6. Heuring, V. P., "The Automatic Generation of Fast Lexical Analyzers," *Software— Practice & Experience 16*, 9 (Sep. 1986), 801–808.
7. Jensen, K., Wirth, N., Mickel, A. B., and Miner, J. F., *Pascal User Manual and Report*, Springer Verlag, New York, 1985. Third Edition.
8. Johnson, W. L., Porter, J. H., Ackley, S. I., and Ross, D. T., "Automatic Generation of Efficient Lexical Processors Using Finite State Techniques," *Comm. of the ACM 11*, 12 (Dec. 1968), 805–813.
9. Kernighan, B. W. and Ritchie, D. M., *The C Programming Language*, Prentice Hall, Englewood Cliffs, NJ, 1978.
10. Knuth, D. E., *Sorting and Searching*, Addison Wesley, New York, 1973.
11. Knuth, D. E., "An Empirical Study of FORTRAN Programs," *Software—Practice & Experience 1* (1971), 105–133.

12. Lesk, M. E., "LEX—A Lexical Analyzer Generator," Computing Science Technical Report 39, Bell Telephone Laboratories, Murray Hill, NJ, 1975.
13. Richards, M., "A Compact Function for Regular Expression Pattern Matching," *Software—Practice & Experience 9*, 7 (July 1979), 527–534.
14. Stone, H. S., *Discrete Mathematical Structures and Their Applications*, Science Research Associates, Chicago, 1973.
15. Thompson, K., "Regular Expression Search Algorithm," *Comm. of the ACM 11*, 6 (June 1968), 419–422.
16. Waite, W. M., "The Cost of Lexical Analysis," *Software—Practice & Experience 16*, 5 (May 1986), 473–488.
17. Waite, W. M., "Treatment of Tab Characters by a Compiler," *Software—Practice & Experience 15*, 11 (Nov. 1985), 1121–1123.
18. Wulf, W. A., Shaw, M., Hilfinger, P. N., and Flon, L., *Fundamental Structures of Computer Science*, Addison Wesley, Reading, MA, 1981.

EXERCISES

3.1 Assume that a basic symbol is represented by the record declaration of Figure 3.1 and an *ExtValue* is represented as shown in Figure 2.4.
  (a) For some machine with a Pascal compiler, compute the amount of storage required for the largest *Token* if the source language is Pascal.
  (b) Complete the enumeration of Figure 3.1 for Pascal and compile the given declarations with the machine's Pascal compiler. How much storage was allocated to the *Token* record?
  (c) Account for any difference between the amount you predicted and the amount allocated by the Pascal compiler. (This exercise can be done with any implementation language substituted for Pascal.)

3.2 Draw a syntax diagram for a FORTRAN real denotation. How does it differ from Figure 3.3b?

3.3 Several languages allow underscores within identifiers to improve readability of programs. Assume that there can be no adjacent underscores, and that the identifier may neither begin with an underscore nor end with an underscore.
  (a) Draw a syntax diagram for identifiers with embedded underscores.
  (b) Develop a finite-state machine that recognizes the character sequences defined by your syntax diagram.

3.4 Consider identifiers with embedded underscores as defined in Exercise 3.3.
  (a) Using only rules (1)-(6) from the beginning of Section 3.2.2, write a regular expression for identifiers with embedded underscores.
  (b) Can you use any of the extensions of the notation to shorten your answer to (a)?
  (c) Relate your answers in (a) and (b) to the syntax diagram of Exercise 3.3a.

3.5 Consider the following regular expression describing a Pascal real denotation:

$$[0-9]^+ \quad (. \ [0-9]^+ \ (\epsilon|E(+|-|\epsilon)[0-9]^+) \quad | \quad E(+|-|\epsilon) \ [0-9]^+)$$

  (a) Use the equivalences of Figure 3.6 to draw a syntax diagram corresponding to this regular expression.
  (b) Compare your syntax diagram with Figure 3.3b. Are the sets of *paths* through the two diagrams the same?

(c) Add a syntax diagram for e^+ to Figure 3.6. Can you use the augmented diagrams to decompose Figure 3.3b? Explain briefly.

3.6 The discussion about skipping spaces that appears in conjunction with Figure 3.7 gives a rationale for storing a nonblank "sentinel" character at the end of each line. Would it be useful for the scanner to *change* this character, depending upon the basic symbol being scanned? (Hint: Consider the process of scanning a Pascal string denotation.)

3.7 Combine the syntax diagrams for FORTRAN integer denotations, FORTRAN real denotations, and the FORTRAN relational operators .EQ. and .NE..
(a) Derive a finite-state machine that will recognize the next basic symbol from this set.
(b) Define the necessary output symbols and write a *complete* interpreter (similar to Figure 3.8) to implement it.

3.8 Consider an interpretive implementation of the finite-state machine discussed in conjunction with Figure 3.8. Assume that the enumerated type *action* is defined as (*none, int, fpt*).
(a) Give Pascal declarations for the arrays *next, output*, and *map*.
(b) Because the computer's memory is a sequence of locations, access to an element *next*[i,j] requires computation of a simple offset from the beginning of the array *next* in storage. Give one possible offset computation.
(c) Using your computation from (b), propose declarations for *next, output*, and *map* that would represent *next* and *output* as one-dimensional arrays and change the code given in Figure 3.8b to the following:

    case *output*[*state* + *map*[*Line*↑.*s*[*temp*]]] **of**

    . . .

    state: = *next*[*state* + *map*[*Line*↑.*s*[*temp*]]];

(d) How does the total storage requirement for the three arrays declared as in (a) compare to the storage requirement for the three arrays declared as in (c)?
(e) How does the cost of the array accesses in Figure 3.8b compare to the cost of the array accesses in (c)?
(f) Suppose that, instead of a single array *map*, we provided separate arrays *mapnext* and *mapoutput*. This would allow us to have *different* sets of identical columns in *next* and *output*. Using this scheme in conjunction with the scheme outlined in (c), compare the total storage for Figure 3.8a to those found in (d).

3.9 Consider the relationship between the interpretive implementation of a finite-state machine (Figure 3.8) and the scanner in which it is embedded (Figure 3.7).
(a) Show that the interaction is not correct if some basic symbol contains an embedded newline character.
(b) Propose a modified interpretive implementation that will work. (Hint: Given that the character set is ASCII, you need only broaden the actions allowed in the **case** statement.)

3.10 In Figure 3.10, states 5 through 10 all have an interesting property: the entry for each column is identical to the entry for every other column. Therefore the action to be taken in each of those states is independent of the input character.
(a) What actions will be performed by the interpretive implementation (analogous to Figure 3.8) of Figure 3.10 when *state* = 1 and *Line*↑.*s*[*start*] = '('?

(b) Show how you could eliminate states 5 through 10 of Figure 3.10 in an interpretive implementation by taking appropriate actions in the **case** statement of Figure 3.8.

3.11 Consider the problem of expanding Figure 3.10 to recognize and discard Pascal comments. (To simplify the problem, assume that comments are invariably opened by (* and closed by *).)
  (a) If a comment cannot cross a line boundary, what is the resulting specification?
  (b) If a comment *can* cross a line boundary, what is the resulting specification?
  (c) Suppose you recognize a comment by recognizing (* and then using direct Pascal code instead of a finite-state machine to find the matching *). What is the appropriate state table and interpreter?

3.12 Describe a set of rules for automatically obtaining a program in the style of Figure 3.11 from a state table such as Figure 3.10a.

3.13 Expand Figure 3.10 to recognize all of the basic symbols of Pascal. Recognize keywords as identifiers, and do not attempt to scan comments.
  (a) Implement the scanner interpretively, using *next* and *output* arrays independently compressed by combining identical columns. (If you have a scanner generator available, use it for this implementation.) Keep track of the amount of time it takes you to do the implementation.
  (b) Implement the scanner as a program in the style of Figure 3.11. Keep track of the amount of time it takes you to do the implementation.
  (c) Use the two programs you developed in (a) and (b) to scan a large Pascal program. Compare the two strategies in terms of programmer effort, size of the resulting scanner, and speed of the resulting scanner.

3.14 Reimplement the loops of your scanner from Exercise 3.13b to use Pascal sets instead of the arrays *Digit* and *LetterOrDigit*, if this is permitted by your Pascal compiler:

  IntegerT: (* Digit—State 2 of Figure 3.10 *)
  begin *SymFound*: = *true*;
  while *Line*↑.*s*[*Current*] **in** [0..9] **do** *Current*: = *Current* + 1;
  end;
  IdentifierT: (* Letter—State 3 of Figure 3.10 *)
  begin *SymFound*: = *true*;
  while *Line*↑.*s*[*Current*] **in** [*a*..*z*,*A*..*Z*,0..9] **do** *Current*: = *Current* + 1;
  end;

  Compare the overall execution times of your scanner with the original arrays and with the sets.

3.15 In your solution to Exercise 3.13b, replace the *Digit* and *LetterOrDigit* arrays by a single array defined as follows:

  continuation: **array** [*char*] **of set of** (*Digit*,*LetterOrDigit*);

  (a) Compare the overall execution time with the times for Exercise 3.12.
  (b) Examine the code generated by your Pascal compiler for the three implementations: Boolean arrays (Exercise 3.13b), sets (Exercise 3.14), and arrays of sets (part *a* of this exercise). Can you account for the differences in execution time?

3.16 Take the fastest of the scanners you developed in Exercise 3.13b, Exercise 3.14 and Exercise 3.15. Measure its execution time with the enumeration defining *SymbolClass* arranged so that the case selectors form a compact group. Rearrange the enumeration to spread the case selectors evenly over the range of a *SymbolClass*, leaving gaps as large as possible between them, and measure the execution time again. If there are differences, examine the code generated by the compiler for the **case** statement in each case and explain the differences. Do they account for the difference in execution times?

3.17 Write a conversion operation for Pascal integer denotations that uses the interface of Figure 3.12.

3.18 Write a conversion operation for Pascal real denotations that uses the interface of Figure 3.12.

3.19 Suppose that you were writing a conversion operation for Pascal string denotations.
   (a) Explain why you cannot determine the amount of space to request from the character pool module without scanning the string.
   (b) Show how to interact with the character pool module so that your routine neither scans the string twice nor retains more character pool storage than necessary to hold the standardized string.

3.20 Consider the definition of a string denotation in C [9]. The statement "a \ and an immediately following newline are ignored" allows strings to be continued over multiple lines by ending each line with "\".
   (a) Draw a syntax diagram that defines C string denotations and derive a finite-state machine that recognizes C string denotations.
   (b) How should this machine be integrated into the scanner of Figure 3.11, in view of the fact that a string denotation may span line boundaries?
   (c) How does the fact that a string spans line boundaries cause difficulties for the representation of an *ExtString* given in Figure 2.4? Briefly explain how these difficulties might be overcome.
   (d) Explain why the conversion operation for a C string denotation cannot obey the interface given in Figure 3.12, and propose a suitable interface for this operation.

3.21 [17] Unix provides a utility program, *col*, that compresses a program by replacing sequences of spaces with horizontal tab characters. Since *col* does not understand the structure of the text it is compressing, it may introduce horizontal tab characters into string denotations. Suppose you wished to replace the horizontal tab characters within string denotations by equivalent sequences of spaces as the program was compiled.
   (a) Why would this be a reasonable thing to do?
   (b) How would you determine the length of an "equivalent sequence of spaces"?
   (c) Would this require any action when a horizontal tab character was found *outside* of a string denotation? Explain briefly.

3.22 Suppose you are writing a compiler for a language that restricts the length of an identifier to six characters.
   (a) How would you detect a violation of this restriction?
   (b) If you wished to place the error message at the seventh character position of a long identifier, how would you specify the coordinates?

3.23 Implement a version of the conversion operation for identifiers based upon the data structures of Figure 3.13a.
   (a) Use Standard Pascal constructs to implement the character sequence comparison. Examine the instructions generated by your Pascal compiler for this comparison, and evaluate its cost relative to the "best" instruction sequence possible.

(b) If your version of Pascal provides a nonstandard character sequence comparison function, change your code to use it and measure the speed of the two versions by carrying out the lexical analysis of a large Pascal program. Account for any differences.

(c) Change the value of *HashConst* from 421 to 256 and measure the speed of the two versions. Add code to print the number of elements on each chain at the end of the analysis. Is the distribution better or worse? Explain briefly.

(d) When *HashConst*=256, does your Pascal compiler implement the **mod** operator specially?

(e) Add special case code to deal with identifiers of length 1 and measure the speed of the two versions. Do you notice any speedup resulting from this modification? Explain briefly.

3.24 Assume that, on the average, 25% of the characters in a program occur within identifiers and keywords and that there are about twice as many identifiers as keywords. Assume further that your comparison procedure spends about 1.5 times as long comparing a character as the scanner spends recognizing it. In addition, your filter reduces the number of character sequences to be compared to an average of 2.5 for each identifier converted.

(a) If you recognize keywords with the identifier conversion operation, as discussed in Section 3.3.2, what will be the relationship between total scanning time for the entire program and total identifier conversion time for the entire program?

(b) Explain why recognizing keywords with the scanner (as illustrated by Figure 3.9) will not change the scanning time.

(c) Suppose the average lengths of identifiers and keywords are the same. What will be the relationship between scanning time and identifier conversion time if keywords are recognized by the scanner?

3.25 Perfect hash functions [3] have been proposed as mechanisms for recognizing keywords quickly during identifier conversion.

(a) Using the assumptions given in Exercise 3.24, show that this strategy will *slow* lexical analysis.

(b) Under what assumptions would a speedup be realized?

3.26 The Pascal standard says that lower case and upper case letters have the same meanings everywhere except in character strings.

(a) On a computer that provides both upper and lower case letters, how many different ways could one write the keyword **begin**?

(b) What is the implication of upper/lower case equivalence for a scanner that recognizes keywords?

(c) What is the implication of upper/lower case equivalence for identifier conversion?

(d) Does upper/lower case equivalence favor one method of recognizing keywords over the other? Explain briefly.

4

Syntactic Analysis

A syntactic analyzer builds the source program tree corresponding to the sequence of basic symbols delivered by the lexical analysis module. Table 1.1 divides this task into two parts: parsing and tree construction. The parser invokes the lexical analyzer to obtain basic symbols and invokes the tree constructor to build nodes. Thus the parser acts as the central control algorithm of the syntactic analysis module. We shall consider the tree construction module and methods for defining the parser's behavior in this chapter. Specific parser implementations are presented in Chapter 5 (recursive descent) and Chapter 6 (shift-reduce).

Section 4.1 presents the operations that the parser uses to construct the source program tree. A complete specification of the parsing process consists of a description of the relationship between invocations of the lexical analyzer (Chapter 3) and invocations of these tree construction operations. Notations used to describe that relationship are explored in Section 4.2. In Section 4.3 we show how operator precedence and association, common structural rules in programming languages, are expressed in parser specifications.

The sequence of tree-building operations invoked by the parser should be consistent, regardless of whether the sequence of basic symbols delivered by the lexical analyzer obeys the rules of the source language. Such a guarantee simplifies the design of the tree construction module and allows detection of additional errors. Section 4.4 explains a strategy by which the parser can continue its task in the face of errors and still guarantee a consistent sequence of tree-building actions.

4.1 HOW TO CONSTRUCT A TREE

In Chapter 1 we decomposed the compilation into three subtasks: structuring, translation, and encoding. The interface between the structuring subtask and the translation subtask was the source program tree; the interface between the translation subtask and the encoding subtask was the target program tree. This section is concerned with the characteristics, representation, and construction of these two trees. All of the discussion will be centered upon the source program tree, since it is the one that is of interest at the moment. Bear in mind, however, that all of the concepts presented here apply directly to the target program tree as well—only the names are changed.

The source program tree is built by the syntactic analyzer and contains all of the information embodied in the source program. This information is coded in the "shape" of the tree (if a is the left operand of a particular + operator, then it is the left child of the construct representing that operator's expression) and in the values stored at the leaves (a leaf representing a contains the integer into which a was converted by the lexical analyzer). We first show how the tree can be stored as a linked data structure, and then discuss how it can be built from the information available in the sequence of basic symbols delivered by the lexical analyzer.

4.1.1 Representing a Tree

A source program tree is composed from *fragments*, each of which represents a single source language construct. Each fragment belongs to a *class* that reflects the properties of the construct it represents. Figure 4.1a shows a subtree of a Pascal source program tree. This subtree is built from the six kinds of fragments shown in Figure 4.1b. It contains two *IdnExpr* fragments, two *IdnLeaf* fragments, and one of each of the others. Four classes are represented in Figure 4.1b. These classes correspond to four distinct Pascal concepts:

- *Identifier*: A basic symbol that is freely chosen by the programmer and given meaning by a declaration.
- *Integer*: A basic symbol that denotes an integer value.
- *Expression*: An executable construct that yields a value.
- *Statement*: An executable construct that does not yield a value.

Three of the fragments in Figure 4.1b are classified as expressions (*IntExpr*, *IdnExpr*, and *PlusExpr*), and one each as an identifier (*IdnLeaf*), an integer (*IntLeaf*), and a statement (*AssignmentStmt*).

A construct places restrictions on the kinds of children it can have by specifying a class for each child. For example, a *PlusExpr* requires that both of its chil-

4.1 HOW TO CONSTRUCT A TREE

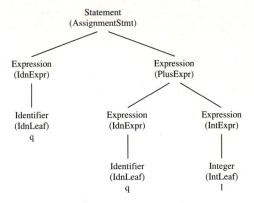

(a) The Pascal source program subtree for "$q := q + 1$"

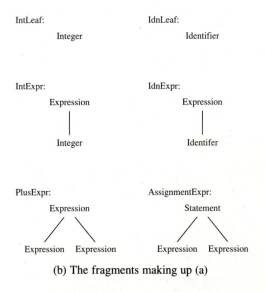

(b) The fragments making up (a)

Figure 4.1
The anatomy of a Pascal source program tree

dren belong to the *Expression* class. The reason for this restriction is that a *PlusExpr* is a Pascal construct that operates on two values to produce a result (the operation might be an integer addition, a real addition, or a set union, depending upon the context). Therefore the children of a *PlusExpr* must yield values for it to operate upon, and *Expression* is exactly the class of constructs that yield values.

Because the mechanism by which the values are obtained is irrelevant, any construct classed as an *Expression* could appear as a child of a *PlusExpr*.

AssignmentStmt is defined to allow any expression as its left child, even though the rules of Pascal do not permit certain expressions to appear on the left-hand side of an assignment. For example, 1 is an expression, but $1 := 2$ is not a legal Pascal assignment. Why is it that we define a tree structure capable of representing invalid programs? Why not recognize two distinct concepts, say an *AddressExpr* and a *ValueExpr*, and demand that the left-hand side of an assignment be a construct classified as the former and the right-hand side be a construct classified as the latter? The answer is that the compiler cannot reliably carry out this classification until the structure of the program is known. For example, consider the assignment $A := 2$. A should be classified as an *AddressExpr* if it is declared as a variable, but as a *ValueExpr* if it is declared as a constant. In order to determine how A was declared, the compiler needs to know the structure of the program. But the purpose of constructing the source program tree is to *determine* the structure of the program!

Our use of a single *Expression* concept instead of distinct *AddressExpr* and *ValueExpr* concepts in the design of the source program tree is a direct consequence of the compilation strategy that we discussed in Chapter 1. Since Pascal requires declaration before use, we could have chosen a different strategy in which partial structural information was used to influence the construction of the source program tree. This strategy is more difficult to understand than the one we chose because it does not permit the designer to separate concerns as cleanly.

While pictures such as those of Figure 4.1 are intuitively appealing, they are difficult to represent in text and hard to reason about. Therefore we adopt a textual notation for describing tree fragments that is similar to the notation used for Pascal function declaration and application. A particular construct is specified by giving its name, the pattern of classes it will accept as children, and its own class. The list of child classes is enclosed in parentheses, and is followed by a colon and the class of the construct. The constructs of Figure 4.1b are described as follows in this notation:

>*IdnLeaf(BasicSymbol)*: *Identifier*
>
>*IntLeaf(BasicSymbol)*: *Integer*
>
>*IntExpr(Integer)*: *Expression*
>
>*IdnExpr(Identifier)*: *Expression*
>
>*PlusExpr(Expression,Expression)*: *Expression*
>
>*AssignmentStmt(Expression,Expression)*: *Statement*

Each of these constructs has a fixed number of children. Many Pascal constructs, such as a procedure call or **case** statement, have an arbitrary number of children. When a construct has an arbitrary number of children, it is convenient to describe those children as a single child that is itself a sequence. The "*" and "+" operators introduced in Section 3.2.2 can be used to indicate a sequence that could be empty and a sequence having at least one element:

4.1 HOW TO CONSTRUCT A TREE

CallStmt(Identifier,Expression*): Statement

CaseStmt(Expression,Case$^+$): Statement

(A procedure might not have any arguments, but a case statement must have at least one alternative.)

In a description of a particular tree, the denotations and identifiers (enclosed in single quotes) appearing in the source program are the arguments to the leaf descriptions. Therefore the tree of Figure 4.1a would be described as:

AssignmentStmt(
  IdnExpr(IdnLeaf('q')),
  PlusExpr(
    IdnExpr(IdnLeaf('q')),
    IntExpr(IntLeaf('1'))))

If an argument is a sequence, then it is surrounded by parentheses, so the source program tree representing *writeln*(4,5) would be described as follows:

CallStmt(
  IdnLeaf('writeln'),
  (IntExpr(IntLeaf('4')), IntExpr(IntLeaf('5'))))

Each fragment of a source program tree is stored as a single Pascal record. The records are linked by pointers to form the complete tree. The data stored in the record are the following:

- Coordinates for error reports involving the construct represented by the fragment.
- A code specifying the fragment corresponding to the record.
- Information relevant to the class to which the fragment belongs.
- Information relevant to the specific fragment (primarily linkage to its children).

Figure 4.2 shows how this record might be declared. (Only a representative sample of the constructs needed to implement Pascal is shown, due to space limitations.)

The fixed field *Coord* and the tag field *Kind* are found in every record. There is then one variant for each class, and the information relevant to the class appears as the fixed part of the corresponding variant. We shall discuss the information relevant to the *Statement* and *Expression* classes in Chapter 7, because it is computed by the translator. *Integer* leaves carry the value of the integer corresponding to the leaf, represented as an *ExtValue* (defined in Figure 2.4). *Identifier* leaves carry the integer value that encodes the identifier corresponding to the leaf, which was determined by the conversion task of the lexical analyzer (Section 3.3.2).

Each class variant of the record has one subvariant for each pattern of children. For example, the constructs *PlusExpr* and *IdnExpr* both belong to the *Expression* class, but the former has two children and the latter only one. Thus *PlusExpr* and *IdnExpr* are represented by different subvariants of the *Expression*

type

    SourceConstruct = ((* Source program constructs *)
      AssignmentStmt,   (* (*Expression,Expression*): *Statement* *)
      CallStmt,   (* (*Identifier,Expression**): *Statement* *)
      PlusExpr,   (* (*Expression,Expression*): *Expression* *)
      IdnExpr,   (* (*Identifier*): *Expression* *)
      IntExpr,   (* (*Integer*): *Expression* *)
      IdnLeaf,   (* (*BasicSymbol*): *Identifier* *)
      IntLeaf);   (* (*BasicSymbol*): *Integer* *)

    Statement = *AssignmentStmt*..*CallStmt*;
    Expression = *PlusExpr*..*IntExpr*;

    SourceTree = ↑*SourceTreeNode*;   (* Representation of the source program tree *)
    SourceSequence = ↑*SourceSequenceElt*; (* Representation of an arbitrary number of child

    SourceTreeNode = **record**
      Coord: *position*;   (* Source text location (Section 2.3.2) *)
      case *Kind*: *SourceConstruct* **of**   (* Construct being represented *)
      AssignmentStmt, *CallStmt*:
        ((* Fields for Statement information (Chapter 7) *
      case *Statement* **of**
      AssignmentStmt: (*Destination,Source*: *SourceTree*);
      CallStmt: (*ProcName*: *SourceTree*; *ProcArguments*: *SourceSequence*));
      PlusExpr, *IdnExpr*, *IntExpr*:
        ((* Fields for Expression information (Chapter 7)
      case *Expression* **of**
      PlusExpr: (*Left,Right*: *SourceTree*);
      IntExpr, *IdnExpr*: (*Child*: *SourceTree*));
      IntLeaf:
        (*Value*: *ExtValue*);   (* Denotation (Section 3.3.1) *)
      IdnLeaf:
        (*LexIdent*: *integer*);   (* Identifier (Section 3.3.2) *)
    end;

    SourceSequenceElt = **record**
      Node: *SourceTree*;   (* Current element of the sequence *)
      Next: *SourceSequence*;   (* Remainder of the sequence *)
    end;

Figure 4.2
Declaring a source tree node

variant. *IdnExpr* and *IntExpr*, on the other hand, are represented by the same subvariant of the *Expression* variant because they have the same pattern of children. Notice that no explicit tag field is necessary for the subvariants, because they are selected by the value of *Kind*.

    A *CallStmt* has one child to represent the procedure being called and an arbitrary number of children to represent the arguments to be passed to that procedure. The arguments are encoded by a *SourceSequence*—a linear list of expressions in this case. If a particular *CallStmt* has no arguments, the *ProcArguments* field of the record will contain **nil**; otherwise it will point to a *SourceSequenceElt* whose *Node* field points to the tree representing the first argument.

Figure 4.3a gives a schematic form for the *SourceTreeNode* record defined in Figure 4.2. These records are used to represent the tree of Figure 4.1 in Figure 4.3b. The coordinate information in the tree specifies that the statement $q := q + 1$ began in column 17 of line 4 and contained no embedded spaces. Identifier q was converted into the integer 108 by the lexical analyzer. Note that the information for *Identifier*- and *Integer*-class nodes has been filled in during tree construction, while the information for *Expression*- and *Statement*-class nodes has not. That information will be computed during semantic analysis by the methods discussed in Chapter 7.

4.1.2 Building a Tree

Trees such as Figure 4.3b are built from information carried by the basic symbols of the source program. The construction process is interleaved with the process of reading the basic symbols. A stack is used to hold pointers to nodes that have been built, but not yet incorporated into the tree. Let's see how this strategy can be used to build Figure 4.3b, given the sequence of basic symbols $q := q + 1$ beginning at column 17 of line 4.

The *Token* (Figure 3.1) corresponding to the first basic symbol, q, carries enough information to build the leftmost leaf:

- It carries the source text coordinates needed for the *Coord* field of the *SourceTreeNode* record.
- It specifies that the basic symbol is an identifier, so the *Kind* field must be set to *IdnLeaf*.
- It carries the integer with which the lexical analyzer has chosen to represent the identifier, needed for the *LexIdent* field.

Therefore the *SourceNode* record representing the leftmost leaf is constructed and a pointer to it is pushed onto the stack. Since this node is the only child of its parent *IdnExpr* node, that node can be constructed next. Its *Coord* field is set from the *Coord* field of its child (which is the top node of the stack), and its *Child* field is set to point to the top node of the stack. Finally, one node is popped off of the stack and a pointer to the *IdnExpr* node is pushed in its place.

The next basic symbol is ":=", which carries the coordinate information for the *AssignmentStmt* node. This node is therefore constructed and a pointer to it is pushed onto the stack. Note that neither of the linkage field values is set at this time.

The second q is processed in exactly the same way as the first, resulting in another *IdnLeaf* node and another *IdnExpr* node. A pointer to the *IdnExpr* node is left on top of the stack at the end of this processing.

The next basic symbol is "+". This basic symbol carries the coordinate information for the *PlusExpr* node, so a *PlusExpr* node is created and a pointer to

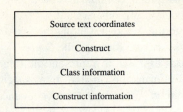

(a) Schematic form of Figure 4.2

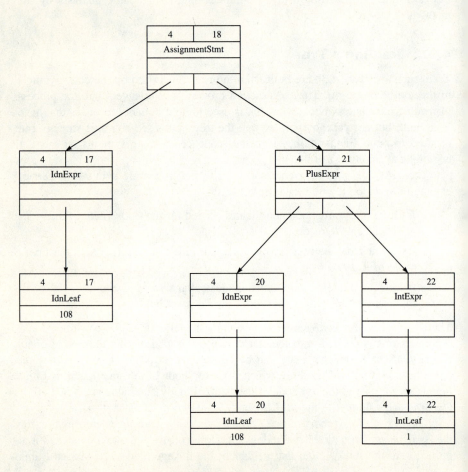

(b) A subtree for $q := q + 1$

Figure 4.3
Representing a tree with linked records

4.1 HOW TO CONSTRUCT A TREE

it is pushed onto the stack. As in the case of the *AssignmentStmt* node, the *Left* and *Right* fields of the *PlusExpr* node are not set at this time.

The last basic symbol in the sequence is 1, from which an *IntLeaf* node and an *IntExpr* node can be constructed in a manner analogous to the construction of the *IdnLeaf* and *IdnExpr* nodes from the basic symbol *q*. After these nodes have been constructed and a pointer to the *IntExpr* node has been pushed onto the stack, the top five locations of the stack contain pointers to the following nodes (1 is the top of the stack):

1. Subtree rooted in an *IntExpr* node with coordinates (4,22).
2. *PlusExpr* node with coordinates (4,21).
3. Subtree rooted in an *IdnExpr* node with coordinates (4,20).
4. *AssignmentStmt* node with coordinates (4,18).
5. Subtree rooted in an *IdnExpr* node with coordinates (4,17).

Elements 1–3 of the stack form the complete subtree rooted in the *PlusExpr* node, so the *Left* field of the second element of the stack can be set to point to the third element, while the *Right* field of the second element can be set to point to the first element. Finally, the top three elements can be removed and a pointer to the *PlusExpr* node pushed onto the stack.

Now the top three elements of the stack form the complete subtree of Figure 4.3b. They can be linked appropriately, removed, and a pointer to the *AssignmentStmt* node pushed to complete the construction of Figure 4.3b.

Figure 4.4 specifies a set of operations to implement this construction process. *SourceTreeInit* establishes an empty stack, *SourceLeaf* creates leaves from the information in a *Token* record, *SourceNode* links subtrees already on the stack to create larger subtrees, and *SourceFinl* delivers the complete source program tree to the translator. The *SourceConstruct* arguments to *SourceLeaf* and *SourceNode* specify the particular node to be built. In order to carry out the construction of the subtree of Figure 4.3b, the compiler would need to make the following sequence of calls:

$$SourceLeaf(IdnLeaf, t_1);$$
$$SourceNode(IdnExpr);$$
$$SourceLeaf(AssignmentStmt, t_2);$$
$$SourceLeaf(IdnLeaf, t_3);$$
$$SourceNode(IdnExpr);$$
$$SourceLeaf(PlusExpr, t_4);$$
$$SourceLeaf(IntLeaf, t_5);$$
$$SourceNode(IntExpr);$$
$$SourceNode(PlusExpr);$$
$$SourceNode(AssignmentStmt);$$

(Here t_i represents the ith *Token* record in the sequence delivered by the lexical analyzer.)

The module interface described by Figure 4.4 can be used for any source tree construction module, but the implementations of *SourceLeaf* and *SourceNode* are specific to a particular tree structure. That tree structure will require that

procedure *SourceLeaf*(*c*: *SourceConstruct*; **var** *l*: *Token*);
   (* Build a leaf of the source program tree
   On entry-
      c = kind of leaf to be built
      l = data to be stored in the leaf
   On exit-
      The constructed leaf has been added to the stack
   *)

procedure *SourceNode*(*c*: *SourceConstruct*);
   (* Build an interior node of the source program tree
   On entry-
      c = kind of node to be built
   On exit-
      The constructed node has replaced its children on the stack
   *)

procedure *EmptySourceSeq*;
   (* Build an empty sequence of source program tree nodes
   On exit-
      An empty sequence has been added to the stack
   *)

procedure *ExtendSourceSeq*;
   (* Add a source program tree node to an existing sequence
   On exit-
      The extended sequence has replaced its components on the stack
   *)

procedure *SourceTreeInit*;
   (* Initialize the source program tree construction module *)

procedure *SourceTreeFinl*;
   (* Finalize the source program tree construction module *)

Figure 4.4
Source tree construction module interface

SourceLeaf, *SourceNode*, *EmptySourceSeq*, and *ExtendSourceSeq* be invoked in a particular sequence to place nodes, subtrees, and sequences onto the stack in the correct order. Figure 4.4 says nothing about this invocation sequence, and therefore does not constitute an adequate interface specification for the module.

The invocation sequence cannot be defined in isolation—a source program tree can be built only as the information about its structure becomes available from the sequence of basic symbols that makes up the source program. Therefore the invocations of the operations listed in Figure 4.4 must be interspersed with invocations of *Lexical* (Section 3.2.3) to obtain basic symbols. Figure 4.5 shows how these operations are used to build a source program subtree for

```
var t: Token;
  . . .
Lexical(t); SourceLeaf(IdnLeaf,t);            (* a *)
SourceNode(IdnExpr);
Lexical(t); SourceLeaf(AssignmentStmt,t);     (* := *)
Lexical(t);                                   (* ( *)
Lexical(t); SourceLeaf(IdnLeaf,t);            (* b *)
SourceNode(IdnExpr);
Lexical(t); SourceLeaf(PlusExpr,t);           (* + *)
Lexical(t); SourceLeaf(SetExpr,t);            (* [ *)
EmptySourceSeq;
Lexical(t); SourceLeaf(IdnLeaf,t);            (* c *)
SourceNode(IdnExpr);
ExtendSourceSeq;
Lexical(t);                                   (* , *)
Lexical(t); SourceLeaf(IdnLeaf,t);            (* d *)
SourceNode(IdnExpr);
ExtendSourceSeq;
Lexical(t);                                   (* , *)
Lexical(t); SourceLeaf(IdnLeaf,t);            (* e *)
SourceNode(IdnExpr);
ExtendSourceSeq;
Lexical(t);                                   (* ] *)
SourceNode(SetExpr);
SourceNode(PlusExpr);
Lexical(t);                                   (* ) *)
SourceNode(AssignmentStmt);
```

Figure 4.5
Sequence of operations constructing a source program tree for $a := (b + [c,d,e])$

$a := (b + [c,d,e])$. This subtree contains a construct with an arbitrary number of children:

SetExpr(Expression*): Expression

EmptySourceSeq establishes an empty sequence, and that sequence is extended each time a subtree belonging to it has been completed.

In the next section we shall show how to relate the invocations of the source program tree construction operations to recognition of basic symbols, thereby both completing the interface specification of Figure 4.4 and defining the parsing task.

4.2 HOW TO SPECIFY THE PARSING TASK

Figure 4.5 is the sequence of observable actions that should be taken by a parser for Pascal when the compiler is presented with the input $a := (b + [c,d,e])$. Presumably the parser will also perform tests on the input and make decisions about which tree construction operations to invoke, what their arguments should be, and when to invoke the lexical analyzer. Such tests and decisions are carried out solely within the parsing module, however, and they can affect the remainder of the compiler only by affecting the sequence of invocations of the tree construction and lexical analyzer operations. The parsing task is completely specified, therefore, if the sequence of invocations of the tree construction and lexical analyzer operations is specified for every possible source program. Any interesting source language is capable of expressing an infinite number of programs; thus, you must specify an infinite number of invocation sequences to completely specify the parsing task. In order to be useful, the specification itself must be finite.

Section 4.2.1 provides an analogy between the infinite sets of invocation sequences that specify the parsing task and the infinite sets of character sequences that specify the scanning task. This analogy can then be used to apply the specification techniques of Chapter 3 to give a finite description of the parsing task. Sections 4.2.2 and 4.2.3 explain the extensions that are needed to the syntax diagram and regular expression notations in order to make them capable of describing the parsing task. A third descriptive technique, the context-free grammar, is introduced in Section 4.2.4.

4.2.1 Activity Sequences

The first step in specifying the parser's task is to define a set of "basic invocations" from which all possible sequences can be built. Basic invocations are the "characters" that make up the vocabulary of the parser specification. There are three kinds of basic invocations, all of which are illustrated by single lines in Figure 4.5:

- *Basic symbol*: Accept a specific basic symbol, but do not invoke the tree construction module (as is done in Figure 4.5 by the line with the comment "(* (*)").
- *Symbol connection*: Accept a basic symbol from a given class and invoke the tree construction operation *SourceLeaf* (as is done in Figure 4.5 by the line with the comment "(* a *)").
- *Structure connection*: Invoke one of the tree construction operations *SourceNode*, *EmptySourceSeq*, or *ExtendSourceSeq* (as is done in Figure 4.5 by the lines without comments).

The observable behavior of the parser when parsing a particular source program can always be described by a finite sequence of these basic invocations. This finite sequence of basic invocations is called an *activity sequence*.

An activity sequence can be thought of as a string in a language whose vocabulary is just the set of basic invocations. Let's call this language the "parsing language" of the compiler, to distinguish it from the source language and the target language. The parsing language is the set of activity sequences that describe the observable behavior of the parser when parsing source programs. If the parser is presented with a program in the source language, then its observable behavior will correspond to an activity sequence in the parsing language. Conversely, every activity sequence in the parsing language describes the observable behavior of the parser when it is presented with *some* program in the source language.

It is convenient to describe a particular activity sequence simply by listing its basic invocations. A basic symbol is delimited by apostrophes, a symbol connection appears as the desired construct applied to the basic symbol, and a structure connection appears simply as the desired construct (if the operation is *SourceNode*), *EmptySourceSeq*, or *ExtendSourceSeq*. Using these conventions, the activity sequence describing the observable behavior of the parser as it processed $a := (b + [c,d,e])$ (recall Figure 4.5) could be written as follows:

IdnLeaf('a')   IdnExpr   AssignmentStmt(':=')   '('   IdnLeaf('b')   IdnExpr   PlusExpr('+')
SetExpr('[')   EmptySourceSeq
IdnLeaf('c')   IdnExpr   ExtendSourceSeq   ','   IdnLeaf('d')   IdnExpr   ExtendSourceSeq   ','
IdnLeaf('e')   IdnExpr   ExtendSourceSeq   ']'   SetExpr   ')'   PlusExpr   AssignmentStmt

If all of the connections (but not the arguments of symbol connections) are deleted from an activity sequence, what remains is the sequence of basic symbols constituting the source program being compiled:

'a'   ':='   '('   'b'   '+'   '['   'c'   ','   'd'   ','   'e'   ']'   ')'

If all of the basic symbols (including arguments of symbol connections) are deleted from an activity sequence, and the names *SourceLeaf* and *SourceNode* are added to construct names denoting symbol connections and structure connections respectively, what remains is the sequence of tree construction operations invoked by the parser to build the source program tree:

SourceLeaf(IdnLeaf)   SourceNode(IdnExpr)   SourceLeaf(AssignmentStmt)
SourceLeaf(IdnLeaf)   SourceNode(IdnExpr)
SourceLeaf(PlusExpr)   SourceLeaf(SetExpr)   EmptySourceSeq
SourceLeaf(IdnLeaf)   SourceNode(IdnExpr)   ExtendSourceSeq
SourceLeaf(IdnLeaf)   SourceNode(IdnExpr)   ExtendSourceSeq
SourceLeaf(IdnLeaf)   SourceNode(IdnExpr)   ExtendSourceSeq
SourceNode(SetExpr)   SourceNode(PlusExpr)   SourceNode(AssignmentStmt)

The activity sequence thus describes the interleaving in time of the "input" and "output" operations of the parser.

4.2.2 Syntax Diagrams

Figure 4.6 gives syntax diagrams describing the parsing language for a small subset of Pascal assignment statements (sufficient to describe the behavior shown in Figure 4.5). It introduces a new notation—the rectangular box—that does not appear in Chapter 3. Rectangular boxes represent complete syntax diagrams.

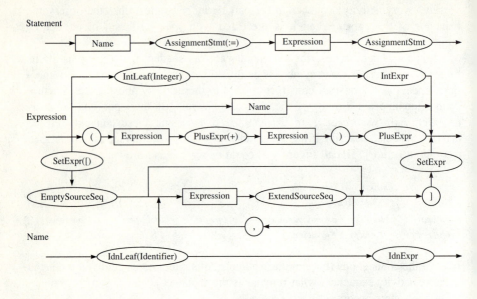

Figure 4.6
A syntax diagram for some Pascal assignment statements

When a rectangular box is encountered during the traversal of a syntax diagram, the syntax diagram named in the box must be traversed.

Round and oval boxes have meanings analogous to those of their counterparts in the syntax diagrams of Chapter 3. When a round box is encountered during the traversal of a syntax diagram, the particular basic symbol it specifies is added to the activity sequence. When an oval box is traversed, the connection it specifies is added to the activity sequence. If the oval box represents a symbol connection, some basic symbol from the given set must be selected as its argument. For example, the first oval box of the *Name* diagram in Figure 4.6 represents a symbol connection. In order to generate an element of an activity sequence from that box, you must pick an element of the set of identifiers. If you chose the identifier *a*, then the generated element of the activity sequence would be *IdnLeaf('a')*.

In Figure 4.6 the left-hand side of the assignment statement is generated by traversing the *Name* diagram, while the right-hand side is generated by traversing the *Expression* diagram. The *Name* diagram can generate an activity sequence consisting only of an *IdnLeaf* symbol connection and an *IdnExpr* structure connection. This restricts the expression trees that can appear as left children of the *Assignment* construct to *IdnExpr* fragments. An *IntExpr* fragment could never appear as the left child of an *Assignment* construct, because the parsing language described by Figure 4.6 does not contain any activity sequences of the following form:

IntLeaf(*integer*)   *IntExpr*   · · ·

If we wished to expand Figure 4.6 to define a parsing language for a larger subset of Pascal assignment statements, we might do so by expanding the *Name* diagram to describe the parsing of more constructs (such as subscripted variables) that can appear on the left-hand side of an assignment. Notice that this automatically would allow such constructs on the right-hand side as well, since one way to traverse the *Expression* diagram is to traverse the *Name* diagram.

It is worthwhile emphasizing that a parsing language is the set of activity sequences that can be derived from a particular description, *not* the description itself. Two descriptions are equivalent if they generate the same set of activity sequences. A given set of activity sequences can be generated by many equivalent descriptions, and each description may have other properties that make it appropriate for a particular task. For example, a description must have a certain property if a parser is to be constructed from it according to the methods of Chapter 5. When a description does not have appropriate properties for a given task, it can sometimes be transformed into an equivalent description that does have those properties.

A syntax diagram can be substituted for a rectangular box containing the name of that diagram without changing the set of activity sequences described. It's easy to see why this is so: If you encountered the rectangular box while traversing the diagram and generating an activity sequence, the rules require that you traverse the diagram named in the box. When that diagram has been substituted for the rectangular box, you will simply traverse it without further ado. Since the rectangular box itself contributes nothing to the activity sequence, you will produce the same sequence whether you encounter the rectangular box or the diagram it names.

If, after a diagram has been substituted for a rectangular box that names it, no rectangular boxes contain the name of that diagram, then the entire diagram can be deleted. The reason is that it is impossible to reach a diagram (other than the "top-level" diagram) unless some reachable diagram contains a rectangular box naming it. For example, if the *Name* diagram of Figure 4.6 is substituted for the rectangular boxes in the *Statement* and *Expression* diagrams that contain the name *Name*, then there will be no rectangular box containing the name *Name*; thus, the *Name* diagram cannot be reached from the *Statement* diagram. Since it is not reachable, it can be deleted (Figure 4.7a).

Generally, it is not possible to remove *all* rectangular boxes by substitution. If all rectangular boxes could be removed, then the activity sequences could be described by the techniques of Chapter 3. In Figure 4.7, for example, any substitution of the *Expression* diagram for a rectangular box containing the name *Expression* will result in *more* rectangular boxes containing the name *Expression*!

A part of an existing diagram can also be split off as a new diagram without changing the set of activity sequences described (Figure 4.7b). Again, the subdiagram will be traversed whether it is included directly or named by a rectangular box that stands in its place. Since the rectangular box itself adds nothing to the activity sequence, its presence cannot be detected by examining the sequence.

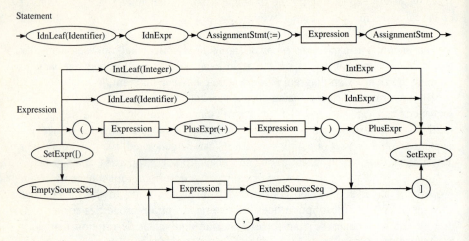

(a) Figure 4.6 modified by deleting the *Name* diagram

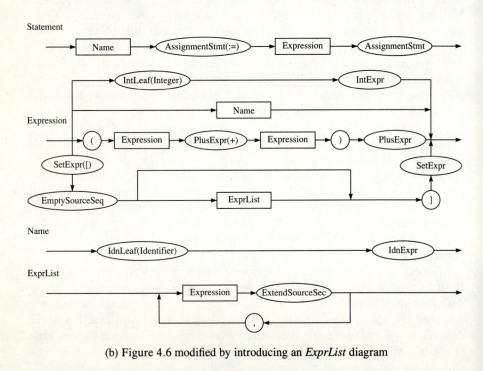

(b) Figure 4.6 modified by introducing an *ExprList* diagram

Figure 4.7
Syntax diagrams equivalent to Figure 4.6

The bottom path through the *Expression* diagram in Figure 4.7b forks just to the right of the second oval box (Figure 4.8a). Suppose that the diagram were redrawn with the fork just to the left of the first oval box, and the oval boxes were duplicated so that they appeared on each of the branches leaving the fork as shown in Figure 4.8b. This transformation does not alter the set of activity sequences the diagram describes. In Figure 4.8a, you would generate the symbol connection *SetExpr*([) followed by the structure connection *EmptySourceSeq*. Then, you would either traverse the *ExprList* diagram or not, depending upon the path you selected. In Figure 4.8b, you would select one of the two paths first. No matter which you selected, however, you would have to generate the symbol connection *SetExpr*([) and the structure connection *EmptySourceSeq* before continuing. Therefore, with either diagram the generated activity sequence would be the same. Clearly, the opposite transformation—from Figure 4.8b to Figure 4.8a— also leaves the set of activity sequences unchanged.

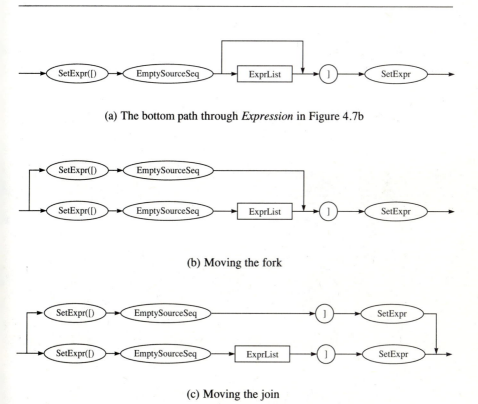

(a) The bottom path through *Expression* in Figure 4.7b

(b) Moving the fork

(c) Moving the join

Figure 4.8
Transformations that move forks and joins leaving the activity sequence unchanged

A similar transformation allows one to move a point at which two paths join past a box. Figure 4.8 illustrates this situation as well. After either traversing or skipping the *ExprList* diagram in Figure 4.8b, you must generate the basic symbol "]" and the structure connection *SetExpr* because the two paths join before the round box. In Figure 4.8c the join has been moved past these two boxes, which now appear on both paths leading to it. Again, no matter which path you selected, you must generate "]" and *SetExpr*. If two identical boxes precede a join, as in Figure 4.8c, the diagram can be transformed by merging them and moving the join to before the merged box (as shown in Figure 4.8b), without changing the set of activity sequences.

The *ExprList* diagrams in Figure 4.7b and Figure 4.9 also generate the same activity sequences. Consider the version in Figure 4.7b (the *iterative* version). This diagram can be traversed by simply passing through from left to right without traversing the loop at all. In Figure 4.9 (the *recursive* version), the top path of the *ExprList* diagram will generate an equivalent activity sequence. *Any*

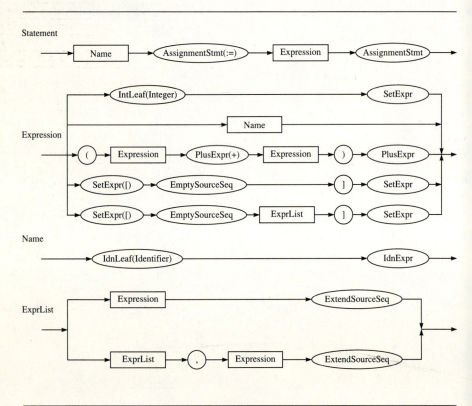

Figure 4.9
Syntax diagrams with parallel paths

traversal of the *ExprList* diagram of Figure 4.7b reaches the fork just before reaching the exit. Therefore, the set of activity sequences generated by traversals reaching the fork is exactly the same as the set of activity sequences generated by traversals reaching the exit. But the set of activity sequences generated by traversals reaching the exit is just the set of activity sequences generated by traversing the diagram named *ExprList*. Once you have reached the fork, you can complete a traversal of the *ExprList* diagram by traversing the loop once. This path is the bottom one of the *ExprList* diagram in Figure 4.9: The leftmost box describes all of the activity sequences that can be generated in reaching the fork, while the remainder of the path describes the activity sequences generated by traversing the loop once.

Another way to explain the equivalence of the *ExprList* diagrams in Figure 4.7b and Figure 4.9 is to think about generating an expression list that contains a specific number of commas. First consider an expression list with no commas. In Figure 4.7b you would select the straight-through path at the fork; in Figure 4.9 you would select the top path at the fork. An expression list with one comma requires you to select the loop the first time you reach the fork in Figure 4.7b and the straight-through path the second time. You would select the bottom path on entering the diagram in Figure 4.9 for the first time, and the top path on entering it for the second time. Note the analogy—"reaching the fork" in the iterative version (Figure 4.7b) is analogous to "entering the diagram" in the recursive version (Figure 4.9). If you want to generate a list with n commas, you make one selection the first n times you "reach the fork" (iterate) or "enter the diagram" (recurse) and the other selection the $n+1^{st}$ time.

The syntax diagrams in Figure 4.9 contain no loops. Each diagram has at most one fork, which immediately follows the entry point, and at most one join, which immediately precedes the exit point. It is important to note that *any* set of syntax diagrams can be transformed into a set having these properties, without changing the parsing language that it describes.

4.2.3 Extended Regular Expressions

Figure 4.10 uses extended regular expressions to describe the activity sequences represented in Figure 4.6. The extension from the regular expression notation of Chapter 3 is to associate a name with a regular expression by writing "name = expression", and then to allow the name to be used to represent the entire expression. This extension is exactly the extension made to the syntax diagrams in the previous section.

A specific basic symbol is represented by enclosing the characters of that basic symbol in single quotes, while connections are represented by names or names applied to arguments. Although connections and regular expression names have the same form, they can be distinguished on the basis of context: A regular expression name must appear on the left-hand side of a definition of the form "name = expression", while a connection name will never appear in this context. Thus *Statement*, *Expression*, and *Name* must be regular expression names in Figure 4.10, while *IdnExpr*, *EmptySourceSeq*, and *AssignmentStmt* represent connections.

```
        Statement  =  Name  AssignmentStmt(':=') Expression AssignmentStmt
        Expression =  IntLeaf(Integer) IntExpr
                   |  Name
                   |  '(' Expression PlusExpr('+') Expression ')' PlusExpr
                   |  SetExpr('[') EmptySourceSeq
                      (ε | Expression ExtendSourceSeq (',' Expression ExtendSourceSeq)*)
                      ']' SetExpr
        Name       =  IdnLeaf(Identifier) IdnExpr
```

a) A definition equivalent to Figure 4.6

```
Name AssignmentStmt(':=') Expression AssignmentStmt
IdnLeaf(Identifier) IdnExpr AssignmentStmt(':=') Expression AssignmentStmt
IdnLeaf('a') IdnExpr AssignmentStmt(':=') Expression AssignmentStmt
IdnLeaf('a') IdnExpr AssignmentStmt(':=')
  '(' Expression PlusExpr('+') Expression ')' PlusExpr AssignmentStmt
IdnLeaf('a') IdnExpr AssignmentStmt(':=')
  '(' IdnLeaf('b') IdnExpr PlusExpr('+') Expression ')' PlusExpr AssignmentStmt
IdnLeaf('a') IdnExpr AssignmentStmt(':=')   '(' IdnLeaf('b') IdnExpr PlusExpr('+')
  SetExpr('[') EmptySourceSeq (ε | Expression ExtendSourceSeq (',' Expression ExtendSourceSeq
  ']' SetExpr
  ')' PlusExpr AssignmentStmt
IdnLeaf('a') IdnExpr AssignmentStmt(':=')   '(' IdnLeaf('b') IdnExpr PlusExpr('+')
  SetExpr('[') EmptySourceSeq Expression ExtendSourceSeq
  (',' Expression ExtendSourceSeq)* ']' SetExpr
  ')' PlusExpr AssignmentStmt
IdnLeaf('a') IdnExpr AssignmentStmt(':=')   '(' IdnLeaf('b') IdnExpr PlusExpr('+')
  SetExpr('[') EmptySourceSeq IdnLeaf('c') IdnExpr ExtendSourceSeq
  ',' Expression ExtendSourceSeq
  ',' Expression ExtendSourceSeq ']' SetExpr
  ')' PlusExpr AssignmentStmt
IdnLeaf('a') IdnExpr AssignmentStmt(':=')   '(' IdnLeaf('b') IdnExpr PlusExpr('+')
  SetExpr('[') EmptySourceSeq
  IdnLeaf('c') IdnExpr ExtendSourceSeq ',' IdnLeaf('d') IdnExpr ExtendSourceSeq
  ',' IdnLeaf('e') IdnExpr ExtendSourceSeq
  ']' SetExpr ')' PlusExpr AssignmentStmt
```

b) Deriving an activity sequence from (a)

Figure 4.10
Extended regular expressions

An activity sequence is produced from the right-hand side of the *Statement* expression by a series of simple transformations. Each transformation rewrites one symbol or chooses a specific alternative. Expression names can be rewritten by replacing the name with the expression it names, and symbol connections can be rewritten by replacing a symbol class with a specific member of that class (thus *IdnLeaf(Identifier)* can be rewritten as *IdnLeaf('a')*). Figure 4.10b shows how the activity sequence for $a := (b + [c,d,e])$ could be produced. (Some of the

4.2 HOW TO SPECIFY THE PARSING TASK

detail has been omitted to save space. For example, two simple transformations are required to go from the fourth line to the fifth: replacing *Expression* with *IdnLeaf(Identifier) IdnExpr* and then selecting the element *'b'* of the class *Identifier*.) The simple transformations can be applied in any order, and the process terminates when no further transformations are possible.

Just as it is possible to alter a syntax diagram without changing the parsing language it describes, extended regular expressions can be transformed without changing their meaning. For example, the parsing language is not altered if a regular expression is substituted for its name or if parts of a regular expression are named. These transformations are the regular expression analogs of substituting a diagram for a rectangular box and substituting a rectangular box for a subdiagram, respectively (Figure 4.7). Other identities for regular expressions are summarized in Figure 4.11. Many of these identities are analogous to those of numeric expressions, with "|" playing the role of "+", concatenation playing the role of "×", and "ϵ" playing the role of "1". The identities involving "*" and idempotence are new, and concatenation is not commutative.

To illustrate the use of the identities given in Figure 4.11, consider the following transformation:

$ExprList$ = *Expression ExtendSourceSeq* (',' *Expression ExtendSourceSeq*)*

= *Expression ExtendSourceSeq* $\qquad\qquad$ (1)

(ϵ | (',' *Expression ExtendSourceSeq*)* (',' *Expression ExtendSourceSeq*))

$$e_1 | e_2 = e_2 | e_1 \quad \text{(commutative)}$$

$$(e_1 | e_2) | e_3 = e_1 | (e_2 | e_3)$$
$$(e_1 e_2) e_3 = e_1 (e_2 e_3) \quad \text{(associative)}$$

$$e_1 (e_2 | e_3) = e_1 e_2 | e_1 e_3$$
$$(e_1 | e_2) e_3 = e_1 e_3 | e_2 e_3 \quad \text{(distributive)}$$

$$e_1 \epsilon = \epsilon e_1 = e_1 \quad \text{(identity)}$$

$$e_1 | e_1 = e_1 \quad \text{(idempotent)}$$

$$(e^*)^* = e^*$$
$$e^* = \epsilon | e e^* = \epsilon | e^* e$$
$$e^* = e | e^*$$

$$\epsilon^* = \epsilon$$

Figure 4.11
Identities for regular expressions

= *Expression ExtendSourceSeq* ε

| *Expression ExtendSourceSeq* (',' *Expression ExtendSourceSeq*)*

(',' *Expression ExtendSourceSeq*)

= *Expression ExtendSourceSeq*

| *Expression ExtendSourceSeq* (',' *Expression ExtendSourceSeq*)*

(',' *Expression ExtendSourceSeq*)

= *Expression ExtendSourceSeq* | *ExprList* ',' *Expression ExtendSourceSeq*   (2)

The last transformation is simply a substitution of the name *ExprList* for the regular expression that defines it in (1).

We say that (2) is *left recursive* because the name of the regular expression appears at the left end of a term. There is also an equivalent *right recursive* form:

ExprList = *Expression ExtendSourceSeq* | *Expression ExtendSourceSeq* ',' *ExprList*

Left or right recursion can always be replaced by iteration, and vice versa, using the identities of Figure 4.11. If the recursion is neither left nor right, as in the fourth line of Figure 4.10a, then it cannot be replaced by iteration.

The relationships between regular expressions and syntax diagrams described in Figure 3.8 continue to hold between extended regular expressions and syntax diagrams with rectangular boxes. In addition, a regular expression name in an extended regular expression is equivalent to a rectangular box in a syntax diagram. The identities of Figure 4.11 therefore have counterparts in the notation of syntax diagrams. It is usually easier, however, to transform syntax diagrams by writing the equivalent extended regular expressions, transforming them, and then constructing the equivalent syntax diagrams.

4.2.4 Context-Free Grammars

It is possible to give a finite description of an infinite set of sequences via a "rewriting system" that uses only one operation—substitution—to generate sequences in the set it describes. Activity sequences can be generated by a restricted form of rewriting system called a *context-free grammar*. A context-free grammar has a vocabulary made up of two disjoint sets of symbols called *nonterminals* and *terminals*. Nonterminals are like the names of the regular expressions in the last section—each is defined by a sequence of symbols. Figure 4.12a shows the nonterminal symbols of a grammar that describes the parsing language we have been discussing. The terminal symbols are possible activity sequence elements (Figure 4.12b).

Rewriting rules, called *productions*, define the nonterminal symbols by sequences of terminal and nonterminal symbols. The productions shown in Figure 4.12c are "context-free" because each has only a single nonterminal appearing on the left-hand side. That means that any production for a given nonterminal can

Statement   Expression   Name   ExprList

a) Nonterminal symbols

IdnLeaf(Identifier)   IntLeaf(Integer)   AssignmentStmt(':=')   '('   PlusExpr('+')   ')'   SetExpr('[')   ']'
AssignmentStmt   IntExpr   PlusExpr   IdnExpr   SetExpr   EmptySourceSeq   ExtendSourceSeq

b) Terminal symbols

Statement	→	*Name AssignmentStmt(':=') Expression AssignmentStmt*
Expression	→	*IntLeaf(Integer) IntExpr*
Expression	→	*Name*
Expression	→	*'(' Expression PlusExpr('+') Expression ')' PlusExpr*
Expression	→	*SetExpr('[') EmptySourceSeq ']' SetExpr*
Expression	→	*SetExpr('[') EmptySourceSeq ExprList ']' SetExpr*
Name	→	*IdnLeaf(Identifier) IdnExpr*
ExprList	→	*Expression ExtendSourceSeq*
ExprList	→	*ExprList ',' Expression ExtendSourceSeq*

c) Productions

Statement

d) Start symbol

Figure 4.12
Example of the components of a context-free grammar

be used to rewrite any occurrence of that nonterminal, regardless of the context—the symbols surrounding the occurrence.

Finally, there is a distinguished nonterminal symbol called the *start symbol*, or *axiom* (Figure 4.12d), with which all derivations begin. Here is a derivation of the activity sequence for $a := 27$:

Statement

Name AssignmentStmt(':=')   Expression AssignmentStmt

IdnLeaf(Identifier)   IdnExpr AssignmentStmt(':=')   IntLeaf(Integer)   IntExpr AssignmentStmt

IdnLeaf('a')   IdnExpr AssignmentStmt(':=')   IntLeaf('27')   IntExpr AssignmentStmt

A rewriting step consists of copying the string as it stands, substituting the right-hand side of some production for the nonterminal appearing on its left-hand side. Thus, in the first step *Statement*, which appears on the left-hand side of only one production, was replaced by the right-hand side of that production. This single derivation step can be described using the "derives" operator $\Rightarrow$ as follows:

Statement $\Rightarrow$ *Name AssignmentStmt(':=')   Expression AssignmentStmt*

By analogy to the conventions of regular expressions, a nonempty *sequence* of derivations is usually described by adding a "+" to the operator; if the sequence of derivations might be empty, then a "*" is added. Thus, the derivation given above can be summarized by writing the following:

Statement $\Rightarrow^+$ *IdnLeaf*('a') *IdnExpr AssignmentStmt*(':=') *IntLeaf*('27') *IntExpr AssignmentStmt*

Formally, a grammar is defined as a quadruple $G = (N,T,P,S)$, with N being the set of nonterminal symbols, T the set of terminal symbols, P the set of productions, and $S \in N$ the start symbol. G defines a *language*, L, which is the set of strings of terminal symbols that can be derived by rewriting the start symbol:

$$L(G) = \{s \in T^* \mid S \Rightarrow^+ s\}$$

Here T^* is the "Kleene closure" of the set T. It is the set of all possible sequences of terminal symbols (including the empty sequence). Each sentence, s, in the language must therefore consist only of terminal symbols and must be derivable via some sequence of rewriting steps from S. The sequence of rewriting steps cannot be empty because S is a nonterminal, s must consist only of terminals, and the sets of nonterminals and terminals are disjoint.

Converting a grammar to a set of syntax diagrams is quite straightforward. Each production corresponds to a single path through the syntax diagram whose name is the left-hand side nonterminal symbol. This path consists of a sequence of boxes, one for each symbol on the right-hand side of the production, in order from left to right. Each nonterminal symbol corresponds to a rectangular box and each terminal symbol corresponds to either a round box (if it represents a basic symbol) or an oval box (if it represents a connection). If the right-hand side of the production is empty, the path is a direct connection (without any boxes) from the entry of the syntax diagram to the exit. Using these rules, you can see that the grammar of Figure 4.12 is equivalent to the set of syntax diagrams shown in Figure 4.9.

Transformation of a set of syntax diagrams to a grammar is simplified if each syntax diagram is first converted to a collection of simple parallel paths, as in Figure 4.9. Then each path corresponds to a single production for the nonterminal that is the name of the diagram containing the path.

4.3 OPERATOR PRECEDENCE AND ASSOCIATION

Figure 4.13 extends the parsing language of Figure 4.10a to accept expressions with operators other than +. The symbol connections appearing in the definition of *Operator* build nodes that carry the coordinates of the operator and specify the appropriate construct. Pointers to these nodes are pushed onto the stack, but they are not linked to their children at the time they are created. (Recall the discussion at the end of Section 4.1.2.)

Dyadic is a structure connection that is invoked when the top three stack locations point to the components of a dyadic expression. The top element of the stack points to the subtree for the operator's right operand, the second element to

```
Statement   = Name AssignmentStmt(':=') Expression AssignmentStmt
Expression  = IntLeaf(Integer)   IntExpr
            | Name
            | '(' Expression Operator Expression ')' Dyadic
            | SetExpr('[')  EmptySourceSeq (ε | Expression ExtendSourceSeq
              (',' Expression ExtendSourceSeq)*) ']' SetExpr
Name        = IdnLeaf(Identifier)   IdnExpr
Operator    = PlusExpr('+') | MinusExpr('-')
            | StarExpr('*') | SlashExpr('/') | DivExpr('div') | ModExpr('mod')
```

Figure 4.13
Parsing language for a subset of Pascal assignment statements

the node built by the operator's symbol connection, and the third element to the subtree for the operator's left operand. An expression subtree can be built by linking the nodes pointed to by these three elements, removing the elements from the stack, and pushing a pointer to the resultant subtree. This processing is completely independent of the particular operator.

Thus, *Dyadic* effectively represents a subclass of expressions consisting of two operands operated upon by an operator. Although *Dyadic* is a value of type *SourceConstruct*, it will never be stored in the *Kind* field of a *SourceTreeNode* (Figure 4.2) because that field will always specify a particular construct in the subclass represented by *Dyadic*. Judicious introduction of *SourceConstruct* values that represent subclasses of source tree nodes allow us to simplify the description of an activity sequence. For example, if *Dyadic* were not used in Figure 4.13, then the third alternative of *Expression* would have to be replaced by one alternative for every operator:

| '(' Expression PlusExpr('+')   Expression ')' PlusExpr
| '(' Expression MinusExpr('-')   Expression ')' MinusExpr
...

One of the activity sequences that can be derived from Figure 4.13 is:

IdnLeaf('T')   IdnExpr AssignmentStmt(':=') '(' IdnLeaf('M')   IdnExpr PlusExpr('+')

'(' IntLeaf('60')   IntExpr StarExpr('')   IdnLeaf('H')   IdnExpr Dyadic ')' Dyadic ')'*

AssignmentStmt

Deleting all of the structure connections and symbol connection names leaves the following sequence of input symbols:

'T'   ':='   '('   'M'   '+'   '('   '60'   ''   'H'   ')'   ')'*

Although this sequence is correct Pascal, most programmers would omit the parentheses and write simply $T := M + 60 * H$. The two expressions are equivalent because the Pascal multiplication operator has a "higher precedence" than the Pascal addition operator. Similarly, the FORTRAN assignment $J = 2**3**2$ (** is the FORTRAN exponentiation operator) is equivalent to $J = (2**(3**2))$ because the exponentiation operator "associates to the right."

Operator precedence and association rules are introduced into a language to determine the structure of an expression when parentheses are omitted. A user can override these rules by introducing explicit parentheses, as in $T := (M + 60)*H$ or $J = (2**3)**2$. Since operator precedence and association rules are used to determine the structure of an expression, they must be incorporated into the description of the parsing task. The purpose of this section is to show how that is done.

Figure 4.13 describes the behavior of a parser that *requires* every expression to be enclosed in parentheses. Suppose for the moment that the terms '(' and ')' were simply removed from Figure 4.13. The result would describe a parser that *prohibited* any expression from containing parentheses. In order to allow parentheses as an option, another alternative could be added to the definition of *Expression* as shown in Figure 4.14a.

The two activity sequences shown in Figures 4.13b and c can be derived from Figure 4.14a. As can easily be seen by deleting connections, both of these activity sequences correspond to the following input sequence of basic symbols:

$$'T' \quad ':=' \quad 'M' \quad '+' \quad '60' \quad '*' \quad 'H'$$

The two activity sequences will result in *different* sequences of invocations of tree construction operations, however. Thus the specification of the parser's behavior is ambiguous. If the input sequence $T := M + 60*H$ is presented to the parser, the specification does not determine which of the two trees shown in Figure 4.15 will actually be constructed.

Note that the ambiguity arises precisely because Figure 4.14a does not embody the operator precedence and association rules of Pascal. Since multiplication has a higher precedence than addition, the tree on the right in Figure 4.15 is the desired one. The description of the parsing language must be revised so that the activity sequence of Figure 4.14b is illegal, since that is the sequence that leads to the erroneous tree.

The strategy is to replace the description of *Expression* by several extended regular expressions. Each of these new regular expressions will represent a Pascal expression that contains an operator at a particular precedence level. Figure 4.16 shows an example. Here *Expression* has been replaced by three names: *Sum*, *Product*, and *Primary*. *Sum* represents Pascal expressions that contain addition operators (+ and −). These operators have the same precedence level, which is lower than that of the multiplication operators (*, /, **div**, and **mod**). *Product* represents Pascal expressions that contain multiplication operators, and *Primary* represents Pascal expressions that do not directly contain any operators. (An expression in parentheses may contain operators, but the parentheses "isolate" these operators so that they do not interact directly with the surroundings of the parenthesized expression.)

In addition to the alternative containing the operator, each rule has an alternative that handles Pascal expressions without operators at the given precedence

```
Statement   = Name AssignmentStmt(':=') Expression AssignmentStmt
Expression  = IntLeaf(Integer)  IntExpr
            |  Name
            |  Expression Operator Expression Dyadic
            |  '(' Expression ')'
            |  SetExpr('[')  EmptySourceSeq (ϵ | Expression ExtendSourceSeq (',' Expression ExtendSourceSeq)*) ']' SetExpr
Name        = IdnLeaf(Identifier)  IdnExpr
Operator    = PlusExpr('+') | MinusExpr('−')
            | StarExpr('*') | SlashExpr('/') | DivExpr('div') | ModExpr('mod')
```

a) A description of the parsing language

```
IdnLeaf('T')    IdnExpr AssignmentStmt(':=')  IdnLeaf('M')    IdnExpr  PlusExpr('+')
    IntLeaf('60')   IntExpr Dyadic StarExpr('*')   IdnLeaf('H')   IdnExpr Dyadic
    AssignmentStmt
```

b) An activity sequence described by (a)

```
IdnLeaf('T')    IdnExpr AssignmentStmt(':=')  IdnLeaf('M')    IdnExpr  PlusExpr('+')
    IntLeaf('60')   IntExpr StarExpr('*')   IdnLeaf('H')   IdnExpr Dyadic Dyadic AssignmentStmt
```

c) Another activity sequence described by (a)

Figure 4.14
Optional parentheses

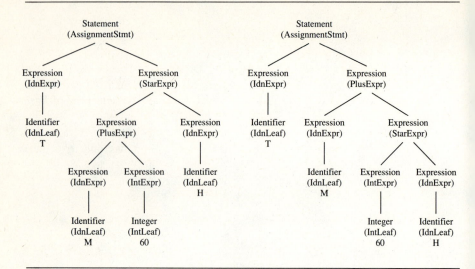

Figure 4.15
Two possible trees for $T := M + 60 * H$

```
Statement = Name AssignmentStmt(':=') Sum AssignmentStmt
      Sum = Sum AddOp Product Dyadic | Product
  Product = Product MulOp Primary Dyadic | Primary
  Primary = IntLeaf(Integer)   IntExpr
          | Name
          | '(' Sum ')'
          | SetExpr('[')   EmptySourceSeq
            (ε | Sum ExtendSourceSeq (',' Sum ExtendSourceSeq)*)
            ']' SetExpr
     Name = IdnLeaf(Identifier)   IdnExpr
    AddOp = PlusExpr('+') | MinusExpr('−')
    MulOp = StarExpr('*') | SlashExpr('/') | DivExpr('div') | ModExpr('mod')
```

Figure 4.16
Specifying operator precedence and association

---

level. Thus to obtain an activity sequence corresponding to an assignment statement that had no addition operator, you could select the second alternative for *Sum*. Note that the second alternative contains no connections or basic symbols. Use of the second alternative therefore adds nothing to the activity sequence. The second alternative has the effect of "equating" the *Sum* and *Product* expressions as far as the activity sequence is concerned.

4.3 OPERATOR PRECEDENCE AND ASSOCIATION

Figure 4.14a defines a parser that accepts a certain source language, but has ambiguous behavior for certain sequences of basic symbols in that language. Figure 4.16 defines a parser that accepts the same source language as the parser defined by Figure 4.14a. However, it can be proven that the parser defined by Figure 4.16 has unambiguous behavior for all sequences of basic symbols in that language. In other words, if you were to delete all connections from two distinct activity sequences defined by Figure 4.16, then the resulting sequences of basic symbols would be different.

Assume you have a definition of a parsing language, but that definition does not include operator precedence and association rules. It has only one name representing an expression and one name representing all operators. (Figure 4.14a satisfies these assumptions.) Here is a general procedure for introducing operator precedence and association rules:

1. Let E_i be a new name defined to represent an expression whose operator is on precedence level i and let E_{max} (where *max* is one greater than the largest i) be a new name defined to represent an expression without an operator.
2. Collect all of the alternatives that contain operators at precedence level i and transform each according to the following rules:

    (a) If *op* is left-associative

    Expression op Expression   becomes E_i *op* E_{i+1}.

    (b) If *op* is right-associative

    Expression op Expression   becomes E_{i+1} *op* E_i.

    (c) If *op* is nonassociative (i.e., two successive occurrences of *op* are not allowed— < is nonassociative in Pascal because $A < B < C$ is illegal)

    Expression op Expression   becomes E_{i+1} *op* E_{i+1}.

3. Combine the transformed alternatives into a rule of the form

    $$E_i = \cdots \mid E_{i+1}.$$

    Here $\cdots$ represents the transformed alternatives.
4. Collect all of the alternatives that do not contain operators and combine them into a rule defining E_{max}.
5. If precedence and association can be overridden by parentheses, add an alternative '(' E_1 ')' to the E_{max} rule.
6. Finally, replace all remaining occurrences of *Expression* with E_1.

Let's see how this procedure was used to transform Figure 4.14a into Figure 4.16. The source language has only two precedence levels, with "multiplication operators" having a higher precedence than "addition operators." *Sum* was chosen as E_1, *Product* as E_2, and *Primary* as E_{max}. All of the operators are left-associative, so the result of step (3) is the expressions shown in Figure 4.16 for *Sum* and *Product*. Step (4) gives the expression defining *Primary*, and the alternative involving parentheses is included by step (5). The occurrence of *Expression* in the definition of a statement was replaced by *Sum* at step (6).

4.4 SYNTACTIC ERROR RECOVERY

If the sequence of basic symbols input to the parser cannot be obtained from any activity sequence, then the program contains a syntactic error. Typical syntactic errors are unbalanced parentheses and missing semicolons. Almost invariably, the error involves an improper delimiter. An incorrect identifier is not a syntactic error according to this definition: The activity sequence requires only *an* identifier, not a *particular* identifier, in some position.

The symptom of a syntactic error is called a *parser-defined* error, and its position does not necessarily coincide with that of the actual error. For example, consider the following incorrect Pascal statement:

$$writeln(sin(x0,x,cos(y),y,exp(z),z); \qquad (1)$$

Presumably the error here is the substitution of 0 for). (The presumption is greatly strengthened by the fact that "0" shares a key with ")" on standard keyboards.) However, since $sin(x0,x,cos(y),y,exp(z),z)$ is a *syntactically* valid Pascal expression, the parser-defined error will be a missing ")" at the end of the statement. (Note that other kinds of errors that might be reported, such as "Undeclared identifier x0" or "Too many arguments for sin" cannot be detected by the parser because they depend on contextual information. These errors must be reported after parsing is complete, using the techniques discussed in Chapter 7.)

In general, a parser-defined error is reported at the leftmost basic symbol that could not be part of a sentence in the language: ";" is the leftmost basic symbol that could not be part of the Pascal statement (1). Up to that point the sequence constituted a valid Pascal statement, with $x0$ a correct identifier. In fact, if there had been a second ")" before the semicolon, then the statement *would* have been syntactically correct. Thus it would be *wrong* to report an error at an earlier point.

A compiler should detect as many errors as possible in a single run; therefore, it should be able to recover from the effects of a syntactic error and continue to analyze the program. After reporting the missing right parenthesis in the statement above, for example, the parser could continue as though it had been present. Effectively, the parser has *repaired* the error by inserting a right parenthesis. It is important to note the distinction between this repair (which allows the analysis to continue) and a *correction* (which makes the program conform to the programmer's intent). The repaired program is probably *not* what the programmer intended in this case.

The most important characteristic of any strategy for recovering syntactic errors is a guarantee that the parser's behavior will always correspond to a legal activity sequence. Only with this guarantee can we be certain that the sequence of tree construction operations is always consistent. If a sequence of tree construction operations is inconsistent, data structures used during tree construction may become corrupted. Since these data structures often have complex internal linkage via pointers, data structure corruption may lead to invalid memory accesses and abnormal termination by the operating system. But if the operating system aborts the compiler, the error module will not be finalized and therefore the error reports may not be output!

4.4.1 A General Error Recovery Strategy

You can think of the sequences of basic symbols derived from valid activity sequences as points in space. The "distance" between these points is a measure of the number of changes required to make one into the other. For example, the following two sequences would be considered "close" because only a single change would make one into the other:

$$'T' \quad ':=' \quad 'M'$$
$$'T' \quad ':=' \quad '60'$$

Two other sequences that are close together, but farther from those above, are:

$$'T' \quad ':=' \quad 'M' \quad '+' \quad '60' \quad '*' \quad 'H'$$
$$'T' \quad ':=' \quad 'M' \quad '*' \quad '60' \quad '+' \quad 'H'$$

Sequences of basic symbols and symbol connections *not* derivable from valid activity sequences also correspond to points in this space. They represent syntactically incorrect programs, while the points corresponding to sequences that are derived from valid activity sequences represent syntactically correct programs.

Since the reason for doing syntactic error recovery is to continue the analysis in order to find more errors, the recovery should perturb the program as little as possible. In other words, the recovery should repair the syntactically incorrect program by changing it into a syntactically correct program that is "close" in the sense of the last paragraph. (Actually, of course, the recovery mechanism does not *change* the source text at all; it simply makes the parser *behave* as though the input had been the correct program.) Figure 4.17 illustrates the process. Figure 4.17a is the basic symbol sequence that would be submitted to a parser for Pascal assignments if the source text were the syntactically incorrect program $T := M; 60 * H$. (You should verify that this sequence cannot be generated from any of the activity sequences described by Figure 4.16.) The error could be recovered by making the parser behave as though it had either the sequence of Figure 4.17b or the sequence of Figure 4.17c as input. Both of these sequences can be derived from activity sequences described by Figure 4.16.

$$'T' \quad ':=' \quad 'M' \quad ';' \quad '60' \quad '*' \quad 'H'$$

(a) A syntactically incorrect basic symbol sequence

$$'T' \quad ':=' \quad 'M' \quad '+' \quad '60' \quad '*' \quad 'H'$$

(b) A correct sequence that is close to (a)

$$'T' \quad ':=' \quad 'M' \quad ';' \quad 'x' \quad ':=' \quad '60' \quad '*' \quad 'H'$$

(c) A correct sequence that is farther from (a)

Figure 4.17
Repairing a syntactic error

It is not practical to consider the whole source program when looking for a replacement. Instead, the recovery mechanism examines a "window" of basic symbols around the parser-defined error.

The simplest strategy is to confine the window to the parser-defined error and an arbitrary number of basic symbols occurring to its right. The general repair strategy consists of three steps:

1. Possibly ignore some sequence of input basic symbols, the first of which is the parser-defined error.
2. Possibly insert some sequence of basic symbols to the left of the input text remaining after step (1).
3. Continue parsing the sequence resulting from step (2).

Table 4.1 gives several examples of this strategy applied to our subset of Pascal assignment statements. (The basic symbol *EOPT*, defined in Chapter 3, has been used to indicate the end of the statement.) In each example, the input sequence is split into three parts: the text successfully parsed before the error was detected (*left context*), the parser-defined error, and the text not yet examined (*right context*). The "Recovery" column gives the basic symbol sequence to be deleted in step (1) and the basic symbol sequence to be inserted in step (2).

Two of the insertions given in Table 4.1 are arbitrary. In the third line any operator could have been inserted, and in the last line either an identifier or an integer could have been inserted. Insertions should be chosen to minimize the possibility of so-called avalanche errors: The remainder of the compiler must perform additional analysis on the source program tree, and inserted basic symbols should minimize the probability of spurious error reports from that analysis. For example, suppose that a Pascal parser inserted an arbitrary identifier into an expression to repair a syntactic error. Name analysis would report that this identifier was undefined. To avoid the problem, the parser should insert a special identifier that the name analysis process can recognize as being inserted.

4.4.2 Implementing the General Strategy

A valid continuation of the activity sequence preceding the parser-defined error is specified by a path through the syntax diagrams that begins at the error detection

TABLE 4.1 EXAMPLES OF THE SIMPLE ERROR RECOVERY STRATEGY

Input Sequence	Left Context	Error	Right Context	Recovery	
				Delete	Insert
$a:=(b+c$	$a:=(b+c$	*EOPT*			)
$a:=b+c)$	$a:=b+c$	)	*EOPT*	)	
$a:=b)c$	$a:=b$	)	c	)	—
$a:=+c$	$a:=$	+	c		Identifier

point and ends at the exit of the diagram for the start symbol. It takes into account the (recursive) nesting of the diagrams determined by the left context of the parser-defined error. The error recovery process must be able to follow this path without making any decisions, since it has no reliable information at its disposal other than the syntax diagrams themselves. (Remember that the input text is incorrect!)

Two classes of path segments can be distinguished:

1. Segments leading from an error detection point within a syntax diagram to the exit of that diagram.
2. Segments leading from the entrance of a diagram to the exit of that diagram.

A segment of class (2) cannot recursively enter the diagram it is traversing, for if it does then the error recovery process will never terminate. Segments of both classes must be acyclic for the same reason.

Figure 4.18 is a set of syntax diagrams for a Pascal assignment parsing language. (They correspond to the unambiguous specification of Figure 4.16.) An integer labels each of the points that corresponds to one of the parser-defined errors shown in Table 4.1. The parser-defined error illustrated in the first row of Table 4.1 corresponds to the point labeled 1, and so forth. The error illustrated in the third row could be recovered by inserting *any* operator. Thus the entry to the *MulOp* box also could have been chosen for the label 3. You should verify that in each case the indicated point could be reached by the parser if it were presented with the left context listed for the error in Table 4.1. At the indicated point the error symbol cannot be accepted by the parser, and therefore that symbol is a parser-defined error.

First consider the situation described by the first row of Table 4.1. Because it has parsed the left context of the error, the parser must have been nested inside of *Statement*, *Sum*, *Product*, and *Primary* at the time it detected the error. Therefore the continuation includes the path from the error detection point (marked 1 in Figure 4.18) to the end of *Primary*, from the rectangular *Primary* box to the end of *Product*, from the rectangular *Product* box to the end of *Sum*, and from the rectangular *Sum* box to the end of *Statement*. In each case the segment leading from the error detection point to the end of the diagram is acyclic.

There might be only one path through a particular diagram, and if so that path must be the segment from the entrance of the diagram to the exit of that diagram used in the continuation. If there are several paths, then one must be chosen. In Figure 4.18 the lower path must be chosen as the segment from entry to exit in both the *Sum* and the *Product* diagrams. The upper path recursively enters the diagram it is traversing in each case. The third path through the *Primary* diagram cannot be used as the entry-to-exit segment because it recursively enters the *Primary* diagram: It enters the *Sum* diagram, whose entry-to-exit segment enters the *Product* diagram. But the *Product* diagram's entry-to-exit segment enters the *Primary* diagram.

Three candidates for entry-to-exit segments through the *Primary* diagram remain after discarding recursive and cyclic paths. A choice can be made among

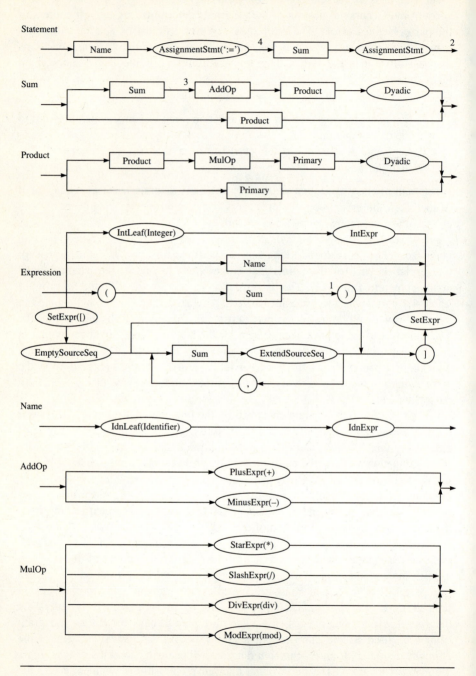

Figure 4.18
Where the errors of Table 4.1 are detected

them on the basis of the symbol connections they contain. In order to understand the criterion, we need to review the effect of syntactic error recovery on the remainder of the compiler.

Whenever the parser reaches a symbol connection during error recovery, it must invoke *SourceLeaf* with a symbol that did not actually appear in the source program. The generated symbol may not satisfy all of the conditions required by the context, and if it doesn't, the compiler will report further errors involving it. Those error reports are spurious, and serve only to confuse the programmer. They can be suppressed if the rest of the compiler *knows* that the symbol involved was generated.

The three candidates for the entry-to-exit segment through the *Primary* diagram are the top path (which requires that an integer be generated), the second path (which requires that an identifier be generated), and the bottom path with its upper segment (which requires that "[ ]" be generated). There is clearly no way to inform the remainder of the compiler that the sequence "[ ]" was generated rather than being found in the input text, because both basic symbols are delimiters. If we chose the top path, we would be in one of the situations mentioned at the end of Section 2.4.1: The compiler needs an external value but is unable to obtain one. By using the value of the variable *NoExtValue* (Figure 2.6), the error recovery module can inform the remainder of the compiler that the integer is missing. Since identifiers are being represented by unique integers, but the particular set of unique integers is arbitrary, it is also easy to set aside one integer value to mean "a generated identifier." (Conventionally, zero is used for this purpose, with identifiers actually appearing in the program being represented by 1, 2, 3, etc.) Thus either the top path or the second one should be chosen as a continuation in this case.

Both the *AddOp* and the *MulOp* diagrams in Figure 4.18 have multiple candidates for their entry-to-exit segments, and there is really no reason to prefer one over another. We shall assume that the bottom path has been chosen in each case.

Once a valid continuation is known, it is possible to determine the set of basic symbols (called *anchors*) that could be accepted while parsing some continuation of the error's left context. Any basic symbol that is not in the anchor set can't be accepted, and therefore should be deleted. The anchor set is used to control the deletion process.

Only two symbols, ")" and the end-of-statement marker *EOPT*, could be accepted along the continuation just determined for the error in the first row of Table 4.1. The set of anchors is therefore {')' *EOPT*}. Notice that *EOPT* will always belong to any anchor set, since it can always be accepted at the end of any source program. You should convince yourself that *EOPT* is the *only* member of the anchor set for the error described by the second row of Table 4.1.

Input symbol deletion can be implemented by repeatedly invoking the lexical analyzer until some member of the anchor set is reached:

while not (current symbol **in** anchors) **do**
    Obtain a new symbol from the lexical analyzer;

Initially the error symbol itself is the "current symbol." If the error symbol happens to be an anchor, then no input symbols will be deleted. The loop will always terminate because *EOPT* is always a member of the anchor set and the lexical analyzer will eventually return that symbol.

Since *EOPT* is in the anchor set for recovering from the error described by the first row of Table 4.1, and *EOPT* is the error symbol itself, no input symbols are deleted to recover this error. On the other hand, the error symbol doesn't belong to the anchor set for the error described by the second row of Table 4.1. Thus the error symbol will be deleted when recovering from that error.

The sequence of symbols to be inserted can be determined by advancing the parser along the continuation that was used to determine the anchors:

> **while** (parser cannot accept the current symbol) **do**
> **begin**
> Generate the next symbol of the continuation;
> Parse the generated symbol;
> **end**

Notice that the sequence is not really inserted into the input. The parser simply *behaves* as it would have if the insertion had been made. Recovery is complete when the parser is able to accept the current symbol.

When recovering the error described in the first row of Table 4.1, the insertion loop is entered with *EOPT* as the current symbol. Since the parser cannot accept *EOPT* at the position marked 1 in Figure 4.18, it must generate the basic symbol ")" and parse it. It can then follow the continuation until it reaches the end of the *Statement* diagram, since there are no more basic symbols or symbol connections. At this point it can accept the anchor, and recovery is complete. In the recovery from the error described by the second row of Table 4.1 the current symbol is *EOPT* after deletion of ")", and *EOPT* can be accepted immediately. Therefore no symbols are inserted in recovering from the error in the second row of Table 4.1.

The precise implementation of the error recovery strategy depends on the parsing technique, to be discussed in Chapters 5 and 6. Three key questions must be answered:

1. How is the continuation specified?
2. How should the anchor be found?
3. How should generated symbols be introduced?

Error recovery should be designed to minimize the penalty for correct programs. Remember that even though most compilations will report errors, the density of those errors will be low. Therefore most of the text parsed is correct, and should be dealt with efficiently. Expensive processes should be invoked only when an error is actually detected.

4.5 SUMMARY

Syntactic analysis determines the structure of the source program, given its basic symbols. The central algorithm is a parser that invokes the lexical analyzer to obtain basic symbols of the source program and invokes operations of the tree construction module to build the source program tree. The task of the parser is specified by defining the relationship between the sequence of lexical analyzer invocations and the sequence of tree construction operations. This relationship is described by an infinite set of activity sequences, each of which represents the time sequence of actions taken by the parser in parsing a particular sentence of the source language.

Any technique for giving a finite description of an infinite set of sequences can be used to give a finite description of a parser. Syntax diagrams and regular expressions, introduced in Chapter 3 as finite descriptions of infinite sets of basic symbol sequences, can be extended to describe activity sequences. The extensions are required because activity sequences involve nested constructs that have no counterpart in the description of basic symbols. A third notation, context-free grammars, can also be used to describe activity sequences. Context-free grammars are particularly useful in constructing the shift-reduce parsers discussed in Chapter 6.

The basic description is determined by the constructs of the source language. In order to provide an unambiguous structure for expressions without requiring that they be fully parenthesized, most source languages have operator precedence and association rules. These rules can be incorporated into the basic description by a mechanical transformation.

Syntactic errors appear as sequences of basic symbols that cannot be generated from any legal activity sequence by deleting connections. The parser should repair each error in an attempt to detect as many errors as possible. Each repair conceptually alters the source program, converting it to a "similar" program that does not contain the syntactic error being repaired. Repairs are *not* corrections—they do not fulfill the intent of the programmer, generally. The effect of a syntactic error is confined to the parser by this approach.

A general repair strategy involves replacing some sequence of input symbols following the point of error with some other sequence. The new sequence, followed by the undeleted portion of the program, is always a legal continuation of the text preceding the error. This strategy is guaranteed to construct a tree that corresponds to a valid program. Therefore the remainder of the compiler is guaranteed to have consistent data presented to it. Implementation details depend upon the specific parser, and are therefore deferred to Chapters 5 and 6.

NOTES

A description of the source program tree is called the *abstract syntax* of the source language [13, 16, 15]. It generally describes source program trees that cannot be derived from any legal source program. For example, an abstract syntax for Pascal in terms of the concepts and constructs of Figure 4.1b would describe a tree in which a *IntExpr* appeared as the left child of an *AssignmentStmt*. As was pointed out in Section 4.1, however, such a tree could not be derived from any legal Pascal program. The legal sentences of the source language are described by the *concrete syntax* of the language. A parser can be thought of as relating the concrete syntax to the abstract syntax by constructing a tree according to the abstract syntax when given a sequence of basic symbols that is legal according to the concrete syntax. Thus, the definition of the parsing language, which is also a definition of the parser's behavior, formally specifies the relationship between the abstract syntax and the concrete syntax. Interactive tools that allow a designer to derive the parsing language definition from the definitions of the source language abstract and concrete syntaxes are available [4].

Most authors concentrate on the description of basic symbol sequences, confining their discussion initially to parsers as recognizers. They introduce connections as an afterthought when they need to obtain information about the structure recognized. Lewis, Rosenkrantz, and Stearns [11] developed activity sequences to describe the relationship between basic symbol sequences and connection sequences. Activity sequences are important because they allow the designer to regard the parser as a translator from the beginning. If one thinks of the parser first as a recognizer, one often falls into the trap of transforming its description and then being unable to decide where connections should be inserted. Activity sequences allow the designer to introduce the connections when it is obvious where they should be placed. Language-preserving transformations of the description then leave the set of activity sequences invariant. The connections are transformed along with the rest of the description and need not be introduced when the transformation is finished.

Historically, context-free grammars have been used to describe syntactic analysis. Extensive theoretical results are available for context-free grammars [9], and for their application to parsing [2]. Strict production notation must use recursion to describe iterative constructs, however, which seems unnatural in certain cases. The result is that many authors *really* use the extended regular expression notation discussed here, although they *call* it "extended BNF" and preserve the fiction that they are using a context-free grammar [1]. Context-free grammars and extended regular expressions are equivalent in expressive power, and a description couched in terms of one can be mechanically transformed into the other. Thus the one that is most natural in a given context should be used.

Syntax diagrams give many people an intuitive feeling for the generation and recognition processes. They are almost as venerable as context-free grammars [6], and they have the same power [12]. Syntax diagrams can be transformed into extended regular expressions or context-free grammars, and vice versa, so there is no reason not to take advantage of their intuitive appeal. Given the increasing use of bit-mapped displays with pointing devices, we can, in the not-too-distant future, expect to see syntax-diagram editors and parser generators that take syntax diagrams as input.

Much of the literature on syntactic error recovery [8] is concerned with ad hoc methods that attempt to make "corrections" rather than "repairs." Ad hoc methods cannot guarantee a consistent sequence of tree construction operations. The general scheme presented here [10, 7] can be applied automatically [14], and guarantees a consistent connection sequence. It adds minimal overhead when parsing a correct program, as we shall see in Chapters 5 and 6. By increasing the overhead, it is possible to make repairs that are more nearly corrections [5].

REFERENCES

1. Aho, A. V., Sethi, R., and Ullman, J. D., *Compilers*, Addison Wesley, Reading, MA, 1986.
2. Aho, A. V. and Ullman, J. D., *The Theory of Parsing, Translation, and Compiling*, Prentice Hall, Englewood Cliffs, 1972.
3. "FORTRAN," X3.9-1978, American National Standards Institute, New York, 1978.
4. Bahrami, A., "CAGT—An Automated Approach to Abstract and Parsing Grammars," MS Thesis, Department of Electrical and Computer Engineering, University of Colorado, Boulder, CO, 1986.
5. Burke, M. G. and Fischer, G. A., "A Practical Method for LR and LL Syntactic Error Diagnosis and Recovery," *Trans. Prog. Lang and Systems 9*, 2 (Apr. 1987), 198–234.
6. Conway, M. E., "Design of a Separable Transition-diagram Compiler," *Comm. of the ACM 6*, 7 (July 1963), 396–408.
7. Gries, D., *Compiler Construction for Digital Computers*, John Wiley & Sons, New York, 1971.
8. Gries, D., "Error Recovery and Correction—An Introduction to the Literature," in *Compiler Construction—An Advanced Course*, vol. 21, F. L. Bauer and J. Eickel (editor), Springer Verlag, Berlin, 1976, 627–638.
9. Harrison, M. A., *Introduction to Formal Language Theory*, Addison Wesley, Reading, MA, 1978.
10. Irons, E. T., "An Error Correcting Parse Algorithm," *Comm. of the ACM 6*, 11 (Nov. 1963), 669–673.
11. Lewis, P. M., Rosenkrantz, D. J., and Stearns, R. E., *Compiler Design Theory*, Addison Wesley, Reading, MA, 1976.
12. Lomet, D. B., "A Formalization of Transition Diagram Systems," *J. ACM 20*, 2 (Apr. 1973), 235–257.
13. McCarthy, J., "Towards a Mathematical Theory of Computation," in *Information Processing 1962*, North-Holland, Amsterdam, 1963, 21–28.
14. Rohirich, J., "Methods for the Automatic Construction of Error Correcting Parsers," *Acta Inf. 13*, 2 (Feb. 1980), 115–139.
15. Schmidt, D. A., *Denotational Semantics*, Allyn and Bacon, Newton, MA, 1986.
16. Tennent, R. D., *Principles of Programming Languages*, Prentice Hall, London, 1981.
17. Wulf, W. A., Shaw, M., Hilfinger, P. N., and Flon, L., *Fundamental Structures of Computer Science*, Addison Wesley, Reading, MA, 1981.

EXERCISES

4.1 Draw a source program subtree for each of the following Pascal fragments, and also describe the subtree using the textual notation introduced in Section 4.1.1.
   (a) $a := [1,2]$;
   (b) $a := [1]$;
   (c) $a := [\ \ ]$;

4.2 Consider an implementation of a module to implement the connections of the activity sequences defined by Figure 4.6. The module's operations are to be those given in Figure 4.4.
  (a) Modify Figure 4.2 to describe the source tree nodes for this problem.
  (b) Design a data structure to represent the stack and write a rationale for your decisions. What, if any, limits does your design place upon the stack size?
  (c) Define appropriate invariants for your stack data structure and implement the initialization and finalization operations in a manner consistent with those invariants.
  (d) Implement *EmptySourceSeq* and *ExtendSourceSeq* in a manner consistent with both the interface descriptions given in Figure 4.4 and the invariant you defined for the stack.
  (e) Implement *SourceLeaf* and *SourceNode* in a manner consistent with the interface descriptions given in Figure 4.4, the invariant you defined for the stack, and the pattern of invocations guaranteed by Figure 4.6.

4.3 Suppose that the output of the syntactic analyzer were to be a postfix string [17] instead of a tree.
  (a) Would the activity sequence defining the parser differ from that used when the tree was being constructed? Explain briefly.
  (b) Would the tree construction module differ from that used when the tree was being constructed? Explain briefly.

4.4 It is not strictly true that every activity sequence corresponds to a legal source program. The *structure* of the source program is guaranteed to be legal, but identifier uses might not agree with their declarations.
  (a) Write a Pascal program that has a legal structure but is nevertheless not a legal program.
  (b) Is it possible to define syntax diagrams that describe only legal source programs? Explain briefly.
  (c) Relate the syntax diagrams that appear in this chapter to those appearing in textbooks that describe source languages. Briefly explain any differences.

4.5 Use regular expression algebra to derive a right-recursive description of *ExprList* (Section 4.2.3).

4.6 Use the grammar of Figure 4.12 to derive an activity sequence corresponding to Figure 4.5.
  (a) Derive the activity sequence by rewriting the leftmost nonterminal at each step. This derivation is called a *leftmost derivation*.
  (b) Derive the activity sequence by rewriting the rightmost nonterminal at each step. This derivation is called a *rightmost derivation*.

4.7 Show that if all recursion in a set of extended regular expressions can be replaced by iteration, then the set of expressions is equivalent to a single expression using the notation of Chapter 3. (In other words, the extension of regular expressions discussed in this chapter is necessary only to describe essential recursion.)

4.8 Give an algorithm that constructs a grammar from an arbitrary set of extended regular expressions.

4.9 Prove that the set of syntax diagrams corresponding directly to a grammar will not contain any loops.

4.10 Add the FORTRAN exponentiation operator ** to the expressions defined by Figure 4.14a and produce an unambiguous description analogous to Figure 4.16. Use the operator precedence and association rules of the FORTRAN Standard [3].

4.11 Given that the error recovery process does not examine the input sequence, explain why a continuation path from the entry of a diagram to its exit must be acyclic. (Hint: Attempt to describe the code that advances the parser along the continuation.)

4.12 Suppose there is only one path from the entry of a particular diagram to its exit. Prove that this path does not involve recursion.

4.13 Consider the problem of determining valid continuations for a parser that implements the parsing language described by Figure 4.18.
   (a) Where could errors be detected?
   (b) Determine a class (1) segment for each position at which an error could be detected.
   (c) Determine a class (2) segment for each syntax diagram. Is more than one such segment possible in every diagram? Explain briefly.

4.14 Consider the recovery from the error described by the third line of Table 4.1.
   (a) Determine the continuation to be followed.
   (b) Explain why ")" will be deleted.
   (c) Explain why a symbol will be inserted. Is the particular symbol important in this case? Relate the choice of " − " to the determination of the class (2) segments.

5
Recursive Descent Parsing

A parser can be implemented by writing one procedure for each syntax diagram of the parsing language that defines the activity sequence. Each box of the diagram corresponds to a code fragment within the procedure: Code corresponding to a round box absorbs the appropriate basic symbol. Code corresponding to an oval box that is a symbol connection absorbs the appropriate basic symbol and invokes *SourceLeaf*, while code corresponding to an oval box that is a structure connection simply invokes *SourceNode*, *EmptySourceSeq*, or *ExtendSourceSeq*. Code corresponding to a rectangular box invokes the procedure for the specified syntax diagram. Code for boxes connected "in series" is sequential, while code for boxes connected "in parallel" is preceded by tests to determine which of the paths should be taken. A label and **goto** implement a loop in the syntax diagram.

Figure 5.1, which implements the parsing language described in Figure 4.6, illustrates all of the basic concepts. The parser effectively "descends" into the set of syntax diagrams, and since any syntax diagram may specify itself to describe one or more of its components, the procedures must be recursive. Hence the name "recursive descent."

Figure 5.1 has been written with redundant code to emphasize the correspondence between boxes in the syntax diagram and code fragments. The code fragment corresponding to a round box or a symbol connection always begins with an **if** statement and ends with an invocation of *Lexical* in Figure 5.1. Some of the tests are unnecessary, because they immediately follow another test of the current token's symbol class. Elimination of the redundant tests is a straightforward optimization.

Implementation of a recursive descent parser, given a set of syntax diagrams, is not always a trivial process. If any of the syntax diagrams are left-recursive, then they must be transformed to eliminate that left recursion. Even when no diagram is left-recursive, it is not always possible to select the proper path to follow for a particular input sequence. Finally, the parser must be written to recover from syntactic errors. (Figure 5.1 simply gives up when it detects an error.) Left recursion, decision making, and error recovery in recursive descent parsers are considered in detail in this chapter.

5.1 LEFT RECURSION

A syntax diagram such as *Sum* in Figure 5.2 cannot be implemented as it stands in a recursive descent parser, because it will lead to an infinite recursion. Suppose that *Sum* is invoked and the first unaccepted basic symbol is such that the upper path is selected. *Sum* will thus be invoked again with the same first unaccepted basic symbol. Hence the upper path will be chosen again, and so forth.

Syntax diagrams having this problem correspond to left-recursive regular expressions. The regular expressions for diagrams *Sum* and *Product* in Figure 5.2 are:

$$Sum = Sum\ AddOp\ Product\ Dyadic\ |\ Product$$

$$Product = Product\ MulOp\ Primary\ Dyadic\ |\ Primary$$

These two expressions are equivalent to the iterative expressions:

$$Sum = Product\ (AddOp\ Product\ Dyadic)*$$

$$Product = Primary\ (MulOp\ Primary\ Dyadic)*$$

The easiest way to demonstrate the equivalence is to use regular expression algebra to convert the iterative forms to the recursive forms. Figure 5.3 shows the syntax diagrams corresponding to the iterative forms.

Figure 5.2 illustrates a particularly obvious form of the left recursion problem, in which *Sum* invokes itself directly. In more subtle cases there is a chain of procedure invocations, none of which accepts the first unaccepted token. Here is a set of expressions that exhibits such "indirect" left recursion:

$$A_1 = B_1\ |\ A_2 C_1$$
$$A_2 = B_2\ |\ A_3 C_2 \quad\quad (1)$$
$$A_3 = B_3\ |\ A_1 C_3$$

Indirect left recursion is handled by converting it to "direct" left recursion and then applying the equivalence discussed above. Thus, (1) can be converted to direct left recursion in two steps. First, substitute the definition of A_1 into the third expression:

procedure *Parser*;
(* Parse a program in the language of Figure 4.6 *)

var *t*: *token*;   (* First unaccepted basic symbol *)

procedure *Name*;
begin
  if *t.kind* <> *IdentifierT* **then**
    Report(*DEADLY*, 2(*Identifier expected*), *t.coord*, 0); *SourceLeaf*(*IdnLeaf,t*); *Lexical*(*t*);
  SourceNode(*IdnExpr*);
end;

procedure *Expression*;
label 1;
begin
  if *t.kind* = *IntegerT* **then**
  begin
    if *t.kind* <> *IntegerT* **then**
      Report(*DEADLY*, 15(*Integer expected*), *t.coord*, 0); *SourceLeaf*(*IntLeaf,t*); *Lexical*(*t*);
    SourceNode(*IntExpr*);
  end
  else if *t.kind* = *IdentifierT* **then**
    Name;
  else if *t.kind* = *LeftParenT* **then**
  begin
    if *t.kind* <> *LeftParenT* **then**
      Report(*DEADLY*, 9(*'(' expected*), *t.coord*, 0); *Lexical*(*t*);
    Expression;
    if *t.kind* <> *PlusT* **then** *Report*(*DEADLY*, 22(*'+' expected*), *t.coord*, 0); *SourceLeaf*(*PlusExpr*); *Lexical*(*t*);
    Expression;
    if *t.kind* <> *RightParenT* **then** *Report*(*DEADLY*, 4(*')' expected*), *t.coord*, 0); *Lexical*(*t*);
    SourceNode(*PlusExpr*);
  end

112

```
        else
          begin
          if t.kind <> LeftBracketT then
            Report(DEADLY, 5(*'['expected*), t.coord, 0); SourceLeaf(SetExpr,t); Lexical(t);
          EmptySourceSeq;
          if t.kind <> RightBracketT then
            begin
         1: Expression;
            ExtendSourceSeq;
            if t.kind = CommaT then begin Lexical(t); goto 1 end;
            end;
          if t.kind <> RightBracketT then Report(DEADLY, 10(*']'expected*), t.coord, 0); Lexical(t);
          SourceNode(SetExpr);
          end;
        end;

procedure Statement;
  begin
  Name;
  if t.kind <> ColonEqT then
    Report(DEADLY,51(*':='expected*),t.coord,0); SourceLeaf(AssignmentStmt,t); Lexical(t);
  Expression;
  SourceNode(AssignmentStmt);
  end;

begin
Lexical(t);                               (* Obtain the first basic symbol of the program *)
Statement;
if t.kind <> EOPT then Report(DEADLY, 23(*End-of-file expected*), t.coord, 0);
end;
```

Figure 5.1
A simple recursive descent parser

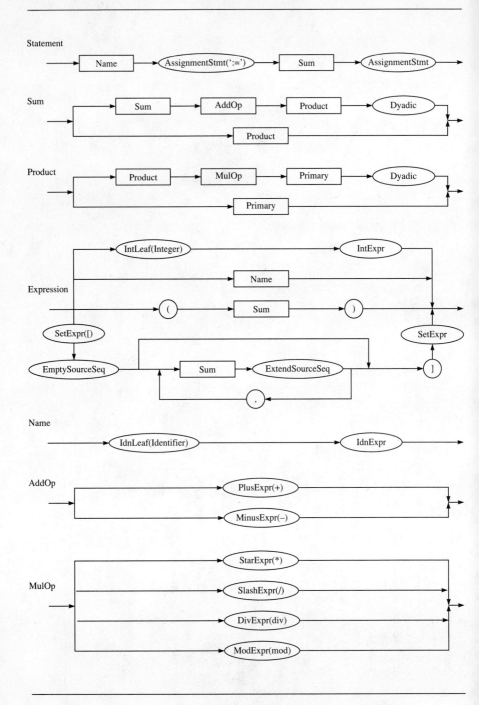

Figure 5.2
Syntax diagrams for a subset of Pascal assignment statements

$$A_1 = B_1 \mid A_2 C_1$$
$$A_2 = B_2 \mid A_3 C_2$$
$$A_3 = B_3 \mid B_1 C_3 \mid A_2 C_1 C_3$$

Next, substitute the definition of A_2 into the new third expression:

$$A_1 = B_1 \mid A_2 C_1$$
$$A_2 = B_2 \mid A_3 C_2$$
$$A_3 = B_3 \mid B_1 C_3 \mid B_2 C_1 C_3 \mid A_3 C_2 C_1 C_3$$

Note that the first two expressions are unchanged by this process, there is no indirect left recursion in the result, and the third expression is directly left-recursive.

The final step is to transform the direct left recursion to iteration:

$$A_3 = (B_3 \mid B_1 C_3 \mid B_2 C_1 C_3)(C_2 C_1 C_3)*$$

5.2 DECISION MAKING

A recursive descent parser must be able to make the proper decision at each fork in the syntax diagram. These decisions are often obvious because the first box on each path specifies a basic symbol of the source language, and at each fork the symbols specified by those boxes are different. All that is necessary is to check the symbol class of the first unaccepted symbol and then follow the path that will accept it. The decision is less obvious in the diagram for *Sum* in Figure 5.3. If the first unaccepted symbol is "+" then it is clearly possible to traverse the *AddOp-Product-Dyadic* cycle, but is that the only possibility? Might it not also be possible to leave the *Sum* diagram? In this case the answer is no, as some additional analysis shows: If *Sum* had been entered because the first *Sum* box in *Primary* had been reached, the only symbol that could be accepted upon leaving it would be ")"; if it had been entered via the second *Sum* box in *Primary*, either "," or "]" could be accepted after leaving it. The only acceptable symbol after leaving the *Sum* box in *Statement* would be the end-of-statement marker *EOPT*. The *Sum* boxes in *Primary* and *Statement* are the only ways of entering the *Sum* diagram, so *Sum* can be left only if the first unaccepted symbol is in the following set:

$$\{')' \quad ',' \quad ']' \quad EOPT\}$$

The parser cannot leave the *Sum* diagram when the first unaccepted symbol is "+".

The set of basic symbol classes that could possibly be accepted next when a particular path of the syntax diagram is traversed is called the *director set* for the path, because it is used to direct the behavior of the parser. In Figure 5.3, the director sets for the four paths of the *Primary* diagram are (from top to bottom) {*Integer*}, {*Identifier*}, {'('}, and {'['}. Since any traversal of the *Primary*

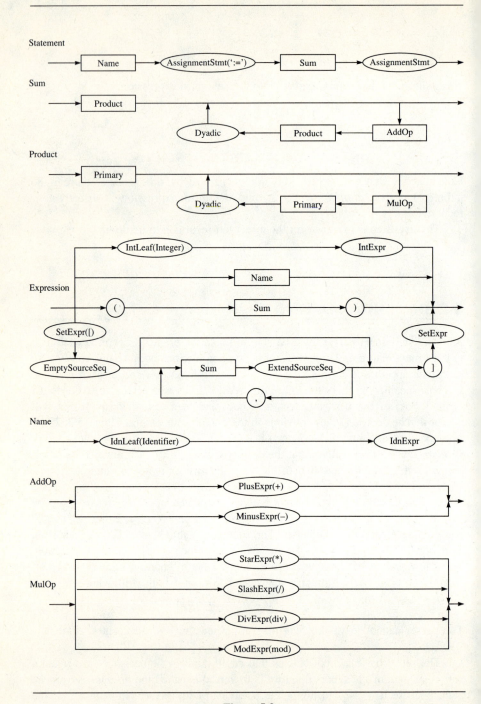

Figure 5.3
An iterative version of Figure 5.2

diagram must traverse one of these four paths, the director set of the path entering the *Primary* box in the *Product* diagram is the union of their director sets:

$$\{Integer \quad Identifier \quad '(' \quad '[' \}$$

The director set for the path leaving the *Product* diagram is:

$$\{'+' \quad '-' \quad ')' \quad ',' \quad ']' \quad EOPT\}$$

This set must be determined by exploring the possible paths that could be followed after leaving *Product*. The only places that *Product* can be called are in *Sum*, and the paths leaving the two calls join. (Since the structure connection *Dyadic* does not accept a basic symbol, it doesn't contribute to the director set.) One possible continuation is to accept a plus or minus (by traversing the *AddOp* box), and hence the first two elements of the director set have been found. The other possible continuation is to leave *Sum*, and we have already determined that the next symbol must be in the set $\{')' \quad ',' \quad ']' \quad EOPT\}$ in that case.

If the parser reaches a point at which a decision must be made, and if the director sets of the paths leaving that point are not disjoint, then the parser will be unable to decide which path to follow. This condition is known as a *director set overlap*. Figure 5.4 shows a set of syntax diagrams with a director set overlap. The language is almost equivalent to the one described by Figure 5.3—the only difference is that assignments can occur *within* other expressions. Thus $a:=b:=3$ would be a legal statement. (Its meaning would be to store the value 3 into the variable b, then into the variable a.)

Figure 5.4 was constructed by the technique presented in Section 4.3. The symbol ":=" was considered to be a right-associative operator with a lower precedence than "+." *Assign* was the name given to expressions that contain assignment operators. Because the operator was right-associative, the rules given in Section 4.3 require that the name (*Sum*) of the expression containing the next-higher-precedence operator appears to the right of ":=". The structure connection builds an expression node with two children to represent the "assignment expression." *Sum* must be an alternative, in case the expression has no assignments.

The director set overlap occurs at the first fork in the *Assign* diagram. *Sum* begins with the things *Product* begins with, and *Product* begins with the things *Primary* begins with. Therefore the director set for the lower path is {*Integer*, *Identifier*, '(', '['}. But the director set of the upper path is {*Identifier*}, so the two director sets have an element in common. The parser will not be able to decide which path to follow if an identifier is the first symbol it encounters.

One way to deal with a director set overlap is to transform the specification to remove it. Such transformations are more easily carried out on the regular expression form of the specification than on the syntax diagrams. The regular expressions that correspond to the interesting diagrams in Figure 5.4 are:

$$Assign = Name \; ':=' \; Assign \; AssignExp \; | \; Sum$$
$$Sum = Product \; (AddOp \; Product \; Dyadic)^*$$
$$Product = Primary \; (MulOp \; Primary \; Dyadic)^*$$

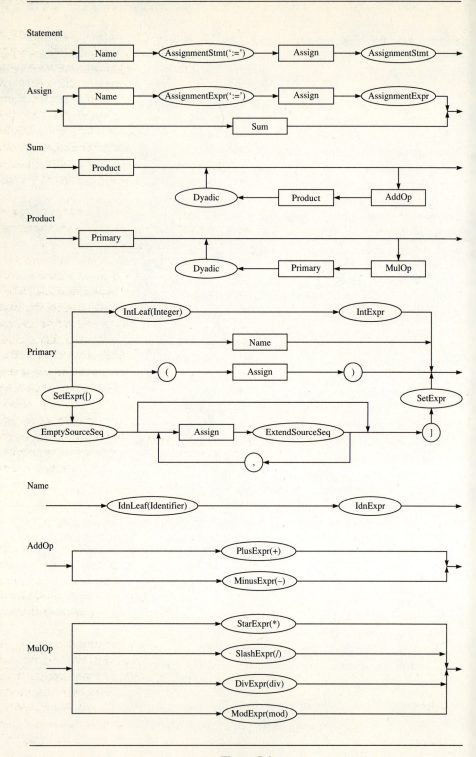

Figure 5.4
Multiple assignment

$Primary$ = $IntLeaf(Integer)$ $IntExpr$ | $Name$ | $'('$ $Assign$ $')'$

| $SetExpr('[')$ (ϵ | $Assign$ $SetExpr$ $(','$ $Assign$ $SetExpr)*)$ $']'$

Defining $(AddOp\ Product\ Dyadic)*$ and $(MulOp\ Primary\ Dyadic)*$ as S and P respectively, and substituting the definitions for Sum, $Product$, and $Primary$ into the equation for $Assign$ yields:

$Assign$ = $Name$ $':='$ $Assign$ $AssignExp$

| ($IntLeaf(Integer)$ $IntExpr$ | $Name$ | $'('$ $Assign$ $')'$

| $SetExpr('[')$ (ϵ|$Assign$ $SetExpr$ $(','$ $Assign$ $SetExpr)*)$ $']'$) P S

Using the distributive law of Figure 4.7 and rearranging the terms:

$Assign$ = $Name$ $':='$ $Assign$ $AssignExp$

| $Name$ P S

| $IntLeaf(Integer)$ $IntExpr$ P S

| $SetExpr('[')$ (ϵ | $Assign$ $SetExpr$ $(','$ $Assign$ $SetExpr)*)$ $']'$ P S

| $'('$ $Assign$ $')'$ P S

This expression brings the director set overlap into sharp focus, and also makes clear how it can be eliminated. All that is necessary is to apply the distributive law to the first two alternatives:

$Assign$ = $Name$ $(P\ S$ | $':='$ $Assign$ $AssignExp)$

| $IntLeaf(Integer)$ $IntExpr$ P S

| $SetExpr('[')$ (ϵ | $Assign$ $SetExpr$ $(','$ $Assign$ $SetExpr)*)$ $']'$ P S

| $'('$ $Assign$ $')'$ P S

Effectively, the decision about which path to take is deferred until the initial *Name* has been accepted. Figure 5.5 shows a set of syntax diagrams that correspond to these equations.

The "dangling **else**" in Pascal illustrates a director set overlap that cannot be removed by transforming the specification. One of the paths through the syntax diagram for a Pascal *Statement* appears in Figure 5.6. Clearly there will be a director set overlap at the decision point in this diagram: The director set of the bottom path is $\{'else'\}$, while that of the top path is the set of source language basic symbols that can follow a *Statement*. But this diagram fragment itself guarantees that **else** can follow a *Statement*!

Actually, Figure 5.6 describes an ambiguous parsing language. It will associate two activity sequences with the following Pascal statement:

$$\text{if } e_1 \text{ then if } e_2 \text{ then } s_1 \text{ else } s_2; \qquad (1)$$

The two activity sequences are those that would correspond to:

$$\text{if } e_1 \text{ then begin if } e_2 \text{ then } s_1 \text{ else } s_2 \text{ end}; \qquad (2)$$

$$\text{if } e_1 \text{ then begin if } e_2 \text{ then } s_1 \text{ end else } s_2; \qquad (3)$$

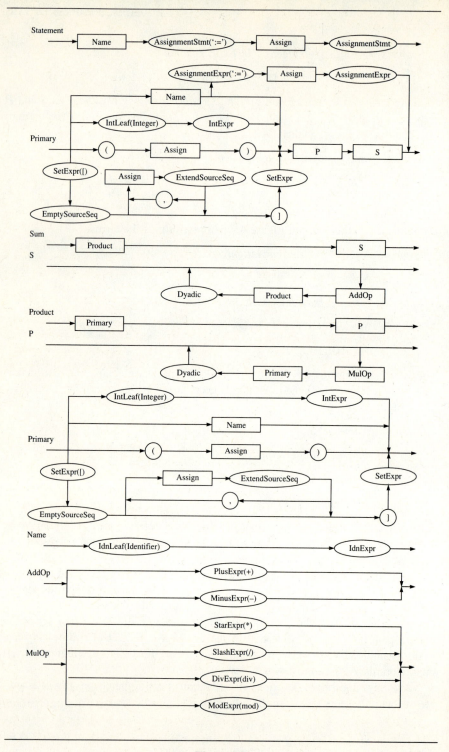

Figure 5.5
Removing director set overlap

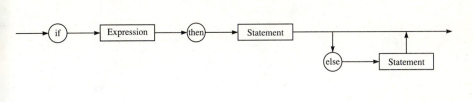

Figure 5.6
The Pascal conditional statement

The Pascal standard contains a paragraph describing the ambiguity and stating that (1) should always be interpreted as though it had the form of (2). This interpretation requires that the lower path of Figure 5.6 always be taken when the first unaccepted symbol is **else**. It has the effect of removing **else** from the director set of the upper path, and hence resolves the director set overlap.

The resolution of Pascal's dangling **else** shows that an ambiguous parsing language can be used to define a deterministic parser. The ambiguity manifests itself in a director set overlap, and it is removed by simply deleting the overlapping element from one set. If an overlapping element is deleted from a director set, the parser will *not* recognize all activity sequences defined by the syntax diagrams. Thus director set overlaps should not be removed by this method unless an ambiguity is being resolved.

5.3 ERROR RECOVERY IN A RECURSIVE DESCENT PARSER

Section 4.4 described a general strategy that enables a parser to recover from syntactic errors and construct a consistent source program tree. In order to implement this strategy, *continuation* paths must be selected from each basic symbol or symbol connection to the end of the current syntax diagram, and from the entry point of each syntax diagram to its exit point. Once the paths are selected, Section 4.4.2 pointed out that there are three parser-dependent questions to be answered in implementing the syntactic error recovery:

1. How is the continuation specified?
2. How should the anchor be found?
3. How should generated symbols be introduced?

In this section we work through a complete example, selecting continuations and then showing how the three questions are answered for a recursive descent parser.

Our example is a parser for the simple subset of Pascal assignments introduced in Section 4.1. The parser's behavior is defined by the syntax diagrams of Figure 5.7, which is identical to Figure 4.6. Figure 5.1 gave a recursive-descent implementation of this parser that terminated the compilation when a syntax error was detected.

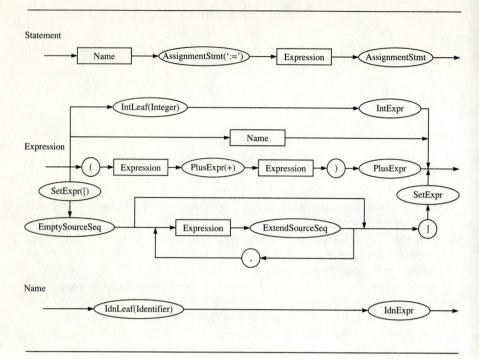

Figure 5.7
A parser definition

5.3.1 How to Specify Continuations

There is only one path through the *Statement* diagram in Figure 5.7, and one path through the *Name* diagram. These two paths must therefore be the continuations from the entry point to the exit point of their respective diagrams.

Since the continuation path through a diagram must be acyclic, the continuation path through the *Expression* diagram cannot involve the box accepting the basic symbol ",". Since it must be nonrecursive, it cannot pass through any of the *Expression* boxes. Of the three remaining paths, the criteria of Section 4.4.2 lead us to select the path through the *Name* box in order to minimize the probability of avalanche errors.

In addition to a continuation path from the entry point of each diagram to the exit point, we need a continuation path from each box accepting a basic symbol to the end of the diagram containing that box. (Don't forget that symbol connections also accept basic symbols!) There are only two boxes in Figure 5.7 that accept basic symbols and have more than one possible path to the exit points of the syntax diagrams containing them—the *SetExpr* symbol connection (which accepts "[") and the box accepting ","—both in the *Expression* diagram. The continuation from the *SetExpr* symbol connection should skip the *Expression* box to minimize the number of generated symbols. The continuation from the round box accepting a comma may not reenter that box because the path must be acyclic.

5.3 ERROR RECOVERY IN A RECURSIVE DESCENT PARSER

It is easy to show that all continuation paths passing through a given fork can follow the same exit from that fork. Each fork in the syntax diagram corresponds to an **if-then-else** construct in the recursive descent implementation of that diagram. We therefore specify continuations in a recursive descent parser by making the last alternative of the **if-then-else** construct specify the exit from the fork that will be followed by the continuation paths. The last alternative is used because that is the alternative that will be reached normally when the current basic symbol is not in any of the director sets.

The continuation specification can be incorporated in the syntax diagram that describes the parsing language by defining an ordering on the paths leaving a fork: Count them clockwise from the arc that enters the fork. Figure 5.8 is a rearrangement of Figure 5.7 such that the last path to leave a fork (counting clockwise from the arc that enters the fork) is always the continuation.

5.3.2 How to Find an Anchor

An anchor is a basic symbol that could be accepted as the parser moves along the continuation from the point where the error was detected to the end of the axiom's diagram. Thus it is necessary to know which symbols could be accepted along the entire continuation, part of which is fixed when the parser is written and part of which depends upon the execution history of the parse.

We begin by determining, for each syntax diagram, the set of basic symbols that the parser could accept when following the continuation path from the entry point of that syntax diagram to the exit point. That set is the union of the sets for each of the boxes along the path and the director sets of all paths leaving the continuation at a fork. (It is important to realize that the anchor set may contain symbols that would take the parser *off* of the continuation, but they must be acceptable at some point *on* the continuation.) Each round box and symbol connection has a singleton set containing the symbol that it accepts. Each structure connection has an empty set. Each rectangular box has a set containing the set of basic symbols that could be accepted along the continuation from the entry point of the diagram named in that box to its exit point.

The algorithm for computing the anchor sets begins with the diagram for the axiom. Assume that all director sets have already been computed. If the continuation path contains a rectangular box for which no anchor set has been computed, suspend the current computation and compute the set for that box. Because a continuation path from the entry point of a diagram to its exit point cannot recursively enter that diagram, we can guarantee that this algorithm will terminate.

For example, computation of the sets for the diagrams of Figure 5.8 begins with computation of the set for *Statement*. Since the continuation path contains a rectangular box for *Name*, for which no set value has yet been computed, the computation for *Statement* must be suspended while a value for *Name* is computed:

$$\{Identifier\} \cup \{\} = \{Identifier\}$$

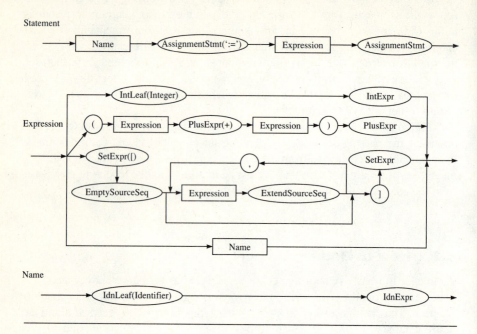

Figure 5.8
The forks of Figure 5.7 rearranged to specify continuations

Similarly, it is necessary to compute a value for *Expression* before the value for *Statement* can be completed.

The continuation from the entry point of *Expression* to its exit point passes the fork at the left of the diagram, and then passes through a rectangular box specifying the *Name* diagram. Because the set for *Name* has already been computed, the set for *Expression* can be obtained without further ado by taking the union of the director sets that lead off of the continuation at the fork and the set for *Name*, which is the only box lying on the continuation:

$$\{Integer\} \cup \{'('\} \cup \{'['\} \cup \{Identifier\} = \{Integer \quad '(' \quad '[' \quad Identifier\}$$

Finally, the set for the *Statement* diagram can be computed as follows:

$$\{Identifier \quad ':=' \quad Integer \quad '(' \quad '['\}$$

A syntactic error is detected when the parser cannot accept the next basic symbol of the source program. Error detection is therefore associated with round boxes or symbol connections in the syntax chart describing the parsing language. When an error is detected, the recovery procedure needs to know the appropriate anchor set in order to decide whether to skip symbols. In Figure 5.9, each round box and symbol connection of Figure 5.8 has been decorated with the set of symbols that the parser could accept when following the continuation path from that

5.3 ERROR RECOVERY IN A RECURSIVE DESCENT PARSER

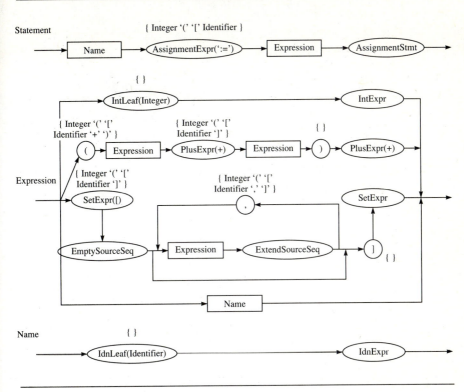

Figure 5.9
Symbols acceptable before reaching the end of the current diagram

box to the end of the diagram that contains it. These decorations were computed by taking the union of the sets for the boxes along the continuation path and the director sets of the arcs leading off of the continuation from a fork that lies on the continuation. They are the part of the anchor set that is dependent upon the current diagram.

The complete anchor set appropriate for an error detected at one of the round boxes or symbol connections of Figure 5.9 is the union of the set decorating that box and the set of symbols that could be accepted after leaving the chart containing that box. This latter set depends upon the left context of the error (Table 4.1), and cannot be determined at the time the parser is written. In order to make the complete anchor set available at the point of error, we add a parameter to each of the procedures of the recursive descent parser. That parameter is exactly the set of symbols that the parser can accept after the procedure has returned. For example, after the parser has returned from the procedure implementing the *Statement* diagram of Figure 5.9, the source program has been completely analyzed—the only symbol that the parser can accept is *EOPT*. Therefore the *Statement* procedure is called with the set {*EOPT*} as its parameter.

126 CHAPTER 5 RECURSIVE DESCENT PARSING

Every rectangular box represents a procedure call. The set of symbols that can be accepted after return from that procedure call is the union of the set of symbols that can be accepted along the continuation from that rectangular box to the end of the current diagram, as well as the set of symbols that can be accepted after leaving the current diagram. In Figure 5.10 each rectangular box of Figure 5.8 has been decorated with the symbols that can be accepted between that box and the end of the diagram containing it. The union of this set and the set passed to the diagram procedure must be used as the argument of the call to which the box corresponds.

5.3.3 How to Introduce Generated Symbols

Generated symbols are most easily introduced by interposing operations of an error recovery module between the parser and the lexical analyzer. Figure 5.11a gives an interface for this module. *Synterr* is invoked by the parser whenever the current basic symbol is not the one required, as shown in Figure 5.11b. Figure 5.11b corresponds to the *Name* diagram of the parser we have been discussing,

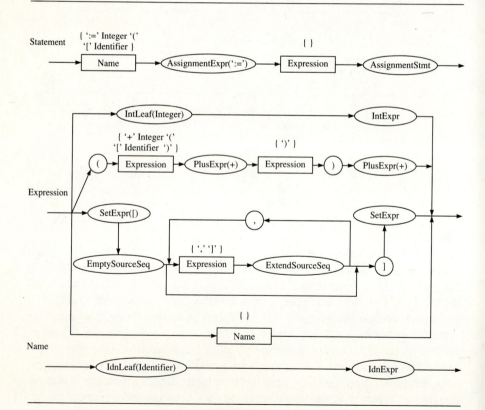

Figure 5.10
Symbols to add to the anchor set parameter

5.3 ERROR RECOVERY IN A RECURSIVE DESCENT PARSER

type
   anchors =   (* Specification of an anchor set *)
     set of *SymbolClass*;

procedure *Synterr*(**var** *t*: *token*; *need*: *SymbolClass*; *r*: *integer*; *cand*: *anchors*);
   (* Deal with an erroneous symbol
     On entry-
       t describes the first unaccepted basic symbol
       need = basic symbol class expected (*EOPT* if unknown)
       r = number of the report text
       cand = set of possible anchors at this position
     On exit-
       t describes a basic symbol of the expected class
  *)

procedure *Accept*(**var** *t*: *token*);
   (* Accept the current basic symbol
     On entry-
       t describes the basic symbol accepted by the parser
     On exit-
       t describes the first unaccepted basic symbol
  *)

procedure *SynterrInit*;
   (* Initialize the syntax error reporting module *)

                      (a) The module's interface specification

```
1    procedure Name(cand: anchors);
2    begin
3      if t.kind < > IdentifierT then Synterr(t,IdentifierT,2(*Identifier expected*),cand);
4      SourceLeaf(IdnLeaf,t); Accept(t);
5      SourceNode(IdnExpr);
6    end;
```
                                (b) A use of the module

Figure 5.11
An error recovery module

and the **if**-statement implements the *IdnLeaf* symbol connection of that diagram. If the current basic symbol (stored in the global variable *t*) is not an identifier, then a syntax error has been detected. An identifier is required in this context, as specified by the second argument of the *Synterr* call, and the appropriate error report is "Identifier expected." According to Figure 5.9, no symbols can be accepted along the continuation from this symbol connection to the end of the *Name* diagram, so the set of possible anchors is just the set of symbols that could be accepted after leaving the diagram. That set is exactly the value of the *cand* argument of *Name*.

    Figure 5.11a guarantees that, after return from *Synterr*, *t* will describe an identifier. (The *need* argument to the *Synterr* call specified that an identifier was expected, and the interface guarantees that t describes a basic symbol of the expected class on exit.) Thus t always describes an identifier upon arrival at line 4 of Figure 5.11b. That identifier might be the current basic symbol of the source program, it might be the first basic symbol following some sequence of symbols deleted by the error recovery module, or it might be a generated identifier. In any of these cases, the parser builds a leaf of the source program tree for that identifier and accepts it by invoking the *Accept* operation of Figure 5.11a.

Consider the following syntactically incorrect assignment:

$$a := (b + , (c+d)) \qquad (1)$$

The simplest way to recover from this error would be to delete the comma, but this recovery requires some additional code in the procedure implementing the *Expression* diagram (Figure 5.12). An additional test (line 4) has been inserted to detect an error before selecting which branch to follow from the fork. This test is not necessary for the correct behavior of the parser and cannot be deduced from any of the material presented so far. It affects only the way in which the parser will recover from certain errors.

You can verify from Figure 5.10 that if the erroneous assignment (1) is presented to our parser, *Expression* will be entered with t describing the comma and *cand* specifying the anchor set $\{')'\ EOPT\}$. Suppose for a moment that Figure 5.12 did not contain lines 4 and 5. None of the tests on lines 6, 11, or 23 would be satisfied, so *Name* would be invoked on line 40 with t describing the comma and *cand* specifying the anchor set $\{')'\ EOPT\}$. Figure 5.11b then shows that *Synterr* would be invoked and told that an identifier is expected. Since *Synterr* implements the general error recovery process, it deletes symbols from the input until it reaches either the expected symbol or a symbol in the anchor set. For our example, this means that "," and "(" would be deleted. *Synterr* would then set t to describe c and return. This identifier would be accepted by *Name*, which would return to *Expression* at line 41 of Figure 5.12, with t describing "+". But then *Expression* would return to its invoker, and "+" could not be accepted. The final effect is that the parser would construct a tree for $a:=(b+c)$, instead of one for the closer approximation $a:=(b+(c+d))$.

The test in line 4 of Figure 5.12 verifies that the basic symbol described by t will be accepted by *some* path leaving the fork. It succeeds when *Expression* is entered with t describing the comma and *cand* specifying the anchor set $\{')'\ EOPT\}$, detecting the error before the parser has committed itself to one of the four paths available. Notice that when the test succeeds, indicating that the current basic symbol cannot be accepted by any of the paths leaving the fork, *Synterr* is called (on line 5) with $need = EOPT$. According to Figure 5.11a, $need = EOPT$ indicates that the expected symbol class is unknown. *Expression* could accept an integer, left parenthesis, or identifier at this point, so the expected symbol class really *is* unknown. The set of possible anchors provided to *Synterr* as its fourth argument is the union of the normal anchor set and the director sets of all paths leaving the fork. *Synterr* will therefore delete "," and set t to describe "(", then return. Now *Expression* will select the second alternative via the test at line 11 and parse $(c+d)$. The desired recovery has been achieved.

5.3 ERROR RECOVERY IN A RECURSIVE DESCENT PARSER   129

Suppose that the input had been $a:=(b+,)$. *Expression* would again be entered with *t* describing the comma and *cand* specifying the anchor set $\{$ $')'$ *EOPT*$\}$, and again the test on line 4 would succeed. This time *Synterr* would return with *t* describing ")". The symbol ")" is in the anchor set, but it cannot be accepted immediately. The tests at lines 6, 11, and 23 would therefore fail, and *Name* (Figure 5.11b) would be invoked at line 40 with *t* describing the right parenthesis and *cand* specifying the anchor set $\{$ $')'$ *EOPT*$\}$. *Name* would again invoke *Synterr*. This invocation *demands* an identifier, so *Synterr* will create one in *t*.

Clearly the invocation of *Synterr* from within *Name* does not represent a new error in this case, but rather a continuation of a previously initiated error recovery. Therefore, *Synterr* should not make a new report; it should simply generate the necessary symbol. To implement this behavior, the error recovery module must have an internal state that determines whether a recovery is in progress. This is the reason for requiring an initialization operation.

Lines 31 and 32 of Figure 5.12 provide better recovery when the comma between set elements is omitted. The test on line 31 checks whether the next symbol is one that could begin an expression. If so, then it cannot be either of the symbols (",", or "]") acceptable at this point in the parse. *Synterr* is called on line 32 with *need*=*CommaT*, under the assumption that a comma has been omitted. Note that the fourth argument to *Synterr* is a singleton set consisting of the current symbol's class; this guarantees that *Synterr* will not delete the basic symbol already assumed to start the next expression. On return from *Synterr*, the interface specification of Figure 5.11a guarantees that *t.kind*=*CommaT*. This causes the parser to go back to the beginning of the loop and accept the next expression as part of the list.

The error recovery module (Figure 5.13) encapsulates all necessary manipulation of the basic symbol sequence, skipping to an anchor as well as generating symbols. When an error is detected, *Synterr* has enough information to issue the error report and skip symbols if necessary to obtain an anchor. If the anchor found is the symbol needed, or if the symbol needed is unknown, *Synterr* copies the anchor into *t* and returns. Otherwise, *Synterr* generates an acceptable symbol. (Figure 5.13 does not specify how an appropriate value is produced for a generated identifier or denotation. That depends on the particular source language, target language, and compilation strategy.)

Variables *gen* and *recover* encode the internal state of the module. When *Accept* is invoked, its behavior is determined by the state. If the module is not in the process of recovering from an error, *Accept* simply obtains a new basic symbol from the lexical analyzer. Otherwise, if the symbol accepted by the parser was the anchor, then the error recovery is complete and *Accept* will also obtain the next basic symbol. If the symbol accepted was a generated symbol, however, recovery is not complete. *Accept* copies the anchor into *t* and returns. Thus, the error recovery module will keep serving up the anchor to the parser until it is finally accepted.

If the anchor is not acceptable at the current point in the parse, *Synterr* will be invoked again. Thus, *Synterr*'s behavior must also be determined by the

```
 1   procedure Expression(cand: anchors);
 2   label 1;
 3   begin
 4     if not (t.kind in [IntegerT,LeftParenT,LeftBracketT,IdentifierT]) then
 5       Synterr(t,EOPT,2(*Identifier expected*),[IntegerT,LeftParenT,LeftBracketT,IdentifierT]+cand);
 6     if t.kind = IntegerT then
 7       begin
 8         SourceLeaf(IntLeaf,t); Accept(t);
 9         SourceNode(IntExpr);
10       end
11     else if t.kind = LeftParenT then
12       begin
13         Accept(t);
14         Expression([PlusT,IntegerT,LeftParenT,LeftBracketT,IdentifierT,RightParenT]+cand);
15         if t.kind <> PlusT then
16           Synterr(t,PlusT,22(*'+' expected*),[IntegerT,LeftParenT,LeftBracketT,IdentifierT,RightParenT]+cand);
17         SourceLeaf(PlusExpr,t); Accept(t);
18         Expression([RightParenT]+cand);
19         if t.kind <> RightParenT then Synterr(t,RightParenT,4(*')' expected*),cand);
20         Accept(t);
21         SourceNode(PlusExpr);
22       end
```

```
23    else if t.kind = LeftBracketT then
24      begin
25        SourceLeaf(SetExpr,t); Accept(t);
26        EmptySourceSeq;
27        if t.kind <> RightBracketT then
28          begin
29   1:     Expression([[CommaT,RightBracketT]+cand);
30          ExtendSourceSeq;
31          if t.kind in [IntegerT,LeftParenT,LeftBracketT,IdentifierT] then
32            Synterr(t,CommaT,20(*','expected*),[t.kind]);
33          if t.kind = CommaT then begin Accept(t); goto 1 end;
34          end;
35        if t.kind <> RightBracketT then Synterr(t,RightBracketT,10(*']'expected*),cand);
36        Accept(t);
37        SourceNode(SetExpr);
38      end
39    else
40      Name(cand);
41    end;
```

Figure 5.12

Using *EOPT* as an argument to *Synterr*

```
var
   anchor: token;                    (* Recovery point in the input *)
   gen: boolean;                     (* True if the current symbol was generated *)
   recover: boolean;                 (* True if recovering *)

procedure Synterr(var t: token; need: SymbolClass; r: integer; cand: anchors);
   (* Deal with an erroneous symbol
      On entry-
         t describes the first unaccepted basic symbol
         need = basic symbol class expected (EOPT if unknown)
         r = number of the report text
         cand = set of possible anchors at this position
      On exit-
         t describes a basic symbol of the expected class
   *)

   begin
   if not recover then
      begin Report(FATAL,r,t.coord,0);
      while not(t.kind in cand+[need]) do Lexical(t);
      anchor: = t;  recover: = true;
      end;
   if(need = EOPT) or (need = anchor.kind) then t: = anchor
   else
      begin gen: = true;
      t.coord: = anchor.coord;  t.kind: = need;
      (* Generate an appropriate value in t if necessary *);
      end;
   end;

procedure Accept(var t: token);
   (* Accept the current basic symbol
      On entry-
         t describes the last basic symbol accepted by the parser
      On exit-
         t describes the first unaccepted basic symbol
   *)

   begin
   if gen then begin gen: = false; t: = anchor end
   else
      begin
      if recover then begin recover: = false; Report(INFO,49(*Analysis continued here*),t.coord,0) end
      Lexical(t);
      end;
   end;

procedure SynterrInit;
   (* Initialize the syntax error reporting module *)

   begin
   recover: = false;  gen: = false;
   end;
```

Figure 5.13
Implementation of the error recovery

module's state: It must not report an error if an error recovery is still in progress. If the state indicates that recovery is not yet complete, *Synterr* merely generates the required symbol. That symbol will drive the parser one step further along the continuation path.

5.4 SUMMARY

A recursive descent parser is constructed by writing one procedure for each syntax diagram of a parsing language. Recursive descent is usually used when writing a compiler by hand.

Left recursion must be removed from any parsing language that is implemented by a recursive descent parser. Syntax diagrams are tedious to manipulate, but the extended regular expression form is usually easy to transform appropriately. The important relationship is the one that relates left recursion and iteration. It was discussed in detail in Section 4.1.2.

Even if there is no left recursion, the parsing language may not be suitable for direct encoding by recursive descent. The parser must be able to decide on a unique path at every point in the syntax diagram where paths diverge. A set of basic symbols, the director set, is associated with each path. If the parser takes a particular path, the first symbol that it accepts as it traverses the path will be one of the symbols in the director set. To make a decision about which path to take, therefore, the parser peeks at the next input symbol and takes the path having that symbol in its director set. If a particular symbol belongs to more than one director set, the parser will be unable to choose a path. Thus, a parsing language that has director set overlaps must be transformed before being implemented by a recursive descent parser.

Substitution and the distributive law are the transformations usually used to remove director set overlap. These transformations of the specification do not change the language it describes. Therefore the activity sequences defined by the transformed specification are identical to the activity sequences described by the original. This means that a parser implementing the transformed specification will invoke the same operations in the same order as one implementing the original specification (if such a parser could have been constructed).

Error recovery is handled by a separate module that deletes input symbols and generates symbols to move the parser along the continuation discussed in Section 4.3. The continuation is defined by the order in which alternatives are written in the parser. Each procedure of the parser is passed an argument that specifies the set of basic symbols that could be accepted along the continuation after that procedure is left. The anchor set is specified to the recovery module as a union of this argument with the set of symbols that could be accepted along the continuation from the code reporting the error to the end of the procedure containing that code. Additional tests and invocations of the error recovery module may be inserted into parsing procedures to improve the recovery in certain cases.

NOTES

Recursive descent parsers have a long history [4, 7]. They are easy to build by hand, and quite efficient [9].

Most left recursion in parsing languages is direct, and can be removed by transforming it to iteration as discussed in Section 5.1. In the rare cases where indirect left recursion appears, a couple of obvious substitutions usually suffice to reduce it to direct left recursion. There is also a general technique for left recursion removal that can be applied to any context-free grammar [6, 10], and is guaranteed to succeed. Thus, in stubborn cases, the specification can be cast as a context-free grammar and the left recursion removed.

If all director set overlaps can be removed from a parsing language, then that specification can be described by a special kind of context-free grammar called an *LL(1)* grammar [8]. An arbitrary grammar can be checked to see whether it is LL(1). If the test fails, it points out the director set overlaps, which can then be attacked by a combination of substitution and factoring as illustrated in Section 5.2. At least one tool has been built to automate these transformations [3]. Unfortunately, such a tool cannot be guaranteed to work in all cases because the existence of an LL(1) grammar for a given language is undecidable [8].

The method of computing the anchor sets for error recovery is due to Ammann [1]. It is straightforward, but unpleasant because it slows the processing of *correct* programs. At each call, the parsing procedure must construct and pass a relatively large set. If the parser did not use individual procedures to implement the recursive descent, but rather used a single procedure that maintained its own stack, then the overhead could be eliminated. *Synterr* could examine the explicit stack and build the anchor set from the sequence of calls [5].

REFERENCES

1. Ammann, U., "Die Entwicklung eines PASCAL-Compilers nach der Methode des Strukturierten Programmierens," Ph.D. Thesis, Eidgenössischen Technischen Hochschule Zürich, Zürich, 1975.
2. Dijkstra, E. W., "Go To Statement Considered Harmful," *Comm. of the ACM 11*, 3 (Mar. 1968), 147–148.
3. Foster, J. M., "A Syntax Improving Program," *Computer J. 11*, 1 (May 1968), 31–34.
4. Grau, A. A., "Recursive Processes and ALGOL Translation," *Comm. of the ACM 4*, 1 (Jan. 1961), 10–15.
5. Gray, R. W., "Generating Fast, Error Recovering Parsers," MS Thesis, Dpt. of Computer Science, University of Colorado, Boulder, CO, Apr. 1987.
6. Harrison, M. A., *Introduction to Formal Language Theory*, Addison Wesley, Reading, MA, 1978.
7. McClure, R. M., "An Appraisal of Compiler Technology," in *Spring Joint Computer Conf.*, vol. 40, AFIPS Press, Montvale, NJ, 1972.
8. Rosenkrantz, D. J. and Stearns, R. E., "Properties of Deterministic Top-Down Grammars," *Inf. and Control 17* (1970), 226–256.
9. Waite, W. M. and Carter, L. R., "The Cost of a Generated Parser," *Software—Practice & Experience 15*, 3 (Mar. 1985), 221–239.

10. Waite, W. M. and Goos, G., *Compiler Construction*, Springer Verlag, New York, NY, 1984.

EXERCISES

5.1 Eliminate the unnecessary tests from Figure 5.1.

5.2 Consider the structure of procedure *Expression* in Figure 5.1.
   (a) Show how to eliminate the label and **goto** statement by using a **while** statement.
   (b) What is the cost of this change?
   (c) Does it make the procedure easier to understand?
   (d) Draw the syntax diagram that corresponds most directly to the restructured procedure. Is this syntax diagram easier to understand than the one given in Figure 4.6?
   (e) Comment on the structured programming concept "**goto** considered harmful" [2] in light of this example.

5.3 Write a tree construction module in which each operation simply prints its arguments. Combine this module with Figure 5.1 and an appropriate lexical analyzer, and execute it on appropriate input data.
   (a) Compare the list of calls for a given program to the sequence of operations you would have to carry out to evaluate that program on a pocket calculator that uses postfix operations.
   (b) What changes would you need to make to Figure 5.1 and the connection procedures to produce an *exact* description of the sequence of pocket calculator operations?

5.4 Why does left recursion arise naturally in the definition of a language? (Hint: Reread Section 4.3.)

5.5 Context-free grammars can describe iteration by right recursion. In order to do this, they need "helper" nonterminals that do not appear in the corresponding syntax diagram.
   (a) Write a context-free grammar corresponding to Figure 5.3.
   (b) Identify all of the "helper" nonterminals. Can you relate these nonterminals to the concept of "being at a particular place" in a traversal of the syntax diagram?
   (c) Write a set of recursive procedures, one per nonterminal of the grammar you described in (a). Compare these procedures with a set of procedures written directly from the diagrams, with labels and **goto**s implementing the iterations. Can you relate the procedures for "helper" nonterminals to labels?
   (d) How does the depth of procedure nesting at execution time grow in the case of the procedures written directly from the grammar? How does it grow in the case of the procedures written directly from the diagram?

5.6 Write a context-free grammar corresponding to Figure 5.2 [6, 10].
   (a) Compare your grammar to the grammar you wrote for Exercise 5.5a. Can you see a general transformation that will change direct left recursion into right recursion without altering the language defined by the grammar? (Since Figure 5.2 and Figure 5.3 define the same activity sequences, your grammar must be equivalent to the grammar you wrote for Exercise 5.5a.)
   (b) Can you state a general transformation that will convert indirect left recursion into direct left recursion?

5.7 The *Assign* diagram in Figure 5.5 duplicates three of the paths from the *Primary* diagram.
   (a) Implement the *Assign* diagram as a procedure that does *not* duplicate these three paths. Instead, invoke the *Primary* procedure. How must you define the director sets to make this possible?
   (b) Can you use reasoning similar to that of (a) to further simplify the *Assign* procedure?

5.8 The Pascal dangling **else** can be resolved by writing a more complex parsing language description:

$$Statement = \textbf{if } Expression \textbf{ then } Statement \mid Balanced$$

$$Balanced = \textbf{if } Expression \textbf{ then } Balanced \textbf{ else } Balanced$$

$$\mid UnconditionalStatement$$

(Here *UnconditionalStatement* represents all of the statement forms that do not contain **if**.) This parsing language is unambiguous.
   (a) Show that there is a director set overlap between the alternatives of *Statement*.
   (b) Show that substitution and use of the distributive law will always result in a director set overlap.
   (c) Can this description ever be used as the basis of a recursive descent parser? Explain briefly.

5.9 The decision procedure described in Section 5.2 depends on a single-symbol lookahead: Each director set specifies the symbols that could be accepted next along the corresponding path. In the example of Figure 5.4, the director set overlap could have been avoided if each director set specified the *pairs* of symbols that could be accepted next along the corresponding path.
   (a) Write a director set whose elements are symbol pairs for each path leaving a fork in Figure 5.4, and show that there is no overlap.
   (b) How does the size of the director set's base type grow with the number of terminal symbols of the language? Do you foresee problems in implementing director sets in the form of pairs for a language such as Pascal?

5.10 Instead of implementing all director sets as sets of pairs, one might use a function to look further ahead in exactly those cases where director sets based on a single lookahead overlapped:

function *Peek*(*k*: integer): *SymbolClass*;

This function would return the class of the kth basic symbol that had not yet been accepted.
Because *Peek* may have advanced the lexical analyzer beyond the first unaccepted basic symbol, the parser cannot call *Lexical* directly. Instead, it must call another procedure that delivers the first unaccepted token:

procedure *Accept*(**var** *t*: *token*);

This procedure sets *t* to the first token the parser has not yet accepted.
   (a) Implement the *Assign* procedure of Figure 5.4 using *Peek* and *Accept*.
   (b) Write a module that implements *Peek* and *Accept* in terms of *Lexical*. Do you need an initialization operation for this module? Do you need a finalization operation? Explain briefly.

(c) What is the relationship of the *Peek—Accept* module to the remainder of the compiler? (For example, where should it be visible? Where would you invoke its initialization and finalization operations, if they exist?)

5.11 Consider the combination of multisymbol lookahead (Exercise 5.10) and syntactic error recovery.
 (a) Define a single module that provides *Peek*, *Accept*, and *Synterr*.
 (b) What set of basic symbols should be tested *before* any choice?
 (c) How should the path be determined when $Peek(k)$ selects some set of paths, but $Peek(k+1)$ is not valid for any of them?
 (d) Write an error-recovering parser for Figure 5.5 that uses 2-symbol lookahead to decide which path to follow in *Assign*.

5.12 The variables *gen* and *recover* in Figure 5.13 determine the internal state of the error recovery module.
 (a) How many internal states are possible? Are any of these states "final" in the sense of Section 3.2.1?
 (b) The internal state of the module is changed by invocations of *Synterr* and *Accept*. Write a regular expression describing the possible sequences of *Synterr* and *Accept* invocations.
 (c) Draw a state diagram for the error recovery module. Label each state with the values of *gen* and *recover* that define it. Label each arc with the invocation that causes the transition. Explain why you need to distinguish two kinds of *Synterr* invocations.
 (d) Show that the distinction between the two kinds of *Synterr* invocations is always well-defined.

5.13 Replace the comment in the *Synterr* procedure of Figure 5.13 with code that generates appropriate values for Pascal basic symbols.
 (a) Which symbol classes must these values be generated for?
 (b) Could existing operations of other modules, possibly with slightly altered interfaces, be invoked to actually carry out the generation? (Hint: Review Section 3.3.)
 (c) Would it be more consistent with the compiler structure presented in Chapter 1 to alter and invoke existing operations, or to place the generation code directly into Figure 5.13? Briefly justify your answer.
 (d) Briefly assess the performance impact of altering existing operations versus placing the generation code directly into Figure 5.13.

5.14 Consider the following erroneous Pascal assignment:

$$S := [a,b \ c,d]$$

 (a) At what point in the parser of Figure 5.12 is the error detected, and what report is given?
 (b) Suppose that the additional test had not been included before the test for *CommaT* at the end of the loop in Figure 5.12. At what point would the error have been detected, and what report would have been given?
 (c) At what point will the parser of Figure 5.12 resume parsing this erroneous assignment? At what point would the parse resume if the additional test was not included?
 (d) State the general rule for including tests that improve error recovery when a list separator is omitted.

5.15 Rewrite the *Parser* procedure of Figure 5.1 so that it recovers from syntactic errors instead of terminating. Your answer should incorporate the code from Figure 5.11b and Figure 5.12.

5.16 Each of the procedures (*Name*, *Expression*, and *Statement*) used to construct your answer to Exercise 5.15 has as its argument a set of basic symbols that could be accepted by the parser after that procedure returns. These argument values must be computed at each procedure call by taking the union of the current procedure's parameter and a set determined at the time the parser was designed (Figure 5.10). The computations place a significant overhead on the parsing of correct programs in order to prepare for a possible error. This exercise outlines an alternative implementation.

(a) Define a variable for each *distinct* set of information specified in Figure 5.10. These variables are local to procedure *Parser*. Add code to the body of *Parser* to initialize the variables.

(b) Replace the *cand* parameter of each parsing procedure (*Expression*, *Assignment*, and *Statement*) and the *Synterr* procedure (Figure 5.11) by two parameters:

> **var** *local*: anchors; **procedure** *outer*

(c) Within each parsing procedure, define a local procedure that has the following interface:

> **procedure** *Build*(**var** *a*: anchors);
> (* Add symbols to an anchor set
>   On entry-
>   *a* contains a partial set of anchors
>   On exit-
>   The anchors specified by the my parent's *local* argument
>   have been added to *a*
>   My parent's *outer* argument has been applied to *a*
> *)

At each call of a parsing procedure, pass the variable specifying the symbols to be added to the candidates (see part b of this exercise) and the local *Build* procedure.

(d) Add a local variable *cand*, of type *anchors*, to *Synterr*. Just before the **while** statement, obtain the candidates for the anchor by executing the code:

> *cand*: = *local*; *outer*(*cand*);

Explain how this statement sequence obtains the set of candidates.

(e) Request a listing of the machine code output of your Pascal compiler and compare the overheads for correct programs using the *Parser* procedure developed in this exercise and the *Parser* procedure developed in Exercise 5.14.

6

Shift-Reduce Parsing

A parser can be implemented by defining a finite-state machine that is based upon the set of syntax diagrams describing the parsing language in much the same way as the lexical analyzer is based upon the set of syntax diagrams describing the basic symbols of the source language. Each state corresponds to some set of box entries or diagram exits, and each output corresponds to invocation of a tree-building operation. When the machine makes a state transition, the current state is pushed onto a stack instead of being lost, as it was in the machines of Section 3.3.1. Upon reaching a state whose set contains a diagram exit, the machine must decide whether the construct corresponding to that exit has actually been recognized. If so, then it pops the stack by the number of components of that construct, and the current state becomes the state at the top of the stack. This process gives the appearance of "shifting" symbols from the input to the stack and periodically "reducing" the size of the stack, hence the name "shift-reduce parsing."

Section 6.1 reviews the derivation of a finite-state machine from syntax diagrams, pointing out the places where parser derivation differs from scanner derivation, and shows how the machine is implemented as a program. A typical Pascal parsing machine has over 300 states, so shift-reduce parsing is a viable technique only when a parser generator is available. The general characteristics of shift-reduce parser generators are discussed in Section 6.2. Section 6.3 shows how the error recovery process of Section 4.4 can be incorporated into a shift-reduce parser.

6.1 HOW TO CONSTRUCT A SHIFT-REDUCE PARSER

The syntax diagrams in Figure 6.1a describe a subset of Pascal assignment statements. They were derived from Figure 4.9 by removing all joins, so that each path through a chart has a unique exit. This modification does not alter the parsing language described by the diagrams. A label has been attached to each symbol and symbol connection box, and to each chart exit. Oval boxes that represent structure connections are not associated with any input symbols; they are therefore "transparent" to the labeling process and remain unlabeled.

The transition table shown in Figure 6.1b was derived from Figure 6.1a by almost exactly the technique described in Section 3.2.1. Each state corresponds to a set of box labels from Figure 6.1a. State 1 corresponds to the set of labels that can be reached from the start of the *Statement* diagram, without passing through any boxes. Clearly, label a must belong to the set of labels for state 1. Label r can also be reached without going *through* any boxes, since the parser can reach the rectangular *Name* box, and r labels the entry point of the *Name* diagram. (This is a general property of the rectangular box—when the parser reaches a label attached to a rectangular box, it automatically reaches the label on the entry of the diagram that box names.) Note that rectangular boxes also act like single basic symbols. One element of the label set represented by state 1 is a, so that the parser has reached the *Name* box when the machine is in state 1. Therefore, when a *Name* is found in state 1, the parser can traverse the *Name* box and the next state of the machine will be the state having b in its label set (state 3).

State 3 represents the label set $\{b\}$. The only possible input at label b is ": = "; thus, only the column for ": = " has an entry in the row for state 3. If the parser traverses the ": = " box at label b, it reaches label c. But since c labels an *Expression* box, it has also reached the entry of the expression diagram. From the entry of the *Expression* diagram, the parser can reach labels $d, e, f, l,$ and n without passing through any boxes. Because e labels a rectangular box containing the name of the *Name* diagram, the parser has reached the entry of the *Name* diagram and hence label r. The entire set of labels reachable from b by passing through the ": = " box is therefore $\{c\ d\ e\ f\ l\ n\ r\}$, which corresponds to state 4.

Figure 6.2 shows how the parser interprets the transition table *next*. Compare this implementation with that of Figure 3.8b. Here *state* is a stack, rather than a simple variable. The stack is pushed on each state transition, so the previous state of the machine is not lost. An error is reported if an input symbol causes the machine to enter its trap state.

Both Figure 6.1b and Figure 6.2 are silent about the machine's behavior in states such as 2 and 7, which indicate that the end of a syntax diagram has been reached. In those situations, the machine removes elements from the stack before making a transition. The "input" symbol controlling the transition is the name of the syntax diagram just completed (e.g., one of the rightmost three column headings in Figure 6.1b). Let's examine a specific example.

Suppose the machine implementing Figure 6.1a attempts to parse the Pascal assignment $T := (M + 60)$. The lexical analyzer will have recognized T and M

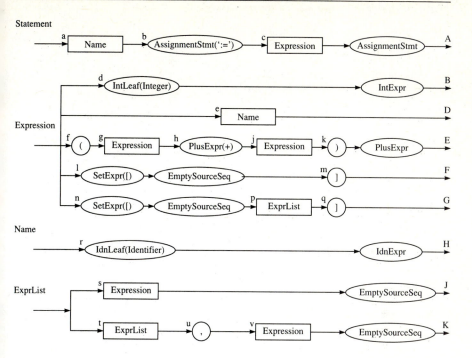

(a) A syntax diagram for some Pascal assignment statements

		Identifier	(	[	Integer	:=	+	,	]	)	Name	Expression	ExprList
	0	0	0	0	0	0	0	0	0	0	0	0	0
{a r}	1	2	0	0	0	0	0	0	0	0	3	0	0
{H}	2	0	0	0	0				0	0	0	0	0
{b}	3	0	0	0	0	4	0	0	0	0	0	0	0
{c d e f l n r}	4	2	5	6	7	0	0	0	0	0	8	9	0
{d e f g l n r}	5	2	5	6	7	0	0	0	0	0	8	10	0
{d e f l m n p r s t}	6	2	5	6	7	0	0	0	11	0	8	12	13
{B}	7	0	0	0	0	0				0	0	0	0
{D}	8	0	0	0	0	0				0	0	0	0
{A}	9	0	0	0	0	0	0	0	0	0	0	0	0
{h}	10	0	0	0	0	0	14	0	0	0	0	0	0
{F}	11	0	0	0	0	0				0	0	0	0
{J}	12	0	0	0	0	0	0		0	0	0	0	0
{q u}	13	0	0	0	0	0	0	15	16	0	0	0	0
{d e f j l n r}	14	2	5	6	7	0	0	0	0	0	8	17	0
{d e f l n r v}	15	2	5	6	7	0	0	0	0	0	8	18	0
{G}	16	0	0	0	0	0				0	0	0	0
{k}	17	0	0	0	0	0	0	0	0	19	0	0	0
{K}	18	0	0	0	0	0	0		0	0	0	0	0
{E}	19	0	0	0	0	0				0	0	0	0

(b) A transition table derived from (a)

Figure 6.1
Deriving a shift-reduce parser

procedure *Parser*;
  (* Table-driven shift-reduce parser *)

  const
    MaxParseDepth = 200;   (* Size of the parser's stack *)

  var
    t: *Token*;   (* First unaccepted basic symbol *)
    state: (* Stack of states *)
      array [1..*MaxParseDepth*] **of** *integer*;
    depth: 0..*MaxParseDepth*;

  begin
  Lexical(*t*); *depth*: = 1; *state*[*depth*]: = 1;
  repeat
    if *next*[*state*[*depth*],*t.kind*] = 0 **then**   (* The current symbol is not acceptable *)
      Report(*DEADLY*,22(*Syntax error*), *t.coord*,1);
    if *depth* = *MaxParseDepth* **then**   (* Compiler limit exceeded *)
      Report(*DEADLY*,397(*Parse stack overflow*), *t.coord*,0);
    depth: = *depth* + 1; *state*[*depth*]: = *next*[*state*[*depth* − 1],*t.kind*];
    Lexical(*t*);
  until ··· ;
  end;

Figure 6.2
Interpreting the transition table

as identifiers and 60 as an integer. Thus, the sequence of input symbols for the parsing machine will be as follows:

  Identifier := (*Identifier* + *Integer*)

Figure 6.3 shows the state transitions described by Figure 6.1b (*shift* operations) and also the *reduce* operations that occur whenever the end of a path in the syntax diagram is reached. You should be able to understand the shift operations from Figure 6.2 and your experience with scanners.

After the first shift operation, the machine is in state 2, which represents the end of the path through the syntax diagram for *Name* in Figure 6.1a. This means that the machine has recognized all of the components of a *Name*. The particular path taken through the *Name* diagram has one symbol connection box, no round boxes, and no rectangular boxes. In following this path, therefore, the machine has pushed exactly one state onto the stack (state 2). If this state is popped off of the stack, the state at the top will be the state the machine was in at the time it started to traverse the *Name* diagram (state 1). Since the machine has recognized all of the components of a *Name*, it should make the transition demanded for a *Name* by state 1. Figure 6.1b indicates that this transition should be to state 3. Therefore, the reduce operation pops one element from the stack and then pushes state 3, resulting in the situation shown in the third line of Figure 6.3.

6.1 HOW TO CONSTRUCT A SHIFT-REDUCE PARSER

Operation	Resulting Stack	Resulting Input
	1	T := (M + 60)
Shift	1 2	:= (M + 60)
Reduce	1 3	:= (M + 60)
Shift	1 3 4	(M + 60)
Shift	1 3 4 5	M + 60)
Shift	1 3 4 5 2	+ 60)
Reduce	1 3 4 5 8	+ 60)
Reduce	1 3 4 5 10	+ 60)
Shift	1 3 4 5 10 14	60)
Shift	1 3 4 5 10 14 7	)
Reduce	1 3 4 5 10 14 17	)
Shift	1 3 4 5 10 14 17 19	
Reduce	1 3 4 9	
Halt		

Figure 6.3
Behavior of Figure 6.1b for the input sequence T := (M + 60)

Starting with the input ":=" in state 3, Figure 6.1b shows that the machine will perform three shift operations, ending up in state 2. The reduce operation described in the last paragraph is then carried out again. This time, however, popping state 2 off of the stack reveals state 5 as the state in which the machine started to traverse the *Name* diagram. Figure 6.1b specifies state 8 as the destination for a transition on *Name* in state 5, so "8" must be pushed onto the stack.

State 8 represents the end of one path through the *Expression* diagram in Figure 6.1a. The machine has therefore recognized an *Expression*. There is one rectangular box, no round box, and no symbol connection along the path defined by state 8. Thus the machine must have pushed one element onto the stack while traversing this path, and popping that element will reveal the state the machine was in when it started to traverse the path. This is the state in which an *Expression* transition must be taken. For our example, the state revealed is 5, and Figure 6.1b specifies that an *Expression* causes a transition from state 5 to state 10.

After several more shifts and reductions, the machine reaches state 19. State 19 represents the end of a path through the *Expression* diagram, but this path includes two round boxes, two rectangular boxes, and a symbol connection. The machine must therefore have added five elements to the stack while traversing the path. In order to reveal the state in which the *Expression* transition must be taken, five elements must be popped off of the stack. An expression transition in state 4, according to Figure 6.1b, leads to state 9.

State 9 represents the end of the path through the *Statement* diagram. Two rectangular boxes and one symbol connection make up this path, so three elements must be removed from the stack. At this point, the entire input has been parsed and the machine halts.

The shift operations of Figure 6.3 are carried out by the code shown in Figure 6.2. That code is an interpretive implementation of a finite-state machine (Section 3.2.3). In order to implement the reduce operations, we need two more tables. Both of these tables are one-dimensional arrays indexed by paths through the syntax diagrams. One, *PathLength*, specifies the number of elements that must be popped off of the stack by the reduce operation. The other, *DiagramName*, provides the name of the diagram containing the path. Figure 6.4a shows these two tables for the example of Figure 6.1.

The paths are numbered in Figure 6.4a in the order they appear in Figure 6.1a. (We have included the label for each path to the left of the arrays.) These

		PathLength	DiagramName
{A}	1	3	Statement
{B}	2	1	Expression
{D}	3	1	Expression
{E}	4	5	Expression
{F}	5	2	Expression
{G}	6	3	Expression
{H}	7	1	Name
{J}	8	1	ExprList
{K}	9	1	ExprList

(a) Tables for implementing reduce operations

repeat
  if *next*[*state*[*depth*],*t.kind*] =0 **then**   (* The current symbol is not acceptable *)
    Report(*DEADLY*,22(*Syntax error*), *t.coord*,1);
  if *next*[*state*[*depth*],*t.kind*] >0 **then**   (* Shift operation *)
  begin
    if *depth* = *MaxParseDepth* **then**
      Report(*DEADLY*,397(*Parse stack overflow*), *t.coord*,0);
    depth: = *depth* +1; *state*[*depth*]: = *next*[*state*[*depth* − 1],*t.kind*];
    Lexical(*t*);
  end
  else   (* Reduce operation *)
  begin *path*: = − *next*[*state*[*depth*],*t.kind*];
    depth: = *depth* − *PathLength*[*path*];
    depth: = *depth* + 1;
    if *path* =1 **then** *state*[*depth*]: =0   (* The parse is complete *)
    else *state*[*depth*]: = *next*[*state*[*depth* − 1],*DiagramName*[*path*]];
  end;
until *state*[*depth*] =0;
if (*depth* < >2) **or** (*t.kind* < > *EOPT*) **then**
  Report(*DEADLY*,22(*Syntax error*), *t.coord*,2);

(b) The complete interpretation code

Figure 6.4
Reductions

numbers are used as subscripts in the code of Figure 6.4b. Note that the negatives of the path numbers are placed into the previously unspecified elements of Figure 6.1b. Thus the empty columns of the row for state 2 will contain "-7". By using negative values, we allow the body of the loop to make the initial decision about whether to execute a shift operation or a reduce operation.

In Section 3.2.3 we showed how to associate output actions with the transitions of a finite-state machine. The same technique can be used to invoke tree-building actions during shift-reduce parsing. Another table, *output*, of the same shape as Figure 6.1b would be used to hold elements of an enumerated type. Two **case** statements would be added to Figure 6.4b, one immediately preceding the invocation of *Lexical* in the code for the shift operation, and the other just before the stack is pushed in the reduce operation. These **case** statements would have one alternative for each of the possible sequences of table construction operations, selected by the appropriate element of *output*.

6.2 SHIFT-REDUCE PARSER GENERATORS

Parser generators accept context-free grammars, not syntax diagrams, as specifications of the parsing task. We discussed the equivalence of syntax diagrams and context-free grammars in Chapter 4. From that discussion, you can easily verify that Figure 6.5a describes the syntax diagrams of Figure 6.1a.

The presence of symbol and structure connections in a grammar leads to a host of caveats and complications for the analysis tool. Fortunately, however, it is possible to transform them into nonterminals in a straightforward manner. The basic idea is to replace each symbol connection by a nonterminal defined by a production whose right-hand side is the terminal that was the symbol connection's argument. Each structure connection is replaced by a nonterminal defined by a production whose right-hand side is empty. If a symbol connection and a structure connection have the same name, then one of them must be renamed. If the same symbol connection is used with several arguments, then several distinct nonterminal names must be used. Figure 6.5b shows the result of transforming Figure 6.5a in this way.

Every reduce operation carried out by the parser corresponds to recognition of a segment of the input sequence described by one of the rules of the context free grammar. (Note that the segment might be of zero length—an infinity of zero-length sequences appears between every pair of input symbols.) If the reduce operation recognizes a sequence described by one of the rules for *IntLeaf* through *ExtendSourceSeq*, then the parser must invoke a tree-building action. For example, a reduction recognizing an *IntLeaf* will invoke *SourceLeaf(IntLeaf,t)*, where *t* is the token for the integer constituting the segment of the input sequence described by the *IntLeaf* rule. Similarly, a reduction recognizing an *AssignmentStmt* will invoke *SourceNode(AssignmentStmt)*.

A parser generator analyzes the grammar, effectively determining the set of box entries and diagram exits corresponding to each state. It verifies that only a single action is possible for each state/input pair. (If more than one action were

Statement	→	Name AssignmentStmt(':=') Expression AssignmentStmt
Expression	→	IntLeaf(Integer) IntExpr
Expression	→	Name
Expression	→	'(' Expression PlusExpr('+') Expression ')' PlusExpr
Expression	→	SetExpr('[') EmptySourceSeq ']'
Expression	→	SetExpr('[') EmptySourceSeq ExprList ']'
Name	→	IdnLeaf(Identifier) IdnExpr
ExprList	→	Expression ExtendSourceSeq
ExprList	→	ExprList ',' Expression ExtendSourceSeq

(a) A grammar describing Figure 6.1a

Statement	→	Name AssignmentOp Expression AssignmentStmt
Expression	→	IntLeaf IntExpr
Expression	→	Name
Expression	→	'(' Expression PlusOp Expression ')' PlusExpr
Expression	→	SetExprSym EmptySourceSeq ']'
Expression	→	SetExprSym EmptySourceSeq ExprList ']'
Name	→	IdnLeaf IdnExpr
ExprList	→	Expression ExtendSourceSeq
ExprList	→	ExprList ',' Expression ExtendSourceSeq
AssignmentOp	→	':='
IntLeaf	→	Integer
PlusOp	→	'+'
SetExprSym	→	'['
IdnLeaf	→	Identifier
AssignmentStmt	→	
IntExpr	→	
PlusExpr	→	
IdnExpr	→	
EmptySourceSeq	→	
ExtendSourceSeq	→	

(b) The connections of (a) transformed to nonterminals

Figure 6.5
Describing syntax diagrams to a parser generator

possible for a particular pair, then the parser would not be able to make a decision when it was in the pair's state and given the pair's input.) In the absence of such conflicts, the parser generator will construct transition and output tables for a deterministic finite-state machine that parses the language described by the grammar and invokes appropriate tree-building operations.

It is surprisingly difficult to construct a parsing grammar that has no conflicts. This means that most of your interactions with a parser generator will involve analysis of conflicts and attempts to avoid them in various ways. To carry out this task effectively, you must understand what the parser generator is trying to tell you when it reports a conflict. The remainder of this section is therefore concerned with conflict reporting and resolution.

6.2 SHIFT-REDUCE PARSER GENERATORS

Our first example is a highly simplified grammar for Pascal conditionals:

Program	→	Statement
Statement	→	'if' Identifier 'then' Statement
Statement	→	'if' Identifier 'then' Statement 'else' Statement
Statement	→	Identifier ':=' Identifier

Figure 6.6a is the set of syntax diagrams corresponding to this grammar, and the transition table for the parsing machine is shown in Figure 6.6b.

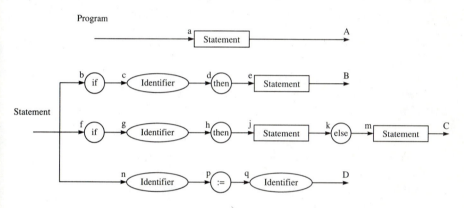

(a) Syntax diagrams for simplified Pascal conditional statements

		if	then	else	Identifier	:=	EOPT	Statement
	0	0	0	0	0	0	0	0
{a b f n}	1	2	0	0	3	0	0	4
{c g}	2	0	0	0	5	0	0	0
{p}	3	0	0	0	0	6	0	0
{A}	4	0	0	0	0	0	−1	0
{d h}	5	0	7	0	0	0	0	0
{q}	6	0	0	0	8	0	0	0
{e j b f n}	7	2	0	0	3	0	0	9
{D}	8	0	0	−4	0	0	−4	0
{B k}	9	0	0	?	0	0	−2	0
{m b f n}	10	2	0	0	3	0	0	11
{C}	11	0	0	−3	0	0	−3	0

(b) A transition table derived from (a)

Figure 6.6
The origin of a shift-reduce conflict

State 9 of the machine represents the label set {B k}. Thus, when the machine reaches state 9, it has either recognized a conditional statement that has no **else**-part, or it is in the process of recognizing a conditional statement that does have an **else**-part. If the next input symbol is **else**, the machine cannot distinguish these two possibilities because the grammar is ambiguous; the following string can be parsed in two different ways:

$$\text{if } a \text{ then if } b \text{ then } c := d \text{ else } e := f$$

If the "?" in Figure 6.6b were replaced by "10", the parser would recognize **if** b **then** $c := d$ **else** $e := f$ as a *Statement*; if it were replaced by "−2 ," the parser would recognize **if** b **then** $c := d$ as a *Statement*.

Most parser generators use a notation based on the input grammar to report conflicts such as the one illustrated in Figure 6.6. Each production of the grammar corresponds to a single path through a syntax diagram. For example, the production

$$\textit{Statement} \rightarrow \textit{'if' Identifier 'then' Statement}$$

corresponds to the path (b, c, d, e, B). A particular box on the path is indicated by inserting "•" into the production just before the symbol corresponding to that box. Thus

$$\textit{Statement} \rightarrow \textit{'if' Identifier} \bullet \textit{'then' Statement} \tag{1}$$

indicates the round box containing "then" on that path. Thus (1) has the same meaning as label d has in Figure 6.6a. A state is described by a set of marked productions such as (1) in exactly the same way as it is described by a set of labels.

In order to report a conflict, (1) must be augmented by the set of symbols that could follow a segment of the input sequence described by (1):

$$\textit{Statement} \rightarrow \textit{'if' Identifier} \bullet \textit{'then' Statement} \quad \{\textit{'else' EOPT}\}$$

The set is determined by the parser generator in the course of its analysis of the grammar.

State 9 of Figure 6.6b represents the set of positions {B k} in the syntax diagrams of Figure 6.6b. The parser generator would therefore provide the following information when reporting the conflict:

Statement → *'if' Identifier 'then' Statement* •   {*'else' EOPT*}
Statement → *'if' Identifier 'then' Statement* • *'else' Statement*   {*'else' EOPT*}

It would also describe the conflict as a "shift-reduce conflict" (meaning that it could not decide whether to shift or reduce), and report that the input symbol causing the conflict was "else."

Another kind of conflict is illustrated by the following grammar:

Program	→	*Block*
Block	→	*Declarations Statements*
Block	→	*Statements*

6.2 SHIFT-REDUCE PARSER GENERATORS

Declarations →

Declarations → *Declarations Decl* ';'

Statements →

Statements → *Statements Stmt* ';'

The parser generator would report a "reduce-reduce conflict" caused by symbol "EOPT," and give the following additional information:

Declarations → • {*EOPT Decl Stmt*}

Statements → • {*EOPT Stmt*}

Here, the problem is that the parser knows it has recognized a segment of the input sequence, but it cannot decide which of two rules describe that segment.

This reduce-reduce conflict, like the shift-reduce conflict discussed earlier, reflects an ambiguity in the grammar. If the machine solves the conflict by recognizing a *Declarations*, then a program will always be considered to have a list of declarations. That list of declarations may, of course, be empty. On the other hand, if the machine solves the conflict by recognizing a *Statements*, then a program may or may not have a list of declarations. A list of declarations can never be empty, however. Which choice should be taken depends upon the semantics of the language, and we do not have enough information here to make a decision.

Some parser generators accept ambiguous grammars and either make an arbitrary resolution or allow the user to provide additional information that resolves the ambiguity. For example, all shift-reduce conflicts might be resolved by doing the shift. This behavior is correct for the Pascal conditional statement example of Figure 6.6. Reduce-reduce conflicts might be resolved by reducing according to the production that appeared first in the grammar. This behavior would mean that all programs would have declaration lists in the example given above.

If the parser generator does not accept ambiguous grammars, or if the resolution of an ambiguity does not yield the desired activity sequence, then the grammar must be rewritten to remove the ambiguity. Section 4.2.2 discussed removal of certain ambiguities by introduction of operator precedence and association rules. Unfortunately, there are no systematic procedures for ambiguities that do not involve operators, although some general hints are possible.

There are two basic approaches to conflict resolution: eliminating configurations from the state and eliminating symbols from the list of followers. Configurations are eliminated from a state by "splitting" some nonterminal that lies to the left of "•" into two or more distinct nonterminals. The productions for the conflicting configurations are written to use distinct nonterminals, so they no longer appear in the same state.

The ambiguity in Figure 6.6 can be resolved by splitting the nonterminal *Statement* (which lies to the left of "•" in the conflicting situations) into *Statement* and *S*1:

Program → *Statement*

Statement → 'if' *Expression* 'then' *Statement*

Statement → 'if' *Expression* 'then' *S*1 'else' *Statement*

$$
\begin{aligned}
Statement &\rightarrow Identifier\ ':='\ Identifier \\
S1 &\rightarrow 'if'\ Expression\ 'then'\ S1\ 'else'\ S1 \\
S1 &\rightarrow Identifier\ ':='\ Identifier
\end{aligned}
$$

There is no effective way to eliminate symbols from the list of followers by manipulating the grammar. Some parser generators, however, allow the user to supply extra information about symbols to be deleted from certain follower sets. Other parser generators allow the user to specify the resolution of each conflict directly.

Some conflicts do not reflect any actual ambiguity in the grammar. Instead, the problem is that the designer is trying to distinguish two possibilities before the information needed to make that distinction becomes available:

$$
\begin{aligned}
S &\rightarrow Q \\
Q &\rightarrow A\ x\ y \\
Q &\rightarrow B\ x\ x \\
A &\rightarrow C\ a\ b \\
B &\rightarrow C\ a\ b \\
C &\rightarrow c
\end{aligned}
$$

Here the grammar is not ambiguous, but the fact that the shift-reduce parser can look only at the symbol immediately following the segment of the input sequence described by a rule means that it cannot decide between the rule for A and the rule for B. Two symbols must be examined to make the distinction.

6.3 ERROR RECOVERY IN A SHIFT-REDUCE PARSER

Section 4.4 described a general strategy that enables a parser to recover from syntactic errors and construct a consistent source program tree. In order to implement this strategy, *continuation* paths must be selected from each basic symbol or symbol connection to the end of its current syntax diagram, and from the entry point of each syntax diagram to its exit point. Once the paths are selected, Section 4.4.2 pointed out that there are three parser-dependent questions to be answered in implementing the syntactic error recovery:

1. How is the continuation specified?
2. How should the anchor be found?
3. How should generated symbols be introduced?

Although it is possible to answer these questions for a shift-reduce parsing machine, we are at the mercy of the parser generator when it comes to providing the necessary information.

6.3.1 How to Specify Continuations

When a shift-reduce parser detects an error, it is in some state, and the stack has some contents. This is the only information available on which to base decisions about the continuation, because the input has been proven unreliable by the fact of

6.3 ERROR RECOVERY IN A SHIFT-REDUCE PARSER 151

the error. The problem is that a state and stack contents do not uniquely determine a particular point in the set of syntax diagrams.

Section 4.4.2 pointed out that continuation paths must be acyclic, and the path from the entry point of a diagram to its exit point cannot reenter that diagram. None of the paths in a set of diagrams describing a shift-reduce parser can be cyclic, because there are no joins. Therefore, all that we need to worry about is recursion. In order to characterize a path with respect to recursion, we can define a *depth* for that path: A path that does not pass through any rectangular box has depth 0. A path passing through a rectangular box named X has a depth one greater than the minimum-depth path through the syntax diagram for X.

The path depths for an arbitrary set of syntax diagrams can be computed iteratively by associating a depth number with each box as follows:

1. Set the depth number of each nonrectangular box to 0, and the depth number of each rectangular box to ∞.
2. Choose a rectangular box whose depth number is ∞. Sum the depth numbers of the boxes along each path in the syntax diagram for that box. If any of the sums is finite, set the depth number of the rectangular box to one larger than the minimum sum.
3. Carry out step (2) repeatedly until all boxes have finite depth numbers.

This procedure will always result in finite depth numbers for all rectangular boxes if it is possible to generate an activity sequence from the syntax diagrams. For the syntax diagrams of Figure 6.1, the depth numbers will be: *Expression* $= 1$, *Name* $= 1$, *ExprList* $= 2$, and *Statement* $= 3$.

Each state of the machine corresponds to a set of points in the syntax diagram, and each point lies on exactly one path. Thus, a state corresponds to a set of paths. For example, consider state 6 of Figure 6.1b. It corresponds to the set of points $\{d\ e\ f\ l\ m\ n\ p\ r\ s\ t\}$, each of which defines exactly one of the nine paths in Figure 6.1a. Several of the points define the same path: Points l and m define path F, and points n and p define path G. Thus the set of paths corresponding to state 6 is $\{B\ D\ E\ F\ G\ H\ J\ K\}$.

For each state, choose one of the paths with the minimum depth for that state. The continuation for the state is the symbol that will advance the parser along the chosen path. Both path B and path H have depth 0 in this example; all of the other paths have larger depth. Thus either the symbol *Integer*, which would advance the parser along path B, or the symbol *Identifier*, which would advance the parser along path H, could be chosen as the continuation for state 6.

6.3.2 How to Find an Anchor

An anchor is a basic symbol that could be accepted as the parser moves along the continuation from the point where the error was detected to the execution of the Halt operation. As the parser moves along the continuation, it enters a sequence of states. Each state is capable of accepting a certain set of input symbols. The anchor set is the union of the sets for all states that the parser will pass through.

The input symbols that can be accepted in a particular state are those having positive, nonzero entries for that state in their transition table columns. State 1 of the machine defined by Figure 6.1 can accept only an *Identifier*, whereas state 6 can accept *Identifier*, ' (', ' [', *Integer*, and '] '. Note that when finding anchors, we are interested only in input symbols, not in the names of rectangular boxes. This means that only the first nine columns of Figure 6.1b are examined. Note also that *EOPT* is always an anchor.

The anchors useful for a particular error recovery must be determined after the error is detected, because they depend on the state of the stack. When an error is detected, the error recovery routine makes a copy of the parse stack and then runs the parser. At each step, the input symbol is assumed to be the continuation symbol associated with the current state. As the parser is run, the anchor set is constructed by taking the union of the symbol sets for the states encountered. Once this process is complete, the current input symbol is checked against the computed anchor set. If the input symbol is not in the anchor set, the lexical analyzer is invoked to obtain the next input symbol. This process will ultimately terminate, because *EOPT* is in the anchor set, and eventually the lexical analyzer is guaranteed to return *EOPT*.

6.3.3 How to Introduce Generated Symbols

Figure 6.7 shows how generated symbols are introduced to force the parser into a state where it can accept the anchor. *RecoverSyntacticError* is declared local to *Parser* (Figure 6.2). It therefore has access to the local variables *t*, *state*, and *depth*, and to the constant *MaxParseDepth*. A call to *RecoverSyntacticError* replaces the deadly error report in Figure 6.2.

RecoverSyntacticError first determines the anchor set as discussed in Section 6.3.2. (This code has been replaced by a comment in Figure 6.7, because the details do not illuminate any error recovery principles.) After obtaining the set of possible anchors, *RecoverSyntacticError* uses *Lexical* to obtain a symbol of that set. It places the anchor symbol into the parser's variable *t* and copies that symbol's coordinates to the local variable *gen*. Then it checks whether the anchor symbol is acceptable in the current state, and if so, it simply returns control to the parser. The exit condition of *RecoverSyntacticError* is satisfied, because *t* specifies a symbol that is acceptable in the current state.

If the symbol is not acceptable in the current state, *RecoverSyntacticError* sets the *kind* field of *gen* to specify the *SymbolClass* of the continuation symbol for the state. The *coord* field of *gen* specifies the coordinates of the anchor, i.e., the current position in the input sequence. Up to this point, the actions taken are independent of the source language. In order to complete the *Token* (Figure 3.1) that describes the generated symbol, however, properties of the source language's basic symbol set must be used. This action is therefore isolated in *GenerateToken* to preserve *RecoverSyntacticError*'s language independence.

GenerateToken deduces the necessary information from the *kind* field of its argument. If the desired basic symbol is a delimiter, nothing is to be done. If it is an identifier, *GenerateToken* sets its *idn* field to the value defining the special "inserted" identifier discussed at the end of Section 4.4.1. If it is a denotation (Section 3.1), *GenerateToken* sets its *val* field appropriately.

6.3 ERROR RECOVERY IN A SHIFT-REDUCE PARSER

---

procedure *RecoverSyntacticError*;
  (* Recover a syntactic error
    On entry-
      $t=$ An unacceptable symbol in *state[depth]*
    On exit-
      $t=$ An acceptable symbol in *state[depth]*
  *)

var
  temp: (* Copy of the state stack *)
    array [1..*MaxParseDepth*] **of** *integer*;
  tdepth: 0..*MaxParseDepth*;
  anchors: (* Symbols that could be accepted along the continuation *)
    set of *SymbolClass*;
  gen: *Token*;   (* Generated input symbol *)

begin
(* Obtain the set of anchors as discussed in Section 6.3.2 *)
while not *t.kind* **in** *anchors* **do** *Lexical*(*t*);
gen.coord: = *t.coord*;
while *next*[*state*[*depth*],*t.kind*] = 0 **do**
  begin
  gen.kind: = *Continuation*[*state*[*depth*]]; *GenerateToken*(*gen*);
  if *next*[*state*[*depth*],*gen.kind*] > 0 **then**   (* Shift operation *)
    begin
    if *depth* = *MaxParseDepth* **then**
      Report(*DEADLY*,397(*Parse stack overflow*), *t.coord*,0);
    depth: = *depth* + 1; *state*[*depth*]: = *next*[*state*[*depth* − 1],*gen.kind*];
    (* Invoke tree-building operation if necessary *)
    end
  else   (* Reduce operation *)
    begin *path*: = − *next*[*state*[*depth*],*gen.kind*];
    depth: = *depth* − *PathLength*[*path*];
    (* Invoke tree-building operation if necessary *)
    depth: = *depth* + 1;
    if *path* = 1 **then** *state*[*depth*]: = 0   (* The parse is complete *)
    else *state*[*depth*]: = *next*[*state*[*depth* − 1],*DiagramName*[*path*]];
    end;
  end;
end;

Figure 6.7
Error recovery in a shift-reduce parser

The remainder of the **while** statement in *RecoverSyntacticError* is identical to the normal parsing code in Figure 6.4b, except that it refers to the generated symbol whose token is stored in *gen*, instead of to the anchor stored in *t*. It advances the parser one step, updating the state and possibly invoking tree-building operations. When the step is complete, *RecoverSyntacticError* checks whether the parser has now reached a state that allows it to accept the anchor *t*.

6.4 SUMMARY

A shift-reduce parser is implemented by a finite-state machine that pushes its states onto a stack instead of overwriting them. Except for this feature, the parsing machine is very similar to the scanning machines discussed in Section 3.2.3. Basically the same technique is used to construct the two kinds of machine, given syntax diagrams that specify the problem.

For practical languages, shift-reduce parsing machines are too complex to construct by hand. This parsing technique is therefore viable only if a parser generator, a program that carries out the construction, is available. Parser generators accept context-free grammars as descriptions of sets of syntax diagrams. Connections are represented by nonterminals in these grammars, and the parser generator provides some notation for specifying which tree building actions are to be invoked when certain nonterminals are recognized.

When a parser generator cannot generate a deterministic parsing machine, it reports a conflict and gives the user information about the problem in terms of the grammar and input symbols. Conflicts may arise either from grammars that are ambiguous, or from attempts to distinguish cases before the necessary information has appeared in the input sequence. Standard resolutions might be provided by the generator itself, there might be a possibility for the user to specify the resolution directly, or the user may be required to rewrite the grammar to remove the problem.

Automatic error recovery can easily be provided for shift-reduce parsers. Unfortunately, the information to support it must be obtained by the parser generator, and many parser generators overlook this crucial task.

NOTES

The technique that we have termed "shift-reduce parsing" was first described by D. E. Knuth [6]. There were practical difficulties with the original method that prompted DeRemer to study a series of special cases [2, 1]. One of these cases, termed "LALR(1)", forms the basis of most current parser generators [5, 3].

It is not clear why people find specification of conflict-free parsing grammars so difficult. One of the main problems seems to be discovering the source of the conflict from the information provided by the parser generator. When the grammar is genuinely ambiguous it is hard to discover examples of the ambiguity, given the generator output. When the grammar is not ambiguous, production of examples is even harder. There are some systematic techniques for delaying decisions and then performing surgery on the constructed tree [4]. They can be used to automatically generate a parser in many cases where the grammar is not genuinely ambiguous. Thus they simplify the problem by reducing the number of conflicts that must be considered by the designer.

REFERENCES

1. DeRemer, F. L., "Practical Translators for LR(k) Languages," MAC-Tech. Rep.-65, MIT, Cambridge, MA, 1969.
2. DeRemer, F. L., "Simple LR(k) Grammars," *Comm. of the ACM 14*, 7 (July 1971), 453–460.
3. Dencker, P., Dürre, K., and Heuft, J., "Optimization of Parser Tables for Portable Compilers," *Trans. Prog. Lang and Systems 6*, 4 (Oct. 1984), 546–572.
4. Harford, A. G., "A New Parsing Method for Non-LALR(1) Grammars," MS Thesis, Dpt. of Computer Science, University of Colorado, Boulder, CO, 1990.
5. Johnson, S. C., "Yacc—Yet Another Compiler-Compiler," Computer Science Technical Report 32, Bell Telephone Laboratories, Murray Hill, NJ, July 1975.
6. Knuth, D. E., "On the Translation of Languages from Left to Right," *Inf. and Control 8*, 6 (Dec. 1965), 607–639.

EXERCISES

6.1 Describe the behavior of Figure 6.1b (augmented by the necessary reduce operations) for each of the following input sequences. Use a form similar to that of Figure 6.3.
  (a) $a := [\ ]$
  (b) $b := (c + [d,e])$
  (c) $f := (g + 1$ (* Note that there is no closing parenthesis on this expression. *)

6.2 Consider the inclusion of tree-building actions in the parser of Figure 6.1.
  (a) Draw the *output* table, which has the same shape as Figure 6.1b.
  (b) Write the two **case** statements that must be included in Figure 6.4b.
  (c) Suppose the oval box *EmptySourceSeq* had been omitted in path F of Figure 6.1a. Would this cause any difficulty in invoking the tree-building actions? Explain briefly.

6.3 Present the grammar of Figure 6.5 to your local shift-reduce parser generator.
  (a) How did you specify that tree-building actions were to be invoked?
  (b) How did you manage to obtain information about the correct tokens for *SourceLeaf*?

6.4 Submit the following grammar to your local shift-reduce parser generator:

$$S \rightarrow A$$
$$A \rightarrow b\ B$$
$$B \rightarrow c\ C$$
$$B \rightarrow c\ C\ f$$
$$B \rightarrow b$$
$$C \rightarrow d\ A$$

  (a) Give an intuitive explanation for the conflict.
  (b) Transform the grammar so that it has no conflicts, but describes the same language.

6.5 Submit the following grammar to your local shift-reduce parser generator:

$$
\begin{align*}
S &\rightarrow A \\
A &\rightarrow a\ B\ c\ B \\
A &\rightarrow B \\
A &\rightarrow D \\
B &\rightarrow b \\
B &\rightarrow F\ f \\
D &\rightarrow d\ E \\
E &\rightarrow F\ c\ A \\
E &\rightarrow F\ c\ E \\
F &\rightarrow b
\end{align*}
$$

(a) Give an intuitive explanation for the conflict.
(b) Transform the grammar so that it has no conflicts, but describes the same language.

6.6 Specify a continuation for every state in Figure 6.1b.

7

Managing Contextual Information

According to the scope rules of Pascal, the occurrence of *A* on line 10 of Figure 7.1 is a use of the variable declared on line 5. On line 12, *A* refers to a field of the record pointed to by *P*. The identifier *B*, on the other hand, refers to a field of the record *R* (declared on line 6) on both lines. Figure 7.2 gives the two source program tree fragments that represent lines 10-12 of Figure 7.1. These fragments are the internal representations of two of the statements in the compound statement forming the body of the program. Note that the subtrees for the statements on lines 10 and 12 are identical in structure, even though their meanings are quite different.

Our compilation strategy, discussed in Chapter 1, separates the task of determining structure from the task of determining meaning. Structure is embodied in an explicit source program tree. Meaning is determined by traversing that tree, gathering and distributing contextual information. This strategy enables us to separate concerns of determining structure from concerns of computing information based upon structure.

Both translation and encoding (Table 1.1) depend upon contextual information. To implement them, we need techniques for gathering that information, for computing values on the basis of it, and for saving some of those values for other tasks. Contextual information obtained by processing the source program tree is used to check whether the program obeys the source language definition, and to

```
1   program Context(input,output);
2   const C=1.2;
3   type T=record A,B,C: integer end;
4   var
5     A: real;
6     R: T;
7     P: ↑T;
8   begin
9     new(P); readln(R.B,R.C,P↑.C);
10    A:=R.B+C;
11    with P↑ do (* Redefines A B C *)
12      A:=R.B+C;
13    R:=P↑; writeln(A,R.A);
14  end.
```

Figure 7.1
A Pascal program

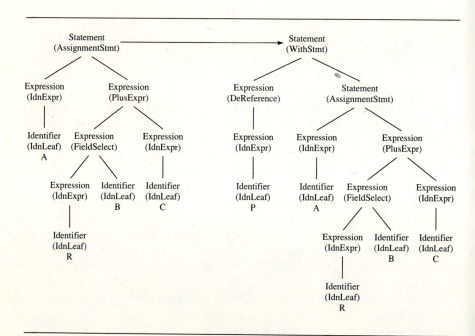

Figure 7.2
Source program tree for $A:=R.B+C;$ **with** $p\uparrow$ **do** $A:=R.B+C;$

guide the transformation task in its construction of the target program tree. Information obtained by processing the target program tree is used to guide the encoding task in its construction of the target text.

Section 7.1 considers a general strategy for designing programs that gather contextual information by traversing trees. Name analysis, the first subtask of semantic analysis given in Table 1.1, is used to illustrate this strategy. The strategy itself is much more general than name analysis, however, being used in the design of all of the compiler tasks that process contextual information.

Name analysis must be performed by a compiler for any language allowing user-defined identifiers. It associates each occurrence of an identifier with the definition of the entity that occurrence represents. The properties of the entities are stored in a data base, called the *definition table*, which is discussed in Section 7.2. An integer *key* is used to access a particular entry in the definition table.

It is important to note the difference between the definition table and the identifier table introduced in Section 3.3.2. The identifier table has one entry for each textually distinct identifier, while the definition table has one entry for each distinct entity defined in the program. Figure 7.3 illustrates the difference between identifiers and entities. A, B, and C are distinct identifiers, and there would be a single entry for each in the identifier table. A is defined as a field of a record on line 3 of Figure 7.3, and as a real variable on line 5. The record field and real variable are two distinct entities, so there would be two entries in the definition table for them. Bold superscripts in Figure 7.3 indicate the definition table keys for the defined entities (these keys were assigned arbitrarily for illustrative purposes only). As discussed in Section 3.3.2, each identifier is also represented internally by an integer. The integer representing A might or might not be the same as one of the bold superscripts in Figure 7.3; integers representing identifiers and integer definition table keys are generated by different modules at different times, and no attempt is made to coordinate them in any way.

```
 1   program Context(input,output);
 2   const C¹ = 1.2;
 3   type T² = record A³,B⁴,C⁵: integer end;
 4   var
 5      A⁶: real;
 6      R⁷: T;
 7      P⁸: ↑¹²T;
 8   begin
 9   new(P); readln(R.B,R.C,P↑.C);
10   A: = R.B + C;
11   with P↑ do (* Re-defines A⁹ B¹⁰ C¹¹ *)
12      A: = R.B + C;
13   R: = P↑; writeln(A,R.A);
14   end.
```

Figure 7.3
Figure 7.1 with definition table keys shown as superscripts

Definition table keys 1 through 11 in Figure 7.3 represent entities that are named by identifiers. There is no identifier, however, that names the pointer type represented by definition table key 12. This example illustrates that some entities whose properties are stored in the definition table are *anonymous*. It reinforces the fact that the identifier table and definition table are distinct, and that definition table keys and internal representations of identifiers are different things, even though both are coded as integers.

Although Figure 7.3 illustrates definition table keys in the context of Pascal, this concept is applicable to any language in which entities become defined as the compiler processes the source program.

The information gathering strategy described in Section 7.1 requires an amount of compilation time that grows linearly with the size of the program. If the compiler has to invoke computations at individual nodes of the tree, and if each of those computations requires an amount of time that also grows with the size of the program, then the overall compilation time will grow much faster with increasing program size. Section 7.3 gives two implementations of the basic name analysis computations, showing the impact of each on the overall compilation time.

7.1 HOW TO GATHER CONTEXTUAL INFORMATION

The general strategy for gathering contextual information has three tactical components:

- *Computation of values and verification of conditions*: The tactics of computing values, given appropriate contextual information, and verifying conditions based upon these values.
- *Tree traversal*: The tactics of moving from one node of the tree to another, and choosing the sequence in which nodes are visited.
- *Information storage*: The tactics of accessing contextual information and storing temporary results.

Each of these components will be discussed in the context of a Pascal compiler's name analysis task. Figure 7.4 shows the effects of Pascal name analysis on the source tree fragments representing lines 10-12 of Figure 7.3. Initially the only decoration is the unique internal representation for each identifier, computed by the lexical analyzer as discussed in Section 3.3.2. (These unique internal representations are really integers; they appear as identifiers in Figure 7.4 in order to make the example more understandable. Throughout the examples in this chapter, we shall use source program identifiers instead of the integers that encode them.)

At each identifier leaf in Figure 7.4a, the name analyzer must compute the definition table key that is associated with that leaf's identifier. In order to do so, it must first have computed the set of associations that is valid at that leaf. According to the visibility rules of Pascal, the set of associations valid inside a **with** statement is different from the set of associations valid outside that statement. Therefore, the name analyzer must compute a new set of associations for each **with**

7.1 HOW TO GATHER CONTEXTUAL INFORMATION

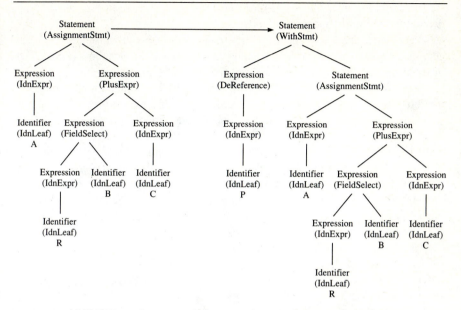

(a) Undecorated source tree fragments input to the semantic analyzer

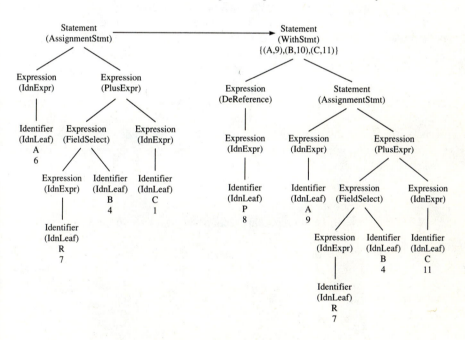

(b) The result of name analysis on (a)

Figure 7.4
Name analysis

statement. In Figure 7.4b, the result of this computation is shown as an additional decoration on the **with** statement node.

In order to compute the additional decorations shown in Figure 7.4b, the compiler must visit the nodes at which the necessary information resides. The order of these visits is determined by the availability of the information. For example, in the right-hand statement tree of Figure 7.4a, the compiler must visit the left-hand expression component in order to determine the type of the record before it can compute any new associations for identifiers in the **with** statement's body. Because the record type is the one declared on line 3 of Figure 7.3, new associations are needed for the field identifiers A, B, and C.

The trees of Figure 7.4a are elements of the list of statements making up the compound statement that is the program body of Figure 7.3. A depth-first, left-to-right traversal of the source program tree for Figure 7.3 would therefore visit the left tree of Figure 7.4a, and then visit the right tree. Each tree would be traversed depth-first, left-to-right. Such a traversal would visit the nodes of Figure 7.4a in an order compatible with the dependence among the computations. In particular, the type of the **with** statement's expression component would be available before it was necessary to compute new associations for identifiers appearing in the **with** statement's statement component.

Computation of the key associated with an identifier requires two pieces of information—the unique integer representing the identifier and a set of associations between identifiers and keys. The unique integer is stored at the identifier node, but how can the compiler access the set of associations? This is a question of information storage, and can be answered once the tree traversal is known.

If a depth-first, left-to-right traversal is used, the current set of associations can be accessed via a global variable. When a node such as the **with** statement node is visited, the content of the variable can be saved, a new set of associations computed, and access to them stored in the same global variable. When the visit to the **with** statement terminates, the saved value is restored. The computation of the key associated with an identifier always accesses the global variable to obtain the set of valid associations.

This example shows that a tree decoration strategy can be developed in three steps:

1. Decide what computations are needed in order to support the decisions that must be made.
2. On the basis of dependence among the computations, determine a sequence of visits guaranteeing that all information is available when it is needed for some computation or decision.
3. Decide how to store the contextual information so that it is accessible to the computations that need it.

Initially, we asserted that the necessary computations for the Pascal name analysis problem were those to determine the key associated with each identifier in the program. In order to support those computations, the type returned by an expression and sets of associations between identifiers and definition table keys had to be computed. The information flow among these computations was compatible with a depth-first, left-to-right traversal of the source tree. Finally, use of a global variable whose value was periodically saved and restored made it simple to access the appropriate set of associations.

The remainder of this section explores in detail each of the three steps used to develop a strategy for gathering contextual information. We will present a general approach to each set of tactical decisions. Although name analysis is used as the running example, you should not conclude that this section teaches you how to do name analysis only! The techniques are applicable to *any* tree decoration problem.

7.1.1 Computation of Values

The values that decorate a tree are computed on the basis of contextual information derived during the tree traversal. It is useful to separate the actual computations from the process of determining the inputs to those computations. This is achieved by encapsulating the computations in a module that provides each relevant operation as a simple call.

Name analysis is based upon the environment module whose interface is given in Figure 7.5. (We shall study possible implementations of this module in Section 7.3.) A value of type *Environment* represents the associations between identifiers and definitions that are established in a particular region of the program text. For example, there are six associations established in the "program" region in Figure 7.6a; the declarations appear on lines 2, 3 (the definition of *T*), and 5-7. The environment showing these associations would therefore be as follows:

$$\{(C,1)\ (T,2)\ (A,6)\ (R,7)\ (P,8)\}$$

The component statement of the *WithStmt* construct is a region that contains definitions and is completely enclosed by the "program" region. The environment showing the associations between identifiers and definitions that are established in the component statement of the *WithStmt* construct is as follows:

$$\{(A,9)\ (B,10)\ (C,11)\}$$

Pascal environment values form a tree, with the children of an environment being the environments for the immediately contained regions, as shown in Figure 7.6b. The environment value returned by *NewEnv* (Figure 7.5) is the root of the tree, and contains associations for the predefined identifiers. (According to the Pascal standard, predefined identifiers "are used as if their defining-points have a region enclosing the program.") The program environment is a child of the root. The **with**-statement environment is a child of the program environment because the region in which it describes the relationship between identifiers and definitions is nested directly within the "program" region.

The function *NewScope* of Figure 7.5 creates an empty environment that is a child of the environment specified by its argument. Thus, an empty environment for the program would be created by applying *NewScope* to the value returned by *NewEnv*, and an empty environment for the component statement of the *WithStmt* construct would be created by applying *NewScope* to the program environment.

type
  Environment = ↑*EnvImpl*;   (* Private type *)

function *NewEnv*: *Environment*;
  (* Establish a new environment
    On exit-
      NewEnv = new environment
  *)

function *NewScope*(*env*: *Environment*): *Environment*;
  (* Establish a new scope within an environment
    On exit-
      NewScope = new environment that is a child of *env*
  *)

function *DefineIdn*(*env*: *Environment*; *idn*: *integer*): *DefTableKey*;
  (* Define an identifier in a scope
    If *idn* is defined in *env* then on exit-
      DefineIdn = key for *idn* in *env*
    Else let *n* be a previously unused definition table key
    Then on exit-
      DefineIdn = *n*
      idn is defined in *env* with the key *n*
  *)

function *KeyInEnv*(*env*: *Environment*; *idn*: *integer*): *DefTableKey*;
  (* Find the key for an identifier in an environment
    If *idn* is defined in *env* then on exit-
      KeyInEnv = key for *idn* in *env*
    Else if *env* was created by *NewScope*(*parent*) then on exit-
      KeyInEnv = *KeyInEnv*(*parent*,*idn*)
    Else on exit-
      KeyInEnv = special key that represents no definition
  *)

function *KeyInScope*(*env*: *Environment*; *idn*: *integer*): *DefTableKey*;
  (* Find the key for an identifier in a scope
    If *idn* is defined in *env* then on exit-
      KeyInScope = key for *idn* in *env*
    Else on exit-
      KeyInScope = special key that represents no definition
  *)

Figure 7.5
Environment module interface

DefineIdn is used by the name analyzer when processing a *defining occurrence* of an identifier. (A defining occurrence is one like *A* in line 5 of Figure 7.6a. It defines an identifier's meaning. All other occurrences, in which the meaning is not defined, are called *applied occurrences*.) *DefineIdn* searches the given environment for the given identifier, returning the associated definition table

7.1 HOW TO GATHER CONTEXTUAL INFORMATION

```
1   program Context(input,output);
2   const C¹ = 1.2;
3   type T² = record A³,B⁴,C⁵: integer end;
4   var
5       A⁶: real;
6       R⁷: T;
7       P⁸: ↑T;
8   begin
9       new(P); readln(R.B,R.C,P↑.C);
10      A: = R.B + C;
11      with P↑ do (* Redefines A⁹ B¹⁰ C¹¹ *)
12          A: = R.B + C;
13      R: = P↑; writeln(A,R.A);
14  end.
```

(a) The identifier/key associations of Figure 7.3

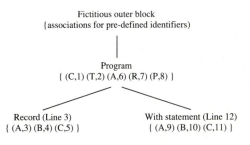

(b) The tree of *Environment* values corresponding to (a)

Figure 7.6
Relationships between Pascal *Environment* values

key if the environment contains an association for that identifier. If no association is found, *DefineIdn* obtains a new key from the definition table module and adds an association between that key and the given identifier to the given environment, as well as returning the new key. Thus *DefineIdn* has a side effect on its environment argument if there is no association for the identifier argument. (Section 7.2.1 shows how to report multiple declarations as errors.)

The name analyzer uses *KeyInEnv* when processing most applied occurrences of identifiers. *KeyInEnv* first examines the given environment, returning the associated definition table key if the environment contains an association for the given identifier. If no association is found, *KeyInEnv* is applied to the parent of the given environment. Only if no association can be found in the given environment or any of its ancestors will *KeyInEnv* deliver a special key that means the identifier is undefined.

KeyInScope is used when it is inappropriate to search the parent of the current environment if there is no definition for the identifier in the current environment itself. An example of such a situation is the applied occurrence of *B* in line 10 of Figure 7.6a. Here the search should take place in the environment associated with the record definition from line 3. If the identifier is not found in that environment, then the parent environment (in this case the program—see Figure 7.6b) should *not* be searched.

7.1.2 Tree Traversal

A tree traversal is made up of a sequence of visits to nodes. At the start of a visit, the compiler assumes that certain information is available. The purpose of the visit is to make some additional information available, so the compiler should be able to assume the availability of that information when the visit is complete. We shall restrict the tree traversal algorithms we discuss in this book to those implementable by procedures that perform computations and visit children of the current node. This restriction prevents the compiler from arbitrarily jumping around in the tree; it may move only from one node to a neighboring node. The restriction does *not* limit the number of times a node can be visited, nor does it require "regular" traversals such as depth-first, left-to-right.

We have seen (in the example of Figure 7.4) that a depth-first, left-to-right traversal is compatible with name analysis of correct Pascal programs. Unfortunately, certain errors are difficult to detect when such a traversal is used. For example, some Pascal compilers fail to report errors in Figure 7.7, even though it is an incorrect program: The identifier *integer* is declared on line 23 as a function name. This declaration supersedes the normal interpretation of *integer* as a type identifier within the body of the program. Since there are no other declarations of the identifier *integer* in Figure 7.7, every other occurrence of *integer* must be an applied occurrence of the function name. The occurrence of *integer* on line 8 is therefore in error on two counts—it is an applied occurrence that precedes its defining occurrence, and it is a function name appearing in a context requiring a type.

Let's see how a carelessly implemented compiler could overlook these errors. A depth-first, left-to-right traversal of Figure 7.7 will encounter the applied occurrence of *integer* on line 8 before encountering its defining occurrence on line 23. If name analysis is carried out during such a traversal, the applied occurrence on line 8 will be erroneously given the key for the predefined type *integer*, since that association will be found by *KeyInEnv*.

One way to avoid this mistake is to visit all of the defining occurrences of identifiers in a given region before visiting any applied occurrences or nested regions. Since the defining occurrence of *integer* on line 23 is in the program region, it will be visited before any occurrences inside the *DotProduct* region are visited. Therefore, when the applied occurrence of *integer* on line 8 is finally visited, the proper association will be in the environment, and the definition on line 23 will be identified.

Using these tactics, a compiler would process this program by first visiting all of the identifier declarations in the program region and associating the identifiers they define with definition table keys. These declarations are represented by nodes

```
 1    program UseBeforeDef(input,output);
 2    const MaxIndex = 2;
 3    type  Index = 1..MaxIndex; Vector = array [Index] of real;
 4    var v1,v2: Vector; x: real;
 5    function DotProduct: real;
 6      var i: Index; result: real;
 7      procedure Average(var v: Vector);
 8        var i: Index; n: integer; d,sum: real;
 9        begin
10        for i: = 1 to MaxIndex do
11          begin n: = 0; sum: = 0.0;
12          while not eoln(input) do begin read(d); sum: = sum + d; n: = n + 1 end;
13          readln;
14          if n < > 0 then v[i]: = sum/n else v[i]: = 0.0;
15          end;
16        end;
17      begin (* DotProduct *)
18      Average(v1); Average(v2);
19      result: = 0;
20      for i: = 1 to MaxIndex do result: = result + v1[i]*v2[i];
21      DotProduct: = result;
22      end; (* DotProduct *)
23    function integer(x: real): boolean;
24      begin integer: = round(x) = x end;
25    begin
26    if integer(DotProduct) then writeln('integer') else writeln('not integer');
27    end.
```

Figure 7.7
A use-before-definition error in Pascal

2 through 8 in Figure 7.8. Since these nodes are classified as declarations, the procedure invoked for each would be *DeclarationVisit*1 (Figure 7.9). The entry condition of this procedure describes the information that the compiler will assume to be available at the start of its first visit to a declaration node, and the exit condition describes the information provided by the visit.

*DeclarationVisit*1 is invoked to visit each of nodes 2 through 8, even though these nodes do not all require the same processing. For example, node 4 represents a type declaration, whose left child is a single identifier, and node 5 represents a variable declaration, whose left child is a list of identifiers. To distinguish the appropriate actions, the body of a visit procedure uses a **case** statement with one alternative for each source construct of the appropriate class. There are ten Pascal source constructs that are classed as declarations: *LabelDecl, ConstantDecl, TypeDecl, VariableDecl, FunctionDecl, ProcedureDecl, ValParameterDecl, VarParameterDecl, RoutineParameterDecl,* and *FieldDecl.* The body of *DeclarationVisit*1 consists of a **case** statement with only nine alternatives, however, because *FunctionDecl* and *ProcedureDecl* are processed in much the same way. Three of the nine alternatives are described in Figure 7.9.

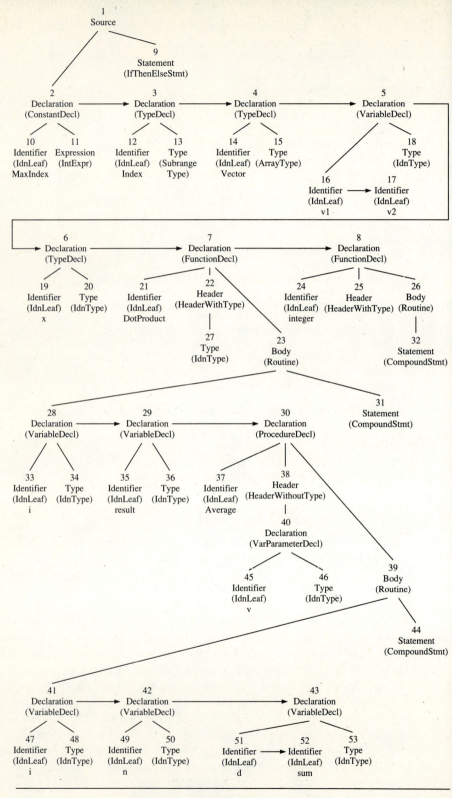

Figure 7.8
Partial source program tree for Figure 7.7

LabelDecl,ConstantDecl,TypeDecl,FieldDecl,VariableDecl,
RoutineDecl,FunctionDecl,ProcedureDecl,
VarParameterDecl,ValParameterDecl,RoutineParameterDecl:
  (
  case *Declaration* **of**
  ConstantDecl,TypeDecl: (*DeclaredId,Declarer*: *SourceTree*);
  FieldDecl,VariableDecl,VarParameterDecl,ValParameterDecl:
    (*Names*: *SourceSequence*; *DeclaredType*: *SourceTree*);
  FunctionDecl,ProcedureDecl: (*RoutineDeclName,RoutineDeclHeader,RoutineDeclBody*: *SourceTree*);
  );
IdnLeaf:
  (*Definition*: *DefTableKey*;   (* Access to properties (Section 7.2.1) *)
  LexIdent: *integer*);   (* Identifier (Section 3.3.2) *)

       (a) Source tree node record (see Figure 4.2) additions for name analysis

procedure *TypeVisit*1(*n*: *SourceTree*);
  (* Obtain keys for all defining occurrences of identifiers in a type
    On entry-
      The environment for the current region has been established
    On exit-
      A key has been associated with each defining occurrence of an identifier in this type
  *)
  . . .

procedure *DeclarationVisit*1(*n*: *SourceTree*);
  (* Obtain keys for all defining occurrences of identifiers in a declaration
    On entry-
      The environment for the current region has been established
    On exit-
      A key has been associated with each defining occurrence of an identifier in this declaration
  *)
  var *t*: *SourceSequence*;
  begin
  case *n*↑.*Kind* **of**
    . . .
    TypeDecl: (* (*Identifier,Type*): *Declaration* *)
      begin
      (* Code to associate a definition table key with the *Identifier* child goes here *)
      *TypeVisit*1(*n*↑.*TypeValue*);
      end;
    VariableDecl: (* (*Identifier*$^+$,*Type*): *Declaration* *)
      begin
      t:=*n*↑.*VariableNames*;   (* Scan the *Identifier* list *)
      while *t*<>**nil do**
        begin
        (* Code to associate a definition table key with the current list element goes here *)
        t:=*t*↑.*Next*;
        end;
      *TypeVisit*1(*n*↑.*VariableType*);   (* Visit the *Type* child *)
      end;
    FunctionDecl,ProcedureDecl: (* (*Identifier,Header,Body*): *Declaration* *)
      begin
      (* Code to associate a definition table key with the *Identifier* child goes here *)
      end;
    end;
  end;

                     (b) The structure of a visit procedure

Figure 7.9
Tree traversal

Figure 7.9 does not show how the operations of the environment module discussed in the last section are invoked to actually associate definition table keys with the identifiers. Instead, comments indicate where those computations take place. Our intent here is to concentrate on the tree traversal tactics. In the next section, after we present the tactics of information storage, we will show how to invoke these operations.

The *Type* component of a type or variable declaration might contain an enumeration such as (*red, yellow, blue*). According to the Pascal standard, *red, yellow,* and *blue* are defining occurrences and their definitions hold in the "closest-containing" block. This means that the compiler must visit the *Type* component of a type or variable declaration in order to process all defining occurrences in the current region. That is the reason for the invocation of *TypeVisit*1 in the *TypeDecl* and *VariableDecl* alternatives. A routine header, on the other hand, does not contain any defining occurrences of identifiers for the current region. (If there are parameters, then they are defining occurrences for the region of the routine itself, not for the region in which the routine is defined.) Since the semantic analyzer will visit all defining occurrences in one region before visiting any applied occurrences or nested regions, the alternative in Figure 7.9 that processes *FunctionDecl* and *ProcedureDecl* nodes does not visit any of the children of those nodes.

7.1.3 Information Storage

Some of the information obtained by the semantic analyzer is used only in computing other information, while some must be kept for use during transformation. Some, such as the environment established for a procedure, applies to a large subtree; some, such as the type of an expression, is interesting only in a narrow context. These characteristics of the information being processed—lifetime and context—influence the choice of data structures to hold that information.

Information used during tree decoration can be stored in the tree or in variables of the module that is decorating the tree. If variables of the decoration module are used, they may be declared as local variables of a specific visit procedure, or as variables global to all visit procedures.

When information is stored in the tree, it is associated with a specific node independently of any possible visit sequence, it exists until the tree is destroyed, and it is available to any module that can access the tree. The internal representations of identifiers are therefore stored in the tree because they are determined during lexical analysis and used during semantic analysis. Definition table keys are also stored in the tree, because they are used at arbitrary points in the visit sequence (see Figure 7.9a).

If a variable is declared local to a particular visit procedure, then it exists only during a single visit to a particular node. Moreover, it is not accessible during visits to the children of that node unless it is explicitly passed as an argument to other visit procedures. If a variable is declared global to all visit procedures, then it exists during the entire sequence of visits and is accessible during any visit. The name analyzer must be able to access the current environment whenever it processes either a defining occurrence or an applied occurrence of an identifier, so

7.1 HOW TO GATHER CONTEXTUAL INFORMATION

it is reasonable to declare a variable global to all visit procedures for holding the current environment value. When processing a nested region, the environment value for the outer region must be saved; a local variable of *DeclarationVisit2* could be used for this purpose.

Figure 7.10 illustrates these information storage considerations in the context of name analysis. The variable *Env* holds the current environment value; it is glo-

---

var *Env*: *Environment*;   (* Current environment value *)
...

procedure *TypeVisit2*(*n*: *SourceTree*; **var** *TypeKey*: *DefTableKey*);
  (* Establish the definition table key representing the type for this node
    On entry-
      A key has been associated with each defining occurrence of an identifier in this region
      A key has been associated with every type whose definition textually precedes the one corresponding to this node
    On exit-
      TypeKey = definition table key representing the type of this node
  *)
...

procedure *DeclarationVisit2*(*n*: *SourceTree*);
  (* Establish all of the properties of defined identifiers
    On entry-
      A key has been associated with each defining occurrence of an identifier in this region
    On exit-
      All of the properties of every identifier with a defining occurrence in this definition have been established
  *)
var
  t: *SourceSequence*;
  SaveEnv: *Environment*;
  TypeKey: *DefTableKey*;
begin
case *n1*.*Kind* **of**
  TypeDecl: (* (*Identifier*,*Type*): Declaration *)
    begin
    TypeVisit2(*n1*.*TypeValue*,*TypeKey*);   (* Visit the *Type* child *)
    (* Code to set the identifier's type property goes here *)
    end;
  VariableDecl: (* (*Identifier*,*Type*): Declaration *)
    begin
    TypeVisit2(*n1*.*VariableType*,*TypeKey*);   (* Visit the *Type* child *)
    t: = *n1*.*VariableNames*;   (* Scan the *Identifier* list *)
    while *t* < > **nil do**
      begin
      (* Code to set the variable's type property goes here *)
      t: = *t1*.*Next*;
      end;
    end;
  FunctionDecl,*ProcedureDecl*:   (* (*Identifier*,*Header*,*Body*): Declaration *)
    begin
    SaveEnv: = *Env*; *Env*: = *NewScope*(*Env*);
    HeaderVisit1(*n1*.*RoutineDeclHeader*,*TypeKey*); (* Visit the *Header* child *)
    (* Code to set the routine's type property goes here *)
    BodyVisit(*n1*.*RoutineDeclBody*); *HeaderVisit2*(*n1*.*RoutineDeclHeader*);
    Env: = *SaveEnv*;
    end;
  end;
end;

Figure 7.10
Information storage

bal to all of the visit procedures because it must be accessible wherever an environment operation must be invoked. *DeclarationVisit2* invokes *HeaderVisit1*, *BodyVisit*, and *HeaderVisit2* to process the nested region corresponding to a procedure or function body. The current environment during this processing must be the environment of the routine itself, not the environment containing the routine. However, when processing is completed the environment must be restored to its current value. Thus *DeclarationVisit2* saves the current environment value in the local variable *SaveEnv* before using *NewScope* to create a new environment value for the routine. The new environment value becomes the current one (because it is assigned to *Env*) while the routine is being visited. After both visits to the *Header* child and the visit to the *Body* child have terminated, *DeclarationVisit2* restores the previous environment value from *SaveEnv*. *SaveEnv* can be a local variable of *DeclarationVisit2* because it is never accessed outside of that procedure.

The local variable *TypeKey* is used to extract information from the visit to a *Type* child or a routine header. This information, the definition table key representing the type described by the child, is used only to establish the type property of the identifier. It is of interest only during the second visit to a particular definition node, so it is implemented as a local variable. However, it is set as a result of processing a child of that definition node, so it must be made available to the appropriate visit procedure as a **var** parameter.

7.2 THE DEFINITION TABLE

The definition table is a data base in which the compiler stores properties of defined entities. Different kinds of entities have different properties, and the properties are determined at various times by various parts of the compiler. For example, one of the properties of a real constant declared by the programmer is its value, and this property is determined by the semantic analyzer when it visits the value component of the constant declaration. One of the properties of a real variable is its location in the target machine's memory, and this property is determined by the data mapping subtask of the transformation process described in Chapter 8.

Entities are represented by integer definition table keys. Each entity is represented by a unique key. Identifier definitions are also represented by definition table keys. Some entities are invariably created by an identifier declaration; others may be created without being associated with an identifier. For example, the following variable declaration defines an identifier and creates a variable associated with that identifier, but also creates a type that is not associated with any identifier:

$$\textbf{var } I: 1..10;$$

The compiler can use one key for the definition of *I* and the variable, since variables are created only in conjunction with identifier declarations. It must use a separate key for the subrange type, however, since types can be created without declaring any identifier.

An identifier declaration always associates that identifier with some entity. One of the properties that is stored in the definition table for every identifier definition is the kind of entity with which the identifier is associated. Figure 7.11 defines *EntityClass* as an enumeration of the kinds of entities that can be named by identifiers in Pascal. When the compiler encounters a use of an identifier, it can extract the value of the entity class property of the identifier's definition to verify that the use is correct. For example, while processing a constant declaration, the compiler would store *ConstantName* as the entity class property of the definition table key associated with the constant identifier. At an applied occurrence of that identifier, the compiler would request the value of the entity class property for the associated key from the definition table and verify that entities of that class are allowed in the current context.

A definition table is simply a general data base, and therefore its characteristics are independent of any particular compiler. The set of properties and the representation of those properties will vary from one compiler to another, but this does not affect the underlying concepts. Section 7.2.1 presents a generic interface that can be specialized easily to handle the properties required for a particular compiler. This section also discusses how the interface is used. Section 7.2.2 provides general criteria for selecting an appropriate set of properties. An implementation of the definition table module is given in Section 7.2.3.

7.2.1 The Definition Table Interface

Figure 7.12 shows an interface to a definition table that stores only one property—the entity class specified in Figure 7.11. The module exports a definition table key that represents "no definition," and an operation for creating new keys. *NoKey* and *NewKey* must be exported by *any* definition table module, regardless of the properties that it must store. The environment module operation *DefineIdn* obtains a new definition table key from *NewKey* to associate with an identifier that has not previously been defined in the given environment; *KeyInEnv* (Figure 7.5) returns *NoKey* when the identifier it has been asked to find has no

```
EntityClass = (                          (* Classification of defined entities *)
    NotDefined,                          (* No definition for this entity *)
    LabelName,                           (* Label *)
    ConstantName,                        (* Constant *)
    TypeName,                            (* Type *)
    FieldName,                           (* Field of a record *)
    VariableName,                        (* Variable *)
    FuncName, ProcName,                  (* Function or procedure *)
    ValParameterName, VarParameterName,  (* Formal parameter to a routine *)
    MultiplyDefined );                   (* Two or more definitions for this entity *)
```

Figure 7.11
Entities that can be named in Pascal

const
    NoKey=0;   (* Definition table key with no properties *)

type
    DefTableKey=*integer*;   (* Definition table keys are represented by integers *)

function *NewKey*: *DefTableKey*;
    (* Deliver a new definition table key
      On exit-
        NewKey=a previously unused definition table key
    *)

procedure *DefInit*;
    (* Initialize the definition table module *)

function *GetEntityClass*(*key*: *DefTableKey*, *default*: *EntityClass*): *EntityClass*;
    (* Get the value of the entity class property
      On entry:
        key specifies the definition whose entity class property is sought
      If (*key*=*NoKey*) or (*key* does not have the entity class property) then on exit-
        GetEntityClass=*default*
      Else on exit-
        GetEntityClass=value of the entity class property of definition *key*
    *)

procedure *SetEntityClass*(*key*: *DefTableKey*, *add*,*change*: *EntityClass*);
    (* Set the value of the entity class property
      On entry:
        key specifies the definition whose entity class property is to be set
      If *key*=*NoKey* then on exit-
        The definition table is unchanged
      Else if *key* does not have the entity class property then on exit-
        The entity class property has been added to definition *key* with value *add*
      Else on exit-
        The value of the entity class property for definition *key*
          has been changed to *change*
    *)

Figure 7.12
A simple definition table interface

definition in the given environment. Other clients of the definition table module may also use *NoKey* and *NewKey*.

The definition table module exports two operations for each property that it has been asked to store. Since the definition table of Figure 7.12 is asked to store only one property, it exports only two operations in addition to *NewKey*. When the compiler needs to obtain the class of an entity, it invokes *GetEntityClass*. This operation queries the data base, returning the entity class value found. The data base query will fail if the item sought is not in the data base, and in that case the value returned by *GetEntityClass* is the value supplied as the *default* argument. Notice that it is not an error to invoke *GetEntityClass* with *NoKey* as the *key* argument. *NoKey* is a perfectly valid key, it simply never has any properties. Therefore any query with *NoKey* as a key will always return the value supplied as the *default* argument.

SetEntityClass allows the compiler to enter a value of the entity class property into the definition table. Two arguments in addition to the key are supplied, and they may in fact be the same value. If its *key* argument is *NoKey*, then *SetEntityClass* has no effect, because *NoKey* can never have any properties. Given any other key value, *SetEntityClass* queries the data base to determine whether it already contains an entity class property value for that key. If there is no entity class value for the given key, then the value of the *add* argument is entered. If an entity class value for the given key is found in the data base, then that value is changed to the value of the *change* argument.

Figure 7.13 shows how the entity class property can be used by a Pascal semantic analyzer to detect multiply-defined identifiers, undefined identifiers, and identifiers whose class does not match the context in which they are used. The three procedures all make visits to source tree nodes classified as *Identifier* leaves. The context in which an *Identifier* leaf occurs classifies it as being a defining occurrence or an applied occurrence, so the visit procedure for a construct with an *Identifier* child need make no run-time tests to determine which of the procedures in Figure 7.13 to invoke.

*DefiningOccurrence*1 is called to implement the first visit to each defining occurrence. The definition table key returned by *DefineIdn* is a new key if the identifier has not previously been defined in the current environment. Since the key is new, there will be no value of the entity class property stored in the definition table for that key. Therefore *SetEntityClass* will set the value of the entity class property for the key to the value of the *kind* parameter. If the identifier *has* previously been defined in the current environment, *DefineIdn* will return the key of the previous definition. Then the definition table is guaranteed to contain an entity class property value for the key of a previous definition. Therefore *SetEntityClass* will set the value of the entity class property for that key to *MultiplyDefined*.

Recall from Section 4.4.2 that zero is conventionally reserved to represent an identifier generated in order to recover from a syntactic error. An occurrence of a generated identifier cannot be reliably associated with any other identifier occurrences, so there is no point in providing it with any properties. The missing identifier has already been reported during syntactic analysis, and further error reports involving an entity corresponding to that missing identifier are at best needless and at worst confusing. Thus, both *DefiningOccurrence*1 and *AppliedOccurrence* associate *NoKey* with generated identifiers.

In Figure 7.9, *DeclarationVisit*1 is responsible for associating a definition table key with each defining occurrence of an identifier in the declaration it is processing. It can do this simply by invoking *DefiningOccurrence*1. For example, the complete code for the *TypeDecl* alternative in Figure 7.9 could be:

```
TypeDecl:                                       (* (Identifier,Type): Declaration *)
  begin
  DefiningOccurrence1(n↑.DeclaredId,TypeName);  (* Associate a key with the Identifier child *)
  TypeVisit1(n↑.TypeValue);                     (* Visit the Type child *)
  end;
```

If all defining occurrences in a region of the program are visited once before any is visited for the second time, then the definition table must contain a value of the entity class property for each definition. This value will be *MultiplyDefined* (indicating that an error has been made) if there is more than one definition of the identifier in the region; it will be the appropriate class, otherwise. Thus, on the second visit to a defining occurrence, *DefiningOccurrence*2 can determine which identifiers are multiply defined by checking this property. Again using the *TypeDecl* alternative as an example, the complete code would be (see Figure 7.10):

```
TypeDecl:                                       (* (Identifier,Type): Declaration *)
  begin
  DefiningOccurrence2(n↑.DeclaredId);           (* Check the Identifier child for multiple definition *)
  TypeVisit2(n↑.TypeValue,TypeKey);             (* Visit the Type child *)
  SetTypeKey(n↑.DeclaredId↑.Definition,TypeKey,NoKey);
  end;
```

This illustrates not only the use of *DefiningOccurrence*2, which was not mentioned in Figure 7.10, but also another definition table access function. *SetTypeKey* defines the identifier's type property, as indicated by the comment in Figure 7.10. If the identifier is multiply defined, it will already have a type property and *SetTypeKey* will replace that property's value with *NoKey* to indicate an unknown type.

If all defining occurrences are visited once before any applied occurrences are visited, *AppliedOccurrence* can check for undefined identifiers and also verify that the class of an identifier is compatible with the context of its use. There are many places in a Pascal program where several different classes of identifier could be used. In an expression, for example, an identifier representing a constant, a variable, a parameter, or a routine would be acceptable. That is the reason for providing *kinds* as a set.

7.2.2 Definition Table Design Criteria

Clearly, there are many properties that might be of interest to a compiler. A Pascal compiler needs to know the type and value of a constant. More information is needed for a variable: its type, the static nesting level of the procedure containing

procedure *DefiningOccurrence1(n: SourceTree; kind: EntityClass);*
  (* Obtain a key for a defining occurrence of an identifier
    On entry-
      kind = entity class determined by context
      The environment for the current scope has been established
    On exit-
      A key has been associated with identifier node *n*
      The entity class property for that key has been set
  *)
begin
if *n↑.LexIdent* = 0 **then** *n↑.Definition*: = *NoKey*
else *n↑.Definition*: = *DefineIdn(Env,n↑.LexIdent);*
SetEntityClass(n↑.Definition,kind,MultiplyDefined);
end;

procedure *DefiningOccurrence2(n: SourceTree);*
  (* Report a multiply-defined identifier if necessary
    On entry-
      All defining occurrences in the current and enclosing regions
        have been visited for the first time
  *)
begin
if *GetEntityClass(n↑.Definition,NotDefined)* = *MultiplyDefined* **then**
  *Report(FATAL,*101(*Multiply-declared identifier*)*,n↑.Coord,*0);
end;

procedure *AppliedOccurrence(n: SourceTree; kinds: EntityClassSet);*
  (* Obtain a key for an applied occurrence of an identifier
    On entry-
      kinds = entity classes permitted by the context
      All defining occurrences in the current and enclosing regions
        have been visited for the first time
    On exit-
      A key has been associated with identifier node *n*
      An error report has been issued if the entity class property
        of that key is not in *kinds*
  *)
var *kind: EntityClass;*
begin
if *n↑.LexIdent* = 0 **then** *n↑.Definition*: = *NoKey*
else
  begin
  n↑.Definition: = *KeyInEnv(Env,n↑.LexIdent);*
  kind: = *GetEntityClass(n↑.Definition,NotDefined);*
  if *kind* = *NotDefined* **then**
    *Report(FATAL,*104(*Undeclared identifier*)*,n↑.Coord,*0)
  else if not (*kind* **in** *kinds*) **then**
    *Report(FATAL,*103(*Identifier is not of the appropriate class*)*,n↑.Coord,*0);
  end;
end;

Figure 7.13
Verifying the class of Pascal identifiers

its declaration, and where it is located in the target machine's memory. The compiler designer must decide how to represent this information.

One possibility is to define a single variant record to implement a definition table entry. The primary variant selector for this record would specify the kind of entity, and some kinds of entities might have further variants. For example, a record representing a type would have variants to describe enumerated types, record types, etc. The obvious disadvantage of this idea is that it does not separate concerns. Everything is defined in one place, even though the various properties are quite distinct and are used by distinct compiler modules. A change to a property of *any* client of the definition table module requires that *every* client must be recompiled!

There is a more subtle problem with the single-record approach: Because properties of an entity are determined at different times by different modules, fields of the record will be undefined for various periods during its lifetime. The first visit to a *VariableDecl* would set the entity class property, but it would not be able to set the property that describes the variable's location in the target machine. If, through an oversight in the design, the compiler accesses one of these undefined fields, then it may very well crash. Such errors are often extremely difficult to diagnose, and the compiler development time is thus increased unnecessarily.

A better approach is to group related information that is obtained at a particular point in the compilation as a single property, and to leave unrelated information or information that is obtained at several different points as separate properties. Each property is then associated with a pair of definition table operations such as *GetEntityClass* and *SetEntityClass*, which are used to query and set values of that property. Concerns are separated because a particular module has to know about only those properties relevant to it. A change to a property of one client requires only recompilation of that client and the definition table module itself. Finally, when a property value is set, that value is complete (if any information was not available at the time, it would have been treated as a separate property), and any query must supply a consistent default value to be returned in case the desired property is not available.

We shall describe definition table properties in conjunction with the modules that use them. The values of each property will be represented by a specific data type, which we will define in our description of the property. We will then assume without further comment that the definition table module exports two operations for that data type, just as Figure 7.12 exports the operations *GetEntityClass* and *SetEntityClass*. If the name of the property is *Property*, and its type is *PropertyType*, then the headers of these two operations will be:

>**function** *GetProperty*(*key*: *DefTableKey*; *default*: *PropertyType*): *PropertyType*;

>**procedure** *SetProperty*(*key*: *DefTableKey*; *add,change*: *PropertyType*);

7.2.3 Implementing the Definition Table Module

Figure 7.14 shows the data structure that implements the definition table. The key is an index to an array of lists. Each list element stores a single property and an

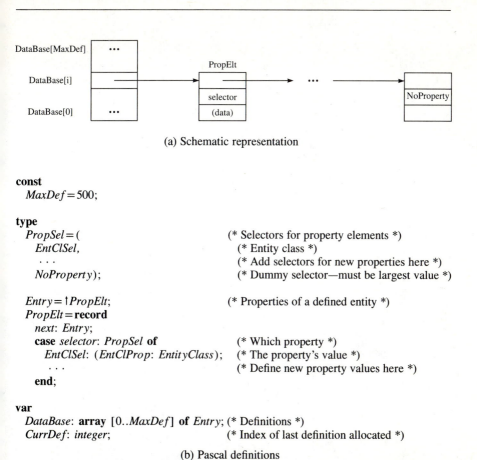

Figure 7.14
The definition table data structure

integer that specifies which property is being stored. When a query is made, the list indexed by the given key is searched for the requested property. To speed up the search, each list is sorted in order of increasing selector values and terminated by a "sentinel" with an impossibly large selector (recall the discussion of search loops in Section 3.2.3).

Note that the initialization and searching of the lists are independent of the number of properties and of the property value types. The variant part of a *PropElt* record depends upon the property value types, but the variant part is not used during initialization or searching. Thus the initialization and searching operations are implemented in exactly the same way for any definition table module. Figure 7.15a gives a Pascal implementation of the property-independent definition table code. The function *find* is not exported, but is used by the property-specific operations to locate the desired property list element.

```
function NewKey: DefTableKey;
  (* Establish a new definition *)
  begin
  if CurrDef = MaxDef then Report(DEADLY,1003(*Definition table overflow*),NoPosition,0);
  CurrDef: = CurrDef + 1; new(DataBase[CurrDef]);
  with DataBase[CurrDef]↑ do begin next: = nil; selector: = NoProperty end;
  NewKey: = CurrDef;
  end;


procedure DefInit;
  (* Initialize the Definition Table *)
  begin CurrDef: = -1; CurrDef: = NewKey end;


function find(key: DefTableKey; p: PropSel; var r: Entry; add: boolean): boolean;
  (* Obtain a relation for a specific property of a definition
      On entry-
        key = definition whose property relation is to be obtained
        p = selector of the desired property
      If the definition does not have the desired property then on exit-
        find = false
        if add then r points to a new entry for the property
        else r points to the entry following the entry for the property
      Else on exit-
        find = true
        r points to the current entry for the property
  *)
  var t: Entry;
  begin
  if (key < NoKey) or (key > CurrDef) then
    Report(DEADLY,1004(*Invalid definition table key*),NoPosition,0);
  r: = DataBase[key]; while r↑.selector < p do r: = r↑.next;
  if r↑.selector = p then find: = true
  else
    begin find: = false;
    if add then begin new(t); t↑: = r↑; r↑.next: = t; r↑.selector: = p end;
    end;
  end;
```

(a) Property-independent part


```
function GetEntityClass(key: DefTableKey; default: EntityClass): EntityClass;
  var r: Entry;
  begin
  if find(key,EntClSel,r,false) then GetEntityClass: = r↑.EntClProp
  else GetEntityClass: = default;
  end;


procedure SetEntityClass(key: DefTableKey; added,changed: EntityClass);
  var r: Entry;
  begin
  if key > NoKey then if find(key,EntClSel,r,true) then r↑.EntClProp: = changed else r↑.EntClProp: = added;
  end;
```

(b) Property-dependent part

Figure 7.15
Definition table implementation

Given *find*, the code for a property routine is almost trivial. The implementations of *GetEntityClass* and *SetEntityClass* are shown in Figure 7.15b. All property routines have exactly the same form as *GetEntityClass* and *SetEntityClass*. Only four things vary:

- The routine names.
- The argument and result types for the get routine and the argument type for the set routine.
- The property selector used as the second argument to *find* (*EntClSel* in Figure 7.15b).
- The field name used to access the property value (*EntClProp* in Figure 7.15b).

All that is needed to add a new property is to define the two routines analogous to *GetEntityClass* and *SetEntityClass*, add a variant to the *PropElt* record of Figure 7.14, and recompile the definition table module. No clients of the definition table module need be changed.

Pascal places one restriction on the types of properties that can be stored directly in the definition table: The result of a function cannot be of a structured type (array, record, set or file). When information that is represented by a structured type must be stored, therefore, the property must be defined as a pointer to the value rather than the value itself.

7.3 THE COST OF GATHERING CONTEXTUAL INFORMATION

Any compiler will require more time to process long programs than to process short programs; the interesting question is how the compilation time grows. Since the compiler must examine the entire program, the best we can hope for is a compilation time that is some linear function of program size. If we choose the wrong algorithms for implementing some of the compiler's subtasks, however, the growth in compilation time could be much faster. In this section we study the effect of gathering contextual information on the rate at which compilation time grows with program size.

When gathering contextual information, the compiler makes some fixed number of visits to each node of the tree. Therefore, the time spent carrying out visits must be a linear function of the number of nodes in the tree. When visiting a node, the semantic analyzer invokes operations of various modules, each of which involves some amount of time. For example, at the first visit to the defining occurrence of an identifier, the compiler invokes the environment module operation *DefineIdn*. The time required to execute *DefineIdn* must therefore be "charged" to the first visit of that defining occurrence.

Suppose that the time required to execute *DefineIdn* were a linear function of the program size. Then as the program size increased, both the number of defining occurrences and the time to process each would increase linearly—the overall increase in compilation time would be quadratic. It is therefore important for the compiler designer to be aware of the computational complexity of the individual computations used in gathering contextual information. Here we illustrate the kind of analysis required by examining two implementations of the environment module whose interface was given in Figure 7.5. Section 7.3.1 discusses a simple implementation in which the time required to carry out the most commonly used computations grows linearly with program size. If a compiler uses this implementation, overall compilation time will grow as the square of the program size. A more complex implementation is developed in Section 7.3.2 to preserve the overall linear growth in compilation time.

7.3.1 A Simple Implementation of the Environment Module

The simplest implementation of the environment module is a direct encoding of the tree of environment values (Figure 7.6b). Each node of the tree has a list of relations attached to it and provides a pointer to its parent node. The parent pointer of the root is **nil**. Figure 7.16 shows how the necessary types might be defined in Pascal, and gives a schematic representation of the complete environment structure for the program of Figure 7.3. Given this data structure, the coding of the module's operations is quite straightforward (Figure 7.17).

How does the cost of *KeyInEnv* increase with increasing program size? Each invocation involves a search that checks the given identifier against each of the identifiers visible at that point in the program. As the program size increases, so will the number of identifiers visible at a particular point. If N is the number of basic symbols in the program, it is reasonable to assume that the number of identifiers will be $C \times N$, where C is some small constant fraction. The number of basic operations (e.g., comparisons) that *KeyInEnv* must make is therefore proportional to N.

The case is less clear for *DefineIdn* and *KeyInScope*, since these two operations search only a single scope. We might choose to assume that the average number of identifiers in a single scope remains roughly constant as program size increases. In other words, the increase in program size introduces more scopes, but does not increase the size of each. For the moment, however, let us assume the worst case—that the number of identifiers in a given scope is also proportional to N. Therefore the number of basic operations executed during a single invocation of *DefineIdn* or *KeyInScope* is proportional to N.

We use the notation "$O(N)$" to indicate that the number of basic operations is proportional to N. In this case, N is the number of basic symbols in the source program. We say that *DefineIdn*, *KeyInEnv*, and *KeyInScope* are all $O(N)$ in the worst case. Clearly, a single invocation of *NewEnv* or *NewScope* executes the same number of basic operations regardless of the size of the program. We therefore say that the worst case behavior of these two operations is $O(1)$.

Now consider the complete process of name analysis. Either *KeyInEnv* or *KeyInScope* is invoked once for each applied occurrence of an identifier. The

7.3 THE COST OF GATHERING CONTEXTUAL INFORMATION

```
type
    Environment = ↑EnvImpl;      (* Set of Identifier/Definition relationships *)
    Scope = ↑RelElt;             (* Single scope *)
    EnvImpl = record             (* Addressing environment *)
        parent: Environment;     (* Enclosing environment *)
        relate: Scope;           (* Current scope *)
        end;
    RelElt = record
        idn: integer;            (* Identifier *)
        nxt: Scope;              (* Next element of the current scope *)
        key: DefTableKey;        (* Definition table key *)
        end;
```

(a) Types implementing the environment

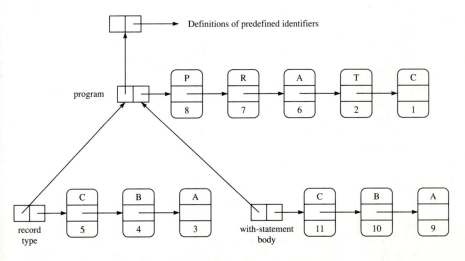

(b) The complete data structure for Figure 7.3

Figure 7.16
An environment data structure

number of applied occurrences of identifiers is certainly proportional to N, the number of basic symbols. But the number of basic operations executed for each invocation of either of these operations is also proportional to N. Therefore the number of basic operations needed to complete the name analysis is proportional to N^2.

Our conclusion is that name analysis is an $O(N^2)$ process when the environment module is implemented as shown in Figure 7.17. That means that the time required to compile a program may grow as the square of the program's size. Of course the implementation of some other algorithm could cause it to grow faster, but there is no hope of guaranteeing that the compilation time is only a linear function of the program size.

```
function NewEnv: Environment;
  var e: Environment;
  begin
  new(e); e↑.relate:=nil; e↑.parent:=nil; NewEnv:=e;
  end;


function NewScope(env: Environment): Environment;
  var e: Environment;
  begin
  if env=nil then Report(DEADLY,1006(*invalid environment*),NoPosition,1);
  new(e); e↑.relate:=nil; e↑.parent:=env; NewScope:=e;
  end;


function DefineIdn(env: Environment; idn: integer): DefTableKey;
  label 1;
  var r: Scope; p: DefTableKey;
  begin
  if env=nil then Report(DEADLY,1006(*invalid environment*),NoPosition,2);
  r:=env↑.relate;
  while r<>nil do if r↑.idn<>idn then r:=r↑.nxt else begin p:=r↑.key; goto 1 end;
  p:=NewKey;
  new(r); r↑.idn:=idn; r↑.key:=p; r↑.nxt:=env↑.relate; env↑.relate:=r;
1: DefineIdn:=p;
  end;


function KeyInEnv(env: Environment; idn: integer): DefTableKey;
  label 1;
  var r: Scope; p: DefTableKey;
  begin
  if env=nil then Report(DEADLY,1006(*invalid environment*),NoPosition,2);
  repeat r:=env↑.relate;
    while r<>nil do if r↑.idn<>idn then r:=r↑.nxt else begin p:=r↑.key; goto 1 end;
    env:=env↑.parent;
  until env=nil;
  p:=NoKey;
1: KeyInEnv:=p;
  end;


function KeyInScope(env: Environment; idn: integer): DefTableKey;
  label 1;
  var r: Scope; p: DefTableKey;
  begin
  if env=nil then Report(DEADLY,1006(*invalid environment*),NoPosition,4);
  r:=env↑.relate;
  while r<>nil do if r↑.idn<>idn then r:=r↑.nxt else begin p:=r↑.key; goto 1 end;
  p:=NoKey;
1: KeyInScope:=p;
  end;
```

Figure 7.17
Environment operations on the data structure of Figure 7.16

Some care must be taken in drawing conclusions from this analysis. Remember that the constant of proportionality may be small, so that for programs of normal size the compilation time never becomes burdensome. Also, we have assumed the worst-case program structure. If the number of identifiers in a scope is independent of the program size, and if most references are to local variables, then the compilation time will not grow so fast. Therefore it is not necessary to reject the simple implementation out of hand. Nevertheless, we should be on the lookout for $O(1)$ implementations of the environment module operations. This is the subject of the next section.

7.3.2 A Second Implementation of the Environment Module

By using a more complex data structure, it is possible to avoid searches in the implementations of *DefineIdn* and *KeyInEnv*. The basic idea is quite simple: Identifiers are represented internally by small positive integers. Use these integers to index an array, and arrange that the array element corresponding to an identifier specifies the currently valid definition for that identifier. If an identifier has no definition, its array element specifies the constant *NoKey*. *KeyInEnv* can be implemented as an array access, returning the value specified by the element that *KeyInEnv*'s *idn* argument indexes.

The array idea is a normal time/space trade-off. In the implementation of Figure 7.16, one list element is stored for each identifier/key pair, and access to a particular pair requires a search. In the proposed array implementation, an array capable of holding the maximum number of identifiers the compiler could ever accept is stored, and access to a particular pair is direct. Since the array must be large enough for the maximum number of identifiers that we will allow in *any* program, it occupies more space than the solution of Figure 7.16; since the lists of Figure 7.16 must be searched for each pair, that solution requires more time than the array solution.

In order to make the array implementation work, there must be additional code to guarantee that the array's content reflects the situation in the environment specified by the *env* argument of *KeyInEnv*. For example, when the name analyzer is processing line 10 of Figure 7.3 (reproduced here as Figure 7.18), the array element for the identifier *A* must contain the definition table key 6. When the name analyzer is processing line 12, the same array element must contain the definition table key 9. Then, when the name analyzer is processing line 13, that element must contain the definition table key 6 again.

Some thought will show that each identifier corresponds to a *stack* of definitions. At line 10 of Figure 7.18 the only definition for *A* is the one with key 6. When the name analyzer is processing line 12, this definition has been temporarily superseded by the one with key 9. Effectively, definition 9 has been pushed onto *A*'s stack. (The "current" definition is always the one on the top of the stack.) When the name analyzer leaves the statement component of the *WithStmt* construct, definition 9 is no longer valid for *A*—it has been popped off of *A*'s stack and the definition with key 6 has again become current.

```
 1    program Context(input,output);
 2    const C¹ = 1.2;
 3    type T² = record A³,B⁴,C⁵: integer end;
 4    var
 5        A⁶: real;
 6        R⁷: T;
 7        P⁸: ↑T;
 8    begin
 9    new(P); readln(R.B,R.C,P↑.C);
10    A: = R.B + C;
11    with P↑ do (* Redefines A⁹ B¹⁰ C¹¹ *)
12        A: = R.B + C;
13        R: = P↑; writeln(A,R.A);
14    end.
```

Figure 7.18
A program corresponding to the data structure of Figure 7.16b

Implementation of *DefineIdn* requires that each definition specify the environment in which it is effective as well as its definition table key. Remember that *DefineIdn* seeks a match for its *idn* argument only in the environment specified by its *env* argument. Unlike *KeyInEnv*, it does not search ancestors of that environment. The currently valid definition for a particular identifier might, however, be from the environment specified by the *env* argument or any of its ancestors. (For example, when *DefineIdn* seeks a match for C in line 3 of Figure 7.18, the currently valid definition for C is that on line 2. But that definition is not from the record's environment; it is from the program environment, the parent of the record environment.) *DefineIdn* must therefore be able to test the definition to determine which environment it belongs to. If that environment is the same as *DefineIdn*'s *env* argument, then *DefineIdn* will return the definition table key; otherwise it will obtain a new definition table key, change the identifier's currently valid definition, and return the new key.

Most of the information that the environment module needs to guarantee that the array's content reflects the *env* argument of *KeyInList* or *DefineIdn* would be provided by the data structure of Figure 7.16. Therefore, the new implementation incorporates that data structure as well as the access array. There may be several trees of environment values, each having a distinct root created by a distinct call to *NewEnv*. Each of these trees has its own access array.

Figure 7.19a gives the complete set of types used by the constant-time access implementation, and Figure 7.19b is a snapshot of the state of the data structure when the compiler is analyzing line 12 of Figure 7.18. (Only two identifier stacks are shown in detail; the others are omitted to avoid cluttering the diagram.)

The tree that is the left part of Figure 7.19b is virtually identical to Figure 7.16. Instead of being searched, however, this tree is accessed via an array. The dotted box on the right side of Figure 7.19b is the *AccessMechanism* record declared at the bottom of Figure 7.19a. It has two fields: the access array itself,

type
   $Environment = \uparrow EnvImpl;$ (* Set of Identifier/Definition pairs *)
   $Scope = \uparrow RelElt;$ (* Single region *)
   $Access = \uparrow AccessMechanism;$ (* Current access state *)
   $EnvImpl =$ **record**   (* Addressing environment *)
     $state: Access;$ (* Constant-time access to identifier definitions *)
     $parent: Environment;$ (* Enclosing environment *)
     $relate: Scope;$ (* Current region *)
   end;
   $RelElt =$ **record**
     $idn: integer;$ (* Identifier *)
     $nxt: Scope;$ (* Next identifier/definition pair for the current region *)
     $key: DefTableKey;$ (* Definition *)
   end;
   $StkPtr = \uparrow StkElt;$ (* List implementing a definition stack *)
   $StkElt =$ **record**
     $out: StkPtr;$ (* Superseded definitions *)
     $key: DefTableKey;$ (* Definition *)
     $env: Environment;$ (* Environment containing this definition *)
   end;
   $AccessMechanism =$ **record**   (* Current state of the access mechanism *)
     $IdnTbl:$ **array**   (* Stacks of definitions *)
       $[0..MaxIdn]$ **of** $StkPtr;$
     $CurrEnv: Environment;$ (* Environment represented by the array state *)
   end;

(a) Data objects for the constant-time access function

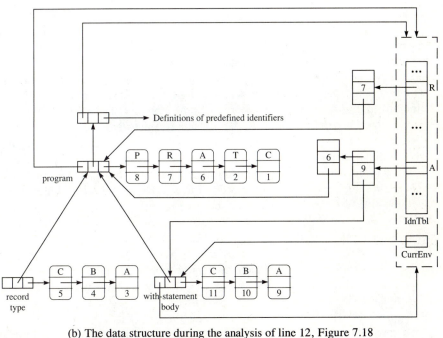

(b) The data structure during the analysis of line 12, Figure 7.18

Figure 7.19
The constant-time access function

and a pointer to the *EnvImpl* record for the "innermost" region whose identifiers are on the identifier stacks. This is the environment that is reflected in the state of the access mechanism.

The only information that must be added to the data structure of Figure 7.16 is the *state* field of the *EnvImpl* record. This field reflects the state of the access mechanism, relative to the environment value represented by the *EnvImpl* record. If the identifiers defined in that environment are on the identifier stacks addressed by the array, then the *state* field contains a pointer to the access mechanism.

In Figure 7.19b, *CurrEnv* is pointing to the *EnvImpl* record for the **with** statement body, which is the environment appropriate for line 12 of Figure 7.18. The identifiers defined in the **with** statement and the identifiers defined in the program are on the identifier stacks. Therefore the *state* fields of the *EnvImpl* records corresponding to those two regions point to the access mechanism. The *state* field of the *EnvImpl* record corresponding to the body of the record declared on line 3 of Figure 7.18 is **nil**, because the field identifiers are *not* on the identifier stacks.

Figure 7.20 gives Pascal code that implements the environment access functions *DefineIdn* and *KeyInEnv*. Both begin by making certain that the array reflects the situation in the environment specified by the *env* argument. *SetEnv*, *EnterEnv*, and *LeaveEnv* are all private procedures of the environment module. They are used to set up the array so that its state reflects a given environment, and are invoked only if some sort of change is necessary.

EnterEnv assumes that the state of the array reflects the parent of the environment to be entered. It scans that environment, pushing a new definition onto the stack for each identifier in the environment. *LeaveEnv* reverses this operation, removing the top definition from the stack for each identifier in the current environment, and thus restoring the state of the array to reflect the parent of the current environment. *SetEnv* decides on a sequence of leave and enter operations that will change the state of the array to reflect the desired environment. If definitions for the desired environment are on the identifier stacks, but the desired environment is not the current one, *SetEnv* simply leaves environments until the desired environment is reached. Otherwise, *SetEnv* sets the environment to the parent of the desired one and then enters the desired environment.

What is the time complexity of the implementation shown in Figure 7.20? Clearly, *DefineIdn* and *KeyInEnv* are $O(1)$ if the state of the array reflects the *env* argument. In order to account for the time required to maintain the array's state, we need to examine the global behavior of the name analyzer. The fundamental question that must be answered is "How often is a particular region considered during name analysis?" The array state must be changed only when the name analyzer shifts its attention from one region to another. As long as the name analyzer remains within a single region, no change in the array is required; *DefineIdn* and *KeyInEnv* execute in constant time.

Figure 7.20 will support a name analyzer that shifts its attention arbitrarily among regions. Since each node in the tree is visited a fixed number of times, independent of the size of the program, the tree traversal can enter a particular region only a fixed number of times. If the name analyzer shifts its attention from one region to another only when the tree traversal actually moves from one region

```
procedure EnterEnv(env: Environment);
  (* Make the state of the array reflect env
     On entry-
       The state of the array reflects the parent of env
  *)
  var r: Scope; s: StkPtr;
  begin r: = env↑.relate;
  env↑.state: = env↑.parent↑.state;
  with env↑.state↑ do
    begin
    while r<>nil do
      begin new(s); s↑.env: = env; s↑.key: = r↑.key; s↑.out: = IdnTbl[r↑.idn]; IdnTbl[r↑.idn]: = s; r: = r↑.nxt; end;
    CurrEnv: = env;
    end;
  end;
procedure LeaveEnv(env: Environment);
  (* Make the state of the array reflect the parent of env
     On entry-
       The state of the array reflects env
  *)
  var r: Scope; s: StkPtr;
  begin r: = env↑.relate;
  with env↑.state↑ do
    begin
    while r<>nil do begin s: = IdnTbl[r↑.idn]; IdnTbl[r↑.idn]: = s↑.out; dispose(s); r: = r↑.nxt end;
    CurrEnv: = env↑.parent;
    end;
  env↑.state: = nil;
  end;
procedure SetEnv(env: Environment);
  (* Make certain that the state of the array reflects env *)
  begin
  if env=nil then Report(DEADLY,1004(*Invalid environment*),NoPosition,1);
  if env↑.state = nil then begin SetEnv(env↑.parent); EnterEnv(env) end
  else with env↑.state↑ do while CurrEnv<>env do LeaveEnv(CurrEnv);
  end;
function KeyInEnv(env: Environment; idn: integer): DefTableKey;
  begin SetEnv(env);
  with env↑.state↑ do
    if IdnTbl[idn] = nil then KeyInEnv: = NoKey else KeyInEnv: = IdnTbl[idn]↑.key;
  end;
function DefineIdn(env: Environment; idn: integer): DefTableKey;
  var found: boolean; p: DefTableKey; r: Scope; s: StkPtr;
  begin SetEnv(env);
  with env↑.state↑ do
    begin
    if IdnTbl[idn] = nil then found: = false else found: = IdnTbl[idn]↑.env = env;
    if found then DefineIdn: = IdnTbl[idn]↑.key
    else
      begin p: = NewKey;
      new(r); r↑.idn: = idn; r↑.key: = p; r↑.nxt: = env↑.relate; env↑.relate: = r;
      new(s); s↑.env: = env; s↑.key: = p; s↑.out: = IdnTbl[idn]; IdnTbl[idn]: = s;
      DefineIdn: = p;
      end;
    end;
  end;
```

Figure 7.20
Environment access operations

to another, then *EnterEnv* and *LeaveEnv* will be executed only a fixed number of times for each region. Both *EnterEnv* and *LeaveEnv* execute a constant number of basic operations for each element of the region's *relate* list, which has one entry for each defining occurrence in the region.

Consider a particular region, R. Suppose that R is entered and left T times. Each time the region is entered, E basic operations are executed for each element of $R.relate$ (Figure 7.19a); each time it is left, L operations are executed for each element of $R.relate$. Therefore, the total number of basic operations executed during the entire compilation for each element of $R.relate$ would be $T \times (E + L)$. We can therefore "charge" the time required to execute $T \times (E + L)$ basic operations to each defining occurrence in R. This shows that we can ignore the costs of *EnterEnv* and *LeaveEnv*, because their only effect is to increase the cost of *DefineIdn* by a constant amount.

All of the operations of the environment module except *KeyInScope* are $O(1)$ in the worst case when implemented as shown in Figure 7.20. *KeyInScope* would also be $O(1)$ if the compiler entered the appropriate region before *KeyInScope* was applied. Then all that would be needed would be to verify that the association at the top of the stack was defined in that region, just as *DefineIdn* does. Taking this approach, however, would mean that applied occurrences of field identifiers in Pascal constructs such as $R.B$ would require the name analyzer to shift its consideration from the current region to the region of a record definition and then immediately shift it back again. Although Figure 7.20 is quite capable of doing this, it violates our assumption that the number of times the name analyzer shifts its attention to a given region is independent of the program size. Thus it makes the cost of *EnterEnv* and *LeaveEnv* impossible to ignore.

In order to salvage our earlier analysis, we must charge the cost of an *EnterEnv* operation followed by a *LeaveEnv* operation to the invocation of *KeyInScope* that processes $R.B$. But since that cost is proportional to the number of fields in R, and the cost of *KeyInScope* as implemented in Figure 7.17 is also proportional to the number of fields in R, nothing has been gained. Since the search operation is simpler than *EnterEnv* followed by *LeaveEnv*, *KeyInScope* should not use the array access mechanism.

For most programs, field references such as $R.B$ are a small fraction of the total number of identifier occurrences. Moreover, the number of fields in a record does not usually grow with overall program size. We can conclude that the implementation of Figure 7.20 gives essentially $O(1)$ complexity for every operation of the environment module, so the actual growth of the name analysis time with program size is $O(N)$ rather than the $O(N^2)$ obtained from the implementation of Figure 7.17.

7.4 SUMMARY

Several compiler subtasks gather contextual information, compute values based on that information, and check constraints involving those computed values. When designing such processes, we separate concerns by considering the tactics of the computations, tree traversal, and information storage independently. Computations are embodied in modules whose operations are invoked during visits to the nodes of the tree. The sequence of visits is determined by the dependence relations that exist among items of information—a visit that computes an item of information must be carried out before a visit that uses that information. Information is stored in nodes of the tree, in the definition table, and in variables that are either local or global to the individual visit procedures. Considerations of lifetime and context govern the choice of storage for each item of information.

The definition table is a central data base accessible to all compiler tasks. It is used to hold properties of entities that are defined by the user and created by the compiler. Entities are represented throughout the compiler by definition table keys. Each property stored in the definition table is associated with a function to access the value of that property for a given key, and a procedure to set that property for a given key. This strategy simplifies the design and maintenance of the compiler itself by making the clients of the definition table module independent of the properties they do not use. In order to avoid the common error of accessing an undefined data item, any function that extracts information from the definition table module must be provided with a default result value on every call. If the desired property is not defined for the item whose key was specified, the function returns this default result.

The time required to gather contextual information grows linearly with the size of the program when only the cost of tree traversal is considered, because every node is visited a fixed number of times. In order to make the time for a complete compilation grow no faster than linearly with program size, we must ensure that individual computations are independent of the program size. A simple implementation of the environment module results in individual computations whose execution time is a linear function of program size, because they involve searches through all existing identifiers. This means that the total compilation time will grow at least as fast as the square of the program size. By increasing the complexity of the data structure that supports the environment module, we can implement these operations so that each requires constant time.

NOTES

Section 6.2 of the Pascal Standard[2] clearly disallows the program shown in Figure 7.7, yet several Pascal compilers accept it. The visibility rules implemented by these compilers are not the visibility rules of Pascal. Whereas the scope of a function identifier in Pascal is the block in which it was declared, the scope implemented by these compilers begins at the point of the function declaration and continues to the end of the block. It is difficult to determine whether the authors of these compilers made a conscious decision to deviate from the definition of Pascal, or whether they simply did not understand that definition. In either case, the resulting compiler is incorrect and should be repaired. We need to emphasize over and over that a compiler writer must *understand* and *adhere to* the definition of the source language.

Tree decoration can be described formally by an attribute grammar [10]. The structure of the tree is described by the context-free productions of the grammar, and the computations of the values that decorate it are described by the attribution rules attached to those productions. A significant advantage of attribute grammars is that the tree traversal strategy need not be stated explicitly. It can be derived mechanically from the dependence relations induced by the specified computations [15]. Tools are available [12, 17, 4] to analyze attribute grammars and produce visit procedures that implement the decorations they describe.

Our compilation strategy builds a complete source program tree and then decorates that tree. Sometimes the computations that decorate the tree can be carried out as the tree is being built [9, 7], and there may be no need to build the tree at all. A decoration algorithm that does not require an explicit source program tree is not as general as the algorithms discussed in this chapter. It is significantly more difficult to design such an algorithm than it is to design one that does require an explicit source program tree. The primary design issues become the constraints on availability of information, and these constraints permeate all aspects of the design. The Whetstone compiler for ALGOL 60 is a fascinating example of this phenomenon [11]. Randell and Russell's excellent description of Whetstone ALGOL is full of clever solutions to problems that vanish completely if a source program tree is built.

When faced with the need to implement a compiler on a machine with limited memory, a designer has two basic choices:

- Avoid building the source program tree.
- Build a linearized form of the source program tree in secondary storage.

The Whetstone compiler designers made the first choice, and the designers of the GIER ALGOL 60 compiler made the second [8]. More recently, the Zurich Pascal compiler [3] (which served as the basis for the popular UCSD microcomputer implementation) avoids building a source program tree, and the Concurrent Pascal compiler [6] uses a linearized source program tree in secondary storage. The descriptions of the Whetstone and GIER compilers, and of the Concurrent Pascal compiler, are all very readable and quite informative for any compiler designer faced with a memory constraint.

While computational complexity is covered in many computer science texts [14, 16, 5], some are devoted exclusively to that topic [1]. It goes under several aliases, such as "algorithmic efficiency," "efficiency of computations," "order of execution time," and "asymptotic execution time properties." The purpose of determining computational complexity is to have an objective measure for comparison between algorithms or between implementations of algorithms. Either time or space, or some combination, can be assessed.

Suppose that $f(n)$ describes the true time or space requirement of an algorithm as a function of some measure, n, of the size of its input. (In Section 7.3 we used the number of basic symbols in the source program as our size metric.) The notation $O(g(n))$ means that there exists some constant c such that for all positive values of n (except possibly a finite number), $f(n) \leqslant c \times g(n)$. We use this notation because often it is not feasible to obtain the exact function f, and in fact what we are really interested in is how the function grows, rather than its precise value. As we pointed out in the text, however, the asymptotic behavior doesn't tell the whole story. Sometimes an algorithm with poorer asymptotic behavior outperforms a "better" algorithm in practice, because the normal input size is small and the "better" algorithm is much more complex.

REFERENCES

1. Aho, A. V., Hopcroft, J. E., and Ullman, J. D., *The Design and Analysis of Computer Algorithms*, Addison Wesley, Reading, MA, 1974.
2. "Pascal Computer Programming Language," ANSI/IEEE 770 X3.97-1983, American National Standards Institute, New York, NY, Jan. 1983.
3. Ammann, U., "The Method of Structured Programming Applied to the Development of a Compiler," in *Proc. of the International Computing Symp. 1973*, North-Holland, Amsterdam, 1974, 94-99.
4. Farrow, R., "LINGUIST-86: Yet Another Translator Writing System Based on Attribute Grammars," *SIGPLAN Notices 17*, 6 (June 1982), 160-171.
5. Gries, D., *The Science of Programming*, Springer Verlag, 1981.
6. Hartmann, A. C., *A Concurrent Pascal Compiler for Minicomputers*, Springer Verlag, Heidelberg, 1977.
7. Koskimies, K., "A Specification Language for One-Pass Semantic Analysis," *SIGPLAN Notices 19*, 6 (June 1984), 179-189.
8. Naur, P., "The Design of the GIER ALGOL Compiler," *Annual Review in Automatic Programming 4* (1964), 49-85.
9. Purdom, P. and Brown, C. A., "Semantic Routines and LR(k) Parsers," *Acta Inf.*, 1980, 299-316.
10. Räihä, K., "Bibliography on Attribute Grammars," *SIGPLAN Notices 15*, 3 (Mar. 1980), 35-44.
11. Randell, B. and Russell, L. J., *ALGOL 60 Implementation*, Academic Press, London, 1964.
12. Saarinen, M., Soisalon-Soininen, E., Räihä, K., and Tienari, M., "The Compiler Writing System HLP (Helsinki Language Processor)," Report A-1978-2, Dept. of Computer Science, Univ. of Helsinki, Helsinki, Finland, Mar. 1978.
13. Sale, A. H. J., "A Note on Scope, One-Pass Compilers, and Pascal," *Pascal News 15* (1979), 62-63.
14. Schneider, G. M. and Bruell, S. C., *Advanced Programming and Problem Solving with Pascal*, John Wiley & Sons, New York, NY, 1981.
15. Waite, W. M. and Goos, G., *Compiler Construction*, Springer Verlag, New York, NY, 1984.
16. Wulf, W. A., Shaw, M., Hilfinger, P. N., and Flon, L., *Fundamental Structures of Computer Science*, Addison Wesley, Reading, MA, 1981.
17. Zimmermann, E., Kastens, U., and Hutt, B., *GAG: A Practical Compiler Generator*, Springer Verlag, Heidelberg, 1982.

EXERCISES

7.1 Draw a source program tree that represents the statements on line 13 of Figure 7.3, showing the decorations involved in name analysis. (See Figure 7.4 for an example of name analysis decorations.)
  (a) Which of your decorations were provided when the tree was built, and which were computed during a traversal of the tree?
  (b) For each identifier in your tree, state where the association you used to obtain its definition table key was defined.

7.2 Pascal labels are subject to the same visibility rules as Pascal identifiers; therefore, the same sort of analysis should be applied to them. If we represent labels with integer values, they could be passed to the operations of Figure 7.5 in exactly the same way as identifiers.
  (a) Suppose we represent each label by its integer value. Explain why the set of integers representing labels would then overlap the set of integers representing identifiers. What problems would this cause in analyzing label visibility? How could those problems be avoided?
  (b) Suppose we represent each label by an integer that is generated by a *CvtLbl* operation analogous to the *CvtIdn* operation discussed in Section 3.3.2. Which module should provide the *CvtLbl* operation? Explain briefly.
  (c) Define an appropriate interface for the *CvtLbl* operation. (Remember that *CvtLbl* must return distinct integers to represent distinct labels. Be sure you understand when two labels are considered distinct, according to the definition of Pascal, before you design your interface!)

7.3 According to Section 6.6.3.1 of the Pascal standard [2], the formal parameter list of a procedure is a region separate from the region constituting the body of that procedure. A defining occurrence of an identifier in the formal parameter list is considered to be both a defining occurrence in the formal parameter list region and in the region constituting the body. Consider the program shown in Figure 7.21.

```
1   program try(input,output);
2   var b: boolean; c: integer;
3   function f(a: integer): boolean;
4     type integer=boolean;
5     var result: integer;
6     begin
7       result:=(a=2);
8       f:=result or b;
9     end;
10  begin
11    b:=false;
12    read(c); b:=f(c);
13    read(c); if f(c) then writeln('yes') else writeln('no');
14  end.
```

Figure 7.21
Redeclaring a parameter type

(a) Explain why the occurrence of *integer* on line 3 is not a use of the type declared on line 4.
(b) Explain why the occurrence of *a* on line 7 has the same type as the constant 2, but not the same type as the variable *result*.
(c) Draw a tree of *Environment* values similar to Figure 7.6b for the program of Figure 7.21.

7.4 Replace the first ellipses (· · ·) in the **case** statement of Figure 7.9 with a combination of comments and code that explains the actions for constant declarations.

7.5 Our treatment of routine declarations did not consider the Pascal *forward* declaration. *Forward* declarations modify the interpretation of the *Identifier* child of a *FunctionDecl* or *ProcedureDecl* node (Figure 7.9): This identifier is a defining occurrence if the *Body* child of the node is a *forward* directive, or if the identifier was not previously declared forward. Otherwise, it is an applied occurrence.
(a) Notice that the interpretation of the *Identifier* child of a *FunctionDecl* or *ProcedureDecl* node may depend on previous occurrences of that identifier in the current region. How can the compiler keep track of such occurrences?
(b) Modify the *FunctionDecl*, *ProcedureDecl* alternative of *DeclarationVisit*1 (Figure 7.9) to determine whether the *Identifier* child is a defining or applied occurrence, and to invoke *DefiningOccurrence*1 only in the former case.
(c) Modify the *FunctionDecl*, *ProcedureDecl* alternative of *DeclarationVisit*2 (Figure 7.10) to invoke *DefiningOccurrence*2 only if the *Identifier* child is a defining occurrence.
(d) Is there any advantage in invoking *AppliedOccurrence* for an *Identifier* child of a *FunctionDecl* or *ProcedureDecl* node? Explain briefly.

7.6 Consider a compiler that achieves the effect of the visit sequence discussed in Section 7.1.2 by doing two complete depth-first, left-to-right traversals of the tree of Figure 7.8.
(a) What tasks would be carried during each of the two traversals?
(b) Can the current environment still be stored in a global variable? Is any additional storage necessary for environments when these new tactics are used? Explain briefly.
(c) Make appropriate changes to Figure 7.9 and Figure 7.10 to implement the new tactics.

7.7 Replace the first ellipses (· · ·) in the **case** statement of Figure 7.10 with a combination of comments and code that explains the actions for constant declarations.

7.8 The *Header* child of a *forward* declaration will give the parameter and result types (if any), and the *Body* child will be the directive "forward." The *Header* child of the second declaration node for the routine will be an empty header, and the *Body* child will be a block.
(a) Figure 7.10 establishes a new environment before visiting the *Header* child of the *forward* declaration for the first time. During the first visit to the *Header* child, associations between the parameter identifiers and definition table keys are entered into this environment. How can this information be made available to the routine's block, which is the *Body* child of the *second* declaration node?
(b) There is no need for *DeclarationVisit*2 to create a new environment for the routine at the second declaration node, although it does no harm. Can you prevent this by some sort of test in *DeclarationVisit*2? Would it be more appropriate to move the environment processing to the header visit routines? Be sure that your

solution also correctly handles parameterless procedures that are *not* forward-declared, such as the following:

procedure *Update*; **begin** $x := x + 1$ **end**;

7.9 Section 6.8.1 of the Pascal Standard[2] defines the conditions under which a **goto** statement can refer to a particular label.
   (a) Cast these rules in terms similar to those of name analysis: Define the region over which a particular statement label can be reached, describe a tree-structured hierarchy of these regions, and determine the analogs of "defining occurrences" and "applied occurrences."
   (b) Define a variable *Reachable*, of type *Environment*, and implement the analysis of label reachability in *StatementVisit*1 and *StatementVisit*2.

7.10 Consider the detection and reporting of definition-before-use errors in Pascal programs. Suppose that it is desirable to report both the use that precedes the definition and the definition that follows the use.
   (a) Define a *Location* property that is a pointer to a *position* (Figure 2.3), and specify interfaces for the appropriate definition table functions.
   (b) Modify Figure 7.13 to make the required reports.
   (c) Suppose there are many uses of a particular identifier that all precede the same definition of that identifier. How could you suppress all but one of the messages attached to the definition?

7.11 Will the entity class *NotDefined* ever appear as an argument of *SetEntityClass*? Explain briefly.

7.12 Consider the response of the operations of Figure 7.13 to source program errors.
   (a) Suppose the source program contained an identifier with two declarations in the same region of the program. List *all* of the error reports that would be issued by these routines for that identifier. Are all of the reports relevant? Explain briefly.
   (b) Suppose the programmer omitted an identifier from an expression (e.g., $a := b+$;). This will be reported as a syntactic error (Section 4.3); what additional reports will be issued by the routines of Figure 7.13? Are these reports relevant? Explain briefly.
   (c) Rewrite the routines in Figure 7.13 to eliminate irrelevant error reports.

7.13 Could the *Location* information introduced in Exercise 7.10 be lumped with the *EntityClass* information as a single property of an identifier definition? Discuss your answer in terms of the criteria presented in Section 7.2.2.

7.14 Modify the definition table implementation of Figure 7.15 to support the *Location* property you defined in Exercise 7.10.

7.15 Complete the procedures *DeclarationVisit*1 (Figure 7.9) and *DeclarationVisit*2 (Figure 7.10).

7.16 The left-hand side of a Pascal assignment statement must always specify an entity to which a value can be assigned. In Chapter 4 we pointed out that it was not possible to check this requirement syntactically.
   (a) Write a procedure *ExpressionVisit* that determines whether the expression node it visits represents an entity to which a value can be assigned. Return the answer via a Boolean **var** parameter.

(b) Write the *AssignmentStmt* case of a visit procedure for statement nodes, showing how an error report would be issued when the left-hand side of an assignment statement could not have a value assigned to it.

7.17 [13] Suppose a Pascal compiler is restricted to a single depth-first, left-to-right traversal of the source program tree. There is thus just one visit procedure for each node class.
   (a) Write a procedure *DeclarationVisit* that merges the functionality of *DeclarationVisit1* and *DeclarationVisit2*.
   (b) Write a procedure *DefiningOccurrence* that merges the functionality of *DefiningOccurrence1* and *DefiningOccurrence2*, except that it reports only the second and subsequent definitions of a multiply-defined identifier.
   (c) Define a global integer variable, *StaticNestingDepth*, whose value is the length of the path from the current environment value to the root of the tree of environment values. (For example, while processing line 12 of Figure 7.6a *StaticNestingDepth* = 2, because the length of the path from the lower right-hand node in Figure 7.6b to the root is 2.) Modify your procedure *DefiningOccurrence* from (b) to set the *DefDepth* property of each definition to the static nesting depth at which that definition occurs, and modify the procedure *AppliedOccurrence* to set the *UseDepth* property of each definition to the static nesting depth at which the last use of the identifier occurred.
   (d) Show that a use-before-definition error can be detected when processing a defining occurrence as follows: Before defining the identifier, obtain the current definition of that identifier. If the *DefDepth* property of that definition is lower than the current static nesting level, and the *UseDepth* property of that definition is equal to or higher than the current static nesting level, then an error has occurred.

7.18 Draw a picture similar to that of Figure 7.16b for the program of Figure 7.7.

7.19 Give implementations of *NewEnv* and *NewScope* for the data structures of Figure 7.19a.

7.20 Draw a picture similar to that of Figure 7.19b for the program of Figure 7.7, assuming that the name analyzer is processing line 13.

7.21 Suppose a compiler was constructed to use a name analysis module with the interface of Figure 7.5, implemented around the data structure of Figure 7.17. After completion, measurements determined that the compiler's performance on large programs was unsatisfactory. Moreover, the data showed that the environment module was a bottleneck for large programs. Therefore it was decided to reimplement the environment module around the data structure of Figure 7.19.
   (a) Which modules, other than the environment module, would need to be recompiled when making this change? Explain briefly.
   (b) If modules other than the environment module had to be recompiled, would that recompilation change their object code? Explain briefly.
   (c) What properties of the compiler's implementation language (Pascal in this text) affected your answers to (a) and (b)?

8
Types and Data Mapping

The translation task of a compiler analyzes the source program tree to determine the meaning of the algorithm expressed by the programmer, and then it decides how to implement that algorithm in terms of target language concepts. Any algorithm has two parts: a description of the actions to be performed and a description of the data to be manipulated by those actions. Both the actions and the data are described by the programmer in terms of source language concepts. In this chapter we are concerned with the implementation of an algorithm's data; Chapter 9 considers implementation of actions.

Figure 8.1 shows an algorithm, expressed in Pascal, that converts an integer to a sequence of digit characters and stores the sequence in an array. The Pascal concepts used to describe the data in Figure 8.1 are the predefined simple types *integer* and *char*, simple types specified as subranges, structured types specified by the **record** and **array** constructors, and procedure parameters. A Pascal-to-VAX compiler must implement these concepts in terms of VAX memory, deciding how many memory elements should be allocated to each simple and structured type, how the fields of the record relate to one another, and how the procedure parameters can be made accessible to the operations that use them. The decisions are made on the basis of contextual information gathered from the source program tree as described in Chapter 7. For example, the compiler needs to know the value of the constant *MaxLength* in order to determine the number of elements in the

```
const
  MaxLength = 136;                (* Maximum length of a string *)

type
  String = record                 (* Representation of a variable-length string *)
    n: 0..MaxLength;              (* Number of characters currently in the string *)
    s: array [1..MaxLength] of char;   (* s[1..n] = string value *)
  end;

procedure IntegerToString(data: integer; var result: String);
  (* Convert an integer to a sequence of digits *)

  procedure ConvertDigits(i: integer);
    (* Build a sequence of digits *)
    begin
    if i >= 10 then ConvertDigits(i div 10);
    result.n := result.n + 1; result.s[result.n] := chr((i mod 10) + ord('0'));
    end;

  begin
  result.n := 0;
  if data < 0 then begin result.n := 1; result.s[1] := '-'; data := -data end;
  ConvertDigits(data);
  end;
```

Figure 8.1
A Pascal fragment

subrange $1..MaxLength$. This number, in conjunction with the amount of memory needed to represent a value of type *char*, allows the compiler to determine how much memory will be devoted to the array.

Section 8.1 discusses ways in which Pascal data concepts can be implemented on the VAX. Although the details are VAX-specific, the approach is one that must be taken with any machine. From this analysis we learn what contextual information the compiler must gather from the declarations. In Section 8.2 we show how this information can be represented as properties of the types, both predefined and user-defined, appearing in the source program. Section 8.3 uses the methods of Chapter 7 to formulate a strategy for obtaining the necessary contextual information and storing it for later use.

8.1 HOW TO REPRESENT PASCAL DATA ON THE VAX

VAX memory is a sequence of 8-bit *bytes*, each with an integer *address* in the range $[0, 2^{32} - 1]$. Data stored in memory occupies one or more contiguous bytes, and is accessed via the address of the first of these bytes. The memory subsystem of the machine gives faster access to some data if its address is divisible by 4. We say that such data is *aligned*.

The compiler designer must decide how each of the predefined types of Pascal is to be represented as a byte sequence, and how the byte sequences representing structured objects will be built from the byte sequences of their components. Factors taken into consideration are the normal uses of these types and the operations provided by the VAX hardware. In the remainder of this section we shall design a particular implementation of Pascal data on the VAX. Our intent is to provide a general approach to the design of such implementations and a specific example of that approach in action. This implementation will also serve as the basis for the implementation of Pascal actions by VAX instructions in Chapter 9.

We begin by deciding on an implementation of Pascal's simple types in Section 8.1.1. Section 8.1.2 then shows how the type construction rules of Pascal can be implemented. Finally, Section 8.1.3 discusses the way in which storage is allocated dynamically for the parameters and variables declared by the programmer.

8.1.1 Simple Types

A simple type in Pascal is one of the predefined types *integer*, *real*, *boolean*, or *char*, or a type defined by an enumeration or subrange constructor. We will also consider pointer types as simple types for this discussion, although they are treated separately in the Pascal Standard.

The VAX hardware provides the normal operations of addition, subtraction, multiplication, and division on 1-, 2-, and 4-byte integers. Since memory addresses are 4-byte integers, there is a special operation for pushing 4-byte integers onto the stack, and it is possible to carry out 4-byte addition as a part of accessing a memory location. The range of signed integer values provided by the 1-byte representation is [−128,127], too small for useful computation. Integers are used mainly for counting and for array indexing, so even the range [−32768,32767] that is provided by the 2-byte representation is apt to pinch programs with large data structures. Therefore, we shall choose the 4-byte representation for integers. A group of four consecutive bytes on the VAX is called a *longword*.

Four forms of floating-point numbers are available for implementing the Pascal *real* data type. They differ only in range and precision, so the choice depends on the kind of numerical calculations for which the compiler will be used. Without any information about the kinds of applications, we shall choose the so-called F-format because it is the only one of the four that occupies 4 bytes. Having the same storage requirements for the *integer* and *real* data types simplifies discussion of the data mapping problem.

We shall require that both *integer* and *real* values be stored at addresses divisible by 4. As noted earlier, this is not an absolute necessity for the VAX, but it will make programs run somewhat faster and it will enable us to show how the compiler handles alignment constraints.

Boolean and *char* values will each occupy one byte, with no restriction on the address. The VAX does not provide convenient operations for accessing single bits. Even though we could save data storage by devoting only one bit to a *boolean* value, the space required for the access instructions would cost more than the space saved.

The minimum amount of storage required for values of an enumerated type is determined by the number of constants of that type. Each of the n constants must be assigned a unique bit pattern; therefore, 2^k must not be less than n if k bits are allocated. Pascal also requires that the constants can be mapped onto consecutive nonnegative integers starting from zero. This mapping must actually be carried out when a constant of the enumerated type is used to access an array or set, or is the argument of the required function *ord*.

Because an integer is represented by a 4-byte VAX longword, one of the criteria for choice of a representation for enumerated types should be easy conversion of that representation to a longword value. The VAX provides instructions (MOVZBL, MOVZWL) for converting bytes and 2-byte *words* to longwords by filling the value with zero bits on the left. Since enumerated constants map to nonnegative integer values, this is exactly the behavior desired. Therefore we shall represent enumerated types with 256 or fewer constants by a byte, those with more than 256 but not more than 65536 constants by a word, and those with more than 65536 constants by a longword. Both the byte and word (2-byte) representations will have alignment 1; the longword representation will have alignment 4. Enumerated types with more than 2^{31} constants cannot be represented using this scheme because their bit patterns correspond to negative integers, but it is highly unlikely that such types will ever occur in practice.

A subrange type can be given the storage requirement of its host type, or the compiler may make an attempt to reduce the storage requirement on the basis of the values given as the subrange bounds. Like enumerated constants, values of subrange type must be convertible to integers. Subrange values may be signed, however. The VAX provides instructions (CVTBL, CVTWL) for converting signed values from bytes or words to longwords by extending the sign bit to the left. Thus bytes, words, or longwords are reasonable representations for subrange types. In order to simplify the compiler's task, we will represent objects of a subrange type in the same way as objects of that subrange's host type. Thus, the compiler will not check the bounds of a subrange to determine the storage requirement for that subrange.

A Pascal pointer value can point only to objects created by the required procedure *new*. Therefore, a pointer is always the address of some location in memory. VAX addresses are always represented by longwords, so every pointer type has size 4 and alignment 4. It is important to note that the storage requirement of a pointer type *does not depend on the type pointed to*.

8.1.2 Structured Types

A Pascal user can define structured types as records, arrays, files, and sets. Any one of these structured types can be specified as "packed." The packed qualifier implies that the user is concerned about the amount of memory allocated to the structured type, but not about the time required to access its components. There is no requirement that the compiler take account of the packed qualifier when allocating storage, although there are several semantic constraints involving it that must be checked. (For example, components of a packed object cannot be passed to procedures as **var** parameters.) We shall ignore the packed qualifier when allocating storage.

A record type is a collection of fields. Storage for the fields of a record is usually allocated in the order the fields were declared, although this is not required by the Pascal Standard. The left declaration in Figure 8.2a defines a record with three fields. These fields might be laid out in storage as shown in the left diagram of Figure 8.2b. Suppose that V was a variable of type R, stored at address a. Then the address of $V.B$ would also be a, that of $V.C$ would be $a + 1$, and that of $V.I$ would be $a + 4$. In order to guarantee that $a + 4$ was divisible by 4, thus satisfying the alignment constraint for integers, a must be divisible by 4. Therefore the record type will inherit the most stringent alignment of any of its fields.

Another record definition is shown at the right of Figure 8.2a. There are two possible layouts for this record, depending upon which variant is chosen, as shown to the right of Figure 8.2b. If the programmer were to declare a variable V of type $\uparrow R$, then the statement $new(V, false)$ would allocate eight bytes laid out according to the first of these two diagrams, while $new(V, true)$ would allocate two bytes laid out according to the second. In both cases the tag field, $V\uparrow.B$, occu-

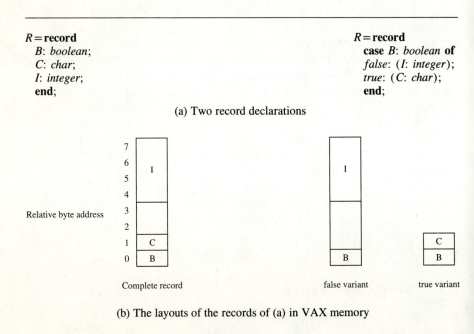

(a) Two record declarations

(b) The layouts of the records of (a) in VAX memory

Figure 8.2
Storage allocation for records

pies the first byte. Finally, the statement *new(V)* would allocate eight bytes laid out according to the leftmost diagram—exactly the same storage allocation that is required for the left record in Figure 8.2a.

Note that in each case the record was built in the order of increasing byte addresses, and the order in which the fields were allocated memory was the order in which they appeared in the record declaration. A field was allocated the first relative byte address that did not overlap previous fields and was divisible by the alignment constraint of the field's type. Variants were allocated individually, starting at the beginning of the record.

The storage requirement for a Pascal array depends upon the number of elements and the storage requirement of each element. Multidimensional array declarations in the source program are considered abbreviations for one-dimensional array declarations, so one-dimensional arrays are the only ones processed by the compiler. For example, the compiler would treat the declaration (1) below as though it had been written as shown in (2):

$$\textbf{array } [1..10, 2..20] \textbf{ of } \textit{integer} \quad (1)$$

$$\textbf{array } [1..10] \textbf{ of array } [2..20] \textbf{ of } \textit{integer} \quad (2)$$

Elements are stored contiguously in memory, and a linear function of the subscript values is used to compute the relative address of the desired element. The linear function subtracts the lower bound from the subscript and multiplies by the element size. Thus, if the array were declared as

$$\textbf{array } [1..10] \textbf{ of } \textit{integer},$$

then the relative address would be calculated from the subscript by

$$\textit{RelativeAddress} := (\textit{subscript} - 1) \times 4.$$

Since the elements are stored contiguously, one may need to adjust the apparent size of an element in order to meet alignment constraints. For example, consider an element type whose storage requirement specifies a size of 5 and an alignment of 4:

$$\textbf{array } [1..10] \textbf{ of record } i: \textit{integer}; \ c: \textit{char} \textbf{ end}$$

If the alignment of the array itself is 4, then the first element will be properly aligned. The second element cannot be stored at relative address 5 (i.e., immediately following the first element), however, because its alignment constraint will then not be met. Relative address 8 is the first location beyond the first element of the array that meets the alignment constraint. The effect is one of increasing the apparent size of an element from 5 to 8.

We shall implement a set type as a sequence of bits, one per element of the set's base type. If there are n elements in the base type, then the set occupies $(n + 7) \div 8$ bytes. Membership can be checked with a VAX bit test instruction. Set union and set difference can be implemented by bit set and bit clear respectively; intersection requires two instructions.

Objects of a file type need space for a buffer and space for status information. The storage requirement of the status information is fixed by the design of the

Pascal input/output support software. The buffer may be a part of the file-type object, or it may be allocated dynamically. We shall assume that it is allocated dynamically, and therefore is not part of the storage requirement of the file-type object. This means that the storage for the file-type object consists only of the status information, and it is therefore independent of the file's component type.

8.1.3 Parameters and Variables

Figure 8.3b shows the assignments and procedure calls executed when *IntegerToString* (Figure 8.3a) is called with the integer -789 and a variable v of type *String*. The right-hand side of each assignment and the arguments of each call have been evaluated to show the data flow within the algorithm. Actions taken within the activation of a procedure are indented below the call that invoked that procedure. Thus, line 1 contains the initial call, and lines 2-9 represent the activation of *IntegerToString* and other activations resulting from it.

Notice that several independent activations of *ConvertDigits* may be in progress simultaneously. At line 7 in Figure 8.3b, for example, three activations are in progress: those begun by the calls on lines 4, 5, and 6, respectively. When several activations of a routine (procedure or function) may be in progress simultaneously, the storage for that routine's parameters and local variables must be allocated dynamically. Because of this dynamic allocation, the compiler cannot know the addresses of the parameters and local variables; nevertheless, it must be able to produce code to access them.

Each activation of a procedure is associated with a (possibly empty) argument list, some housekeeping information, and a (possibly empty) area of memory used for local storage. This collection of storage is called an *activation record*. Conventionally, two of the VAX's sixteen general-purpose registers are set aside to provide access to the current activation record. AP (register 12) contains the address of the argument list, and FP (register 13) addresses the longword just beyond the area of memory used for local storage. Figure 8.4 shows the activation records for two of the procedure invocations of Figure 8.3b. In order to make the example concrete, we have assumed specific memory addresses for these storage areas.

AP and FP address the components of the *current* activation record, but a procedure may require access to the activation records of other procedures. For example, *ConvertDigits* refers to an argument of *IntegerToString* in Figure 8.3a. This argument is not part of the activation record of any activation of *ConvertDigits*. *ConvertDigits* must therefore be able to access the activation record of the correct activation of *IntegerToString* (there may be more than one in progress) to obtain the address of this argument.

In Pascal, the visibility rules allow a routine to access its own parameters and local variables, and the parameters and local variables of any routine containing its declaration. Thus, in Figure 8.3a, *ConvertDigits* is allowed to access the parameters and local variables of *IntegerToString*, as well as those of the routine in which *IntegerToString* was declared, the routine in which *that* routine was declared, and so forth. Because all of the activation records containing that infor-

8.1 HOW TO REPRESENT PASCAL DATA ON THE VAX

```
const
    MaxLength = 136;                (* Maximum length of a string *)

type
    String = record                 (* Representation of a variable-length string *)
        n: 0..MaxLength;            (* Number of characters currently in the string *)
        s: array [1..MaxLength] of char;  (* s[1..n] = string value *)
    end;

procedure IntegerToString(data: integer; var result: String);
    (* Convert an integer to a sequence of digits *)

    procedure ConvertDigits(i: integer);
        (* Build a sequence of digits *)
        begin
        if i >= 10 then ConvertDigits(i div 10);
        result.n:=result.n+1; result.s[result.n]:=chr((i mod 10) + ord('0'));
        end;

    begin
    result.n:=0;
    if data < 0 then begin result.n:=1; result.s[1]:='-'; data:=-data end;
    ConvertDigits(data);
    end;
```

(a) The Pascal fragment of Figure 8.1

```
1    IntegerToString(-789,v)
2        result.n:=0
3        result.n:=1; result.s[1]:='-'; data:=789
4        ConvertDigits(789)
5            ConvertDigits(78)
6                ConvertDigits(7)
7                    result.n:=2; result.s[2]:='7'
8                result.n:=3; result.s[3]:='8'
9            result.n:=4; result.s[4]:='9'
```

(b) The sequence of assignments and procedure calls executing *IntegerToString*(−789,s)

Figure 8.3
Procedure activation

mation are allocated dynamically, the compiler must generate code to find them at run time. The information used by this code is called the *static chain*: Each activation record contains the address of the memory used for local storage by the activation of the containing routine. We use the last longword of the local storage area to hold this address. Therefore, the last longword of the local storage area in

206 CHAPTER 8 TYPES AND DATA MAPPING

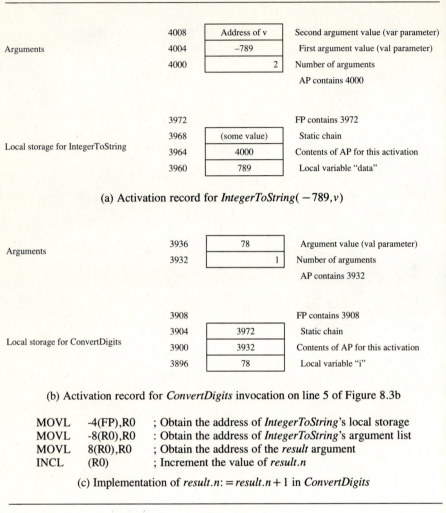

Figure 8.4
Activation record addressing on the VAX

Figure 8.4b contains the address just above the local storage area in Figure 8.4a, because Figure 8.4a is the activation record of *IntegerToString*, and *IntegerToString* is the routine containing the definition of *ConvertDigits*.

There is no fixed relationship between the address of the local storage area for a routine activation and the address of the argument list for that same activation. Thus, the local storage area must contain the address of the corresponding argument list in order to allow access to arguments by nested routines. We use the longword immediately below the static chain for this purpose. Figure 8.4c shows how *ConvertDigits* could access *result.n*, a field of an argument of *IntegerToString*, using this mechanism. First the content of the longword whose address is 4 less than the address in FP is moved to R0. (If the current activation of *Convert-Digits* were the one resulting from the invocation on line 5 of Figure 8.3b, FP would contain 3908. Therefore, R0 would be set to 3972.) R0 then addresses the local storage of *IntegerToString* (Figure 8.4a). The longword whose address is 8 less than the address in R0 is then moved to R0, so that R0 addresses the argument list. The first longword of the argument list specifies the number of arguments, and successive longwords specify the argument values in order from left to right. Since *result* is the second argument, its address is the content of the longword whose address is 8 greater than the address of the argument list. Finally, since *n* is the first field of the record, its address is the same as the record address.

By convention, every argument is represented by a longword on the VAX. If an argument is passed by value, and that value can be expressed in 4 bytes or less, we will store the value itself in the argument list. Otherwise, we will store the address of the value in the argument list. The value of the first argument to *IntegerToString* is therefore stored in the argument list, because it is a value parameter and it can be expressed in 4 bytes. *IntegerToString*'s second argument is a **var** parameter, so its address is stored in the argument list. If it had been a value parameter, its address still would have been stored, because objects of type *String* cannot be represented in 4 bytes or less.

According to the Pascal Standard, every value parameter is associated with a local variable of the routine. Assignments to a value parameter, such as the assignment $data := -data$ in *IntegerToString*, are thus perfectly legal. The standard VAX routine calling conventions do not permit values in an argument list to be altered by the called routine, however. We will therefore copy the values of all value parameters to the local storage area just after entering a routine, and then treat them as though they had been declared to be local variables. In Figure 8.4a, the value of the *data* parameter is stored in the longword whose address is 12 less than the address in FP.

8.2 THE COMPILER'S TYPE SYSTEM

A compiler embodies its understanding of source language data types and their implementations in a *type system*. The concept of a type is used to encapsulate many of the properties of a value, so they need not be restated with every instance of the value. The compiler designer's requirements are often different from those of the language designer; therefore, the "types" recognized by a compiler may differ slightly from the "types" familiar to someone who programs in the source language accepted by the compiler.

The compiler's type system should guarantee that every value has a *single* type. A language designer, on the other hand, may allow a value to belong to several different classes, because all of the operations of those classes are applicable to the value. For example, the Pascal value **nil** is a member of all pointer types, and the Pascal value [ ] is a member of all set types. The designer of a Pascal compiler would probably make each of these values the lone member of its class. Thus, **nil** might be considered by the compiler to be of type *NilType*. A value of type *NilType* could be converted to a value of any pointer type, just as a value of type *integer* can be converted to a value of type *real*.

The reason for insisting upon a single type for every value is to simplify the compiler's data structures. Each type, whether predefined or defined by the user, is associated with a unique definition table key. The type returned by an expression is specified by the definition table key representing that type. If **nil** could be of any pointer type, then its type would have to be specified by a list of the definition table keys for *all* pointer types. Because type conversion is a process that must be carried out anyway (the compiler needs to be able to convert *integer* to *real*), it is more convenient to represent **nil**'s type by a single definition table key, and to use type conversion to obtain the pointer type required by the context.

Another important criterion in the design of the compiler's type system is unification of concepts. In Pascal, functions and procedures are distinguished. These two constructs both represent abstraction, and the compiler could handle them in the same way. Since the only difference is that functions return a value and procedures do not, the compiler designer might choose to unify the concepts of a procedure and a function by defining a *VoidType* to represent "no value." A procedure then becomes a function returning a value of type *VoidType*.

Finally, the compiler must be capable of dealing with erroneous programs. If a program contains an undefined identifier, the type of value represented by that identifier may be impossible to determine. (Perhaps some information could be obtained from the context in which the identifier is used.) The fatal error "Identifier not declared" has already been reported by the name analyzer when type analysis of the expression begins. Thus, there is no point in reporting that the type of the identifier is wrong. What is needed is a distinguished *UnknownType* that can be converted to any type required by the context. We shall see that another distinguished type, *ErroneousType*, is also useful for preventing spurious error messages. Any type can be converted into *ErroneousType*.

Figure 8.5 classifies the types recognized by a Pascal compiler. The classification follows the principles stated above: Every value in a Pascal program can be assigned a single type; procedures and functions have been unified; and types are provided for dealing with erroneous programs. No two classes have exactly the same properties, so none of the classes are redundant.

Any number of properties can be stored in the definition table and accessed via the type's definition table key. The criteria presented in Section 7.2 state that distinct items of information should be combined into a single property only if they are related, and if they become available at the same time. The *TypeDescriptor* record of Figure 8.5 summarizes the items of information that can be deduced solely from the appearance of a new type in the source program tree, and are used during the semantic analysis of expressions. There is no need to have the *TypeDescriptor* record of one type available in order to construct a *TypeDescriptor* record for another. The *TypeDescriptor* record will therefore be stored in the definition table as a single property of a type. Given the type's definition table key, values of this property would be set via a procedure *SetTypeDescriptor* and queried via a function *GetTypeDescriptor* provided by the definition table module as discussed in Section 7.2.

```
TypeClass = (                                    (* Classification of types *)
  UnknownType,                                   (* Type about which nothing is known *)
  BooleanType,CharType,IntegerType,RealType,     (* Required simple types *)
  EnumeratedType,SubrangeType,                   (* User-defined simple types *)
  TextType,                                      (* Required structured type *)
  ArrayType,RecordType,SetType,FileType,         (* User-defined structured types *)
  PointerType,                                   (* User-defined pointer type *)
  NilType,                                       (* Type of the value nil *)
  EmptySetType,                                  (* Type of the value [ ] *)
  ProcType,                                      (* Type of a function or procedure *)
  VoidType,                                      (* Type of the value returned by a procedure *)
  StringType,                                    (* Type of a character constant *)
  ErroneousType);                                (* Type known to be in error *)
DefList = ↑DefListElement;                       (* List of definitions *)
DefListElement = record
  Definition: DefTableKey;                       (* Current list element *)
  Next: DefList;                                 (* Remainder of the list *)
  end;
TypeDescriptor = ↑TypeDesc;                      (* Description of a type value *)
TypeDesc = record
  case Class: TypeClass of;                      (* Class of the type described *)
  UnknownType,BooleanType,CharType,
  IntegerType,RealType,EnumeratedType,
  TextType,NilType,EmptySetType,VoidType
  ErroneousType: ( );
  SubrangeType:
    (First,Last: ExtValue;                       (* Limits of the subrange *)
    Host: DefTableKey);                          (* Host type for the subrange *)
  ArrayType:
    (Index,Element: DefTableKey);                (* Array index and element types *)
  RecordType:
    (FieldIds: Environment;                      (* Field identifiers *)
    Fields: DefList);                            (* Field definitions *)
  SetType,FileType:
    (Base: DefTableKey);                         (* Base type *)
  PointerType:
    (PointsTo: DefTableKey);                     (* Identifier of the type pointed to *)
  ProcType:
    (Parameters: DefList;                        (* Parameter definitions *)
    Result: DefTableKey);                        (* Result type *)
  StringType:
    (Length: ExtValue);                          (* Number of characters *)
  end;
```

Figure 8.5
Type system for a Pascal compiler

Other properties of types are also stored in the definition table. Each type must have a property describing its storage requirements, enumerated types must have a property describing the number of elements, and structured types must have a property describing whether they are packed. This additional information is not used for the same purpose as the *TypeDescriptor* record, so it is stored in separate definition table properties.

Every property of a type must be determined and stored in the definition table before it can be used. The information required to construct a *TypeDescriptor* record is primarily structural, and can be obtained directly from contextual information using the techniques discussed in Chapter 7. Storage requirements are also determined from contextual information, using operations provided by the storage module presented in Section 8.3.1. In Section 8.3.2 we consider the design of the visit sequence that actually constructs the *TypeDescriptor* records and sets the properties of each type.

8.3 TYPE DECLARATIONS AND STORAGE ALLOCATION

A definition table key is established for each new type during the second visit to the source program tree node describing that type. (As discussed in Chapter 7, the first visit to a source program tree node describing a type establishes definition table keys for any enumerated constant identifiers defined within the type, and enters associations between the identifiers and those keys in the environment for the routine containing the new type.) The *TypeDescriptor* record is also constructed during the second visit and stored as a property of the new type. Finally, the visit determines the storage requirements of the type. Thus the second visit to a *Type*-class node of the source program tree is itself a rather complex process of gathering contextual information and acting upon that information. It provides us with a second example of how the general methodology introduced in Chapter 7 is applied in compiler design.

The major computations determine the storage requirements for a structured type, given the storage requirements of its components. Those computations are embodied in a module whose interface and implementation are discussed in Section 8.3.1. Section 8.3.2 develops an appropriate visit sequence, given that module, to implement the second visit to a *Type*-class node of the source program tree.

8.3.1 The Storage Module

The basic computational task of the data mapper is to determine the storage requirement of a composition of two objects, each of which has its own storage requirement. There are two distinct composition strategies: concatenation and overlaying. When two objects are concatenated, they are allocated adjacent areas of memory; when they are overlaid, they share memory. For example, Figure 8.6a shows a Pascal variant record to be mapped onto VAX memory.

8.3 TYPE DECLARATIONS AND STORAGE ALLOCATION 211

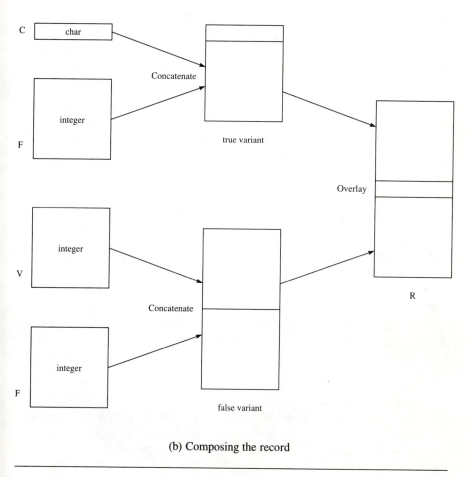

```
R = record
   F: integer           (* Fixed field has its own storage *)
   case boolean of      (* Untagged variant -- no tag field *)
   false: (V: integer); (* These variants may share storage *)
   true: (C: char)
   end;
```

(a) A Pascal record definition

(b) Composing the record

Figure 8.6
Storage composition strategies

There are two variants of the record R. One is formed by concatenating fields F and V, the other by concatenating fields F and C (see Figure 8.6b). Only one of these two variants is possible at any particular point in the execution of the program, so the storage requirement of any object of type R is the result of overlaying them. Because of the way in which the variants were constructed, the fixed field *F* occupies the same relative position in each variant. (Addresses are assumed to increase from the bottom to the top in this and subsequent figures depicting VAX memory.)

The address of the character field in Figure 8.6b is the address of its byte, and the address of the integer field is the address of its first byte. Thus, each of these objects has as its address the address of the first byte belonging to it. If the storage required for a local variable were being concatenated to the local storage area of an activation record, however, the local variable would be addressed by the address of its first byte and the local storage area would be addressed by the address of the first byte above it (Figure 8.7).

The box on the left in Figure 8.7b represents the activation record of procedure *p*. It contains the local variables of *p*, in the same way that the box at the right of Figure 8.6b contains the fields of the record *R*. Activation record storage requirements are determined in exactly the same way as the storage requirements of user-declared record types—by combining the storage requirements of the components. Figure 8.7b shows how the storage requirement for variable *T* is added to the storage requirement for the activation record containing space for the static chain (since *p* has no arguments, there is no need for the address of an argument list) and the local variable *A*, to form the complete activation record for procedure *p*.

Three pieces of information are needed to define the storage requirements of an object: the number of bytes it occupies, the number by which its address should be divisible, and whether its address is the address of its first byte or the address of the first byte above it. These pieces of information are given by fields of the *StorageRequired* record type exported by the storage module (Figure 8.8). Each of the two composition operations exported by the module accepts two *StorageRequired* objects as arguments. The storage defined by the second argument is either concatenated to or overlaid upon the storage described by the first. As a result of that operation, the *size* and *alignment* fields of the first argument may be modified. Neither operation ever modifies the *topaddress* field. The storage requirement of the composite block is described by the modified first argument of the operation.

After either operation, the address of the component represented by the first argument is the address of the composite object. The component represented by the second argument, however, must now be addressed relative to the address of the composite object. For example, suppose that argument *a* to *Concatenate* described the storage requirement of an activation record fragment containing only the static chain pointer and variable *A* (the top box on the right in Figure 8.7), and argument *b* to *Concatenate* described the storage requirement of variable *T* (the bottom box on the right in Figure 8.7). On return from *Concatenate*, argument *a* would describe the storage requirement of the complete activation record shown at the left of Figure 8.7b. The address of the activation record fragment containing *A* has not been changed by this operation, but variable *T* must now be addressed relative to the activation record address. The required offset (-16 in this case) is returned as the value of the *Concatenate* function.

8.3 TYPE DECLARATIONS AND STORAGE ALLOCATION

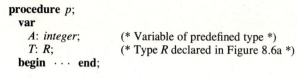

```
procedure p;
  var
    A: integer;      (* Variable of predefined type *)
    T: R;            (* Type R declared in Figure 8.6a *)
  begin  ···  end;
```

(a) A Pascal procedure definition

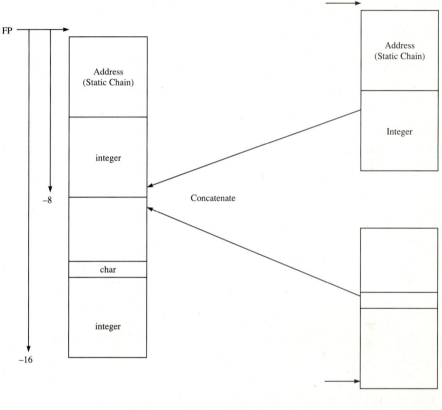

(b) Layout of the variables in memory

Figure 8.7
Storage for Pascal local variables

When *a.topaddress* = *b.topaddress*, the value returned by the *Overlay* function is always 0. Figure 8.6b provides an example. The variants were overlaid so that they shared the same address. On the other hand, if one of the two storage areas is addressed by its first byte, while the other is addressed by its last + 1 byte, they cannot share both storage and an address! Thus the value returned by the *Overlay* function is never 0 if *a.topaddress* ≠ *b.topaddress*.

type
  StorageRequired = **record**   (* Storage requirement *)
    size,   (* Number of bytes *)
    alignment: *integer*;   (* Number that must divide the address *)
    topaddress: *boolean*;   (* True if addressed by the last+1 location *)
  end;

function *Concatenate*(**var** *a*: *StorageRequired*; *b*: *StorageRequired*): *integer*;
  (* Extend the storage requirement for an object by concatenating another object
    On entry-
      a describes the object to be extended
      b describes the object to be concatenated to *a*
    On exit-
      a describes the storage required by the extended object
      Concatenate = offset of the address of *b* from the address of *a*
  *)
  var *offset*: *integer*;
  begin
  if *a.topaddress* = *b.topaddress* **then**
    begin *offset*: = ((*a.size* + (*b.alignment* − 1)) **div** *b.alignment*)**b.alignment*;
    a.size: = *offset* + *b.size*; **end**
  else
    begin *offset*: = ((*a.size* + *b.size* + (*b.alignment* − 1)) **div** *b.alignment*)**b.alignment*;
    a.size: = *offset*; **end**;
  if *a.alignment* < *b.alignment* **then** *a.alignment*: = *b.alignment*;
  if *a.topaddress* **then** *Concatenate*: = −*offset* **else** *Concatenate*: = *offset*;
  end;

function *Overlay*(**var** *a*: *StorageRequired*; *b*: *StorageRequired*): *integer*;
  (* Extend the storage requirement for an object by overlaying another object
    On entry-
      a describes the object to be extended
      b describes the object to be overlaid on *a*
    On exit-
      a describes the storage required by the extended object
      Overlay = offset of the address of *b* from the address of *a*
  *)
  var *tmp*: *StorageRequired*;
  begin
  if *a.topaddress* = *b.topaddress* **then** *Overlay*: = 0
  else begin *tmp*: = *a*; *tmp.size*: = 0; *Overlay*: = *Concatenate*(*tmp,b*); *b*: = *tmp* **end**;
  if *a.size* < *b.size* **then** *a.size*: = *b.size*;
  if *a.alignment* < *b.alignment* **then** *a.alignment*: = *b.alignment*;
  end;

Figure 8.8
The storage module

The heart of the concatenation operation is an expression to determine the next available address having a particular alignment. Let x be an address. Then the smallest address divisible by y that is not smaller than x can be computed by

8.3 TYPE DECLARATIONS AND STORAGE ALLOCATION

the following expression:

$$\mathit{Align}(x,y) \;=\; ((x+(y-1))\;\textbf{div}\;y)\;\times\;y$$

For a particular concatenation, the arguments of this operation depend upon whether *a.topaddress* = *b.topaddress*. In Figure 8.9a, the relative address of the storage for *b* must be the first location beyond the end of *a* that is divisible by *b.alignment*. In Figure 8.9b, however, the relative address of the storage for *b* lies at the "far end" of the composite area. Therefore, it must be the first location, far enough from the beginning of *a* to accommodate *both* storage areas, that is divisible by *b.alignment*.

If *a.topaddress* = *b.topaddress*, the overlay operation simply guarantees that the composite storage area has the same size as the larger of its two components. When *a.topaddress* ≠ *b.topaddress*, however, the composite storage area may contain additional space required to satisfy an alignment constraint. *Overlay* obtains this extra space by concatenating *b* to an empty area, and then overlaying *a* with the result.

All of the alignment calculations assume that the address of *a* is divisible by both the alignment of *a* and the alignment of *b*. The alignment of the composite storage area must satisfy that assumption. For most machines, all alignments are powers of 2. Therefore, the maximum of two alignments is divisible by either. In other cases, a more complex calculation would be needed to set the alignment of the composite area to the least common multiple of the alignments of its components.

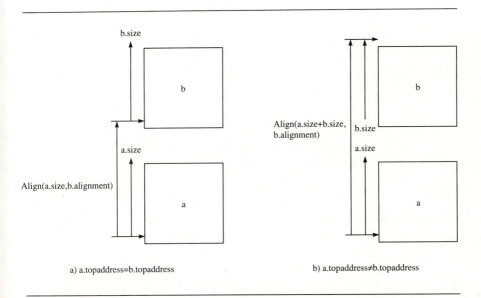

a) a.topaddress=b.topaddress

b) a.topaddress≠b.topaddress

Figure 8.9
The Operation of *Concatenate(a,b)*

8.3.2 Visit Sequence Design

Tipe-class nodes are used in the source program tree to represent every Pascal type construct, from the simplest type identifier reference to the most complex variant record. In every case, the second visit to the *Type*-class node must produce the same overall results: a definition table key must be associated with the type, and the appropriate properties for that key must be set. The "appropriate properties" depend upon the particular type construct—every type has a *TypeDescriptor* property and a *StorageRequirement* property, but only enumerated types have an *ElementCount* property, and only structured types have an *IsPacked* property.

Our basic strategy will be to make the second visit to each *Type*-class node in the order in which the type constructs they represent appear in the source program text. When the type construct is a reference to a type identifier, *TypeVisit2* simply accesses the definition table key previously associated with that identifier (Figure 8.10). If every textually preceding *Type* node has been visited for the second time, then the use-before-definition rule of Pascal guarantees that every correctly used type identifier (except one following "↑" in a declaration of a pointer type) will have its *Type* property set. Therefore the value of *TypeKey* can be set from that property, because the current *Type*-class node is simply a reference to a previously defined type.

A *PackedTypeNode* represents a packed qualifier attached to a type constructor. That type constructor is represented by the *Type*-class node that is the child of the current node. The desired *TypeKey* is the *TypeKey* for the constructed type, which can be obtained by visiting the child for the second time. After that visit, the type's *TypeDescriptor* and *StorageRequirement* properties have been set. Since it must be a structured type (the concrete grammar would reject any attempt to attach a packed qualifier to a simple type), it has no *ElementCount* property.

The *IsPacked* property has a Boolean value. Suppose that every query of this property has the following form:

GetIsPacked(k, false)

If the property's value has not been set, this query will return the value *false*. The query would also return *false* if the property's value had been set to *false*. If "*false*" means "this type is not packed," then there is no point in setting the *IsPacked* property of a type that is not packed. Choosing to represent one value of *IsPacked* by not setting the property at all simplifies the compiler—there is no need to set the *IsPacked* property in each alternative that corresponds to a structured type. It does not complicate the query, because "unpacked" is a reasonable default assumption when nothing is known about a type.

All *Type*-class nodes other than type identifiers and packed qualifiers represent new types in Pascal. Therefore *NewKey* is used to obtain a new definition table key, and records are allocated for a new type descriptor and a new storage requirement. Notice that both the *TypeDescriptor* property and the *StorageRequirement* property are actually pointers to the respective records, in keeping with the restriction that structured types may not be stored directly in the definition table (Section 7.2.3).

```
                                    (* Pointers to be stored in the definition table *)
                                    (* Current storage requirement *)
type Storage = ↑StorageRequired; TypeDescriptor = ↑TypeStructure;
var CurrentStorage: StorageRequired;
procedure TypeVisit2(n: SourceTree; var TypeKey: DefTableKey);
   (* Establish the definition table key representing the type for this node
      On entry-
         A key has been associated with each defining occurrence of an identifier in this region
         Every Type node textually preceding the current one has been visited for the second time
      On exit-
         TypeKey = definition table key representing the type for this node
         The TypeDescriptor, StorageRequirement, and ElementCount properties have been set
   *)
   var
      t: SourceSequence; i: integer; TypeDesc: TypeDescriptor;
      SaveStorage: StorageRequired; StorageProperty: Storage;
   begin
   if n↑.Kind = IdnType then                        (* Applied occurrence of a type identifier *)
      begin AppliedOccurrence(n↑.TypeIdn,[TypeName]);
      TypeKey: = GetType(n↑.TypeIdn↑.Definition,NoKey) end
   else if n↑.Kind = PackedTypeNode then            (* Packed qualifier *)
      begin TypeVisit2(n↑.UnpackedType,TypeKey); SetIsPacked(TypeKey,true,true) end
   else                                             (* Type constructor *)
      begin
      TypeKey: = NewKey;
      new(TypeDesc); SetTypeDescriptor(TypeKey,TypeDesc,nil);
      new(StorageProperty); SetStorageRequirement(TypeKey,StorageProperty,nil);
      case n↑.Kind of
         EnumeratedTypeNode:                        (* (Identifier⁺): Type *)
            begin TypeDesc↑.Class: = EnumeratedType;
            t: = n↑.EnumList; i: = 0;               (* Scan the Identifier list *)
            while t < > nil do
               begin DefiningOccurrence2(t↑.Node);  (* Visit the current Identifier *)
               with t↑.Node↑ do
                  begin SetTypeKey(Definition,TypeKey,TypeKey); SetOrdinal(Definition,i,i) end;
               i: = i + 1; t: = t↑.Next;
               end;
            SetElementCount(TypeKey,i,0);
            if i ⩽ 256 then begin StorageProperty↑.size: = 1; StorageProperty↑.alignment: = 1 end
            else if i ⩽ 65536 then begin StorageProperty↑.size: = 2; StorageProperty↑.alignment: = 1 end
            else begin StorageProperty↑.size: = 4; StorageProperty↑.alignment: = 4 end;
            StorageProperty↑.topaddress: = false;
            end;
         RecordTypeNode:                            (* (FieldList): Type *)
            begin TypeDesc↑.Class: = RecordType; TypeDesc↑.FieldEnv: = n↑.RecordEnv;
            SaveStorage: = CurrentStorage;
            CurrentStorage.Size: = 0; CurrentStorage.Alignment: = 1; CurrentStorage.topaddress: = false;
            FieldListVisit2(n↑.RecordFields); StorageProperty↑: = CurrentStorage;
            CurrentStorage: = SaveStorage;
            end;
         PointerTypeNode:                           (* (Identifier): Type *)
            begin TypeDesc↑.Class: = PointerType;
            AppliedOccurrence(n↑.PntrType,[TypeName]);
            TypeDesc↑.PointsTo: = n↑.PntrType↑.Definition;
            StorageProperty↑.Size: = 4; StorageProperty↑.Alignment: = 4;
            StorageProperty↑.topaddress: = false;
            end;
         end;
      end;
   end;
```

Figure 8.10
Constructing a type

The storage requirements of a record are actually determined by several distinct visit procedures, as we shall see later in this section. Therefore, the criteria of Section 7.1.3 suggest that a variable global to all visit procedures be used to store the relevant information. *Storage* must be saved and restored by *TypeVisit2* because Pascal allows type constructors to be nested.

The treatment of enumerated types gives the flavor of a visit to a type constructor. First the *Class* field of the type descriptor is set, and then the children of the node are visited to gather relevant information for the type descriptor and any other properties. In the case of an enumeration, there is no additional information needed in the type descriptor. All of the enumerated constant identifiers must be visited because they are defining occurrences, quite apart from any information required by the enumeration itself. After visiting each enumerated constant identifier, its *Type* and *Ordinal* properties are set. The value of the enumerated type's *ElementCount* property is obtained by counting the enumerated constant identifiers. That count is also used to determine the storage requirement for values of the enumerated type, as discussed in Section 8.1.1.

The identifier following "↑" in a pointer type declaration might not have a type associated with it at the time the *PointerTypeNode* is visited for the second time. Therefore, the type descriptor for the pointer type cannot specify the type pointed to. The type identifier's definition table key, on the other hand, *is* guaranteed to be available when the *PointerTypeNode* is visited for the second time—one of the entry conditions for *TypeVisit2* is that all defining occurrences have been visited once. Therefore, the entry condition for *AppliedOccurrence* (Figure 7.13) is met, and that routine can be invoked to place the type identifier's definition table key into the *Identifier* child of the pointer type declaration.

The actual type pointed to is not needed until expressions are being analyzed, and at that time the identifier will certainly be associated with a type. Therefore, the compiler can access the type information via the identifier found in the type descriptor by querying its type property. If desired, the definition table key for the type can then be stored as a separate property of the pointer type to speed access.

Figure 8.11 shows the source program tree structure for a typical record declaration. Four additional source tree node classes—*FieldList*, *RecordSection*, *Tag*, and *Variant*—appear in the tree of Figure 8.11b. Each of these node classes must be associated with one or more visit procedures. Note that a node from any of these classes might have a *Type*-class node as a descendant. Since *Type*-class nodes must be visited twice, *FieldList*, *RecordSection*, *Tag*, and *Variant*-class nodes must also be visited at least twice in order to reach their *Type*-class descendants.

The *RecordTypeNode* alternative of the **case** statement in *TypeVisit2* invokes *FieldListVisit2* (Figure 8.12) after establishing the storage requirement of an empty record. A *FieldList* node always has at least one child, the fixed part of the record, which is a list of record sections. (The list might be empty.) *FieldListVisit2* visits each element of the list to assign field offsets and concatenate the fields to the growing record.

If the field list has variants, the tag is visited next. A tag may or may not occupy storage, but in either case it specifies a type key to be used in verifying the

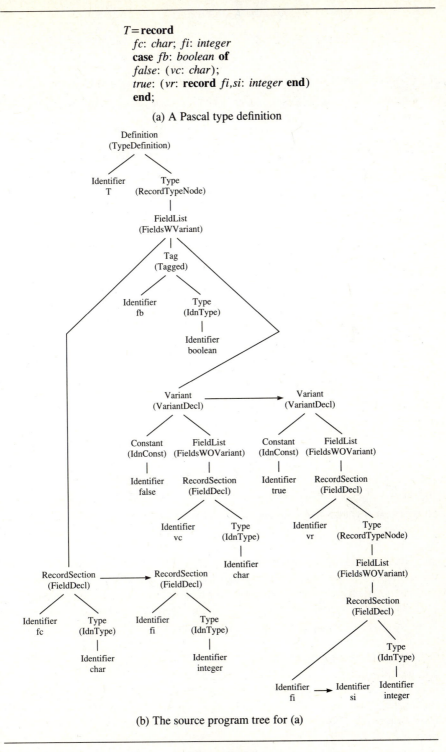

```
T = record
  fc: char; fi: integer
  case fb: boolean of
  false: (vc: char);
  true: (vr: record fi,si: integer end)
end;
```

(a) A Pascal type definition

(b) The source program tree for (a)

Figure 8.11
A typical record type

procedure *FieldListVisit2*(*n*: *SourceTree*);
  (* Establish storage for a *FieldList*
    On entry-
      A key has been associated with each defining occurrence of an identifier in this region
      Every *Type* node textually preceding the current one has been visited for the second time
      CurrentStorage reflects the storage allocation for all fields textually preceding this *FieldList*
    On exit-
      CurrentStorage has been updated to include the storage required for this *FieldList*
  *)
  var
    t: *SourceSequence*; *i*: *integer*; *TypeKey*: *DefTableKey*;
    CompleteStorage, *CommonStorage*: *StorageRequired*;
  begin
  t: = *n*↑.*FixedPart*;
  while *t* < > **nil do begin** *RecordSectionVisit2*(*t*↑.*node*); *t*: =*t*↑.*Next* **end**;
  if *n*↑.*Kind* = *FieldsWVariant* **then**
    begin *TagVisit2*(*n*↑.*Tag*,*TypeKey*);
    CompleteStorage: = *CurrentStorage*; *CommonStorage*: = *CurrentStorage*;
    t: = *n*↑.*VariantPart*;
    while *t* < > **nil do**
      begin *CurrentStorage*: = *CommonStorage*;
      VariantVisit2(*t*↑.*Node*,*TypeKey*); *i*: = *Overlay*(*CompleteStorage*,*CurrentStorage*);
      t: = *t*↑.*Next*;
      end;
    CurrentStorage: = *CompleteStorage*;
    end;
  end;

Figure 8.12
Processing a *FieldList*

constants associated with each variant. Thus, *TagVisit2* is invoked with a **var** parameter to pick up the key. Upon return from *TagVisit2*, storage for the tag field has been added to the growing record if necessary.

After the *Tag* node has been visited, *CurrentStorage* specifies the storage requirement of the part of the record common to all variants. This requirement is the starting point for each variant, and so *FieldListVisit2* saves it in local variable *CommonStorage*. Before visiting each variant, *CurrentStorage* is reset from this local variable. Thus, each variant starts out with the common storage requirement and builds upon it.

The storage requirement of the complete record is obtained by overlaying the requirements of the variants: After the second visit to each variant, *Overlay* is invoked to combine the storage requirement of that variant with the storage requirements of all previous variants. The result is kept in the local variable *CompleteStorage*, which is copied to *CurrentStorage* after all of the variants have been visited.

RecordSectionVisit2 (Figure 8.13) illustrates the use of default values for properties as well as showing how storage is allocated for fields. After visiting the record section's *Type* child to obtain the field type's definition table key,

procedure *RecordSectionVisit2*(*n*: *SourceTree*);
(* Establish storage for a *RecordSection*
   On entry-
     A key has been associated with each defining occurrence of an identifier in this scope
     Every *Type* node textually preceding the current one has been visited for the second time
     CurrentStorage reflects the storage allocation for all fields
        textually preceding this *RecordSection*
   On exit-
     CurrentStorage has been updated to include the storage required for this *RecordSection*
     The *Type* and *Offset* properties of all fields in this *RecordSection* have been set
*)
var
  t: *SourceSequence*; *i*: *integer*; *TypeKey*: *DefTableKey*;
  TypeStorageProperty: *Storage*;
begin *TypeVisit2*(*n*↑.*DeclaredType*,*TypeKey*);
TypeStorageProperty: = *GetStorage*(*TypeKey*,**nil**);
t: = *n*↑.*Names*;
while *t* < > **nil do**
  begin
  DefiningOccurrence2(*t*↑.*node*);
  with *t*↑.*Node*↑ **do**
    begin *SetTypeKey*(*Definition*,*TypeKey*);
    if *TypeStorageProperty* < > **nil then**
      SetOffset(*Definition*,*Concatenate*(*CurrentStorage*,*TypeStorageProperty*↑));
    end;
  t: = *t*↑.*Next*;
  end;
end;

Figure 8.13
Processing a *RecordSection*

RecordSectionVisit2 accesses the *Storage* property. This property is a pointer to the storage requirement for the field type. Every field defined in the record section needs storage satisfying that requirement.

The elements of the record section's identifier list are all defining occurrences. After visiting one of these defining occurrences for the second time, *RecordSectionVisit2* sets the corresponding field's *Type* property. If the storage requirement for that type is known, *RecordSectionVisit2* also uses *Concatenate* to add memory for the field to the storage requirement of the record and to determine the field's offset. If the storage requirement for the field type is unknown (because of some programming error), then the earlier call to *GetStorage* would have yielded the default value **nil**. In that case, no storage is allocated. The field identifier is defined and given a *Type* property, however.

8.4 SUMMARY

In order to determine implementations for the simple types of a programming language on a particular machine, the compiler writer must study the properties of the instruction set and of the applications of the language. The chosen implementation will balance considerations of efficiency with those of capability: There is no point in having an implementation generating small, fast programs that can solve only a small subset of the interesting problems. Nor is there any point in an implementation that is capable of solving every problem, but takes so much time and space that it cannot be used.

Structured types obey certain common rules in programming languages, and once the implementations for the simple types are determined, there is little creative work in defining the structured types.

Storage for parameters and local variables of Pascal routines must be allocated dynamically, because several activations of a routine may exist simultaneously. This means that access to data involves run-time computation to determine the address of the proper activation record. The data to support that run-time computation must be made available from standard places (such as registers) and as linkages stored in the activation records themselves. Hardware manufacturers often specify conventions for routine invocation that provide the necessary information.

Source language data types are represented by definition table keys, and properties common to all objects of a particular type are accessed via that key. The compiler usually uses a set of keys that does not correspond exactly to the set of source language types. Type keys are chosen to guarantee that every object is associated with exactly one key, and also to simplify compiler algorithms.

One of the properties of a type is its storage requirement. The storage requirements of predefined types are established by the compiler designer, and the compiler uses these in constructing requirements for user-defined types. A machine-independent module can be used to compute new storage requirements by concatenating and overlaying known requirements. This module represents a storage requirement as a size, an alignment, and an indication of whether the address of the storage area is that of its first memory element or the address of the first memory element above it.

To establish the properties of all types, a Pascal compiler might visit type definitions twice during depth-first, left-to-right traversals of the program. The first visit is used to associate all defining occurrences of identifiers with definition table keys; the second is used to associate types with definition table keys and determine the relevant properties.

NOTES

A compiler designer must have access to definitive information about the architecture of the target machine. As with programming languages, it is not sufficient to rely on textbooks for this information. We used the 1981 Edition of the VAX Architecture Handbook [2] as the source for all of the information we present in this text. Later editions are not as technically oriented, and do not provide all of the material a compiler writer needs. Digital Equipment Corporation has seemingly followed the lead of IBM in distributing the pertinent information among a variety of documents, complicating the compiler designer's research task.

Textbooks about the target machine are useful as overviews, giving a broad picture of the architecture and allowing the compiler designer to identify the sticky points that must be pursued in the manufacturer's documentation. They also describe typical ways to implement various operations, providing hints for data representation and code sequences. The compiler designer should be wary of these hints, however, because they often fail for extreme values due to simplifications for pedagogical purposes.

An exhaustive treatment of strategies for record storage allocation has been given for PL/1 [6]. That paper proposed several methods, including ones that do not require the alignment of a composite object to be the least common multiple of the alignments of its components. Often it is possible to save space by removing the least common multiple requirement, but the resulting map makes input/output difficult, and has other nasty side effects as well. The approach we presented in Section 8.1.2 is a reasonable one under a variety of assumptions.

Alignment constraints can cause "holes"—memory that lies within the bounds of an object, but is not used to store information belonging to that object. If the source language allows rearrangement of record fields and local variables, the amount of space wasted by holes can sometimes be reduced. For the special case in which a machine has only alignments 1 and 2 (such as the Digital PDP-11 or Intel 8086), a linear algorithm can be used to obtain optimum packing. If you attempt optimization of record layout, the choice of layout should be kept separate from the routines *Concatenate* and *Overlay* of Figure 8.8.

Often, conventions for procedure calling, parameter passing, and variable addressing are proposed by the hardware manufacturer. (The material in Section 8.1.3 follows the VAX Procedure Calling and Condition Handling Standard [2].) Most of these conventions are very similar in design, being based upon the model described by Dijkstra as a technique for implementing ALGOL 60 [3, 4]. This technique was named the "contour model" by Johnston [5], and has been discussed by a number of authors [8, 7].

REFERENCES

1. "Pascal Computer Programming Language," ANSI/IEEE 770 X3.97-1983, American National Standards Institute, New York, NY, Jan. 1983.
2. *VAX Architecture Handbook*, Digital Equipment Corporation, Concord, MA, 1981.
3. Dijkstra, E. W., "Recursive Programming," *Numerische Mathematik 2* (1960), 312-318.
4. Dijkstra, E. W., "An ALGOL 60 Translator for the X1," *Annual Review in Automatic Programming 3* (1963), 329-345.
5. Johnston, J. B., "Contour Model of Block Structured Processes," *SIGPLAN Notices 6*, 2 (Feb. 1971), 55-82.
6. McLaren, M. D., "Data Matching, Data Alignment, and Structure Mapping in PL/I," *SIGPLAN Notices 5*, 12 (Dec. 1970), 30-43.
7. Pratt, T. W., *Programming Languages Design and Implementation*, Prentice Hall, Englewood Cliffs, NJ, 1975.

8. Randell, B. and Russell, L. J., *ALGOL 60 Implementation*, Academic Press, London, 1964.

EXERCISES

8.1 The Pascal Standard [1] requires that the predefined constant *maxint* have the following properties:

- All integral values in the closed interval from $-maxint$ to $+maxint$ are values of the integer type.
- Any monadic operation performed on an integer value in this interval is correctly performed according to the mathematical rules for integer arithmetic.
- Any dyadic integer operation on two integer values in this interval is correctly performed according to the mathematical rules for integer arithmetic, provided that the result is also in this interval.
- Any relational operation on two integer values in this interval is correctly performed according to the mathematical rules for integer arithmetic.

Given our choice of representation for integer values, what is the largest possible value for *maxint*? Explain briefly.

8.2 Consider the relationship between integers and real numbers.
  (a) Given our representations for types *integer* and *real*, is it possible to represent every integer exactly as a real number? Explain briefly.
  (b) If your answer to (a) is "no," does that mean our implementation is in violation of the Pascal Standard [1]?

8.3 Suppose we represented a *boolean* value by a single bit, instead of by a byte. Write a sequence of VAX instructions that implements the Boolean assignment "$a:=b;$" where a occupies bit 3 of a particular byte and b occupies bit 5. Assume the remaining bits of the byte are occupied by other Boolean variables whose values must not be altered by this assignment statement.

8.4 Suppose we chose whether to use a byte, word, or longword to implement a subrange on the basis of the bounds, rather than the host type. Write specific conditions that would allow you to determine the implementation, given the bounds.

8.5 What would the storage layout for each of the following Pascal records be if the target machine was the VAX?
  (a) R = **record** C: *char*; I: *integer* **end**
  (b) R = **record** I: *integer*; C: *char* **end**

8.6 Exercise 8.5 shows that the amount of storage required by a record depends upon the order in which the fields are declared.
  (a) Do you think it would be feasible for the compiler to attempt to rearrange the fields to minimize storage? Explain briefly.
  (b) What effect does wasted space have on simple code to compare two records for equality?
  (c) Does Pascal allow a user to compare two records for equality? Quote from the Pascal Standard [1] to support your answer.

8.7 Assume the target machine has only alignments 1 and 2. (The Digital Equipment PDP-11 and the Intel 8086 have this property.) We need a linear algorithm for minimizing the amount of space taken up by holes in a record laid out on such a machine. The algorithm will consider each of the fields in the order in which they were declared. For each field, it will perform one of three actions: immediately concatenate it to the current partial record, save it temporarily, or immediately concatenate a saved field to the current partial record and then concatenate the current field.

(a) Every field of a record can be characterized by whether its alignment is even or arbitrary and whether its size is even or odd. Which class (or classes) of fields can be concatenated to the current partial record whenever they are encountered, with no possibility of creating a hole?

(b) Each of the classes whose members cannot always be concatenated to the current partial record with no possibility of creating a hole must have an associated local variable. How many elements of each such class must be retained until they can be concatenated to the current partial record in combination with a newly encountered field?

(c) Define an interface for a storage optimization module that can be invoked during the traversal of the source program tree. Does this module need an initialization procedure? Does it need a finalization procedure? Explain briefly.

(d) Implement the module whose interface you gave in (c).

8.8 Consider the following record declaration:

```
R = record
    F: integer              (* Fixed field has its own storage *)
    case T: boolean of      (* Tagged variant—explicit tag field *)
    false: (V: integer);    (* These variants may share storage *)
    true: (C: R)
end;
```

(a) Try to draw the layout of this record in VAX memory. Will this definition cause a problem for a Pascal compiler? Explain briefly.

(b) Is the declaration legal in Pascal? Quote from the Pascal standard [1] to support your answer.

8.9 Figure 8.9b illustrates the case in which *a.topaddress* is false and *b.topaddress* is true. Draw a similar diagram for the case in which *a.topaddress* is true and *b.topaddress* is false. Does *Concatenate* yield the correct result in this case?

8.10 We said that in order to guarantee alignment of all of the fields, we would
- Make the relative address of each field divisible by the alignment of that field.
- Make the address of the record divisible by the "most stringent" of the field alignments.

Then the address of a field (which is the sum of the address of the record and the relative address of the field) would be divisible by the alignment of that field.

(a) Suppose the field alignments could be arbitrary integers. Show that this condition is satisfied if the record address is divisible by the least common multiple of the field alignments.

(b) Suppose the field alignments are powers of 2. Show that this condition is satisfied if the record address is divisible by the maximum of the field alignments.

8.11 Draw a snapshot of the set of activation records stored in memory during the execution of line 7 in Figure 8.3b. Make up appropriate addresses, under the assumptions that a new activation record is stored below existing ones and that the local storage area for an activation is stored below the argument list for that activation.

CHAPTER 8 TYPES AND DATA MAPPING

8.12 Look up the descriptions of the VAX CALLG and CALLS instructions in the VAX Architecture Handbook or in some textbook that discusses VAX architecture and assembly language.
   (a) Either attack or defend our assumption that there is no necessary relationship between the address of the argument list and the address of the local storage area.
   (b) Suppose that a requirement for our Pascal compiler was that modules written in Pascal could be invoked by programs written in other languages. Would that requirement affect your answer to (a)? Explain briefly.
   (c) Why do we require that the called routine make no changes in the argument list? (Hint: An attempt to write into the area of memory containing the program itself will cause the program to abort.)

8.13 A Pascal **with** statement creates pseudo variables corresponding to the fields of the record variable specified by that statement. These pseudo variables are accessed relative to the address of a record variable. Because the record variable is often the result of some computation, the compiler cannot assume that the address will be known at compile time. Suppose the address of the record variable of a **with** statement is stored in the local storage area of the current activation record, just as though it were a local variable of pointer type.
   (a) Explain why the number of bytes that must be reserved is independent of the type of the record variable.
   (b) How many bytes of VAX memory must be reserved to address the record variables for the statement **with** *a,b,c* **do** *S*?
   (c) During what part of the execution will the space reserved in the local storage area to address record variables contain useful information?
   (d) How many bytes of VAX memory must be reserved to address the record variables for the following sequence of **with** statements?

   with *a,b,c* **do** *S*; **with** *d,e* **do** *T*

8.14 For most machines, all alignments are powers of 2. Show how $Align(x,y)$, the basic computation of the *Concatenate* operation, can be implemented by an addition and a bitwise-and in this case.

8.15 Write code for the storage-allocation visits to an *ArrayTypeDef* construct.
   (a) How will you obtain the bounds of the array?
   (b) What information must be computed before the storage-allocation visit *begins*?
   (c) Show that your implementation is compatible in terms of information flow with the visit to a *RecordTypeDef* defined in Figure 8.7.

8.16 According to the Pascal standard, the identifiers *light*, *intensity*, and *filter* are defined in the region consisting of lines 3 through 8 in Figure 8.14. Similarly, *color* and *opacity* are defined in the region consisting of lines 6 and 7. All of the enumerated constant identifiers are defined in the region consisting of lines 1-10.
   (a) Draw the source program tree that the compiler would derive from Figure 8.14.
   (b) The interface for *TypeVisit*1, given in Figure 7.9, asserts that on entry to the routine the environment for "the current region" has been established. What is "the current region" when the compiler visits the *Type* node derived from lines 3-9 of Figure 8.14?
   (c) *TypeVisit*1 contains a **case** statement with one alternative for each construct that is classed as a *Type*. Write the code for the *EnumeratedTypeNode* alternative. How will this code access the environment corresponding to the region consisting of lines 1-10 from Figure 8.14?

```
1   procedure P;
2     type T = record
3       light: (red,green,blue);
4       intensity: real;
5       filter: record
6         color: (magenta,yellow,cyan);
7         opacity: real;
8       end;
9     end;
10  end;
```

Figure 8.14
A Pascal record declaration

- **(d)** Explain why the *RecordTypeNode* alternative must invoke *FieldListVisit1*.
- **(e)** Should *TypeVisit1* establish a new scope before invoking *FieldListVisit1* in the alternative for a *RecordTypeNode*? Explain briefly.
- **(f)** Implement the procedures *FieldListVisit1*, *RecordSectionVisit1*, *TagVisit1*, and *VariantVisit1*.

8.17 Implement the *SubrangeTypeNode* case for procedure *TypeVisit2* (Figure 8.10).

8.18 Consider the procedure *VariantVisit2* that is invoked in Figure 8.12.
- **(a)** What should the interface for *VariantVisit2* be?
- **(b)** How many times should the list of constants that is the left child of a *Variant*-class node be visited? Explain briefly.
- **(c)** Give an interface specification for each procedure that visits constant children of a *Variant*-class node.
- **(d)** Write the body of *VariantVisit2*.

9
Action Mapping and the Target Program Tree

The assignment statement of Figure 9.1a can be implemented as the VAX instruction sequence shown in Figure 9.1c, given the data mapping of Figure 9.1b. Let's examine the decision process that a compiler could follow to arrive at this implementation. Relative addresses for the parameter and variables are calculated by the data mapping task and left in the definition table, as discussed in Chapter 8. Based upon the operand types, the compiler can deduce that each "+" must be implemented by a VAX floating-point addition operation, the "−" by a floating-point subtraction, and the "/" by a floating-point division. The data flow (i.e., which operations result in operands of the division, and where the result of the division is used) can be determined from the structure of the source program tree. Data flow relationships provide a partial evaluation order. (In this case, $y - 1.0$ and $z + 1.0$ must be evaluated before the division, but the address of q could be evaluated before, after, or between those two evaluations.) The compiler must select a total order for the evaluations that is compatible with this partial order and allocate VAX registers to hold the intermediate results. Finally, specific instructions must be selected to implement the desired operations. Some operations (such as the 32-bit integer addition needed to calculate the field address) may be implemented as parts of operand access functions, rather than by separate instructions.

```
type r = record a,b:real end;
procedure p(var q: r);
  var x,y,z: real;
  begin
    ...
    x:=q.b+(y−1.0)/(z+1.0);
    ...
  end;
```

(a) A Pascal program fragment

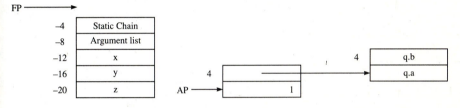

(b) The result of the data mapping task

```
SUBF3   #1.0,−16(FP),R0         y−1.0
ADDF3   #1.0,−20(FP),R1         z+1.0
DIVF2   R1,R0                   (y−1.0)/(z+1.0)
MOVL    4(AP),R1                Address of q
ADDF3   R0,4(R1),−12(FP)        x:=q.b+(y−1.0)/(z+1.0)
```

(c) A possible implementation of the assignment statement from (a)

Figure 9.1
Implementing an algorithm

Clearly, the decision process is a rather complex one. In order to control this complexity, the compiler model of Table 1.1 separates the concerns of mapping source language constructs into equivalent target language constructs from the concerns of allocating target machine resources and selecting specific instructions. Action mapping, a subtask of translation, deduces the target machine operations (such as floating-point addition) that must be used to implement the source language operations. It creates a target program tree that embodies the data flow relationships among these operations, decorating the leaves of that tree with operand access functions deduced from the results of data mapping. Determination of the final execution order, allocation of registers for intermediate results, and selection of instructions or access functions to realize the target operations are all left to the code generator.

The separation of concerns between the action mapper and the code generator is not arbitrary; it arises naturally from the origins of those concerns. For example, the concerns leading the compiler to map real addition into floating-point addition stem from the relationship between Pascal and the VAX, while those leading it to implement that addition with an ADDF3 instruction stem from the properties of VAX floating-point addition.

Section 9.1 develops a target program tree structure from a particular separation of concerns, using this development to illustrate general design principles. The constructs of the source language can be expressed in terms of this target tree structure, as shown in Section 9.2. Examples of more complex target program tree design are discussed in Section 9.3, emphasizing that target program tree structure is *not* completely independent of the source language.

In this chapter we simplify the action mapping problem by assuming that every operator in the source language describes only one operation. For example, we assume that "+" can describe only the "integer addition" operation. In most programming languages, however, "+" describes at least the two operations "integer addition" and "real addition." We say that "+" is *overloaded* when it describes more than one operation.

It turns out that the presence of overloading can be handled in a very general way by some additional computations on contextual information. These computations are rather complex, but they do not affect the overall process of mapping actions. We therefore defer consideration of overloaded operators to Chapter 10.

9.1 THE TARGET PROGRAM TREE

When discussing source program trees in Chapter 4, we could refer to a language definition that was itself couched in terms of trees. Although we made some small adjustments in the source language structure to simplify the compiler's task, basically we encoded the model provided by the language designer. The situation is quite different with respect to target program constructs. Machine architects do not think in terms of trees, and target machine descriptions don't mention them. Therefore, this section develops a rationale for the target program tree structure.

The basis for a target program tree design is the desired separation of concerns between the translator and the code generator: Certain decisions will be made during translation and others during code generation. Because the target program tree is the interface between these two processes, it must reflect the decisions made by the former and provide information to support the decisions made by the latter.

In this book we shall defer three classes of decision to the code generator:
- Allocation of machine resources to intermediate results.
- Selection of particular instructions to implement target operations.
- Determination of the order in which to evaluate operands of an operator.

The first class of decision is illustrated by the allocation of R0 to hold the value of $(y - 1.0)$ in Figure 9.1c. Selection of DIVF2 (rather than, say, DIVF3) to implement the VAX floating point division illustrates the second class of deferred decision. Determining that the division will occur before the computation of the address of $q.b$ is a decision of the third class. Each of the next three subsections is devoted to one class of decision and how that class affects the design of the target program tree.

9.1.1 Resource Allocation Decisions

In order to allocate resources to intermediate results, the code generator must know where each such result is created and where it is used. Intermediate results are created by VAX operations such as floating-point addition; they are *not* created by operations such as jumps. Every VAX operation can be classified according to whether it yields a value, and only those operations classified as yielding values can create intermediate results. Moreover, if an operation yields a value, then that value will *always* be considered an intermediate result; the action mapping task must arrange to have that result used by some other operation.

Every node of the target program tree corresponds to some operation of the target program. If an operation yields a value, then the corresponding node is classified as a *Datum* node; otherwise it is classified as an *Item* node. Thus, the code generator knows that every intermediate result for which it must allocate resources is created at a *Datum*-class node, and that every *Datum*-class node creates an intermediate result. The intermediate result created by a *Datum*-class node will be used by the parent of that node, and not by any other nodes.

Figure 9.2 shows a possible target program tree for the assignment statement from Figure 9.1. The node corresponding to the floating-point subtraction (*SubF*) translating ($y - 1.0$) is a *Datum*-class node because it corresponds to an operation yielding a value. That value must be considered an intermediate result by the code generator. It is used as an operand of the division operation (*DivF*), the parent of the node corresponding to the floating-point subtraction. On the other hand, the node corresponding to the floating-point move operation (*MovF*) translating the assignment to x is an *Item*-class node, because it corresponds to an operation that does not yield a value.

Notice that the order of the children in Figure 9.2 is the order in which the corresponding operands appear in the VAX instruction (see Figure 9.1c). Thus, #1.0 is the left child of the *SubF* node and the *SubF* node is the right child of the *DivF* node. This order is exactly the reverse of the order in which the source language operands are written. Establishing the proper order for a node's children is part of the process of mapping from Pascal concepts to VAX concepts.

It is important to realize that the order of the children of a target tree node does not necessarily determine the order in which the values represented by those nodes are computed. Thus, Figure 9.2 does not assert that the *AddF* operation is carried out before the *SubF* operation. It merely specifies that the result of the *AddF* is the first operand of the *DivF* and the result of the *SubF* is the second. We will discuss the question of evaluation order further in Section 9.1.3.

We require that a value represented by a *Datum*-class node must be directly usable by a target machine operation. This constrains the kinds of value that *Datum*-class nodes can represent. Each of the following kinds of value can be directly used by some VAX operation:

- Integer values of length 1, 2, 4, or 8 bytes
- Floating-point values of length 4, 8, or 16 bytes

These seven kinds of value are therefore the only ones that can be yielded by the *Datum*-class nodes of a VAX target program tree. For example, the leaves of Fig-

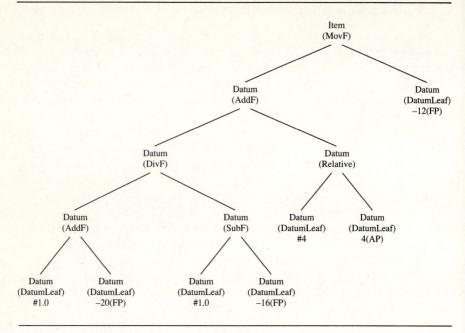

Figure 9.2
A target program tree fragment for $x := q.b + (y - 1.0)/(z + 1.0)$

ure 9.2 that correspond to the parameter q and the local variables x, y, and z all yield 4-byte integer values that will be interpreted as memory addresses by the operations that use them. The interior node corresponding to the *Relative* operator also yields a 4-byte integer value that will be interpreted as a memory address; all other *Datum*-class nodes in Figure 9.2 yield 4-byte floating-point values.

Machine instructions are constrained not only in the kinds of values they can use, but also in the places from which they can obtain those values. Each instruction is capable of accessing some number of operands, and each operand can be accessed via one of a specified set of *access functions*. An access function has two parts: an *addressing mode*, which defines the way in which the operand value will be obtained, and zero or more *parameters*, which define a particular operand. For example, the SUBF3 instruction in Figure 9.1c is capable of accessing three operands. The first two operands can be accessed via any VAX access function. In Figure 9.1c, the first operand's access function consists of the "literal" addressing mode and the parameter "1.0". This means that the value 1.0 will be obtained from the instruction itself (as defined by the literal addressing mode). The second operand's access function consists of the "displacement" addressing mode and two parameters "-16" and "13". This means that -16 will be added to the contents of register 13 (the frame pointer) and the result used as a memory address to access the operand value.

The third operand of a SUBF3 instruction can be accessed only by a "write" access function—one that specifies a register or a memory location. Thus, an access function with the literal addressing mode would be illegal for the third operand of SUBF3. In Figure 9.1c, the third operand's access function consists of the "register" addressing mode and the parameter "0". This means that the result of the floating-point subtraction will be written into register 0.

Because every value yielded by a *Datum*-class node must be directly usable by a VAX instruction, any intermediate result can be described completely by a VAX access function. VAX access functions are represented internally by objects of type *Operand* (Figure 9.3). *Operand* is a complex data structure because the VAX provides a rich set of access functions for its instructions. Three of these access functions were described in the previous paragraphs. We shall discuss each of the others in detail when we first use it in representing a source language construct. You should not try to master all of the addressing modes in Figure 9.3 at this point.

Access functions that describe leaf values are provided by the action mapper; those describing values at interior nodes are determined during code generation. Consider the rightmost leaf of Figure 9.2, which represents an access to x. X is a local variable of the procedure, and Figure 9.1b shows that its address is 12 bytes lower than the address contained in the frame pointer register FP. The VAX's displacement addressing mode (*disp* in Figure 9.3) specifies an address as an offset from the contents of a register. Field n of the *Operand* record gives the register parameter of this access function, and field *offset* gives the offset parameter. Thus, the action mapper will represent x by an *Operand* with $mode = disp$, $n = 13$ (register 13 is the frame pointer FP), and $offset = -12$. The leaves representing accesses to local variables y and z are decorated by the action mapper with similar *Operand* values, differing only in the content of the *offset* field.

Figure 9.1b shows that the parameter list of a procedure is accessed via the argument pointer AP (register 12) rather than the frame pointer FP. The displacement addressing mode is still used, so the leaf representing q is decorated by an *Operand* with $mode = disp$, $n = 12$, and $offset = 4$. Again, this decoration is provided by the action mapper at the time the target program tree is built. Thus, the translator makes decisions about how Pascal local variables and parameters are to be mapped onto the memory model of the target machine and transmits those decisions to the code generator via the leaf access functions. Decisions about how resources are allocated to intermediate results are not made by the translator—it does not decorate interior nodes of the tree with access functions.

9.1.2 Instruction Selection Decisions

The usual reason for deferring a decision about instruction selection is that the best instruction in a given context is determined by the pattern of machine resources allocated to its operands. But those operands are often intermediate results, and allocation of machine resources to intermediate results is carried out

```
type
  AddressingMode = (                          (* VAX addressing modes *)
    lit,                                      (* Literal value *)
    ref,                                      (* Symbolic label *)
    reg,                                      (* Rn *)
    regdef,regdefndx,                         (* (Rn), (Rn)[Rx] *)
    autodecr,autodecrndx,                     (* -(Rn), -(Rn)[Rx] *)
    autoincr,autoincrndx,                     (* (Rn)+ , (Rn)+[Rx] *)
    autoincrdef,autoincrdefndx,               (* @(Rn)+ , @(Rn)+[Rx] *)
    disp,dispndx,                             (* offset(Rn), offset(Rn)[Rx] *)
    dispdef,dispdefndx,                       (* @offset(Rn), @offset(Rn)[Rx] *)
    symb,symbndx,                             (* place(Rn), place(Rn)[Rx] *)
    symbdef,symbdefndx);                      (* @place(Rn), @place(Rn)[Rx] *)

  Operand = record                            (* Description of an operand *)
    case mode: AddressingMode of
      lit: (v: ExtValue);                     (* Literal value (see Figure 2.4) *)
      ref: (lbl: ExtValue);                   (* Symbolic label *)
      reg,regdef,autodecr,autoincr,
      autoincrdef,disp,dispdef,symb,symbdef,
      regdefndx,autodecrndx,autoincrndx,
      autoincrdefndx,dispndx,dispdefndx,
      symbndx,symbdefndx:                     (* Register or memory access *)
        (n,x: integer;                        (* Base and index registers *)
         case AddressingMode of
           reg,regdef,autodecr,autoincr,
           autoincrdef,
           regdefndx,autodecrndx,autoincrndx,
           autoincrdefndx:
             ;                                (* No displacement *)
           disp,dispdef,dispndx,dispdefndx:
             (offset: ExtValue);              (* Absolute displacement *)
           symb,symbdef,symbndx,symbdefndx:
             (place: ExtValue);               (* Symbolic displacement *)
         end);
    end;
```

Figure 9.3
Description of a target operand

by the code generator. Therefore, the information necessary to select the appropriate instruction is simply not available to the action mapper. We can conclude that the decision to defer instruction selection is a consequence of the decision to defer resource allocation.

Even though the action mapper cannot determine the best *instruction* to carry out a given task, it must determine the correct machine *operation*. Longword addition (*AddL*, Table 9.1) is a typical VAX operation that can be implemented by a variety of VAX instructions. It performs a two's-complement addition of two 4-byte values and yields a 4-byte value as its result. The most general implementation of longword addition is the ADDL3 instruction, which accepts two arbitrary

9.1 THE TARGET PROGRAM TREE

TABLE 9.1 SOME VAX TARGET TREE NODES ILLUSTRATING INSTRUCTION SELECTION

Construct	Structure
AddL	(*Datum,Datum*): *Datum*
CvtBL	(*Datum*): *Datum*
Indirect	(*Datum*): *Datum*
MovB	(*Datum,Datum*): *Item*
MovF	(*Datum,Datum*): *Item*
MovL	(*Datum,Datum*): *Item*
MovW	(*Datum,Datum*): *Item*
NegL	(*Datum*): *Datum*
Relative	(*Datum,Datum*): *Datum*

operands and stores their sum in an arbitrary register or memory location. If the same machine resource can be allocated to the right operand and to the result, then ADDL2 provides a slightly cheaper implementation of *AddL*. When the left operand of an ADDL2 is "1", the still cheaper INCL can be used.

It is important to understand the distinction made in the last paragraph between *AddL*, which represents an operation that the VAX is capable of carrying out, and (say) ADDL3, which is a particular instruction that implements the *AddL* operation. The action mapper would select the *AddL* operation to implement a source language construct such as Pascal integer addition. This selection is based on the relationship between Pascal and the VAX. Selection of the instruction to implement the *AddL* operation, however, is based on the locations of the operands of that *AddL* operation. (We will always use *italics* for the names of operations and CAPS for the names of instructions.)

Remember that the target program tree must reflect the decisions made by the action mapper and provide information to support the decisions made by the code generator. The action mapper determines the VAX operation to be used in each computation and provides these operations to the code generator by building specific target program tree nodes. Table 9.1 gives the structure of some typical operation nodes built by the action mapper. Each of these operations is representative of a class of "similar" operations—operations with the same structure and overall behavior. For example, *AddL* is typical of a wide variety of arithmetic operations that accept two values and calculate a third. This class contains other operations on longwords (such as *SubL* and *MpyL*), as well as the same operation on operands with different lengths (such as *AddB* and *AddW*). We will discuss each of the operations that appears in Table 9.1, and leave you to extend those discussions to similar operations.

If an operation can be implemented only by one target machine instruction, then the target program tree node alone provides enough information to support the code generator's instruction selection decision. *CvtBL* (Table 9.1) is an example of a VAX operation that can be implemented only by one particular VAX instruction. It converts the byte representation of a value to the longword representation of the same value, and it is implemented by the VAX instruction CVTBL.

If an operation can be implemented by any one of several instructions, as is the case for the *AddL* operation, then the code generator must use other information available in the target program tree to make its decision. The target program tree node specifies the operation, and this limits the set of candidate instructions. The particular instruction is then determined by decorations of the node and its children. We will discuss this decision process in detail in Chapter 11.

There is only one VAX instruction that can implement each of the operations *MovB*, *MovF*, *MovL*, and *MovW* (Table 9.1). Nevertheless, instruction selection decisions are required of the code generator for these target program tree nodes: Depending upon the pattern of operands, it may be possible to combine the operation described by, say, a *MovF* node with that of its left child. The generation of the instruction sequence of Figure 9.1c from the target program tree of Figure 9.2 is an example of this combination. The ADDF3 instruction at the end of the sequence in Figure 9.1c stores its result in the location specified by the right child of the *MovF* node at the top of Figure 9.2, thus implementing both the *AddF* operation and the *MovF* operation. (We shall discuss how the code generator makes this decision in Chapter 11.)

The child of an *Indirect* node always represents the address of a memory location containing a 4-byte integer that is itself a memory address. *Indirect* yields the address stored at the location addressed by its child. The left child of a *Relative* construct is an integer and the right child is an address. *Relative* yields the address that is the sum of the values of its children. Each of these operations can be implemented by a single VAX instruction, but might also be implementable by an access function. For example, the *Relative* operation in Figure 9.2 is implemented in Figure 9.1c by the access function "4(R1)". The decision about whether an *Indirect* or *Relative* operation can be implemented via an access function depends upon the resources allocated to the children, and therefore must be deferred to the code generator.

Any integer or floating-point value can be negated; *NegL* (Table 9.1) is typical of these unary negation operations (one for each of the seven kinds of value that a *Datum*-class node can yield). There is only one VAX instruction implementing each negation operation.

9.1.3 Execution-Order Decisions

When a target program is finally executed, its instructions are carried out in a particular order. This order is the result of decisions made by the action mapper, decisions made by the code generator, and decisions made by the program itself. For example, consider the program fragment shown in Figure 9.4. The action mapper decides on the basic "shape" of the code to implement the Pascal statement **while** *B* **do** *S*:

        Jump to L2
L1:   Instruction sequence implementing the statement *S*
L2:   Instruction sequence implementing a jump to L1 if condition *B* is true

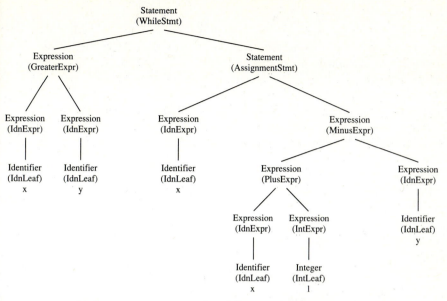

(a) A source program tree for **while** $x > y$ **do** $x := (x+1) - y$;

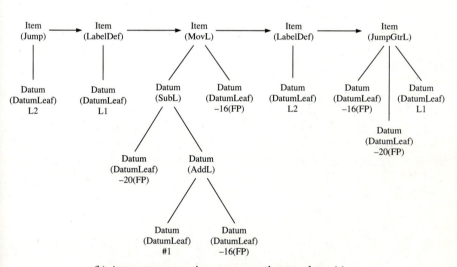

(b) A target program item sequence that translates (a)

```
        BR      L2
L1:     ADDL3   #1,-16(FP),R0           ; x+1
        SUBL3   -20(FP),R0,-16(FP)      ; x:=(x+1)-y
L2:     CMPL    -16(FP),-20(FP)         ; x>y
        BGTR    L1
```

(c) An instruction sequence that implements (b)

Figure 9.4
Decisions about sequencing

The code generator determines the order of the operations making up the assignment statement, and the jump instructions control the final execution sequence. How is each of these decisions expressed, and how is support for future decisions provided?

The structure of the target program tree reflects the execution-order decisions made by the action mapper. Notice in Figure 9.4b that the action mapper has produced a sequence of five subtrees. The code generator is constrained to produce instructions for the elements of a sequence in the order in which the elements appear in that sequence. Thus, the instruction implementing the *Jump* operation must precede the implementation of the *LabelDef* operation for L1; this, in turn, must precede the instructions implementing the tree rooted in the *Item*-class *MovL* construct, and so forth.

Decisions about the order in which the instructions implementing the assignment statement will be written are deferred to the code generator by expressing that construct as a tree rather than a sequence. The code generator may produce instructions for the nodes of a tree in any order compatible with the tree's structure: Instructions implementing the child of a node must precede instructions implementing the node itself, but no order is implied among unrelated nodes.

The labels L1 and L2 are used to establish cross-references between an instruction and a memory location to which that instruction refers, so that execution-order decisions can be taken as the program runs. They are represented in the target program tree by *ref*-class *Operand* records (Figure 9.3). These records are used to decorate *Datum* leaves appearing as children of constructs like those listed in Table 9.2.

LabelDef marks the destination for one or more jump instructions. This target program tree construct does not correspond to any VAX instruction; it is used by the code generator simply to provide information to the assembly module. The compiler designer must make a *LabelDef* construct available, regardless of the machine for which the target program tree is being specified.

The labels in Figure 9.4b implement *internal* cross-references, in which the instruction and the location to which it refers are in the same program. Programmer-defined labels in Pascal are also internal cross-references. Internal

TABLE 9.2 SOME VAX TARGET TREE NODES USED IN ESTABLISHING INSTRUCTION ORDER

Construct	Structure
Calls	(*Datum,Datum*): *Item*
Jump	(*Datum*): *Item*
JumpGtrL	(*Datum,Datum,Datum*): *Item*
LabelDef	(*Datum*): *Item*
SequenceDatum	(*Item$^+$,Datum*): *Datum*

cross-references can be established by the compiler, since it knows about both the instruction and the location to which it refers. All that is needed is a unique name for the referenced location. This can be provided by associating a unique external integer value with each location, and storing that value in the *ref*-class *Operand* representing the label.

A call to a library routine involves an *external* cross-reference. The call instruction is in the program being compiled, but the location to which it refers is not. Since the compiler knows nothing about the location referred to by the instruction, it cannot establish the cross-reference. An analogous situation arises when a library routine (*sqrt*, for example) is being compiled. Here the compiler knows about a location that will be referred to by instructions in other programs (the entry point of *sqrt*), but it cannot establish the cross-reference because it does not know about the various instructions referring to that location (the callers of *sqrt*).

Like an internal cross-reference, an external cross-reference must associate a unique name with each referenced location. External integers cannot be used for this purpose, however, because there would be no way to guarantee that the same integer value would be associated with a particular location in several compilations. The solution is to store the symbol string ("sqrt," for example) as an external string value in the *ref*-class *Operand* representing the label.

Our compiler will always implement a conditional transfer of control by a comparison or test instruction, followed by a conditional jump instruction. Because these instructions are invariably paired, the sequence is represented in the target program tree by a single operation. The *JumpGtrL* construct listed in Table 9.2 is typical of comparison operations, which provide each of the six relations on each of the seven kinds of integer and floating-point values. *Jump* is used to describe an unconditional transfer of control.

One straightforward implementation of a function call on the VAX involves the following sequence of actions:

1. Evaluate the function's arguments in reverse order, pushing each onto the stack as it is obtained.
2. Execute the CALLS instruction, with the address of the called function and the number of arguments as operands.
3. On completion of the function, execute the instruction following CALLS; the function's value can be found in R0.

Figure 9.5 illustrates this implementation.

Figure 9.5 introduces a new interaction between execution-order decisions and resource allocation decisions: The action mapper must guarantee that the arguments of the function are evaluated and placed on the stack in a certain order—the order expected by the function body (see Section 8.1.3). The code generator, on the other hand, must be able to decide when the function invocation should take place relative to the other computations in the expression containing it. Thus, the fixed-order argument evaluation must be treated as a unit in the arbitrary-order expression evaluation. To express this relation, there must be a

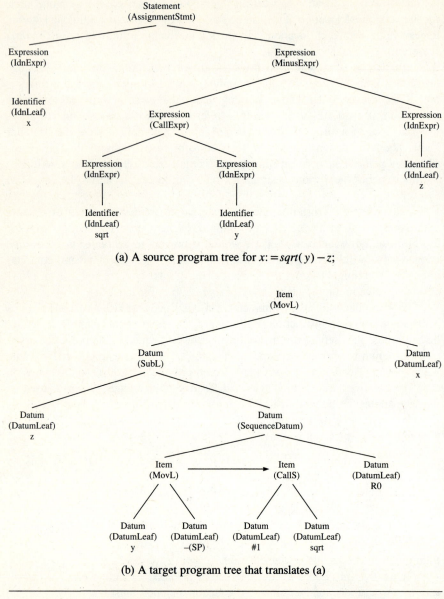

Figure 9.5
A sequence as a component of a tree node

way to describe a sequence of *Item*-class nodes and a *Datum*-class node as a single *Datum*-class construct.

SequenceDatum (Table 9.2) provides the necessary description mechanism. The code generator is constrained to implement the code for the component item sequence, followed by code for the component datum. (When producing the code for the sequence, the normal constraints for sequences apply, preserving the argument evaluation order.) Thus, in Figure 9.5b, the code generator will decide when to generate code for the *SequenceDatum* node relative to the leaf nodes for z and x. (Code for the *SequenceDatum* node must be generated before code for the *SubL* node, because it is a child of that node.) The code for the *SequenceDatum* node consists of the following sequence, assuming that y is a local variable with offset -16:

MOVL	-16(FP),$-$(SP)	; Push y onto the stack
CALLS	#1,sqrt	; Invoke the routine
		; ('sqrt' is an external cross-reference)
		; The routine leaves its result in R0

($-$(SP) specifies that register 14, the stack pointer, will be decremented by the length of the operand, and then the operand's value will be stored at the location addressed by the result.) Notice that there is no code generated for the leaf describing R0. This leaf merely establishes the location where the result will be found.

9.2 HOW TO CONSTRUCT A TARGET PROGRAM TREE

The target program tree is constructed by a module whose interface (Figure 9.6) is identical to that of the source program tree construction module (Figure 4.4), except for the routine names. You should review Section 4.1 for a discussion of the general techniques by which trees are represented and constructed, as this material applies to target tree construction as well as source tree construction.

TargetConstruct is an enumerated type specifying all of the possible target program tree constructs. The identifiers appearing in the first columns of Table 9.1 and Table 9.2 (*AddL*, *Jump*, etc.) are all elements of *TargetConstruct*. We will not define *TargetConstruct* completely in this text. From time to time we will introduce target program tree constructs and give them names; you should simply assume that all such names are elements of the enumerated type *TargetConstruct*.

Target tree construction operations are invoked during a traversal of the source program tree. They must be invoked in the proper order, because the children of a node must be placed on the target tree construction module's internal stack in the proper order. For simplicity, we assume that the source program tree traversal during which the target program tree is generated does nothing else. It is this traversal that carries out the action mapping task, and the collection of visit procedures used during this traversal constitute the action mapper. In this book, the name of the action mapping procedure for source program tree node class C will always be *MapC*. Thus, all nodes of class *Expression* will be mapped by the procedure *MapExpression*, while all nodes of class *Statement* will be mapped by procedure *MapStatement*. The entry condition for an action mapping procedure is always that all necessary contextual information is available to that procedure. If a

procedure *TargetLeaf*(*c*: *TargetConstruct*; **var** *l*: *Operand*);
    (* Build a leaf of the target program tree
        On entry-
            c = kind of leaf to be built
            l = data to be stored in the leaf
        On exit-
            The constructed leaf has been added to the stack
    *)

procedure *TargetNode*(*c*: *TargetConstruct*);
    (* Build an interior node of the target program tree
        On entry-
            c = kind of node to be built
        On exit-
            The constructed node has replaced its children on the stack
    *)

procedure *EmptyTargetSeq*;
    (* Build an empty sequence of target program tree nodes
        On exit-
            An empty sequence has been added to the stack
    *)

procedure *ExtendTargetSeq*;
    (* Add a target program tree node to an existing sequence
        On exit-
            The extended sequence has replaced its components on the stack
    *)

procedure *TargetTreeInit*;
    (* Initialize the target program tree construction module *)

procedure *TargetTreeFinl*;
    (* Finalize the target program tree construction module *)

Figure 9.6
Target tree construction operations

mapping procedure constructs a subtree rooted in a *Datum*-class node, that node is left at the top of the target tree construction module's internal stack on exit from the mapping procedure. If a mapping procedure constructs a sequence of subtrees rooted in *Item*-class nodes, those nodes have been added to an item list that is at the top of the target tree construction module's internal stack on exit from the mapping procedure.

No additional source program errors will be detected during action mapping, and thus there is no reason to map the actions if fatal errors have already been detected. The error module maintains a count of the errors that have been detected at each severity level (array *ErrorCount*, Figure 2.3), so the translation module can avoid entering the action mapping task if the source program has fatal errors.

9.2 HOW TO CONSTRUCT A TARGET PROGRAM TREE

This means that no error recovery code need be included in the action mapping procedures. If an inconsistency is uncovered during action mapping (such as an attempt to map an undefined identifier), that inconsistency stems from a mistake in the compiler itself, and should lead to a deadly error report.

We consider the mapping of a simple subset of Pascal constructs in the remainder of this section. Our intent is to show how we represent source language constructs, given a target program tree structure designed according to the principles of Section 9.1, and how that representation is actually built. Section 9.2.1 covers statement mapping, Section 9.2.2 deals with expressions, and Section 9.2.3 discusses identifiers.

9.2.1 Statement Mapping

Figure 9.7a shows a fragment of a Pascal source program tree. Assume that all of the identifiers have been declared as local integer variables. The target program tree of Figure 9.7b represents a VAX algorithm that has the same meaning as the Pascal algorithm represented by Figure 9.7a. (Leaves of Figure 9.7b are marked with identifiers, rather than the corresponding *Operand* values, to simplify the discussion.)

Consider for a moment the relationship between Figure 9.7a and Figure 9.7b. The top-level structure of Figure 9.7b is a list of six items whose meanings can be described as follows:

A conditional jump implementing the test of the **if** statement

The implementation of the **then** part

An unconditional jump skipping the **else** part

A label definition that names the **else** part

The implementation of the **else** part

A label definition that names the continuation of the program

A little thought will show that the target program tree fragment corresponding to *any* Pascal **if**-**then**-**else** statement can be described in exactly this way. Of course, the condition, **then** part, and **else** part may each be implemented with a longer list, but the overall structure will remain the same. Effectively, the list of six items constitutes a "template" specifying the relationships among the labels and jumps that implement the conditional statement. A similar template for the **while** statement can be deduced from Figure 9.4:

An unconditional jump skipping the body of the **while** statement

A label definition that names the body

The implementation of the body

A label definition that names the condition of the **while** statement

A conditional jump implementing the test of the **while** statement

The template for the **repeat** statement is almost identical to that for the **while**. It is missing the jump skipping the body and the label naming the condition, and the

244   CHAPTER 9   ACTION MAPPING AND THE TARGET PROGRAM TREE

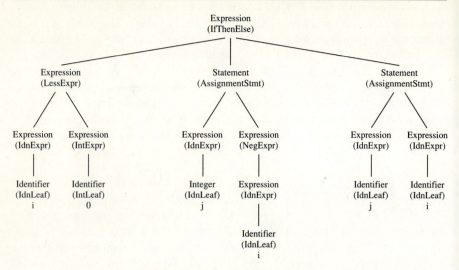

(a) A source program tree fragment for **if** $i<0$ **then** $j:=-i$ **else** $j:=i$;

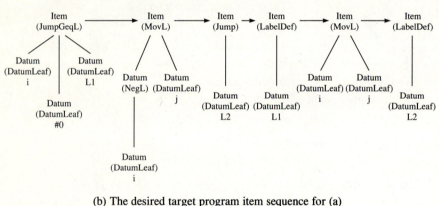

(b) The desired target program item sequence for (a)

Figure 9.7
The representation of a Pascal conditional statement

conditional jump transfers when the condition is false (in the **while** it transfers when the condition is true).

Figure 9.8 shows how these templates are incorporated into the *MapStatement* procedure, which constructs the target program tree fragment for a *Statement*-class source program tree node. As with all visit procedures, the body of *MapStatement* consists of a **case** statement with one alternative for each source construct in the class that it processes. The *IfThenElse* alternative implements the template illustrated by Figure 9.7b. First, *MapStatement* must generate label operands L1 and L2. Each of the remaining lines produces one of the six elements

procedure *GenerateLabel*(**var** *newlbl: Operand*);
(* Generate a new label operand *)
. . .

procedure *MapStatement*(*n: SourceTree*);
(* Create a target tree fragment corresponding to a statement
  On entry-
    An item sequence is being built
  On exit-
    The item sequence has been extended to include the implementation
      of the statement represented by node *n*
*)
var
  L1,L2: Operand;
  s: SourceSequence;
begin
case *n*↑.*Kind* **of**
  IfThenStmt:
    begin *GenerateLabel*(*L1*);
    MapCondition(*n*↑.*IfExpr,false,L1*);
    MapStatement(*n*↑.*ThenPart*);
    TargetLeaf(*DatumLeaf,L1*); *TargetNode*(*LabelDef*); *ExtendTargetSeq*;
    end;
  IfThenElseStmt:
    begin *GenerateLabel*(*L1*); *GenerateLabel*(*L2*);
    MapCondition(*n*↑.*IfExpr,false,L1*);
    MapStatement(*n*↑.*ThenPart*);
    TargetLeaf(*DatumLeaf,L2*); *TargetNode*(*Jump*); *ExtendTargetSeq*;
    TargetLeaf(*DatumLeaf,L1*); *TargetNode*(*LabelDef*); *ExtendTargetSeq*;
    MapStatement(*n*↑.*ElsePart*);
    TargetLeaf(*DatumLeaf,L2*); *TargetNode*(*LabelDef*); *ExtendTargetSeq*;
    end;
  WhileStmt:
    begin *GenerateLabel*(*L1*); *GenerateLabel*(*L2*);
    TargetLeaf(*DatumLeaf,L2*); *TargetNode*(*Jump*); *ExtendTargetSeq*;
    TargetLeaf(*DatumLeaf,L1*); *TargetNode*(*LabelDef*); *ExtendTargetSeq*;
    MapStatement(*n*↑.*WhileBody*);
    TargetLeaf(*DatumLeaf,L2*); *TargetNode*(*LabelDef*); *ExtendTargetSeq*;
    MapCondition(*n*↑.*WhileExpr,true,L1*);
    end;
  . . .
  CompoundStmt:
    begin *s*: = *n*↑.*StatementList*;
    while *s* < > **nil do begin** *MapStatement*(*s*↑.*Node*); *s*: = *s*↑.*Next* **end**;
    end;
  AssignmentStmt:
    begin
    MapExpression(*n*↑.*Source*);
    if (*n*↑.*Source.ExprTypeKey* = *IntegerType*) **and**
          (*n*↑.*Destination.ExprTypeKey* = *RealType*) **then**
      TargetNode(*CvtLF*);
    MapExpression(*n*↑.*Destination*);
    if (*n*↑.*Destination.ExprTypeKey* = *BooleanType*) **then** *TargetNode*(*MovB*)
    else if (*n*↑.*Destination.ExprTypeKey* = *IntegerType*) **then** *TargetNode*(*MovL*)
    else *TargetNode*(*MovF*);
    ExtendTargetSeq;
    end;
  end;
end;

Figure 9.8
Statement mapping

of the template. *MapCondition* is invoked to build the first element, and *MapStatement* to build the second. The third element of the template is constructed directly: *MapStatement* builds the label leaf specifying L2, builds a *Jump* operation using that leaf as an operand, then adds the resulting item to the current item list. Construction of the remainder of the sequence is handled in a similar fashion, the label definitions being built directly and *MapStatement* being used for the **else**-part.

MapCondition is used to create a conditional transfer of control. Its parameters are the node describing the Boolean expression that defines the condition, the value of that expression that should result in a jump, and the label of the instruction to which the jump should occur. (Note that the condition of the **if**-statement must transfer control when the expression yields *false*, but the condition of the **while**-statement must transfer control when the expression yields *true*.)

For the moment, assume that the Boolean expression contains a single relational operator, no Boolean operators, and only integer subexpressions. (Chapter 10 shows how the general case is handled.) The *Expression* child of *n*, the source program tree node being mapped by *MapStatement*, will then be a construct representing a relational operator (e.g., *GreaterExpr*, *LessExpr*—see Figure 9.4a and Figure 9.7a).

Figure 9.9 sketches the implementation of *MapCondition*. It first builds target program tree nodes for the two integer expressions whose values are to be compared. Unlike *MapStatement*, which adds *Item*-class nodes to an existing sequence, *MapExpression* simply creates a *Datum*-class node and leaves it on the target program tree construction module's stack. Thus, after the first three lines of *MapCondition*, the three children of the conditional jump construct occupy the top three locations of the target program tree construction module's stack. The **case** statement then selects the proper conditional jump, based upon the source language construct being mapped and whether the transfer is to take place when the condition is true or when it is false. (If the relational operator is "<" and the transfer is to take place when the condition is false, then the target program construct must jump when the first expression's value is greater than or equal to the second expression's value.) Finally, since the condition is represented by an *Item*-class node, it must be added to the current sequence.

Often, the statement components of a structured statement are compound statements, represented in the source program tree by a sequence of *Statement*-class nodes. The *CompoundStmt* alternative of *MapStatement* (Figure 9.8) deals with this situation, simply applying *MapStatement* to each member of the sequence in turn. Notice that no new sequence is started in the target program tree; the compound statements lose their identities as the *Item*-class nodes implementing them are added to the target program tree.

An assignment statement translates into a single *Item*-class node, as shown in several of the examples we have been discussing (Figure 9.7 was the most recent). The left child of the *MovL* node describes the value to be moved, and the right child describes the address at which that value must be stored. But the value to be moved is the value yielded by the *right* child of the source program tree node representing the assignment. Thus, *MapExpression* must be applied first to the

```
procedure MapCondition(n: SourceTree; when: boolean; where: Operand);
    (* Create a target tree fragment corresponding to a condition
        On entry-
            An item sequence is being built
        On exit-
            The item sequence has been extended to include the implementation
                of the condition represented by node n
    *)

begin
    MapExpression(n↑.Left);
    MapExpression(n↑.Right);
    TargetLeaf(DatumLeaf,where);
    case n↑.Kind of
        LessExpr:
            if when then TargetNode(JumpLssL)
            else TargetNode(JumpGeqL);
            ...

        GreaterExpr:
            if when then TargetNode(JumpGtrL)
            else TargetNode(JumpLeqL);
            ...

    end;
    ExtendTargetSeq;
end;
```

Figure 9.9
Condition mapping

right child of the *AssignmentStmt* node and then to the left child in order to leave the target program tree fragments on the stack in the right order.

The left-hand side of a Pascal assignment statement might specify a real variable while the right-hand side yielded an integer value. In this case, the longword value resulting from the translation of the right-hand side must be converted to the equivalent floating-point value. Moreover, the proper move operation must be selected to carry out the assignment. For simplicity, we assume in Figure 9.8 that only *boolean*, *integer*, and *real* assignments are possible. This restriction will be lifted in Chapter 10.

9.2.2 Expression Mapping

In this section we assume a subset of Pascal that includes only boolean, integer, and real values, and in which all of the values within an expression must be of the same type. Type conversion is allowed as part of an assignment operation only. The point of these restrictions is to simplify the problem of deciding which target construct corresponds to each source construct. Chapter 10 presents a general method for solving this decision problem; all of the restrictions will be lifted there.

The compiler creates a target program tree for an expression by first creating target program trees for any subexpressions, then building the node for the expression's top-level construct. Children of the construct are mapped in the order required by the top-level construct, as shown in Figure 9.10. Remember from Figure 9.2 that the target tree generated from the right child of a *MinusExpr* construct in the source program tree is the left child of the corresponding *SubL* construct in the target program tree. Therefore, *MapExpression* must first be applied to the right child of *n* in the *MinusExpr* alternative of Figure 9.10.

The *UpArrowExpr* alternative of Figure 9.10 (which maps a pointer reference) illustrates the simpler case of a unary operator. There is only one child to be mapped, and then the *Indirect* construct of Table 9.1 is built.

The *CallExpr* alternative of *MapExpression* illustrates the production of a *SequenceDatum* construct. It first creates a new, empty sequence for argument evaluation items and invokes *MapArgumentList* to create those items.

```
procedure MapExpression(n: SourceTree);
  (* Create a target tree fragment corresponding to an expression *)

procedure NumArgValue(k: DefTableKey);
  (* Create a target tree node for the number of arguments of a function *)
  . . .

  begin
  case n↑.Kind of
    MinusExpr:                    (* Left − Right *)
      begin
      MapExpression(n↑.Right); MapExpression(n↑.Left);
      if n↑.ExprTypeKey = IntegerType then TargetNode(SubL)
      else TargetNode(SubF);
      end;
    . . .
    UpArrowExpr:                  (* Child↑ *)
      begin
      MapExpression(n↑.Child);
      TargetNode(Indirect);
      end;
    CallExpr:                     (* CalledName(ActualParamList) *)
      begin
      EmptyTargetSeq;
      MapArgumentList(n↑.ActualParamList,n↑.CalledName↑.ExprTypeKey);
      NumArgValue(n↑.CalledName↑.ExprTypeKey); MapIdentifier(n↑.CalledName);
      TargetNode(Calls); ExtendTargetSeq;
      rand.mode: = reg; rand.n: = 0; TargetLeaf(DatumLeaf,rand);
      TargetNode(SequenceDatum);
      end;
    IdnExpr:
      MapIdentifier(n↑.Child);
    end;
  end;
```

Figure 9.10
Expression mapping

MapArgumentList must produce one kind of code for arguments corresponding to **var** parameters and another kind for arguments corresponding to value parameters. Since the argument list itself does not distinguish these two cases, *MapArgumentList* needs access to the type key for the procedure. Upon return from *MapArgumentList*, the (possibly empty) sequence of argument evaluations is the top element of the target tree construction module's stack. *MapExpression* therefore builds the *Item*-class *Calls* construct and adds it to the sequence. Finally, it creates a target leaf specifying the register addressing mode with 0 as a parameter and builds the *SequenceDatum* construct with the sequence as its left child and this leaf as its right (see Figure 9.5b).

NumArgValue is typical of a procedure used to obtain information about the source program that is needed for the mapping. Although it would be possible to implement *NumArgValue* directly by a sequence of Pascal statements in the *CallExpr* alternative of *MapExpression*, making it a separate procedure does improve readability. The operation is sufficiently complex that it "pays for itself" in the sense of Section 2.1, so there is no significant performance penalty due to use of a procedure.

When *NumArgValue* is invoked, it is passed the key that represents the type of the routine being called. This type key was stored at the source program tree node corresponding to the routine call as part of the contextual information management process discussed in Chapter 7. One of the properties of a type is the *TypeDescriptor* defined in Figure 8.5, so *NumArgValue* can access this property and use it to obtain the *ExtValue* containing the number of arguments. *NumArgValue* can then invoke *TargetLeaf*, passing it an *Operand* specifying this external value.

9.2.3 Identifier Mapping

Only one source construct, *IdnLeaf*, is classed as an *Identifier*. This construct might represent a constant, a variable, a parameter, a field, or a routine name. The identifier's *EntityClass* property (Figure 7.11) is used to distinguish the various possibilities. Arithmetic constants and field identifiers are simple to map—each results in a *DatumLeaf* with a literal-mode *Operand* (Figure 9.3). The value stored in the *v* field of the *Operand* is the constant's value, or the offset of the field. String constants of length 1 are converted to integer values and treated as integer constants. A longer string constant cannot be used directly as an operand of the VAX instructions used to implement Pascal operations, so it is represented by an *Operand* with *mode=ref* and *lbl* referencing the location at which the string value is stored. We will consider this case more carefully in Chapter 11.

A local variable address is represented in the target program tree by a *DatumLeaf* whose *Operand* specifies a displacement from register *FP*. This representation is possible because *FP* holds the address of the current activation record, within which the storage for the local variable has been allocated. Nonlocal variables cannot be represented in this way because their activation record addresses are not directly available.

250   CHAPTER 9   ACTION MAPPING AND THE TARGET PROGRAM TREE

A nonlocal variable address must be represented by a target tree fragment that computes it. Recall the discussion of the static chain from Section 8.1.3: The longword at relative address -4 in the current activation record contains the address of the activation record for the enclosing procedure. To compute the address of a variable in the enclosing procedure, therefore, the compiler can access the address found at $FP-4$ and then add the variable's relative address from the definition table (Figure 9.11a). As Figure 9.11b shows, access to parameters in the enclosing procedure requires an extra indirection to obtain the base address of the argument list.

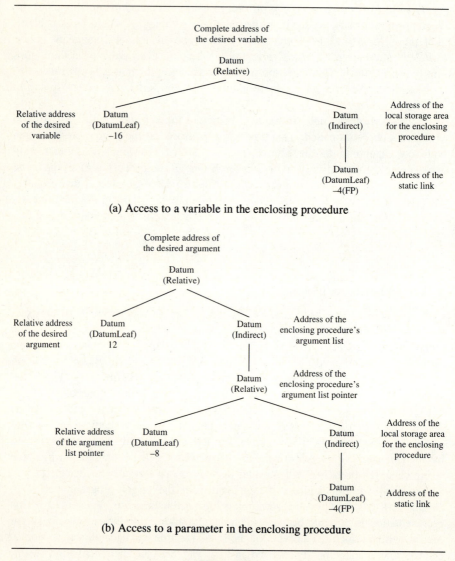

Figure 9.11
Accessing nonlocal variables and parameters

Figure 9.12 is a partial definition of the mapping routine for Pascal identifiers, showing the different ways in which field identifiers and variable identifiers are mapped.

The leaf representing a field identifier can be built directly from the definition table information associated with that identifier. In order to distinguish local variables from non-local variables, the compiler must associate a "level" with each procedure. This is an integer value that specifies how deeply each procedure definition is nested. The main program and all of the library procedures are at level 0, because they are not nested within any other definition. A procedure whose definition appears within the definition of a procedure at level k is at level $k+1$. The *Level* property of every variable declared within a procedure at level k is set to k, and *CurrentLevel* is a global variable of the action mapper that gives the level of the procedure currently being mapped. Therefore, a variable is local if the value of its *Level* property is equal to the value of *CurrentLevel*.

9.3 CASE STUDIES IN TARGET PROGRAM TREE DESIGN

In Section 9.1 we developed the structure of the target program tree from the set of implementation decisions that were to be deferred during action mapping. Operand leaves represented target machine access functions, and interior nodes represented operations deduced from the target machine instruction set. The examples we used to illustrate these principles were straightforward. They represented constructs that appear in a wide variety of languages and are implemented directly on most computers.

Unfortunately, the complete design of a mapping from source language concepts to target machine concepts is *not* straightforward. It demands a good understanding of the source language semantics and the exact behavior of the target machine instructions. A complete treatment of the idiosyncrasies of even a single source language/target machine pair is beyond the scope of this book. Here we cover three important cases to show the depth of understanding required.

Section 9.3.1 discusses the implementation of array indexing operations. Indexing is a frequently executed operation in scientific programs, and it is often supported by special hardware. Another construct that may be supported by special hardware is the **for** statement, whose implementation is covered in Section 9.3.2. The **for**-statement implementation also illustrates the need to consider carefully the effect of the finite representation of integer values. In Section 9.3.3 we show an example of the need for a new target program structuring mechanism to support a class of source language constructs that do not appear in Pascal.

9.3.1 Array Indexing

Figure 9.13a shows three Pascal array declarations. Those arrays would be mapped onto VAX storage by the data mapping task as discussed in Section 8.1.2, resulting in the memory layouts shown in Figure 9.13b.

procedure *MapIdentifier(n: SourceTree);*
  (* Create the target tree fragment corresponding to an identifier *)

  var
    rand: Operand;
    class: EntityClass;
    level: integer;

  begin
  class:= GetEntityClass(n↑.Definition,NotDefined);
  case *class* **of**
    NotDefined,LabelName,TypeName,MultiplyDefined:
      *Report(DEADLY,*3001(*Mapping error*)*,n↑.Coord,*0);
    FieldName:
      begin
      *rand.mode:= int; rand.v:= GetOffset(n↑.Definition,*0);
      TargetLeaf(DatumLeaf,rand);
      end;
    VariableName, ParameterName:
      begin *rand.mode:= disp; rand.n:= FP; rand.x:=*0;
      level:= GetLevel(n↑.Definition,CurrentLevel);
      if *level = CurrentLevel* **then**   (* Local variable or parameter *)
        begin *rand.offset:= GetOffset(n.Definition,*0);
        if *class = Parameter* **then** *rand.n:= AP;*
        TargetLeaf(DatumLeaf,rand);
        end
      else   (* Nonlocal variable or parameter *)
        begin *rand.offset:= −*4;
        TargetLeaf(DatumLeaf,rand); TargetNode(Indirect);
        *rand.mode:= int; rand.v:= −*4;
        level:= level + 1;
        while *level < CurrentLevel* **do**
          begin
          TargetLeaf(DatumLeaf,rand); TargetNode(Relative); TargetNode(Indirect);
          level:= level + 1;
          end;
        if *class = ParameterName* **then**
          begin *rand.v:= −*8;
          TargetLeaf(DatumLeaf,rand); TargetNode(Relative); TargetNode(Indirect);
          end;
        *rand.v:= GetOffset(n↑.Definition,*0);
        TargetLeaf(DatumLeaf,rand); TargetNode(Relative);
        end;
      end;
    . . .
  end;
end;

Figure 9.12
Mapping source program identifiers

9.3 CASE STUDIES IN TARGET PROGRAM TREE DESIGN

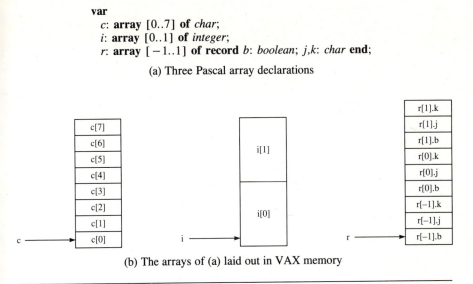

    var
        c: **array** [0..7] **of** char;
        i: **array** [0..1] **of** integer;
        r: **array** [−1..1] **of record** b: boolean; j,k: char **end**;

(a) Three Pascal array declarations

(b) The arrays of (a) laid out in VAX memory

Figure 9.13
How arrays are stored

Each element of array c occupies one cell of the VAX memory. Moreover, the first element of the array is the element with subscript 0. This means that the value of c's subscript can be used directly as the relative address of the subscripted array element: c[0] has address 0, relative to the base address of the array c; c[1] has address 1, relative to the base address of the array c, and so forth.

An element of array i, however, occupies four cells of the VAX memory. The first element of the array is the element with subscript 0, but i's subscript cannot be used directly as the relative address of the subscripted array element. As discussed in Section 8.1.2, the subscript must be multiplied by the element length to obtain the relative address. Thus the address of i[1], relative to the base address of the array i, is 4.

The first element of array r is the element with subscript −1. In order to obtain the relative address of a subscripted element we must first subtract −1 (the subscript of the array's first element), and then multiply the difference by the length of an element. Thus the address of r[1], relative to the base address of the array r, is $(1 − (−1)) \times 3 = 6$.

In order to access an array element, the compiler must obtain its address. This is done by converting the subscript into a relative address and adding that relative address to the base address of the array. Suppose that c has offset −16 in the current activation record. The base address of c is then the value of the VAX access function $-16(\text{FP})$; an access function with displacement addressing mode and parameters $-16, 13$ (remember that the frame pointer FP is register 13). To access a particular element of array c, we need an access function that uses the sum of this base address and the subscript to determine an address.

The VAX *index* addressing mode takes a register and an access function as parameters. It evaluates the access function to obtain a base address, shifts the content of the register left, and adds the result to the base address. The sum is then used to access memory. Shifting a binary number left by n places has the effect of multiplying that number by 2^n. Thus the index addressing mode multiplies the subscript value in the "index" register by a power of 2 before adding it to the base address calculated from the access function. This is exactly the behavior needed to access an element of c or i. In the case of an access to an element of c, we need a multiplication by $2^0 = 1$ (no shift), while in the case of an access to an element of i we need a multiplication by $2^2 = 4$.

Access functions using the index addressing mode do *not* specify the amount that the index register will be shifted. The shift value is determined from the operation using the access function. If an operation is using the access function to access a byte, then the content of the index register will not be shifted (i.e., the shift will be 0). If it is being used to access a word (a two-byte value), then the content of the index register will be shifted one place to the left, and so forth. Note that it is the *specific access* that controls the shift. An instruction such as CVTBL, for example, accesses a byte with its first operand and a longword with its second. Thus, the index register content of an index addressing mode access function appearing as the first operand would not be shifted, but the index register content of an index addressing mode access appearing as the second operand would be shifted two places to the left.

Table 9.1 defined a *Relative* operation that took an integer as its left operand and an address as its right operand. It yielded the address that was the sum of its operands, and we pointed out that it could be implemented either by a longword addition instruction or by an access function using the displacement addressing mode. In order to have the possibility of producing an access function using the index addressing mode, an additional operation is necessary. This new operation, which we shall call *Element*, takes two integers and an address as its operands. It multiplies the value of its first operand by the value of its second operand and yields the address that is the sum of this product and the value of its third operand.

Element is needed because the implementation of the index multiplication depends not only on the value of the multiplier, but also on the resources allocated to the operands. Since the resource allocation decisions have been deferred to the code generator, the action mapper does not have enough information to decide how the index multiplication and subsequent addition should be coded. If the multiplier is 1, 2, 4, 8, or 16, then an index-mode access function should be used. An index-mode access function should also be used for the addition in other cases if the operands are in certain places. We shall explore this point further in Chapter 11.

9.3 CASE STUDIES IN TARGET PROGRAM TREE DESIGN

Figure 9.14 shows how an assignment statement involving references to elements of the arrays defined in Figure 9.13 could be represented as a target program tree. For concreteness, Figure 9.14 assumes that i has offset -24 and r has offset -40. The local integer variables x and y have offsets -44 and -48, respectively.

The lower left *Element* node implements $i[y]$: The leftmost child defines the subscript with a displacement-mode access function that specifies the location of y

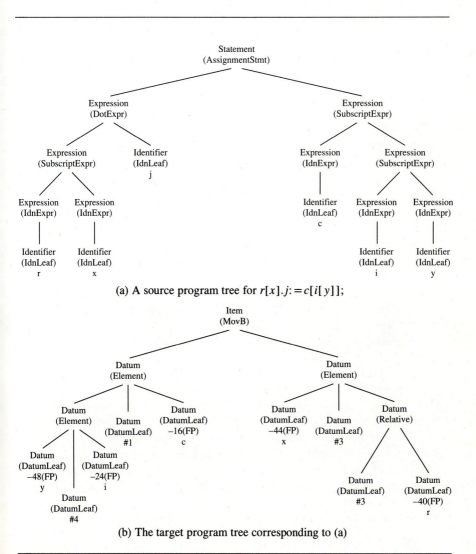

Figure 9.14
Representing indexed references on the VAX

in the activation record. (We have added the identifiers to the leaf nodes to clarify the example; those identifiers would not be present in the actual tree.) A literal-mode access has been used in the second child to specify the length of each element of array i. This length is the multiplier for the value yielded by the leftmost child, and it is 4 in this case because the elements of i are longwords. The third child defines the base address of the array with a displacement-mode access function that specifies the location of the first element of i in the activation record.

Array r has lower bound -1, and this is reflected in the third child of the rightmost *Element* node in Figure 9.14b. This child specifies a base address that is not the location of the first element of r in the activation record, but rather a location three cells higher. Recall from the discussion in Section 8.1.2 that an array element address is determined by computing a relative address from the subscript value and adding that relative address to the address of the array's first element:

$ElementAddress := AddressOfFirstElement + (Subscript - LowerBound) \times ElementSize$

$ElementAddress := AddressOfFirstElement + Subscript \times ElementSize - LowerBound \times ElementSize$

$ElementAddress := (AddressOfFirstElement - LowerBound \times ElementSize) + Subscript \times ElementSize$

When the lower bound of the array is not 0, then a *Relative* construct is used to obtain the value of $AddressOfFirstElement + (-LowerBound \times ElementSize)$, and this value becomes the base address for the *Element* construct. Since the lower bound of r is -1 and the element size is 3, $-LowerBound \times ElementSize = 3$.

Figure 9.15 shows how an array reference is handled by *MapExpression*. (*MapExpression* was introduced in Figure 9.10.) The variables of Figure 9.15a hold information extracted from the array type entry in the definition table by *ArrayInfo*. This information is used by the *SubscriptExpr* alternative of *MapExpression*'s **case** statement (Figure 9.15b) to build the necessary tree fragment.

After obtaining the lower bound and element size, Figure 9.15b creates the first child of the *Element* construct by mapping the subscript expression. The second child, the multiplier, is generated directly by building a literal-mode operand specifying the element size and creating a target leaf. One of the two forms shown in Figure 9.14b must now be selected for the third child, based upon whether the lower bound of the array is 0. If the lower bound is 0, the base address for the *Element* operation is the address of the first element of the array; otherwise, it is the address obtained by adding $-LowerBound \times ElementSize$ to the address of the first element. The address of the first element of the array is obtained by mapping the left child of the source program *SubscriptExpr* node. Figure 9.15b either uses this target program tree directly, or builds a *Relative* node with it as the right child and the value of $-LowerBound \times ElementSize$ as the left child.

9.3.2 Count-Controlled Iteration

The Pascal **for** statement implements an iteration. A variable, called the *controlled* variable, is set to an initial value and tested against a limit. The body of the

9.3 CASE STUDIES IN TARGET PROGRAM TREE DESIGN 257

```
var
    rand: Operand;                          (* Space for building constants *)
    LowerBound,ElementSize: ExtValue;       (* Array characteristics *)

procedure ArrayInfo(var bound,element: ExtValue; k: DefTableKey);
    (* Obtain information about an array
        On entry-
            k specifies the array type
        On exit-
            LowerBound = lower bound of the array
            ElementSize = size of an array element
    *)
```

(a) Obtaining and holding information needed for subscript expressions

```
SubscriptExpr:                              (* Left[Right] *)
    begin ArrayInfo(LowerBound,ElementSize,n↑.ExprTypeKey);
    MapExpression(n↑.Right);
    rand.mode: = lit; rand.v: = ElementSize; TargetLeaf(rand);
    if ExtEqual(LowerBound,IntegerZero) then MapExpression(n↑.Left)
    else
        begin rand.v: = IntegerZero;
        dummy: = ExtSub(rand.v,LowerBound); dummy: = ExtMpy(rand.v,ElementSize);
        TargetLeaf(rand); MapExpression(n↑.Left); TargetNode(Relative);
        end;
    TargetNode(Element);
    end;
```

(b) Constructing the target program tree fragment

Figure 9.15
Mapping an array element reference

---

iteration is executed if the variable has not passed the limit, the variable's value is advanced, and the test is repeated. (An "advance" may either increase or decrease the controlled variable.)

Statements such as the Pascal **for**, which effectively use a counter to control an iteration, are often mapped incorrectly by compiler designers who fail to consider machine limitations on integer values. It is important to understand why the "obvious" implementation (Figure 9.16a) of **for** $i:=E_1$ **to** E_2 **do** S is incorrect. This implementation requires that the controlled variable be advanced *beyond* the limit. When the value of E_2 happens to be the largest possible integer ($2^{31} - 1$ on the VAX), that advance cannot yield a larger value to cause loop termination. On the VAX, adding 1 to $2^{31} - 1$ results in -2^{31}. Since this value is certainly less than or equal to the value of *final* (-2^{31} is the smallest representable integer), the loop will run forever.

To correct the flaw, rearrange the loop and add a label and unconditional jump as shown in Figure 9.16b. Now the controlled variable is advanced only if it is less than the limit, so the advance is guaranteed to be well defined. The extra

```
        i := E₁;                        (* Initial value *)
        final := E₂;                    (* Final value (final is a generated variable) *)
        if i > final then goto 2;       (* Test for zero-trip case *)
    1:  S
        i := i+1;                       (* Advance the controlled variable *)
        if i ≤ final then goto 1;       (* If more trips *)
    2:
```

(a) An incorrect implementation of **for** $i := E_1$ **to** E_2 **do** S;

```
        i := E₁;                        (* Initial value *)
        final := E₂;                    (* Final value (final is a generated variable) *)
        if i > final then goto 2;       (* Test for zero-trip case *)
        goto 1;                         (* Enter the loop *)
    3:  i := i+1;                       (* Advance the controlled variable *)
    1:  S
        if i < final then goto 3;       (* If more trips *)
    2:
```

(b) A correct implementation of **for** $i := E_1$ **to** E_2 **do** S;

```
        i := E₁;                        (* Initial value *)
        final := E₂;                    (* Final value (final is a generated variable) *)
        if i > final then goto 2;       (* Test for zero-trip case *)
        count := f(i, final);           (* Compute an appropriate counter value *)
    1:  S
        i := i+1;                       (* Advance the controlled variable *)
        count := g(count);              (* Modify the counter *)
        if h(count) then goto 1;        (* If more trips *)
    2:
```

(c) Another correct implementation

Figure 9.16
Implementations of a **for**-statement

jump is executed only once, not once for each trip around the loop. (This is the same pattern that we saw when realizing the **while** statement).

Like many machines, the VAX provides instructions that modify a counter, test the result, and transfer control based upon the outcome. These instructions are designed expressly to implement **for** statements, so it would be nice to make use of them. Figure 9.16c is an implementation that controls the number of trips around the loop with a counter distinct from the controlled variable. The functions f, g, and h are determined by the semantics of the particular machine operation used. They must guarantee that the loop will be executed the number of times required by the source language.

Note that i will be incremented past the limit by Figure 9.16c. The Pascal Standard states that the value of the controlled variable is undefined after a normal exit from the **for** statement, however, so the actual content is irrelevant. Since i is not being used to control the loop, an incorrect value is harmless unless the computation of that value causes an interrupt that aborts the program. On the VAX, integer arithmetic operations set the V bit of the condition code if the result is not representable. It is possible to cause an interrupt and abort the program whenever the V bit is set, but this is usually not done. Assuming that the integer overflow interrupt is not enabled, incrementing the controlled variable past the largest possible integer causes no difficulty on the VAX.

What are the relative costs of Figure 9.16b and Figure 9.16c? Both implementations must preserve one integer value (*final* or *count*) over the body of the loop. The counter implementation has one less jump, but some operation is required to initialize the counter. Neither the eliminated **goto** nor the counter initialization lies within the loop. The key performance question concerns the additional operation (to modify the counter) executed on each trip around the loop by Figure 9.16c. If this operation is bundled with the comparison and jump as a single instruction, it will probably be faster than the sequence of a compare instruction and a jump instruction needed to implement the test in Figure 9.16b.

Regardless of which implementation is chosen, neither *final* nor *count* is used within the body of the loop. They are therefore intermediate results, and resources should be allocated to them by the code generator because we have decided to defer allocation of resources to intermediate results. In order to do this allocation effectively, the code generator must have available to it all of the resource allocation information for the body of the loop. If the loop body does not use all of the registers, for example, then *final* or *count* could be allocated a register.

The necessary information can be conveyed to the code generator by a target construct *ForLoop* with the structure:

$$(Datum, Datum, Datum, Datum, Item*): Item$$

The first *Datum*-class child is the controlled variable, the second the initial value, the third the final value, and the fourth the step. (In Pascal, the step is either 1 or -1, depending on whether **to** or **downto** was specified by the **for** statement. Other languages permit arbitrary step values.) S is implemented by the sequence of *Item*-class nodes. Figure 9.17a gives an example. (All of the identifiers in Figure 9.17a except a are assumed to correspond to local variables of type *integer*; a is a local array of integers with lower bound 0. Since the precise access functions for the variables are irrelevant for this example, we have replaced them with the corresponding identifiers.)

The *ForLoop* node is constructed by *MapStatement*, as shown in Figure 9.17b. Note that a new item sequence is begun before invoking *MapStatement* to map the controlled statement. If this were not done, the interface specification for *MapStatement* would be violated—a sequence would not lie at the top of the stack.

Notice that none of the functions f, g, and h specified in Figure 9.16c appear in the target program tree of Figure 9.17a. The action mapper, implemented by Figure 9.17b, does not generate them. Their implementation has therefore been deferred to the code generator. This decision is not mere whim; the implementations of f, g, and h depend upon the precise instruction selected to carry out the increment, test, and branch operation. Since instruction selection is deferred, implementation of f, g, and h must also be deferred.

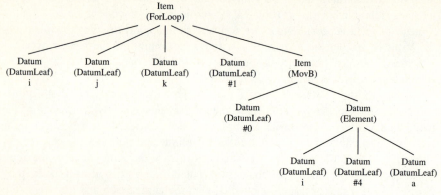

(a) A target program tree for **for** $i := j$ **to** k **do** $a[i] := 0$;

ForUpStmt,   (* **for** *ForControl* := *ForStart* **to** *ForEnd* **do** *ForBody*; *)
ForDownStmt: (* **for** *ForControl* := *ForStart* **downto** *ForEnd* **do** *ForBody*; *)
  begin
  MapIdentifier(n↑.*ForControl*);
  MapExpression(n↑.*ForStart*);
  MapExpression(n↑.*ForEnd*);
  rand.mode := *lit*; *rand.v* := *IntegerOne*;
  if n↑.*Kind* = *ForDownStmt* **then** *dummy* := *ExtNegate*(*rand.v*);
  TargetLeaf(*DatumLeaf*,*rand*);
  EmptyTargetSeq; *MapStatement*(n↑.*ForBody*);
  TargetNode(*ForLoop*);
  end;

(b) The code used by *MapStatement* to translate a **for**-statement

Figure 9.17
Mapping a **for**-statement

9.3.3 Expressions with Alternatives

Pascal provides two constructs to express alternative courses of action selected during program execution: the **if** statement and the **case** statement. Figure 9.7 showed how an **if** statement could be implemented by a sequence of subtrees rooted in *Item*-class nodes. A **case** statement is implemented in a similar fashion, except the selection of the appropriate alternative is handled by a *CaseL* (or *CaseW* or *CaseB*) operation, instead of a conditional jump operation. The important point here is that the alternatives are *statements* in the source language, and therefore they do not yield values. Thus, each can be represented in the target program tree by an *Item*-class node.

Many languages have expression constructs that express alternative computations. For example, the following conditional expression is legal in ALGOL 60:

(**if** $a > 0$ **then** a **else** $-a$) + (**if** $b > 0$ **then** b **else** $-b$) + c

9.3 CASE STUDIES IN TARGET PROGRAM TREE DESIGN

The effect of this expression is to sum the absolute values of a and b and add the value of c to the result (ALGOL 60 requires that expressions be evaluated strictly from left to right). A more compact version of the same expression can be written in C:

$$(a > 0 \: ? \: a : -a) \: + \: (b > 0 \: ? \: b : -b) \: + \: c$$

Here there is no restriction on the order of evaluation of the summands.

When alternative computations can appear in an expression, each alternative yields a value. Therefore it is not possible to express them in the target program tree with *Item*-class nodes, because an *Item*-class node does not yield a value. We need a target program tree construct that embodies a sequence of *Datum*-class nodes in order to express alternative computations within an expression. Figure 9.18a illustrates the use of a new construct called *AlternativeDataL* to describe the VAX program implementing the C conditional expression discussed above. (Variable names are attached to the leaves representing source program variables to make the tree easier to read. They would not actually be present in the tree created by the compiler.)

A conditional expression of the form (e_1 ? e_2 : e_3) in C has the value of e_2 if e_1 yields a nonzero value; it has the value of e_3, otherwise. Moreover, only one of the two expressions e_2 and e_3 is evaluated. When such an expression is translated to VAX machine code, therefore, the final algorithm must evaluate e_1, test the result, and then transfer control to the appropriate code for evaluating either e_2 or e_3. Regardless of which of the two expressions is evaluated, the result must end up in a specific place so that it can be used by the parent of the conditional expression.

Because resource allocation for intermediate results is deferred, the translator cannot determine the "specific place" where the results of both e_2 and e_3 should be stored. According to our previous conventions, subtrees with *Datum*-class roots must be created for each of these expressions and made children of a *Datum*-class node that represents the single result. This is the purpose of the *AlternativeDataL* construct. Exactly one of the children of an *AlternativeDataL* node will be executed, and the result it yields will be left in the place specified by the *Operand* decoration of the *AlternativeDataL* node itself. (That decoration will, of course, be established by the code generator.)

The children of an *AlternativeDataL* node form a sequence, and therefore we require that instructions selected for them be written in the order in which they appear in that sequence. Since the code for only one of the children can be executed, there will be a jump to the end of the construct generated after the code for each child, except the last. But this means that each child, except the first, must be labeled. The label definition and the following computation constitute a unit that must be kept together as a single child of the parent *AlternativeDataL*, thus, the use of *SequenceDatum* to describe these components.

Notice that there is one alternative data construct for each of the seven kinds of VAX value, but there is only a single *SequenceDatum* construct. The reason is that the code generator does not need to produce any value-manipulation instructions for the *SequenceDatum* construct. Thus, it does not need to know what kind of value is being represented. With the alternative data, however, the code generator must guarantee that the result ends up in the "specific place." That may require generation of a move instruction, so the code generator must know what kind of value is to be moved. Our convention has always been that the construct specifies the kind of operation and the *Operand* record specifies the access function.

Figure 9.18b shows the code that might be produced by the code generator from Figure 9.18a. The first two instructions implement the leftmost *JumpLeqL* operation. Since the second operand of this operation is 0, the normal CMPL instruction can be replaced by the cheaper TSTL. R0 is the "specific place" chosen by the code generator to hold the result of the leftmost *AlternativeDataL* construct. The *Operand* specified by the first node in the sequence child of this construct shows that b is not in R0, so the code generator had to emit a MOVL instruction to place it there. A MOVL was chosen because the construct is *AlternativeDataL*; if the construct had been, say, *AlternativeDataB*, then MOVB would have been used. Only one of the subtrees in the sequence child of *AlternativeDataL* can be executed. The code generator has therefore created a label L3 and inserted a branch to that label following the code for the first element of the sequence. L1, the label for the second element of the sequence, was created by the action mapper and incorporated into Figure 9.18a. It must be known to the action mapper because it cross-references the code for the second element with the *JumpLeqL* construct. Notice that the second element of the sequence involves a computation, and the code generator arranges that the result be left in the "specific place" so that no additional move instruction is required.

9.4 SUMMARY

The action mapping task is concerned with converting source language constructs into equivalent target language constructs and determining access functions for memory and constant operands. It creates a target program tree that embodies these decisions. The possible forms of target program tree are determined by the kinds of decisions made by the action mapper and the kinds of decisions deferred to the code generator. In this book, we defer decisions about evaluation order within expressions, register allocation, and instruction selection. That choice leads to target trees whose nodes may be classified as data (constructs yielding values used by other constructs) and items (constructs not yielding values used by other constructs).

The target program tree is constructed in much the same way as the source program tree was constructed. There is a module embodying a stack and exporting operations that build tree nodes. These operations are invoked in a particular order, building the target program tree bottom-up and from left to right. Target tree construction takes place during a single traversal of the source program tree,

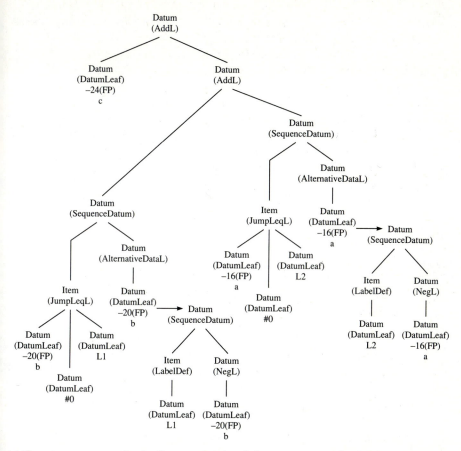

(a) Target program tree for the C expression $(a>0 \:?\: a \:: -a) + (b>0 \:?\: b \:: -b) + c$

```
          TSTL    -20(FP)         ; b>0
          BLEQ    L1
          MOVL    -20(FP),R0      ; b
          BR      L3              ; Jump produced by the code generator
L1:       MNEGL   -20(FP),R0      ; -b
L3:       TSTL    -16(FP)         ; a>0
          BLEQ    L2
          MOVL    -16(FP),R1      ; a
          BR      L4              ; Jump produced by the code generator
L2:       MNEGL   -16(FP),R1      ; -a
L4:       ADDL2   R1,R0           ; (a>0 ? a : -a) + (a>0 ? a : -a)
          ADDL2   -24(FP),R0      ; (a>0 ? a : -a) + (b>0 ? b : -b) + c
```

(b) VAX assembly code implementation of (a)

Figure 9.18
Additional target program tree structuring constructs

carried out by visit procedures of the sort discussed in Chapter 7. No additional source program errors are detected during target program tree construction, so there is no point in carrying out this process if fatal errors have been detected earlier in the compilation. This means that a consistent source program tree can be assumed, and any inconsistency must reflect an error in the compiler itself.

A compiler designer must understand the semantics of both the source language and the target machine, and be careful to verify that the action mapper implements the relationship between them correctly. Some of the subtle interactions that must be taken into account are illustrated by the implementation of array references on the VAX. The issue is the surprising behavior of the index addressing mode, which incorporates a multiplication by the array element length in certain cases. Implementation of the Pascal **for**-statement illustrates the importance of "end effects" resulting from the finite representation of integers. It also shows how special instructions may be accommodated by more complex target program tree constructs. Complex target tree constructs may also be required by source language facilities, as illustrated by the conditional expression of ALGOL 60 or C. This emphasizes the fact that the form of the target program tree is not completely independent of the source language.

NOTES

Target program tree structures are usually referred to as "intermediate languages" in the literature. Criteria given for their designs vary widely, with the most popular being some form of machine independence [9, 2]. The goal of a "universal" intermediate language is an old one [7, 11, 10, 4, 6], and seems to be one of those ideas that is rediscovered by each new generation of programmers. Our approach to target tree design—determine the characteristics of the tree on the basis of the decisions made by the action mapper and the decisions deferred to the code generator—is implicit in all of these papers. We believe that it is important for the designer to lay out the division of labor in the decision process explicitly.

Because the correctness of the action mapping depends so strongly on a thorough understanding of subtleties of the source language and target language semantics, it is imperative for the compiler designer to consult authoritative sources. The Pascal standard [1] and the 1981 edition of the VAX Architecture Handbook [5] were used in preparing this text. (Later editions of the VAX Architecture Handbook are public relations documents that do not provide sufficient information for compiler designers.)

The existence of standard implementations for structured statements has been noted often in the literature. Although most authors agree on the basic "shape" of these implementations, specific machines may require additional thought [3]. Of all of the structured statements, the **for** statement and its analogs seem to be the most difficult to implement correctly [8].

REFERENCES

1. "Pascal Computer Programming Language," ANSI/IEEE 770 X3.97-1983, American National Standards Institute, New York, NY, Jan. 1983.
2. Ammann, U., Nori, K. V., Jensen, K., Jacobi, C., and Nägeli, H. H., "The Pascal-P Compiler: Implementation Notes," Bericht 10, Eidgenössische Technische Hochschule, Zurich, July 1976.
3. Baskett, F., "The Best Simple Code Generation Technique for WHILE, FOR and DO Loops," *SIGPLAN Notices 13*, 4 (Apr. 1978), 31-32.
4. Coleman, S. S., Poole, P. C., and Waite, W. M., "The Mobile Programming System, Janus," *Software—Practice & Experience 4*, 1 (1974), 5-23.
5. *VAX Architecture Handbook*, Digital Equipment Corporation, Concord, MA, 1981.
6. Haddon, B. K. and Waite, W. M., "Experience with the Universal Intermediate Language Janus," *Software—Practice & Experience 8* (1978), 601-616.
7. Mock, O., Olsztyn, J., Strong, J., Steel, T. B., Tritter, A., and Wegstein, J., "The Problem of Programming Communications with Changing Machines: A Proposed Solution," *Comm. of the ACM 1*, 2 (Feb. 1958), 12-18.
8. Newey, M. C. and Waite, W. M., "The Robust Implementation of Sequence-Controlled Iteration," *Software—Practice & Experience 15*, 7 (July 1985), 655-668.
9. Richards, M., "The Portability of the BCPL Compiler," *Software—Practice & Experience 1* (1971), 135-146.
10. Steel, T. B., "UNCOL. The Myth and the Fact," *Annual Review in Automatic Programming 2* (1961), 325-344.
11. Steel, T. B., "UNCOL, Universal Computer Oriented Language Revisited," *Datamation 6* (1960), 14-20.

EXERCISES

9.1 Suppose the variables y and z had been declared *integer* in Figure 9.1a, and the assignment statement had been:

$$x := q.b + (y - 1)/(z + 1);$$

Draw a target program tree fragment similar to Figure 9.2 for this statement. What decisions of the translator caused the differences between your tree and that of Figure 9.2? *Be specific.*

9.2 Why does Figure 9.3 distinguish between absolute and symbolic displacements? Under what circumstances might a symbolic displacement be used? (Hint: Think about how you might implement FORTRAN COMMON storage.)

9.3 List *all* of the VAX operations that you would need to implement the arithmetic operations of Pascal. Show which VAX operation implements each Pascal operation. Be sure to account for any necessary type conversions, but do not include field selection, array indexing, or pointer dereferencing.

9.4 Draw the target program tree fragment that implements the Pascal statement **repeat** S_1; $\cdots$ S_n **until** e;

9.5 The *sqrt* routine is a Pascal library function that expects a value parameter. Change Figure 9.5b to describe the invocation of a function f that expects a **var** parameter.

9.6 Suppose r is a record variable with size 8 and alignment 4 at offset -30 in the current activation record. The compiler is translating the statement $p(r)$. It will implement the procedure invocation by a *Calls* operation. The argument list must be a single longword that is placed on the stack prior to executing the *Calls* operation. (See Figure 9.5 for an example of a routine call.)
   (a) Draw the source program tree for the statement $p(r)$.
   (b) Assume the procedure p was declared to have a **var** parameter, and draw the target program tree fragment implementing $p(r)$.
   (c) Assume the procedure p was declared to have a value parameter, and draw the target program tree fragment implementing $p(r)$.
   (d) Draw the target program tree fragment that must be generated within the procedure p to handle the value parameter in case (c). (Hint: In Pascal, a value parameter is defined to be a local variable whose value is initialized to the value of the corresponding argument.)
   (e) Would your answers to (b), (c), and (d) have been any different if r had been defined as an integer variable and the procedure declaration changed accordingly? Explain briefly.

9.7 Define the *RepeatStmt* alternative of *MapStatement* (Figure 9.8).

9.8 Suppose the data mapping task allocates space for the address yielded by the expression component of a Pascal **with**-statement in the current activation record, just as though it were a local pointer variable.
   (a) Is there any need for a special target program tree construct to implement the **with**-statement? Explain briefly.
   (b) Define the *WithStmt* alternative of *MapStatement* (Figure 9.8).

9.9 Explain why there is no need for the *AssignmentStmt* alternative of *MapStatement* (Figure 9.8) to test for the condition:

$(n\uparrow.Source.ExprTypeKey = RealType)$ **and** $(n\uparrow.Destination.ExprTypeKey = IntegerType)$

9.10 Define the *EqualExpr* alternative of *MapCondition* (Figure 9.9).

9.11 Define the *DotExpr* alternative of *MapExpression* (Figure 9.10). (A *DotExpr* construct is used for a field reference such as $r.f$).

9.12 Write the function *NumArgValue*, whose interface is specified in Figure 9.10.

9.13 Assume the following code fragment:

   procedure p;
     var i: *integer*;
     procedure q;
       procedure r;
         begin $i:=1$ **end**;

Draw the target program tree describing the assignment statement.

9.14 Why does the *LabelName* alternative of *MapIdentifier* (Figure 9.12) lead to a deadly error? How can a *DatumLeaf* for a user-defined label be created?

9.15 The standard routine calling conventions for the VAX prohibit a routine from changing values that appear in the argument list. Pascal, on the other hand, specifies that value parameters are initialized local variables, and therefore their values can be changed by the routine.
  (a) Propose a way of reconciling these two conflicting requirements.
  (b) Does your solution have any impact on *MapIdentifier* (Figure 9.12)? Explain briefly.

9.16 Consider the implementation of the Pascal statement $A[i,j,k] := '''';$, assuming that A is declared by

  var A: **array** $[10..20]$ **of array** $[-5..0, 1..5]$ **of** *char*;

  (a) Explain why the assignment is correct according to the definition of Pascal.
  (b) Draw the complete target program tree fragment representing the statement.

9.17 The VAX INDEX instruction [5] performs a bounds check in addition to multiplying the subscript value by the element size and adding the result to the base address of the array.
  (a) Define a target operation corresponding to the INDEX instruction. Explain why a single operation is sufficient.
  (b) Draw a target program tree similar to Figure 9.14b, but using the operation you defined in (a).
  (c) Do Exercise 9.16b using the operation you defined in (a).
  (d) Rewrite Figure 9.15b to generate the operation you defined in (a).

9.18 Consider the VAX CASE instruction [5].
  (a) Define VAX operations similar to those of Table 9.1 for the various forms of the CASE instruction.
  (b) Show how the following Pascal **case** statement could be represented by a target tree fragment that uses the operations you defined in (a):

  case a **of** *red*: $b := 3$; *yellow*: $b := 4$; *blue*: $b := 5$; **end**;

  Assume the declarations

  var a: (*red, yellow, blue*); b: *integer*;

  (c) Write the *CaseStmt* alternative of *MapStatement*.

9.19 Suppose a language defined a **case**-expression similar to the conditional expression discussed in Section 9.3.3:

  $b :=$ **case** a **of** *red*: 3; *yellow*: 4; *blue*: 5; **end** $+ 14$;

  Show how this expression could be represented by a target program tree. If you use any additional constructs, specify their semantics and briefly justify the need for them.

10

Operator Identification

Many languages, Pascal included, use one basic symbol to denote several distinct operations. This technique is known as *overloading*, and the basic symbol is called an *overloaded operator*. For example, the basic symbol "*" is overloaded in Pascal. It can be used in a program to denote integer multiplication, real multiplication, or set intersection. The purpose of the operator identification subtask of semantic analysis is to resolve overloading. Overloading has been resolved when every node of the source program tree that describes an operation has been decorated with the proper operator. Thus, when overloading has been resolved, a *StarExpr* node of a Pascal source program tree might be decorated with the integer multiplication operator.

Operator identification must decorate the nodes of the source program tree *consistently*: If a *StarExpr* node is decorated with the integer multiplication operator, then the children of that node must be decorated with operators whose results are integer values. Similarly, the parent of the *StarExpr* node must be decorated with an operator that will accept an integer value as its operand. The problem of finding a consistent decoration is complicated by the presence of *coercions*. A coercion is a type conversion operation that the compiler is allowed to insert into a computation without an explicit request from the programmer. In Pascal, for example, an integer value can be converted to a real value by the compiler, if necessary. Suppose that one child of some *StarExpr* node yielded a value of type *integer* and the other yielded a value of type *real*. The Pascal compiler is allowed to insert an integer-to-real conversion operator and then decorate the *StarExpr* node with a real multiplication operator.

Section 10.1 discusses the problem of overload resolution and describes a general approach to its solution. In Section 10.2 we incorporate this solution into the action mapping task, removing the restrictions on Pascal expressions introduced in Chapter 9. The implementation of the operator identification module that embodies the solution is sketched in Section 10.3.

10.1 OVERLOAD RESOLUTION

When resolving the overloading of source language operator symbols, the operator identification process must answer two distinct questions:

1. Is the use of this particular operator symbol in this context consistent with the rules of the source language?
2. How should this source language construct be implemented as a target program tree fragment?

Although the questions are different, the answers to both are determined by the operator that embodies the meaning of the construct. For example, the operator symbol "*" that appears in the Pascal expression $i*j$ is consistent with the Pascal definition when i is a local variable of type *integer* and j is a local variable of type *real*. In this case the expression must be translated into a *MulF* construct for the VAX, with a *DatumLeaf* describing the access function for j as its left child and a *CvtLF* construct as its right child. The child of the *CvtLF* construct would be a *DatumLeaf* describing the access function for i.

In order to resolve overloading, the compiler must be provided with a set of distinct operators that distinguish all of the various meanings of source language operator symbols. One of these operators is the so-called *invalid operator*, and is used to represent constructs that are inconsistent with the rules of the source language. Exactly one of the operators in the set must be associated with each operator construct in the source program tree. If the invalid operator is associated with a construct, then question (1) is answered in the negative and a fatal error has occurred. As discussed in Chapter 9, the compiler will not attempt to map a source program containing a fatal error, so the answer to question (2) is irrelevant in this case.

Section 10.1.1 explains how the set of operators is designed, and how the necessary information about their meanings is maintained. These operators are used to decorate nodes of the source program tree. Such a decoration must be "consistent," as defined in Section 10.1.2. The actual computation of a consistent decoration is based on a module in much the same way as the name analysis computation in Chapter 7. Section 10.1.3 defines the interface for this module and shows how the computation is carried out during visits to the source program tree nodes.

10.1.1 How to Characterize an Operator

In order to answer the two questions posed at the beginning of Section 10.1, we need to distinguish all of the valid meanings for source language constructs. Some of those meanings can be deduced from the source language definition, others from the relationship between the source language and the target machine. For example, the Pascal standard says that the operator symbol "*" can stand for integer multiplication, real multiplication, or set intersection.

We have chosen to implement integer values with VAX longwords (Section 8.1.1). There are three VAX instructions that accept longword operands and perform integer multiplication: MULL3, MULL2, and EMUL. MULL3 and MULL2 have the same semantics, differing only in the pattern of operand access functions. As discussed in Section 9.1.2, therefore, we defer selection of one of these instructions to the code generator by defining the VAX operation *MulL*. EMUL, on the other hand, delivers its result as a *quadword*—an 8-byte integer value—and therefore embodies a different operation, *Emul*.

Why would it be useful for the compiler to allow the Pascal operation symbol "*" to stand for either of two integer multiplication operations, one yielding a longword and the other yielding a quadword? Assume that all of the identifiers in Figure 10.1 represent integer variables. The Pascal **mod** operation is most easily implemented by the VAX EDIV instruction, which expects a quadword integer as its second operand. In the **then** part of Figure 10.1, the *StarExpr* node is the left child of a *ModExpr* node; its result will therefore be the second operand of an EDIV instruction. If the *StarExpr* is implemented by an *Emul* operation in this context, the result can be used immediately by the EDIV instruction. If the *StarExpr* were implemented by a *MulL* operation, on the other hand, the result would have to be converted to a quadword before being used.

The parent of the *StarExpr* in the **else** part of Figure 10.1 is a *PlusExpr* node. This node represents an integer addition, implemented by a VAX operation requiring longword operands. It would thus be incorrect to implement the *StarExpr* by an *Emul* operation in this context, because *Emul* yields a quadword result. That result would then have to be *shortened* to satisfy the VAX integer addition operation using it.

Each source language construct that represents an operation is associated with a set of operators, any one of which might describe the meaning of that construct. Clearly, these operators must differ in some way. Otherwise, there would be no way to decide which of them actually did describe the construct's meaning in a particular context. The primary feature distinguishing one operator of the set from another is its *signature*—the pattern of operand types it requires and the result type it delivers. For example, the integer multiplication operator expects two integer operands and delivers an integer result; the real multiplication operator expects two real operands and delivers a real result. These two members of the set of operators that could describe the meaning of a Pascal *StarExpr* thus have distinct signatures:

$$(integer, integer): integer$$

$$(real, real): real$$

10.1 OVERLOAD RESOLUTION

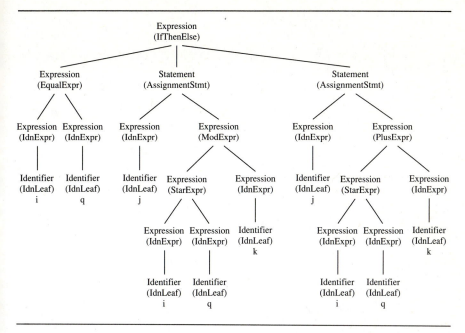

Figure 10.1
A source program tree fragment for **if** $i=q$ **then** $j:=i*q$ **mod** k **else** $j:=i*q+k$;

Recall that in Section 8.2 we pointed out that the compiler's type system might differ slightly from that of the source language. There we introduced types to describe the values **nil** and [ ]. An additional type must now be introduced to distinguish the signatures of the two VAX integer multiplications:

$$(integer, integer):integer$$

$$(integer, integer):quadint$$

Types such as *quadint* always correspond directly to data objects defined by the target machine. In effect, this extension of the type system is used to allow the compiler to represent the union of source language and target machine data objects. The action mapping task, since it embodies the relationship between source language concepts and target machine concepts, must have access to this union.

A signature is only one property of an operator. Integer addition and integer multiplication both have the same signature, but they are implemented by different target machine operations. Thus, another property of the operator is the target machine operation that implements it.

At first glance it might seem that the target machine operation completely characterizes an operator, but that is not the case. Consider two Pascal set types, declared as follows:

hue = **set of** (*red, yellow, blue*);
$schedule$ = **set of** (*sun, mon, tue, wed, thu, fri, sat*);

According to Section 8.1.2, each of these set types will have its values represented by single bytes. Therefore, the target machine operation implementing intersection of two *hue* values will be exactly the same as the target machine operation implementing intersection of two *schedule* values. They are not the same operators, however, because they have distinct signatures:

$$(hue,hue):hue$$

$$(schedule,schedule):schedule$$

If these two signatures were not distinguished by the compiler, it would not be able to detect an error if the programmer tried to compute the intersection of a *hue* value with a *schedule* value.

What, then, *is* an operator? It doesn't correspond precisely to the notion of a source language operation—a Pascal-to-VAX compiler recognizes two distinct operators that implement the Pascal integer multiplication operation. It also doesn't correspond precisely to the notion of a target language operation, because the Pascal-to-VAX compiler uses the same VAX operation to implement two distinct set intersection operators.

The compiler's set of operators, like its set of types (Section 8.2), embodies an understanding of both the source language and the target machine and therefore cannot be deduced solely from either. Each distinct operator is represented by a distinct definition table key, and the properties of that operator (such as the signature and corresponding target machine operation) can be accessed via that key. A set of definition table keys representing operators is then associated with each source language construct as the set of its possible meanings.

10.1.2 How to Obtain a Consistent Labeling

The decorations attached to source program tree nodes during overload resolution must be "consistent" in the sense mentioned at the beginning of this chapter: If a node is decorated with an operator whose signature is $(t_1, \ldots, t_n):t_0$, then the node must have n children. The leftmost child must yield a value whose type is coercible to t_1, the next child must yield a value whose type is coercible to t_2, and so forth. Finally, t_0 must be coercible to the type required by the construct's parent.

Coercions are operators just like any other operators. They all have one operand, and each may or may not have a corresponding target machine operation. For example, a user-defined subrange $'a'..'z'$ is distinct from the Pascal predefined type *char*, and the compiler is allowed to convert a value of the subrange type into a value of type *char*. Thus, there must be a coercion, but since a value of the subrange type is implemented identically to the equivalent value of type *char*, there is no need for any conversion instruction.

Figure 10.2a shows some possible overloadings of the Pascal constructs *PlusExpr*, *StarExpr*, and *ModExpr* in a compiler whose target machine is the VAX. It also shows some of the allowable coercion operators, which are not associated with particular source constructs. Only the signature and target construct

10.1 OVERLOAD RESOLUTION 273

Source construct	Operator	Signature	Target construct
PlusExpr	Op1 Op2	(integer,integer): integer (real,real): real	AddL AddF
StarExpr	Op3 Op4 Op5	(integer,integer): quadint (integer,integer): integer (real,real): real	Emul MulL MulF
ModExpr	Op6	(quadint,integer): integer	Ediv
	Op7 Op8	(integer): quadint (integer): real	CvtLQ CvtLF

(a) Some overloadings in a Pascal/VAX compiler

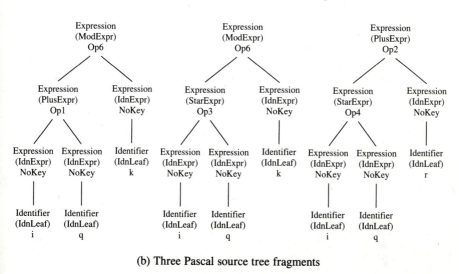

(b) Three Pascal source tree fragments

Figure 10.2
Consistent labelings

properties of each operator are shown. The signature is the property of interest when discussing consistent renamings.

Three source program tree fragments involving the Pascal constructs of Figure 10.2a and *IdnExpr* constructs are shown in Figure 10.2b. Each *Expression* node has been labeled with one of the associated operators. An *IdnLeaf* produces a value determined by the type associated with the identifier in the definition table. Assume that in this example all of the identifiers except *r* denote variables of type *integer*; *r* denotes a variable of type *real*.

In the leftmost tree fragment of Figure 10.2b, the *PlusExpr* has two children producing *integer* values. Figure 10.2a shows that one of the meanings of *PlusExpr* is an operator, *Op*1, that has two *integer* operands and produces an *integer* result. If the *PlusExpr* node is decorated with this operator (as indicated in Figure 10.2b), both children of the *ModExpr* node would produce *integer* values. Since an *integer* can be coerced into a *quadint*, *ModExpr* can be decorated by the operator *Op*6. Thus the decorations on the operator nodes of the leftmost tree in Figure 10.2b are consistent—each operator produces a result that can be coerced to the value required as an operand by the parent of that operator.

The second tree fragment of Figure 10.2b represents a more complex situation because there are two consistent labelings: *StarExpr* could also yield an *integer* result, and that *integer* value could be coerced into a *quadint* value. One less coercion operation is required by the labeling of Figure 10.2b, however, and therefore this solution is the preferred one. Two consistent labelings are possible in the third fragment as well. One of the meanings of *StarExpr* expects *real* operands and produces a *real* result. This meaning could be used instead of the one given in Figure 10.2b, because the values yielded by the leaves are coercible to *real*, and the operator decorating *PlusExpr* can accept a *real* result from *StarExpr*. The Pascal standard prohibits this interpretation, however, by stating that if both operands of "*" are of type *integer*, then the result is of type *integer*.

Let's see how we can use the information from Figure 10.2a to obtain the decorations shown in Figure 10.2b. We first compute a set of possible meanings for each *Expression* node on the basis of that node's operator (if any) and the possible types of its children. The context in which the node appears is not considered when computing these sets of possible meanings. Thus, the computation proceeds "bottom up," starting with the lowest *Expression* nodes in the tree.

In each tree fragment of Figure 10.2b, the lowest expression nodes are the *IdnExpr* nodes, thus the computation of possible meanings begins with these. Each of the *IdnExpr* constructs except the rightmost could produce an *integer* result directly, because we have assumed that i, k, and q are all integer variables. According to Figure 10.2a, however, it is possible to coerce an *integer* into either a *quadint* or a *real*. Therefore, each of these *IdnExpr* constructs could also produce a *quadint* or a *real* result via a coercion.

We can represent the possible meanings of each of the *IdnExpr* constructs in Figure 10.2b, except the rightmost, by a set of triples:

$$\{ (integer, NoKey, 0) \; (quadint, Op7, 1) \; (real, Op8, 1) \} \qquad (1)$$

There is one triple for each of the possible result types that the node could produce. Each triple specifies that result type, an operator that could be identified for the construct, and the "cost" of producing a value of the specified result type.

The three triples of (1) specify the three possible types of value that could be produced by the *IdnExpr* constructs, as discussed above. Because the *IdnExpr* construct describes an integer variable, no operation is required to produce a value of type *integer*. Therefore, the operator in the first triple is represented by *NoKey*, the distinguished definition table key that has no properties. A value of type *quadint* could be produced from the integer variable by applying *Op*7, and a value of type *real* could be produced by applying *Op*8.

The costs given in the triples of (1) simply count the number of operators needed to produce a value of the specified type: An *integer* value can be produced directly from an integer variable, so no operators are needed. That integer value could be converted into a *quadint* by applying a single coercion operator, at a total cost of 1 for the coercion. Similarly, conversion of the *integer* value to a *real* value involves one coercion operator.

If a sequence of operators must be applied to yield a value of a particular type, only the first appears in the triple. Suppose, for example, that a type *complex* were defined and a coercion from *real* to *complex* provided. Then it would be possible to produce a *complex* value from an *integer* value by first coercing the integer to a real and then coercing the real to a complex. A sequence of two operators must therefore be applied to yield the complex value. Set (1) would have a fourth triple that specified *complex* as the possible result type, $Op7$ (the first operator in the sequence) as the operator and 2 as the cost.

The rightmost *IdnExpr* construct in Figure 10.2b cannot produce an integer because r was assumed to be a *real* variable. Pascal does not permit coercion of *real* values to type *integer*, so the possible meanings for the rightmost *IdnExpr* construct in Figure 10.2b are represented by a singleton triple set:

$$\{ (real, NoKey, 0) \} \qquad (2)$$

Possible meanings for the other *Expression* nodes in Figure 10.2b are determined from the possible meanings of their operands and the operators associated with their constructs. In the leftmost fragment, *PlusExpr* can yield an *integer* result via the $Op1$ operation. $Op1$ requires two *integer* operands, and the possible meaning sets of both children specify that *integer* values can be provided at a cost of 0. The total cost of producing an *integer* result from this *PlusExpr* node is the cost of the $Op1$ operation itself (1), plus the total cost of producing the required *integer* operands (0).

The *integer* result produced by the *PlusExpr* construct at a total cost of 1 can be coerced to *quadint*, so this *Expression* node could also produce a *quadint* result at a total cost of 2.

There are two ways in which the *PlusExpr* could yield a *real* value: the result of $Op1$ could be coerced to *real* at a total cost of 2, or $Op2$ could be used. $Op2$ requires two *real* operands, and the possible type sets of both children specify that *real* values can be provided at a cost of 1. The total cost of producing a *real* result in this manner is therefore the cost of the $Op2$ operation itself (1), plus the total cost of producing the required *real* operands (2). Clearly, it is more expensive to produce a *real* result using an $Op2$ operation (cost 3) than it is to produce a *real* result by coercing the result of $Op1$ (cost 2). Only the cheapest of these alternatives need be retained, because the more expensive can never lead to a cheaper overall implementation. Therefore, the set of possible meanings for the *PlusExpr* in the leftmost tree fragment of Figure 10.2b is as follows:

$$\{ (integer, Op1, 1) \; (quadint, Op1, 2) \; (real, Op1, 2) \} \qquad (3)$$

By similar reasoning, we can determine the set of possible types and costs for the *ModExpr* node at the root of the leftmost tree fragment:

$$\{ \ (integer, Op6, 3) \ (quadint, Op6, 4) \ (real, Op6, 4) \ \} \qquad (4)$$

Notice that no coercion operators are specified in the triples of sets (3) and (4), because if a coercion is required, it is the second or subsequent operator in a sequence. For example, to produce a *quadint* value from the *PlusExpr* node, we must first execute $Op1$ and then apply $Op7$ to the result. The second and subsequent operators in such a sequence are always coercions. In order to determine a set of possible meanings for each expression, the compiler need know only whether a particular coercion is allowed, and how much it will cost. The actual sequence of operators needed to carry it out is irrelevant. Once the final meaning of the expression has been decided upon, the mapping process discussed in Section 10.2.1 generates the appropriate coercion sequence.

Suppose the leftmost tree fragment in Figure 10.2b represented the right-hand side of a Pascal assignment statement whose left-hand side was an integer variable. In that case, the *integer* result of *ModExpr* must be used for the leftmost tree fragment. We therefore say that *integer* is the *final type* of the *Expression* node at the root of that fragment. Once the final type and the set of possible meanings are known for an *Expression* node, the compiler can identify the operator that should decorate that node and determine the final types of the operands.

Since *integer* is the final type for the *ModExpr* node, $Op6$ must decorate it. The signature of $Op6$ specifies that the operator's left operand must be a *quadint* and its right operand must be an *integer*. Therefore, the final type of the left child of the node decorated by $Op6$ must be *quadint* and the final type of the right child must be *integer*.

Exactly the same reasoning can now be applied to the *PlusExpr* node in the leftmost tree fragment of Figure 10.2b, because its final type and set of possible meanings are known. The set of possible meanings is (3) above, and the final type is *quadint*. According to (3), the node can produce a *quadint* via a sequence beginning with $Op1$. $Op1$'s signature demands that the final types of the children of any node decorated by $Op1$ be *integer*.

Finally, set (1) requires that each of the *IdnExpr* nodes be decorated with *NoKey*, the empty operator. Since the *IdnExpr* nodes do not have *Expression*-class descendants, this completes the operator identification process for the leftmost tree in Figure 10.2b. You should check your understanding by verifying the operators identified in the other two trees, assuming that the final type of each root is *integer*.

10.1.3 How to Use the Operator Identification Module

As with any tree decoration task, we separate the concerns of computation, tree traversal, and information storage as discussed in Chapter 7. The major computations used during operator identification determine the set of possible meanings on the basis of the construct and the possible meanings of its children, and identify the operator on the basis of the final type and the set of possible meanings of the construct itself. It is also necessary to extract information from the signature of the identified operator in order to determine the final types of the operands.

Figure 10.3 encapsulates these operations. The operators and result types are represented by definition table keys so that they may have arbitrary properties associated with them. An *Indication* is a unique integer representing a construct to be identified. By defining it as an integer, we make the definition of the operator identification module independent of the definition of the set of constructs to be identified.

PossibleMeanings is a private type of the operator identification module; it represents a set of triples like (1)–(4) in Section 10.1.2.

The signature of an operator is represented as an array, indexed from zero to the maximum number of operands, of types. Element 0 is the result type, elements 1 through n the operand types. Since the maximum number of operands is probably 2, there is little point in trying to vary the storage requirements of a signature. Remember, because of the limitations of Pascal, the *Signature* property value must be a pointer to the actual array (Section 7.2.3).

Clearly, two operators can share the same *Signature* property value if they have the same signature (e.g., $Op1$ and $Op4$ in Figure 10.2a). Perhaps not so obvious is that a signature property can sometimes be shared between two operators with different numbers of operands. Consider, for example, $Op3$ and $Op7$ from Figure 10.2a. Elements 0 and 1 of the signatures for these two operators are identical. Because the code that interrogates the signature invariably knows the number of operands to check, the content of element 2 of the signature is irrelevant for $Op7$. Thus, $Op3$ and $Op7$ can share the same *Signature* property value.

The relationship between source language constructs and operators is embodied in a set of lists within the operator identification module. Each element of this set corresponds to a distinct source language construct. The element itself is a list of the operators that could possibly implement the corresponding source language construct.

The result types, operators, and coercions needed for a particular translation are usually not fixed at the time the translator is written. For example, a user can define additional types in a Pascal program. Depending upon the compilation strategy chosen, user-defined types may introduce additional coercions. Other languages allow the user to define operators as well as types. Even if the set of operators and types is fixed at the time the compiler is designed, the data structures required for operator identification must be initialized.

New result types and operations can easily be created and their properties specified via the definition table operation *NewKey* and the *Set* procedures for the relevant properties. Figure 10.4 shows the operations provided by the operator identification module to insert these entities into that module's internal data structures. Let's see how these operations would be used to establish the information summarized in Figure 10.2a.

Figure 10.2a has eight operators whose signatures are based on three distinct types, *integer*, *quadint*, and *real*. *AddType* will therefore have to be called three times to tell the operator identification module that these three types are the allow-

```
const
    MaxOpnd = 2;                              (* Maximum number of operands for any operator *)

type
    Indication = integer;                     (* Representation of a construct to be identified *)
    Operator = DefTableKey;                   (* Representation of an identified operator *)
    ResultType = DefTableKey;                 (* Representation of a kind of result *)
    PossibleMeanings = ???;                   (* Private type representing a set of possible meanings (Section 10.3.2) *)
    MeaningSetArray =                         (* Possible operand types *)
        array [1..MaxOpnd] of PossibleMeanings;
    Signature = ↑Sig;
    Sig = array [0..MaxOpnd] of ResultType;   (* Operator signature *)

var
    InvalidOperator: Operator;

function CoercibleFrom(T: ResultType): PossibleMeanings;
    (* Compute the possible meanings for a non-operator node
       On entry-
         T = a priori type of the value represented by the node
       On exit-
         CoercibleFrom represents the possible meanings for the construct
    *)

function ResultsOf(Node: Indication; n: integer; var MeaningSet: MeaningSetArray): PossibleMeanings;
    (* Determine the possible meanings for a computation
       On entry-
         Node represents the construct to be identified
         n = number of operands
         MeaningSet[1..n] = operand meaning sets
       On exit-
         ResultsOf represents the possible meanings
    *)
```

function *IdentifyOperator*(*Final: ResultType; Possible: PossibleMeanings*): *Operator*;
(* Identify the operator decorating an *Expression* node
   On entry-
      Final represents the result type required by the node's parent
      Possible represents the possible meanings for the node
   If the construct has no valid operator in the given context then on exit-
      IdentifyOperator = InvalidOperator
   Else on exit-
      IdentifyOperator represents the operator that should decorate the node
*)

function *SignatureElt*(*Op: Operator; ArgIndex: integer*): *ResultType*;
(* Obtain an element of a signature
   On entry-
      Op is an operator
      ArgIndex = index of the argument whose type is desired
         (0 indexes the result type, 1 the leftmost argument type, etc.)
   On exit-
      SignatureElt = type of the indexed argument
*)

Figure 10.3
Operator identification computations

procedure *AddType(T: ResultType);*
  (* Add an element to the allowed result types
    On entry-
      T=type to be added
  *)

procedure *AddOperator(Ind: Indication; Op: Operator);*
  (* Add an operator to the possible identifications for a source construct
    On entry-
      Ind=indication of the source construct
      Op=new operator associated with that construct
  *)

procedure *AddCoercion(CoerceOp: Operator);*
  (* Add an operator to the coercion graph (Figure 10.15a)
    On entry-
      CoerceOp=coercion to be added
  *)

Figure 10.4
Modifying the data structures for operator identification

able result types. Each call will specify the definition table key of one of the types as its argument. The compiler needs global variables containing the definition table keys for Pascal's predefined types. Types defined by the compiler writer, such as *quadint*, must also have corresponding global variables. These global variables serve as the source of the definition table keys passed to *AddType*.

Six of the eight operators in Figure 10.2a (*Op*1-*Op*6) are possible decorations for *Expression*-class source nodes. *AddOperator* must be used to associate the definition table keys for these operators with the source constructs they might decorate. *Op*7 and *Op*8 are coercions, and *AddCoercion* must therefore be used to make them known to the operator identification module. Figure 10.5 shows the details.

All of the information appearing in Figure 10.2a is known at the time the compiler is written; therefore, all operators and relationships can be established by a single procedure. In general, however, new types, operators, and relationships must be established during the compilation on the basis of declarations encountered. To handle this task, code fragments such as those appearing in the body of *Makeops* should be included in declaration visit procedures.

It is important to note that all of the types, operators, and relationships must be established before any operator identification is attempted. The operator identification module will report a deadly error and terminate the compilation if any of the routines of Figure 10.4 is invoked after some routine listed in Figure 10.3. Thus, the operator identification module places a constraint on the tree traversal strategy in much the same way as the scope rules of a source language do (recall Section 7.1.2).

```
procedure Makeops;
(* Define operators and establish relationships *)

var
  i: integer;
  CurrSig: Signature;
  CurrOp: DefTableKey;

begin
  AddType(IntegerType);                                                              (* integer *)
  new(CurrSig); for i:=0 to MaxOpnd do CurrSig↑[i]:=IntegerType;                     (* (integer,integer):integer *)
  CurrOp:=NewKey; SetSignature(CurrOp,CurrSig,CurrSig); SetOpCost(CurrOp,1,1);       (* Op1 *)
  SetTargetConstruct(CurrOp,AddL,AddL); AddOperator(ord(PlusExpr),CurrOp);
  CurrOp:=NewKey; SetSignature(CurrOp,CurrSig,CurrSig); SetOpCost(CurrOp,1,1);       (* Op4 *)
  SetTargetConstruct(CurrOp,MulL,MulL); AddOperator(ord(StarExpr),CurrOp);

  AddType(RealType);                                                                 (* real *)
  new(CurrSig); for i:=0 to MaxOpnd do CurrSig↑[i]:=RealType;                        (* (real,real):real *)
  CurrOp:=NewKey; SetSignature(CurrOp,CurrSig,CurrSig); SetOpCost(CurrOp,1,1);       (* Op2 *)
  SetTargetConstruct(CurrOp,AddF,AddF); AddOperator(ord(PlusExpr),CurrOp);
  CurrOp:=NewKey; SetSignature(CurrOp,CurrSig,CurrSig); SetOpCost(CurrOp,1,1);       (* Op5 *)
  SetTargetConstruct(CurrOp,MulF,MulF); AddOperator(ord(StarExpr),CurrOp);
  new(CurrSig); CurrSig↑[0]:=RealType; CurrSig↑[1]:=IntegerType;                     (* (integer):real *)
  CurrOp:=NewKey; SetSignature(CurrOp,CurrSig,CurrSig); SetOpCost(CurrOp,1,1);       (* Op8 *)
  SetTargetConstruct(CurrOp,CvtLF,CvtLF); AddCoercion(CurrOp);

  AddType(QuadType);                                                                 (* quadint *)
  new(CurrSig); CurrSig↑[0]:=QuadType; CurrSig↑[1]:=IntegerType; CurrSig↑[2]:=IntegerType;  (* (integer,integer):quadint *)
  CurrOp:=NewKey; SetSignature(CurrOp,CurrSig,CurrSig); SetOpCost(CurrOp,1,1);       (* Op3 *)
  SetTargetConstruct(CurrOp,Emul,Emul); AddOperator(ord(StarExpr),CurrOp);
  CurrOp:=NewKey; SetSignature(CurrOp,CurrSig,CurrSig); SetOpCost(CurrOp,1,1);       (* Op7 *)
  SetTargetConstruct(CurrOp,CvtLQ,CvtLQ); AddCoercion(CurrOp);
  new(CurrSig); CurrSig↑[0]:=IntegerType; CurrSig↑[1]:=QuadType; CurrSig↑[2]:=IntegerType;  (* (quadint,integer):integer *)
  CurrOp:=NewKey; SetSignature(CurrOp,CurrSig,CurrSig); SetOpCost(CurrOp,1,1);       (* Op6 *)
  SetTargetConstruct(CurrOp,Ediv,Ediv); AddOperator(ord(ModExpr),CurrOp);
end;
```

Figure 10.5
Establishing operators and relationships

Operator identification is carried out during two visits to *Expression* nodes. The first of these visits computes the set of possible meanings for each construct, while the second determines the construct's operator and the final types of its children. Before the possible meanings of *IdnExpr* constructs can be determined, a definition table key must be associated with each identifier, and the definition table must specify the identifier's *Type* property.

Each of the three values computed during operator identification—the possible meaning set, the final type, and the operator—should be stored in the *Expression* node with which they are associated. The set of possible meanings is determined during the first of the two operator identification visits, and is then used during the second. The final type for an *Expression* node is determined during the second of the two visits to the parent of that node, and we shall see in Section 10.2.1 that it is needed when the target program tree is actually generated. Finally, the identified operator is also needed when producing the target program tree. Figure 10.6a shows how this information might be stored in the source program tree node partially defined by Figure 4.2.

The code that actually performs the operator identification is given in Figure 10.6b (computation of the set of possible meanings during the first operator identification visit) and Figure 10.6c (identification of the operator and computation of the final types of the children during the second operator identification visit).

An *IntExpr* construct is always implemented by an *integer*. Thus, the compiler needs the definition table key for the predefined Pascal *integer* type whenever it is visiting an *IntExpr* construct. *IntegerType* is the global variable initialized to that definition table key (recall Figure 10.5). The type naturally delivered by an *IdnExpr*, on the other hand, must be obtained by querying the *Type* property of the particular identifier.

Before the possible result types of a *PlusExpr* can be computed, the possible result types of the children must be obtained by visiting them. Similarly, after the final types of the children of a *PlusExpr* have been computed, they must be visited to identify their operators. Recall from Figure 10.3 that *ResultsOf* requires a unique integer representation for a source construct. This is obtained in Figure 10.6b by simply applying *ord* to the construct name.

10.2 ACTION MAPPING AND OPERATOR IDENTIFICATION

The action mapping procedures discussed in Chapter 9 performed a very limited kind of operator identification, using nested conditional statements. We placed heavy restrictions on the kinds of expressions that could be translated in order to reduce the complexity of these tests. The techniques of Section 10.1, however, allow us to decorate each node of the source program tree with a definition table key that describes precisely the operation corresponding to that node. Thus, no complex testing is required—all that is necessary is to access the appropriate information via the specified key. We will now explore the information that must

```
PlusExpr,IdnExpr,IntExpr:
    (pt: PossibleMeanings;              (* Set of possible meanings *)
    ExprTypeKey: ResultType;            (* Final type *)
    op: Operator;                       (* Identified operator *)
    case Expression of
    PlusExpr: (Left,Right: SourceTree);
    IntExpr,IdnExpr: (Child: SourceTree)  );
IdnLeaf:
    (Definition: DefTableKey;           (* Access to properties (Section 7.2.1) *)
    LexIdent: integer);                 (* Identifier (Section 3.3.2) *)
```

(a) Source tree node record (see Figure 4.2) augmented with operator identification values

```
procedure ExpressionVisiti(n: SourceTree);
    (* First of two operator identification visits
        On exit-
            n↑.pt describes the possible meanings for node n
    *)
    var opnd: MeaningSetArray;
    begin
    case n↑.Kind of
      IntExpr: n↑.pt: = CoercibleFrom(IntegerType);
      IdnExpr: n↑.pt: = CoercibleFrom(GetType(n↑.Child↑.Definition,NoKey));
      PlusExpr,MinusExpr, . . . , OrExpr:
        begin ExpressionVisiti(n↑.Left); ExpressionVisiti(n↑.Right);
        opnd[1]: = n↑.Left↑.pt; opnd[2]: = n↑.Right↑.pt;
        n↑.pt: = ResultsOf(ord(n↑.Kind),2,opnd);
        end;
      end;
    end;
```

(b) Code for the first operator identification visit

```
procedure ExpressionVisitj(n: SourceTree);
    (* Second of two operator identification visits
      On entry-
        n↑.pt describes the possible result types and costs of node n
        n↑.ExprTypeKey describes the final type of node n
      On exit-
        n↑.op describes the operator of node n
    *)
    begin
    case n↑.Kind of
      IntExpr, IdnExpr: ;
      PlusExpr,MinusExpr, . . . , OrExpr:
        begin n↑.op: = IdentifyOperator(n↑.ExprTypeKey,n↑.pt);
        n↑.Left↑.ExprTypeKey: = SignatureElt(n↑.op,1); n↑.Right↑.ExprTypeKey: = SignatureElt(n↑.op,2);
        ExpressionVisitj(n↑.Left); ExpressionVisitj(n↑.Right);
        end;
      end;
    end;
```

(c) Code for the second operator identification visit

Figure 10.6
Invoking the operator identification computations

be accessible via the operator's key, and we will consider how the action mapping routines use that information.

Section 10.2.1 shows that both target constructs and processing methods must be selected via an operator's key; Section 10.2.2 and Section 10.2.3 give complete examples to illustrate the power of the approach.

10.2.1 How to Interpret an Operator

Operators are interpreted at the time a source construct is mapped to a target construct. At that time, the action mapper must be able to discover how to build a target program tree fragment implementing the operator. In the most general case, therefore, the operator would have a procedure that builds the appropriate target program tree fragment as its only property.

Because of the regularity of languages and machines, many of the target program tree construction procedures attached to operators would be virtually identical. If the complete procedure were stored with every operator (or made an alternative of some **case**-statement whose selector was stored with the operator), storage would be wasted by redundant code. To avoid this redundancy, a single procedure is defined to build target program tree fragments corresponding to a set of operators. Each operator then has properties that define the parameters needed to make this common procedure build the specific fragment for that operator. Notice that this approach is used solely for space reasons—the fundamental concept remains a distinct construction procedure for each operator.

It is difficult to state general principles for deciding what sets of operators should be grouped together and handled by a single procedure, and what the parameters for that procedure should be. This is basically a design question, and there is no "right" partition. We will give several examples here to illustrate the possibilities.

Our first example is the "normal" dyadic computational operators such as integer addition and real subtraction. If the source language does not overload the operator symbols for these operators with operators on large data structures (such as sets), all operators corresponding to these constructs can be translated in the same way. The only property that the individual operator must provide is its corresponding *TargetConstruct* (Section 9.2). Pascal's "/", "**div**", and "**mod**" satisfy these conditions.

When a source construct is overloaded with operators requiring different kinds of processing, then each must have a property that defines the kind of processing it requires. Pascal set operations on sets over base types with more than 32 elements require different processing than arithmetic operations on integers and reals. Since Pascal overloads the operator symbols "+", "−", and "*" with operators of both kinds, these operators must be distinguished by a "processing" property.

Note, however, that *all* operators on long sets can be processed in the same way, as can all arithmetic operators: The generated fragments are identical, except for the particular target construct. The processor for each of these sets of operators thus needs to have a *TargetConstruct* as a parameter, so the operator needs a *TargetConstruct* property.

10.2 ACTION MAPPING AND OPERATOR IDENTIFICATION

Figure 10.7 shows the alternatives for the **case**-statement in *MapExpression* (Figure 9.10) that handle the constructs discussed so far. The three constructs that have no meaning for sets are mapped by first mapping their children and then building a target program tree node to represent the appropriate target operation. Only the *TargetConstruct* value distinguishes the three operators, so that property is obtained from the definition table by invoking *GetTargetConstruct* with the key for the identified operator. *NoInstruction* is a distinguished *TargetConstruct* value that will cause *TargetNode* to terminate with a deadly error, thus detecting uninitialized operator entries in the definition table.

A long set value must always be stored in memory, and operations on long sets involve loops that iterate over the bytes of the set's representation. The counters for those iterations, as well as any memory required to hold intermediate results, are machine resources whose allocation is deferred to the code generator. Target constructs that describe dyadic long set operations have three children, the two operands and a *DatumLeaf* that defines the set size. The **if**-statement in the second alternative of Figure 10.7 uses *GetMappingProcess* to distinguish long set operations and invoke a procedure to construct the extra child before building the target program tree node representing the operator itself.

Note that the fact that long set operators have a "mapping process" property does not imply that arithmetic operators and operators on short sets must also have this property. If the identified operator has no mapping process property, *GetMappingProcess* will return *NoMapping*. Since this value is clearly not equal to *LongSetOperator*, the extra child will not be created.

Both alternatives in Figure 10.7 end with an invocation of *MapCoercion*. The purpose of this procedure is to insert code that transforms the value created by the current operation into the representation required by the context in which that result is required. *SignatureElt*($n\uparrow.op$,0) gives the type of the operator's result.

SlashExpr,DivExpr,ModExpr:
  begin
    MapExpression($n\uparrow.Right$); *MapExpression*($n\uparrow.Left$);
    TargetNode(*GetTargetConstruct*($n\uparrow.op$,*NoInstruction*));
    MapCoercion(*SignatureElt*($n\uparrow.op$,0),$n\uparrow.ExprTypeKey$);
  end;
PlusExpr,MinusExpr,StarExpr:
  begin
    MapExpression($n\uparrow.Right$); *MapExpression*($n\uparrow.Left$);
    if *GetMappingProcess*($n\uparrow.op$,*NoMapping*) = *LongSetOperator* **then**
      MapSetSize($n\uparrow.op$);
    TargetNode(*GetTargetConstruct*($n\uparrow.op$,*NoInstruction*));
    MapCoercion(*SignatureElt*($n\uparrow.op$,0),$n\uparrow.ExprTypeKey$);
  end;

Figure 10.7
Mapping Pascal expression constructs

The final type, $n\uparrow.ExprTypeKey$, decorating the source program tree node is the type required by the context. If no fatal errors were reported during operator identification, then we can guarantee that either these two types are the same, or that a sequence of coercion operators can be applied to a value of the result type in order to transform it to the type required by the context. (When translating Pascal for the VAX, the sequence never contains more than one operation; other language/machine pairs require longer sequences.) Figure 10.8 gives the details.

The information decorating the source program tree nodes alone is not sufficient for *MapCoercion* to determine the appropriate operators. An additional operation (Figure 10.8a) must be provided by the operator identification module to extract those operators from its internal data structures. In this way we avoid the need for additional source program tree decorations to specify coercion

---

function *Coercion*(**var** *have*: *ResultType*; *need*: *ResultType*): *Operator*;
  (* Obtain a coercion operator
    On entry-
      have describes the type of object available
      need describes the type of object desired
    On exit-
      Coercion describes the coercion operation that must be applied to the available object
      have describes the type of object resulting from the application of *Coercion* to
        the available object
  *)

(a) Additional operator identification module operation

procedure *MapCoercion*(*have*,*need*: *ResultType*);
  (* Provide any necessary coercions
    On entry-
      have describes the kind of value computed
      need describes the kind of value demanded by the context
  *)
  var *op*: *DefTableKey*;
begin
  while *have* < > *need* **do**
    begin *op*: = *Coercion*(*have*,*need*);
    case *GetMappingProcess*(*op*,*NoMapping*) **of**
      NoMapping:
        ;
      OneChild:
        TargetNode(*GetTargetConstruct*(*op*,*NoInstruction*));
      ...
    end;
  end;
end;

(b) Creating the type transformation nodes

Figure 10.8
Generating type transformation code

sequences. The **while**-loop in *MapCoercion* (Figure 10.8b) applies this operation repeatedly to deliver the complete sequence.

MapCoercion examines the mapping process property of the operator to select appropriate generation code. If the mapping process is *NoMapping*, this is taken to mean that the coercion generates no code. Most coercions that do generate code are implemented by a single target program tree node with one child, but some are more complex.

10.2.2 Jump Cascades

A *jump cascade* is a technique for efficiently implementing a Boolean expression, based upon relations, whose value is used to control the flow of execution. Figure 10.9 illustrates this technique with a small example. Notice that the Boolean operators in Figure 10.9a do not correspond to any VAX instructions in Figure 10.9c; their effect is obtained by the arrangement of the conditional jumps (hence the term "jump cascade").

Both $a<0$ and $c<0$ will be represented by *LessExpr* constructs in the source program tree for Figure 10.9a, but $a<0$ must be translated into a *JumpLssL* target construct while $c<0$ must be translated into a *JumpGeqL* construct (Figure 10.9b). The decision is based upon the relationship between the *LessExpr* constructs and their parents in much the same way as the decision to translate a *StarExpr* into a *MulL* or *Emul* is based upon the relationship between that node and its parent. Therefore, the same technique, operator identification, is applicable.

In order to apply operator identification to the production of jump cascades, we need to extend the type system to name the kinds of results produced by the relational operators. These results are not bit patterns stored in registers of the target machine, but represent patterns of jumps. We shall therefore define the type *truejump* to indicate the situation in which a jump occurs when the relational operator yields a true result, and the type *falsejump* to indicate the situation in which a jump occurs when the relational operator yields a false result. Both of these new types are "refinements" of the Pascal type *boolean*. They are related to *boolean* in the same way that *quadint* (Section 10.1.1) is related to *integer*.

Figure 10.10 shows some of the overloadings for jump cascade generation. (There must be additional overloadings for relations on reals, sets, and so forth.) Each line of Figure 10.10 represents a distinct operator. Although they are distinct operators, several may have the same value for their target construct properties. For example, both *Op9* and *Op12* have *JumpLssL* as the value of their target construct property. The reason is that if we need to transfer control when *LessExpr* yields the value *true* (*Op9*), then we need a *JumpLssL*. If we need to transfer control when *GreaterEqualExpr* yields *false* (*Op12*), then we also need a *JumpLssL*.

Because the **and**, **or**, and **not** operations do not correspond to any VAX instructions (see Figure 10.9c), the operators identified for them do not need any target construct property. Their signatures, however, must be arranged to yield the pattern of jumps having the effect of the operator. *NotExpr* is the simplest: If the effect of *NotExpr* is to be a transfer of control to a particular location when

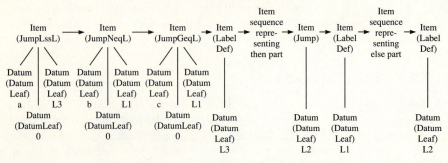

if $(a<0)$ **or** $(b=0)$ **and** $(c<0)$ **then** $\cdots$ **else** $\cdots$;

(a) A typical **if** statement

(b) The desired target program item sequence for (a)

```
            TSTL    -12(FP)    ; a<0
            BLSS    L3         ; Transfer to then if true
            TSTL    -16(FP)    ; b=0
            BNEQ    L1         ; Transfer to else if false
            TSTL    -20(FP)    ; c<0
            BGEQ    L1         ; Transfer to else if false
     L3:
                               ; Code for the then part
            BR      L2         ; Skip the else part
     L1:
                               ; Code for the else part
     L2:
```

(c) Possible VAX assembly code corresponding to (b)

Figure 10.9
Jump cascades

the expression yields *true* (the first signature), then that effect will be obtained if the same transfer occurs when *NotExpr*'s child yields *false*. Thus, the final type of the child should be *falsejump* when the final type of the *NotExpr* itself is *truejump*, as expressed by the first signature. Similar reasoning yields the second signature, and exhausts the possibilities.

Both *AndExpr* and *OrExpr* have two children. If the first child transfers control to a particular location, the second child will not be evaluated. Thus, if a transfer occurs, the value yielded by the first child determines the value of the entire expression. The value of an *AndExpr* is guaranteed to be *false* if the value yielded by the first child is *false*; if the first child yields *true*, then the value of the *AndExpr* cannot be determined without evaluating the second child. Thus, both of the signatures describing possible meanings of *AndExpr* specify *falsejump* as the final type of the first child—only when the first child yields *false* can we skip the evaluation of the second child. Similar reasoning leads to a final type of *truejump* for the first child of *OrExpr*.

10.2 ACTION MAPPING AND OPERATOR IDENTIFICATION 289

Source construct	Operator	Signature	Target construct
LessExpr	$Op9$ $Op10$	(integer,integer):truejump (integer,integer):falsejump	JumpLssL JumpGeqL
GreaterEqualExpr	$Op11$ $Op12$	(integer,integer):truejump (integer,integer):falsejump	JumpGeqL JumpLssL
GreaterExpr	$Op13$ $Op14$	(integer,integer):truejump (integer,integer):falsejump	JumpGtrL JumpLeqL
LessEqualExpr	$Op15$ $Op16$	(integer,integer):truejump (integer,integer):falsejump	JumpLeqL JumpGtrL
EqualExpr	$Op17$ $Op18$	(integer,integer):truejump (integer,integer):falsejump	JumpEqlL JumpNeqL
NotEqualExpr	$Op19$ $Op20$	(integer,integer):truejump (integer,integer):falsejump	JumpNeqL JumpEqlL
AndExpr	$Op21$ $Op22$	(falsejump,truejump):truejump (falsejump,falsejump):falsejump	
OrExpr	$Op23$ $Op24$	(truejump,truejump):truejump (truejump,falsejump):falsejump	
NotExpr	$Op25$ $Op26$	(falsejump):truejump (truejump):falsejump	
	$Op43$ $Op44$	(boolean):falsejump (boolean):truejump	JumpEqlB JumpNegB

Figure 10.10
Operator overloading for jump cascades

If the first child of *AndExpr* or *OrExpr* does not determine the value, so that the second child must be evaluated, then the behavior of the second child should be exactly the same as the behavior of the entire construct. Thus the final type of the second child in every signature for these two constructs is exactly the same as the final type of the construct itself.

Figure 10.11 shows the source program tree for the condition of the **if** statement from Figure 10.9a. The final type of the root of Figure 10.11 is *falsejump* because control should transfer when the condition of an **if** statement yields *false*. (If Figure 10.11 was the condition of a **while** statement, then the final type would be *truejump*—see Section 9.1.3.) Thus $Op24$ is identified for the root node, making the final type of the root's left child *truejump* and the final type of the root's right child *falsejump*. This, in turn, requires that $Op9$ be identified for the left child and $Op22$ for the right child. You should verify the identifications for the remaining nodes.

Note that the complete operator identification process is carried out by the same code (Figure 10.6) that handles dyadic arithmetic constructs. No special tests or computations are needed. All that remains is to map Figure 10.11 into the first part of the item sequence shown in Figure 10.9b.

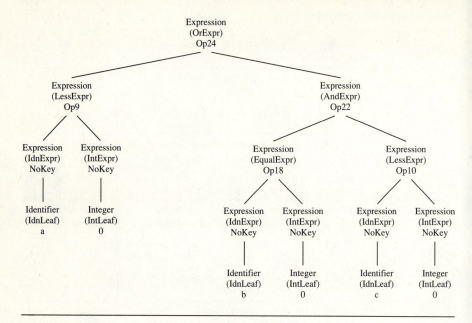

Figure 10.11
Operator identification for a jump cascade

In Section 9.2.1 we introduced a procedure *MapCondition* (Figure 9.9) to create a conditional transfer of control. Its parameters were the node describing the Boolean expression defining the condition, what value of that expression should result in a jump, and the label of the instruction to which the jump should occur. If we implement a Boolean expression with a jump cascade as discussed here, the final type of the expression tells the compiler what value of that expression should result in a jump (if the final type is *truejump*, then the jump should occur when the expression yields *true*). Thus, the second parameter to *MapCondition* in Figure 9.9 is no longer necessary (Figure 10.12).

If the condition is a reference to a Boolean variable, then *MapCondition* generates a conditional jump testing that variable's value against 0. The actual target construct is obtained from the proper coercion operator. Otherwise, the condition must be the result of a Boolean or relational operation. Relational operators have no special mapping requirements; after invoking *MapExpression* for each operand, *MapCondition* generates a leaf for the destination of the conditional jump and then the conditional jump itself.

Recall that the code generated by the first child of an *AndExpr* or *OrExpr* may transfer control. If the condition under which the child transfers control is the same as the condition under which the entire construct transfers control, then it is sufficient to simply invoke *MapCondition* recursively. When the conditions are different, however, the first child must transfer to the end of the code implementing the second child. The reason is that the condition under which the child transfers is the condition under which the entire transfer does *not* transfer—the condition under which control arrives at the instruction following the entire construct.

When the first child must transfer to the end of the construct, *MapCondition* must generate a destination label for the first child and define that label as the location of the first instruction following the second child. This is shown in the last alternative of the **case**-statement in Figure 10.12.

Invoking *MapCondition* with the root of Figure 10.11 as its first argument and the operand L1 as its second results in the creation of the first four items in Figure 10.9b. When $Op24$ was created (in the manner illustrated at the end of Section 10.1.3), its *MappingProcess* property was set to *AndOrOperator*. Recall that the final type of the root node of Figure 10.11 is *falsejump*, and note from Figure 10.10 that the left operand of $Op24$ must be of type *truejump*. Thus, the condition of the **if** statement in the *AndOrOperator* case of Figure 10.12 yields *false*, and *MapCondition* generates a label (assumed to be "L3" in Figure 10.9b). It then invokes itself on each of the two children of the root, creating the first three *Item* trees in Figure 10.9b and adding them to the current item sequence. Finally, it builds the fourth *Item* tree and adds it to the item sequence.

When *MapCondition* is applied to the left child of the root, its second argument is the operand L3. $Op9$ was not created with any *MappingProcess* property, so the default *NoMapping* is returned by the *GetMappingProcess* call in the **case** selector of Figure 10.12. This leads *MapCondition* to invoke *MapExpression* on each of its children, creating the *Datum* leaves for *a* and 0, and to build a *Datum* leaf referring to L3 (the *where* argument). According to Figure 10.10, the target construct for $Op9$ is *JumpLssL*. *MapCondition* therefore generates a *JumpLssL* node, which takes the three *Datum* nodes as children, and adds it to the current *Item* sequence. You should follow through the remainder of the mapping traversal to convince yourself that the result is, in fact, Figure 10.9b.

10.2.3 Voiding

Pascal makes a clear distinction between expressions and statements. Expressions are constructs that return values; statements do not. It is never possible to use an expression in a context that demands a statement, or vice versa. Other languages do not take such a rigid view. In C, for example, an expression can be used in a statement context—the expression's value is simply discarded. This process of discarding an expression's value is called *voiding* the expression.

If an expression's value is going to be thrown away, why should we bother to compute it? If the only effect of an expression is to yield its value, and that expression is voided, then there is no need whatsoever to carry out the computation that the expression describes. On the other hand, if the expression has a "side effect," then the compiler must generate code for at least a part of the computation. An assignment, for example, is an expression in C. It yields the value of its right-hand side and has the side effect of storing that value into memory at the address specified by its left-hand side. Assignments are often used in statement contexts in C, even though they are expressions, just as assignment statements are

procedure *MapCondition*(*n*: *SourceTree*; *where*: *Operand*);
  (* Create a target tree fragment corresponding to a condition
     On entry-
       An item sequence is being built
     On exit-
       The item sequence has been extended to include the implementation
         of the condition represented by node *n*
  *)

var
  rand: *Operand*;
  have: *DefTableKey*;

begin
if *n*↑.*Kind* = *IdnExpr* **then**
  begin
  MapIdentifier(*n*↑.*Child*);
  rand.mode: = *lit*; *rand.v*: = *IntegerZero*; *TargetLeaf*(*DatumLeaf,rand*);
  TargetLeaf(*DatumLeaf,where*);
  have: = *BooleanKey*;
  TargetNode(*GetTargetConstruct*(*Coercion*(*have,n*↑.*ExprTypeKey*),*NoInstruction*));
  ExtendTargetSeq;
  end;
else
  case *GetMappingProcess*(*n*↑.*op,NoMapping*) **of**
    NoMapping: (* Relational operator *)
      begin
      MapExpression(*n*↑.*Left*); *MapExpression*(*n*↑.*Right*); *TargetLeaf*(*DatumLeaf,where*);
      TargetNode(*GetTargetConstruct*(*n*↑.*op,NoInstruction*)); *ExtendTargetSeq*;
      end;
    NotOperator: (* **not** *)
      MapCondition(*n*↑.*Child,where*);
    AndOrOperator: (* **and** or **or** *)
      if *SignatureElt*(*n*↑.*op*,1) = *n*↑.*ExprTypeKey* **then**
        begin *MapCondition*(*n*↑.*Left,where*); *MapCondition*(*n*↑.*Right,where*) **end**
      else
        begin *GenerateLabel*(*rand*);
        MapCondition(*n*↑.*Left,rand*); *MapCondition*(*n*↑.*Right,where*);
        TargetLeaf(*DatumLeaf,rand*); *TargetNode*(*LabelDef*); *ExtendTargetSeq*;
        end;
    end;
end;

Figure 10.12
Translating jump cascades

used in Pascal. The result of an assignment is discarded, but code must be generated for that assignment so that the side effect of storing the value occurs.

In order to handle voided expressions correctly, we need to define several new types and operators. Figure 10.13a illustrates the process with the source constructs of Figure 10.2a, plus the assignment construct *AssignExpr*. The types *vinteger* and *vreal* keep track of the original types of voided values. This is impor-

Source construct	Operator	Signature	Target construct
PlusExpr	Op1 Op27 Op2 Op28	(integer,integer): integer (vinteger,vinteger): vinteger (real,real): real (vreal,vreal): vreal	AddL AddF
StarExpr	Op3 Op4 Op27 Op5 Op28	(integer,integer): quadint (integer,integer): integer (vinteger,vinteger): vinteger (real,real): real (vreal,vreal): vreal	MulL Emul MulF
ModExpr	Op6 Op27 Op28	(quadint,integer): integer (vinteger,vinteger): vinteger (vreal,vreal): vreal	Ediv
AssignExpr	Op29 Op30 Op31 Op32 Op33 Op34 Op35 Op36	(integer,integer): void (real,real): void (integer,real): void (real,integer): void (integer,integer): integer (real,real): real (integer,real): real (real,integer): integer	MovL MovF CvtFL CvtLF StoreL StoreF StoreFL StoreLF
	Op7 Op8 Op37 Op38 Op39 Op40	(integer): quadint (integer): real (integer): vinteger (real): vreal (vinteger): void (vreal): void	CvtLQ CvtLF

(a) Some overloadings

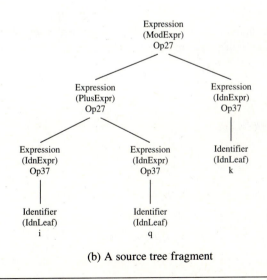

(b) A source tree fragment

Figure 10.13
Consistent labelings when voiding is allowed

tant in order to be able to verify the consistency of source types, even though the entire expression will be discarded. *Void* is the final type of any expression that appears in a statement context.

Notice that *Op*27 and *Op*28 are both associated with more than one source construct. These operators indicate that the computation is to be discarded, and so their effect is independent of the source construct. Thus, there is no need to have more than one such operator for each signature.

The costs of *Op*27, *Op*28, and *Op*37 − *Op*40 are all zero because none of them represents any code. Assuming that all of the other operators in Figure 10.13 have cost 1, the possible meanings of the *IdnExpr* nodes in the tree fragment of Figure 10.13b are as follows:

$$\{ (integer, NoKey, 0)\ (quadint, Op7, 1)\ (real, Op8, 1)\ (vinteger, Op37, 0)\ (vreal, Op8, 1) \\ (void, Op37, 0) \} \quad (5)$$

The following possible meanings describe the *PlusExpr* node and the *ModExpr* node, respectively:

$$\{ (integer, Op1, 1)\ (quadint, Op1, 2)\ (real, Op1, 2)\ (vinteger, Op27, 0)\ (vreal, Op1, 1) \\ (void, Op27, 0) \} \quad (6)$$

$$\{ (integer, Op6, 3)\ (quadint, Op6, 4)\ (real, Op6, 4)\ (vinteger, Op27, 0)\ (vreal, Op6, 1) \\ (void, Op27, 0) \} \quad (7)$$

If the expression represented by Figure 10.13b appears in a statement context, then the final type of the root node will be *void*. *Op*27 will be identified as the operator for both the *PlusExpr* node and the *ModExpr* node, as shown in Figure 10.13b.

Figure 10.14 shows how the expression mapping described in Figure 10.7 must be modified to handle voiding. The only change is that *all* operators associated with expression constructs have a *MappingProcess* property. *Op*27 and *Op*28 use *NoMapping* to indicate that no code is generated, while the other operators use *DyadicOperator* to indicate the processing discussed in Section 10.2.1.

```
SlashExpr,DivExpr,ModExpr,PlusExpr,MinusExpr,StarExpr:
   begin
   MapExpression(n↑.Right); MapExpression(n↑.Left);
   process: = GetMappingProcess(n↑.op,NoMapping);
   if process< >NoMapping then
      begin
      if process = LongSetOperator then MapSetSize(n↑.op);
      TargetNode(GetTargetConstruct(n↑.op,NoInstruction));
      MapCoercion(SignatureElt(n↑.op,0),n↑.ExprTypeKey);
      end;
StarExpr
   end;
```

Figure 10.14
Mapping voided expression constructs

10.3 IMPLEMENTING THE OPERATOR IDENTIFICATION COMPUTATIONS

The operator identification computations operate on representations of operators, result types, and sets of possible meanings. We have chosen to represent operators and result types as definition table keys, so that we can use the mechanisms discussed in Section 7.2 to associate arbitrary properties with these entities. For example, we have seen that some operators are associated with target constructs, whereas others are not.

Possible meanings are represented by triples specifying a result type, an operator, and an integer cost as illustrated in Section 10.1.2. Operator identification is based on sets of these triples. Each set defines all the possible meanings of some source construct.

There are several standard methods for representing sets of objects. Each of these methods has advantages and disadvantages, and a choice must be made on the basis of the required operations. Section 10.3.1 therefore describes the operator identification computations in terms of set operations. In Section 10.3.2, we examine the properties of those set operations and choose an appropriate data structure.

10.3.1 The Computation Algorithms

The operator identification module makes eight operations (in addition to its initialization operation) available to its clients. These operations, whose interfaces are discussed in Section 10.1.3, are:

> *SignatureElt*(*Op*: *Operator*; *ArgIndex*: *integer*): *ResultType*
> *AddType*(*T*: *ResultType*)
> *AddCoercion*(*CoerceOp*: *Operator*)
> *CoercibleFrom*(*T*: *ResultType*): *PossibleMeanings*
> *Coercion*(**var** *have*: *ResultType*; *need*: *ResultType*): *Operator*
> *IdentifyOperator*(*Final*: *ResultType*; *Possible*: *PossibleMeanings*): *Operator*
> *ResultsOf*(*Node*: *Indication*; *n*: *integer*; **var** *MeaningSet*: *MeaningSetArray*): *PossibleMeanings*
> *AddOperator*(*Indication*: *Indication*; *Op*: *Operator*)

SignatureElt is nothing but a convenient mechanism for accessing the *Signature* property of an operator. It uses only definition table operations, and will not be discussed further in this section.

The type universe in which operator identification takes place can be defined by a graph that has one node for each type. If a coercion operator converting values of type t_1 to values of type t_2 exists, then there is an arc from node t_1 to node t_2. Figure 10.15a shows such a graph for the type universe discussed in this chapter.

A type graph can be represented internally by a set of possible meaning sets, one for each node. The set of possible meanings for a particular node contains one triple for each arc leaving that node. Each triple specifies the destination of the arc, the operator implementing the arc, and the cost of executing that operator. It

296 CHAPTER 10 OPERATOR IDENTIFICATION

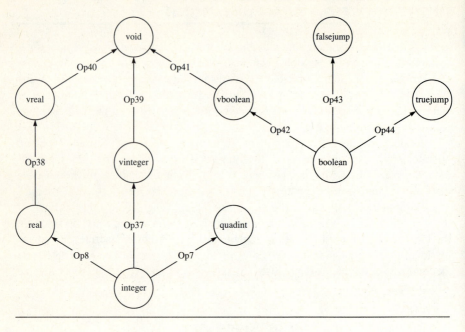

(a) A type graph

{ (*integer,NoKey*,0) (*real,Op*8,1) (*vinteger,Op*37,0) (*quadint,Op*7,1) }
{ (*real,NoKey*,0) (*vreal,Op*38,0) }
{ (*quadint,NoKey*,0) }
{ (*boolean,NoKey*,0) (*vboolean,Op*42,0) (*falsejump,Op*43,1) (*truejump,Op*44,1) }
{ (*vinteger,NoKey*,0) (*void,Op*39,0) }
{ (*vreal,NoKey*,0) (*void,Op*40,0) }
{ (*vboolean,NoKey*,0) (*void,Op*41,0) }
{ (*void,NoKey*,0) }
{ (*falsejump,NoKey*,0) }
{ (*truejump,NoKey*,0) }

(b) Definition of (a) in terms of possible meaning sets

{ (*integer,NoKey*,0) (*real,Op*8,1) (*vinteger,Op*37,0) (*quadint,Op*7,1) (*vreal,Op*8,1) (*void,Op*37,0) }
{ (*real,NoKey*,0) (*vreal,Op*38,0) (*void,Op*38,0) }
{ (*quadint,NoKey*,0) }
{ (*boolean,NoKey*,0) (*vboolean,Op*42,0) (*falsejump,Op*43,1) (*truejump,Op*44,1) (*void,Op*42,0) }
{ (*vinteger,NoKey*,0) (*void,Op*39,0) }
{ (*vreal,NoKey*,0) (*void,Op*40,0) }
{ (*vboolean,NoKey*,0) (*void,Op*41,0) }
{ (*void,NoKey*,0) }
{ (*falsejump,NoKey*,0) }
{ (*truejump,NoKey*,0) }

(c) Possible meaning sets representing the shortest paths in (a)

Figure 10.15
A type universe for operator identification

10.3 IMPLEMENTING THE OPERATOR IDENTIFICATION COMPUTATIONS

is convenient to augment this description with a triple indicating that a value of the type corresponding to the node itself can be obtained at no cost by applying no operator. Figure 10.15b shows how Figure 10.15a would be represented by possible meaning sets.

Figure 10.15b is created by the *AddType* and *AddCoercion* operations. *AddType* adds a node to the universe and associates a singleton possible meaning set with that node:

Add type T to the type universe
$temp := \emptyset$; $INSERT((T, NoKey, 0), temp)$;
$SetTypeSet(T, temp, temp)$;

The *INSERT* operation adds the element given by its first argument to the set given by its second argument (in this case, adding the element $(T, NoKey, 0)$ to the empty set $\emptyset$).

AddCoercion inserts the triple describing the conversion operator into the set for the type node of the operator's argument:

$temp := GetTypeSet(SignatureElt(CoerceOp, 1), \emptyset)$;
$INSERT((SignatureElt(CoerceOp, 0), CoerceOp, GetCost(CoerceOp, 0)), temp)$;
$SetTypeSet(SignatureElt(CoerceOp, 1), temp, temp)$;

CoercibleFrom returns a set of triples describing the possible coercions of values of type T. The set of types to which a value of type T can be coerced is the set of nodes in the type graph that are reachable from node T. If a node t is reachable from node T, then there must be one or more paths in the graph from node T to node t. The sequence of arcs forming these paths represent sequences of operations that can be used to convert a value of type T into a value of type t. There is a cost associated with each operation, and the compiler should choose the cheapest sequence of operations when performing the conversion.

Figure 10.15c shows sets that define the possible coercions of values of each type in Figure 10.15a. Each possible coercion is represented by a triple that specifies the type to which the value will be coerced, the first operator of the coercion sequence, and the total cost of the coercion. These sets of possible coercions are exactly those introduced in Section 10.1.2. They can be constructed from the sets representing the type graph (Figure 10.15b) as follows:

for $t_i, t_j \in TypeUniverse$ do
$\quad M^0_{t_i t_j} := MEMBER(t_j, GetTypeSet(t_i, \emptyset))$;
for $k := 1$ to $|TypeUniverse|$ do
$\quad$ for $t_i, t_j \in TypeUniverse$ do
$\quad\quad$ begin $x := 0$;
$\quad\quad$ if $M^{k-1}_{t_i t_j} \neq M_\emptyset$ then $x := x+1$;
$\quad\quad$ if $(M^{k-1}_{t_i t_k} \neq M_\emptyset)$ and $(M^{k-1}_{t_k t_j} \neq M_\emptyset)$ then
$\quad\quad\quad$ begin $x := x+2$; $newcost := M^{k-1}_{t_i t_k}.cost + M^{k-1}_{t_k t_j}.cost$ end;
$\quad\quad$ if $x=3$ then if $M^{k-1}_{t_i t_j}.cost \leqslant newcost$ then $x := 1$ else $x := 2$;

case x **of**
  0: $M^k_{t_i t_j} := M_\varnothing$;
  1: $M^k_{t_i t_j} := M^{k-1}_{t_i t_j}$;
  2: $M^k_{t_i t_j} := (t_j, M^{k-1}_{t_i t_k}.op, newcost)$;
  end;
end;
for $t_i \in TypeUniverse$ **do**
  begin $temp := \varnothing$;
  for $t_j \in TypeUniverse$ **do**
    if $M^n_{t_i t_j} \neq M_\varnothing$ **then** $INSERT(M^n_{t_i t_j}, temp)$;
  $SetTypeSet(t_i, temp)$;
  end;

A MEMBER operation obtains the element specified by its first argument from the set given by its second argument. Only the type component of the triple is considered by *MEMBER* in determining set membership in this application. (Technically, a *MEMBER* operation yields a Boolean value, determining only whether a particular value is an element of the set. Here, we need a slightly more complex version that yields the element itself if it is present, and $M_\varnothing$ otherwise.)

Remember that the operator identification module requires that all *AddType*, *AddOperator*, and *AddCoercion* invocations must precede any invocations of the other operations. Thus the module has two internal states: one in which it builds its data structures, the other in which it uses those data structures. It enters the "build" state when initialized, and makes a transition to the "use" state when *CoercibleFrom* is invoked in the "build" state. The shortest-path algorithm, described in the previous paragraph, is executed as part of this state transition.

Note that the shortest-path computation stores the possible meaning set representing the types to which a value can be coerced as the *TypeSet* property of that type. The result of *CoercibleFrom*(t) is therefore simply the value of the *TypeSet* property of t. No set operations are needed to implement *CoercibleFrom*.

Coercion accesses the *TypeSet* property of its *have* argument and returns the *Operator* component of the *need* element:

$M := MEMBER(need, GetTypeSet(have, \varnothing))$;
if $M = M_\varnothing$ **then** $Coercion := InvalidOperator$
else begin $Coercion := M.operator$; $have := SignatureElt(M.operator, 0)$ **end**;

IdentifyOperator accesses its *Possible* argument and returns the *Operator* component of the *Final* element:

$M := MEMBER(Final, Possible)$;
if $M = M_\varnothing$ **then** $IdentifyOperator := InvalidOperator$
else $IdentifyOperator := M.operator$;

ResultsOf must search the list of possible identifications for its *Node*, checking to see whether each is applicable given the possible operand values represented by *MeaningSet*. The search is tedious, but straightforward: Each element of the list is an operator, whose signature specifies the types of operands it requires. If all of the operator's operand types are elements of the corresponding

10.3 IMPLEMENTING THE OPERATOR IDENTIFICATION COMPUTATIONS

MeaningSet sets, then the operator is a possible result of identifying the construct in this context. Thus *ResultsOf*, like *Coercion* and *IdentifyOperator*, uses *MEMBER* on sets of possible meanings.

Each time the search in *ResultsOf* discovers a possible operator, it must merge the set of meanings for that operator into the set of possible meanings of the source construct. Let *PossibleOp* be the possible operator and *TreeCost* be the cost of using it, calculated by adding the operand evaluation costs obtained from the *MeaningSet* elements to the cost property of *PossibleOp* extracted from the definition table. *Merged* (initially empty) is the possible meaning set being constructed. The merge operation can then be described as follows:

for $M \in CoercibleFrom(SignatureElt(PossibleOp,0))$ **do**
  begin
  $t := M.type;\ TotalCost := M.cost + TreeCost;$
  $M_t := MEMBER(t, Merged);$
  if $M_t = M_\emptyset$ **then** $INSERT((t, PossibleOp, TotalCost), Merged)$
  else if $M_t.cost > TotalCost$ **then**
    begin $DELETE(t, Merged);\ INSERT((t, PossibleOp, TotalCost), Merged)$ **end**;

The merge operation uses *DELETE* in addition to *INSERT* and *MEMBER*. *DELETE* removes the element specified by its first argument from the set given by its second argument.

AddOperator simply adds an element to the list of possible identifications for a construct.

10.3.2 The Underlying Data Structure

Section 10.3.1 has shown that the only operations needed on possible meaning sets are *MEMBER*, *INSERT*, and *DELETE*. A set on which *MEMBER*, *INSERT*, and *DELETE* operations are allowed is called a *dictionary*. There are a number of common implementations for a dictionary; we have seen one, the hash table, in Section 3.3.2.

It is interesting to note that, despite the searches and merging, the computation performed by *ResultsOf* must be considered a constant-time operation! Remember that when we analyze the computational complexity of the compiler, we are interested in how the compilation time grows with the size of the program. But the cost of *ResultsOf* depends only on the number of operators and result types. Even in languages that allow user-defined types, the number of types and operators does not grow at the same rate as the overall program length. This means that no reasonable implementation of the possible meaning sets will disturb the $O(N)$ asymptotic behavior of the compiler.

The simplest representation of a set is a bit vector. One bit in the vector corresponds to each value of the base type, and this bit is 1 if and only if the corresponding value is an element of the set. $MEMBER(a,S)$ is implemented by testing the bit of set S that corresponds to the value a. $INSERT(a,S)$ is implemented by setting that bit, and $DELETE(a,S)$ is implemented by clearing that bit. In Section 8.1.2 we implemented Pascal sets by bit vectors.

A bit vector representation is unsatisfactory for possible meaning sets because *MEMBER(a,S)* must return the triple whose type component is the value *a*, rather than simply testing for membership. This could be done by using a vector of pairs *(operator,cost)* instead of a bit vector. A distinguished pair, perhaps *(NoKey,* −1*)*, could be used to indicate that triple is not a member of the set. *MEMBER(a,S)* would then be implemented by testing the *cost* field of the pair of set *S* that corresponds to the value *a*. *INSERT(a,S)* would be implemented by storing values in that pair, and *DELETE(a,S)* would be implemented by storing −1 in the *cost* field of that pair.

A linear list of the triples representing the elements is another simple implementation of a possible meaning set. The linear list representation and the pair vector representation imply a time/space trade-off. *MEMBER* and *DELETE* must both search a linear list in order to find the specified element, whereas they can compute the proper location in a pair vector. (This computation would involve accessing an integer *PairIndex* property of a *ResultType*, in our case.) On the other hand, a pair vector must have a position for every type, even though most sets have only a small number of elements.

For typical compilers, the linear list representation of possible meaning sets seems to be most appropriate. The lists are typically very short—the five-element set (5) in Section 10.2.3 is one of the longer ones—even though the total number of types can be quite large. Lists are short because the type graphs for most languages are sparse. In Figure 10.15a, for example, the arithmetic and Boolean types form almost disjoint subgraphs.

10.4 SUMMARY

Programming language designers overload operator symbols with a variety of meanings. In order to resolve this overloading, the compiler must determine whether the meaning of a particular source construct is consistent with the context in which it is used and decide how to implement that meaning as a target program tree fragment. Each meaning is characterized by an operator that is represented by a definition table key. The keys are distinguished by signature properties that specify the context in which the meaning is applicable. It is possible to access information about how to implement the construct's meaning via the definition table key representing the operator.

Each node in the source program tree that might have several meanings is decorated with a particular operator by the compiler. This "labeling" of the tree must be consistent: The signature of the operator decorating a node must specify a number of operands equal to the number of children the node has, and the result type of the operator decorating each child must be coercible to the corresponding operand type.

A consistent labeling is obtained by determining a set of possible meanings for each source program leaf, based upon the type of entity the leaf represents and the available coercions. Sets of possible meanings for interior nodes are then determined on the basis of the sets of possible operand types and the construct represented by the node. The total cost of the computation also enters into the determination of possible meanings.

Once the possible meanings are available, a final type is selected for the root of each tree fragment. Given the final type and the possible meaning set at a node, the compiler identifies the operator that embodies the meaning of that node. The final types of the node's children are then the operand types found in the signature associated with the identified operator.

A language- and machine-independent operator identification module can be defined to carry out the computations that determine the consistent labeling. The module provides additional operations used to build internal data structures, and clients are constrained to complete all invocations of these operations before invoking any of the analysis operations. This constraint may affect the traversal strategy if the source language allows user-defined types and operators.

If a consistent labeling can be found, then the program conforms to the rules of the source language. The nodes have been decorated with the keys describing their meanings, and the corresponding target program tree can be built. This process is carried out in essentially the manner described in Chapter 9. Use of operator identification as a uniform decision procedure, with the keys giving direct access to specific mapping processes, simplifies the structure of the code and lifts the restrictions imposed in Chapter 9.

Boolean expressions are most frequently used to determine alternate computations—for example, as the condition of an **if** statement or **while** statement in Pascal. The translation of such statements involves conditional jumps to alter the normal sequential execution of an *Item* sequence. Moreover, the expressions themselves are often based upon relations rather than Boolean variables. A special implementation technique, the jump cascade, is useful when relations can be implemented on the target machine by conditional jumps. Operator identification can be used to obtain the contextual information necessary for supporting jump cascades.

When expressions are allowed in statement contexts, the values they compute are discarded. It may be that some or all of the computations described by the expression are irrelevant when the expression is voided in this manner. Operator identification can be used to determine which computations are necessary and which are not.

Operator identification computations are carried out via operations on sets that can be implemented in several standard ways. Although these operations involve searches, the search costs do not depend upon the length of the program. Therefore, operator identification does not increase the computational complexity of the compiler.

NOTES

Compile-time analysis of types and automatic insertion of type conversion operators was first described in conjunction with the CPL compiler [5]. CPL used a type graph to express the relations among types, augmenting it with two special types—*unknown* and *general*. A value of type *unknown* could be converted to a value of any other type, and a value of any type could be converted to a value of type *general*. Because the graph is acyclic, addition of these two types allows the type system to satisfy the axioms of an algebraic structure known as a lattice [8].

The operator identification strategy we have discussed in this chapter was originally described as an algorithm for optimal code generation [1]. A modified form, in which there are no costs associated with the possible types, is used to resolve overloading in Ada [7]. A directly executable version of the *ResultsOf* algorithm has been presented by Emmelmann and his colleagues [4].

Implementation strategies for sets and for the shortest path algorithm can be found in most books on data structures [2].

REFERENCES

1. Aho, A. V. and Johnson, S. C., "Optimal Code Generation for Expression Trees," *J. ACM 23*, 3 (July 1976), 488-501.
2. Aho, A. V., Hopcroft, J. E., and Ullman, J. D., *The Design and Analysis of Computer Algorithms*, Addison Wesley, Reading, MA, 1974.
3. "Pascal Computer Programming Language," ANSI/IEEE 770 X3.97-1983, American National Standards Institute, New York, NY, Jan. 1983.
4. Emmelmann, H., Schrör, F., and Landwehr, R., "BEG—A Generator for Efficient Back Ends," *SIGPLAN Notices 24*, 7 (Sep. 1989), 227-237.
5. Hext, J. B., "Compile-Time Type Matching," *Computer J. 9*, 4 (Feb. 1967), 365-369.
6. "Revised Report on the Algorithmic Language ALGOL 60," *Comm. of the ACM 6*, 1 (Jan. 1963), 1-17.
7. Persch, G., Winterstein, G., Dausmann, M., and Drossopoulou, S., "Overloading in Preliminary Ada," *SIGPLAN Notices 15*, 11 (Nov. 1980), 47-56.
8. Stone, H. S., *Discrete Mathematical Structures and Their Applications*, Science Research Associates, Chicago, 1973.

EXERCISES

10.1 Consider the Pascal operator symbols +, −, *, /, **div**, and **mod**.
  (a) Briefly explain why operations on subranges of *integer* (such as 1..10) do not constitute overloadings for these operator symbols in Pascal. (Hint: See Section 6.7.1 of the Pascal Standard [3].)
  (b) Is is possible to list *all* of the overloaded meanings of these operator symbols? Explain briefly.
  (c) Is it possible to list all of the distinct target program tree fragments that must be used to implement overloaded meanings of these operator symbols? Explain briefly.

10.2 Consider only the arithmetic operations that overload the Pascal operator symbols +, −, *, /, **div**, and **mod**. Construct a matrix, each of whose rows corresponds to a distinct signature, and each of whose columns corresponds to one of the six operator symbols. Place a cross in the matrix elements that correspond to Pascal operations. Your matrix should be based solely on the rules of Pascal.
  (a) Are there any elements that should have two or more crosses? If so, how can the compiler distinguish the operations represented by these crosses?

(b) If there are elements that have no crosses, briefly explain why Pascal does not define these operations. Do any other languages that you know of define them?

10.3 Do Exercise 10.2, considering the relationship between Pascal and some machine with which you are familiar. This means that you can construct signatures from machine types as well as Pascal types. Instead of crosses, place machine operators in the matrix elements.

10.4 Suppose that q was declared as a variable of type *real*. For each of the tree fragments given in Figure 10.2b, either show a consistent labeling or briefly explain why one is not possible. If a consistent labeling is not possible, show that the source language expression violates the rules of Pascal.

10.5 The text points out that there is another consistent labeling of the rightmost tree fragment in Figure 10.2b that is illegal according to the rules of Pascal.
  (a) Given our choice of decisions to defer (see the beginning of Section 9.1), what are the possible cost values that could be used in operator identification? Explain briefly.
  (b) Adjust the costs of the operators and coercions so that the procedure discussed in Section 10.1.2 will yield the illegal labeling of the rightmost tree fragment in Figure 10.2b.
  (c) Is it possible to adjust costs so that the labeling yielded by the procedure discussed in Section 10.1.2 is *not* consistent? Explain briefly.
  (d) Is it possible to adjust the costs so that the compiler cannot decide between two consistent labelings? Explain briefly.
  (e) What should be the primary criterion for selecting costs? Explain briefly.

10.6 Why is it important to make the operator identification module independent of the definition of the set of constructs to be identified? (This was the reason for representing an *Indication* by an integer—see the beginning of Section 10.1.3.)

10.7 Consider the *SignatureElt* operation defined in Figure 10.3. *Must* this operator be defined by the operator identification module, or could it be exported by some other module? Explain briefly.

10.8 Write the alternatives for *NotExpr* in Figure 10.6b and Figure 10.6c. Could this code be used for other constructs? Explain briefly.

10.9 Consider the C conditional expression, described in Section 9.3.3. (Figure 9.18 shows an example of this construct and its implementation.)
  (a) Why must the values of e_2 and e_3 be coerced to the same type in $(e_1 \ ? \ e_2 \ : \ e_3)$?
  (b) What operation could be applied to the sets of possible types and costs decorating the roots of the tree fragments for e_2 and e_3 in order to obtain the type to which both should be coerced?
  (c) Why is it necessary to have the operator identification module provide an operation with the following interface to carry out this operation?

function *Balance(Opnd1,Opnd2: PossibleMeanings): PossibleMeanings*;
  (* Compute the possible result types and costs when two constructs must yield the same kind of result
   On entry-
     $Opnd_i$ describes the possible result types and costs of the ith construct
   On exit-
     Balance describes the possible common result types and costs
  *)

10.10 In Section 10.2.1 we pointed out that the only property of an operator is (theoretically) the procedure that builds the appropriate target program tree fragment.
  (a) Why isn't it possible to store a mapping procedure in the definition table as a property of an operator when the implementation language for the compiler is Pascal?
  (b) Suppose the compiler implementation language was object-oriented. In that case, the constructor for the target program tree fragment could be a method of the operator's object. Would it be possible to use the inheritance mechanism of the language to reduce the amount of code needed? Explain in detail either how the reduction would be achieved or why it is not possible.

10.11 Consider the mapping of Pascal simple types to the VAX that was discussed in Section 8.1.1. Give an example of a legal coercion from one simple type to another that does not require any VAX instruction to be generated.

10.12 Suppose that f and g are functions with side effects (each sets the global variable A to the argument of the function), and consider the following Pascal conditional statement:

  if $(f(1)<3)$ **and** $(g(7)>5)$ **then** *writeln(A)* **else** *writeln(−A)*;

  (a) What (if anything) can be said about the value written? Quote the Pascal Standard [3] to support your answer.
  (b) Is a jump cascade a possible implementation of this conditional statement? Explain briefly, in light of your answer to (a).
  (c) This statement also happens to be legal ALGOL 60 [6]. Quote the ALGOL 60 Report to answer the question posed in (a).
  (d) Explain why the following sequence could be used in place of the given statement in either Pascal or ALGOL 60:

  $temp1:=f(1)$; $temp2:=g(7)$;
  if $(temp1<3)$ **and** $(temp2>5)$ **then** *writeln(A)* **else** *writeln(−A)*;

  (Here *temp1* and *temp2* are appropriately declared variables that are not used anywhere else in the program.)
  (e) Use your answer to (d) to show how a jump cascade can *always* be used to implement a Boolean expression that controls the flow of control.

10.13 Consider the following Pascal conditional statement:

  if $(a<0)$ = $(b<0)$ **then** $\cdots$ **else** $\cdots$;

  (a) Write VAX assembly code similar to that of Figure 10.9c to implement this conditional statement.
  (b) On the basis of your answer to (a), augment the overloading specification of Figure 10.10.
  (c) Do you have to add any new target constructs to build a target program tree for this conditional? Explain briefly, justifying any added target constructs that do not correspond to VAX instructions.

10.14 Consider the implementation of a type set as a linear list.
  (a) Define the type *PossibleMeanings* of Figure 10.3.
  (b) Implement *MEMBER(a,S)*, *INSERT(a,S)*, and *DELETE(a,S)* in terms of the type you defined in (a).

(c) Compare your implementation to the definition table implementation shown in Figure 7.15. Can you identify the *MEMBER*, *INSERT*, and *DELETE* operations in Figure 7.15?

(d) The expected number of comparisons executed by *find* (Figure 7.15a) is $n/2$, where n is the number of properties the given definition table key has. What is the expected number of comparisons executed by *MEMBER* or *DELETE* in your implementation? How does the expected number of comparisons executed by *MEMBER* or *DELETE* relate to the cost of executing *INSERT*?

10.15 *ResultsOf* is the most expensive operation exported by the operator identification module. In practice, particular source constructs are often used with similar operands. This means that *ResultsOf* is forced to do the same computation many times.

(a) How could you characterize a particular *ResultsOf* computation so that it could be recognized easily when it arose again? (Hint: Under what circumstances will two invocations of *ResultsOf* yield the same set of possible meanings?)

(b) One simple way to avoid the computation is to build a dictionary of the characterizations you identified in (a). The entry for each characterization gives the set of possible meanings yielded by the characterized *ResultsOf* computation. Would all of the operations *MEMBER*, *INSERT*, and *DELETE* be applied to this dictionary? Explain briefly.

(c) [2] Propose a suitable implementation technique for the dictionary discussed in (b).

10.16 [8] Figure 10.15a is a directed acyclic graph (each edge has a direction, indicated by the arrow, and it is not possible to find a path along these directed edges from a node to itself).

(a) If we were to draw a graph like Figure 10.15a that showed all of the coercions allowed by Pascal, would it also be a directed acyclic graph? Explain briefly.

(b) Fortran, unlike Pascal, allows the assignment $I=R$ where I is a variable of type *integer* and R is a variable of type *real*. Does this assignment involve a coercion? Explain briefly.

(c) If we were to draw a graph like Figure 10.15a that showed all of the coercions allowed by FORTRAN, would it also be a directed acyclic graph?

(d) Does your answer to (b) affect your answer to (c)? Explain briefly.

11
Code Generation

Code generation produces a sequence of target machine instructions to implement the algorithm described by a target program tree. The structure of the code generator is similar to the structure of the translator: It accepts a tree with information stored at the leaves, decorates that tree, and then uses the decorated tree to construct a new representation of the program. Although the specific decorations and computations differ in the two cases, we can use the same basic design methodology for both.

Three major decisions must be made during code generation:

- The order in which to evaluate children of most nodes.
- Where to hold intermediate values yielded by *Datum*-class constructs.
- Selection of specific instructions to implement target operations.

All three of these decisions involve the set of intermediate values yielded by the *Datum*-class constructs of the target program tree. Operand evaluation order is chosen to minimize the number of values that exist simultaneously. Registers are used to hold the values wherever possible, and specific registers are chosen to simplify the instructions that operate on the values. Finally, instructions are selected to provide the cheapest implementation for each target operation, given the locations of its operands and result. It is therefore not surprising that the entire code generation process revolves around calculation and use of *Operand* values associated with the *Datum*-class constructs.

A value of type *Operand* will ultimately be stored at each *Datum*-class node in the target program tree to define the result yielded by that node. Recall that the action mapper provided a value of type *Operand* for each leaf at the time it built the tree (see the interface specification for *TargetLeaf* in Figure 9.6). The code generator will supply the remaining values during its contextual analysis of the target program tree.

We shall consider the three major code generation decisions in the order given. Section 11.1 explains how to choose an operand evaluation order that minimizes the number of intermediate values existing simultaneously, and how to decide which intermediate values should be held in registers and which should be stored in memory. In Section 11.2, this information—plus properties of the target operations—is used to complete *Operand* decorations for interior *Datum*-class nodes of the target program tree. The *Operand* decorations are used to select instructions that implement each operation as shown in Section 11.3, which also discusses the operations used by the compiler to output the target program.

11.1 OPERAND EVALUATION ORDER

Figure 11.1a shows a fragment of a target program tree. It is a translation of the Pascal expression $(z - 1.0)/(z + 1.0) + a*b$, in which a, b, and z are all local variables of type *real*. According to the rules of Pascal, it is immaterial whether $(z - 1.0)/(z + 1.0)$ is evaluated before $a*b$ is evaluated, or vice versa. Both values must, of course, be available before the final value of the expression can be computed. This partial order among the subexpressions is embodied in the structure of the target tree: children must be evaluated before their parents, but the order in which siblings are to be evaluated is unspecified.

Figure 11.1b shows a possible sequence of instructions that simply evaluates the subexpressions in the order in which they are encountered during a depth-first, left-to-right traversal of Figure 11.1a. This sequence of instructions needs three registers to store its intermediate values. If the computations were done in a different order (Figure 11.1c), only two registers would be needed to store intermediate values. Thus the number of registers required during the evaluation of an expression may depend upon the order in which the components of that expression are evaluated.

Section 11.1.1 shows a general method by which the compiler can determine an evaluation order that minimizes the number of intermediate values existing simultaneously during the evaluation of an expression. This general method must be adapted to the specific characteristics of the target machine, as discussed in Section 11.1.2, in order to decide which of these intermediate values can be held in registers and which must be stored in memory. Section 11.1.3 sketches an implementation strategy that carries out these computations within the target tree construction module.

308   CHAPTER 11   CODE GENERATION

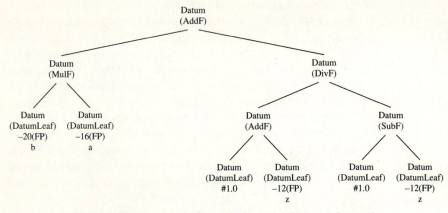

(a) A target program tree fragment for $(z-1.0)/(z+1.0)+a*b$

MULF3	-20(FP),-16(FP),R1	; R1:=$a*b$
ADDF3	#1.0,-12(FP),R2	; R2:=$z+1.0$
SUBF3	#1.0,-12(FP),R0	; R0:=$z-1.0$
DIVF2	R2,R0	; R0:=$(z-1.0)/(z+1.0)$
ADDF2	R1,R0	; R0:=$(z-1.0)/(z+1.0)+a*b$

(b) Depth-first, left-to-right evaluation

ADDF3	#1.0,-12(FP),R1	; R1:=$z+1.0$
SUBF3	#1.0,-12(FP),R0	; R0:=$z-1.0$
DIVF2	R1,R0	; R0:=$(z-1.0)/(z+1.0)$
MULF3	-20(FP),-16(FP),R1	; R1:=$a*b$
ADDF2	R1,R0	; R0:=$(z-1.0)/(z+1.0)+a*b$

(c) A different evaluation order

Figure 11.1
The effect of evaluation order on register requirements

11.1.1 Determining the Evaluation Order

Figure 11.1b differs from Figure 11.1c in the order of evaluation of the two children of the root. The crucial factor in this choice is the number of registers required to evaluate each of those children. Notice that only one register is required during evaluation of the left child (to hold the result of the *MulF* operation), while two are required during evaluation of the right child (to hold the results of the *AddF* and *SubF* operations). If the subexpression with the larger register requirement is evaluated first, then the total register requirement is minimized. Therefore, the compiler needs to compute the register requirements of the children in order to determine which should be evaluated first.

If every intermediate value occupies exactly one register, and if no intermediate values are to be stored in memory, then the minimum number of registers required to evaluate the expression rooted in some node is equal to the maximum number of intermediate values that can exist simultaneously during that evaluation: Intermediate values that exist simultaneously cannot share storage. Because no intermediate values are to be stored in memory, all of them must be stored in registers. Each intermediate value requires exactly one register, so the number of registers needed is equal to the number of intermediate values.

The maximum number of intermediate values that must exist simultaneously during evaluation of an expression is often called the *Sethi-Ullman number* of the expression, after the authors of the most complete description of how to compute it. A Sethi-Ullman number can be computed for a node in a tree if the characteristics of the computation and the Sethi-Ullman numbers of the children are known.

Computation of Sethi-Ullman numbers for *Datum*-class nodes is based on several assumptions:

- Leaves of the target program tree represent values that need not be computed; therefore, the Sethi-Ullman number of a leaf is 0.
- The result of a computation is considered to be an intermediate value, so the Sethi-Ullman number of a *Datum*-class node representing a computation is always at least 1.
- The result of a computation is *not* considered to exist simultaneously with the values of any of the operands of that computation.

These assumptions arise from the characteristics of target program trees and computer hardware. Target program leaves represent values that are either in memory or in the instruction stream, for which no registers need be allocated. (The base register of the local activation record is not considered an allocatable register. We shall return to this point in Section 11.1.2.) As discussed in Section 9.1.1, the result of a computation is always an intermediate value and must be consumed by the parent of that computation's node. On most machines an instruction may overwrite one of its operands with its result; therefore, the operand and result do not exist simultaneously.

The Sethi-Ullman number of a computation represented by a node with one child is the maximum of 1 and the Sethi-Ullman number for that node's child. (A computation's Sethi-Ullman number must be at least 1, and the number of intermediate values that must exist simultaneously when evaluating an expression cannot be smaller than the number of intermediate values that must exist simultaneously when evaluating any of that expression's operands.)

When the number of operands of a node is two or more, the Sethi-Ullman number for the node may depend on the order in which the operands are evaluated. Let's consider the two-operand situation first. If the Sethi-Ullman number of one child is 0 (as is the case with the *MulF* construct in Figure 11.1a), the reasoning of the previous paragraph leads to the conclusion that the Sethi-Ullman number of the node is the maximum of 1 and the Sethi-Ullman number of the other child. Thus, the Sethi-Ullman number of the *MulF* node in Figure 11.1a is 1, as are the Sethi-Ullman numbers of the two children of *DivF*.

Two cases must be considered if both children have nonzero Sethi-Ullman numbers:

1. The Sethi-Ullman numbers of the children are equal.
2. One child has a higher Sethi-Ullman number than the other.

In Figure 11.1, both children of the *DivF* node have Sethi-Ullman number 1, so this node is an example of case (1). After discussing this case, we shall see that the Sethi-Ullman number of the *DivF* node is 2. Since the Sethi-Ullman number of the *MulF* node is 1, the root node of Figure 11.1 is an example of case (2).

In case (1), either operand can be computed first. The number of simultaneous intermediate results required for the first computation is the Sethi-Ullman number, i, of that operand's node. A single intermediate value, the result of the operand computation, remains after the computation has been completed. That intermediate value cannot be discarded until the computation for the node itself has been carried out. But first the other operand must be computed. By hypothesis, the Sethi-Ullman number of that operand's node is also i. Therefore $i+1$ intermediate values must exist simultaneously during the second operand computation (i due to the computation itself, and the one that was the result of the first operand computation). We conclude that the Sethi-Ullman number of the node must be $i+1$. In Figure 11.1a, the *DivF* node satisfies case (1) with $i=1$, so its Sethi-Ullman number is 2.

In case (2), let the Sethi-Ullman numbers attached to the operand nodes be i and j, with $i>j$. Suppose that the operand with the larger Sethi-Ullman number, i, is evaluated first. As in the previous case, i intermediate values must exist simultaneously during this computation, and a single value remains when it is finished. During the second operand computation, $j+1$ intermediate values must exist simultaneously (j due to the computation, and the one that was the result of the first operand computation). But remember that $i>j$, so $i\geqslant j+1$. Therefore, at most, i intermediate values must exist simultaneously during the entire computation, and the Sethi-Ullman number of the node is i. In Figure 11.1a, the root node satisfies case (2) with $i=2$, $j=1$, so its Sethi-Ullman number is 2.

It is easy to show (by reasoning analogous to that of the previous paragraph) that the number of intermediate values that must exist simultaneously will be one higher if the operand with the smaller Sethi-Ullman number is evaluated first. Thus, the decision about the evaluation order of the operands depends in part upon the Sethi-Ullman numbering: Always evaluate the operand with the largest Sethi-Ullman number first. When the Sethi-Ullman numbers of the operands are equal, either operand can be evaluated first.

If an operator has more than two operands, more than one intermediate value must be saved during operand evaluation. The operands should be evaluated in order of decreasing Sethi-Ullman number. Let this sequence be

$$e_{i_0}, e_{i_1}, \ldots, e_{i_n}$$

If the Sethi-Ullman number of e_{i_j} is S_{i_j}, then the Sethi-Ullman number of the result is as follows:

$$\max_{j=0,\ldots,n} (S_{i_j}+j)$$

Here the term S_{i_j} accounts for the intermediate results that must be held simultaneously in order to compute the operand value, and j accounts for the previously computed operand values that must be held for the parent operator.

Item-class nodes do not have results that are considered intermediate values, so even those carrying out computations might have Sethi-Ullman numbers of 0. For example, consider a *JumpGtrL* construct (Table 9.2) that transfers control if the value of a variable is greater than 0. Both the variable and the value 0 are leaves, whose Sethi-Ullman numbers are 0. The comparison on which the jump is based does not create a result, so this computation can be carried out without intermediate values. Therefore, the Sethi-Ullman number of the *JumpGtrL* node is 0. In general, the Sethi-Ullman number of an *Item*-class node that has *Datum*-class children is the maximum of the Sethi-Ullman numbers of those children.

Chapter 9 defined two *Datum*-class constructs that had sequences as subtrees:

SequenceDatum $(Item^+, Datum):Datum$ (Table 9.2)
AlternativeDataL $(Datum^+):Datum$ (Section 9.3.3)

In each case, the Sethi-Ullman number of the corresponding node is the maximum of the Sethi-Ullman numbers of its children, because no intermediate values from one child must be retained during evaluation of another child. Only one of the children of *AlternativeDataL* will be evaluated during any given evaluation of *AlternativeDataL*. No intermediate values are retained from evaluation of one *Item* to the next in a *SequenceDatum*, nor are any retained between evaluation of any *Item* and evaluation of the *Datum*.

The *ForLoop* construct defined in Section 9.3.2 is a somewhat more complex case. Because it is an *Item*-class node, it returns no value. However, it must retain a local value (*counter*, in the implementation of Figure 9.16c) during the execution of its *Item*$^+$ child. Given the implementation of Figure 9.16c, the Sethi-Ullman number of the *ForLoop* is:

$$\max(\max_{i=1,\ldots,4} (D_i), \max_{i=1,\ldots,n} (I_i) + 1) \quad (1)$$

Here D_i is the Sethi-Ullman number of the ith *Datum*-class child of the *ForLoop*, and I_i is the Sethi-Ullman number of the ith element of the component *Item*-sequence. The 1 accounts for *counter*, which must exist during execution of the entire sequence of items constituting the loop body.

Note that (1) is valid *only* for the implementation shown in Figure 9.16c. If the implementation were changed, an analysis like the one given in the previous paragraph must be carried out to determine the appropriate computation.

11.1.2 Determining the Register Requirements

Section 11.1.1 showed how to compute a Sethi-Ullman number for every node of the target program tree. Sethi-Ullman numbers specify the maximum number of intermediate values that must exist simultaneously during evaluation of a subtree, and they help to determine the evaluation order of an expression's operands.

Unfortunately, the simple computation discussed in Section 11.1.1 must be modified according to the characteristics of the target machine before it can completely satisfy the requirements of the code generator.

The code generator must ultimately associate some of a target program's intermediate values with registers and others with storage (because the target machine may not have enough registers to hold the maximum number of intermediate values that must exist simultaneously). Sethi-Ullman numbers computed by the method discussed in Section 11.1.1 give the number of intermediate values that must exist simultaneously during the evaluation of an expression, but some intermediate values (such as the result of the VAX *Emul* operation) may occupy more than one register. In order to determine the number of registers required to evaluate an expression, the computation of Section 11.1.1 must be modified to account for multiple-register intermediate values.

If a target construct *produces* a multiple-register intermediate value, then a register count is determined by the method appropriate for its operands. The total register count is the maximum of this value and the number of registers required to hold the operator's result.

If a target construct *uses* a multiple-register intermediate value, then more cases must be considered to determine the number of registers needed to compute the operands. Here we restrict ourselves to two operands, one of which is a two-register intermediate value. Let i be the number of registers needed to evaluate the operand yielding the two-register intermediate value, and j be the number of registers needed to evaluate the operand yielding the single-register intermediate value. (Note that, because of the postulated sizes of the intermediate values, i must be at least 2 and j must be at least 1.) There are four distinct cases, and each can be analyzed as described in Section 11.1.1. The cases and the results of the analysis are as follows:

Case	Evaluation order	Total Registers
$i < j$	One-register operand first	j
$i = j$	One-register operand first	$i+1$
$i = j+1$	Either operand first	$i+1$
$i > j+1$	Two-register operand first	i

Some operators destroy registers other than those used for their operands and result. These "scratch" registers are accounted for in different ways, depending upon whether they must be distinct from the registers used to hold operands, and whether they must be distinct from the registers used to hold results. Scratch registers that must be distinct from operand registers are treated as extra operands whose register counts are 1, and scratch registers that must be distinct from result registers are treated as extra registers. A register count, C, for the node is then determined as usual. The total register requirement is given by:

$$\max(C, ScratchRegisters)$$

ScratchRegisters is the number of scratch registers that need not be distinct from either operands or results.

Another factor that complicates the register counting process is that some constructs use *fixed* registers for certain purposes. For example, a function returns its value in R0. Thus R0 must be available to any subtree that contains a function call. Similarly, the VAX character string operations use registers R0 through R5 as scratch registers; these registers must be available to any subtree containing character string operations.

Fixed registers are, of course, included in the count of registers required for the construct that uses them. Unfortunately, a simple register count for each child no longer suffices to determine the register requirement of the parent node. Consider a node with two children. Assume that the node requires one register for its result, uses no scratch registers, and has no fixed register requirement. If the left child requires 2 registers and the right child requires 1, the register requirement of the node should be 2. Suppose, however, that the left child contained operations that used R0 and R1, while the right child contained an instruction that used R12. The register requirement of the node itself would then be 3.

If hardware characteristics or operating system conventions dictate the use of fixed register by certain constructs, each node must carry a register set in addition to the register count. This register set contains the fixed registers required to evaluate the subtree rooted in the node. It is computed by taking the union of the sets for the children and the set of fixed registers (if any) used by the node itself. The node's register count is the maximum of the count determined as discussed earlier in this section and the number of registers in the node's fixed register set. For our example, the fixed register set is [R0, R1, R12]; therefore, the node's count must be 3.

If the total number of registers required to evaluate an expression exceeds the number of registers available for allocation, then some intermediate value must be stored during the computation of that expression. Let N be the number of registers that the compiler designer is willing to allocate to hold intermediate values. N is almost certainly *not* equal to the total number of target machine registers, because some of the registers must be reserved for special purposes. For example, the VAX has sixteen registers, but four are used in particular ways by the hardware and the operating system: Register 15 is the program counter, register 14 is the stack pointer, register 13 holds the address of the current activation record, and register 12 holds the address of the current argument list. Thus the hardware and operating system place an upper limit of 12 on the value of N.

A target machine's hardware also places a lower limit on the value of N, because N must always provide enough registers so that any operation can be carried out when all of its operands are initially in memory. VAX character string instructions use six scratch registers, so if the compiler will generate these instructions then $N \geq 6$ for the VAX.

Suppose that every intermediate value occupies one register, and no operation uses scratch registers, so that the Sethi-Ullman number of a node is also its register count. Suppose further that the maximum number of operands of any operation is two. Under these assumptions, the lowest-level subtree that can require more than N registers is rooted in a node with two operands, and each of those operands requires N registers for its evaluation. But this expression could be evaluated with only N registers as follows:

1. Evaluate one of the operands (say, the left one). This evaluation can be done with N registers, and its result occupies one register.
2. Store the result of the evaluation in memory. All N registers are now free.
3. Evaluate the other operand (the right one, in this case). This evaluation can be done with N registers, and its result occupies one register.
4. Evaluate the operation, using the value stored in memory and the value left in the register by the second operand evaluation.

The argument of the previous paragraph can be extended to any number of operands and operators with scratch registers or multiple-register intermediate values. It is necessary to store only enough of the operands to free the number of registers required to carry out the operation. (Remember that the lower limit on N discussed above guarantees that this is always possible.) Therefore the register requirement of any node will be less than or equal to N, and the process of computing this register requirement has the side effect of marking certain intermediate values as being stored in memory.

Item-class nodes may also produce intermediate results that must be stored in memory to avoid exceeding the number of registers available for allocation. The *ForLoop* construct is a typical example. Suppose that N registers are required during execution of a subtree rooted in one of the *Item* nodes in the body of the **for**-statement. Since *counter* (Figure 9.16) retains its value during the entire body, resources devoted to it cannot be used during execution of any component node of the body. If *counter* occupies a register in this case, there won't be enough registers to implement the body. Thus, the code generator must allocate a memory location to *counter* instead of allocating a register to it.

11.1.3 Determining Operand Classes During Tree Construction

We have seen in Section 11.1.1 and Section 11.1.2 that all of the information about storage requirements for intermediate values can be obtained by working up the tree from the leaves. This means that the computation can be done as the tree is being built. By combining target program tree construction and determination of some of the contextual information, we can use that contextual information to modify the tree structure. This modification will simplify later code generation tasks.

A value of type *Operand*, describing a VAX access function, is stored at each *Datum*-class node of the target program tree. (*Operand* values are defined by Figure 9.3, which is reproduced here as Figure 11.2 for easy reference.) The action mapping task determines the *Operand* value for every target program tree leaf as discussed in Section 9.1.1, and passes it as an argument to the *TargetLeaf* operation of the target tree construction module. *Operand* values for interior nodes of

```
type
  AddressingMode = (                      (* VAX addressing modes *)
    lit,                                  (* Literal value *)
    ref,                                  (* Symbolic label *)
    reg,                                  (* Rn *)
    regdef,regdefndx,                     (* (Rn), (Rn)[Rx] *)
    autodecr,autodecrndx,                 (* -(Rn), -(Rn)[Rx] *)
    autoincr,autoincrndx,                 (* (Rn)+, (Rn)+[Rx] *)
    autoincrdef,autoincrdefndx,           (* @(Rn)+, @(Rn)+[Rx] *)
    disp,dispndx,                         (* offset(Rn), offset(Rn)[Rx] *)
    dispdef,dispdefndx,                   (* @offset(Rn), @offset(Rn)[Rx] *)
    symb,symbndx,                         (* place(Rn), place(Rn)[Rx] *)
    symbdef,symbdefndx);                  (* @place(Rn), @place(Rn)[Rx] *)

  Operand = record                        (* Description of an operand *)
    case mode: AddressingMode of
      lit: (v: ExtValue);                 (* Literal value (see Figure 2.4) *)
      ref: (lbl: ExtValue);               (* Symbolic label *)
      reg,regdef,
      autodecr,autoincr,autoincrdef,
      disp,dispdef,symb,symbdef,
      regdefndx,autodecrndx,
      autoincrndx,autoincrdefndx,
      dispndx,dispdefndx,
      symbndx,symbdefndx:                 (* Register or memory access *)
        (n,x: integer;                    (* Base and index registers *)
        case AddressingMode of
          reg,regdef,
          autodecr,autoincr,autoincrdef,
          regdefndx,autodecrndx,
          autoincrndx,autoincrdefndx:
            ;                             (* No displacement *)
          disp,dispdef,dispndx,dispdefndx:
            (offset: ExtValue);           (* Absolute displacement *)
          symb,symbdef,symbndx,symbdefndx:
            (place: ExtValue);            (* Symbolic displacement *)
        end);
    end;
```

Figure 11.2
Description of a target operand

the tree are determined partially as the tree is being built, and partially by the register allocator (Section 11.2).

Other values computed as the tree is being built are the integer register count introduced in Section 11.1.2, the set of fixed registers required by a subtree, and an indication of the order in which code for a node's children should be generated. A register count and fixed register requirement set are stored at every target tree node, regardless of its class. Order specifications are stored only when the order is not fixed by the definition of the construct itself. Figure 11.3 shows how the tar-

```
type
  TargetConstruct = (                       (* Target program constructs *)
    MovL,                                   (* (Datum,Datum): Item *)
    LabelDef,                               (* (Datum): Item *)
    Jump,                                   (* (Datum): Item *)
    AddL,                                   (* (Datum,Datum): Datum *)
    Relative,                               (* (Datum,Datum): Datum *)
    Indirect,                               (* (Datum): Datum *)
    DatumLeaf);                             (* Datum *)

  Item = MovL..Jump;
  Datum = AddL..DatumLeaf;

  TargetTree = ↑TargetTreeNode;             (* Representation of the source program tree *)
  TargetSequence = ↑TargetSequenceElt;      (* Representation of an arbitrary number of children *)

  TargetTreeNode = record
    Count: integer;                         (* Register count *)
    FixedRegisters: RegisterSet;            (* Specific registers used *)
    case Kind: TargetConstruct of           (* Construct being represented *)
    MovL,LabelDef,Jump:
      (                                     (* Fields for Item information *)
      case Item of
        MovL: (From,To: TargetTree);
        LabelDef,Jump: (Child: TargetTree)
      );
    AddL,Relative,Indirect,DatumLeaf:
      (                                     (* Fields for Datum information *)
      Value: Operand;                       (* Intermediate value *)
      case Datum of
        AddL,Relative:
          (LeftThenRight: boolean;          (* Evaluation order *)
           Left,Right: TargetTree);
        Indirect: (Address: TargetTree);
        DatumLeaf: ()
      );
  end;

  TargetSequenceElt = record
    Node: TargetTree;                       (* Current element of the sequence *)
    Next: TargetSequence;                   (* Remainder of the sequence *)
  end;
```

Figure 11.3
Declaring a target tree node

get tree node might be declared. (Only a representative sample of the constructs needed to describe VAX programs is shown, due to space limitations.) Compare Figure 11.3 to Figure 4.2, which describes the source program tree nodes. The general outline for the two data structures is the same, because the processing strategies are the same.

Recall that our VAX compiler will use registers 12–15 for special purposes, and will never allocate them to hold intermediate values. These registers are therefore excluded from consideration as "registers" by the code generator, so the type *RegisterSet* is defined as a set over the base type 0..11.

The target leaf construction operation, *TargetLeaf* (Figure 9.6), sets the *Value* field to the *Operand* supplied as an argument. If the access function defined by this *Operand* requires one or more fixed registers, the number of fixed registers is stored in the leaf's *Count* field, and a set specifying them is made the value of the *FixedRegisters* field. Otherwise, *Count* is set to 0 and *FixedRegisters* is set to [ ]. For the right child of the *SequenceDatum* node in Figure 9.5b (which represents the result of a function call), *Value.mode* = *reg* and *Value.n* = 0. R0 is therefore required by the corresponding target program leaf, and *TargetLeaf* sets *Count* = 1 and *FixedRegisters* = [0]. The rightmost leaf in Figure 11.1a, on the other hand, does not require any of the allocatable registers (the frame pointer, FP, is never used for intermediate results by the code generator). *Count* = 0 and *FixedRegisters* = [ ] for this leaf.

The behavior of *TargetNode*, the construction operation for interior nodes of the target program tree, is determined by the particular construct for which a node is being generated. Whenever possible, *TargetNode* should generate a leaf having the same meaning as the construct. The reason is that a leaf represents an access function rather than an instruction. Access functions require less space in the target program than instructions and take less time to execute.

Suppose that *TargetNode(Relative)* was invoked when the topmost stack element was a *DatumLeaf* with *Value.mode* = *lit* and *Value.v* = 14, and the second element was a *DatumLeaf* with *Value.mode* = *disp*, *Value.n* = 13 (specifying FP), and *Value.offset* = −36. This construct yields the address 14, relative to the address −36 in the current activation record. Clearly, the result will be the address −22 in the current activation record. Instead of creating a *Relative* node whose children are the top two stack elements, *TargetNode* should delete those elements and push a newly created *DatumLeaf* with *Value.mode* = *disp*, *Value.n* = 13, and *Value.offset* = −22. The *Count* and *FixedRegisters* field of the leaf will contain 0 and [ ] respectively, because no allocatable registers are used in its access function.

A similar situation would arise if *TargetNode(SubL)* were invoked with two *DatumLeaf* operands that specify literal addressing modes. This means they are constant values, and *TargetNode* itself can compute the result of the *SubL* operation. *TargetNode* should therefore remove the two leaves from the stack and push a leaf specifying a *Value* field with *mode* = *lit* and *v* equal to the difference of the values specified by the operands (computed using the *ExtSub* operation shown in Figure 2.6).

With any other operand subtrees, *TargetNode(SubL)* must construct a *SubL* node with the operand subtrees as children. Suppose for the moment that the *Count* field of at least one of these children is less than N, the maximum number of registers available. The *Value* field of the generated *SubL* node should then have *mode* = *reg*, but the *n* field (which specifies the register to be used) should be set to −1 to indicate that the register is yet unknown. Thus, the fact that the result will be in a register is noted as the tree is being built, but the particular register to be used is left open. It will be filled in by the register allocator (Section 11.2). The value of the *Count* field is computed on the basis of the *Count* fields of the children, as discussed in Section 11.1.2. Figure 11.4a illustrates this situation.

If the *Count* fields of both children are N, as shown in Figure 11.4b, the value produced by the first child evaluated must be stored in memory while the second evaluation takes place. As soon as the second evaluation has been completed, the value stored in memory will be used by the *SubL* operation. The memory location will therefore be free, because every intermediate value is used exactly once. One can easily show that the memory in which intermediate values are stored is used in a last-in, first-out manner, and can therefore be implemented by a stack.

A value is conventionally pushed onto the VAX's run time stack by using an *auto-decrement* access function that specifies the stack pointer (register 14). Register 14 (also known as SP) contains the address of the lowest stack element. The auto-decrement access function first decrements the content of SP by the length of the operand being accessed (determined by the operation). This effectively allocates a new stack element. The result is then stored in this new element. An *auto-increment* access function specifying SP is used to fetch the value and remove the stack element that contained it.

TargetNode indicates that the value computed by the left child should be stored by making it the child of a newly created target tree construct having the following signature:

$$\text{Stack }(Datum):Datum$$

This construct's root *Operand* has *Value.mode* = *autoincr* and *Value.n* = 14. The new construct is used as the left child of the *SubL* node (see Figure 11.4b). *Count* = N for the *SubL* node itself; *SubL*'s *Operand* value specifies *Value.mode* = *reg* and *Value.n* = -1.

A *Stack* construct is also generated when both operands of a construct such as *SubL* specify the same register. This situation arises on the VAX when the operands are both function calls. Because calls always leave their result in R0, the result of the first function computed must be pushed onto the stack during the computation of the second. In this case, *Count* will not necessarily be N for the *SubL* node; it will depend on the *Count* fields of the two children in the normal way. *SubL*'s *Operand* value still specifies *mode* = *reg* and $n = -1$.

There is a problem with pushing intermediate values onto the stack when they are computed and then popping them off when they are used: If the expression evaluation is not completed, a value may be pushed but not popped. The only way to avoid completing an expression evaluation in Pascal is to execute a jump out of a function invoked in that expression. This means that control must arrive at a label. Since Pascal does not allow labels within an expression, the compiler can assume that any intermediate values on the stack when control arrives at a label are no longer interesting. They can be removed by adjusting the stack pointer. This stack pointer adjustment is necessary only at a label that can be reached from a jump out of a function, and must be inserted into the target program tree by the action mapper as explicit *MovL* constructs following such labels.

11.1 OPERAND EVALUATION ORDER

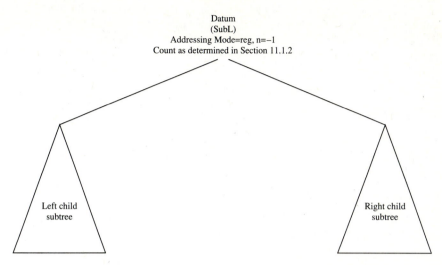

(a) At least one of the top two stack elements nonconstant, one with *Count* < *N*

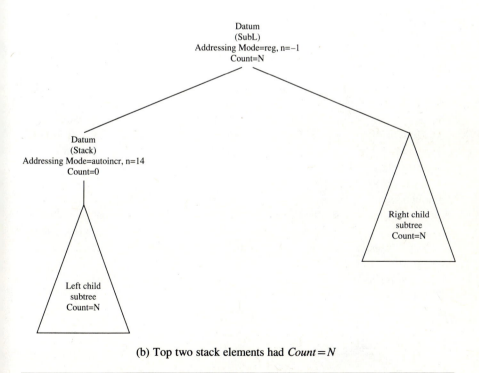

(b) Top two stack elements had *Count* = *N*

Figure 11.4
Subtrees possibly resulting from *TargetNode(SubL)*

Item-class constructs, such as the *ForLoop*, may also have intermediate results that must be stored in memory. These intermediate results must *not* be pushed onto the stack, but must be allocated in the activation record. The reason is that jumps can be made both within and out of the components of an *Item*-class node. A jump out of the construct requires that intermediate results be discarded; jumps within the construct require that they be retained. Thus there would be no simple strategy for maintaining the stack if such values were pushed onto it.

A number of target program tree constructs would require no instructions if particular relationships held between their operand and result access functions. For example, suppose the two children of a *MovL* construct had identical *Value* fields. This means that the source and destination of the move instruction are identical; a MOVL instruction would be superfluous. Another example is a *Stack* construct whose child has *Value.mode = autodecr* and *Value.n* = 14. This access function says that the operand has already been pushed onto the stack, so no additional instructions are needed to accomplish that task.

TargetNode should attempt to create such relationships wherever possible. Two tactics can be used:

- Generate an access function for the created node that bears a useful relationship to the given operand access function(s).
- Change an operand access function to establish a useful relationship.

Both of these tactics can be used when creating VAX target program trees.

As an example of the tactic of generating an appropriate access function for a result, suppose that *TargetNode(Relative)* were invoked with the second stack element a *DatumLeaf* having *Value.mode = lit* and *Value.v* = -4, while the topmost element was an *Indirect* having *Value.mode = regdef* and *Value.n* = -1. (This situation arises when a non-local variable is referenced—see Figure 9.11b.) *TargetNode* should create a *Relative* node with *Value.mode = disp*, *Value.n* = -1, and *Value.offset* = -4. If the register allocator (Section 11.2) allocates the same register for the access functions of the *Indirect* and *Relative* nodes, then no code need be generated for the *Relative* node.

It is always possible to change the *Value* field of a child specifying an unknown register (*mode = reg, n* = -1) to specify any register or memory access function. Unknown registers are always the result of some computation, and any VAX operation that leaves its result in a register can also leave its result in memory. Suppose that *TargetNode(MovL)* were invoked with the topmost stack element a *DatumLeaf* and the second element specifying an unknown register value. *TargetNode* could then copy the *Value* field from the topmost stack element into the second stack element before generating the *MovL* node. No code would be generated for this *MovL*.

11.2 RESOURCE ALLOCATION

The methods of Section 11.1 determine which intermediate values must be stored in memory during a computation, and which can be held in registers. They do not, however, associate intermediate values with *specific* registers, or allocate memory for values that must be held in the activation record.

Particular relationships among the registers used for the operands and result of an operation may be enforced by the target machine instruction set. For example, an instruction might deliver its result by modifying one of its operands. In that case, the same register must be associated with the modified operand and the result. This section shows how the compiler can associate a specific register with each intermediate result that is to be held in a register, taking instruction-dependent constraints into account, and how it can allocate activation record storage for the intermediate results of *Item*-class constructs.

As with any problem involving contextual information, we consider the computation, traversal, and storage aspects separately. Section 11.2.1 deals with the computations needed to support register allocation. The traversal strategy that makes the information available to individual nodes is presented in Section 11.2.2, and we discuss storage of information during the traversal in Section 11.2.3.

11.2.1 Computations for Resource Allocation

Register allocation is based upon sets of registers. It must be possible to request an element of a set, and to create a new set from an old one by deleting an element. (Note that the operation requesting an element does *not* remove any elements from the set.) Figure 11.5 gives an implementation of the request operation using Pascal sets. *Select* simply searches its argument until an element is found. The deadly error report is a compiler debugging aid; *Select* will never be called when *s* is empty if the compiler is correct.

A new set can be created by deleting elements of an existing set via the Pascal set difference operator, so there is no need for a special implementation of that operation. Pascal set union operations can be used to combine register sets, so the

---

```
const
    N = 11;                              (* Topmost register to be allocated *)

type
    RegisterSet = set of 0..N;           (* Allocatable registers *)

function Select(s: RegisterSet): integer;
    (* Select an available register
        On exit-
            Select = an element of s
    *)
    label 1;
    var temp: integer;
    begin
    for temp: = 0 to N do if temp in s then goto 1;
    Report(DEADLY,3004(*Compiler error - register sets*),NoPosition,0);
1:  Select: = temp;
    end;
```

Figure 11.5
Computations for register allocation

register allocation module does not have to export a union operation. Notice that if the implementation language were C, rather than Pascal, the register allocation module would need to export a full complement of set operations.

Allocation of activation record storage is handled by the storage module discussed in Chapter 8; no new operations are required.

11.2.2 Resource Allocation Traversal Strategy

Resource allocation for the VAX can be carried out during a single traversal of the target program tree, if it has been constructed as discussed in Section 11.1.3. When a node is visited, its parent provides it with a set of registers that are available for use within the subtree rooted at that node. The parent also provides an activation record to which temporaries used by the subtree rooted at that node can be added. If the node is a *Datum*-class node, its parent guarantees that the node's *Value* field specifies a complete access function.

The visit procedure allocates scratch registers, if any, for the node being visited and completes the *Value* fields of that node's *Datum*-class children. It then visits all of the children, providing a set of available registers and an activation record to each. The precise resources available to each child depend upon the properties of the node. Here is a general strategy that can be followed during a visit to a construct with *Datum*-class children:

1. Examine the children in reverse order of execution, computing the union of their fixed register sets. Define a register set *Prohibited* for each child as the union of the fixed register sets of the children evaluated after it.
2. If the construct is one in which a certain register allocation might simplify the code, attempt to make such an allocation. (We give an example of this process below.) This step may change the values of *Prohibited* sets.
3. Examine the children in order of execution, completing each result access function. The registers used to complete the access function must belong to the set of available registers provided to the node, must not be elements of *Prohibited*, and must not have been allocated to the result access function of a previously evaluated child of this node.
4. When a child's access function has been completed, visit that child. Provide it with the set of registers provided to the node, less the registers used in result access functions for previously computed children.

Note that the register set provided to a child contains the registers allocated to its own result access function. Only the registers appearing in the result access functions of *previously evaluated* children of the same node are excluded.

As an example, consider a visit to a *SubL* node. Assume that both of the operands and the result are intermediate values stored in registers. When the *SubL* node is visited, its parent has completed the access function for its result. Thus the *Value* field of the *SubL* node specifies that the result is to be left in a particular register, which we will denote by r. Neither operand access function has been completed, so each specifies that the value is to be found in an unknown register ($mode = reg, n = -1$).

The first step is to compute a *Prohibited* set for each operand. This depends on the operand evaluation order determined during tree construction. Since the operand to be evaluated second has no evaluations following it, its *Prohibited* set is empty. The *Prohibited* set for the operand to be evaluated first is just the set specifying the fixed register requirements of the operand to be evaluated second.

A *SubL* operation, neither of whose operands is a constant, can be implemented by either a SUBL2 or a SUBL3 instruction on the VAX. The SUBL3 instruction is completely general: It can use any access functions for its operands, and any access function defining a writable location for its result. SUBL2, on the other hand, stores its result using the access function that it used to obtain its right operand. SUBL2 is cheaper than SUBL3 because only two access functions need be computed when the instruction is fetched. Step (2) of the general strategy given above therefore attempts to arrange that the right operand of the node is stored in the same register as the result.

We have assumed that the result access function of the right operand of this *SubL* node specifies "register unknown." If r, the register holding the result of the *SubL*, is not in the *Prohibited* set of the right operand, step (2) completes the access function by setting $Value.n := r$. If r is in the *Prohibited* set (or if the access function had not been "register unknown") step (2) does nothing. The procedure is the same for any non-commutative computational operation on the VAX.

If the access function for the right child of the *SubL* node was completed by setting $Value.n := r$, r was made a fixed register requirement of the right child: Register r must be available for use by the right child, otherwise the right child could not store its result in r. But this means that if the left child is computed before the right child, r must be added to the *Prohibited* set of the left child. Remember that the *Prohibited* set of a child is a set of registers that cannot be used in the access function for the child's result. The result access functions of all children must exist simultaneously, so the registers they employ must be distinct.

When the result access function of a child is completed during step (2), only the *Prohibited* sets of children evaluated before that child must be modified. Step (3) ensures that result access functions of children evaluated after that child will not use the registers of its result access function.

Step (2) for a commutative operation such as *AddL* is almost the same as step (2) for a noncommutative operation such as *SubL*. The only difference is that if r is in the *Prohibited* set of the right operand (or if the access function for the right operand is not "register unknown"), step (2) attempts to complete the access function of the left operand by setting $Value.n := r$. Exactly the same conditions (access function must be "register unknown" and r must not be in the *Prohibited* set) are checked. The reason for this additional test is that the operands of a commutative operator can be exchanged, and a two-address instruction used. (Section 11.3.2 shows how the exchange is made.)

Suppose that step (2) completed the access function of the right operand of our example *SubL* construct. The left operand access function is still "register unknown." If the left operand is to be evaluated before the right operand, then r has been added to the left operand's *Prohibited* set. Otherwise, the *Prohibited* set of the left operand is unchanged by step (2).

The general strategy outlined above now examines the two operands in execution order (step 3). Assume that the right operand is to be evaluated first. Its access function is complete, so step (4) can be carried out. Since there are no previously evaluated children, the set of registers available to the child is the set of registers that was available to the *SubL* node itself. When the left operand is examined, the code generator finds that its access function is not complete. A register is selected from the set available to the *SubL* node, less register r, because r has been allocated to the result access function of a previously evaluated node. Let this set, from which the allocation is made, be S. S is also provided to the left child when it is visited during step (4).

Suppose that the left operand were to be evaluated first. The code generator would find that its access function is not complete, and would select a register from the set available to the *SubL* node, less the registers in the left child's *Prohibited* set. Since there are no previously evaluated children, the set of registers available to the child is the set of registers that was available to the *SubL* node itself. Note that r, being in the left child's *Prohibited* set, would not be allocated to complete the result access function. Register r would, however, be a member of the set of registers available to the subtree rooted in the left child. When the right operand is examined, the code generator finds its access function is complete. The set made available to the subtree rooted in the right child is the set available to the *SubL* node itself, less the register allocated to the left child's result access function.

The *SubL* example considered register-mode access functions, but the resource allocation traversal may also need to allocate registers for use in access functions with other addressing modes. For example, the index register of the access function yielded by the *Element* construct will usually not be defined when the tree is constructed. A register must be allocated and *Value.x* changed from -1 to the number of the allocated register in order to complete that access function.

11.2.3 Storage Used During Resource Allocation

During the resource allocation traversal, a set of available registers is computed for each subtree. These sets are not used during any other traversal, so there is no reason to store them in the target program tree nodes. Each set is specific to a particular visit; child visits get sets that are modifications of those used for the parent visits. Thus, sets are not used over wide areas of the tree, and global variables are inappropriate. The best choice seems to be to use local variables and parameters of the visit procedures for both the available and the prohibited register sets.

Most results of register allocation are stored in the tree as completed access functions. The register numbers allocated to scratch registers must also be stored in the tree, as must the offsets of storage areas allocated in the activation record, if instruction selection takes place during a separate traversal.

Finally, allocation of activation record storage involves two global variables of type *StorageRequired* (Figure 8.8) to keep track of the allocation state. One of them, *ActivationRecord*, specifies the complete storage requirements known so far. The other, *CurrentAR*, defines the area that is currently in use. Figure 11.6

```
procedure ItemVisit(node: TargetTree; Available: RegisterSet);
  (* Allocate resources to temporaries
    On entry-
      Available describes the registers available for use in this subtree
      ActivationRecord describes the total activation record storage
      CurrentAR describes the activation record storage in use
         before executing the code generated from this subtree
    On exit-
      Registers have been assigned to all register intermediate values in the subtree
      ActivationRecord describes the total activation record storage
      CurrentAR describes the activation record storage in use
         after executing the code generated from this subtree
  *)
  var
    i,maxcount: integer;
    fixed,NowAvailable: RegisterSet;
    SaveAR: StorageRequired;
    t: TargetSequence;

  begin
  case node↑.Kind of
    . . .
    ForLoop:
      begin SaveAR:=CurrentAR;
      DatumVisit(node↑.First,Available);
      DatumVisit(node↑.Limit,Available);
      maxcount:=0; fixed:=[ ]; t:=node↑.Body;
      while t<>nil do
        begin
        with t↑.Node↑ do
          begin
          if Count>maxcount then maxcount:=Count;
          fixed:=fixed+FixedRegisters;
          end;
        t:=t↑.Next;
        end;
      if maxcount<N then              (* Put counter in a register *)
        begin
        node↑.LoopCounter.mode:=reg;
        node↑.LoopCounter.n:=Select(Available−fixed);
        NowAvailable:=Available−[node↑.LoopCounter.n];
        end
      else                            (* Put counter in the activation record *)
        begin
        node↑.LoopCounter.mode:=disp;
        node↑.LoopCounter.n:=13;
        node↑.LoopCounter.offset:=Concatenate(CurrentAR,LongwordStorage);
        i:=Overlay(ActivationRecord,CurrentAR);
        NowAvailable:=Available;
        end;
      t:=node↑.Body;
      while t<>nil do begin ItemVisit(t↑.Node,NowAvailable); t:=t↑.Next end;
      CurrentAR:=SaveAR;
      end;
    . . .
    end;
  end;
```

Figure 11.6
Allocating resources to a *ForLoop*

illustrates the use of these variables to allocate space for the *counter* value of a *ForLoop*.

The amount of activation record storage that is in use at the end of the **for** statement is identical to the amount in use at the beginning, because if activation record storage is needed for *counter*, it will no longer be needed after the loop has been exited. Thus the value of *CurrentAR* is saved at the beginning of the visit and restored at the end.

Only two of the *Datum* children of the *ForLoop* construct could possibly require resources. (The controlled variable and the step are *DatumLeaf* constructs with complete access functions provided by the action mapper.) Figure 9.16c shows that *counter* does not exist during execution of either of these children, so their resource allocation does not reflect the resources devoted to *counter*. Resource allocation for the *Item* nodes making up the body, however, does need to reflect the resources devoted to *counter*.

Counter is needed during execution of the **for** statement body, so it cannot be stored in any register required by the body. If the body does not need all N registers, then a register is available for *counter*. The register chosen, however, cannot be one of those specifically required in the body. If the body does need all N registers, then *counter* must be stored in the activation record. Space for a longword is concatenated onto the storage currently in use, and the updated block overlaid on the total storage requirement.

As discussed above, the specification of *counter* itself is stored in the tree as the field *LoopCounter*, of type *Operand*. (*LoopCounter* is a field of the *TargetTreeNode* record, which was partially specified in Figure 11.3.) *NowAvailable* defines the set of registers that can be used by each of the subtrees rooted in the *Item*-class nodes of the loop body. If *counter* was allocated a register, that register does not appear in *NowAvailable*; otherwise *NowAvailable* contains all of the registers provided to the *ForLoop* construct by its parent.

Figure 11.7 shows how registers are allocated to a computational operation. The three-step strategy used was discussed in Section 11.2.2. Figure 11.7 employs the same tactics for propagating the result register for both commutative and noncommutative operations. Thus, if the result register of a *SubL* cannot be used for the right operand, it may be used for the left operand. There is no particular advantage in this register assignment, but there is no disadvantage either. By using the same tactics in both cases we simplify the code, and do not incur any penalty.

CompleteAccessFunction guarantees that an arbitrary access function is complete, and returns the set of allocatable registers used in that access function. If the addressing mode of the *rand* argument to *CompleteAccessFunction* does not use any registers, or if the fields that describe the register(s) it uses specify valid register numbers, then *rand* represents a complete access function. When *rand*'s addressing mode uses registers, but the corresponding fields (n and/or x) contain -1, then *CompleteAccessFunction* uses *Select* to obtain one or two registers from its *available* argument and completes the access function. When *CompleteAccessFunction* has a complete access function, it checks whether that access function uses allocatable registers. If so, then it stores the set of allocatable registers used in its *used* argument and exits.

procedure *CompleteAccessFunction*(**var** *rand*: *Operand*; *available*: *RegisterSet*; **var** *used*: *RegisterSet*);
(* Complete an access function
   On entry-
      rand is the access function to be completed
      available = registers that could be used in the access function
   On exit-
      used = registers used in the completed access function
*)
. . .

procedure *DatumVisit*(*node*: *TargetTree*; *Available*: *RegisterSet*);
(* Allocate registers to temporaries
   On entry-
      Available describes the registers available for use in this subtree
      ActivationRecord describes the total activation record storage
      CurrentAR describes the activation record storage in use
         before executing the code generated from this subtree
   On exit-
      Registers have been assigned to all register intermediate values in the subtree
      ActivationRecord describes the total activation record storage
      CurrentAR describes the activation record storage in use
         after executing the code generated from this subtree
*)
var
   RightProhibited,LeftProhibited,UsedHere: *RegisterSet*;
begin
case *node*↑.*Kind* **of**
   . . .
   AddL,SubL:
      begin
      if *LeftThenRight* **then**   (* Step 1: Determine *Prohibited* sets *)
         begin *LeftProhibited*: = *node*↑.*Right*↑.*FixedRegisters*; *RightProhibited*: = [ ] **end**
      else
         begin *LeftProhibited*: = [ ]; *RightProhibited*: = *node*↑.*Left*↑.*FixedRegisters* **end**;
      if *node*↑.*Value.mode* = *reg* **then**   (* Step 2: Facilitate two-address instruction *)
         begin
         if (*node*↑.*Right*↑.*Value.mode* = *reg*) **and** (*node*↑.*Right*↑.*Value.n* = −1)
               and not (*node*↑.*Value.n* **in** *RightProhibited*) **then**
            begin *node*↑.*Right*↑.*Value.n*: = *node*↑.*Value.n*;
            if *LeftThenRight* **then** *LeftProhibited*: = *LeftProhibited* + [*node*↑.*Value.n*];
            end
         else if (*node*↑.*Left*↑.*Value.mode* = *reg*) **and** (*node*↑.*Left*↑.*Value.n* = −1)
               and not (*node*↑.*Value.n* **in** *LeftProhibited*) **then**
            begin *node*↑.*Left*↑.*Value.n*: = *node*↑.*Value.n*;
            if not *LeftThenRight* **then** *RightProhibited*: = *RightProhibited* + [*node*↑.*Value.n*];
            end;
         end;
      if *LeftThenRight* **then**   (* Steps 3 and 4: Complete access functions and visit children *)
         begin
         CompleteAccessFunction(*node*↑.*Left*↑.*Value,Available* − *LeftProhibited,UsedHere*);
         DatumVisit(*node*↑.*Left,Available*);
         Available: = *Available* − *UsedHere*;
         CompleteAccessFunction(*node*↑.*Right*↑.*Value,Available* − *RightProhibited,UsedHere*);
         DatumVisit(*node*↑.*Right,Available*);
         end
      else
         begin
         CompleteAccessFunction(*node*↑.*Right*↑.*Value,Available* − *RightProhibited,UsedHere*);
         DatumVisit(*node*↑.*Right,Available*);
         Available: = *Available* − *UsedHere*;
         CompleteAccessFunction(*node*↑.*Left*↑.*Value,Available* − *LeftProhibited,UsedHere*);
         DatumVisit(*node*↑.*Left,Available*);
         end;
      end;
   . . .
   end;
end;

Figure 11.7
Allocating resources to a computational operation

Step (3) uses *CompleteAccessFunction* to allocate registers to the children of the node if necessary. In Figure 11.7, if the left operand should be evaluated before the right operand, then any of the registers available to the parent node, less the fixed registers required by the right child, could be used in the left child's access function. (*LeftProhibited* specifies the fixed register requirement of the right child.) Allocatable registers used in the left child's access function, defined by *UsedHere* on return from *CompleteAccessFunction*, cannot be used in the right child's access function or its computation.

11.3 INSTRUCTION SELECTION

Once the target program tree has been decorated with *Operand* values, instructions can be selected to implement each operator. As the instructions are selected, they are added to the target program by invoking operations of the assembly module (Figure 11.8). The rationale for the assembly module interface is discussed in Section 11.3.1. Section 11.3.2 is concerned with how to select instructions, given the decorated target program tree. In Section 11.3.3 we show how the code generator controls the layout of the program in memory in order to conform to the requirements of other system components.

11.3.1 Rationale for the Assembly Module Interface

In Section 9.1 we derived the characteristics of the target program tree from the set of decisions that the action mapper deferred to the code generator. A similar situation arises in the design of the assembly module interface. Two decisions are deferred by the code generator's instruction selection task:

- Encoding of instructions and data as bit patterns.
- Determination of absolute memory addresses.

The nature of those decisions determines the interface of the assembly module.

The *OpCode* enumeration in Figure 11.8 represents the set of encoding decisions that the assembly module is prepared to make. Most of them correspond to specific VAX instructions that the *Assemble* operation will convert into the bit patterns describing those instructions to the control unit of the VAX. Operands of the instructions, if any are required, are specified by records of type *Operand* (Figure 11.2). As noted in Section 9.1, a literal-mode instruction operand must be representable by a 1-, 2-, 4-, or 8-byte integer, or a 4-, 8-, or 16-byte floating point number.

Other elements of *OpCode* (such as BYTE) request that *Assemble* simply encode the data that is being supplied in the *opnd* argument, without generating any bits to define an instruction. The *Operand* records supplied with these requests must have literal or reference addressing mode, since they represent values known to the compiler.

MarkPosition is the operation that allows the code generator to defer determination of absolute memory addresses. Its argument is a reference-mode operand

11.3 INSTRUCTION SELECTION

```
const
    MaxArity=6;              (* Maximum number of operands for any encoding operation *)

type
    OpCode=(                 (* Encoding operations *)
        ADDB2,ADDW3,         (* Addition *)
        ...
        JLSS,JGEQ,           (* Conditional jump *)
        ...
        BYTE,WORD,LONG,      (* Data generation *)
        ...
        CODE,DATA,SPACE);    (* Control Sections (Section 11.3.3) *)

    arity=0..MaxArity;

    OpndArray=               (* Operand specification *)
        array [1..MaxArity] of Operand;

procedure Assemble(op: OpCode; n: arity; var opnd: OpndArray);
    (* Encode information in the target program
        On entry-
            op = encoding operation to be performed
            n = number of operands
            opnd = operand specifications
    *)

procedure MarkPosition(x: Operand);
    (* Mark a position for cross-referencing
        On entry-
            x is a valid reference-mode operand
        On exit-
            The operand described by x references the current address
    *)

procedure AssemInit;
    (* Initialize the assembly module *)

procedure AssemFinl;
    (* Finalize the assembly module *)
```

Figure 11.8
The assembly module interface

that the compiler wishes to use as a cross-reference. Invocation of *MarkPosition* causes the operand to refer to the next location that *Assemble* will use to store encoded information. When that operand is passed to *Assemble*, it will be interpreted as the address of that location. The invocation of *MarkPosition* defining a reference-mode operand need not precede an invocation of *Assemble* using it.

Conditional jump operations such as *JumpLssL* are implemented by VAX branch instructions. Unfortunately, conditional branch instructions can specify a transfer only to a location within approximately 128 bytes. The unconditional transfer instruction JMP can transfer control to an arbitrary memory location, however, so it is possible to construct a conditional transfer to an arbitrary location by reversing the condition and skipping a JMP instruction (Figure 11.9). The code generator does not have sufficient information to select the proper instruction sequence, because determination of the actual machine addresses has been deferred to the assembly module.

As a consequence of deferring the decision about address values, the code generator must request that conditional jump operations (rather than conditional branch instructions) be encoded by the assembly module. This requirement is analogous to the requirement that the action mapper specify VAX operations such as *AddL* instead of VAX instructions such as ADDL3. In each case a decision has been deferred; thus, the information needed to make another decision has become unavailable.

JLSS is an example of an encoding operation whose result depends on the length of the transfer. It might produce the bit pattern implementing either of the instruction sequences shown in Figure 11.9; the selection will be made by the assembly module on the basis of the location of the jump and the location of the instruction transferred to.

11.3.2 How to Select and Encode Instructions

To encode an instruction, the code generator must set up the necessary operand descriptions in an array of type *OpndArray* and then invoke *Assemble* with the appropriate *OpCode* value. The operand descriptions are obtained from the target program tree nodes that describe the construct being encoded. An *Operand* value is simply copied from each of the relevant nodes into the appropriate element of an *OpndArray* local to the encoding procedure.

Most *Item*-class nodes represent exactly one instruction or sequence of instructions, so instruction selection for an *Item*-class node usually involves no decisions. Encoding of most *Item*-class nodes is therefore a straightforward matter of setting up operand values and invoking *Assemble* (Figure 11.10).

Neither *Jump* nor *LabelDef* has any children that must be evaluated at target program execution time. *EncodeItem* produces a JMP instruction for the *Jump* construct by invoking *Assemble* with the destination address as the only operand.

Short distance	Long distance
BLSS destination skip:	BGEQ skip JMP destination

Figure 11.9
Instruction selection for *JumpLssL*

11.3 INSTRUCTION SELECTION

```
procedure EncodeItem(node: TargetTree);
  (* Encode an Item node
    On entry-
      The target program tree has been decorated with operand values
    On exit-
      The code for node has been passed to the assembly module
  *)

  var
    Rand: OpndArray;

  begin
  case node↑.Kind of
    Jump:
      begin Rand[1]:=node↑.Child↑.Value; Assemble(JMP,1,Rand) end;
    LabelDef:
      MarkPosition(node↑.Child↑.Value);
    MovL:
      begin
      if node↑.To↑.Count>node↑.From↑.Count then
        begin EncodeDatum(node↑.To); EncodeDatum(node↑.From) end
      else
        begin EncodeDatum(node↑.From); EncodeDatum(node↑.To) end;
      Rand[1]:=node↑.From↑.Value; Rand[2]:=node↑.To↑.Value;
      if not EqualOperands(Rand[1],Rand[2]) then Assemble(MOVL,2,Rand);
      end;
      . . .
    end;
  end;
```

Figure 11.10
Encoding *Item* constructs

A *LabelDef* node does not result in any code, so *EncodeItem* does not invoke *Assemble*. Instead, it uses *MarkPosition* to establish the address referred to by the label as the next location to be filled with encoded information by *Assemble*.

The *MovL* construct has two children that may require code to be generated. *EncodeItem* generates code for the child requiring the most registers first, and if the children have the same register requirement, it generates code to evaluate the source operand first. Each child is a *Datum*-class node, so *EncodeDatum* is invoked for this purpose. After the code for both children has been generated, we are guaranteed that the access functions given by their *Value* fields define the source value and destination address respectively. If these access functions are not identical, then *EncodeItem* uses *Assemble* to create a MOVL instruction; otherwise, no instruction is needed.

Datum-class constructs can often be implemented by any one of several instructions, depending upon the access functions of the operands and result. The required tests on the access function properties can be arbitrarily complex. Each test controls a single decision in a so-called *decision tree*. Figure 11.11a shows a

332 CHAPTER 11 CODE GENERATION

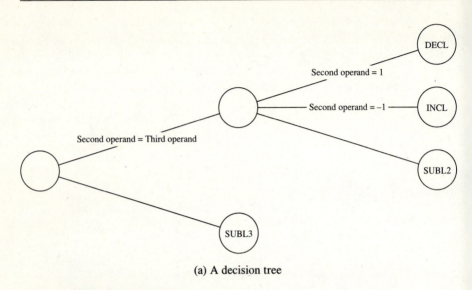

(a) A decision tree

(* *Rand*[2] − *Rand*[1] → *Rand*[3] *)
if *EqualOperands*(*Rand*[2],*Rand*[3]) **then**
  if *PlusOneOperand*(*Rand*[1]) **then begin** *Rand*[1]:=*Rand*[2]; *Assemble*(*DECL*,1,*Rand*) **end**
  else if *MinusOneOperand*(*Rand*[1]) **then begin** *Rand*[1]:=*Rand*[2]; *Assemble*(*INCL*,1,*Rand*) **end**
  else *Assemble*(*SUBL2*,2,*Rand*)
else *Assemble*(*SUBL3*,3,*Rand*);

(b) Implementation of (a) as a set of nested conditional statements

Figure 11.11
Decision trees

decision tree for the *SubL* operation. The compiler selects an instruction to implement the *SubL* operation by starting at the root and progressing to a leaf. A branch can be traversed if its test yields *true*; branches that do not specify a test can be traversed unconditionally. At each node, the selection process follows the first possible branch (counting clockwise from the 12 o'clock position). It is easy to see that a decision tree corresponds to a set of nested conditional statements (Figure 11.11b).

In Figure 11.11b, *Rand* is the *OpndArray* into which the *Operand* values from the tree have been stored. *EqualOperands*, *PlusOneOperand*, and *MinusOneOperand* are Boolean functions that test properties of *Operand* values; the particular operations required depend on the target machine instruction set. On the VAX, for example, a two-operand instruction can be used when the subtrahend and the difference are the same *Operand* value. Therefore, the code generator needs an operation to compare two *Operand* values for equality.

The operand values for a *SubL* construct are always copied from the tree to the array in a particular way: *Rand*[1] is set to the *Operand* value from the left child, *Rand*[2] is set to the *Operand* value from the right child, and *Rand*[3] is set to the *Operand* value from the root node of the construct. When a construct represents a commutative operator (e.g., *AddL*), it is appropriate for the compiler to vary the way in which the operands are copied to the array: If the *Operand* value of the left child is the same as the *Operand* value of the construct's root node, then it should be copied to *Rand*[2]; otherwise, it should be copied to *Rand*[1]. The *Operand* value of the right child is then copied to the other of *Rand*[1] or *Rand*[2], and *Rand*[3] is set to the *Operand* value from the root node of the construct. This simplifies generation of a two-operand instruction (Figure 11.12).

11.3.3 Control Sections

Most compiled programs are used as parts of larger systems, and are combined with one another by a separate program called a *loader*, or a *link editor*. The compiler must provide additional information in the program it generates in order to support this combining process. Most of the details can be hidden in the assembly module; one problem, that of the division of memory into regions with different properties, must be dealt with explicitly if it occurs.

The memory of the target machine is often divided into regions by the loader, which then puts a part of each compiled program into each region. A common division is into three regions:

- Program instructions. The loader must place information (the generated instructions) into this region. No writes will be permitted into this region during execution of the program.
- Initialized variables. The loader must place information (the initial values) into this region. Writes will be permitted into this region during execution of the program.
- Uninitialized variables. No information need be placed into this region by the loader, although the region's size must be determined. Writes will be permitted into this region during execution of the program.

Note that the instructions of *all* programs will be placed into the instruction region, and the initialized variables of *all* programs into the initialized variable region. Thus, the instructions and initialized variables of a single program may be separated from one another by an arbitrary distance. This division allows memory protection to be applied to a contiguous block of storage (the program instructions), and allows a compact representation of initialization values.

In order to support this facility of the loader, the compiler must divide a program that it is compiling into three regions. These regions are called *control sections*. Three of the encoding operations listed in Figure 11.8—CODE, DATA, and SPACE—are used for control section management. When *Assemble* is invoked with the operation CODE, it is taken by the assembly module as a signal that encoded information should be added to the "program instruction" region until further notice. DATA and SPACE are signals to switch to the "initialized

procedure *EncodeDatum*(*node*: *TargetTree*);
  (* Encode a datum node
    On entry-
      The target program tree has been decorated with operand values
    On exit-
      The code for *node* has been passed to the assembly module
  *)

var *Rand*: *OpndArray*;

procedure *EncodeChildren*(*node*: *TargetTree*);
  (* Encode the children in the proper order *)
  begin
  if *node*↑.*LeftThenRight* **then**
    begin *EncodeDatum*(*node*↑.*Left*); *EncodeDatum*(*node*↑.*Right*) **end**
  else
    begin *EncodeDatum*(*node*↑.*Right*); *EncodeDatum*(*node*↑.*Left*) **end**
  end;

procedure *Commutative*(*node*: *TargetTree*);
  (* Arrange the operands of a commutative operator
    On exit-
      Rand[1] and *Rand*[2] are set appropriately
  *)
  begin
  if *EqualOperands*(*node*↑.*Left*↑.*Value*,*node*↑.*Value*) **then**
    begin *Rand*[1]:=*node*↑.*Right*↑.*Value*; *Rand*[2]:=*node*↑.*Left*↑.*Value* **end**
  else
    begin *Rand*[1]:=*node*↑.*Left*↑.*Value*; *Rand*[2]:=*node*↑.*Right*↑.*Value* **end**
  end;

begin
case *node*↑.*Kind* **of**
  DatumLeaf: ;
  AddL:
    begin *EncodeChildren*(*node*);
    Commutative(*node*);
    Rand[3]:=*node*↑.*Value*;
    if *EqualOperands*(*Rand*[2],*Rand*[3]) **then**
      if *PlusOneOperand*(*Rand*[1]) **then begin** *Rand*[1]:=*Rand*[2]; *Assemble*(*INCL*,1,*Rand*) **end**
      else if *MinusOneOperand*(*Rand*[1]) **then begin** *Rand*[1]:=*Rand*[2]; *Assemble*(*DECL*,1,*Rand*) **end**
      else *Assemble*(*ADDL2*,2,*Rand*)
    else *Assemble*(*ADDL3*,3,*Rand*);
    end;
  SubL:
    begin *EncodeChildren*(*node*);
    Rand[1]:=*node*↑.*Left*↑.*Value*; *Rand*[2]:=*node*↑.*Right*↑.*Value*;
    Rand[3]:=*node*↑.*Value*;
    if *EqualOperands*(*Rand*[2],*Rand*[3]) **then**
      if *PlusOneOperand*(*Rand*[1]) **then begin** *Rand*[1]:=*Rand*[2]; *Assemble*(*DECL*,1,*Rand*) **end**
      else if *MinusOneOperand*(*Rand*[1]) **then begin** *Rand*[1]:=*Rand*[2]; *Assemble*(*INCL*,1,*Rand*) **end**
      else *Assemble*(*SUBL2*,2,*Rand*)
    else *Assemble*(*SUBL3*,3,*Rand*);
    end;
    . . .
  end;
end;

Figure 11.12
Encoding *Datum* constructs

11.3 INSTRUCTION SELECTION

variables" and "uninitialized variables" regions, respectively. There is no restriction on the number of times the region can be switched, and each region grows monotonically.

As an example of the need for the compiler to deal with different memory regions, consider the translation of the Pascal statement

$$writeln(f, \text{'}Distance=\text{'}, rate*time)$$

The source program tree for this statement is shown in Figure 11.13a. One of the argument expressions in this statement is a string constant, which must be stored somewhere. It is inconvenient to store such constants among the instructions of a program, because then some arrangement must be made to avoid executing them. The ideal place for them is the area used by the loader for initialized variables. Figure 11.13b shows how the expression mapping routine (*MapExpression*, Figure 9.10) uses the assembly module to achieve this effect.

The code of Figure 11.13b is executed when *MapExpression* visits the *StrExpr* construct of Figure 11.13a. "*'Distance='*" is stored at that node as an *ExtValue*, the content of the *Value* field (Figure 4.2). This string cannot be represented directly by any of the seven kinds of value that can act as an operand of a VAX instruction. Therefore, the *StrExpr* node is mapped into a target leaf

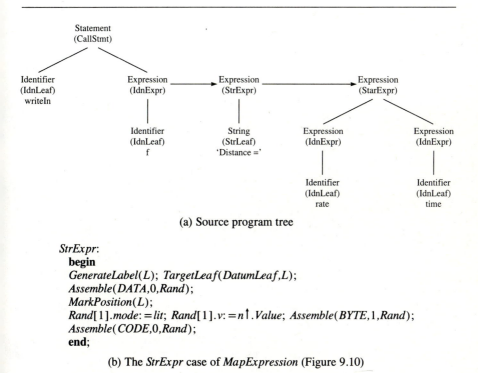

(a) Source program tree

```
StrExpr:
    begin
    GenerateLabel(L); TargetLeaf(DatumLeaf,L);
    Assemble(DATA,0,Rand);
    MarkPosition(L);
    Rand[1].mode:=lit; Rand[1].v:=n↑.Value; Assemble(BYTE,1,Rand);
    Assemble(CODE,0,Rand);
    end;
```

(b) The *StrExpr* case of *MapExpression* (Figure 9.10)

Figure 11.13
Use of control sections

specifying a label that cross-references the address where the string can be found in memory. Figure 11.13b uses the *GenerateLabel* procedure (Figure 9.8) to create a new label for this purpose, and then invokes *TargetLeaf* to produce the target program tree node.

Once the target program tree node has been created, Figure 11.13b must define the generated label and store the character of the string into the target program. DATA (Figure 11.8) tells the assembly module to add future information to the "initialized variables" region of the target program. This operation requires no operands. After invoking *Assemble* to switch to the initialized variable region, Figure 11.13b marks the current position in that region with the generated label and then encodes the characters of the string. The BYTE encoding operation, when provided with an *ExtString* operand, places each character into a single byte of the current region in the target program. Finally, Figure 11.13b returns to the instruction region by using the encoding operation CODE.

11.4 SUMMARY

The code generator first estimates the number of intermediate values that must exist simultaneously during the computation represented by each target program tree node. This estimation is carried out as the tree is being built. *Datum*-class nodes that do not involve run-time computation are never added to the target program tree, so the estimate is not inflated by the presence of intermediate values that can be calculated by the compiler. The results of the estimation determine which intermediate values must be stored in memory and which can be held in registers. Operand evaluation order is also determined, since the estimate depends upon a specific evaluation order.

Given the set of intermediate values that are to be held in registers, the code generator associates each with a specific register. It also allocates space in the activation record for any intermediate values that cannot be placed on the stack. The assignment of registers depends not only on the estimate of total register usage, but also on any fixed register requirements imposed by hardware characteristics or software conventions. One tree traversal is used to carry out the resource allocation.

Each subtree of the target program tree is allocated a set of registers by its parent, with the root being allocated the complete set. These registers are available for the subtree code to use in any way, and their number is guaranteed to be sufficient for the subtree's needs. At each node, the access functions of all children are completed, and the available registers are apportioned among the children for use in evaluating their subtrees. When a node represents an operation that could be implemented more efficiently with certain register assignments, the allocator attempts to make those assignments.

Finally, instructions are selected to implement each target construct. Instruction selection requires a single execution-order traversal of the decorated target program tree. At each node, the cheapest instruction is selected on the basis of the operation to be performed and the characteristics of the operands and result. The instructions are output via the assembly module as they are selected.

The assembly module provides facilities for encoding target instructions as bit patterns and for marking specific locations with labels. Since most programs are combined with separately-compiled code (such as library routines) before being run, the assembly module also allows its clients to partition the compiled code in accordance with the requirements of the operating system.

NOTES

The fact that the amount of temporary storage required to evaluate an expression depended upon the order in which the operands were evaluated was first noted by Floyd [6]. Nakata [10] introduced the idea of labeling each tree node with the number of registers needed to evaluate the expression rooted in that node, and stated the rules for determining the best evaluation order and computing the label values. Nakata's method was extended to operators with more than two operands by Redziejowski [11], who gave a formal proof that it always led to the minimum register requirement. Sethi and Ullman [12] proved that the earlier algorithms yield the minimum number of operations on any computer with fetch, store, and computation instructions. They incorporated algebraic properties (associativity and commutativity) of the operators into their analysis, and also showed how to account for operations that use scratch registers.

On the basis of the Sethi-Ullman numbers, we choose to evaluate some operand of an operator first. The complete code for this evaluation is generated before any code for another operand is generated. This strategy is called *contiguous evaluation*, because all of the code for one subtree forms a contiguous sequence. It can be shown [2] that if some operators yield intermediate values requiring more than one register, then contiguous evaluation does not always lead to the best code. Recall that the VAX's EMUL instruction, which we use, has exactly that property. Execution-order determination algorithms that take account of multiple-register results are much more complex than the approach we described. In our experience, the loss resulting from use of contiguous evaluation is insignificant in practice.

All of the techniques in this chapter are described in terms of a "general register" machine architecture, in which the processor has access to a number of registers with identical capabilities. The trend in hardware architecture seems to be in the direction of such machines, probably because that organization simplifies both hardware and software design. Another important architecture, used frequently in floating-point coprocessors, is one in which the registers are replaced by a stack. Operations always take their operands from the top n stack locations and return their result to the top of the stack. There is no need for register allocation on a stack machine, and instruction selection is trivial in most cases because each operation is implemented by exactly one instruction. Execution order determination is still important, and the basic ideas of Section 11.1.1 remain valid. The only difference is an additional constraint imposed by the requirement that operands be computed onto the stack in a particular order [3].

When a machine has several different kinds of registers (e.g., index registers and accumulators), the number of registers of each class required by an expression can be computed using the techniques of Section 11.1. By reasoning similar to that used for machines with multiple-register intermediate values, one can show that contiguous evaluation may not be best. Again, the difference is small in practice.

The basic principle used by the code generator in selecting instructions is to first fix the locations of all of an instruction's operands. Once that has been done, the number of choices for the instruction is quite limited [7, 8]. Decision trees provide a natural way of describing the decision process, and they lead to a simple implementation. Tools have been developed to aid the compiler designer in constructing the decision trees and implementing them [4].

"Control section" is a term first introduced in conjunction with IBSYS, an operating system for IBM 7040 and 7090 computers [15]. IBSYS took a very general view of control sections, allowing the loader to insert, delete, and replace them arbitrarily. This flexibility is quite useful for languages such as FORTRAN, which provide many named regions for common data.

Assembly module implementation is basically straightforward [9]. When the target machine places restrictions on the sizes of certain address operands, as in the case of VAX conditional branch instructions, there is additional complexity [14]. Many compiler writers do not bother to write a complete assembly module, but simply have *Assemble* and *MarkPosition* write symbolic assembly code that is then passed to a symbolic assembler. This is a good way to bring a compiler up quickly, but it entails performance penalties due to the volume of character input/output. A better strategy is that taken by the designers of the Edinburgh Multiple Access System—provide an assembly module as part of the standard library [13].

REFERENCES

1. Aho, A. V. and Johnson, S. C., "Optimal Code Generation for Expression Trees," *J. ACM 23*, 3 (July 1976), 488–501.
2. Aho, A. V., Johnson, S. C., and Ullman, J. D., "Code Generation for Machines with Multiregister Operations," *Proc. of the Fourth ACM Symp. on Prin. of Prog. Lang.*, 1977, 21–28.
3. Bruno, J. L. and Lassagne, T., "The Generation of Optimal Code for Stack Machines," *J. ACM 22*, 3 (July 1975), 382–396.
4. Cordy, J. R., "An Orthogonal Model for Code Generation," CSRI-177, Computer Systems Research Institute, Univ. of Toronto, Toronto, Jan. 1986.
5. *VAX Architecture Handbook*, Digital Equipment Corporation, Concord, MA, 1981.
6. Floyd, R. W., "An Algorithm for Coding Efficient Arithmetic Operations," *Comm. of the ACM 4*, 1 (Jan. 1961), 42–51.
7. Horspool, R. N. and Scheuneman, A., "Automating the Selection of Code Templates," *Software—Practice & Experience 15*, 5 (May 1985), 503–514.
8. Horspool, R. N., "An Alternative to the Graham-Glanville Code-Generation Method," *IEEE Software*, May 1987, 33–39.
9. Mealy, G. H., "A Generalized Assembly System," in *Programming Systems and Languages*, S. Rosen (editor), McGraw-Hill, 1967, 535–559.
10. Nakata, I., "On Compiling Algorithms for Arithmetic Expressions," *Comm. of the ACM 10*, 8 (Aug. 1967), 492–494.

11. Redziejowski, R. R., "On Arithmetic Expressions and Trees," *Comm. of the ACM 12*, 2 (Feb. 1969), 81-84.
12. Sethi, R. and Ullman, J. D., "The Generation of Optimal Code for Arithmetic Expressions," *J. ACM 17*, 4 (Oct. 1970), 715-728.
13. Stephens, P. D., "The IMP Language and Compiler," *Computer J. 17* (1974), 216-223.
14. Szymanski, T. G., "Assembling Code for Machines with Span-Dependent Instructions," *Comm. of the ACM 21*, 4 (Apr. 1978), 300-308.
15. Talmadge, R. B., "Design of an Integrated Programming and Operating System Part II. The Assembly Program and its Language," *IBM Systems Journal 2* (1963), 162-179.

EXERCISES

11.1 Consider the computation of Sethi-Ullman numbers.
    (a) Show how to construct an expression with an arbitrarily high Sethi-Ullman number.
    (b) Show how to construct an expression whose Sethi-Ullman number is 1, but which has an arbitrarily large number of operators.
    (c) Figure 8.10 appears to be a rather complex program. What is the maximum Sethi-Ullman number you can find for any expression in Figure 8.10?

11.2 Consider the computation of the Sethi-Ullman number for a construct whose operator has n operands. Assume that the operands are evaluated in the order

$$e_{i_0}, e_{i_1}, \ldots, e_{i_n}$$

and the Sethi-Ullman number for e_{i_j} is S_{i_j}. Prove that the Sethi-Ullman number for the construct is a minimum when

$$S_{i_0} \leqslant S_{i_1} \leqslant \cdots \leqslant S_{i_n}$$

11.3 Consider the question of fixed register requirements on the VAX.
    (a) The routine calling conventions established by the VMS operating system and generally followed elsewhere dictate that a function should return its result in R0 (and R1 if the result is 8 bytes long). What other fixed register requirements are established by the hardware [5]?
    (b) Given your answer to (a), is it possible that the union of fixed register requirement sets at a node will have more elements than indicated by the normal register counting process? Explain briefly.
    (c) If the answer to (b) were "no," does that imply that the fixed register sets need not be computed at all? Explain briefly.

11.4 Registers 12-14 are used for special purposes on the VAX, so we defined a register set over the base type 0..11. Suppose that the special-purpose registers had been 3, 7, 11, and 12. Show how to define register sets and fixed register requirements so all of our existing techniques can be used in this case.

11.5 When an expression requires more than the available number of registers, we advocate inserting stacking code within that expression. It would also be possible to break up the expression by removing subexpressions whose values must be stored, creating assignments that compute the values of those subexpressions, and assigning the results to explicit temporaries. These explicit temporaries would then be referenced in the original expression [1]. Is this strategy ever superior to ours? If so, under what circumstances?

11.6 [2] Consider a machine (such as the Digital PDP-11) in which the result of an integer multiplication occupies two registers and an integer division requires a two-register dividend.

(a) Use the methods of Section 11.1.2 to determine the number of registers required to evaluate the following expression without storing any intermediate values:

$$(((a*b+c*d) \text{ div } e)*f) \text{ div } ((g*h) \text{ div } (i+j))$$

(b) In light of your answer to (a), explain the register usage of the following evaluation strategy:

(R0,R1): = $a*b$
(R2,R3): = $c*d$
(R0,R1): = (R0,R1) + (R2,R3)
R0: = (R0,R1) **div** e
(R2,R3): = $g*h$
R1: = $i+j$
R2: = (R2,R3) **div** R1
(R0,R1): = R0*f
R0: = (R0,R1) **div** R2

11.7 We pointed out in Section 11.1.3 that jumps out of procedures require the action mapper to generate additional code following a label that could be the target of such a jump. This code must delete any stacked temporary results.

(a) Specify the target program tree fragment that the action mapper must generate.

(b) Suppose that, unlike Pascal, the source language being translated allowed the bounds of a local array variable to be specified on procedure entry (both FORTRAN and ALGOL 60 have this property). Would your answer to (a) be affected? Explain briefly.

11.8 Try to devise a strategy that will allow you to store the counter of a *ForLoop* construct implemented according to Figure 9.16c on the stack. Be sure that you handle the following situation correctly:

```
for i:=j to k do
  begin
  S₁; if e₁ then goto 1; S₂;
  for p:=q to r do
    begin
    S₃; if e₂ then goto 1; S₄;
    end;
  S₅; 1: S₆;
  end;
```

Can you state any advantage for storing the counter on the stack?

11.9 Suppose that we chose not to use the VAX EDIV instruction to implement the Pascal **mod** operator.

(a) Write a sequence of VAX operations that implement x **mod** 10 using DIVL, MULL, and SUBL, assuming that x is a local integer variable.

11.4 SUMMARY

(b) Explain why you cannot carry out this implementation with a collection of target operations that represent the individual VAX instructions, but instead must define a single *ModL* construct.

(c) Write the code for the *ModL* case of *TargetNode*. (This code must compute the register requirement of the *ModL* node, given the register requirements of its children.)

11.10 *Relative*, *Element*, and *Indirect* are the three target program constructs that can be implemented as addressing modes.

(a) For each construct, list the addressing modes that could appear as the value of the *mode* field of the construct's *Value*.

(b) For each construct, and each of the values you noted in (a), state the addressing modes that must appear as the value(s) of the *mode* field(s) of the construct's child(ren)'s *Value*(s).

11.11 At the end of Section 11.1.3, we noted that it was always possible to change an access function of a child that specified an unknown register (*Value.mode*=reg, *Value.n*=−1). Is it possible to change the child's access function if it is anything else? Explain briefly.

11.12 We have seen that the selection of addressing modes for *Datum*-class nodes is determined by both the construct and the context. In Chapter 10, the final type for an *Expression*-class node was also determined by both the construct and the context.

(a) Develop an analogy between addressing mode determination for *Datum*-class target program tree nodes and final type determination for *Expression*-class source program tree nodes. What are the analogs of the indication, operator, and possible type set?

(b) Using the analogy you developed in (a), write a set of signatures that describe the addressing mode relationships.

(c) Show how the operator identification module could be used to determine addressing modes.

11.13 Draw the target tree that would be constructed by the technique of Section 11.1 for each of the following expressions. Be sure to show the partial access functions specified by the *Value* fields of the nodes. (Assume that all variables are local.)

(a) $p\uparrow.f$
(b) $p\uparrow[i+17].f$
(c) $a[i][j]$
(d) $a[p\uparrow.f+17]\uparrow+10$

11.14 For each of the trees you drew in Exercise 11.13, apply the register allocation procedure of Section 11.2 to complete the *Value* fields of the nodes.

11.15 Consider the target program tree fragment of Figure 11.4b.

(a) Write the best VAX instruction to implement the *SubL* node.

(b) Suppose the value of the right child, rather than the value of the left child, had been pushed onto the stack. (The *Stack* construct would therefore have been the right child of *SubL*.) Write the best VAX instruction to implement the *SubL* node under these conditions.

(c) In Section 11.1 we stated that either operand could be evaluated first if their register requirements were the same. Given your answers to (a) and (b), would you recommend an alteration in that statement?

11.16 Write the procedure *CompleteAccessFunction* whose interface appears in Figure 11.7.

11.17 Write code for the *Relative* and *Indirect* cases of *DatumVisit* (Figure 11.7).

11.18 Consider the statement $v := v + p.f\uparrow.i$. Assume that all variables are local.
  (a) What sequence of target tree construction operator invocations would be made by the translator in building a target program tree for this expression?
  (b) Draw the target program tree actually produced, showing the information placed into each of the *Value* fields during tree construction.
  (c) Show the complete target program tree decorations after the resource allocation traversal.

11.19 Prove that the register-allocation visit procedure can never provide any of its children with fewer available registers than that child requires.

11.20 Add code for the operation *JumpGtrL* (Table 9.2) to Figure 11.10.

11.21 Consider the encoding of the VAX operation *Relative*.
  (a) Draw a decision tree for this operation. At least one of the leaves of this tree should correspond to "no instruction"; simply leave such leaves blank.
  (b) Add the code for case *Relative* to Figure 11.12.

11.22 In Figure 11.13b, *Assemble* is invoked to switch memory areas both before and after the operations that define the string and its label. Show that these calls could be omitted, and the desired effect achieved by a single *Assemble* invocation before the action mapping traversal and a single *Assemble* invocation after the action mapping traversal.

11.23 Redefine the interface for the assembly module, assuming a machine other than the VAX. Was it necessary to change the structure of the interface? Give a brief rationale for your design.

Appendix

Sample Project Documentation

A typical project in an introductory compiler construction course based on this book implements a compiler that accepts a simple algorithmic language and produces assembly code for an available computer. The source language and target machine should be complex enough to require nontrivial solutions to all of the problems listed in the rightmost column of Table 1.1, yet simple enough so the compiler can be completed within the time available for the course.

The purpose of the project is to familiarize you with the task of constructing a compiler, and to give you a model for compiler design. You should *not* be required to develop the model on your own. This means that the documentation describing the project should define not only the source language, but also the source and target program trees and the relationships among the four representations of the program (source program text, source program tree, target program tree, and target program text). The manufacturer's documentation should be used to define the target machine.

Section A.1 defines C-- (a scaled-down version of C) and Section A.2 discusses three sample programs written in that language. A source program tree structure appropriate for representing C-- programs is specified in Section A.3. Section A.4 adapts the target program tree format presented in Chapter 9 to C-- programs. Some aspects of the mapping from C-- to the VAX are discussed in Section A.5.

A.1 THE DEFINITION OF C--

This section defines the structure and meaning of a C-- program. It has five subsections, each dealing with one aspect of the language: basic symbols, programs, declarations, statements, and expressions. Basic symbols are the indivisible atoms of the language, and their meanings are defined by relating them to our shared experience with programming languages. All other constructs are composite—each is formed by combining parts. Their meanings can thus be defined in terms of the meanings of their components and fundamental concepts such as "sequence of execution."

A.1.1 Basic Symbols

The basic symbols of C-- are its identifiers, denotations, and delimiters. Figure A.1 shows the structure of identifiers and denotations in C--. The set *letter* includes all upper- and lower-case alphabetic characters, plus the underscore "_". Upper- and lower-case versions of the same letter are distinct. The delimiters of the language are the following special characters and keywords:

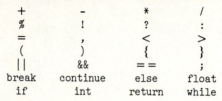

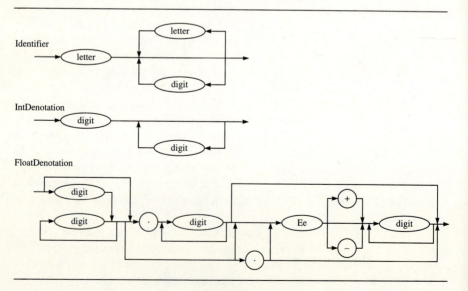

Figure A.1
C-- identifiers and denotations

An identifier is a freely chosen representation for an object. It is given meaning by a construct of the program. The appearances at which an identifier is given a meaning are called *defining occurrences* of that identifier. All other appearances of the identifier are called *applied occurrences*.

Denotations have the usual meanings.

Keywords can be used only as indicated by the syntax diagrams.

Comments are arbitrary sequences of characters beginning with "/*" and ending with "*/". Comments cannot be nested. Comments, spaces, and newlines may not appear within basic symbols. Two adjacent basic symbols must be separated by one or more comments, spaces, or newlines, unless one of the basic symbols is a special character. Otherwise comments, spaces, and newlines are meaningless.

A.1.2 Program Structure

Figure A.2 shows the structure of a C-- program. See Section A.1.3 for types, parameters, and declarations, and Section A.1.4 for statements.

A.1.2.1 Programs A program specifies a computation by describing a sequence of actions. A computation specified in C-- may be realized by any sequence of actions having the same effect as the one described here for the given computation. The meaning of constructs that do not satisfy the rules given here is undefined. Whether, and in what manner, a particular implementation of C-- gives meaning to undefined constructs is outside the scope of this definition.

A program is executed by reading parameter values from the standard input unit and executing the component *Compound*. A *Return* (Section A.1.4.5) must be executed to terminate the program.

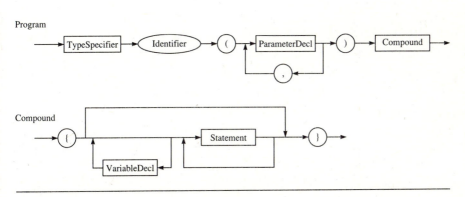

Figure A.2
The structure of a C-- program

A.1.2.2 Compounds The components of a *Compound* are executed in the sequence in which they were written.

A.1.2.3 Visibility Rules Let the term *range* be used to describe either a *Program* or a *Compound* (Figure A.2). The text of a range, excluding the text of ranges nested within it, may contain no more than one defining occurrence of a given identifier. Every applied occurrence of an identifier must *identify* some defining occurrence of that identifier. Unless otherwise stated, the defining occurrence D identified by an applied occurrence A of the identifier I is determined as follows:

1. Let R be the text of A, and let P be the entire C-- program.
2. Let R' be the smallest range properly containing R, and let T be the text of R', excluding the text of all ranges nested within it.
3. If T does not contain a defining occurrence of I, and R' is not P, then let R be R' and go to step (2).
4. If T contains a defining occurrence of I, then let T' be the fragment of T that begins with the first defining occurrence of I and ends at the end of T.
5. If T' does not contain R, and R' is not P, then let R be R' and go to step (2).
6. If T' contains R, then the defining occurrence at the beginning of T' is D.

(For an example of this process, see Section A.2.)

Identifier is a defining occurrence in the syntax diagrams for *Program* (Figure A.2), *ParameterDecl* (Figure A.3), and *VariableDecl* (Figure A.3). All other instances of *Identifier* are applied occurrences.

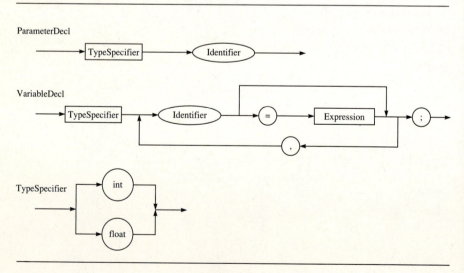

Figure A.3
Declarations

A.1.3 Declarations

Figure A.3 shows the structure of C-- declarations. See Section A.1.5 for Expressions.

A.1.3.1 Values, Types, Objects, and Variables *Values* are abstract entities upon which operations may be performed, *types* classify values according to the operations that may be performed upon them, and *objects* are the concrete instances of values that are operated upon. Two objects are *equal* if they are instances of the same value. A *variable* of type t is a concrete instance of an abstract entity that can *refer to* (or *contain*) an object that is an instance of a value of type t.

Every object and variable has a specified *extent*, during which it can be operated upon. The extents of denotations (see Section A.1.1) are unbounded; the extents of variables are determined by their declarations.

Values of types *int* and *float* have the usual meanings. The range of *int* values, and the range and precision of *float* values, are determined by the particular implementation of C--.

A.1.3.2 Parameter Declarations A variable is created, and the identifier represents this variable. The extent of the created variable is the entire execution history of the program. It refers initially to an object read from the standard input unit before program execution begins. The objects read are referred to by the variables named in the parameter list in order from left to right.

If the parameter declaration has the form

t Identifier

then the created variable can refer to objects of type t.

A.1.3.3 Variable Declarations A variable is created, and the identifier represents this variable. The extent of the created variable begins when the declaration is executed and ends when execution of the smallest *Compound* (Figure A.2) containing the declaration is complete.

If the variable declaration has the form

t Identifier

then the created variable can refer to objects of type t. Initially, it refers to an arbitrary object.

If the variable declaration has the form

t Identifier = Expression

then the created variable can refer to objects of type t. Initially, it refers to the object yielded by the given *Expression*.

A.1.4 Statements

Figure A.4 defines the structure of C-- Statements. See Section A.1.2 for Compounds and Section A.1.5 for Expressions.

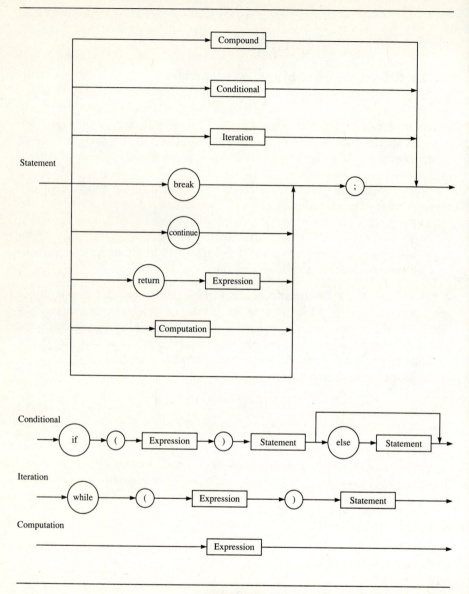

Figure A.4
Statements

A.1.4.1 Conditionals A *Conditional* is executed by first evaluating the component *Expression*, which must yield an object of type *int*. If the result of this evaluation is not 0, the first component *Statement* is executed. Otherwise, if the keyword *'else'* is present, then the second component *Statement* is executed.

A.1 THE DEFINITION OF C-- 349

If the keyword *'else'* is present, then it forms a *Conditional* with the closest preceding *'if'* in the same *Compound*. Therefore the statement

$$\text{if } (e_1) \text{ if } (e_2) \; s_1 \text{ else } s_2$$

is identical in meaning to the statement

$$\text{if } (e_1) \; \{ \text{ if } (e_2) \; s_1 \text{ else } s_2 \; \}$$

A.1.4.2 Iterations
The iteration

$$\text{while } (\, e \,) \; s$$

is identical in meaning to the conditional

$$\text{if } (\, e \,) \; \{ \, s \text{ while } (\, e \,) \; s \,\}$$

A.1.4.3 Break
A break may appear only within the component *Statement* of an iteration. Execution of a break causes termination of the smallest containing iteration.

A.1.4.4 Continue
A continue may appear only within the component *Statement* of an iteration. Execution of a continue causes termination of the component *Statement* of the smallest containing iteration. The component *Expression* of the iteration is evaluated next. Therefore, the continue has the effect of cutting short the current execution of the controlled statement and testing whether another should be commenced. Contrast this behavior with that of the break, which escapes from the iteration entirely.

A.1.4.5 Return
A return is executed by first evaluating the component *Expression*. Execution of the program is then terminated, with the value of the component *Expression* as the result.

A.1.4.6 Computation
A computation is executed by first evaluating the component *Expression*. The result of that evaluation is then discarded.

A.1.5 Expressions

Expression structure in C-- is determined by operator precedence and association in the usual way (see Section 4.3):

> *Expression* = *Identifier* '=' *Expression* | *Condition* .
> *Condition* = *Disjunction* | *Disjunction* '?' *Expression* ':' *Condition* .
> *Disjunction* = *Conjunction* | *Disjunction* '||' *Conjunction* .
> *Conjunction* = *Comparison* | *Conjunction* '&&' *Comparison* .
> *Comparison* = *Relation* | *Relation* '==' *Relation* .
> *Relation* = *Sum* | *Sum* ('<' | '>') *Sum* .
> *Sum* = *Term* | *Sum* ('+' | '−') *Term* .
> *Term* = *Factor* | *Term* ('*' | '/' | '%') *Factor* .
> *Factor* = *Primary* | ('!' | '−') *Factor* .
> *Primary* = *IntDenotation* | *FloatDenotation* | *Identifier* | '(' *Expression* ')' .

Every subexpression (*Condition*, *Disjunction*, *Conjunction*, etc.) may be evaluated to yield an object of a certain type. The operands of an expression are evaluated collaterally unless the expression is a *Condition*, a *Disjunction*, or a *Conjunction* (see Section A.1.5.2). Each operator indication denotes a set of possible operations, with the particular one meant in a given context being determined by the operand types according to Table A.1. When the type of value delivered by an operand does not satisfy the requirements of an operation, a *coercion* (Section A.1.5.1) can be applied to yield a value that does satisfy the requirements. Any ambiguities in the process of selecting computations and coercions is resolved in favor of the choice with the smallest total number of coercions.

It must be possible to determine an operation for every operator indication appearing in a program.

A.1.5.1 Coercions

The context in which an expression appears may permit a stated set of types for the result of that expression, prescribe a single type, or require that the result be discarded. When the a priori type of the result does not satisfy the requirements of the context, coercion is employed. (See Section 10.1.2 for further discussion.)

C-- allows only one coercion operation: Conversion of an integer value to floating point.

A.1.5.2 Operations

An assignment causes the variable represented by the left operand to refer to a new instance of the value yielded by the right operand. The result of the assignment is the value yielded by the right operand.

If the left operand of an assignment represents an integer variable and the right operand yields a floating-point value, then the floating-point value is truncated to an integer by removing any nonzero fractional part. Thus, 3.6 would become 3 and -3.6 would become -3. If the resulting integer is not representable, then the behavior of the assignment is undefined.

A *Condition* containing the '?' and ':' operators is evaluated by first evaluating the component *Disjunction*. If the result is not zero, then the value of the condition is the value of the component *Expression*, and the component *Condition* is not evaluated. Otherwise, the value of the condition is the value of the component *Condition*, and the component *Expression* is not evaluated.

The component *Expression* and component *Condition* of a *Condition* must be *balanced* to ensure that the type of the result yielded is the same, no matter which alternative was chosen. Balancing involves coercing the result of each to a common type. When the type is uniquely prescribed by the context, then this type is chosen as the common result type for all alternatives. If the context of the expression is such that several result types are possible, the one leading to the smallest total number of coercions is chosen.

The expression $e_1 \;||\; e_2$ has the same meaning as the expression

$$e_1 == 0 \,?\, e_2 : 1.$$

The expression $e_1 \;\&\&\; e_2$ has the same meaning as the expression

$$e_1 == 0 \,?\, 0 : e_2.$$

TABLE A.1 OPERATOR IDENTIFICATION

Indication	Operand Type Left	Operand Type Right	Result Type	Operation
=	int	int	int	integer assignment
		float		truncating assignment
	float	float	float	floating assignment
||	int	int	int	disjunction
&&	int	int	int	conjunction
==			int	integer equality
	float	float	int	floating equality
<	int	int	int	integer less than
	float	float	int	floating less than
>	int	int	int	integer greater than
	float	float	int	floating greater than
+	int	int	int	integer addition
	float	float	float	floating addition
−	int	int	int	integer subtraction
	float	float	float	floating subtraction
*	int	int	int	integer multiplication
	float	float	float	floating multiplication
/	int	int	int	integer division
	float	float	float	floating division
%	int			remainder
!		int	int	complement
−		int	int	integer negation
		float	float	floating negation

The expression $!e$ has the same meaning as the expression $e == 0\ ?\ 1 : 0$.

Equality yields the value 1 if its operands have the same value. Otherwise, it yields the value 0.

Relational operators yield the value 1 if the relation they describe is satisfied. Otherwise, they yield the value 0.

The arithmetic operators addition, subtraction, multiplication, floating division, and negation have the usual meaning as long as the values of all operands and results lie in the range permitted by the mapping from C-- objects to target machine objects (Section 8.1.1). Division and remainder are defined only when the value of the right operand is nonzero.

The result of an integer division operation with dividend m and divisor $n \neq 0$ is determined as follows:

1. Let q and $0 \leq r < |n|$ be two integers such that $m = q \times n + r$.
2. If $r = 0$ then the result of m/n is q.
3. Otherwise, if $m > 0$ and $n > 0$ then the result of m/n is q.
4. Otherwise, the result of m/n is either q or $q+1$ at the discretion of the implementor.

The result of the remainder operation $m\%n$ is given by:

$$m - (m/n)*n$$

A.2 SAMPLE C-- PROGRAMS

Figure A.5 shows a C-- program to compute the greatest common divisor of two integers. The initial values of the parameters are read from the standard input device as a part of the initialization process. The result returned by the program is written to the standard output device as a part of the finalization process.

The factorial program of Figure A.6 uses an initialized variable declaration to define the limit imposed by machine arithmetic. If the initial value of v is invalid, the program returns -1 as its answer.

Figure A.7 illustrates the visibility rules of C--. According to Section A.1.2.3, the identification of the identifier v in $v+7$ is carried out as follows:

1. Let R be the identifier v in $v+7$, and let P be the complete text of Figure A.7.
2. Let R' be the compound statement beginning with {, and ending with }; this is the smallest range containing R. Since there are no ranges contained within R', $T = R'$.

```
int
GCD(int x, int y)
{
    while (!(x == y))
        if (x > y) x = x-y;
        else y = y-x;
    return x;
}
```

Figure A.5
GCD in C--

```
int
Factorial(int v)
{
    int limit = 7;

    if (v < 0 || v > limit) return -1;
    {
        int c = 0, fact = 1;

        /* Loop invariant: fact == c! */
        while (c < v) {
            c = c+1; fact = fact*c;
        }
        return fact;
    }
}
```

Figure A.6
Factorial in C--

3. T contains a defining occurrence of v (the variable declarator $v=3$), so we do not return to step (2).
4. Since $v=3$ is the first defining occurrence of v in T, let T' be the fragment of T beginning with $v=3$ and ending with }.
5. T' does not contain R, R' is not P, so we let R be R' and return to step (2).
2'. Since R is now the entire compound statement, the smallest range containing R is P, the whole text of Figure A.7. Therefore $R'=P$. Let T be the lines up to (but not including) {, (because T must exclude the text of the compound statement—a range nested within R').
3'. T contains a defining occurrence of v (the declaration *int v*), so we do not return to step (2).
4'. Since *int v* is the first defining occurrence of v in T, let T' be the fragment of T beginning with *int v* and ending just after }.
5'. T' contains R, so we do not return to step (2).

```
int
Scope(int v)
{
    int limit = v + 7, v = 3;

    return limit-v;
}
```

Figure A.7
Visibility in C--

6. T' contains R, so D is the defining occurrence at the beginning of T'—the v in the parameter declaration.

A similar analysis can be used to show that the v in the return statement identifies the defining occurrence in the variable declaration $v=3$. Thus, the effect of this program is to print an integer larger by 4 than its input parameter.

It is important to note that the visibility rules of C-- make use of an identifier before its definition impossible.

A.3 THE C-- SOURCE PROGRAM TREE

All of the information that the structuring task of the compiler obtains about the source program is embodied in the source program tree (Figure A.8). If a particular item of information cannot be accessed via this tree, then it cannot be obtained at all. Information is encoded in the "shape" of the tree and in values stored at the leaves. See Section 4.1.1 for a general discussion of the structure and content of a source program tree.

This section defines the set of possible source program trees by defining all of the concepts and constructs of the source language.

A.3.1 C-- Concepts

C-- is a rather simple language, having only eight distinct concepts. Each of the eight is described below in a separate subsection. The subsections are ordered according to the order of appearance of the concepts in the C-- definition.

Each node of the source program tree carries the coordinates (see Section 2.2) of the left end of the construct rooted in that node. Since all nodes have this information, which is determined at the time the tree is built, it is not mentioned in the descriptions of the individual concepts below.

A.3.1.1 Identifier An identifier is a freely chosen representation for an object. Its properties are a unique encoding and the definition determined by the visibility rules (Section A.1.2.3). Distinct identifiers have distinct encodings.

Each identifier occurrence in the source program is represented in the source program tree by a leaf. The unique encoding of the identifier represented is stored at that leaf when the source program tree is constructed. All leaves representing occurrences of a particular identifier store the same value; leaves representing occurrences of different identifiers store different values.

The associated definition is determined during semantic analysis; it is not stored at the time the tree is constructed.

A.3.1.2 Integer An integer denotation is a representation of an integer value. Its only property is the value represented. According to the definition of C--, any sign preceding a denotation is not part of that denotation; therefore, only nonnegative values are represented by integer denotations.

```
            int
            GCD(int x, int y)
            {
                while (!(x == y))
                    if (x > y) x = x-y;
                    else y = y-x;
                return x;
            }
```

(a) The source text from Figure A.5

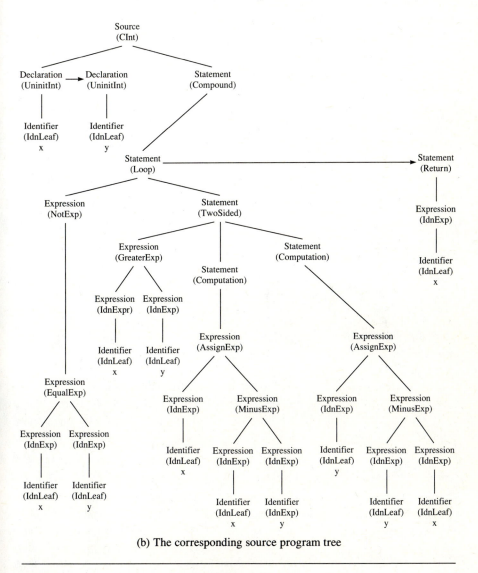

(b) The corresponding source program tree

Figure A.8
The GCD source program

Each integer denotation in the source program is represented in the source program tree by a leaf. The value of the integer represented is stored at that leaf when the source program tree is constructed.

A.3.1.3 Float A floating-point denotation is a representation of a real number. Its only property is the value represented. According to the definition of C--, any sign preceding a denotation is not part of that denotation; therefore, only nonnegative values are represented by floating-point denotations.

Each floating-point denotation in the source program is represented in the source program tree by a leaf. The value of the real number represented is stored at that leaf when the source program tree is constructed.

A.3.1.4 Source A source is a complete C-- program. Its properties are the scope that it provides for parameter definitions and the type of its result.

Both properties are evaluated during semantic analysis; neither is stored at the time the tree is constructed.

A source node is the root of the source program tree, and never appears in any other position.

A.3.1.5 Range A range is a region of the program that contains declarations. Its only property is the scope that it provides for variable definitions.

The scope is evaluated during semantic analysis; it is not stored at the time the tree is constructed.

A.3.1.6 Declaration A declaration is a construct that associates an identifier with an entity. Its only property is the identifier/entity relationship it establishes.

The identifier/entity relationship is established during semantic analysis; it is not stored at the time the tree is constructed.

A.3.1.7 Statement A statement is a construct that carries out an action but does not return a value. It has no additional properties.

A.3.1.8 Expression An expression is a construct that returns a value. Its only property is the type (Section A.1.3.1, Table A.1) of the value it returns.

The type returned by an expression is determined during semantic analysis; it is not stored at the time the tree is constructed.

A.3.2 C-- Constructs

Table A.2 summarizes the constructs of C--. The structure of the subtree for each construct is given in the second column of Table A.2. For example, the "InitFloat" construct appears as a subtree whose root is a *Declaration* node. The *Declaration* node has two children—an *Identifier* node and an *Expression* node. Further structure of the subtree can be determined only when the construct that implements the *Expression* node is known.

TABLE A.2 C-- CONSTRUCTS

Construct	Structure
AndExp	(*Expression,Expression*): *Expression*
AssignExp	(*Expression,Expression*): *Expression*
Block	(*Declaration$^+$,Statement$^+$*): *Range*
BreakStmt	*Statement*
CFloat	(*Declaration$^+$,Statement*): *Source*
CInt	(*Declaration$^+$,Statement*): *Source*
Compound	(*Statement**): *Statement*
Computation	(*Expression*): *Statement*
ContinueStmt	*Statement*
CondExp	(*Expression,Expression,Expression*): *Expression*
EmptyStmt	*Statement*
EqualExp	(*Expression,Expression*): *Expression*
FloatLeaf	*Float*
FloatVal	(*Float*): *Expression*
GreaterExp	(*Expression,Expression*): *Expression*
IdnExp	(*Identifier*): *Expression*
IdnLeaf	*Identifier*
InitFloat	(*Identifier,Expression*): *Declaration*
InitInt	(*Identifier,Expression*): *Declaration*
Inner	(*Range*): *Statement*
IntLeaf	*Integer*
IntVal	(*Integer*): *Expression*
LessExp	(*Expression,Expression*): *Expression*
Loop	(*Expression,Statement*): *Statement*
MinusExp	(*Expression,Expression*): *Expression*
NegExp	(*Expression*): *Expression*
NotExp	(*Expression*): *Expression*
OneSided	(*Expression,Statement*): *Statement*
OrExp	(*Expression,Expression*): *Expression*
PercentExp	(*Expression,Expression*): *Expression*
PlusExp	(*Expression,Expression*): *Expression*
ReturnStmt	(*Expression*): *Statement*
SlashExp	(*Expression,Expression*): *Expression*
StarExp	(*Expression,Expression*): *Expression*
TwoSided	(*Expression,Statement,Statement*): *Statement*
UninitFloat	(*Identifier*): *Declaration*
UninitInt	(*Identifier*): *Declaration*

Most of the constructs have a fixed number of components. Variable numbers of components are indicated in Table A.2 by the notation "*X**", specifying "zero or more" *X*s and "*X$^+$*", specifying "one or more" *X*s. Thus, a Block has one or more *Declaration* components and one or more *Statement* components, while a Compound has zero or more *Statement* components.

The subsections that describe the constructs of Table A.2 are ordered alphabetically. All dyadic expressions (such as an AndExp) are discussed in a single section, as are all monadic expressions (such as NegExp).

A.3.2.1 Block A block declares one or more variables, and executes one or more statements in the context of those declarations.

A.3.2.2 BreakStmt A break terminates the execution of the smallest containing iteration (Section A.1.4.3).

A.3.2.3 CFloat, CInt The component *Declaration*$^{+}$ of the construct is a list that specifies the program's parameter(s), while the component *Statement* is a tree that specifies the program's actions.

The scope associated with the construct is a new environment that contains only the parameter definitions.

A.3.2.4 Compound A compound executes a sequence of zero or more statements.

A.3.2.5 Computation A computation evaluates the component *Expression* and discards the result. Any side effects (such as a change in the value of a variable due to assignment) take place.

A.3.2.6 ContinueStmt A continue terminates the execution of the component *Statement* of the smallest containing iteration (Section A.1.4.4).

A.3.2.7 CondExp A conditional expression evaluates either the second component *Expression* or the third component *Expression*, depending upon the value of the first component *Expression* (Section A.1.5.3).

The type of value returned by the root *Expression* of the "CondExp" construct is the type that results from balancing (Section A.1.5.3) the types returned by the second and third component *Expression*s.

A.3.2.8 Dyadic Expressions A dyadic expression applies a function to two operand values, obtaining a single result. The first component *Expression* of the dyadic expression is the left operand, the second component *Expression* is the right operand. The function to be applied is determined from the types returned by the operand expressions, as shown in Table A.1.

The type returned by the root *Expression* of the dyadic expression is determined by the function, according to Table A.1.

Each component *Expression* must return a value that is compatible with the corresponding argument type of the function, according to Table A.1.

A.3.2.9 EmptyStmt An empty statement does nothing.

A.3.2.10 FloatLeaf A floating-point number is a leaf of the source program tree (Section A.1.1). Its value is established at the time the tree is built

A.3.2.11 FloatVal
A floating-point number may appear as a denotation in an expression.

The type of the value returned by the root *Expression* of the "FloatVal" construct is *float*.

A.3.2.12 IdnExp
An identifier may appear as an operand in an expression. The type of the value returned by the root *Expression* of the "IdnExp" construct is the type of the object related to the identifier by the visibility rules (Section A.1.2.3).

A.3.2.13 IdnLeaf
An identifier is a leaf of the source program tree (Section A.1.1). Its unique encoding is established at the time the tree is built.

A.3.2.14 InitFloat, InitInt
An initialized declaration associates an identifier with a new variable of a specified type. According to Section A.1.3.3, this association holds in the closest ancestor *Range* of the construct. The component *Expression* is a tree that specifies the initial value of this variable.

The relationship of the *Declaration* is a relationship between the new variable and the component *Identifier* of the construct.

A.3.2.15 Inner
An "Inner" construct represents a *Compound* that contains at least one *VariableDecl* (Figure A.2).

The scope of the component *Range* of the "Inner" construct is established within the environment inherited from the construct's closest ancestor *Range*.

A.3.2.16 IntLeaf
An integer is a leaf of the source program tree (Section A.1.1). Its value is established at the time the tree is built

A.3.2.17 IntVal
An integer may appear as a denotation in an expression.

The type of the value returned by the root *Expression* of the "IntVal" construct is *int*.

A.3.2.18 Loop
A loop represents an iteration (Section A.1.4.2). The component *Expression* of the construct is a tree that specifies the iteration's condition, while the component *Statement* is a tree that specifies the statement controlled by that condition.

The type of value returned by the first component *Expression* must be *int*. (Section A.1.4.2 states that the iteration is equivalent to a conditional clause, and Section A.1.4.1 requires that the expression in a conditional clause yield *int*.)

A.3.2.19 Monadic Expression
A monadic expression applies a function to one operand value, obtaining a result. The function to be applied is determined from the type returned by the operand expression as shown in Table A.1.

The type returned by the root *Expression* of the "Monadic" construct is determined by the function, according to Table A.1.

The component *Expression* must return a value that is compatible with the argument type of the function, according to Table A.1.

A.3.2.20 OneSided The "OneSided" construct represents a conditional that has no **else** part (Section A.1.4.1). The component *Expression* of the construct is a tree that specifies the condition, while the component *Statement* is a tree that specifies the statement controlled by that condition.

The type of value returned by the component *Expression* must be *int*.

A.3.2.21 ReturnStmt A return statement terminates execution of the program, delivering the value returned by the component *Expression*. The value of the component *Expression* must be coerced to the type specified by the program's *TypeSpecifier* (see Figure A.2).

A.3.2.22 TwoSided The "TwoSided" construct represents a conditional with an **else** part (Section A.1.4.1). The component *Expression* of the construct is a tree that specifies the condition: the first component *Statement* is a tree that specifies the statement to be executed if that condition does not yield 0; the second component *Statement* is a tree that specifies the statement to be executed if that condition does yield 0.

The type of value returned by the component *Expression* must be *int*.

A.3.2.23 UninitFloat, UninitInt An uninitialized declaration associates an identifier with a new variable of a specified type. According to Section A.1.2.3, this association holds in the closest ancestor *Range* of the construct.

The relationship of the *Declaration* is a relationship between the new variable and the component *Identifier* of the construct.

A.4 THE VAX TARGET PROGRAM TREE

All of the information that the translation task of the compiler provides about the target program is embodied in the target program tree (Figure A.9). If a particular item of information cannot be accessed via this tree, then it cannot be obtained at all. Information is encoded in the "shape" of the tree and in values stored at the leaves. See Section 9.1 for a general discussion of the structure and content of a target program tree.

This section defines the set of possible target program trees by defining all of the concepts and constructs of the target language. (We consider only the concepts and constructs needed to implement C--.)

A.4.1 VAX Concepts

A.4.1.1 Datum A datum is a construct yielding an explicit value that can be stored or used as an operand for other operations. Its only property is a VAX *Operand* (Figure 9.3) describing the machine access to the explicit value yielded.

The *Operand* properties of datum leaves are supplied by the translator when the target program tree is being built; *Operand* properties of interior datum nodes are evaluated during encoding.

A.4 THE VAX TARGET PROGRAM TREE

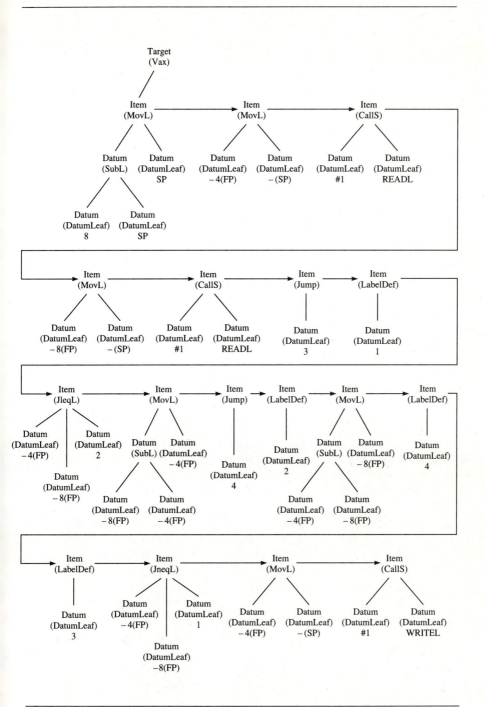

Figure A.9
The GCD target program tree

A.4.1.2 Item An item is a construct that does not yield a value. It has no properties.

A.4.1.3 Target A Target is a complete VAX program. It has no properties.

The Target node is the root of the target program tree, and never appears in any other position.

A.4.2 VAX Constructs

Table A.3 summarizes the constructs of the VAX. The structure of the subtree for each construct is given in the second column of Table A.3.

The following subsections describe the constructs of Table A.3. Some of those constructs represent specific VAX instructions, some represent "generic" operations that can be implemented by any one of several instructions, depending upon the pattern of operands, and others represent collections of instructions that involve related decisions about operand access. Section A.4.2.1 discusses all of the constructs corresponding to specific instructions, and Section A.4.2.2 covers many of those corresponding to generic operations. The remaining subsections are ordered alphabetically by construct name.

A.4.2.1 Specific Instructions "CvtFL," "CvtLF," "Ediv," "Emul," "MnegF," "MnegL," "MovaF," "MovaL," "MovF," "MovL," and "Ret" all correspond to specific VAX instructions. The order of the components in Table A.3 is the order of the corresponding nonresult operands of the instruction as it is described in the VAX Architecture Handbook.

Each of these constructs is encoded by encoding its components and then encoding the instruction that corresponds to the construct itself.

The code generator is free to choose any order of evaluation for the components, based upon their resource requirements.

A.4.2.2 Generic Operations "AddF," "AddL," "DivF," "DivL," "MulF," "MulL," "SubF," and "SubL" all correspond to generic operations that can be implemented by any one of several VAX instructions. The order of the components in Table A.3 is the order of the corresponding nonresult operands of the most general corresponding instruction as it is described in the VAX Architecture Handbook.

Each of these constructs is encoded by encoding its components and then selecting an appropriate instruction. For example, the *AddL* operation can always be implemented by ADDL3. If the *Operand* property of the second component *Datum* of the *AddL* construct is identical to the *Operand* property of the root of that construct, then the cheaper ADDL2 can be used. If this condition is met and the *Operand* property of the first component *Datum* specifies a literal 1, then the still cheaper INCL will implement the operation. See Section 9.1.2 and Section 11.3.2 for further discussion.

TABLE A.3 VAX CONSTRUCTS

Construct	Structure
AddF	(*Datum,Datum*): *Datum*
AddL	(*Datum,Datum*): *Datum*
AlternativeDataF	(*Datum$^+$*): *Datum*
AlternativeDataL	(*Datum$^+$*): *Datum*
CvtFL	(*Datum*): *Datum*
CvtLF	(*Datum*): *Datum*
CvtLQ	(*Datum*): *Datum*
DivF	(*Datum,Datum*): *Datum*
DivL	(*Datum,Datum*): *Datum*
Ediv	(*Datum,Datum*): *Datum*
Emul	(*Datum,Datum*): *Datum*
DatumLeaf	*Datum*
JeqlF	(*Datum,Datum,Datum*): *Item*
JeqlL	(*Datum,Datum,Datum*): *Item*
JgeqF	(*Datum,Datum,Datum*): *Item*
JgeqL	(*Datum,Datum,Datum*): *Item*
JgtrF	(*Datum,Datum,Datum*): *Item*
JgtrL	(*Datum,Datum,Datum*): *Item*
JleqF	(*Datum,Datum,Datum*): *Item*
JleqL	(*Datum,Datum,Datum*): *Item*
JlssF	(*Datum,Datum,Datum*): *Item*
JlssL	(*Datum,Datum,Datum*): *Item*
JneqF	(*Datum,Datum,Datum*): *Item*
JneqL	(*Datum,Datum,Datum*): *Item*
Jump	(*Datum*): *Item*
LabelDef	(*Datum*): *Item*
MnegF	(*Datum*): *Datum*
MnegL	(*Datum*): *Datum*
MovaF	(*Datum,Datum*): *Item*
MovaL	(*Datum,Datum*): *Item*
MovF	(*Datum,Datum*): *Item*
MovL	(*Datum,Datum*): *Item*
MulF	(*Datum,Datum*): *Datum*
MulL	(*Datum,Datum*): *Datum*
Ret	*Item*
SequenceDatum	(*Item$^+$,Datum*): *Datum*
StoreF	(*Datum,Datum*): *Datum*
StoreFL	(*Datum,Datum*): *Datum*
StoreL	(*Datum,Datum*): *Datum*
StoreLF	(*Datum,Datum*): *Datum*
SubF	(*Datum,Datum*): *Datum*
SubL	(*Datum,Datum*): *Datum*
Vax	(*Item$^+$*): *Target*

The code generator is free to choose any order of evaluation for the components, based upon their resource requirements.

A.4.2.3 CvtLQ A "CvtLQ" construct is implemented by an ASHQ instruction. Depending upon the properties of the component *Datum*, this instruction may be preceded by a MOVL instruction to place the 32-bit operand in an appropriate location.

A.4.2.4 DatumLeaf A "DatumLeaf" construct represents a directly accessible value. Its *Operand* property is set by the translator.

A.4.2.5 Conditional Jumps "JeqlF," "JeqlL," "JgeqF," "JgeqL," "JgtrF," "JgtrL," "JleqF," "JleqL," "JlssF," "JlssL," "JneqF," and "JneqL" all represent conditional transfers of control. The order of the first two *Datum* components is the order of the operands of a CMPF or CMPL instruction as they are described in the VAX Architecture Handbook. The third component *Datum* is the label (see Section 9.1.3) to which control may be transferred.

Each of these constructs is encoded by encoding its first two *Datum* components, followed by a CMPF (if the construct name ends in F) or a CMPL (if the construct ends in L) with the results of those *Datum* constructs as operands. Finally, an appropriate conditional jump (JEQL for JeqlF or JeqlL, JNEQ for JneqF or JneqL, etc.) is encoded with the label corresponding to the third component *Datum* of the construct as its operand.

The code generator is free to choose any order of evaluation for the components, based upon their resource requirements.

A.4.2.6 Jump A "Jump" construct is encoded as follows:

JMP *L*

Here *L* is the label (see Section 9.1.3) represented by the component *Datum*.

A.4.2.7 LabelDef A "LabelDef" construct is implemented by invoking the *MarkPosition* operation of the assembly module (see Figure 11.8). The argument of the *MarkPosition* invocation is the label (see Section 9.1.3) specified by the component *Datum*.

A.4.2.8 Alternatives An "AlternativeDataF" or "AlternativeDataL" construct is encoded as follows:

>   Code for $Datum_1$
>   Possible MOVF or MOVL
>   JMP *L*
>   Code for $Datum_2$
>   Possible MOVF or MOVL
>   JMP *L*
>   . . .

>   Code for *Datum*$_n$
>   Possible MOVF or MOVL
> *L*:

Here "*Datum*$_i$" is the ith element of the component *Datum*$^+$ and "*L*:" represents an invocation of the *MarkPosition* operation of the assembly module (Figure 11.8). The argument of the *MarkPosition* call is *L*, an *ExtInteger* generated by the code generator. A move instruction is produced for the ith component if the *Operand* property of *Datum*$_i$ is not identical to the *Operand* property of the alternative construct. In this case the first operand of the move instruction is the *Operand* property of *Datum*$_i$, and the second is the *Operand* property of the alternative construct. See Section 9.3.3 for further discussion.

A.4.2.9 SequenceDatum

A "SequenceDatum" construct is implemented as follows:

>   Code for *Item*$_1$
>   ...
>   Code for *Item*$_n$
>   Code for *Datum*

Here *Item*$_i$ is the ith element of the component *Item*$^+$.

A.4.2.10 StoreF, StoreL

"StoreF" and "StoreL" constructs represent VAX MOVF and MOVL instructions respectively. The root *Datum* has the same *Operand* property as the first component *Datum*. The source operand of the instruction is given by the *Operand* property of the first component *Datum*, the destination operand is given by the *Operand* property of the second component *Datum*.

A.4.2.11 StoreFL

A "StoreFL" construct represents a VAX CVTFL instruction. The root *Datum* has the same *Operand* property as the first component *Datum*. The source operand of the instruction is given by the *Operand* property of the first component *Datum*, the destination operand is given by the *Operand* property of the second component *Datum*.

The first component *Datum* and the root *Datum* of the "StoreFL" construct represent 4-byte floating-point values; the second component *Datum* represents the address of a memory area capable of holding 4-byte integers.

A.4.2.12 StoreLF

A "StoreLF" construct represents a VAX CVTLF instruction. The root *Datum* has the same *Operand* property as the first component *Datum*. The source operand of the instruction is given by the *Operand* property of the first component *Datum*, the destination operand is given by the *Operand* property of the second component *Datum*.

The first component *Datum* and the root *Datum* of the "StoreFL" construct represent 4-byte integer values; the second component *Datum* represents the address of a memory area capable of holding 4-byte floating-point numbers.

A.4.2.13 Vax The encoding of a "Vax" construct depends on the assembler and the operating system in use. The following encoding assumes that the MACRO assembler will be used and the program will be run under VMS:

> .ENTRY   START,4095
> Code for *Item*$_1$
> . . .
> Code for *Item*$_n$
> .END   START

Figure A.10 shows the implementation of the target program tree for GCD (Figure A.9).

A.5 TRANSFORMING C-- SOURCE TREES TO VAX TARGET TREES

The results of the data mapping process (Chapter 8) are reflected in the *Operand* properties of the target program tree's *Datum* leaves, while the results of the action mapping process (Chapter 9) are embodied in the target program tree's structure.

A.5.1 C--/VAX Data Mapping

C-- programs can manipulate only integer and floating-point values; the language provides no mechanism for constructing additional types. It does allow the user to declare parameters and variables. Therefore, a definition of the data mapping

```
        .ENTRY   START,4095
        SUBL2    #8,SP              ; Allocate activation record space
        PUSHAL   -4(FP)             ; Read the value of x
        CALLS    #1,READL
        PUSHAL   -8(FP)             ; Read the value of y
        CALLS    #1,READL
        BR       L3                 ; Invert the test and body of the while
L1:     CMPL     -4(FP),-8(FP)      ; if x > y
        BLEQ     L2
        SUBL2    -8(FP),-4(FP)      ; then x := x - y
        BR       L3
L2:     SUBL2    -4(FP),-8(FP)      ; else y := y - x
L3:     CMPL     -4(FP),-8(FP)
        BNEQ     L1                 ; while not(x = y)
        PUSHL    -4(FP)
        CALLS    #1,WRITEL          ; Write the result
        RET
        .END     START
```

Figure A.10
VAX assembly code for GCD

task must specify how C-- integer and floating-point values are implemented on the VAX, and how storage is allocated for parameters and variables.

A.5.1.1 Simple Types A C-- integer is implemented by a VAX longword (32 bits), and a C-- floating-point number by a VAX F-format (32-bit) value. (See Section 8.1.1 for a discussion of the considerations leading to this decision.)

A.5.1.2 Parameters and Variables Because there is no possibility of recursion in C--, it would be possible to allocate storage for parameters and variables statically. It is simpler, however, to use a standard VAX activation record (see Appendix C of the VAX Architecture Handbook) for the parameters and variables.

The C-- "parameters" really aren't parameters at all—they are top-level variables that must be initialized by reading from the standard input unit before executing the body of the C-- program. Thus they are implemented just like variables.

Storage for all of the variables declared in a C-- program is allocated in a single area of VAX memory. During execution, the frame pointer register FP (register 13) contains the address of the first memory location above this area. Thus, any variable's location can be specified by the sum of a negative number and the content of FP. Since each variable occupies 4 bytes of memory, the negative offsets from the content of FP are all multiples of 4: The topmost variable is accessed via the VAX operand "$-4(FP)$", the next variable by "$-8(FP)$", and so forth.

Given the extent rules for C-- variables (Section A.1.3.3), variables declared in two disjoint ranges (Section A.1.2.3) of a C-- program do not exist at the same time. Such variables may therefore be allocated the same storage. The data mapping takes advantage of this property to reduce the size of the area needed for C-- variables: Storage for parameters is allocated starting at $-4(FP)$ and using successively lower longwords until all parameters have been allocated storage. Storage for variables whose declarations are components of the program's *Compound* (Figure A.2, Figure A.3) are then allocated successively lower longwords. Let the first unallocated longword be f. For each component *Statement* of the program's *Compound* that is itself a *Compound* with *VariableDecl* nodes as children, local variables are allocated f and successively lower longwords. Thus, the storage from f downwards is shared by variables in disjoint ranges of the program's *Compound*.

Each nested *Compound* is treated the same way as the program's component *Compound*, so the storage allocation is similar to that for a Pascal variant record except that it grows toward lower addresses. See Section 8.1.2 for further discussion.

A.5.2 C--/VAX Action Mapping

Most of the C-- constructs map to VAX constructs in an obvious way. Many "DatumLeaf" constructs of the VAX target program tree are derived from simple

C-- *Expressions* on the basis of the results of the data mapping; some are generated by the compiler in the course of translating C-- constructs such as "Loop," "OneSided," and "TwoSided." Other *Datum* nodes are derived from more complex C-- *Expressions* using type information computed during semantic analysis. *Item* nodes are derived from C-- *Statement* constructs.

A.5.2.1 DatumLeaf The "DatumLeaf" construct is used to represent a C-- "FloatVal," "IdnExp," or "IntVal," or a label generated by the compiler (C-- does not permit user-defined labels). A "DatumLeaf" construct representing a C-- identifier or denotation has its *Operand* property set as follows:

C-- construct	*Operand* (Figure 11.2)
FloatVal IntVal	$c = lit$, $v =$ external value from the component leaf
IdnExp	$c = disp$, $n = 13$, $x = 0$, *offset* = relative address

A *DatumLeaf* construct representing a compiler-generated label has its *Operand* property set with $c = ref$. The *lbl* field contains either the external integer that identifies the internal cross-reference (see Section 9.1.3) or the external string that is the name used for global cross-referencing.

A.5.2.2 Arithmetic Operations The arithmetic operations are used to represent the C-- operators in the obvious way. Don't forget, however, that the left operand of a VAX operations is the right operand of the corresponding C-- operator (see the VAX Architecture Handbook).

For example, "PlusExp" is represented by "AddF" if either of its operands is of type *float* (Section A.1.3.1); otherwise, it is represented by "AddL." If e_1 is of type *float* and e_2 is of type *int* in $PlusExp(e_1, e_2)$, t_1 is the translation of e_1, and t_2 is the translation of e_2, then the translation of $PlusExp(e_1, e_2)$ is as follows:

$$AddF(CvtLF(t_2), t_1)$$

Translation of $PercentExp(e_1, e_2)$ is more complex. The types of both e_1 and e_2 must be *int* (see Table A.1), but the translation depends on the left operand construct. The special case follows:

$$PercentExp(StarExp(e_1, e_2), e_3) \rightarrow Ediv(t_3, Emul(t_2, t_1))$$

In all other cases, the translation is given by:

$$PercentExp(e_1, e_2) \rightarrow Ediv(t_2, CvtLQ(t_1))$$

A.5.2.3 Assignment If the result of an assignment is never used, then that assignment is represented by either the "MovL" construct or the "MovF" con-

A.5 TRANSFORMING C-- SOURCE TREES TO VAX TARGET TREES

struct, depending upon the operand types. For example, if e_1 and e_2 have type *int* while e_3 and e_4 have type *float*, then the following translations would be appropriate:

$$Computation(AssignExp(e_1,e_2)) \rightarrow MovL(t_2,t_1)$$
$$Computation(AssignExp(e_1,e_4)) \rightarrow MovL(CvtFL(t_4),t_1)$$
$$Computation(AssignExp(e_3,e_2)) \rightarrow MovF(CvtLF(t_2),t_3)$$
$$Computation(AssignExp(e_3,e_4)) \rightarrow MovF(t_4,t_3)$$

If the result of an assignment *is* used, then that assignment is represented by one of the "store" constructs, depending on the operand types and the type required by the context in which it is used. For example, suppose the result of the assignment is negated in a context requiring a floating-point value. The following translations would be appropriate:

$$NegExp(AssignExp(e_1,e_2)) \rightarrow MnegF(CvtLF(StoreL(t_2,t_1)))$$
$$NegExp(AssignExp(e_1,e_4)) \rightarrow MnegF(StoreFL(t_4,t_1))$$
$$NegExp(AssignExp(e_3,e_2)) \rightarrow MnegF(StoreF(CvtLF(t_2),t_3))$$
$$NegExp(AssignExp(e_3,e_4)) \rightarrow MnegF(StoreF(t_4,t_3))$$

If the context of the negation required an integer value, however, the appropriate translations would be the following:

$$NegExp(AssignExp(e_1,e_2)) \rightarrow MnegL(StoreL(t_2,t_1))$$
$$NegExp(AssignExp(e_3,e_2)) \rightarrow MnegL(StoreLF(t_2,t_3))$$

A.5.2.4 Conditional Expressions

If e_2 and e_3 are both of type *float* in $CondExp(e_1,e_2,e_3)$, then a simple translation is as follows (*L* is a label generated by the compiler):

SequenceDatum(
    JeqlL(t_1,*DatumLeaf*(0),*DatumLeaf*(*L*)),
    AlternativeDataF(t_2,*SequenceDatum*(*LabelDef*(*DatumLeaf*(*L*)),t_3)))

When the types of e_1 and e_2 differ, a "CvtLF" construct must be added to balance the values (see Section A.1.5.2).

Often e_1 is itself a relational operator (an "EqualExp," "GreaterExp," or "LessExp" construct), in which case an extra comparison against 0 is superfluous. For example, consider the following (assume all expressions yield integer values):

CondExp(*EqualExp*(e_1,e_2),e_3,e_4) →
    SequenceDatum(
        JneqL(t_1,t_2,*DatumLeaf*(*L*)),
        AlternativeDataL(t_3,*SequenceDatum*(*LabelDef*(*DatumLeaf*(*L*)),t_4)))

More general conditions, involving the "AndExp," "OrExp," and "NotExp" constructs are implemented by jump cascades (Section 10.2.2). Here is an example:

$$(a<0 \ || \ b==0 \ \&\& \ c>0 \ ? \ 3 \ : \ 4)$$

Figure A.11 shows the translation of this example using a jump cascade. (Figure A.11b assumes that the variables a, b, and c are stored at relative addresses -4, -8, and -12, respectively.)

A.5.2.5 Loop

The "Loop" construct is implemented as follows:

$Loop(e,s) \rightarrow$
    $Jump(DatumLeaf(L_1))$,
    $LabelDef(DatumLeaf(L_2))$, i,
    $LabelDef(DatumLeaf(L_1))$,
    $JneqL(t,DatumLeaf(0),DatumLeaf(L_2))$,
    $LabelDef(DatumLeaf(L_3))$

Here, i is the list of *Item* nodes that is the translation of s, and t is the translation of e. The same considerations apply to the translation of e that apply to the translation of the condition of a conditional expression—the "JneqL" might be replaced by a comparison appearing within e, or by a jump cascade.

L_3 is a label that can be used as the destination of jumps implementing "BreakStmt" constructs within the loop. "ContinueStmt" constructs within the loop are implemented by transfers to L_1.

A.5.2.6 OneSided

The "OneSided" construct is implemented as follows:

$OneSided(e,s) \rightarrow$
    $JeqlL(t,DatumLeaf(0),DatumLeaf(L))$, i, $LabelDef(DatumLeaf(L))$

Here, i is the list of *Item* nodes that is the translation of s, and t is the translation of e. The same considerations apply to the translation of e that apply to the translation of the condition of a conditional expression—the "JeqlL" might be replaced by a comparison appearing within e, or by a jump cascade.

A.5.2.7 TwoSided

The "TwoSided" construct is implemented as follows:

$TwoSided(e, s_1, s_2) \rightarrow$
    $JeqlL(t,DatumLeaf(0),DatumLeaf(L_1))$, i_1, $Jump(DatumLeaf(L_2))$,
    $LabelDef(DatumLeaf(L_1))$, i_2, $LabelDef(DatumLeaf(L_2))$

Here, i_1 and i_2 are the lists of *Item* nodes that are the translations of s_1 and s_2, respectively, and t is the translation of e. The same considerations apply to the translation of e that apply to the translation of the condition of a conditional expression—the "JeqlL" might be replaced by a comparison appearing within e, or by a jump cascade.

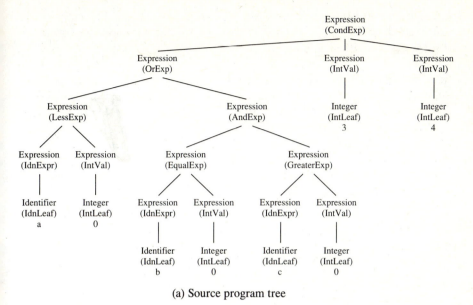

(a) Source program tree

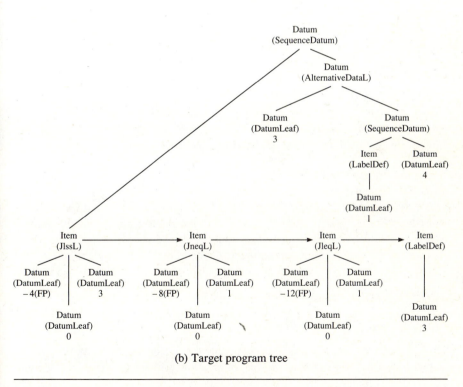

(b) Target program tree

Figure A.11
Translation of $(a<0 \parallel b==0 \ \&\& \ c>0 \ ? \ 3 \ : \ 4)$

A.5.2.8 ContinueStmt, BreakStmt

These constructs are implemented by jumps to either the test of the closest containing iteration (ContinueStmt) or its terminator (BreakStmt).

A.5.2.9 ReturnStmt

The "ReturnStmt" construct is implemented by an invocation of a run-time routine to write the object yielded by the component *Expression*, followed by a "Ret" construct. The component *Expression* must yield an object of type *float* if the root of the source program tree is a "CFloat" construct; it must yield an object of type *int* if the root of the source program tree is a "CInt" construct.

A.5.2.10 InitFloat, InitInt

These constructs are translated as follows:

$$InitFloat(i,e) \rightarrow MovF(t, DatumLeaf(v))$$
$$InitInt(i,e) \rightarrow MovL(t, DatumLeaf(v))$$

Here, v is the operand describing the access to variable i, and t is the translation of e.

A.5.2.11 CFloat, CInt

These constructs are both translated into a "Vax" construct (see Figure A.9). The first element of the component *Item*$^+$ is as follows:

$$MovL(SubL(DatumLeaf(size), DatumLeaf(SP)), DatumLeaf(SP))$$

Here *size* is the number of bytes of memory required by the C-- program, and *SP* is the *Operand* describing register 14 ($c = reg$, $n = 14$—see Figure 11.2). This *Item* reserves the storage for variables. It is followed by elements (one per *ParameterDecl*) that are invocations of a run-time routine to read parameter values from the standard input unit, initializing the variables described by the program's parameter list, and then the sequence of *Item* nodes that translates the component *Compound* of the source program tree root.

A.5.2.12 Invocations of Run-Time Routines

Run-time routines are needed to read parameter values and write results. These routines might have been created specially for this project, or they might be service routines available from the operating system. Figure 9.5b shows the general strategy for invoking a routine that returns a result; our case is a bit simpler because no result is returned. Figure A.10 illustrates the process, using a special routine READL to read a single integer from the standard input unit and a special routine WRITEL to write a single integer to the standard output unit.

NOTES

The key point in selecting a language suitable for an educational compiler project is to illustrate an appropriate set of compilation problems without introducing uninteresting complications. One must also resist the temptation to make the "appropriate set" of problems too large. A variety of criteria for language selection have been stated in the literature [1, 3].

Documentation describing the target machine architecture and the operating system are necessary to support the project. We have found it useful to consult a textbook that discusses assembly language programming for the target machine [4]. This material helps you to understand the rather terse descriptions of instructions given in the machine manual [2].

REFERENCES

1. Atteson, K., Lorenz, M., and Dowling, W. F., "NARPL: A Solution to the Student Compiler Project Problem," *SIGPLAN Notices 24*, 3 (Mar. 1989), 57-66.
2. R. A. Brunner, ed., *VAX Architecture Reference Manual*, Digital Equipment Corporation, Concord, MA, 1991.
3. Lambert, K. A., "Compiling Tinyturing in a Compiler Construction Course," *SIGCSE 22*, 3 (Sep. 1990), 2-6.
4. Levy, H. M. and Jr., R. H. E., *Computer Programming and Architecture: The VAX-11*, Digital Press, Bedford, MA, 1980.

PROJECT EXERCISES

A.1 Specify the scanning problem for C-- and obtain a solution to that problem via the techniques discussed in Section 3.2.1.
  (a) Augment the syntax diagrams in Figure A.1 with diagrams for the special-character delimiters of C-- listed in Section A.1.1 to produce a single diagram defining the C-- scanning task. Assume that keywords will be recognized by the identifier conversion process as discussed in Section 3.3.2, so they will not be defined via syntax diagrams. Don't forget, however, to include facilities for scanning comments.
  (b) Derive a finite-state machine from the syntax diagram you constructed in (a). Express your finite-state machine both as a state table and as a state diagram. Make sure the correspondence between machine outputs and basic symbol classes is obvious!

A.2 Suppose you were going to implement your machine interpretively.
  (a) Assuming one column per ASCII character, what would the *total* space requirement of the machine definition be?
  (b) Assuming that you compress the tables by replacing every set of identical columns by a single column, what would the *total* space requirement of the machine definition be?
  (c) Would it be cost-effective to compress the next state and output arrays separately in this case? Justify your answer.
  (d) Write the **case** statement that you would use in Figure 3.8 for your interpreter.

A.3 The interpretive implementation of a finite-state machine is embedded in the lexical analysis module as shown in Figure 3.7.
  (a) Show that the correctness of the text's implementation depends upon the fact that no basic symbol can contain an embedded newline.
  (b) Given the definition of C-- and the design of your machine, show that the interpretive implementation discussed in the text will fail.
  (c) Propose a modified interpretive implementation that *will* work. (Hint: Given that the character set is ASCII, you need only broaden the actions allowed in the **case** statement.)

A.4 Implement a lexical analyzer for C-- that incorporates a directly executable scanner and conversion operations for identifiers, integer denotations, and floating-point denotations on the basis of your answer to Exercise A.1. Use the interface specification of Figure 3.1, modifying the definitions of *SymbolClass* and *Token* as appropriate.

(a) Modify the skeleton scanner of Figure 3.11 to implement the finite-state machine you described in Exercise A.1b.

(b) Implement the conversion operation for identifiers as discussed in Section 3.3.2. Be sure to initialize the hash table with the keywords listed in Section A.1.1.

(c) Implement the conversion operation for integer denotations as discussed in Section 3.3.1.

(d) Implement the conversion operation for floating-point denotations by a call to *ExtCodeFloat* (Figure 2.5).

A.5 Specify the parsing and tree construction problems for C-- and obtain solutions to those problems via the techniques of Section 4.2.2. (These two problems must be dealt with together because they interact—placement of connections depends on what those connections do.)

(a) Add structure connections to the syntax diagrams of Figure A.2, Figure A.3, and Figure A.4, and to the extended regular expressions given in Section A.1.5. Also, replace terminal symbols with symbol connections where appropriate. Feel free to transform the specifications, using the diagram transformations discussed in Section 4.2.2 or regular expression algebra, if you feel that clarity will be enhanced thereby. Be careful when doing such transformations, however, to obey the rules. If you do not obey the rules, then the transformed specifications may not describe C--.

(b) Briefly describe the action that will be carried out by each structure connection and each symbol connection in your specification.

(c) Each path through a given syntax diagram or alternative of a given regular expression involves a (possibly empty) sequence of connections. Each sequence of connections may result in a change of the tree construction module's internal state. Show that the tree construction module's internal states resulting from following different paths through a diagram, or taking different alternatives in an expression, are consistent with one another.

A.6 Transform the specification you gave as an answer to Exercise A.5 into a form suitable for recursive descent parsing.

(a) Use the techniques of Section 5.1 to remove all left recursion from the specification.

(b) Find the director set of each path leaving a fork in the syntax diagrams, and each alternative in the extended regular expressions. Transform the specification, if necessary, to remove director set overlap, as discussed in Section 5.2.

(c) The error recovery continuation at each fork in a syntax diagram and at each set of alternatives in an extended regular expression must be chosen by the compiler designer. Use the criteria of Section 5.3.1 to make these decisions, and indicate them by arranging forks and alternatives so the continuation is the last.

(d) Determine, for each box in the syntax diagrams and each symbol in the extended regular expressions, the set of basic symbols that the parser could accept when following the continuation path from that box or symbol to the exit of the diagram or end of the expression containing it (Section 5.3.2).

A.5 TRANSFORMING C-- SOURCE TREES TO VAX TARGET TREES

A.7 Implement a recursive descent parser and a tree construction module for C--.
  (a) Code the specification you developed for Exercise A.6, using the mechanical technique illustrated by Figure 5.1, but replacing calls to *Report* and *Lexical* by calls to *Synterr* and *Accept*, respectively. (See Figure 5.12 for an example of that replacement.) *Don't attempt to eliminate redundant code during this process!*
  (b) Modify *Synterr* (Figure 5.13) to generate appropriate values for C-- denotations and identifiers. (Section 4.2.2 gives some hints about the criteria for deciding what values are appropriate.)

A.8 Express your answer to Exercise A.5 as a context-free grammar (Section 4.2.4) and use a parser generator to create a shift-reduce parser from that grammar. Your parser should recover from as many syntactic errors as possible. What guarantees can you make about the source program tree your parser will create? (If an inconsistent tree is possible, you will need to either abandon the compilation if syntax errors are detected, or build further error recovery into later modules.)

A.9 Implement the tree construction module from the descriptions of the connections that you gave in answer to Exercise A.5b.
  (a) Modify the data structures of Figure 4.2 to describe the constructs listed in Table A.2.
  (b) Code the operations given in the tree construction module interface (Figure 4.4). The bodies of *SourceLeaf* and *SourceNode* should each contain a **case**-statement that selects one of the actions you described in Exercise A.5b on the basis of the *SourceConstruct* parameter.

A.10 Implement the name analysis task of the C-- compiler. The result of name analysis should be a definition table key (Section 7.2) stored at each *Identifier* leaf in the source program tree. You should report *all* defining occurrences of multiply-defined identifiers and *all* applied occurrences of undefined identifiers. Do not report applied occurrences of multiply-defined identifiers.
  (a) Note that the visibility rules for C-- (Section A.1.2.3) differ from those of Pascal: In C-- the scope of a definition begins at the declaration and continues to the end of the range; in Pascal, the scope of a definition is the entire range in which it occurs. Show that this difference in visibility rules results in different tree traversals for name analysis.
  (b) Define visit procedure interfaces for name analysis in C--. You should have a distinct procedure for each visit to each of the five kinds of interior node listed in Section A.3.1 (*Source, Range, Declaration, Statement,* and *Expression*). Such interface specifications are illustrated by the definition of *DeclarationVisit*1 in Figure 7.9.
  (c) Describe the contextual information you will need to carry out the name analysis and explain how it will be stored (i.e., what must be stored in the tree, what can be stored in global variables, and what will be stored in local variables of the visit procedures).
  (d) Code the bodies of the visit procedures, using the general structure illustrated by Figure 7.9. Invoke the environment module (Figure 7.5) to carry out the basic computations of name analysis.

A.11 Implement the data mapping task of the C-- compiler. The result of data mapping should be a relative address (Section 8.1.3) for each declared variable and a

specification of the total amount of storage needed during execution of the program. Be sure that you overlay storage for variables that are not active simultaneously.
  (a) Augment the interface specifications of the visit procedures you defined in Exercise A.10 to reflect the data mapping task. Define additional procedures and their interfaces if necessary.
  (b) Describe the contextual information you will need to carry out the data mapping, and explain how it will be stored (i.e., what must be stored in the tree, what can be stored in global variables, and what will be stored in local variables of the visit procedures).
  (c) Modify the bodies of existing visit procedures as necessary and code any additional visit procedures you defined in (b). Invoke the storage module (Figure 8.8) to carry out the basic computations of data mapping.

A.12 Implement a restricted action mapping task of the C-- compiler. The restriction is that the only *Expression* constructs that the source program tree may contain are *FloatVal*, *IdnExp*, and *IntVal*. (See Table A.2 for the definition of the constructs of a C-- source program tree.) The result of action mapping should be a listing of the sequence of target tree construction operations (Figure 9.6) invoked, with the argument values for each invocation.
  (a) Define mapping procedure interfaces for action mapping in C--. You should have a distinct procedure for each of the five kinds of interior node listed in Section A.3 (*Source*, *Range*, *Declaration*, *Statement*, and *Expression*). Such interface specifications are illustrated by the definition of *MapStatement* in Figure 9.8.
  (b) Describe the contextual information you will need to carry out the action mapping, and explain how it will be stored (i.e., what must be stored in the tree, what can be stored in global variables, and what will be stored in local variables of the visit procedures).
  (c) Modify the bodies of existing visit procedures as necessary and code the mapping procedures you defined in (a).

A.13 Complete the action mapping task of the C-- compiler. The result of action mapping should be a listing of the sequence of target tree construction operations (Figure 9.6) invoked, with the argument values for each invocation.
  (a) Use Section A.1.3.1, Section A.1.5.1, the source language considerations discussed in Section 8.2, the target machine considerations discussed in Section 10.1.1, and the needs of jump cascades (Section 10.2.2) to develop a type system for use in the C-- compiler.
  (b) For each C-- construct involving an operation (e.g., *AndExp*, *AssignExp*, *NegExp*, *NotExp*—see Table A.2), specify the overloadings in terms of the type system you defined in (a). (See Figure 10.2a and Figure 10.9 for examples of such specifications.)
  (c) Associate VAX constructs and costs with each signature you specified in (b), as discussed in Section 10.1.2 and Section 10.2.2.
  (d) Augment the interface specifications of the mapping procedures you defined in Exercise A.12 to reflect the operator identification task. Define additional procedures and their interfaces if necessary.
  (e) Modify the bodies of existing mapping procedures as necessary, and code any additional mapping procedures you defined in (d).

A.14 Implement the target tree construction module of the C-- compiler. Your module should determine the register requirement of every subtree of the target program tree (Section 11.1.2) and determine the classes of all operands (Section 11.1.3).

A.5 TRANSFORMING C-- SOURCE TREES TO VAX TARGET TREES

(a) Modify the data structures of Figure 11.3 to describe the constructs listed in Table A.3.

(b) Code the operations given in the tree construction module interface (Figure 9.6).

A.15 Implement the register allocation and instruction selection tasks of the C-- compiler. The output should be VAX assembly code; you should demonstrate the correctness of your compiler by compiling a suite of C-- programs and running them on the VAX.

(a) Define visit procedure interfaces for VAX register allocation and instruction selection. You should have a distinct procedure for each visit to each of the three kinds of node listed in Section A.4.1 (*Target, Item, Datum*). Such interface specifications are illustrated by the definition of *ItemVisit* in Figure 11.6.

(b) Describe the contextual information you will need to carry out the register allocation and instruction selection, and explain how it will be stored (i.e., what must be stored in the tree, what can be stored in global variables, and what will be stored in local variables of the visit procedures).

(c) Code the bodies of the visit procedures, using the general structure illustrated by Figure 11.6. Invoke the assembly module (Figure 11.8) to resolve internal cross-references and deliver completed assembly language instructions.

A.16 Use any performance measurement tools available under your operating system to analyze the execution time and space requirements of your compiler. In order to get meaningful results, you will need to construct a large C-- program. The easiest way to do this is to combine the *Compound* components of all of the programs in your test suite and duplicate the result many times, concatenate the duplicates, and add appropriate parameter declarations to take care of any undefined symbols.

(a) Measure the total elapsed time, storage use, disk reads and writes, and system time for a compilation. Account for the ratio of disk reads to disk writes. On the basis of the measurements of system and user time, do you think that there is any hope of reducing the compilation time by making changes in the compiler? Justify your answer.

(b) Obtain a profile of the compiler's execution time, giving the fraction of the total compilation time that is spent in each routine. Which routines are "hot spots" in this profile? Suppose you reduced to zero the time spent in the routine showing the largest fraction of the execution time. What would the percentage improvement in execution speed be?

(c) Storage allocation often accounts for a significant fraction of the total execution time of a compiler. If this is the case for your compiler, would it be reasonable to attack this bottleneck by reducing the cost of the storage allocation operation itself? Would it be reasonable to try to reduce the number of storage allocation operation invocations? Explain briefly.

Collected Bibliography

Aho, A. V., Johnson, S. C., and Ullman, J. D., "Code Generation for Machines with Multiregister Operations," *Proc. of the Fourth ACM Symp. on Prin. of Prog. Lang.*, 1977, 21–28.

Aho, A. V., Sethi, R., and Ullman, J. D., *Compilers*, Addison-Wesley, Reading, MA, 1986.

Aho, A. V., Hopcroft, J. E., and Ullman, J. D., *The Design and Analysis of Computer Algorithms*, Addison-Wesley, Reading, MA, 1974.

Aho, A. V. and Ullman, J. D., *The Theory of Parsing, Translation, and Compiling*, Prentice Hall, Englewood Cliffs, NJ, 1972.

Aho, A. V. and Johnson, S. C., "Optimal Code Generation for Expression Trees," *J. ACM* *23*, 3 (July 1976), 488–501.

"Ada Programming Language," ANSI/MIL-STD-1815A, American National Standards Institute, New York, NY, Feb. 1983.

"Pascal Computer Programming Language," ANSI/IEEE 770 X3.97–1983, American National Standards Institute, New York, NY, Jan. 1983.

"FORTRAN," X3.9–1978, American National Standards Institute, New York, 1978.

Ammann, U., "Die Entwicklung eines PASCAL-Compilers nach der Methode des Strukturierten Programmierens," Ph.D. Thesis, Eidgenössischen Technischen Hochschule Zürich, Zürich, 1975.

Ammann, U., Nori, K. V., Jensen, K., Jacobi, C., and Nägeli, H. H., "The Pascal-P Compiler: Implementation Notes," Bericht 10, Eidgenössische Technische Hochschule, Zurich, July 1976.

Ammann, U., "The Method of Structured Programming Applied to the Development of a Compiler," in *Proc. of the International Computing Symp. 1973*, North-Holland, Amsterdam, 1974, 94–99.

Atteson, K., Lorenz, M., and Dowling, W. F., "NARPL: A Solution to the Student Compiler Project Problem," *SIGPLAN Notices 24*, 3 (Mar. 1989), 57–66.

Bahrami, A., "CAGT—An Automated Approach to Abstract and Parsing Grammars," MS Thesis, Department of Electrical and Computer Engineering, University of Colorado, Boulder, CO, 1986.

T. O. Barnett, ed., *Modular Programming: Proceedings of a National Symposium, Symposium Preprint*, Information and Systems Press, Cambridge, MA, 1968.

Baskett, F., "The Best Simple Code Generation Technique for WHILE, FOR and DO Loops," *SIGPLAN Notices 13*, 4 (Apr. 1978), 31–32.

Bell, J. R., "Threaded Code," *Comm. of the ACM 16*, 6 (June 1973), 370–372.

R. A. Brunner, ed., *VAX Architecture Reference Manual*, Digital Equipment Corporation, Concord, MA, 1991.

Bruno, J. L. and Lassagne, T., "The Generation of Optimal Code for Stack Machines," *J. ACM 22*, 3 (July 1975), 382–396.

Burke, M. G. and Fischer, G. A., "A Practical Method for LR and LL Syntactic Error Diagnosis and Recovery," *Trans. Prog. Lang and Systems 9*, 2 (April 1987), 198–234.

Carter, L. R., *An Analysis of Pascal Programs*, UMI Research Press, Ann Arbor, MI, 1982.

Cichelli, R. J., "Minimal Perfect Hash Functions Made Simple," *Comm. of the ACM 23*, 1 (Jan. 1980), 17–19.

Coleman, S. S., Poole, P. C., and Waite, W. M., "The Mobile Programming System, Janus," *Software—Practice & Experience 4*, 1 (1974), 5–23.

Conway, M. E., "Design of a Separable Transition-diagram Compiler," *Comm. of the ACM 6*, 7 (July 1963), 396–408.

Coonen, J. T., "Contributions to a Proposed Standard for Binary Floating-Point Arithmetic," Ph.D Thesis, Univ. of California, Berkeley, 1984.

Cordy, J. R., "An Orthogonal Model for Code Generation," CSRI-177, Computer Systems Research Institute, Univ. of Toronto, Toronto, Jan. 1986.

DeRemer, F. L., "Simple LR(k) Grammars," *Comm. of the ACM 14*, 7 (July 1971), 453–460.

DeRemer, F. L., "Practical Translators for LR(k) Languages," MAC-Tech. Rep.-65, MIT, Cambridge, MA, 1969.

Dencker, P., Dürre, K., and Heuft, J., "Optimization of Parser Tables for Portable Compilers," *Trans. Prog. Lang and Systems 6*, 4 (Oct. 1984), 546–572.

Dennis, J. B., "Modularity," in *Advanced Course on Software Engineering*, vol. 81, F. L. Bauer (editor), Springer-Verlag, Heidelberg, 1973, 128–182.

Dewar, R. B. K., "Indirect Threaded Code," *Comm. of the ACM 18*, 6 (June 1975), 330–331.

Dijkstra, E. W., "An ALGOL 60 Translator for the X1," *Annual Review in Automatic Programming 3* (1963), 329–345.

Dijkstra, E. W., "Go To Statement Considered Harmful," *Comm. of the ACM 11*, 3 (March 1968), 147–148.

Dijkstra, E. W., "Recursive Programming," *Numerische Mathematik 2* .if !1960 (1960), 312–318.

Emmelmann, H., Schrör, F., and Landwehr, R., "BEG—A Generator for Efficient Back Ends," *SIGPLAN Notices 24*, 7 (Sep. 1989), 227–237.

Farrow, R., "LINGUIST-86: Yet Another Translator Writing System Based on Attribute Grammars," *SIGPLAN Notices 17*, 6 (June 1982), 160–171.

Floyd, R. W., "An Algorithm for Coding Efficient Arithmetic Operations," *Comm. of the ACM 4*, 1 (Jan. 1961), 42–51.

Foster, J. M., "A Syntax Improving Program," *Computer J. 11*, 1 (May 1968), 31–34.

Goos, G. and Kastens, U., "Programming Languages and the Design of Modular Programs," in *Constructing Quality Software*, P. Hibbard and S. Schuman (editor), North-Holland, Amsterdam, 1977, 153–186.

Grau, A. A., "Recursive Processes and ALGOL Translation," *Comm. of the ACM 4*, 1 (Jan. 1961), 10–15.

Gray, R. W., "A Generator for Lexical Analyzers That Programmers Can Use," *Proc. USENIX Conf.*, June 1988.

Gray, R. W., "Generating Fast, Error Recovering Parsers," MS Thesis, Dept. of Computer Science, University of Colorado, Boulder, CO, April 1987.

Gries, D., *Compiler Construction for Digital Computers*, John Wiley & Sons, New York, 1971.

Gries, D., "Error Recovery and Correction—An Introduction to the Literature," in *Compiler Construction—An Advanced Course*, vol. 21, F. L. Bauer and J. Eickel (editor), Springer-Verlag, Berlin, 1976, 627–638.

Gries, D., *The Science of Programming*, Springer-Verlag, 1981.

Haddon, B. K. and Waite, W. M., "Experience with the Universal Intermediate Language Janus," *Software—Practice & Experience 8* (1978), 601–616.

Harford, A. G., "A New Parsing Method for Non-LALR(1) Grammars," MS Thesis, Dept. of Computer Science, University of Colorado, Boulder, CO, 1990.

Harrison, M. A., *Introduction to Formal Language Theory*, Addison-Wesley, Reading, MA, 1978.

Hartmann, A. C., *A Concurrent Pascal Compiler for Minicomputers*, Springer-Verlag, Heidelberg, 1977.

Helman, P. and Veroff, R., *Intermediate Problem Solving and Data Structures*, Benjamin/Cummings, Menlo Park, CA, 1986.

Heuring, V. P., "The Automatic Generation of Fast Lexical Analyzers," *Software—Practice & Experience 16*, 9 (Sep. 1986), 801–808.

Hext, J. B., "Compile-Time Type Matching," *Computer J. 9*, 4 (Feb. 1967), 365–369.

Horspool, R. N., "An Alternative to the Graham-Glanville Code-Generation Method," *IEEE Software*, May 1987, 33–39.

Horspool, R. N. and Scheuneman, A., "Automating the Selection of Code Templates," *Software—Practice & Experience 15*, 5 (May 1985), 503–514.

"Binary Floating Point Arithmetic," ANSI/IEEE Std. 754-1985, IEEE, New York, NY, 1985.

Irons, E. T., "An Error Correcting Parse Algorithm," *Comm. of the ACM 6*, 11 (Nov. 1963), 669–673.

Jensen, K., Wirth, N., Mickel, A. B., and Miner, J. F., *Pascal User Manual and Report*, Springer-Verlag, New York, 1985. Third Edition.

Johnson, S. C., "Yacc—Yet Another Compiler-Compiler," Computer Science Technical Report 32, Bell Telephone Laboratories, Murray Hill, NJ, July 1975.

Johnson, W. L., Porter, J. H., Ackley, S. I., and Ross, D. T., "Automatic Generation of Efficient Lexical Processors Using Finite State Techniques," *Comm. of the ACM 11*, 12 (Dec. 1968), 805–813.

Johnston, J. B., "Contour Model of Block Structured Processes," *SIGPLAN Notices 6*, 2 (Feb. 1971), 55–82.

Kernighan, B. W. and Ritchie, D. M., *The C Programming Language*, Prentice Hall, Englewood Cliffs, NJ, 1978.

Knuth, D. E., "An Empirical Study of FORTRAN Programs," *Software—Practice & Experience 1* (1971), 105–133.

Knuth, D. E., "On the Translation of Languages from Left to Right," *Inf. and Control 8*, 6 (Dec. 1965), 607–639.

Knuth, D. E., *Seminumerical Algorithms*, Addison-Wesley, New York, 1969.

Knuth, D. E., *Sorting and Searching*, Addison-Wesley, New York, 1973.

Koskimies, K., "A Specification Language for One-Pass Semantic Analysis," *SIGPLAN Notices 19*, 6 (June 1984), 179–189.

Lambert, K. A., "Compiling Tinyturing in a Compiler Construction Course," *SIGCSE 22*, 3 (Sep. 1990), 2–6.

Lesk, M. E., "LEX—A Lexical Analyzer Generator," Computing Science Technical Report 39, Bell Telephone Laboratories, Murray Hill, NJ, 1975.

Levy, H. M. and Jr., R. H. E., *Computer Programming and Architecture: The VAX-11*, Digital Press, Bedford, MA, 1980.

Lewis, P. M., Rosenkrantz, D. J., and Stearns, R. E., *Compiler Design Theory*, Addison-Wesley, Reading, MA, 1976.

Lomet, D. B., "A Formalization of Transition Diagram Systems," *J. ACM 20*, 2 (Apr. 1973), 235–257.

Matula, D. W., "In-and-Out Conversions," *Comm. of the ACM 11*, 1 (Jan. 1968), 47–50.

Matula, D. W., "Base Conversion Mappings," *AFIPS Conf. Proc. 30* (1967), 311–318.

McCarthy, J., "Towards a Mathematical Theory of Computation," in *Information Processing 1962*, North-Holland, Amsterdam, 1963, 21–28.

McClure, R. M., "An Appraisal of Compiler Technology," in *Spring Joint Computer Conf.*, vol. 40, AFIPS Press, Montvale, NJ, 1972.

McLaren, M. D., "Data Matching, Data Alignment, and Structure Mapping in PL/I," *SIGPLAN Notices 5*, 12 (Dec. 1970), 30–43.

Mealy, G. H., "A Generalized Assembly System," in *Programming Systems and Languages*, S. Rosen (editor), McGraw-Hill, 1967, 535–559.

Mock, O., Olsztyn, J., Strong, J., Steel, T. B., Tritter, A., and Wegstein, J., "The Problem of Programming Communications with Changing Machines: A Proposed Solution," *Comm. of the ACM 1*, 2 (Feb. 1958), 12–18.

Nakata, I., "On Compiling Algorithms for Arithmetic Expressions," *Comm. of the ACM 10*, 8 (Aug. 1967), 492–494.

Naur, P., "The Design of the GIER ALGOL Compiler," *Annual Review in Automatic Programming 4* (1964), 49–85.

"Revised Report on the Algorithmic Language ALGOL 60," *Comm. of the ACM 6*, 1 (Jan. 1963), 1–17.

Newey, M. C. and Waite, W. M., "The Robust Implementation of Sequence-Controlled Iteration," *Software—Practice & Experience 15*, 7 (July 1985), 655–668.

Parnas, D. L., "A Technique for Software Module Specification with Examples," *Comm. of the ACM 15*, 5 (May 1972), 330–336.

Parnas, D. L., "On the Criteria to be Used in Decomposing Systems Into Modules," *Comm. of the ACM 15*, 12 (Dec. 1972), 1053–1058.

Persch, G., Winterstein, G., Dausmann, M., and Drossopoulou, S., "Overloading in Preliminary Ada," *SIGPLAN Notices 15*, 11 (Nov. 1980), 47–56.

Pratt, T. W., *Programming Languages Design and Implementation*, Prentice Hall, Englewood Cliffs, NJ, 1975.

Purdom, P. and Brown, C. A., "Semantic Routines and LR(k) Parsers," *Acta Inf.*, 1980, 299–316.

Räihä, K., "Bibliography on Attribute Grammars," *SIGPLAN Notices 15*, 3 (Mar. 1980), 35–44.

Randell, B. and Russell, L. J., *ALGOL 60 Implementation*, Academic Press, London, 1964.

Redziejowski, R. R., "On Arithmetic Expressions and Trees," *Comm. of the ACM 12*, 2 (Feb. 1969), 81–84.

Richards, M., "The Portability of the BCPL Compiler," *Software—Practice & Experience 1* (1971), 135–146.

Richards, M., "A Compact Function for Regular Expression Pattern Matching," *Software—Practice & Experience 9*, 7 (July 1979), 527–534.

Röhrich, J., "Methods for the Automatic Construction of Error Correcting Parsers," *Acta Inf. 13*, 2 (Feb. 1980), 115–139.

Rosenkrantz, D. J. and Stearns, R. E., "Properties of Deterministic Top-Down Grammars," *Inf. and Control 17* (1970), 226–256.

Saarinen, M., Soisalon-Soininen, E., Räihä, K., and Tienari, M., "The Compiler Writing System HLP (Helsinki Language Processor)," Report A-1978-2, Dept. of Computer Science, Univ. of Helsinki, Helsinki, Finland, Mar. 1978.

Sale, A. H. J., "A Note on Scope, One-Pass Compilers, and Pascal," *Pascal News 15*, 1979, 62–63.

Schmidt, D. A., *Denotational Semantics*, Allyn & Bacon, Inc., Newton, MA, 1986.

Schneider, G. M. and Bruell, S. C., *Advanced Programming and Problem Solving with Pascal*, John Wiley & Sons, New York, NY, 1981.

Sethi, R. and Ullman, J. D., "The Generation of Optimal Code for Arithmetic Expressions," *J. ACM 17*, 4 (Oct. 1970), 715–728.

Steel, T. B., "UNCOL, Universal Computer Oriented Language Revisited," *Datamation 6* (1960), 14–20.

Steel, T. B., "UNCOL. The Myth and the Fact," *Annual Review in Automatic Programming 2* (1961), 325–344.

Stephens, P. D., "The IMP Language and Compiler," *Computer J. 17* (1974), 216–223.

Stone, H. S., *Discrete Mathematical Structures and Their Applications*, Science Research Associates, Chicago, 1973.

Szymanski, T. G., "Assembling Code for Machines with Span-Dependent Instructions," *Comm. of the ACM 21*, 4 (Apr. 1978), 300–308.

Talmadge, R. B., "Design of an Integrated Programming and Operating System Part II. The Assembly Program and its Language," *IBM Systems Journal 2* (1963), 162–179.

Tennent, R. D., *Principles of Programming Languages*, Prentice Hall, London, 1981.

Thompson, K., "Regular Expression Search Algorithm," *Comm. of the ACM 11*, 6 (June 1968), 419–422.

Waite, W. M., "Treatment of Tab Characters by a Compiler," *Software—Practice & Experience 15*, 11 (Nov. 1985), 1121–1123.

Waite, W. M., "The Cost of Lexical Analysis," *Software—Practice & Experience 16*, 5 (May 1986), 473–488.

Waite, W. M. and Goos, G., *Compiler Construction*, Springer-Verlag, New York, NY, 1984.

Waite, W. M. and Carter, L. R., "The Cost of a Generated Parser," *Software—Practice & Experience 15*, 3 (Mar. 1985), 221–239.

Wirth, N., *Programming in Modula-2*, Springer-Verlag, Heidelberg, 1985. Third Edition.

Wulf, W. A., Shaw, M., Hilfinger, P. N., and Flon, L., *Fundamental Structures of Computer Science*, Addison-Wesley, Reading, MA, 1981.

Zimmermann, E., Kastens, U., and Hutt, B., *GAG: A Practical Compiler Generator*, Springer-Verlag, Heidelberg, 1982.

Index

* (asterisk) operator,
  See Also operators;
  in context-free grammar rewriting rules; 92
  in regular expressions,
    identities, (figure); 89
    precedence; 49
  in source program tree notation, meaning; 72
  integer multiplication use, reasons for different representations; 270
= > (derives) operator,
  term definition; 91
[] (Pascal empty set),
  source language typing vs compiler typing of; 207
+ (plus) operator,
  in context-free grammar rewriting rules; 92
  in regular expressions; 49
  in source program tree notation; 72
[] (square brackets),
  extending regular expression notation with; 51
| (vertical bar),
  meaning in regular expressions; 49
  precedence in regular expressions; 49
  use in regular expression identities, (figure); 89

A

abnormal termination,
  See Also errors;
  advantages of centralizing it in the error module; 24
  characteristics; 24
abstractions,
  abstract machine, (notes and references); 14
  abstract program, construction by code generator; 11
  abstract syntax, term definition (notes); 105
  functions and procedures as; 208
***Accept* operation,**
  procedure description, (figure); 127, 132
access functions,
  See Also action mapping; machine operations; target program;
  allocation to Datum-class nodes by parent during target program tree traversal; 322
  array indexing, design issues; 254
  characteristics; 232
  completion by *CompleteAccessFunction* operation; 326
  definition table; 174, 179
    use of *SetTypeKey*; 177
  encapsulating data flow relationships in operand; 229
  environment module,
    constant-time data structures and objects, (figure); 187
    constant-time implementation; 188
  for intermediate results, provided by code generator; 233
  index addressing mode, shift amount determined by; 254
  interior node values, provided by code generator; 233
  leaf values, provided by action mapper; 233
  local variables, description; 233
  non-local variables, target tree representation (figure); 250
  register mode, allocating registers for; 324
  representation by *Operand* type, (figure); 234
  requiring fixed registers, effect on target tree construction; 317
  storage of register allocation results as completed access functions; 324
  term definition and examples; 232
  testing during instruction encoding operations; 331
action mapping (transformation subtask),
  See Also mapping; operator identification;
  access functions for leaf nodes provided by; 233
  C-- language to VAX; 367
  (chapter); 228
  deadly error inconsistencies detected during; 242
  defined as collection of source program tree visit procedures; 241

385

386 INDEX

definition table keys operator description,
    components and use by; 282
descriptive overview; 11
establishing order of children as a component
    of; 231
handling type conversions during; 247
naming conventions for procedures that
    implement; 241
operator identification and; 282
role in determining execution order; 236
separation of concerns from code generator;
    229
simplified; 230
structure of operation nodes built by, (table);
    235
target program tree and, (chapter); 228
term definition; 229

activation records,
See Also procedures; storage; variables;
accessing non-current activation records; 204
ActivationRecord variable, monitoring
    allocation state with; 324
addressing; 204
    on the VAX (figure); 206
allocating; 322
    memory for values that must be held in;
        320
    variables used to keep track of; 324
storage,
    of parameters; 204
    requirements; 212
term definition; 204
visibility rules, effect on; 204

activity sequences,
See Also syntactic analysis; syntax diagrams;
characteristics as finite sequence of basic
    invocations; 80
context-free grammar used to generate; 90
deriving,
    (exercise); 108
    from extended regular expressions (figure);
        88
describing by listing basic invocations; 81
equivalence; 83
    (exercise); 108
extending regular expressions to support; 87
generating by rewriting regular expressions;
    88
iterative, transforming into recursive activity
    sequences; 86
significance for parser design; 106
term definition; 80
transformations that move forks and joins
    without changing, (figure); 85

add operations,
See Also nodes;
AddCoercion operation,
    characteristics; 297
    sample use (figure); 280
AddL operation,
    as example of operation combination; 235
    node structure description (table); 235
AddOperator operation,
    characteristics; 299
    sample use (figure); 280
AddType operation,
    characteristics; 297
    sample use (figure); 280

addresses,
See Also external address resolution; internal
    address resolution;
argument list, linking activation record to
    argument list address; 206
array elements; 254
composite objects,
    determination by *Concatenate* operation;
        212
    determination by *Overlay* operation; 213
instruction, determination by code generator;
    11
local storage area, linking activation record to
    argument list address; 206
relative,
    array element computation; 203
    local variable representation by *Operand*
        value; 233
    parameter representation by *Operand*
        value; 233
VAX hardware, data representation concerns;
    200

addressing,
activation records; 204
    on the VAX (figure); 206
modes,
    AddressingMode type definition(figure);
        315
    as component of an access function; 232
    index, accessing array elements with; 254
    VAX, representing with *Operand* type,
        (figure); 234

***AddressingMode* type,**
definition, (figure); 234, 315

algebra,
regular expressions, transforming left-
    recursive regular expressions into
    iterative expressions; 111

algorithms,
See Also computational complexity;
    performance;
anchor set computation; 123

efficiency of, (notes and references); 192
equivalence,
  (notes and references); 14
  term definition; 1
implementing, (figure); 229
integer division example, (figure); 2
operator identification; 295
parser as central control for syntactic
    analysis; 69
shortest-path,
  (notes and references); 301
  use in operator identification; 298
tree traversal; 166
alignment,
See Also data types; storage;
aligned data, term definition; 199
calculations by composition operations in
    determining next available address; 214
constraints,
  impact on storage management, (notes and
    references); 223
  record data type; 202
AlternativeDataL **nodes,**
representing alternative computation
    expressions by; 261
Sethi-Ullman number of; 311
ambiguous parsing language,
See Also parsers;
handling by removing director set overlaps;
    121
anchors,
See Also parsers; syntactic analysis;
anchor sets,
  appropriate for a specific error, character-
    istics of; 125
  computing, (notes and references); 134
  computing, recursive descent parsers; 123
  computing, shift-reduce parsers; 151
  parameter, symbols to add to, (figure);
    126
  procedures for making available to error
    recovery; 125
anchors type, description (figure); 127
generating symbols; 151
term definition; 103
and operation,
generating the effect of; 287
AndExpr **construct,**
operator and signature for, (figure); 289
anonymous entities,
See Also entities;
representation in definition table; 172
storing in definition table; 160
AP register (VAX register 12),
See Also registers;

activation record addressing with; 204
applied occurrence,
See Also identifiers; occurrences (identifier);
AppliedOccurrence operation (semantic
    analysis),
  description; 177
  procedure definition (figure); 176
definition table use in validating; 173
leaf context use to identify; 175
term definition; 164
visiting after defining occurrences; 166
AppliedOccurrence **operation,**
procedure description, (figure); 176
arbitrary sequences,
See Also representation; trees;
source program tree representation; 72
target program tree representation; 238
arguments,
argument lists,
  address, activation record linking local
    storage area address to; 206
  mapping, example description; 248
  procedure activation record, VAX registers
    used to access; 204
representation,
  in source program tree node notation; 72
  on the VAX; 207
arithmetic computation,
See Also computation(s); floating-point;
converting floating-point constants to
    representation for; 31
DatumLeaf node, mapping arithmetic
    constants and field identifiers into; 249
multiple-precision integer arithmetic, (notes
    and references); 35
arity **type,**
definition, (figure); 329
ArrayInfo **operation,**
procedure description, procedure description
    (figure); 257
arrays,
See Also data types;
ArrayInfo operation, procedure description
    (figure); 257
data type, characteristics and representation
    on the VAX; 203
element,
  addresses; 254
  relative address computation; 203
environment module implementation use of;
    185
indexing operations, target program tree
    mapping design issues; 251
OpndArray, copying *Operand* type values
    into during instruction encoding
    operations; 330

388 INDEX

Pascal restrictions on direct storage in definition table; 181
references,
   MapExpression handling of, (figure); 257
   target program tree representation of assignment statements with; 255
   storage in VAX memory, (figure); 253
Assemble operation,
   procedure description, (figure); 329
assembly (encoding subtask),
   Assemble operation, procedure description (figure); 329
   AssemFinl operation, procedure description (figure); 329
   AssemInit operation, procedure description (figure); 329
   module,
      implementation (notes and references); 338
      interface specification (figure); 329
   subtasks of, descriptive overview; 12
***AssemFinl* operation,**
   procedure description, (figure); 329
***AssemInit* operation,**
   procedure description, (figure); 329
assignment statements,
   See Also nodes; operators; statements;
   AssignExpr construct,
      handling voided expression children; 292
      overloading operators and signatures (figure); 293
   AssignmentStmt alternative, mapping assignment statements with; 247
   AssignmentStmt nodes,
      characteristics; 72
      constructing; 75
      textual notation for; 72
   constructing a source tree node for; 75
   finite-state machine example description (figure); 55
   implementing, (figure); 229
   mapping with *AssignmentStmt* alternative of *MapStatement* procedure; 247
   multiple, as example of director set overlap, (figure); 118
   Pascal, syntax diagrams for a subset, (figure); 114
   syntax diagram, examples (figure); 82
   target program tree fragment for, (figure); 232
   with array references, target program tree representation of; 255
association(s),
   See Also definition table; identifiers; keys;
   between identifiers and definitions, representing by *Environment* type value; 163
   compiler types and defintion table keys; 208
   computing the set that is valid at a source program tree leaf; 160
   definition table keys with identifier definition occurrences, example description; 177
   establishing between types and definition table keys; 210
   identifier,
      accessing considerations; 162
      and class of entity it is associated with; 173
   identifier/key,
      establishing by *DefineIdn* function; 164
      establishing by visit to identifier declaration nodes; 166
      finding with *KeyInEnv* function; 165
      storing in global variable; 162
   operator,
      incorporating into parsing specification; 92
      specifying example (figure); 96
   referenced locations with unique names; 239
   rules,
      avoiding parentheses in regular expressions with; 49
      incorporating into parsing specification; 92
      procedures for incorporating into parsing specification; 97
   types with definition table keys; 216
asterisk (*) operator,
   See * (asterisk) operator;
asymptotic execution time properties,
   See computational complexity;
avalanche errors,
   See Also errors; syntactic analysis; syntax errors;
   avoiding in syntax error recovery; 100
axiom,
   anchor defined in terms of; 123
   term definition; 91

B
basic symbols,
   See Also lexical analysis; symbols; syntactic analysis;
   accepting,
      characteristics; 80
      representation in activity sequence descriptions; 81
      syntax diagrams, example (figure); 82
   building source program tree from information contained in; 75
C-- language; 344
classification in,
   Pascal (list); 21
   source language constructs; 70

constructing with syntax diagrams; 42
director set characteristics and use; 115
finding the set that constitute anchors; 123
formal definition,
  graphical notations for; 42
  textual notations for; 48
frequency of occurence, importance to
      efficient scanner implementation; 51
recognizing,
  as lexical analyzer subtask; 38
  (exercise); 66
  with syntax diagrams; 42
representation,
  as leaves of source program tree; 6
  (figure); 40
  in extended regular expressions; 87
  in syntax diagrams by round boxes; 110
scanner,
  construction of, descriptive overview; 5
  operations when recognizing; 41
term definition; 38
Big O,
  See O (N) notation;
bit vectors,
  set representation, characteristics; 299
boolean,
  See Also data types; expressions;
  data type,
    characteristics and representation on the
        VAX; 200
    relationship of *truejump* and *falsejump* type
        to; 287
  expressions,
    implementing with jump cascades; 287
    MapCondition procedure use of; 246
bounds,
  on external values, requirements for; 26
  on internal data structures, deciding
      maximum line length as a problem in
      specifying; 21
boxes,
  See Also syntactic analysis;
  oval,
    characteristics and use; 82
    parser syntax diagrams, unlabeled because
        not associated with input symbols; 140
    structure connections in parser syntax
        diagrams representation by; 110
  rectangular,
    anchor set for; 123
    characteristics and use; 81
    parser finite-state machine example
        description (figure); 141
    procedure calls represented in syntax
        diagrams by; 126

recursion as reason why rectangular boxes
      cannot all be eliminated from syntax
      diagrams; 83
  substituting syntax diagrams for in activity
      sequence syntax diagrams; 83
  syntax diagrams representation in syntax
      diagrams by; 110
round,
  characteristics and use; 82
  representation of basic symbols in syntax
diagrams by; 110
  syntax diagrams, characteristics and use; 81
branching,
  MapCondition procedure use for, (figure);
      247
buffers,
  See Also memory; storage;
  allocating for file data type; 203
***BufferSize* constant,**
  constant definition, (figure); 19
building,
  See constructing;
byte sequences,
  See Also data types;
  representing predefined Pascal data types, q
      design concerns; 200

C
C-- language,
  characteristics; 344
  concepts; 354
  constructs, (table); 357
  declarations, (figure); 346
  identifiers and denotations, (figure); 344
  operator identification, (table); 351
  program structure, (figure); 345
  sample programs; 352
  source,
    constructs and structure; 354
    constructs and structure (table); 357
    program tree (figure); 355
  statements, (figure); 348
  target program tree, (figure); 361
  VAX assembly code, (figure); 366
  VAX constructs, (figure); 363
  visibility in, (figure); 353
***CallExpr* alternative (*MapExpression*
    procedure),**
  mapping routine calls with; 248
***CallStmt* nodes,**
  description, (figure); 74
case sensitivity,
  (exercise); 68
case statement,
  representation by an Item-class node; 260

Chain **type,**
  description, (figure); 61
ChainElt **type,**
  description, (figure); 61
characters,
  See Also data types; types;
  char data type, characteristics and representation on the VAX; 200
  character pool,
    module as example of interface specification, (figure); 19
    storage, allocated by external value module; 29
    storage, use by clients of the external value module; 32
  character sequences,
    describing with syntax diagrams; 42
    extracting from source text with the scanner; 41
    invocation sequences compared with; 80
    notations for describing; 48
  compared with lines as unit of text delivered by source module; 21
  converting to an internal representation; 56
  describing a set of characters with a regular expression; 49
  manipulating, managing literals as a problem of; 26
  obtaining from source text, source module specification; 21
  problems in defining for ASCII and EBCDIC machines; 50
  sentinel, (exercise); 65
  strings, determining the maximum length of; 26
CharPool **type,**
  as example of public data type (figure); 19
children,
  See Also trees;
  linkage to children stored in source node record; 73
  source tree nodes, represented by class subvariants; 73
class,
  See Also source program tree;
  defined entity, verifying context compatibility; 177
  of a tree fragment, term definition; 70
  of an entity; 174
  source node, use in source node textual notation; 72
  variants, of source program tree nodes; 73
classification,
  basic symbols, descriptive overview; 5
  entity associated with an identifier, stored in definition table; 173

Pascal compiler types, (figure); 209
source program tree fragment, stored in Pascal records; 73
client,
  See Also interface; module;
  term definition; 18
closeness,
  in syntactic error recovery, term definition; 99
code generation (encoding subtask),
  access functions for interior nodes provided by; 233
  (chapter); 306
  classes of decision deferred to, (list); 230
  conditional expression code generated from *AlternativeDataL* construct; 262
  determining operand classes during; 314
  instruction sequence production constrained by target program tree structure; 238
  (notes and references); 337
  resource allocation needs, for statements; 259
  role in determining execution order; 238
  separation of concerns from action mapper; 229
  subtasks of, descriptive overview; 12
CoercibleFrom **operation,**
  function definition, (figure); 278
coercion,
  See Also operators;
  C-- language; 350
  CoercibleFrom operation,
    characteristics; 297
    function definition (figure); 278
  Coercion operation,
    characteristics; 298
    function description (figure); 286
  construction from type graph sets; 297
  graph, adding an operator to, procedure definition, (figure); 280
  operators,
    obtaining consistent labeling of source tree nodes for; 272
    reasons for not including in operator triples; 276
  term definition; 268
comments,
  See Also lexical analysis;
  recognizing, (exercise); 66
Commutative **operation,**
  procedure description, (figure); 334
comparison operations,
  See Also action mapping;
  conditional transfer of control implemented by; 239
compilation,
  general model of; 2

model used in this book; 3
    separating from environment concerns; 16
    time, effect of information gathering strategy
        on; 160, 181
compiler,
    characteristics,
        (notes and references); 14
        overview, (chapter); 1
    compiler construction problem, modular
        decomposition of; 17
    controlling behavior with error report
        classification system; 24
    interface, characteristics and specification
        (chapter); 16
    tasks, (table); 3
***CompleteAccessFunction* operation,**
    procedure description, (figure); 327
complexity,
    See computational complexity;
component relations,
    trees as data structures that embody; 4
composition,
    See Also data mapping;
    operations, *StorageRequired* type objects as
        arguments to; 212
    strategies for determining object storage
        requirements; 210
compound statements,
    See Also statements;
    mapping with *CompoundStmt* alternative of
        MapStatement procedure; 246
computation(s),
    See Also code generation;
    allocating registers for, (figure); 327
    arithmetic, converting floating-point constants
        to representation for; 31
    deciding which are needed for tree decoration
        strategy; 162
    dyadic computational operators, as a group;
        284
    efficiency of, (notes and references); 192
    for resource allocation, (figure); 321
    necessary for name analysis; 162
    of identifier key, information required for;
        162
    of values,
        as tactical component of contextual
            information gathering strategy; 160
        decorating a tree; 163
    operator identification; 276
    provided by external value module (figure);
        30
    strict, implication for external value module;
        32
computational complexity,
    See Also performance;

impact on time required to gather contextual
    information; 182
(notes and references); 192
O (N) notation used to measure; 182
***Concatenate* operation,**
    function description, (figure); 214
concatenation,
    composition strategy; 210
    Concatenate operation,
        function description (figure); 214
        relative address determination by; 212
    precedence in regular expressions; 49
    use in regular expression identities, (figure);
        89
concrete syntax,
    See Also syntactic analysis;
    term definition, (notes); 105
Concurrent Pascal compiler,
    (notes and references); 192
conditional,
    See Also action mapping;
    control flow,
        representation in target program tree; 239
        target program tree mapping design issues;
            260
    expressions,
        code generated for; 262
        jump cascade translation in C-- language
            (figure); 371
        mapping, *MapCondition* procedure use for
            (figure); 247
    jump operations,
        circumventing VAX limitations by
            deferring encoding to assembly module;
            329
        implementation on the VAX (figure); 330
    statement (Pascal),
        representation in source and target
            program trees (figure); 244
        source language constructs into target
            language constructs, example descrip-
            tion; 243
        syntax diagram (figure); 121
conflicts,
    conflict-free parsing grammars, (notes and
        references); 154
    eliminating from parser generator grammar,
        example description; 146
    resolution of, approaches to; 149
connections,
    See structure connections; symbol connec-
        tions;
consistency,
    operator labeling of source tree nodes; 272
    overload resolution issue; 269
    verifying for voided expressions; 292

392 INDEX

constant-time access function,
  data structures and objects, (figure); 187
constants,
  See Also denotations; literals; symbols; variables;
  as external values, characteristics; 26
  BufferSize, (figure); 19
  EndOfLineMarker, (figure); 41
  exported, characteristics; 18
  ExtIntegerSize, (figure); 29
  HashConst, (figure); 61
  mapping; 249
  MaxArity, (figure); 329
  MaxBucket, (figure); 61
  MaxDef, (figure); 179
  MaxLength, (figure); 205
  MaxOpnd, (figure); 278
  MaxRadix, (figure); 29
  properties stored in definition table; 172
constructing,
  basic symbols, with syntax diagrams; 42
  source program tree,
    example description (figure); 76
    from source program text; 69
  target program tree; 241
constructs,
  C-- language, (table); 357
context-free grammars,
  See Also grammars;
  as input to parser generators; 145
  characteristics and use in the parsing subtask; 90
  component of, example (figure); 91
  (exercises); 135
  left recursion removal techniques, (notes and references); 134
  rule correspondence to reduce operations; 145
  shift-reduce parser generator use of; 145
  theoretical implications; 106
contextual information,
  See Also information; semantic analysis;
  checking compatibility of entity class with use; 177
  cost of gathering; 181
    analysis of environment module strategies; 182
  data structure design effect on cost of gathering; 185
  determination,
    by semantic analyzer; 8
    of type properties from; 210
  effect on data structure choice; 170
  Identifier leaf, as determiner of applied vs defining occurrence; 175
  managing,
    (chapter); 157
    (exercises); 194
    (notes and references); 191
  modifying target program tree structure with; 314
  strategy for gathering; 160
  use in,
    associating types and definition table keys; 210
    translating data structures into target machine language concepts; 198
contiguous evaluation strategy,
  See Also execution-order determination; operands;
  (notes and references); 337
continuation,
  paths,
    characteristics of activity sequence following a parser-defined error; 101
    (exercise); 109
    specifying anchor sets in terms of; 123
    specifying in recursive descent parsers; 122
    specifying in shift-reduce parser; 150
continuations,
  See Also syntax diagrams;
  specifying by rearranging syntax diagram forks, (figure); 124
contour model,
  (notes and references); 223
control flow,
  See Also operators;
  operators,
    implementing with jump cascades (figure); 288
    that manipulate, jump cascade; 287
  representation in target program tree; 239
control sections,
  characteristics and implementation; 333
  (notes and references); 338
  term definition; 333
  use of; 333
    (figure); 335
  using, (figure); 335
controlling,
  compiler behavior, error report classification use for; 24
conversion (lexical analysis subtask),
  importance of avoiding in floating-point operations (notes and references); 34
  problems for floating-point values; 27
  characteristics; 56
  denotations, algorithm descriptions; 58

description,
  (figure); 57
  overview; 6
floating-point, difficulties with, (notes and references); 34
module, use of hash functions as filters; 60
operation, general form (figure); 58
operations, (exercise); 66
radix, external representation conversion as; 31
reasons for separating from,
  recognition; 57
  scanning operations; 42
term definition; 39
type, See types, conversion of;
ConvertDigits operation,
procedure description, (figure); 205
Coord field,
description, (figure); 74
coordinate system (source text),
combining with error module; 25
contained in basic symbol representation; 75
error reporting design issues; 23
specification of; 24
correctness,
See Also interface; modules;
of a module, as part of meaning of a module; 17
cost component,
of operator representation triple, meaning of; 275
count-controlled iteration,
target program tree mapping design issues; 256
counters,
use in mapping for statements; 258
CPL compiler,
type conversion operators in, (notes and references); 301
cross-references; 239
See Also action mapping;
CurrDef variable,
definition, (figure); 179
Current variable,
description, (figure); 41
CurrentAR variable,
monitoring allocation state with; 324
CurrOp variable,
definition, (figure); 281
CurrSig variable,
definition, (figure); 281
CvtBL operation node,
CvtBL operation, structure description (table); 235

CvtXXX **operation**,
procedure description, (figure); 58

D

dangling else statements,
See Also parsers; statements;
as director set overlap example; 119
data flow,
procedure activation; 204
relationships, encapsulating in operand access functions; 229
term definition; 228
data mapping (transformation subtask),
See Also data types; mapping;
basic computational operation; 210
bibliographic reference; 223
C-- language to VAX; 366
(chapter); 198
descriptive overview; 11
types and, (notes and references); 222
DATA **operation code**,
control section management by; 333
data representation,
See Also data types; representation; source program tree; target program tree;
on target machine, (chapter); 198
data structures,
See Also data types; representation; source language;
choice affected by lifetime and context of the information; 170
compiler; 13
  effect of compiler type system design on; 208
definition table,
  construction and use by semantic analyzer; 9
  (figure); 179
design, effect on cost of gathering contextual information; 185
determination of, as a component of modular decomposition; 17
environment module, (figure); 183, 189
identifier table, (figure); 61
internal, design considerations; 21
linked, trees stored as; 70
modifying for operator identification, (figure); 280
operator identification module,
  characteristics; 299
  states defined in terms of building and use of; 298
program implementation example, (figure); 186

394　INDEX

trees,
　descriptive overview; 4
　source program tree generation overview; 6
　target program tree generation overview; 6
data types,
　See Also representation; types;
　analysis of, descriptive overview; 9
　anonymous, representation in definition table; 172
　array, characteristics and representation on the VAX; 203
　associating with definition table keys; 177
　boolean,
　　characteristics and representation on the VAX; 200
　　relationship of *truejump* and *falsejump* type to; 287
　char, characteristics and representation on the VAX; 200
　CharPool, as example of public data type, (figure); 19
　comparison with compiler type system; 207
　conversion of, effect on compiler type system design; 208
　enumerated,
　　specifying error report severity by; 24
　　VAX representation, design considerations; 201
　file, characteristics and representation on the VAX; 203
　integer, characteristics and representation on the VAX; 200
　limited private, term definition; 20
　packed structured, storage requirement considerations; 201
　Pascal real, characteristics and representation on the VAX; 200
　pointer, characteristics and representation on the VAX; 201
　position, definition, (figure); 25
　predefined,
　　global variables use with; 280
　　Pascal, representation of; 200
　private,
　　characteristics and comparison with public data types; 18
　　information hiding use by; 20
　　limited, term definition; 20
　public,
　　characteristics and comparison with private data types; 18
　　CharPool as example, (figure); 19
　　vs private. considerations for selecting; 20
　record,
　　characteristics and representation on the VAX; 202
　　storage allocation methods; 203
　representing definition table property values by; 178
　set, characteristics and representation on the VAX; 203
　severity, definition, (figure); 25
　simple Pascal, characteristics and representation on the VAX; 200
　source language, representation on target machine; 11
　structured,
　　Pascal, characteristics and representation on the VAX; 201
　　Pascal restrictions on direct storage in definition table; 181
　subrange, storage requirement issues; 201
　Token,
　　fields set by lexical analysis scanner; 41
　　figure; 40
　user-defined, operator identification handling of; 277
database,
　See Also definition table;
***DataBase* variable,**
　definition (figure); 179
***Datum* constructs,**
　encoding, (figure); 334
***Datum* type,**
　definition, (figure); 316
Datum-class nodes,
　access functions allocation to, by parent during target program tree traversal; 322
　AlternativeDataL construct use to embody a sequence of; 261
　characteristics and comparison with Item-class node; 231
　Datum type definition, (figure); 316
　decoration with ref-class *Operand* records; 238
　descriptive overview; 7
　encoding, (figure); 334
　implementing with decision trees, (figure); 332
　instruction encoding from; 331
　intermediate values produced by, role in code generation; 306
　MapExpression creation of; 246
　Sethi-Ullman number of; 309
　stack condition on mapping procedure exit; 242
　target program tree traversal strategy; 322

INDEX **395**

value constraints on; 231
DatumLeaf **node,**
  descriptive overview; 7
  mapping arithmetic constants and field identifiers into; 249
  values obtained from data mapping subtask stored in; 11
DatumVisit **operation,**
  procedure description, (figure); 327
deadly error,
  See Also errors;
  characteristics; 24
  inconsistencies detected during action mapping; 242
  reports, as compiler debugging aid; 321
  uninitialized definition table operator entries; 285
decision,
  making, in recursive descent parsers; 115
  trees,
    access function testing use of; 331
    code generator use in selecting instructions, (notes and references); 338
    implementing Datum-class constructs with (figure); 332
decision trees,
  implementation of, (figure); 332
declarations,
  See Also data mapping; nodes;
  C-- language; 347
    (figure); 346
  Declaration nodes, example illustration in source program tree (figure); 168
  DeclarationVisit1 operation,
    procedure description (figure); 169
    use of *DefiningOccurrence1*, example description; 175
  DeclarationVisit2 operation, procedure description (figure); 171
  identifiers, used in semantic analysis; 8
  identifying nodes that are; 166
  procedures for associating with definition table keys, example description; 177
  variables, establishing associations for; 163
  visiting Type component of; 170
DeclarationVisit1 **operation,**
  procedure description, (figure); 169, 176
DeclarationVisit2 **operation,**
  procedure description, (figure); 171
decoding operations,
  external values, interface specification (figure); 29
decorations,
  See Also code generation; syntactic analysis; trees;

formal descriptions, (notes and references); 192
source program tree,
  identifier associations as; 160
  leaves decorated by syntactic analyzer; 6
  name analysis (exercise); 194
  nodes decorated by semantic analyzer; 8
  operator identification (chapter); 268
  operators; 272
  type information attached to the leaves; 9
storage of information used during; 170
strategy for applying to a tree; 162
target program tree,
  leaf nodes, with access functions; 233
  nodes decorated by code generator; 314
  operand nodes, with machine resource information; 12
default argument,
  entity class, obtaining with *NoKey* key argument; 174
defined entities,
  See Also entities;
  Pascal, (figure); 173
  properties stored in definition table; 172
DefineIdn **operation,**
  associations between identifiers and keys created by; 164
  function description, (figure); 164, 184
  procedure description, (figure); 189
  use of *NewKey* definition table module function; 173
defining occurrences,
  See Also identifiers;
  accessing,
    by visiting identifier declarations; 166
    current environment while processing; 170
  DefiningOccurrence1 operation (semantic analysis),
    associating identifier definitions with definition table keys; 177
    procedure definition (figure); 176
    procedure description, example description; 175
  DefiningOccurrence2 operation (semantic analysis),
    procedure definition (figure); 176
    procedure description, example description; 177
  enumerated constant identifiers, visit sequence; 218
  identified by identifier leaf context; 175
  source program tree visit strategy; 177
  term definition; 164
  visiting,
    before applied occurences; 166

Type component of declarations to process
   all; 170
DefiningOccurrence1 **operation,**
   procedure description, (figure); 176
DefInit **operation,**
   function description, (figure); 174
definition table,
   See Also identifier table; operators; types;
   access functions; 174
   characteristics,
      and use; 172
      as general data base; 173
   compared with identifier table; 159
   construction and use by semantic analyzer; 9
   data structures, (figure); 179
   DefInit operation, procedure description
      (figure); 174, 180
   definition table module,
      environment module use of create key
         operation; 173
      implementing; 178
      interface characteristics; 173
   definitions (source language), establishing
      associations between identifiers and;
      163
   DefTableKey type, definition (figure); 174
   design criteria; 177
   implementation, (figure); 180
   information about data types entered by data
      mapping subtask; 11
   keys,
      associating with type represented by a 1
         Type-class node; 216
      compared with identifier table; 159
      compiler types associated with unique; 208
      computing for identifiers, as name
         analyzer subtask; 160
      implementation of; 179
      operator description, components and use
         by action mapping routines; 282
      reasons for representing operators and
         result types as; 295
      reasons for storing in tree; 170
      representing identifier type, establishing
         during tree decoration; 172
      representing operators with; 272, 277
      representing result types with; 277
      role in determining possible operator
         meanings; 282
      shown as superscripts in a Pascal program
         (figure); 159
      types, source program tree visit that
         establishes; 210
   name analysis use of, descriptive overview; 9
   properties, access and creation functions
      implementation; 179

storing target construct property in; 285
transformation subtask use to build target
   program tree; 11
type analysis use of, descriptive overview; 9
DELETE operation,
   characteristics; 299
delimiters,
   See Also denotations; identifiers; source
      language; syntax diagrams;
   basic symbol, term definition; 39
   compared with denotations and identifiers; 39
   improper, as major cause of syntax errors; 98
   string, conversion of Pascal representation;
      59
   Token data type specification of; 39
denotations,
   See Also constants; lexical analysis;
   basic symbol, term definition; 39
   C-- language, (figure); 344
   compared with, delimiters and identifiers; 39
   converting to an internal representation; 56
      algorithm desciptions; 58
   integer, recognizing with syntax diagrams
      (figure); 43
   real, recognizing with syntax diagrams
      (figure); 43
   representation as leaf arguments in source
      program trees; 73
   string, recognizing with syntax diagrams
      (figure); 43
   syntax diagrams for, (exercise); 64
   Token data type specification of; 39
dependence relations,
   See Also trees;
   computational, tree traversal order relation
      ship to; 162
   tree traversal strategy use of, (notes and
      references); 192
depth,
   continuation paths, computing for shift-reduce
      parsers; 151
derivations,
   See Also operators;
   activity sequences,
      from regular expressions; 88
      start symbol as axiom for; 91
   derives (= >) operator, term definition; 91
deterministic finite automaton,
   See finite-state machines;
dictionary,
   term definition; 299
director set,
   See Also syntactic analysis;
   overlap,
      (exercise); 136

LL(1) grammar use in removing, (notes and references); 134
multiple assignment as example of (figure); 118
removing; 117
term definition; 117
term definition; 115
distinguished objects,
compiler type,
ErroneousType; 208
UnknownType; 208
definition table key, *NoKey*; 274
external value, needed in external value module specification; 28
NoExtValue variable use as generated symbol during syntactic error recovery; 103
nonterminal symbol, start symbol as; 91
value,
identifying generated symbols by use of a; 103
NoInstruction; 285
distributive,
identity, for regular expressions (figure); 89
law, removing director set overlaps using; 119
documentation,
key importance to maintaining interface specification integrity; 34
dyadic,
See Also operators;
computational operators, handled by a single target tree instruction procedure; 284
expression, incorporating into parsing specifications (figure); 93
dynamic allocation,
See Also memory;
implications for compiler storage allocation; 204

E
Edinburgh Multiple Access System,
assembly module implementation strategy, (notes and references); 338
efficiency of computations,
See Also performance;
See computational complexity;
elements,
Element nodes, constructing; 256
Element operation, array indexing use of; 254
ElementCount property, characteristics; 216
empty set,
source language typing vs. compiler typing of; 207
EmptySourceSeq **operation,**
procedure description, (figure); 78

EmptyTargetSeq **operation,**
procedure description, (figure); 242
EncodeDatum **operation,**
procedure description, (figure); 334
EncodeItem **operation,**
procedure description, (figure); 331
encoding (compiler task),
(chapter), code generation; 306
compared with translation compiler task; 6
EncodeChildren operation, procedure description (figure); 334
EncodeDatum operation, procedure description (figure); 334
EncodeItem operation, procedure description (figure); 331
execution order determination compared with that of translation compiler task; 7
subtasks of, descriptive overview; 12
EndOfLineMarker **constant,**
description, (figure); 41
EnterEnv **operation,**
procedure description, (figure); 189
entities,
See Also identifiers; name analysis;
anonymous,
pointer as example of; 160
properties stored in definition table; 172
storing in definition table; 160
class, operation for getting; 174
defined,
properties stored in definition table; 172
verifying context compatibility; 177
EntityClass property,
definition (figure); 173
definition table interface for; 173
extraction from definition table to verify identifier use; 173
property, extraction from definition table to verify identifier use; 173
use in detecting multiply-defined identifiers; 175
enumeration of kinds of that can be named by identifiers, (figure); 173
identifier, classification associated with stored in definition table; 173
multiply-defined, detecting by *DefiningOccurrence2* operation, example description; 177
source program,
determining meanings for (chapter); 157
properties stored in definition table; 159
entry conditions,
action mapping procedures; 241
Entry **type,**
definition, (figure); 179

enumerated,
See Also data types; types;
constant identifier, visit sequence; 218
data type,
specifying error report severity by; 24
VAX representation, design considerations; 201
visit sequence as example of visit to a type constructor; 218
EnumeratedTypeNode alternative (*TypeVisit2* operation), implementation (figure); 217
Env variable,
description, (figure); 171
environment,
See Also interface; modules; variables;
adding identifier/key associations to; 164
compiler interactions with, (chapter); 16
current value,
global variable definition, (figure); 171
reasons for declaring its variable global; 170
empty, creation function description; 163
Env variable, definition (figure); 171
environment module,
access functions, constant-time implementation; 188
complex implementation; 185
data structures (figure); 183
interface, description of components; 163
interface specification (figure); 164
simple implementation; 182
use of *NewKey* operation exported from definition table module; 173
Environment type, definition (figure); 164
operations, function descriptions (figure); 184
restricting search for an identifier key to the current; 165
searching for a given identifier; 164
tree, pre-defined identifier associations contained in the root; 163
values,
description as a tree; 163
direct encoding of tree; 182
relationships between Pascal (figure); 165
***Environment* type,**
description, (figure); 164
EOPT (end-of-statement marker),
as argument to Synterr, (figure); 131
as member of all anchor sets; 103
scanner use of, (figure); 57
syntax error recovery use of; 100
used as an argument to syntax error recovery module; 128
***EqualExpr* construct,**
operator and signature for, (figure); 289

equivalence,
See algorithms;
***ErroneousType* type,**
erroneous program handling with; 208
***ErrorFinl* operation,**
procedure description, (figure); 25
***ErrorInit* operation,**
procedure description, (figure); 25
errors,
See Also interface; modules; syntactic analysis;
avalanche, avoiding in syntax error recovery; 100
classification of; 23
compiler type system handling of; 208
deadly error,
characteristics; 24
inconsistencies detected during action mapping; 242
reports, as compiler debugging aid; 321
uninitialized definition table operator entries; 285
denotation conversion, reporting; 59
detecting,
depth-first left-to-right tree traversal algorithm limitations; 166
in syntax diagrams, example (figure); 102
error module,
(exercise); 36
interface, characteristics; 23
interface, specification example description (figure); 25
ErrorCount variable, definition (figure); 25
ErrorFinl operation description, (figure); 25
ErrorInit operation description, (figure); 25
fatal error, characteristics; 24
information error, characteristics; 23
messages, See errors - reports;
parser-defined, where reported; 98
recovery,
anchor determination, in recursive descent parsers; 123
anchor determination, shift-reduce parsers; 151
continuation path specification, recursive descent parsers; 122
continuation path specification, shift-reduce parsers; 150
error recovery module interface specification (figure); 127
example descriptions (table); 100
identifiers generated during syntactic recovery, recursive descent parser; 126
in a shift-reduce parser (figure); 153

reasons why error recovery code not needed in action mapping procedures; 242
recursive descent parser; 121
shift-reduce parser; 150
strategy descriptions; 99
syntactic analysis, (exercise); 109, 137
syntax errors, general strategy description; 99
syntax errors, general strategy implementation; 101
reporting problem, characteristics; 23
reports,
  classification, (notes and references); 34
  coordinates, as integral part of the mechanism; 26
  encoding compiler task; 11
  lexical analyzer; 6
  modular handling of; 16
  semantic analyzer; 8
  source program tree fragments, storage of; 73
  source text coordinates, stored in Pascal records containing source program nodes; 73
  specifying coordinates for; 24
  syntactic analyzer; 6
syntax,
  detection associated with terminal symbols and; 124
  disadvantages of ad-hoc recovery methods (notes and references); 106
  EOPT used as an argument to error recovery module; 128
  error recovery module implementation (figure); 132
  recovering from in shift-reduce parser; 150
  recovery from; 98
  recovery, strategy implementation questions; 104
  repair constrasted with correction; 99
  strategies for replacing incorrect sequences; 99
  undetectable by the parser; 98
  use-before-definition error (Pascal), problems in detecting, (figure); 167
  warning error, characteristics; 23
evaluation order,
  See Also encoding; execution-order determination; target program tree;
  as a code generation decision; 306
  conditional expressions, specification with *SequenceDatum* construct; 262
  determining; 308
  effect on register requirements, (figure); 308

not necessarily determined by target tree node order; 231
operand,
  determination and implmentation strategy; 307
  Sethi-Ullman number for a node affected by; 309
partial,
  determination during target tree construction; 315
  determined by data flow relationships; 228
execution-order determination (code generation subtask),
  action mapper decisions, effect on target program tree structure; 238
  (chapter); 306
  determination,
    by encoding compiler task; 11
    encoder compared with translator; 7
  effect on design of target program tree; 236
  execution-order determination subtask, descriptive overview; 12
  final, determination by code generation; 229
  (notes and references); 192, 337
  resource allocation relationship to, in function invocation, (figure); 240
exporting,
  term definition; 18
***Expression* operation,**
  procedure description, (figure); 131
expressions,
  Boolean, implementing with jump cascades; 287
  C-- language; 349
  conditional,
    code generated for; 262
    jump cascade translation in C-- language (figure); 371
    representation in the target program tree; 260
  constructing a source tree node for; 75
  dyadic as subclass of; 93
  expression mapping,
    example description; 247
    MapExpression procedure use for (figure); 248
    modifying to handle voiding (figure); 294
  Expression tree fragment class, characteristics; 71
  Expression-class,
    leaves, information not filled in during syntactic analysis, (figure); 76
    nodes, operators that are possible decorations for; 280
    nodes, storing final type in; 282

Pascal constructs, mapping (figure); 285
representation,
    by operator triples; 274
    in a source program tree; 72
    in a source program tree, example description (figure); 5
    in source program tree records; 73
    of alternative computation expressions by *AlternativeDataL* nodes; 261
    return value type specified by definition table key; 208
rewriting; 88
simplifying activity sequence descriptions by use of dyadic; 93
subscript, obtaining and holding information needed for (figure); 257
temporary storage required for evaluation, (notes and references); 337
term definition; 4
tree fragment class, term definition; 70
type analysis,
    descriptive overview; 9
    type determined by, descriptive overview; 9
voided,
    overloading (figure); 293
    types and operators needed; 291
ExpressionVisiti **operation,**
    procedure description, (figure); 283
ExpressionVisitj **operation,**
    procedure description, (figure); 283
ExtAdd **operation,**
    function description, (figure); 33
ExtCodeDigit **operation,**
    procedure description, (figure); 30
ExtCodeFloat **operation,**
    procedure description, (figure); 30
ExtCodeString **operation,**
    procedure description, (figure); 30
ExtDecodeDigit **operation,**
    procedure description, (figure); 30
ExtDecodeFloat **operation,**
    procedure description, (figure); 30
ExtDiv **operation,**
    function description, (figure); 33
extended regular expressions,
    deriving activity sequences from, (figure); 88
    notation, (notes and references); 106
ExtendSourceSeq **operation,**
    procedure description, (figure); 78
ExtendTargetSeq **operation,**
    procedure description, (figure); 242
ExtEqual **operation,**
    function description, (figure); 33

external address resolution (assembly subtask),
    See Also addresses;
    descriptive overview; 13
external cross-references,
    term definition and representation in target program tree; 239
external values,
    See Also types;
    external value module,
        characteristics; 26
        computations (figure); 30
        conversions (figure); 29
    floating-point, representation specification; 31
    integers, representation specification; 30
    management problem, characteristics; 26
    modular handling of; 16
    module, (exercise); 37
    objects, converting denotations into; 56
    operations,
        ExtAdd, function description (figure); 33
        ExtCodeDigit, function description (figure); 30
        ExtCodeFloat, procedure description (figure); 30
        ExtCodeString, procedure description (figure); 30
        ExtDecodeDigit, function description (figure); 30
        ExtDecodeFloat, procedure description (figure); 30
        ExtDiv, function description (figure); 33
        ExtEqual, function description (figure); 33
        ExtInit, function description (figure); 33
        ExtLess, function description (figure); 33
        ExtMod, function description (figure); 33
        ExtMpy, function description (figure); 33
        ExtNegate, function description (figure); 33
        ExtSub, function description (figure); 33
    storage allocation considerations; 28
    string, representation; 31
    types,
        ExtFloating, definition (figure); 29
        ExtInteger, definition (figure); 29
        ExtString, definition (figure); 29
        ExtType, definition (figure); 29
        ExtUnknown, definition (figure); 29
        ExtValue, definition (figure); 29
ExtInit **operation,**
    function description, (figure); 33
ExtIntegerSize **constant,**
    definition, (figure); 29
ExtLess **operation,**
    function description, (figure); 33

ExtMod operation,
   function description, (figure); 33
ExtMpy operation,
   function description, (figure); 33
ExtNegate operation,
   function description, (figure); 33
ExtSub operation,
   function description, (figure); 33

F

F-format (VAX floating-point),
   representing Pascal real data type by; 200
falsejump **type,**
   definition; 287
fatal error,
   characteristics; 24
FieldList **source tree node class,**
   source program tree structure, (figure); 219
FieldListVisit2 **operation,**
   procedure description, (figure); 220
fields,
   See Also records;
   Coord, description, (figure); 74
   identifier, mapping; 249
   Kind, description, (figure); 74
   storage allocation for; 202
      methods; 203
files,
   file data type, characteristics and representation on the VAX; 203
   Pascal restrictions on direct storage in definition table; 181
filters,
   conversion module use of hash functions as; 60
final execution order,
   determination by code generation; 229
final type,
   See Also types;
   storing in *Expression* node; 282
   use in identifying operators; 276
finalization operation,
   characteristics; 18
find **operation,**
   function description, (figure); 180
finite-state machines,
   See Also parsers; syntactic analysis;
   assignment statement example description, (figure); 55
   characteristics,
      and term definition; 44
      and use in lexical analysis scanning subtask; 42
   construction by parser generator; 145

converting syntax diagrams into, example description (figure); 47
describing basic symbols with; 43
example description (figure); 45
(exercise); 64, 65
(notes and references); 62
parser implementation with; 139
scanner implementation,
   directly-executable implementation (figure); 55
   example description (figure); 52
   interpretive implementation (figure); 53
fixed registers,
   See Also registers;
   effects on register requirement calculation; 313
   requirement set, determination during target tree construction; 315
floating-point,
   See Also data types; registers;
   conversion, difficulties, (notes and references); 34
   data type, characteristics and representation on the VAX; 200
   denotations, recognizing with syntax diagrams (figure); 43
   external values,
      determining the maximum range of; 26
      representation issues; 27
      representation specification; 31
      storage allocation considerations; 28
   numbers,
   converting to an internal representation; 58
   VAX representation of Pascal real data type; 200
   operations, (notes and references); 35
   variables, properties stored in definition table; 172
FloatingZero **variable,**
   See Also variables;
   description, (figure); 33
follower set,
   See Also grammars; syntactic analysis;
   parsing grammar, handling conflict resolution by eliminating symbols from; 149
for statement,
   See Also statements;
   implementation of, comparision of correct and incorrect code (figure); 258
   mapping, VAX instructions for modifying counters use in; 258
   resource allocation needs; 259
   target program tree mapping design; 256
forks,
   See Also syntax diagrams;

specifying continuation paths through; 123
transformations that move (figure); 85
ForLoop construct,
allocating resources for, (figure); 325
resource allocation; 324
Sethi-Ullman number of; 311
FP register (VAX register 13),
activation record addressing with; 204
fragments,
See Also trees;
source program tree,
input (figure); 161
record contents description; 73
records, example declaration description (figure); 74
records, example declaration schematic form (figure); 76
textual notation for; 72
target program tree, constructing from operator fragments; 284
tree, term definition; 70
functions,
See Also operations;
calls, implementation of, (figure); 240
compiler type handling of; 208
exported, characteristics; 18

G
generated symbols,
See Also identifiers; symbols;
GenerateLabel operation, (procedure description figure); 245
how to introduce,
recursive descent parser; 126
shift-reduce parser; 151
identifying by use of a distinguished value; 103
NoKey associated with; 175
use during syntax error recovery; 104
***GenerateLabel* operation,**
procedure description, (figure); 245
get operations,
GetEntityClass operation, function description (figure); 174, 180
GetProperty operation, function description; 178
GetTargetConstruct operation, accessing *TargetConstruct* property with; 285
***GetEntityClass* operation,**
function description, (figure); 174, 180
global variables,
See Also variables;
set of associations between identifier and key stored in; 162
visit procedures, reasons for declaring; 170

glossary,
See term definitions;
goto statements,
See Also statements;
Dijkstra's paper arguing against, bibliographic reference; 134
eliminating, (exercise); 135
grammars,
See Also syntactic analysis;
conflict-free parsing,
conflict reporting and resolution; 146
(notes and references); 154
constructing, (exercise); 108
context-free,
as input to parser generators; 145
characteristics and use in the parsing subtask; 90
component of, example (figure); 91
(exercises); 135
left recursion removal techniques, (notes and references); 134
rule correspondence to reduce operations; 145
shift-reduce parser generator use of; 145
theoretical implications; 106
LALR, (notes and references); 154
LL(1), (notes and references); 134
LR(k), bibliographic reference; 155
resolving ambiguities in; 148
rewriting to remove ambiguities; 149
term definition; 92
transforming, syntax diagrams from, principles for; 92
***GreaterEqualExpr* construct,**
operator and signature for, (figure); 289
***GreaterExpr* construct,**
operator and signature for, (figure); 289

H
hash,
functions, use in identifier conversion, example description (figure); 61
HashConst constant, description (figure); 61
HashTbl variable, description (figure); 61
table, as dictionary implementation; 299
***HashConst* constant,**
description, (figure); 61
Header nodes,
example illustration in source program tree, (figure); 168
holes,
term definition; 223
Horner's rule,
use in integer conversion; 58

I

identifier table,
  as example of a dictionary; 63
  compared with definition table; 159
  internals, (figure); 61
  pre-loading by conversion module initialization operation; 60
  use in identifier conversion; 59

Identifier-class nodes,
  See Also nodes;
  detecting invalid identifiers during visits to; 175
  in source program tree, (figure); 168
  information filled in during syntactic analysis, (figure); 76
  leaf values; 73
  source program tree, computing associations valid for; 160

identifiers,
  See Also association(s); definition tables; lexical analysis; nodes; symbols syntactic analysis; variables;
  accessing current environment while processing occurrences of; 170
  advantages of recognizing keywords as; 53
  applied occurrences,
    definition table use in validating; 173
    leaf context use to identify; 175
    term definition; 164
    visiting after defining occurrences; 166
  basic symbol, term definition; 39
  C-- language, (figure); 344
  compared with delimiters and denotations; 39
  constructing a source tree node for; 75
  conversion operations for, (exercise); 67
  converting to an internal representation; 56
    algorithm desciptions; 59
  declarations,
    association properties stored in definition table; 173
    used in semantic analysis; 8
  defining occurrences,
    accessing by visiting identifier declarations; 166
    accessing current environment while processing; 170
    enumerated constant identifiers, visit sequence; 218
    identified by identifier leaf context; 175
    source program tree visit strategy; 177
    term definition; 164
    visiting before applied occurences; 166
    visiting *Type* component of declarations to process all; 170
  definition, use of *NewKey* operation exported from definition table module; 173
  detecting undefined; 165
  enumeration of kinds of entities that can be named by, (figure); 173
  establishing,
    a key for a definition of; 164
    associations between definitions and; 163
  generated,
    during syntactic error recovery; 103
    during syntactic error recovery, recursive descent parser; 126
    during syntactic error recovery, shift-reduce parser; 152
  invalid, detection by semantic analyzer; 175
  key associated with, information required for computation of; 162
  lexical analysis conversion subtask handling of, descriptive overview; 6
  mapping into target program tree,
    example description; 249
    (figure); 252
  name analysis association of use with definition of; 9
  path, representation in reduce operations; 143
  pre-defined,
    associations contained in environment tree root; 163
    compared with keywords; 59
  properties stored in definition table; 172
  recognizing,
    (exercise); 67
    in syntax diagrams (figure); 43
  representation,
    as leaf arguments in source program trees; 73
    in source program tree records; 73
    storing in tree, reasons for; 170
  scope and definition errors, when reported; 9
  syntax diagrams for, (exercise); 64
  Token data type specification of; 39
  tree fragment class, term definition; 70
  type,
    determined by type analysis subtask, descriptive overview; 9
    use by *TypeVisit2* operation; 216
  undefined, checking for; 177
  visiting *Type* component of declarations for; 170

***IdentifyOperator* operation,**
  characteristics; 298
  function definition, (figure); 278

identities,
  regular expressions, (figure); 89

***IdnExpr* node,**
  constructing; 75
  description, (figure); 74
  textual notation for; 72

IdnLeaf **node,**
   See Also nodes;
   constructing; 75
   identifiers represented by; 249
   textual notation for; 72
if **statement,**
   See Also statements;
   representation by an Item-class node; 260
   source program tree fragment, (figure); 271, 290
if-then-else **statement,**
   template description; 243
index,
   addressing mode, accessing array elements with; 254
   indexed references, representation on the VAX (figure); 255
   multiplication, resource allocation impact on; 254
   registers, shifting during array element accessing; 254
Indication **type,**
   definition, (figure); 278
indirect,
   left recursion, procedures for eliminating; 111
   operation nodes, structure description (table); 235
information,
   See Also interface; semantic analysis;
   basic symbols, building source program tree from; 75
   characteristics, effect on choice of data structures; 170
   contextual,
      checking compatibility of entity class with use; 177
      cost of gathering; 181
      cost of gathering, analysis of environment module strategies; 182
      data structure design effect on cost of gathering; 185
      determination by semantic analyzer; 8
      determination of type properties from; 210
      Identifier leaf as determiner of applied vs defining occurrence; 175
      managing (chapter); 157
      managing (exercises); 194
      managing (notes and references); 191
      modifying target program tree structure with; 314
      strategy for gathering; 160
      use in associating types and definition table keys; 210
      use in translating data structures into target machine language concepts; 198
   error characteristics; 23
   hiding,
      See Also computational complexity;
      See Also performance;
      as part of meaning of a module; 17
      private data type use of; 20
      role in deciding whether to make a data type public or private; 20
   information gathering strategy, effect on compilation time; 160
   loss, problem with floating-point values when changing radix; 27
   machine resource, target program tree operand nodes decorations; 12
   source program tree,
      filled in during syntactic analysis (figure); 76
      source program structure embodied in; 70
      storage,
      accessing identifer association set as a question of; 162
      as component of tree decoration strategy; 162
      as tactical component of contextual information gathering strategy; 160
      name analysis (figure); 171
      semantic analyzer, effect of information characteristics on; 170
   type, source program tree decorations; 9
initialization,
   definition table property lists, implementation of; 179
   operation, characteristics; 18
initialized variables memory region,
   characteristics; 333
input symbol,
   manipulation during syntax error recovery; 103
INSERT **operation,**
   characteristics; 297
instruction encoding (assembly subtask),
   Assemble operation (figure); 329
   descriptive overview; 13
instruction selection (code generation subtask),
   action mapper role in; 233
   as code generation subtask; 229
   characteristics and implementation; 328
   descriptive overview; 12
   for *JumpLssL*, (figure); 330
   VAX target tree nodes that illustrate, (table); 235
instructions,
   See Also addresses; code generation; machine; registers;
   addresses, named by code generator; 11

compared with machine operations; 234
jump, providing destination labels for; 238
linking to memory location referenced by; 238
memory region, characteristics; 333
operands,
    determination by code generator; 11
    specification with records of *Operand* type; 328
    specifying access with access functions; 232
sequences,
    assignment statement, (figure); 229
    determination by code generator; 11
    determination by execution-order subtask; 12

integers,
See Also data types; operators; variables; *IntegerOne* variable;
class leaves, information filled in during syntactic analysis (figure); 76
constructing a source tree node for; 75
converting to an internal representation, algorithm desciptions; 58
data type, characteristics and representation on the VAX; 200
denotations,
    recognizing with syntax diagrams; 42
    recognizing with syntax diagrams (figure); 43
determining the maximum range of; 26
external values,
    representation specification; 30
    storage allocation considerations; 28
IntegerOne variable, description (figure); 33
IntegerZero variable, description (figure); 33
machine limitations, effect on count-controlled iteration mapping; 257
multiple-precision integer arithmetic, (notes and references); 35
multiplication operators; 270
representation in source program tree records; 73
tree fragment class,
    leaf values; 73
    term definition; 70

***IntegerToString* operation,**
procedure description, (figure); 205

interface,
See Also information, hiding; performance; trees;
assembly module (figure); 329
between translator and code generator, target program tree use as; 230
character pool module (figure); 19
compiler, characteristics and specification (chapter); 16

definition table, characteristics; 173
definitions, environment module, (figure); 164
environment module description of components; 163
error module characteristics; 23
external value module (figure); 29, 30
lexical analysis module (figure); 40
operator identification module (figure); 278
source module (figure); 22
source tree construction module, (figure); 78
specifications,
    design considerations for; 20
    example description (figure); 19
    (exercises); 36
    (notes and references); 34
    role in structuring modularity of methods; 17
    term definition; 17
storage module (figure); 211
syntax error recovery module (figure); 127
target tree construction module (figure); 242
use of source and target program trees as; 70

interior node values,
access functions, provided by code generator; 233

intermediate,
See Also resource allocation;
results,
    describing by VAX access functions; 233
    generated by Datum-class nodes; 231
    machine register allocation for, descriptive overview; 12
    operations that create; 231
    storage of, as tactical component of contextual information gathering; 160
values,
    multiple-registers, modifying Sethi-Ullman computation to account for; 312
    number existing simultaneously, Sethi-Ullman number of operand effect on; 310
    register requirements, determining when there are not enough registers; 313
    relationship to number of registers needed; 308
    Sethi-Ullman number as specification of maximum simultaneously existing; 309

internal,
cross-references, term definition and target tree representation; 238
state,
    character pool module characteristics; 18
    source module, initialization of; 23

internal address resolution (assembly subtask),

descriptive overview; 13
internal cross-references,
  term definition and representation in target program tree; 239
***IntExpr* node,**
  constructing; 77
  description, (figure); 74
  textual notation for; 72
***IntLeaf* node,**
  constructing; 77
  textual notation for; 72
invalid operator,
  See Also operators; variables;
  inconsistent operator use indicated by; 269
  InvalidOperator variable, operator identification use of (figure); 278
invariants,
  of lexical analysis state variables, (figure); 41
  stack data structure, (exercise); 108
  term definition; 36
***IsPacked* property,**
  characteristics; 216
Item-class node,
  See Also nodes;
  characteristics and comparison with Datum-class node; 231
  creation; 246
  descriptive overview; 7
  encoding *Item* constructs, (figure); 331
  instruction encoding from; 330
  intermediate value storage in; 320
  Item type definition, (figure); 316
  Pascal alternative computation statements represented as; 260
  register requirements, determining when there are not enough registers; 314
  sequences, meaning of; 12
  Sethi-Ullman number of; 311
  stack condition on mapping procedure exit; 242
***ItemVisit* operation,**
  procedure description, (figure); 325
iteration,
  See Also action mapping; recursion;
  count-controlled, target program tree mapping design issues; 256
  transforming iterative activity sequences into recursive activity sequences; 86

J
joins,
  in activity sequences, transformations that move (figure); 85
  removing from syntax diagrams used by shift-reduce parser; 140

jump operations and nodes,
  See Also nodes; translation;
  instructions, providing destination labels for; 238
  jump cascades,
    C-- language example (figure); 371
    implementing Boolean expressions with; 287
    implementing control flow operators with (figure); 288
    term definition; 287
    translating (figure); 292
  Jump nodes, characteristics and structure (table); 238
  JumpEqlB target construct, overloading (figure); 289
  JumpEqlL target construct, overloading (figure); 289
  JumpGeqL target construct, overloading (figure); 289
  JumpGtrL nodes, characteristics and structure (table); 238
  JumpGtrL target construct, overloading (figure); 289
  JumpLeqL target construct, overloading (figure); 289
  JumpLssL target construct,
    instruction selection for (figure); 330
    overloading (figure); 289
    translating Boolean source construct into; 287
  JumpNeqB target construct, overloading (figure); 289
  JumpNeqL target construct, overloading (figure); 289
  operator identification, (figure); 290

K
***KeyEnv* operation,**
  function description, (figure); 184
  procedure description, (figure); 189
***KeyInEnv* operation,**
  function description, (figure); 164, 184
***KeyInScope* operation,**
  function description, (figure); 164
keys,
  See Also identifiers;
  associated with an identifier, information required for computation of; 162
  associating with identifier declaration nodes; 166
  definition table,
    associating with identifier definition occurrences, example description; 177
    associating with type represented by a Type-class node; 216

compiler types associated with unique; 208
computing for identifiers, as name
  analyzer subtask; 160
implementation of; 179
NoKey distinguished object (figure); 174
operation for creating; 173
operator description, components and use
  by action mapping routines; 285
reasons for representing operators and
  result types as; 295
reasons for storing in tree; 170
representing identifier type, establishing
  during tree decoration; 171
representing operators with; 272, 277
representing result types with; 277
role in determining possible operator
  meanings; 282
shown as superscripts in a Pascal program
  (figure); 159
types, source program tree visit that
  establishes; 210
establishing for an identifier definition; 164
KeyInEnv operation,
  finding identifier key with; 165
  function description (figure); 164, 184
  use of *NoKey* definition table module
    value; 173
KeyInScope operation,
  function description (figure); 164, 184
  restricting search for an identifier; 165
NoKey definition table key, obtaining default
  property value with; 175
NoKey distinguished definition table key,
  operator representation triple use of;
  274
types, location in source program tree; 249
keywords,
  compared with pre-defined identifiers; 59
  cost of recognizing in the lexical analysis
    scanner, (figure); 54
  recognizing,
    during identifier conversion operation; 59
    (exercise); 68
***Kind* field,**
  description, (figure); 74
Kleene closure,
  grammar definition use of; 92

L

labelings,
  consistent, when voiding is allowed (figure);
  293
labels,
  consistent labeling,
    obtaining (figure); 273

  when voiding is allowed (figure); 293
LabelDef nodes, characteristics and structure
  (table); 238
parser syntax diagrams, meaning for shift-
  reduce parser generation; 140
source tree nodes, operator consistency
  issues; 272
target program tree, characteristics and
  representation; 238
language,
  defined by a grammar, term definition; 92
LeaveEnv **operation,**
  procedure description, (figure); 189
leaves,
  See Also nodes; trees;
  creating, operation specification (figure); 78
  denotations and identifiers as arguments to
    descriptions of; 73
  Identifier, detecting invalid identifiers during
    visits to; 175
  Sethi-Ullman number of; 309
  source program tree,
    basic symbols represented as; 6
    characteristics; 73
    classes where information is filled in
      during syntactic analysis, (figure); 76
    computing associations valid for; 160
    constructing from basic symbols, example
      description (figure); 76
    decorated by name analysis; 9
    decorated by syntactic analyzer; 6
    descriptive overview; 4
  target program tree,
    access functions for values provided by
      action mapper; 233
    information determined by data mapping
      subtask; 11
  values,
    identifier-class nodes; 73
    integer tree fragment class; 73
left recursion,
  See Also parsers; recursion;
  eliminating in recursive descent parsers; 111
  (exercise); 135
  general technique for removal, (notes and
    references); 134
  term definition; 90
LessEqualExpr **construct,**
  operator and signature for, (figure); 289
LessExpr **construct,**
  operator and signature for, (figure); 289
lexical analysis (structuring subtask),
  calls to interleaved with source tree
    construction during syntactic analysis;
    75

(chapter); 38
(exercises); 64
Lexical operation procedure description,
   (figure); 40, 52
lexical structure,
   describing basic symbols with syntax
      diagrams; 42
   describing with regular expressions; 48
LexInit operation,
   procedure definition (figure); 41
   procedure description (figure); 40
module,
   characteristics; 39
   interface specification, (figure); 40
   scanner characteristics and algorithm
      design principles; 41
(notes and references); 62
operations overview; 38
subtasks of, descriptive overview; 5
LexInit operation,
   procedure description, (figure); 40
library routine calls,
   representation in target program tree; 239
lifetimes,
   See Also information; storage;
   effect on data structure choice; 170
   external values, as factor in allocating
      storage; 27
Limit **variable,**
   description, (figure); 41
limited private data type,
   term definition; 20
linear list of triples,
   set representation; 300
lines,
   See Also *LinePtr* variable; scanning; source
      program; variables;
   characteristics in human vs computer-
      produced source text; 21
   compared with characters as unit of text
      delivered by source module; 21
   Line variable, definition (figure); 22
   LineLng variable, definition (figure); 22
   LineNumber variable, description (figure); 41
   LinePtr variable, definition (figure); 22
linking,
   See Also trees;
   link editor, compiler support for operations
      of; 333
   linked,
      data structures, trees stored as; 70
      records, source program tree represented
         by; 73
   subtrees into tree, operation specification
      (figure); 78

literals,
   See Also constants; symbols; variables;
   as external values, characteristics; 26
   managing; 26
loader,
   compiler support for operations of; 333
local,
   storage, VAX registers used to access; 204
   variables,
      access function description; 233
      mapping; 249
      relative address representation by *Operand*
         value; 233
      storage for (figure); 213
      storage requirements; 212
      visit procedures reasons for declaring
         local; 170
location,
   property, defining, (exercise); 196
   referenced, providing unique names for; 239
   values used by machine instructions,
      specifying with access functions; 232
long set operators,
   mapping into target program tree; 285
longword,
   term definition; 200
loops,
   LoopCounter field of *ForLoop* construct use
      of *Operand* type; 326
   removing from syntax diagrams; 83
   search, technique for speeding up; 52
LowerBound.ElementSize **variable,**
   definition, (figure); 257

M
machine,
   See Also code generation; instructions;
      memory;
   abstract, (notes and references); 14
   architectures,
      general register, (notes and references);
         337
      stack, (notes and references); 337
      understanding of crucial to compiler
         design; 222
   instructions, See instructions;
   limitations, integers, effect on count-
      controlled iteration mapping; 257
   operations,
      compared with machine instructions; 234
      encoded in target program tree by action
         mapper; 233
      that can be implemented by multiple target
         machine instructions, instruction
         selection issues; 235

that can be only implemented by one target machine instruction, example description; 235
resources, resource allocation determination by encoding compiler task; 11
target,
    concepts, mapping source language concepts into; 251
    data representation on (chapter); 198
    generating instructions, (chapter); 306
    operation, operator property characteristics; 271
    resource information, target program tree operand node decorations; 12
    source language data types representation on; 11
    VAX characteristics as a target; 1
Makeops **operation**,
    procedure description, (figure); 281
MapCondition **operation**,
    procedure description, (figure); 247, 292
MapExpression **operation**,
    procedure description, (figure); 248
MapIdentifier **operation**,
    procedure description, (figure); 252
mapping,
    See Also action mapping; data mapping; interface; transformation;
    array element references, (figure); 257
    conditional expressions; 246
    expressions,
        example description; 247
        modifying to handle voiding (figure); 294
    for statement to target program tree, (figure); 260
    identifiers,
        example description; 249
        into target program tree (figure); 252
MapCoercion operation,
    procedure definition (figure); 286
    selecting generation code; 285
MapCondition operation,
    implementation of jump cascade modification of (figure); 292
    procedure description (figure); 247
MapExpression operation,
    array reference handling by; 256
    compared with MapStatement operation; 246
    mapping expressions with; 247
    mapping Pascal expression constructs with, implementation, (figure); 285
    mapping pointer references with; 248
    procedure description (figure); 248
    StrExpr case (figure); 335

MapIdentifier operation, procedure description (figure); 252
mapping process property, selecting generation code with; 285
MapStatement operation,
    compared with *MapExpression* operation; 246
    construction of *ForLoop* by; 259
    procedure description (figure); 245
Pascal expression constructs, (figure); 285
source language,
    concepts into target machine concepts, design issue case studies; 251
    constructs into target language constructs, example description; 243
voided expression constructs, (figure); 294
MapStatement **operation**,
    procedure description, (figure); 245
MarkPosition **operation**,
    procedure description, (figure); 329
MaxArity **constant**,
    definition, (figure); 329
MaxBucket **constant**,
    description, (figure); 61
MaxDef **constant**,
    definition, (figure); 179
MaxLength **constant**,
    description, (figure); 205
MaxOpnd **constant**,
    definition, (figure); 278
MaxRadix **constant**,
    definition, (figure); 29
meanings,
    See Also contextual information; operators;
    determining for source program entities, (chapter); 157
MeaningSetArray type, operator identification use of (figure); 278
of an identifier compared with the meaning of a denotation; 39
operators,
    determining the set of, procedure implementation; 276
    representation of; 295
regular expressions; 49
sets of,
    storing in *Expression* node; 282
    types operator identification (figure); 296
source tree expression constructs, representation by operator triple; 274
MEMBER **operation**,
    coercion operation use of; 298
memory,
    See Also machine; performance; storage;
    addresses, determination of absolute; 328

allocating, for values that must be held in
    activation records; 320
data mapping into, impact of alignment
    constraints on, (notes and references);
    223
initialized variables region, characteristics;
    333
intermediate value storage in; 313
layout; 225
    determination by code generator; 11
    of local variables (figure); 213
location, linking to the instruction that refers
    to it; 238
mapping variant records into; 210
partitioning of, characteristics; 333
protection, facilitation by memory partition
    ing; 333
uninitialized variables region, characteristics;
    333
VAX,
    array storage in (figure); 253
    characteristics; 199
    layout of records in, (figure); 202
mod **operation (Pascal),**
    integer representation required by; 270
ModExpr **construct,**
    overloading operators and signatures,
        (figure); 293
modularity,
    See Also computational complexity;
        performance;
    as a structuring method for complex
        programs; 17
    modular decomposition, characteristics and
        use in compiler design; 17
    (notes and references); 34
modules,
    See Also interface; modularity;
    correctness, as part of meaning of a module;
        17
    information hiding, as part of meaning of a
        module; 17
    term definition and properties; 17
modules (by name),
    assembly,
        implementation, (notes and references);
            338
        interface specification; 328
    character pool,
        as example of interface specification,
            (figure); 19
        interface (figure); 19
        conversion, use of hash functions as filters;
            60

definition table,
    characteristics; 173
    implementation; 178
environment,
    access functions, constant-time implemen-
        tation; 188
    as example of cost of gathering contextual
        information, complex implementation;
        185
    as example of cost of gathering contextual
        information, simple implementation;
        182
    data structures (figure); 183
    interface, description of components; 163
    interface, specification (figure); 164
    use of *NewKey* operation exported from
        definition table module; 173
error,
    characteristics; 23
    (exercise); 36
    interface (figure); 25
error recovery,
    implementation (figure); 132
    interface specification (figure); 127
external values,
    characteristics; 26
    (exercise); 37
    interface (figure); 30
    interface specification; 28
lexical analysis,
    characteristics; 39
    interface specification (figure); 40
operator identification,
    interface specification, (figure); 278
    operations, *Coercion* function, (figure);
        286
    states defined in terms of building and use
        of data structures; 298
register allocation, *Select* operation
    description (figure); 321
source,
    as serious potential hazard for performance
        (notes and references); 35
    characteristics; 20
    (exercise); 37
    interface specification, (figure); 19
source program tree construction, interface
    specification (figure); 78
storage, interface specification and implemen-
    tation (figure); 214
target tree construction, interface specifica
    tion, (figure); 242
translation, characteristics which satisfy
    requirements of a module; 17

INDEX   411

move operation nodes,
  MovB operation nodes, structure description 1(table); 235
  MovF operation nodes, structure description (table); 235
  MovL operation nodes, structure description (table); 235
  MovW operation nodes, structure description (table); 235
multi-symbol lookahead,
  (exercises); 136
multiple definitions,
  entities, detecting by *DefiningOccurrence2* operation, example description; 177
  identifiers, detection by the semantic analyzer, example description; 175
  when reported; 9
multiple-precision integer arithmetic,
  (notes and references); 35

N

name analysis (semantic analysis subtask),
  as an O(N) process, in a more sophisticated environment module implementation; 190
  as an O(N-squared) process, in a simple environment module implementation; 183
  (chapter); 157
  compilation time cost of; 181
  computing the values that decorate the source program tree; 163
  descriptive overview; 9
  detecting multiply-defined identifiers, example description; 175
  information storage issues during; 170
  managing contextual information, (chapter); 157
  (notes and references); 191
  source tree input fragments, (figure); 161
Name operation,
  procedure description, (figure); 127
names,
  See Also syntactic analysis;
  Name operation, procedure description (figure); 127
  regular expressions,
    context-free grammar nonterminals compared with; 90
    distinguishing from symbol connection names; 87
negation operations,
  See Also trees;
  NegL operation nodes, structure description (table); 235

structure of target program tree node that represents, (table); 235
nested,
  regions, processing during tree decoration visits; 172
  routines, accessing arguments of; 206
***NewEnv* operation,**
  environment trees created by; 163
  function description, (figure); 164, 184
***NewKey* operation,**
  creating new result types and operations wtih; 280
  function description, (figure); 174, 180
  obtaining a definition table key for a type with; 216
***NewScope* operation,**
  function description, (figure); 164, 184
  new environments created by; 163
***NextLine* operation,**
  function description, (figure); 52
***nil* value,**
  source language typing vs compiler typing of; 207
nodes,
  See Also trees;
  AddL operation, structure description (table); 235
  AlternativeDataL,
    representing alternative computation expressions by; 261
    Sethi-Ullman number of; 311
  AssignExpr, voided expression handling use of; 292
  AssignmentStmt,
    characteristics; 72
    constructing; 75
    textual notation for; 72
  Body, example illustration in source program tree, (figure); 168
  CallStmt, description, (figure); 74
  Datum-class,
    access functions allocation to by parent during target program tree traversal; 322
    AlternativeDataL construct use to embody a sequence of; 261
    characteristics and comparison with Item-class node; 231
    Datum type definition (figure); 316
    decoration with ref-class *Operand* records; 238
    descriptive overview; 7
    encoding (figure); 334
    implementing with decision trees (figure); 332

412 INDEX

  instruction encoding from; 331
  intermediate values produced by, role in code generation; 306
  MapExpression creation of; 246
  Sethi-Ullman number of; 309
  stack condition on mapping procedure exit; 242
  target program tree traversal strategy; 322
  value constraints on; 231
DatumLeaf,
  descriptive overview; 7
  mapping arithmetic constants and field identifiers into; 249
  values obtained from data mapping subtask; 11
Declaration, example illustration in source program tree , (figure); 168
declaration, identifying; 166
Element, constructing; 256
Expression-class,
  operators that are possible decorations for; 280
  storing final type in; 282
Header, example illustration in source program tree , (figure); 168
Identifier-class,
  detecting invalid identifiers during visits to; 175
  example illustration in source program tree, (figure); 168
  information filled in during syntactic analysis (figure); 76
  leaf values; 73
  source program tree, computing associations valid for; 160
IdnExpr,
  constructing; 75
  description, (figure); 74
  textual notation for; 72
IdnLeaf,
  constructing; 75
  identifiers represented by; 249
  textual notation for; 72
Indirect operation, structure description (table); 235
interior, access functions for provided by code generator; 233
IntExpr,
  constructing; 77
  description, (figure); 74
  textual notation for; 72
IntLeaf,
  constructing; 77
  textual notation for; 72

Item-class,
  characteristics; 231
  creation by *AssignmentStmt* alternative of *MapStatement* operation; 246
  creation by *CompoundStmt* alternative of *MapStatement* operation; 246
  descriptive overview; 7
  instruction encoding from; 330
  intermediate value storage; 320
  Item type definition (figure); 316
  Pascal alternative computation statements represented as; 260
  register requirements; 314
  sequences, meaning of; 12
  Sethi-Ullman number of; 311
  stack condition on mapping procedure exit; 242
Jump, characteristics and structure, (table); 238
JumpCtrL, characteristics and structure, (table); 238
LabelDef, characteristics and structure, (table); 238
leaf, access functions for provided by action mapping; 233
MovB operation, structure description (table); 235
MovF operation, structure description (table); 235
MovL operation, structure description; 235
MovW operation, structure description (table); 235
NegL operation, structure description (table); 235
operation, structure description, (table); 235
PlusExpr,
  constructing; 75
  description, (figure); 74
  determining result types for; 282
  integer representation required by; 270
  overloading operators and signatures (figure); 293
  restrictions on children of; 71
  textual notation for; 72
PointerTypeNode, visit sequence; 218
Relative operation, structure description (table); 235
SequenceDatum,
  characteristics and structure, (table); 238
  conditional expression evaluation order specified with; 262
  including sequences in; 248
  Sethi-Ullman number of; 311
source program tree,

INDEX 413

children represented by class subvariants; 73
classes, (figure); 219
constructing for assignment statements; 75
constructing for expressions; 75
constructing for identifiers; 75
constructing for integers; 75
decorated by semantic analyzer; 8
decorated by type analysis; 9
descriptive overview; 4
example declaration (figure); 74
if statement root, types of; 289
obtaining consistent labeling of for coercion operators; 272
operator labeling of; 272
representation of an arbitrary number of arguments in; 72
restrictions on children of; 71
source language constructs represented in; 70
stored as linked Pascal records; 73
textual notation for; 72
use of stack to hold pointers to unincorporated nodes; 75
Statement-class,
example illustration in source program tree, (figure); 168
mapping into target program tree with *MapStatement* procedure; 244
statements represented by; 4
structure description, (table); 235
target program tree,
building with *MapCondition* procedure; 246
correspondence to operations of the target program; 231
instruction encoding determination by instruction selection subtask; 12
operation (figure); 235
sequences as components of (figure); 240
Sethi-Ullman number calculations for; 308
time cost of visits to; 181
tree traversal as sequence of visits to; 166
Type-class,
characteristics of second visit to; 210
example illustration in source program tree, (figure); 168
impact on record class node visits; 218
Pascal types represented by; 216
setting *TypeKey* variable from *Type* property during second visit to; 216
VAX target tree, examples, (table); 238
WithStmt, associations established in component statement of; 163

NoExtValue variable,
description, (figure); 33
NoInstruction distinguished value (*TargetContruct* type),
deadly error termination with; 285
NoKey value,
constant definition (figure); 174
obtaining default property value with; 175
operator representation triple use of; 274
non-local variables,
mapping; 250
nondeterminism,
See Also finite-state machines; syntax diagrams;
in finite automata, (notes and references); 62
in syntax diagrams, converting into deterministic versions; 43
issues, director set overlap; 117
removing from syntax diagrams, example description (figure); 47
nonterminal symbols,
See Also grammars; symbols;
"helper", use with right recursion in context-free grammars, (exercise); 135
in a context-free grammer, example (figure); 91
relationship to terminal symbols; 90
splitting to reduce grammar ambiguity; 149
transforming symbol and structure connections into; 145
NoPosition variable,
definition, (figure); 25
not operation,
generating the effect of; 287
notation,
arbitrary sequences in source tree fragments; 72
extended regular expressions, (notes and references); 106
O(N),
computational complexity measured in terms of; 182
name analysis as an O(N) process in a more sophisticated environment module implementation; 190
name analysis as an O(N-squared) process en a simple environment module implementation; 183
postfix, impact on syntactic analysis (exercise); 108
regular expressions,
extending with square brackets; 51
extending with unary + operator; 49
lexical analyzer; 48

414 INDEX

state diagrams, comparision of different; 44
syntax diagrams,
  lexical analyzer; 42
  parsing language; 81
textual, source program tree fragments; 72
NotExpr construct,
  operator and signature for, (figure); 289
NullString variable,
  description, (figure); 40
NumArgValue operation,
  procedure description; 249
  (figure); 248
numbers,
  representation, floating-point value problems; 27
numerical analysis,
  managing literals as a problem in; 26

O

O(N) notation,
  See Also computational complexity; notation;
  computational complexity measured in terms of; 182
  name analysis,
    as an O(N) process in a more sophisticated environment module implementation; 190
    as an O(N-squared) process in a simple environment module implementation; 183
objects,
  C-- language; 347
occurrences (identifier),
  See Also identifiers;
  applied,
    definition table use in validating; 173
    leaf context use to identify; 175
    term definition; 164
    visiting after defining occurrences; 166
  defining,
    accessing by visiting identifier declarations; 166
    accessing current environment while processing; 170
    enumerated constant identifiers, visit sequence; 218
    identified by identifier leaf context; 175
    source program tree visit strategy; 177
    term definition; 164
    visiting before applied occurences; 166
    visiting Type component of declarations to process all; 170
OpCode type,
  definition, (figure); 329

Operand type,
  See Also types;
  associated with Datum-class nodes, importance to code generation; 306
  characteristics, (tables); 234
  definition, (figure); 315
  describing VAX access function, storing at Datum-class node of target program tree; 314
  LoopCounter field of *ForLoop* construct use of; 326
  ref-class,
    cross references represented by; 239
    labels represented in target program tree by; 238
  specifying number of arguments for a routine call with; 249
  values,
    copying into *OpndArray* array during instruction encoding operations; 330
    decorating target program tree with; 233
    interior nodes of target program tree, when determined; 314
operands,
  access functions, implementation of some operations by; 228
  evaluation order, determination and implementation strategy; 307
  instructions, determination by code generator; 11
  location, information required to select machine instruction; 235
  nodes,
    Sethi-Ullman number, affected by evaluation order; 309
    Sethi-Ullman number, effect on number of intermediate values existing simultaneously; 310
  sharing signatures between operators with different numbers of; 277
  source language, compared with target program tree order of children; 231
  target, description (figure); 315
operations,
  See Also computations; operator identification;
  Accept, (figure); 127, 132
  AddCoercion, (figure); 280
  AddL, as example of operation combination; 235
  AddOperator, (figure); 280
  AddType, (figure); 280
  AppliedOccurrence, (figure); 176
  ArrayInfo, (figure); 257

INDEX

Assemble, (figure); 329
AssemFinl, (figure); 329
AssemInit, (figure); 329
C-- language, (figure); 350
CoercibleFrom, (figure); 278
Coercion, (figure); 286
Commutative, (figure); 334
CompleteAccessFunction, (figure); 327
composition, *StorageRequired* type objects as arguments to; 212
Concatenate, (figure); 214
conversion; 57
ConvertDigits, (figure); 205
CvtXXX, (figure); 58
DatumVisit, (figure); 327
DeclarationVisit1,
   (figure); 169, 176
   use of *DefiningOccurrence1*, example description; 175
DeclarationVisit2, (figure); 171
decoding of external values, interface specification (figure); 29
DefineIdn,
   associations between identifiers and keys created by; 164
   (figure); 164, 184, 189
   use of *NewKey* definition table module function; 173
DefiningOccurrence1, (figure); 176
DefiningOccurrence2, (figure); 176
DefInit, (figure); 174
Element, array indexing use of; 254
EmptySourceSeq, (figure); 78
EmptyTargetSeq, (figure); 242
EncodeDatum, (figure); 334
EncodeItem, (figure); 331
encoding of external values, interface specification (figure); 29
ErrorFinl, (figure); 25
ErrorInit, (figure); 25
Expression, (figure); 131
ExpressionVisiti, (figure); 283
ExpressionVisitj, (figure); 283
ExtAdd, (figure); 33
ExtCodeDigit, (figure); 30
ExtCodeFloat, (figure); 30
ExtCodeString, (figure); 30
ExtDecodeDigit, (figure); 30
ExtDecodeFloat, (figure); 30
ExtDiv, (figure); 33
ExtendSourceSeq, (figure); 78
ExtendTargetSeq, (figure); 242
ExtEqual, (figure); 33
ExtInit, (figure); 33

ExtLess, (figure); 33
ExtMod, (figure); 33
ExtMpy, (figure); 33
ExtNegate, (figure); 33
ExtSub, (figure); 33
FieldListVisit2, (figure); 220
finalization, characteristics; 18
floating-point, (notes and references); 35
GenerateLabel, (figure); 245
GetEntityClass, (figure); 174, 180
GetTypeDescriptor, accessing *TypeDescriptor* property of a type with; 208
IdentifyOperator, (figure); 278
implementing operator identification computation, characteristics; 295
initialization, characteristics; 18
IntegerToString, (figure); 205
ItemVisit, (figure); 325
KeyEnv, (figure); 189
KeyInEnv,
   (figure); 164, 184
   finding identifier key with; 165
   use of *NoKey* definition table module value; 173
KeyInScope,
   (figure); 164, 184
   restricting search for an identifier; 165
LeaveEnv, (figure); 189
Lexical, (figure); 40, 52
LexInit, (figure); 40
machine, compared with machine instructions; 234
Makeops, (figure); 281
MapCoercion, (figure); 286
MapCondition, (figure); 247, 292
MapExpression,
   array reference handling by; 256
   (figure); 248
MapIdentifier, (figure); 252
MapStatement,
   construction of *ForLoop* by; 259
   (figure); 245, 247
MarkPosition, (figure); 329
Name, (figure); 127
NewEnv,
   environment trees created by; 163
   (figure); 164, 184
NewKey, (figure); 174, 180
NewScope,
   (figure); 164, 184
   new environments created by; 163
NextLine, (figure); 52
NumArgValue, (figure); 248
operation nodes, structure description (table); 235

Overlay, (figure); 214
Parser, (figure); 142
PoolInit, (figure); 19
PoolSpace, (figure); 19
RecordSectionVisit2, (figure); 221
RecoverSyntacticError, (figure); 153
reduce,
    context-free grammar rule correspondence to; 145
    example description (figure); 143
    representation of path identifier and number of elements; 143
Report, (figure); 25
ResultsOf, (figure); 278
Select, (figure); 321
SetEntityClass, (figure); 174, 176, 180
SetEnv, (figure); 189
SetTypeDescriptor, setting *TypeDescriptor* property of a type with; 208
shift,
    example description (figure); 143
    interpretive implementation example; 143
shift-reduce stack, example description (figure); 142
SignatureElt, (figure); 278
SourceInit, (figure); 22
SourceLeaf, (figure); 78
SourceLine, (figure); 22
SourceNode, (figure); 78
SourceTreeFinl, (figure); 78
SourceTreeInit, (figure); 78
Synterr, (figure); 127, 132
SynterrInit, (figure); 127, 132
target program, correspondence of target program tree nodes to; 231
TargetLeaf, (figure); 242
TargetNode, (figure); 242
TargetTreeFinl, (figure); 242
TargetTreeInit, (figure); 242
tree construction,
    invocation as output of a parser finite-state machine; 139
    specifying (figure); 78
    when invoked by a shift-reduce parser; 145
TypeVisit1, (figure); 169
TypeVisit2, (figure); 171, 217
operator association,
    See Also syntactic analysis;
    incorporating into parsing specification; 92
    specifying, example (figure); 96
operator identification,
    See Also action mapping;
    applying to jump cascade production; 287

C-- language,
    (figure); 351
    (table); 351
    (chapter); 268
computation algorithms; 295
implementation, (figure); 283
implementing computations; 295
jump cascade, (figure); 290
merging results into existing set of possible meanings; 299
module,
    interface, (figure); 278
    operations, *Coercion* function, (figure); 286
(notes and references); 301
source tree traversal strategy; 280
strategy, (notes and references); 301
type universe for, (figure); 296
operator precedence,
    See Also syntactic analysis;
    in regular expressions; 49
    incorporating into parsing specification; 92
    specifying, example (figure); 96
Operator **type**,
    operator identification use of, (figure); 278
operators,
    asterisk (*),
        integer multiplication use, reasons for different representations; 270
        meaning and precedence in regular expressions; 49
        meaning in source program tree notation; 72
        use in regular expression identities, (figure); 89
        use with derives operator in context-free grammar rewriting rules; 92
    Boolean expressions, implementing with jump cascades; 287
    building target program tree fragments for; 284
    coercion,
        obtaining consistent labeling of source tree nodes for; 272
        reasons for not including in operator triples; 276
    control flow, implementing with jump cascades (figure); 288
    defining and handling in parsing specification, (figure); 93
    derives (= >), term definition; 91
    distinguishing from source language operations and target language operations; 272

interpreting; 284
invalid, inconsistent operator use indicated
    by; 269
long set, mapping into target program tree;
    285
meanings, determining the set of, procedure
    implementation; 276
overloaded,
    effect on attempt to group; 284
    representation; 269
    term definition; 268
plus (+),
    meaning and precedence in regular
        expressions; 49
    meaning in source program tree notation;
        72
    use with derives operator in context-free
        grammar rewriting rules; 92
principles for combining into sets; 284
properties,
    determining for different classes of; 284
    target machine operation characteristics;
        271
relational, constructs for jump cascade
    implementation; 287
representation; 270
    triples, representing sequences in; 275
    triples, use of *NoKey* distinguished
        definition table key; 274
sets of possible meanings,
    computing; 274
    representing; 274
signature use to distinguish among members
    of a set of; 270
source language constructs relationship,
    representation in operator identification
        module; 277
source program tree decorations; 272
storing in *Expression* node; 282
voided expressions; 292
OpndArray type,
    definition, (figure); 329
    encoding operation use of; 330
or operation,
    generating the effect of; 287
ordering,
    order of children, target program tree
        compared with source language
        operands; 231
    paths leaving a syntax diagram fork, as
        continuation path specification method;
        123
OrExpr construct,
    operator and signature for, (figure); 289

output,
    See Also machine; trees;
    actions, associating with tree-building actions
        during shift-reduce parsing.; 145
    parser finite state machine, meaning of; 139
    tables, construction by parser generator; 146
oval boxes,
    See Also boxes; syntax diagrams;
    structure connections in parser syntax
        diagrams representation by; 110
    syntax diagrams,
        characteristics and use; 82
        unlabeled because not associated with input
            symbols; 140
Overlay operation,
    function description, (figure); 214
    obtaining storage requirement for complete
        record with; 220
    relative address determination by; 213
overlaying,
    composition strategy; 210
    example description; 211
overloading,
    See Also operators; type analysis (semantic
        analysis subtask);
    effect on attempt to group operators; 284
    jump cascade generation, (figure); 289
    obtaining consistent labeling for, (figure);
        273
    resolution of,
        (chapter); 268
        characteristics and issues; 269
        (notes and references); 301
    term definition; 230, 268
    voided expressions, (figure); 293
overloading constructs,
    (figure); 293

P

packed qualifier,
    IsPacked property, characteristics; 216
    PackedTypeNode property, characteristics;
        216
    properties of; 210
    representing by *IsPacked* property; 216
    type representation of; 216
PackedTypeNode property,
    characteristics; 216
parameters,
    See Also access functions; arguments;
    access function description; 233
    activation record storage of; 204
    as component of an access function; 232
    C-- language; 347

418   INDEX

characteristics and representation on the VAX; 204
effect of VAX routine calling conventions on handling of; 207
representation on the VAX; 207
types, redeclaring(figure); 194
var,
   passing limited private type objects as; 20
   representation on the VAX; 207
parentheses,
   use in a parsing language, examples (figure); 95
Parser **operation,**
   procedure description, (figure); 142
parsers,
   See Also errors; syntactic analysis;
   activity sequences significance for parser design; 106
   parser generators,
     describing syntax diagrams to a (figure); 146
     grammar conflict reporting and resolution; 146
   parser-defined errors,
     continuation paths of activity sequence following a , characteristics; 101
     term definition; 98
   recursive descent,
     anchor determination in; 123
     (chapter); 110
     error recovery; 121
     (notes and references); 134
   shift-reduce,
     (chapter); 139
     construction principles; 139
     error recovery; 150
     generators, characteristics; 145
     (notes and references); 154
     term definition; 139
   syntax diagram definition, (figure); 122
parsing (syntactic analysis subtask),
   See Also activity sequences; context-free grammars;
   ambiguous parsing language, handling by removing director set overlaps; 121
   behavior, methods for defining (chapter); 69
   (chapters),
     methods for defining a parser; 69
     recursive descent; 110
     shift-reduce; 139
   descriptive overview; 6
   parser generators,
     describing syntax diagrams to a, (figure); 146
     grammar conflict reporting and resolution; 146

parsing language,
   distinguished from source and target languages; 80
   relationship of activity sequences to; 80
   syntax diagrams characteristics; 81
recursive descent,
   chapter; 121
   characteristics and implementation; 110
   (exercises); 135
   (notes and references); 134
shift-reduce,
   (chapter); 139
   construction principles; 139
   error recovery; 150
   (exercises); 155
   (notes and references); 154
   parser generator characteristics; 145
specifying; 79
partial evaluation order,
   See Also data flow; evaluation order;
   determined by data flow relationships; 228
Pascal,
   compiler type system, (figure); 209
   conditional statement representation in source and target program trees, (figure); 244
   data, representing on the VAX; 199
   expression, representation in a source program tree; 4
   lexical analyzer, characteristics; 5
   name analysis subtask, as illustration of contextual analysis; 160
   program,
     fragment illustrating procedure activation (figure); 199
     illustrating scope rules (figure); 158
     illustrating use-before-definition error (figure); 167
   records, source program tree fragments stored as; 73
   relationships between environment values, (figure); 165
   statement, representation in a source program tree; 4
path segments,
   See Also continuations; errors;
   syntax diagrams, syntax error recovery use of; 101
performance,
   See Also computational complexity;
   effect of gathering contextual information on; 181
   identifier and keyword recognition, importance to string comparison; 60
   importance of scanning algorithm for; 42
   issues, count-controlled iteration target tree mapping; 258

INDEX **419**

lexical analysis, reasons for high cost of; 39
measurement, value in designing good and effective tools (notes and references); 63
modular decomposition issues; 18
role in deciding whether to make a data type public or private; 20
scanner speed crucial to; 51
search loops, technique for speeding up; 52
source module,
    as serious potential hazard for (notes and references); 35
    size of source text unit in; 21
plus (+) operator,
    meaning and precedence in regular expressions; 49
    meaning in source program tree notation; 72
    use with derives operator in context-free grammar rewriting rules; 92
PlusExpr **nodes,**
    See Also nodes;
    constructing; 75
    description, (figure); 74
    determining result types for; 282
    integer representation required by; 270
    overloading operators and signatures, (figure); 293
    restrictions on children of; 71
    textual notation for; 72
pointer(s),
    See Also data types; nodes; types;
    as example of unnamed defined entities whose properties are stored in the definition table; 160
    data type,
        characteristics and representation on the VAX; 201
        visit sequence; 218
    PointerTypeNode alternative (*TypeVisit2* operation), implementation (figure); 217
    PointerTypeNode nodes, visit sequence; 218
    references, mapping; 248
PoolInit **operation,**
    procedure description, (figure); 19
PoolSpace **operation,**
    procedure description, (figure); 19
position data type,
    definition, (figure); 25
PossibleMeanings **type,**
    operator identification use of, (figure); 278
postfix notation,
    impact on syntactic analysis, (exercise); 108
precedence rules,
    See Also operators; syntactic analysis;
    avoiding parentheses in regular expressions with; 49

    incorporating into parsing specification; 92
    procedures for; 97
preprocessors,
    as example of non-human source text producer; 21
principle of the longest match,
    See Also scanning;
    characteristics; 48
private data types,
    See Also data types;
    characteristics and comparison with public data types; 18
    information hiding use by; 20
procedures (source language),
    See Also operations;
    activation,
        data flow; 204
        data flow and actions associated with, (figure); 205
    activation record, VAX registers used to access argument lists; 204
    calls,
        conventions, (notes and references); 223
        represented in syntax diagrams by rectangular boxes; 126
    compiler type handling of; 208
    definitions, nesting level, determining local vs non-local variable; 251
    exported, characteristics; 18
    implementations, *Makeops*, (figure); 281
productions,
    in a context-free grammer, example (figure); 91
    term definition; 90
program(s),
    abstract, construction by code generator; 11
    environment, as a child of the environment value tree; 163
    regions, environment types representing associations between identifiers and definitions in; 163
    size, role in deciding whether to make a data type public or private; 20
program structure,
    C-- program, (figure); 345
Prohibited register sets,
    See Also registers;
    defining during target program tree traversal; 322
properties,
    See Also types;
    associated with a type, storing in definition table; 208
    asymptotic execution time, (notes and references); 192

compiler types, obtaining information necessary to construct; 210
default value use of; 220
defined source program entitites, stored in definition table; 159, 172
definition table,
  access and creation function implementation; 179
  access and definition operations; 178
  Pascal restrictions on direct storage of; 181
determining for different classes of operators; 284
ElementCount, characteristics; 216
entity class,
  obtaining with *GetEntityClass* operation; 174
  storage in definition table; 173
IsPacked, characteristics; 216
location, defining, (exercise); 196
mapping process, selecting generation code with; 285
of a value, encapsulating in a compiler type; 207
operators,
  signature characteristics; 270
  target machine operation characteristics; 271
PackedTypeNode, characteristics; 216
Pascal restrictions on direct storage in definition table; 181
PropElt type, definition (figure); 179
PropSel type, definition (figure); 179
Storage, accessing during field storage requirement determination; 221
storage requirement, definition table storage of; 210
StorageRequirement,
  characteristics; 216
  represented as pointers; 216
TargetConstruct, distinguishing among different operators in a set with; 284
Type, *TypeKey* set from during second visit to Type-class node; 216
TypeDescriptor,
  characteristics; 216
  definition, (figure); 209
  obtaining number of arguments from; 249
  represented as pointers; 216
types,
  associating with definition table key; 210
  identifiers, establishing during tree decoration visit; 172
  setting in definition table; 216
TypeSet, coercion operation use of; 298

public data types,
  See Also data types;
  characteristics and comparison with private data types; 18

Q

quadint **type,**
  characteristics; 271
queues,
  implementing, (exercise); 36

R

radix conversions,
  See Also representation;
  external representation conversion as; 31
  importance of avoiding in floating-point operations, (notes and references); 34
  problems for floating-point values; 27
rand **variable,**
  definition, (figure); 257
  description, (figure); 257
real number,
  See floating-point;
records,
  See Also source program tree;
  data type,
    characteristics and representation on the VAX; 202
    storage allocation methods; 203
  linked, source program tree represented by; 73
  Pascal restrictions on direct storage in definition table; 181
  RecordSection source tree node class, source program tree structure (figure); 219
  RecordSectionVisit2 operation, procedure description (figure); 221
  RecordTypeNode alternative (*TypeVisit2* operation), implementation (figure); 217
  source program tree,
    constructing from basic symbols, example description (figure); 76
    fragments, contents description; 73
    fragments, example declaration description (figure); 74
    fragments, example declaration schematic form (figure); 76
    structure and visit sequence (figure); 219
  storage,
    allocation strategies (notes and references); 223
    layout (exercise); 224
    requirements for complete; 220
    requirements of; 218

RecordSectionVisit2 **operation,**
  procedure description, (figure); 221
RecoverSyntacticError **operation,**
  procedure description, (figure); 153
rectangular boxes,
  See Also boxes; syntax diagrams;
  anchor set for; 123
  parser finite-state machine, example
    description (figure); 141
  procedures calls represented in syntax
    diagrams by; 126
  substituting syntax diagrams for in activity
    sequence syntax diagrams; 83
  syntax diagrams,
    characteristics and use; 81
    representation in syntax diagrams by; 110
recursion,
  See Also parsers;
  as reason why rectangular boxes cannot all be
    eliminated from syntax diagrams; 83
  avoiding in continuation path specification for
    error recovery in shift-reduce parsers;
    151
  continuation paths guaranteed to terminate
    because they may not contain; 123
  indirect left, procedures for eliminating; 111
  left,
    eliminating in recursive descent parsers;
      111
    (exercise); 135
    general technique for removal (notes and
      references); 134
  recursive descent parsers,
    (chapter); 110
    error recovery; 121
    (exercises); 135
    (notes and references); 134
  replacing by iteration, guidelines for when it
    can and cannot; 90
  right, (exercise); 135
  substitution, (exercise); 108
  transforming iterative activity sequences into
    recursive activity sequences; 86
  use in parser design; 110
reductions,
  See Also operations (generic compiler);
  operations,
    context-free grammar rule correspondence
      to; 145
    example description (figure); 143
    representation of path identifier and
      number of elements; 143
    reduce-reduce conflict, reporting by a parser
      generator; 149
    tables and interpretation code, (figure); 144

ref-class *Operand* **record,**
  external cross references represented by; 239
  labels represented in target program tree by;
    238
referenced location,
  providing unique names for; 239
register allocation (code generation subtask),
  (chapter); 306
  descriptive overview; 12
  register allocation module, *Select* operation
    description (figure); 321
register requirements,
  effect of evaluation order on, (figure); 308
registers,
  See Also code generation; instructions;
    machine; types;
  activation record tracking with AP register
    (VAX register 12); 204
  allocating,
    descriptive overview; 12
    for intermediate values; 320
    to a computational operation (figure); 327
    to nodes by parent during target program
      tree traversal; 322
  computation for allocation of, (figure); 321
  count, determination during target tree
    construction; 315
  fixed,
    effects on reqister requirement calculation;
      313
    requirement set determination during target
      tree construction; 315
  register allocation module, *Select* operation
    description(figure); 321
  RegisterSet type, definition (figure); 321
  requirements,
    determining the; 311
    determining when there are not enough
      registers for intermediate values; 313
    determining when there are not enough
      registers for Item-class nodes; 314
    evaluation order effect on, (figure); 308
  scratch, effects on register requirement
    calculation; 312
  sets,
    allocation to nodes during target program
      tree traversal; 322
    storage allocation for; 324
  shifting index, during array element
    accessing; 254
  use for intermediate results; 229
RegisterSet **type,**
  definition, (figure); 321
regular expressions,
  See Also activity sequences; grammars;

422 INDEX

algebra,
  (exercise); 108
  transforming left-recursive regular expressions into iterative expressions; 111
  characteristics and use in lexical analysis scanning subtask; 48
  describing denotations with, (exercise); 64
  extended,
    deriving activity sequences from (figure); 88
    notation (notes and references); 106
    relationship with syntax diagrams; 90
    to support activity sequences; 87
  identities, (figure); 89
  left-recursive, converting to iterative forms; 111
  (notes and references); 62
  relationship to syntax diagrams, (figure); 50
  removing director set overlap by transforming; 117
  rules for defining meaning of; 49
  term definition; 48
relational operators,
  constructs for jump cascade implementation; 287
relative address,
  See Also addresses; external address resolution; internal address resolution;
  computation, array elements; 203
  parameter, representation by *Operand* value; 233
***Relative* operation nodes,**
  structure description, (table); 235
repeat statement,
  template description; 243
***Report* operation,**
  procedure description, (figure); 25
representation,
  access functions, by *Operand* type (figure); 234
  anonymous entities, in definition table; 172
  arbitrary sequences, in source program tree, notation; 72
  arguments,
    arbitrary number of in source program tree node notation; 72
    on the VAX; 207
  array data type, on the VAX; 203
  assignment statements, with array references, in target program tree; 255
  associations between identifiers and definitions in a program region; 163

basic symbols; 39
  as leaves of source program tree; 6
  coordinate system (source text) contained in; 75
  in activity sequence descriptions; 81
  in extended regular expressions; 87
  in syntax diagrams by round boxes; 110
boolean data type, on the VAX; 200
case statement, by an Item-class node; 260
characters,
  char data type on the VAX; 200
  characteristics; 56
conditional control flow, in target program tree; 239, 260
conditional statement (Pascal), in source and target program trees (figure); 244
data, on target machine, (chapter); 198
data types,
  export status as criteria for public vs private designation; 18
  source language, on target machine; 11
denotations,
  as leaf arguments in source program trees; 73
  conversion algorithm descriptions; 58
enumerated data type, on the VAX; 201
expressions,
  by operator triples; 274
  in a source program tree, example description (figure); 5
  in source program tree records; 73
  of alternative computation expressions by *AlternativeDataL* nodes; 261
external,
  cross-references in target program tree; 239
  values exported type and constant definitions, (figure); 29
file data type, on the VAX; 203
floating-point,
  characteristics; 56
  external values; 31
  on the VAX; 200
generated identifiers; 175
identifiers,
  in source program tree records; 73
  storing in tree, reasons for; 170
if statement, by an Item-class node; 260
indexed references, on the VAX (figure); 255
integers,
  in source program tree records; 73
  integer data type on the VAX; 200
  integer external values specification; 30

internal,
   cross-references in target program tree; 238
   of source and target programs, reasons for making explicit; 3
local variable relative address, by *Operand* value; 233
non-local variables,
   access functions, target tree (figure); 250
   in the target program tree; 250
numbers, floating-point value problems; 27
operators; 270
   control flow, target program tree jump cascade (figure); 288
   meanings; 295
   overloaded; 269
   relationship (source language), in operator identification module; 277
   sets of possible meanings for; 274
parameters,
   on the VAX; 204
   relative address by *Operand* value; 233
Pascal,
   conditional statement (figure); 244
   data types; 200
   simple data types, VAX implementation; 200
path identifiers, in reduce operations; 143
pointer data type, on the VAX; 201
properties of a defined entity, design decisions; 177
record data type, on the VAX; 202
schematic, source program tree records (figure); 76
set data type, on the VAX; 203
sets of meanings; 299
source program,
   as tree; 6, 70
   as tree (exercise); 107
   as tree, linked records used for; 73
statements, source program tree, example description (figure); 5
strings,
   characteristics; 56
   external values; 31
structure connections,
   in activity sequence descriptions; 81
   in parser syntax diagrams by oval boxes; 110
symbol connections, in activity sequence descriptions; 81
syntax diagrams,
   in procedures; 110
   loops, in syntax diagrams by rectangular boxes; 110
target program,
   as tree; 6
   machine instructions; 306
target program tree labels; 238
transfer of control, in target program tree; 239
trees; 70
type, of packed qualifier; 216
variables, on the VAX; 204
while statement,
   source program tree (figure); 5
   target program tree (figure); 8
resource allocation,
See Also intermediate results; registers; storage allocation;
conditional expressions, specification with *AlternativeDataL* construct; 261
decisions, effect on the design of the target program tree; 231
determination,
   by encoding compiler task; 11
   by register allocation subtask; 12
effect on instruction selection; 233
execution-order relationship to, in function invocation, (figure); 240
for statements, code generator needs; 259
machine resources; 229
   determination by encoding compiler task; 11
methods for; 320
registers for intermediate results; 229
state, monitoring through activation record global variables; 324
storage used during; 324
to a computational operation, (figure); 327
traversal strategy; 322
***ResultsOf* operation,**
characteristics; 299
function definition, (figure); 278
***ResultType*,**
operator identification use of, (figure); 278
rewriting,
regular expressions, to transform into activity sequences; 88
rules of context-free grammars, characteristics; 90
step, characteristics; 91
right recursion,
See Also parsers; recursion;
(exercise); 135
term definition; 90

round boxes,
See Also boxes; syntax diagrams;
basic symbols representation in syntax diagrams by; 110
syntax diagrams, characteristics and use; 82

S

SaveEnv **variable,**
definition, (figure); 171
scanning (lexical analysis subtask),
basic symbols, reasons for handling separately from conversion; 57
descriptive overview; 5
design principles; 51
developing a scanner, (exercise); 66
finite-state machine,
description (figure); 52
directly-executable implementation; 53
interpretive implementation (figure); 53
lexical analysis module, characteristics and algorithm design principles; 41
problem, characteristics; 46
separation from basic symbol conversion task; 42
term definition; 39
schematic representation,
source program tree records, (figure); 76
scope,
See Also visibility rules;
effect of an increase in number on the time to gather contextual information; 182
establishing a new scope within an environment, environment module function definition, (figure); 164
restricting search for an identifier key to a particular; 165
rules, determining adherence to by semantic analysis of source program tree, (chapter); 157
scratch registers,
effects on register requirement calculation; 312
searching,
definition table property lists, implementation of; 179
speeding up loops, technique for; 52
Select **operation,**
function description, (figure); 321
semantic analysis (translation subtask),
(chapters),
name analysis; 157
operator identification; 268
types and data mapping; 198
Pascal visibility rules diagrams, (figure); 10
subtasks of, descriptive overview; 9

sematic analyzer,
(exercises); 194
sentinel characters,
See Also scanning;
(exercise); 65
separation of concerns,
See Also computational complexity; modularity; performance;
action mapping vs code generation; 229
compilation and environment; 17
computations vs inputs in computation of values to decorate the source program tree; 163
issues in definition table design; 178
lexical analysis, scanner vs conversion subtasks; 42, 57
not possible with coordinate system and error module; 26
operator identification; 276
source module vs error module; 26
structure determination vs computing information based on structure; 157
translator vs code generator, as basis for target tree design; 230
sequences,
activity,
characteristics as finite sequence of basic invocations; 80
context-free grammar use to generate; 90
deriving, (exercise); 108
deriving from extended regular expressions (figure); 88
describing by listing basic invocations, format description; 81
equivalence characteristics of invocation sequence descriptions; 83
(exercise); 108
extending regular expressions to support; 87
generating by rewriting regular expressions; 88
iterative, transforming into recursive activity sequences; 86
significance for parser design; 106
term definition; 80
transformations that move forks and joins without changing (figure); 85
arbitrary,
representation in source program tree records; 73
representation in source program trees; 72
length, compound statements as examples of; 4
byte, representing predefined Pascal data types, design concerns; 200

character,
    describing with syntax diagrams; 42
    extracting from source text with the
        scanner; 41
    invocation sequences compared with; 80
    notations for describing; 48
    storage during lexical analysis conversion;
        56
coercion operators as components of; 276
compared with tree as method of controlling
        execution-order decisions; 238
    including in *SequenceDatum* node; 248
    instructions, determination by code generator;
        11
    invocation of source tree construction,
        and lexical analyzer operations, parsing
        subtask specified in terms of; 79
    operations, specification concerns; 78
Item nodes, execution order determined by; 7
of target program subtrees, effect on
        execution order; 238
representing in operator triples; 275
SequenceDatum nodes,
    characteristics and structure (table); 238
    conditional expression evaluation order
        specified with; 262
    including sequences in; 248
    Sethi-Ullman number of; 311
syntax error recovery, strategy for replacing
        incorrect; 99
target program tree,
    as components of (figure); 240
    (figure); 237
VAX instruction, assignment statement,
        (figure); 229
SetEntityClass operation,
    procedure description, (figure); 174
    function description, (figure); 180
SetEnv operation,
    procedure description, (figure); 189
Sethi-Ullman numbers,
    computation of; 309
    operator evaluation order, (notes and
        references); 337
    term definition; 309
sets,
    implementation strategies for, (notes and
        references); 301
    operations, coercion operator implementation;
        297
    Pascal restrictions on direct storage in
        definition table; 181
    representation of by bit vectors; 299
    set data type, characteristics and representation on the VAX; 203

setting operations,
    See Also types;
    SetElementCount alternative (*TypeVisit2*
        operation), implementation (figure); 217
    SetEntityClass operation, procedure
        description (figure); 174, 180
    SetEnv operation, procedure description
        (figure); 189
    SetProperty operation; 178
    SetTypeKey operation, defining identifier type
        property with; 177
severity data type,
    definition, (figure); 25
shift-reduce,
    See Also parsers;
    conflict,
        origin of(figure); 147
        reporting by a parser generator; 148
    operations,
        example description(figure); 143
        interpretive implementation example; 143
    parsers,
        (chapter); 139
        construction principles; 139
        error recovery; 150
        (exercises); 155
        generators, characteristics; 145
        (notes and references); 154
        term definition; 139
    stack operations, example description
        (figure); 142
shortest-path algorithm,
    (notes and references); 301
    use in operator identification; 298
side effects,
    handling in the implementation of voided
        expressions; 291
SignatureElt operation,
    function definition, (figure); 278
signatures,
    See Also operators; types;
    operators distinguished by; 270
    sharing between operators with different
        numbers of operands; 277
    Signature type, operator identification use of
        (figure); 278
    SignatureElt operation,
        characteristics; 295
        function definition (figure); 278
    term definition; 270
single-record approach,
    definition table design, problems with; 178
size,
    See Also performance;
    program, role in deciding whether to make a
        data type public or private; 20

INDEX

source text unit, performance considerations; 21
source language,
  See Also types;
  constructs,
    C-- language; 356
    operator relationship, representation in operator identification module; 277
    representation in source program tree, descriptive overview; 4
    representation in source program tree, descriptive overview (figure); 5
    representing as tree fragments; 70
  data types, representation on target machine; 11
  relationship with target language determined by translation compiler task; 6
  source text,
    coordinate system use in reporting errors; 23
    input problem characteristics; 20
    modular handling of; 16
  SourceConstruct type, description (figure); 74
  SourceInit operation, procedure description (figure); 22
  SourceLeaf operation,
    invoking during syntactic error recovery; 103
    procedure description (figure); 78
  SourceLine operation, function description (figure); 22
  SourceNode operation, procedure description (figure); 78
  SourceSequenceElt record, description (figure); 74
  SourceTreeFinl operation, procedure description (figure); 78
  SourceTreeInit operation, procedure description (figure); 78
  SourceTreeNode record, description (figure); 74
  standard, crucial importance of understanding for compiler design; 191
  term definition; 1
source module,
  characteristics; 20
  (exercise); 37
  interface specification, example description (figure); 19
source program tree,
  See Also target program tree; trees;
  augmented with operator identification values, (figure); 283
  building, example description (figure); 76
  C-- language; 354
    (figure); 355
    transforming into VAX target program trees; 366
  construction,
    characteristics and; 70
    module interface, operation specifications (figure); 78
    operation invocations, relating to lexical analyzer invocations; 79
  descriptive overview; 4
  example description (figure); 71
  fragments,
    storage and linkage in; 73
    textual notation for; 72
  if statement fragment, (figure); 271
  indexed references representation, (figure); 255
  jump cascade in C-- language, (figure); 371
  leaves, basic symbols represented as; 6
  nodes,
    augmentation with operator identification values, (tables); 282
    classes (figure); 219
    decorated by semantic analyzer; 8
    decorated by type analysis; 9
    example declaration (figure); 74
    operator labeling of; 272
    stored as linked Pascal records; 73
  Pascal program fragment, (figure); 158, 167
  record, additions for name analysis, (figure); 169
  representation of, (exercise); 107
  sequence of operations constructing, (figure); 79
  syntactic analyzer creation of, descriptive overview; 6
  time cost of visits to nodes of; 181
  traversal,
    as tactical component of contextual information gathering strategy; 160
    characteristics and strategy development; 166
    during target tree construction, as the action mapping subtask; 241
    operator identification constraints; 280
  type nodes, visit that establishes definition table key for; 210
  Type-class node visit sequence design; 216
source programs,
  relating legal structures and legal programs, (exercise); 108
  SourceLeaf **operation,**
    procedure description, (figure); 78

***SourceNode* operation,**
procedure description, (figure); 78
***SourceTreeFinl* operation,**
procedure description, (figure); 78
***SourceTreeInit* operation,**
procedure description, (figure); 78
***SPACE* operation code,**
control section management by; 333
specifying,
the parsing subtask; 79
tree-scanning subtask; 42
square brackets ([]),
extending regular expression notation with; 51
stack,
contents after construction of a source tree node; 77
function argument placement and invocation issues; 239
intermediate value storage on; 318
source program tree use of, example description (figure); 76
state, dependence of anchor set determination on; 151
target tree construction module,
condition on Datum-class node mapping procedure exit; 242
condition on Item-class node mapping procedure exit; 242
standards,
source language, crucial importance of understanding for compiler design; 191
***StarExpr* construct,**
overloading operators and signatures, (figure); 293
start symbol,
in a context-free grammer, example (figure); 91
term definition; 91
state(s),
See Also finite-state machines; parsers;
constant-time access implementation; 188
diagrams,
compared with syntax diagrams; 44
comparision of different notations; 44
(notes and references); 62
term definition; 44
finite-state machine,
characteristics; 44
state table characteristics; 44
internal,
character pool module characteristics; 18
initialization of source module; 23
lexical analysis module, embodiment of (figure); 41

operator identification module, characteristics; 298
parser finite-state machine,
example description (figure); 141
implementation as stack; 140
term definition; 139
parser generator determination of components; 145
tables,
characteristics and use (figure); 47
interpreting (figure); 53
term definition; 44
transition,
effect on parser finite-state machine stack; 140
effects on stack; 139
example description (figure); 143
variables,
invariants (figure); 41
lexical analysis module vs source module; 40
statements,
assignment,
constructing a source tree node for; 75
finite-state machine example description (figure); 55
implementing, (figure); 229
mapping with *AssignmentStmt* alternative of *MapStatement* procedure; 247
multiple, as example of director set overlap, (figure); 118
Pascal subset, iterative version syntax diagrams (figure); 116
Pascal, syntax diagrams for a subset, (figure); 114
syntax diagram example; 82
target program tree fragment for, (figure); 232
with array references, target program tree representation of; 255
C-- language, (figure); 348
case, representation by an Item-class node; 260
compound, mapping with *CompoundStmt* alternative of *MapStatement* procedure; 246
conditional,
Pascal, syntax diagrams (figure); 121
source language constructs into target language constructs; 243
target program tree mapping design issues; 260
dangling else, as director set overlap example; 119
for,

mapping, VAX instructions for modifying counters use in; 258
  resource allocation needs; 259
  target program tree mapping design; 256
goto, eliminating, (exercise); 135
if, representation by an Item-class node; 260
if-then-else, template description; 243
mapping, *MapStatement* proceure user for (figure); 245
mapping of,
  example description; 243
  for statements, target program tree design; 256
repeat, template description; 243
representation in source program tree,
  example description (figure); 5
  records; 73
statement class leaves, information not filled in during syntactic analysis, (figure); 76
Statement-class nodes,
  example illustration in source program tree (figure); 168
  mapping into target program tree, with *MapStatement* procedure; 244
  statements represented by; 4
term definition; 4
tree fragment class, term definition; 70
while,
  source program tree representation, (figure); 5
  target program tree representation, (figure); 8
  template description; 243
static chain,
  See Also activation records; code generation;
  term definition; 205
  use in mapping non-local variables; 250
status information,
  allocating for file data type; 203
storage,
  See Also memory;
  allocation,
    See Also resource allocation;
    arrays; 203
    files; 203
    records (figure); 202
    sets; 203
    static chain; 204
    type declarations and; 210
  arrays, in VAX memory, (figure); 253
  character sequences, during lexical analysis conversion; 56
  external values, allocation issues; 27
  intermediate values of Datum-class constructs, as code generation decision; 306

local variables, (figure); 213
requirements,
  activation records; 212
  compiler types, definition table storage of; 210
  composition strategies; 210
  enumerated data type; 201
  external values visible at the interface of external value module; 28
  information needed to define; 212
  Pascal simple data types, VAX implementation; 200
  records; 218
  types, determining; 210
storage module,
  Concatenate operation (figure); 215
  function and type descriptions (figure); 214
  interface specification and characteristics, example description (figure); 211
Storage property, accessing during field storage requirement determination; 221
Storage type, definition (figure); 217
Storage variable, use in determining storage requirements for a record; 218
StorageRequired type,
  activation record global variables; 324
  definition (figure); 214
StorageRequirement property,
  characteristics; 216
  represented as pointers; 216
string external values,
  allocated by external value module; 29
  implications of implementation decisions; 31
***StorageRequired* type,**
  definition, (figure); 214
strict computations,
  implication for external value module; 32
String **type,**
  description, (figure); 205
strings,
  See Also characters; data types; representation;
  comparison operations effect on conversion performance; 60
  converting to an internal representation; 56
  algorithm descriptions; 58
  delimiters, conversion of Pascal representation; 59
  denotations, recognizing with syntax diagrams (figure); 43
  determining the maximum length of; 26
  mapping; 249
  recognizing and converting in C, (exercise); 67

string external values,
   representation; 31
   storage allocation considerations; 28
   storage of, implications of implementation decisions; 31
structure,
   source program tree, source program information embodied in; 70
   target program tree,
     action mapper execution-order decisions reflected in, (figure); 237
     VAX target tree node examples, (table); 238
structure connections,
   See Also symbol connections; symbols; syntactic analysis;
   anchor set for; 123
   context-free grammars handling of; 145
   dyadic, incorporating into parsing specification (figure); 93
   invocations,
     characteristics; 80
     in syntax diagrams example (figure); 82
     representation in activity sequence descriptions; 81
   not part of director sets; 117
   parser syntax diagrams, unlabeled because not associated with input symbols; 140
   syntax diagrams, representation by oval boxes; 110
structured objects,
   representation of; 200
structuring (compiler task),
   (chapters),
     lexical analysis; 38
     syntactic analysis, parsing and tree construction; 69
     syntactic analysis, recursive descent parsing; 110
     syntactic analysis, shift-reduce parsing; 139
   (figure); 5
   modularity of methods, interface specification role in; 17
   problem, requirements for solution; 17
   subtasks of, descriptive overview; 4
subexpressions,
   See Also expressions;
   partial ordering, embodiment in target tree; 307
subscript expressions,
   obtaining and holding information needed for, (figure); 257
substitution,
   See Also grammars;
   context-free grammar rewriting step use of; 90, 91
   in syntax diagrams describing an activity sequence; 83
   syntax error recovery use of; 99
   transforming regular expressions by; 89
subtrees,
   See Also trees;
   resulting from *TargetNode* operation, (figure); 319
symbol connections,
   See Also structure connections; symbols; syntactic analysis;
   anchor set for; 123
   continuation path choice based on; 103
   distinguishing names from regular expression names; 87
   handling in context-free grammars; 145
   invocations,
     characteristics; 80
     in syntax diagrams example (figure); 82
     representation in activity sequence descriptions; 81
   operators, defining and handling in parsing specification (figure); 93
   parser finite-state machine handling, example description (figure); 143
   representation in syntax diagrams by oval boxes; 110
   represented in extended regular expressions; 87
symbols,
   See Also basic symbols; variables;
   acceptable, specifying in a syntax diagram, (figure); 125
   generated,
     how to introduce, recursive descent parser; 126
     how to introduce, shift-reduce parser; 151
     identifying by use of a distinguished value; 103
   NoKey associated with; 175
   use during syntax error recovery; 104
   input, syntax error recovery, implementation of; 103
   nonterminal,
     "helper", use with right recursion in context-free grammars, (exercise); 135
     in a context-free grammer, example (figure); 91
     relationship to terminal symbols; 90
     splitting to reduce grammar ambiguity; 149
     transforming symbol and structure connections into; 145

start,
   in a context-free grammer, example (figure); 91
   term definition; 91
SymbolClass,
   type, description (figure); 40, 57
   value, use during keyword recognition; 59
terminal,
   anchor set for; 123
   as activity sequence elements; 90
   in a context-free grammer example (figure); 91
syntactic analysis (structuring subtask),
   See Also source program tree; (chapters),
      parsing and tree construction; 69
      recursive descent parsing; 110
      shift-reduce parsing; 139
   (notes and references); 105
   subtasks of, descriptive overview; 6
syntax diagrams,
   See Also context-free grammars; finite-state machines; parsers; regular expressions; structure connections; symbol connections;
   advantages and future potential of, (notes and references); 106
   ambiguity determination; 48
   continuation path specifications incorporation in; 123
   continuations specification by rearranging forks, (figure); 124
   converting,
      into deterministic finite state machines, example description (figure); 47
      nondeterministic into deterministic versions; 43
   decision making process analysis, in recursive descent parsers; 115
   error detection in, example (figure); 102
   examples, (figure); 82, 84
   (exercise); 108
   lexical analysis scanning subtask use of; 42
   (notes and references); 62
   parser,
      defining a finite-state machine with; 139
      definition (figure); 122
      describing to a parser generator (figure); 146
      language characteristics; 81
   Pascal assignment statements,
      subset, (figure); 114
      subset, iterative version (figure); 116
   Pascal conditional statements, (figure); 121
   path segments, syntax error recovery use of; 101
   regular expressions,
      extended regular expression relationship with; 90
      relationships, (figure); 50
   representation in syntax diagrams by rectangular boxes; 110
   specifying acceptable symbols, (figure); 125
   state diagrams compared with; 44
   term definition; 42
   transforming,
      to/from grammars, principles for; 92
      with substitution; 83
   with parallel paths, (figure); 86
syntax errors,
   detection associated with terminal symbols; 124
   diagnosis, bibliographic reference; 107
   disadvantages of ad-hoc recovery methods, (notes and references); 106
   recovery; 98
      in shift-reduce parser; 150
      strategy example (table); 100
      strategy for replacing incorrect sequences; 99
      strategy implementation questions; 104
   repairing,
      contrasted with correction; 99
      examples (figure); 99
   Synterr operation, procedure description (figure); 127
   SynterrInit operation, procedure description (figure); 127
***Synterr* operation,**
   procedure description, (figure); 127, 132
***SynterrInit* operation,**
   procedure description, (figure); 127, 132

T

T*,
   Kleene closure of set T in a grammar definition; 92
***Tag* source tree node class,**
   source program tree structure, (figure); 219
   TagVisit1 operation, implementation (exercise); 226
   TagVisit2 operation, implementation (figure); 220
target,
   distinctions between operations and instructions; 234
   language,
      relationship with source language determined by translation compiler task; 6
      term definition; 1

INDEX 431

machine,
  generating instructions, (chapter); 306
  operation, operator property characteristics; 271
operands,
  characteristics (figure); 234
  description (figure); 315
target program tree,
  See Also registers; source program tree; trees;
  action mapper creation of, (chapter); 228
  descriptive overview; 11
  (notes and references); 264
  as interface between translator and code generator; 230
  assignment statement fragment, (figure); 232
  C-- language; 360
    (figure); 361
  characteristics of values represented by leaves of; 309
  constructing,
    by transformation subtask; 11
    (chapter); 228
    for an expression; 248
    operations(figure); 242
    operator fragments; 284
  construction module, interface specification, (figure); 242
  context information that is computed when the tree is being constructed; 314
  creation by translation compiler task, descriptive overview; 6
  Datum-class node, descriptive overview, (figure); 8
  declaring a node, (figure); 316
  decorations, nodes decorated by code generator; 314
  description of operand, (figure); 315
  design,
    case studies in; 251
    characteristics and differences from source program trees; 230
  determining operand classes during construction of; 314
  for statement implementation, (figure); 260
  indexed references representation, (figure); 255
  instruction order nodes, (table); 238
  jump cascade,
    in C-- language (figure); 371
    representation of control flow operators (figure); 288
  leaves, data mapping results attached to; 11
  machine operation encoding by the action mapper; 233
  mapping identifiers into, (figure); 252
  nodes,
    building with *MapCondition* procedure; 246
    correspondence to operations of the target program; 231
    declaring (figure); 316
    instruction encoding determination by instruction selection subtask; 12
    operation (figure); 235
  order of children, compared with source language operands; 231
  register count for constructs, involving multiple-register intermediate values; 312
  resource allocation traversal strategy; 322
  Sethi-Ullman number calculations for the nodes of; 308
  structure, action mapper execution-order decisions reflected in, (figure); 237
  structuring constructs, code and diagram (figure); 263
  TargetConstruct property, distinguishing among different operators in a set with; 284
  TargetConstruct type,
    characteristics; 241
    definition (figure); 316
  TargetLeaf operation,
    Operand value argument use in constructing target program leaves; 317
    Operand value use in determining fixed registers; 317
    procedure description (figure); 242
  TargetNode operation,
    considerations affecting behavior; 317
    procedure description (figure); 242
    subtrees possibly resulting from (figure); 319
  TargetSequence type, definition (figure); 316
  TargetSequenceElt type, definition (figure); 316
  TargetTree type, definition (figure); 316
  TargetTreeFinl operation, procedure description (figure); 242
  TargetTreeInit operation, procedure description (figure); 242
  TargetTreeNode type, definition (figure); 316
  VAX, transforming C-- language source program trees into; 366
TargetConstruct type,
  definition, (figure); 316
TargetLeaf operation,
  procedure description, (figure); 242
TargetNode operation,
  procedure description, (figure); 242

432 INDEX

***TargetSequence* type,**
  definition, (figure); 316
***TargetSequenceElt* type,**
  definition, (figure); 316
***TargetTree* type,**
  definition, (figure); 316
***TargetTreeFinl* operation,**
  procedure description, (figure); 242
***TargetTreeInit* operation,**
  procedure description, (figure); 242
***TargetTreeNode* type,**
  definition, (figure); 316
templates,
  See Also action mapping;
  incorporating into *MapStatement* procedure; 244
  statement,
    if-then-else and while; 243
    repeat; 243
term definitions,
  abstract syntax, notes); 105
  access functions; 232
  action mapping; 229
  activation records; 204
  activity sequences; 80
  aligned data; 199
  anchors; 103
  applied occurrences; 164
  axiom; 91
  basic symbols; 4, 38
  class, of a tree fragment; 70
  client; 18
  closeness, in syntactic error recovery; 99
  coercion; 268
  concrete syntax, notes); 105
  context, of nonterminals; 90
  context-free grammar; 90
  control sections; 333
  conversion(s), lexical analysis subtask; 39
  cross-references; 239
  data flow; 228
  data types,
    limited private; 20
    private; 18
    public; 28
  defining occurrence; 164
  delimiter, basic symbol; 39
  denotation, basic symbol; 39
  = > (derives operator); 91
  dictionary; 63, 299
  director set; 115
  director set overlap; 117
  equivalence; 1
  errors, parser-defined; 98
  exporting; 18

  expressions; 4
  external cross-references; 239
  finite-state machines; 44
  fragments of a tree; 70
  grammars; 92
  holes; 223
  identifier, basic symbol; 39
  interface specification; 17
  internal cross-references; 238
  invariant; 36
  jump cascades; 287
  language, defined by a grammar; 92
  left recursion; 90
  limited private data type; 20
  longword; 200
  modules; 17
  nonterminal symbols; 90
  operator, overloaded; 268
  overloading; 230, 268
  parser-defined errors; 98
  productions; 90
  regular expressions; 48
  right recursion; 90
  scanning, lexical analysis subtask; 39
  Sethi-Ullman number; 309
  shift-reduce parsing; 139
  signature; 270
  source language; 1
  start symbol; 91
  state,
    finite state machine; 43
    parser; 139
  state diagram; 44
  state table; 44
  statements; 4
  statements tree fragment class; 70
  static chain; 205
  syntax diagrams; 42
  target language; 1
  terminal symbols; 90
  token separators; 21
  tree; 4
  tree fragment class; 70
  types,
    compiler; 207
    Environment; 163
  voiding; 291
terminal symbols,
  See Also symbols; syntactic analysis;
  anchor set for; 123
  as activity sequence elements; 90
  in a context-free grammar, example (figure); 91
textual notation,
  for source program tree fragments; 72

time,
  See Also performance;
  asymptotic execution time properties, (notes and references); 192
  compilation, effect of gathering contextual information on; 181
  impact of computational complexity on time required to gather contextual information; 182
  order of execution, (notes and references); 192
Token **data type,**
  See Also data types;
  description, (figure); 40
  fields set by the scanner; 41
  source program tree leaf created from information in; 75
token separators,
  term definition; 21
transfer of control,
  jump cascade handling of; 290
  representation in target program tree; 239
transformation,
  between grammars and syntax diagrams, principles for; 92
  of invocation sequence descriptions into activity sequences; 83
  of regular expressions into activity sequences; 88
  removing director set overlaps with; 119
transformation (translation subtask),
  action mapping, (notes and references); 264
  (chapters),
    action mapping; 228
    data mapping; 198
  data mapping, (notes and references); 222
  subtasks of, descriptive overview; 11
transition,
  See Also parsers;
  finite state machine, output association with; 46
  tables,
    See Also shift-reduce parsers;
    construction by parser generator; 146
    parser finite state machine, example description (figure); 141
    parser interpretation of, (figure); 142
translation (compiler task),
  (chapters),
    semantic analysis, name analysis; 157
    semantic analysis, operator identification; 268
    semantic analysis, types; 198
    transformation, action mapping; 228
    transformation, data mapping; 198

execution-order decisions embodied in Item-class sequences; 12
from source language to target language, example description using Euclid's integer division algorithm, (figure); 2
module, characteristics which satisfy requirements of a module; 17
problem, requirements for solution; 17
subtasks of, descriptive overview; 6
trap state,
  characteristics; 44
tree construction (syntactic analysis subtask),
  (chapter); 69
  descriptive overview; 6
tree traversal,
  algorithms, characteristics; 166
  computational dependency relationship to order of; 162
  computing values that decorate the source program tree; 163
  defining occurrence visit strategy; 177
  depth-first left-to-right,
    compatibility with computation dependence relations; 162
    limitations of; 166
  source program tree,
    as tactical component of contextual information gathering strategy; 160
    importance of target tree construction operator placement; 241
    name analysis, (chapter); 157
    target program tree generation by; 241
    stored identifier-key associations computed during; 162
  target program tree, resource allocation; 322
  visits,
    characteristics and purpose; 166
    defining occurrences before applied occurrences or nested regions; 166
    methods for distinguishing appropriate actions; 167
    procedure design characteristics; 244
    sequence based on computation dependence; 162
    sequence design; 216
    sequence determined by information availability; 162
    source program tree Type-class node, second visit characteristics; 210
    time required for; 181
    to identifier declaration nodes; 166
trees,
  See Also nodes; representation; sequences; source program tree; target program tree;

compared with sequence as method of controlling execution-order decisions; 238
construction operations; 70
  invocation as output of a parser finite-state machine; 139
  specifying, (figure); 78
  when invoked by a shift-reduce parser; 145
direct encoding of environment values, as implementation of environment module, example description; 182
information stored during tree decoration, characteristics; 170
linking subtrees into, operation specification (figure); 78
representation of; 70
storing information in a; 170
term definition; 4
truejump type,
  definition; 287
type analysis (semantic analysis subtask),
  (chapters),
    data mapping and; 198
    operator identification; 268
  data mapping and, (chapter); 198
  descriptive overview; 9
  (notes and references),
    operator identification; 301
    types and data mapping; 222
  operator identification, (chapter); 268
  overloading resolution, (chapter); 268
  types and data mapping, (chapter); 198
Type-class nodes,
  See Also nodes; types;
  characteristics of second visit to; 210
  impact on record class node visits; 218
  Pascal types represented by; 216
  setting *TypeKey* variable from *Type* property during second visit to; 216
types,
  See Also data types;
  AddressingMode, (figure); 234, 315
  arity, (figure); 329
  C-- language; 347
  Chain, (figure); 61
  ChainElt, (figure); 61
  compile-time analysis of, (notes and references); 301
  compiler,
    classification of Pascal, (figure); 209
    comparision with source language data types; 207
    differences from source language types; 271
    extending to encompass both source and target language data objects; 271
    extending to jump cascades; 287
    reasons for enforcing a single type for each value; 208
    term definition and characteristics; 207
  constructing, (figure); 217
  constructors,
    creating structured types with; 216
    visiting; 218
  conversion of,
    coercions as a form of implicit; 268
    effect on compiler type system design; 208
    handling during action mapping; 247
  data mapping and, (notes and references); 222
  Datum, (figure); 316
  declarations, storage allocation and; 210
  definitions, environment module, (figure); 164
  enumerated,
    properties of; 216
    visit sequence as example of visit to a type constructor; 218
  Environment,
    (figure); 164
    term definition; 163
  falsejump, definition; 287
  final,
    operator identification use of; 276
    storing in *Expression* node; 282
  generating transformation code, (figure); 286
  identifier, use by *TypeVisit2* operation; 216
  impact on determination of identifier association set; 162
  implementing the environment, (figure); 183
  Indication, operator identification use of, (figure); 278
  information, source program tree decorations; 9
  key, location in source program tree; 249
  multiply-defined entity, redefining with *SetTypeKey* function; 177
  new, represented by Type-class nodes; 216
  of root of if statement source program tree node; 289
  OpCode,
    definition, (figure); 329
    (figure); 329
  Operand,
    associated with Datum-class nodes, importance to code generation; 306
    (figure); 315
  Operator, operator identification use of, (figure); 278

operator identification graph and meaning
sets, (figure); 296
OpndArray,
encoding operation use of; 330
(figure); 329
pointer, visit sequence; 218
PossibleMeanings, operator identification use
of, (figure); 278
properties of; 216
accessing with *GetTypeDescriptor*; 208
ElementCount property; 216
identifiers, establishing during tree
decoration visit; 172
obtaining information necessary to
construct; 210
packed property; 210
setting with *SetTypeDescriptor*; 208
storage requirement property; 210
stored in definition table; 172
quadint, characteristics; 271
RegisterSet, (figure); 321
relationships among, defining by type graphs;
295
representing in source program tree by Type-
class nodes; 216
Signature, operator identification use of,
(figure); 278
StorageRequired,
activation record global variables; 324
definition, (figure); 214
String, (figure); 205
structured, properties of; 216
SymbolClass, (figure); 57
TargetConstruct,
characteristics; 241
(figure); 316
TargetSequence, (figure); 316
TargetSequenceElt, (figure); 316
TargetTree, (figure); 316
TargetTreeNode, (figure); 316
truejump, definition; 287
type analysis use of definition table,
descriptive overview; 9
Type component, type or variable declaration,
visiting during identifier/key association
definition; 170
type graphs,
CPL compiler use of, (notes and
references); 301
representing the operator identification
types with; 295
Type nodes, example illustration in source
program tree (figure); 168
Type property, *TypeKey* set from during
second visit to Type-class node; 216

TypeDescriptor property,
characteristics; 216
definition (figure); 209
obtaining number of arguments from; 249
represented as pointers; 216
TypeDescriptor record, creation of; 210
TypeKey variable,
definition (figure); 171
setting from Type property during second
visit to Type-class node; 216
TypeSet property, coercion operation use of;
298
TypeVisit1 operation, procedure description
(figure); 169
TypeVisit2 operation, procedure description
(figure); 171, 217
UnknownType, erroneous program handling
with; 208
vinteger, voided expression handling use of;
292
voided expressions; 292
VoidType, use in unifying the handling of
functions and procedures; 208
vreal, voided expression handling use of; 292
TypeVisit1 operation,
procedure description, (figure); 169
TypeVisit2 operation,
procedure description, (figure); 171, 217

U

unconditional transfer of control,
representation in target program tree; 239
undefined identifiers,
compiler type system handling of; 208
detection; 165
by the semantic analyzer, example
description; 175
when reported; 9
unification of concepts,
See Also separation of concerns;
as criterion in compiler type system design;
208
uninitialized variables memory region,
See Also memory; variables;
characteristics; 333
UnknownType **type,**
erroneous program handling with; 208
unpacked qualifier,
as default type assumption; 216
UpArrowExpr **alternative (***MapExpression*
procedure),
mapping pointer references with; 248
use-before-definition error (Pascal),
problems in detecting, (figure); 167

V

validity,
  external values, importance of ascertaining; 32

values,
  See Also constants; symbols; variables;
  [], source language typing vs. compiler typing of; 207
  C-- language; 347
  compiler type relationship to; 207
  computing,
    as tactical component of contextual information gathering; 160
    for source program tree decoration; 163
  Datum-class nodes, constraints on; 231
  default, use of properties; 220
  default property, obtaining with *NoKey* definition table key; 175
  distinguished,
    identifying generated symbols by use of a; 103
    NoExtValue; 33
    NoInstruction; 285
    NoKey; 174
  environment,
    current, global variable definition, (figure); 171
    current, reasons for declaring its variable global; 170
    description as a tree; 163
    direct encoding of tree; 182
    encoding as an array; 185
    relationships between Pascal (figure); 165
  expressions,
    distinguished, from statements by return of; 4
    return value type specified by definition table key; 208
  external,
    converting denotations into objects; 56
    distinguished, needed in external value module specification; 28
    external value module, (exercise); 37
    external value module interface(figure); 30
    floating-point, representation specification; 31
    integers representation specification; 30
    management problem characteristics; 26
    modular handling of; 16
    module interface characteristics; 26
    storage allocation considerations; 28
    string representation; 31
  floating-point,
    determining the maximum range of; 26
    representation issues; 27
  intermediate,
    allocating registersfor; 320
    constructs target program tree register count for that produce multiple-register; 312
    multiple-registers, modifying Sethi-Ullman computation to account for; 312
    number existing simultaneously, Sethi-Ullman number of operand effect on 310
    produced by Datum-class nodes, role in code generation; 306
    register requirements, determining when there are not enough registers; 313
    relationship to number of registers needed; 308
    Sethi-Ullman number as specification of maximum simultaneously existing; 309
    storage in Item-class node; 320
    storage on stack; 318
  leaf,
    access functions provided by action mapper; 233
    identifier-class nodes; 73
    integer-class nodes; 73
  missing, representation issues; 28
  nil, source language typing vs compiler typing of; 207
  node, access functions provided by code generator; 233
  NoExtValue, variable declaration (figure); 33
  NoInstruction value (*TargetConstruct*), signalling uninitialized definition table operator entry with; 285
  NoKey value, constant definition, (figure); 174
  obtained from data mapping subtask, stored in *DatumLeaf* node; 11
  Operand type,
    copying into *OpndArray* array during instruction encoding operations; 330
    interior nodes of target program tree, when determined; 314
  relationships between constructs that produce values and those that consume them, descriptive overview; 7
  representing cost of producing in an operator representation triple; 275
  string, determining the maximum length of; 26
  SymbolClass value, use during keyword recognition; 59
  VAX operation classification according to whether it yields a value or not; 231

INDEX

variables,
See Also symbols;
ActivationRecord, monitoring allocation state with; 324
C-- language; 347
characteristics and representation on the VAX; 204
controlled, taking machine limitations on integers into account in mapping design; 257
CurrDef, definition (figure); 179
Current, (figure); 41
CurrentAR, monitoring allocation state with; 324
CurrOp, definition (figure); 281
CurrSig, definition (figure); 281
DataBase, definition (figure); 179
declarations, establishing associations for; 163
Env,
  definition (figure); 171
  (figure); 171
ErrorCount, definition, (figure); 25
exported, characteristics; 18
floating-point, properties stored in definition table; 172
FloatingZero, (figure); 33
global,
  set of associations between identifier and key stored in; 162
  visit procedures, reasons for declaring global; 170
HashTbl, (figure); 61
initialized variables memory region, characteristics; 333
IntegerOne, (figure); 33
IntegerZero, (figure); 33
InvalidOperator, operator identification use of (figure); 278
Limit, (figure); 41
Line, definition, (figure); 22
LineLng, definition, (figure); 22
LineNumber, (figure); 41
LinePtr, definition, (figure); 22
local,
  access function description; 233
  storage for (figure); 213
  storage requirements; 212
  visit procedures reasons for declaring local; 170
LowerBound.ElementSize, (figure); 257
mapping; 249
NoExtValue,
  (figure); 33
  use as generated symbol during syntactic error recovery; 103

non-local,
  accessing, target tree representation (figure); 250
  mapping; 250
  representation in the target program tree; 250
NoPosition, definition, (figure); 25
NullString, (figure); 33
rand,
  description (figure); 257
  (figure); 257
SaveEnv, definition (figure); 171
state,
  invariants (figure); 41
  lexical analysis module (figure); 41
states, lexical analysis module vs source module; 40
Storage, use in determining storage requirements for a record; 218
storing tree decoration information in; 170
TypeKey,
  definition (figure); 171
  setting from *Type* property during second visit to Type-class node; 216
uninitialized variables memory region, characteristics; 333
var parameters,
  passing limited private type objects as; 20
  representation on the VAX; 207
variants,
implementing definition table entries with, advantages and disadvantages; 178
storage,
  allocation methods; 203
  requirement; 220
variant records, mapping into memory; 210
Variant source tree node class, source program tree structure (figure); 219
VAX,
activation record addressing on, (figure); 206
assembly code, C-- language (figure); 366
characteristics as a target machine; 1
constructs, C-- language (figure); 363
constructs and structure; 360
  (table); 361
instruction sequence, assignment statement, (figure); 229
memory,
  characteristics; 199
  (figure); 202
operations, classifying according to whether they yield a value or not; 231
representation of Pascal data types on; 200
routine calling conventions, effect on value parameter handling; 207

sample assembly code, (table); 366
target program tree,
    nodes examples, (table); 238
    value constraints on Datum-class nodes for; 231

verification,
    of class of Pascal identifiers, (figure); 176
    of conditions based on value computation, as tactical component of contextual information gathering strategy; 160

vertical bar (|),
    in regular expressions; 49

vinteger type,
    voided expression handling use of; 292

visibility rules,
    See Also scope;
    effect on activation records; 206
    identifier associations determined by; 160
    in C-- language; 346
        (figure); 353
    name analysis use of; 9
    (notes and references); 191
    Pascal, semantic analysis diagrams, (figure); 10

visits,
    See tree traversal;

voiding,
    See Also operator identification;
    overloading voided expressions, (figure); 293
    term definition and implementation; 291
    VoidType type, use in unifying the handling of functions and procedures; 208

vreal **type,**
    voided expression handling use of; 292

W

warning error,
    characteristics; 23

Whetstone ALGOL 60 compiler,
    (notes and references); 192

while **statement,**
    source program tree representation, (figure); 5
    target program tree representation, (figure); 8
    template description; 243

WithStmt **nodes,**
    associations established in component statement of; 163

write access function,
    characteristics; 232

Z

zero,
    generated identifiers represented by; 175